Handbook of the Humanities and Aging

Second Edition

Thomas R. Cole, PhD
Robert Kastenbaum, PhD
Ruth E. Ray, PhD
Editors

 Springer Publishing Company

Thomas R. Cole, Ph.D., is Professor and Graduate Program Director at the Institute for the Medical Humanities, University of Texas Medical Branch, in Galveston. He has published many articles and books on the history of aging and humanistic gerontology. His book, *The Journey of Life: A Cultural History of Aging in America* (Cambridge, 1992) was nominated for a Pulitzer Prize. He is senior editor of *What Does It Mean to Grow Old?* (Duke, 1986); the *Handbook of Humanities and Aging,* first edition (Springer, 1992); *Voices and Visions: Toward a Critical Gerontology* (Springer, 1993); *The Oxford Book of Aging* (Oxford, 1995); and the biannual newsletter, *Aging and the Human Spirit.* As a medical humanist, Cole's interest in the life stories of older people has taken him into the history of civil rights in Texas, resulting in a biography, *No Color Is My Kind: The Life of Eldrewey Stearns and the Integration of Houston* (Texas, 1997) and a documentary film, *The Strange Demise of Jim Crow: How Houston Integrated Its Public Accommodations, 1959–1963.* He is currently completing a film, *Anatomy and Humanity: Conversations with Donors and Dissectors,* doing life story work with elders in nursing homes and writing groups, and beginning a study of aging in the Jewish tradition.

Robert Kastenbaum, Ph.D., is Professor of Gerontology in the Department of Communication, Arizona State University. A clinician and researcher, he has also served as director of a geriatric hospital and cofounder of the National Caucus on Black Aging. Kastenbaum is editor of *International Journal of Aging and Human Development,* and *Omega, Journal of Death and Dying.* His books include *The Psychology of Death, Death, Society and Human Experience,* and *Dorian, Graying: Is Youth the Only Thing Worth Having.* He has written the libretto for three operas: Dorian (premiered, 1995); Closing Time (premiered 1999); and American Gothic (for a year 2000 premiere).

Ruth E. Ray, Ph.D., is Associate Professor of English at Wayne State University in Detroit, where she is also faculty associate at the Institute of Gerontology. She is the recipient of a 1994–1997 fellowship from the Brookdale Foundation to study older women's self-representations. Her current research interests include age and auto/biography, women's mid-life and late-life narratives, and spirituality and aging. Her latest book is *Writing a Life: Age, Gender, and Diversity in the Life Story.*

Handbook of the Humanities and Aging

Second Edition

Springer Publishing Company, Inc.
536 Broadway
New York, NY 10012-3955

Acquisitions Editor: Bill Tucker
Production Editor: Janice Stangel
Cover design by James Scotto-Lavino

00 01 02 03 04 / 5 4 3 2 1

Library of Congress Cataloging-in-Publication-Data

Handbook of humanities and aging / Thomas R. Cole, Robert
    Kastenbaum and Ruth E. Ray, editors. — 2nd ed.
      p.   cm.
    Includes bibliographical references and index.
    ISBN 0-8261-6241-X (hardcover)
    1. Gerontology and the humanities. 2. Aging. I. Cole, Thomas
R., 1949–   . II. Kastenbaum, Robert. III. Ray, Ruth E., 1954–
HQ1061.H33654   2000
305.26—dc21   99-41209
                                           CIP

Printed in the United States of America

For David D. Van Tassel—
Who Started Us All Down
This Path 25 Years Ago

Contents

Part III   Humanistic Themes in the Study of Aging

Part IV   Reflections

Contributors

W. Andrew Achenbaum, Ph.D.
Dean of Humanities, Fine Arts
  and Communications
University of Houston
Houston, Texas

Robert C. Atchley, Ph.D.
Professor and Chair
Department of Gerontology
Boulder, Colorado

Ann Davis Basting, Ph.D.
1998 Brookdale Fellow
The University of Wisconsin-
  Milwaukee
Center for Twentieth-Century Studies
Milwaukee, Wisconsin

Harry J. Berman, Ph.D.
Professor of Child, Family,
  and Community Services
Associate Vice Chancellor
  for Academic Affairs
University of Illinois at Springfield
Springfield, Illinois

Anne M. Wyatt-Brown, Ph.D.
Associate Professor of Linguistics
University of Florida
Gainesville, Florida

Thomas R. Cole, Ph.D.
Professor and Graduate Program
  Director
Institute for the Medical Humanities
University of Texas Medical Branch
Galveston, Texas

Margaret M. Gullette, Ph.D.
Harvard University
Cambridge, Massachusetts

Carole Haber, Ph.D.
Professor and Chair
University of Delaware
Department of History
Newark, Delaware

Sheldon R. Isenberg, Ph.D.
Associate Professor
University of Florida
Department of Religion
Gainesville, Florida

Robert Kastenbaum, Ph.D.
Professor of Gerontology
Arizona State University
Department of Communications
Tempe, Arizona

Stephen Katz, Ph.D.
Associate Professor
Department of Sociology
Trent University
Peterborough, Ontario
CANADA

Sharon R. Kaufman, Ph.D.
Professor in Residence
Medical Anthropology Program
Institute for Health and Aging
University of California
Department of Social and Behavioral
  Sciences
San Francisco, California

Melvin A. Kimble, Ph.D.
John L. Rothrock Professor of
  Pastoral Theology and Ministry
Luther Northwestern Theological
  Seminary
St. Paul, Minnesota

Gisela Labouvie-Vief, Ph.D.
Wayne State University
Detroit, Michigan

Teresa Mangum, Ph.D.
Associate Professor
The University of Iowa
Department of English
Iowa City, Iowa

Ronald J. Manheimer, Ph.D.
Research Associate Professor
  of Philosophy and Executive
  Director of the Center for
  Creative Retirement
University of North Carolina
Center for Creative Retirement
Asheville, North Carolina

Laurence B. McCullough, Ph.D.
Professor of Medicine and
  Medical Ethics
Center for Medical Ethics
  and Health Policy
Faculty Associate
Huffington Center on Aging
Baylor College of Medicine
Houston, Texas

Ruth E. Ray, Ph.D.
Associate Professor
Wayne State University
English Department
Detroit, Michigan

Pat M. Thane, Ph.D.
Professor of Contemporary History
University of Sussex
Department of History
Falmer, Brighton
Great Britain, ENGLAND

Leng Leng Thang, Ph.D.
Assistant Professor
National University of Singapore
Department of Japanese Studies
Singapore

Gene R. Thursby, Ph.D.
Associate Professor
University of Florida
Department of Religion
Gainesville, Florida

Steve Weiland, Ph.D.
Professor of Higher Education
  and Director of the Jewish
  Studies Program
University of Michigan
Department of Education
  Administration
East Lansing, Michigan

Robert E. Yahnke, Ph.D.
Professor
General College
University of Minnesota
Minneapolis, Minnesota

Introduction

The first edition of the *Handbook of the Humanities and Aging* (1992) broke new ground in several ways. It established the legitimacy of humanistic gerontology, staked out temporary boundaries of the field, and commissioned several chapters that served not as overviews but as original substantive contributions in their own right. Our purpose was to advance humanities scholarship, and we are pleased to note the remarkable quantity and quality of new work produced in the last seven years. But in retrospect, that first edition did not do much to promote much needed interdisciplinary and collaborative work among humanists, scientists, and practitioners. In fact, it apparently had little impact on mainstream gerontological audiences.

Gerontological knowledge making remains dominated by the paradigm of modern science and its various expressions in the social and medical sciences. This situation must change if gerontology is to fulfill its real potential. In the last quarter of the 20th century it has become clear that scientific and professional gerontology lacks a shared discourse for addressing moral, aesthetic, and spiritual issues or for appreciating their historical and cultural contexts. A flood of work in the humanities and interpretive social sciences has emerged to fill this void. But this latter work has yet to be appropriately integrated into gerontological scholarship, clinical education, policy making, or funding.

The next generation of gerontologists will surely need to embrace a wider range of viewpoints from which to study and shape the multiple meanings of age. We like to think of the second edition of the *Handbook of Humanities and Aging* as a step in this direction—a demonstration and celebration of the interdisciplinary mindset needed for a rich and complex understanding of age.

We offer the *Handbook* as a source for future cross-fertilization and a valuable resource for researchers, practitioners, teachers, and advanced students of gerontology and geriatrics. We also envision it as an authoritative (and well written) reference text for those students and professional humanists just waiting to be lured into gerontology! In order to accommodate important new developments (growing interest in spirituality, cultural studies, film/video, and performance studies), we did have to sacrifice certain valuable features of the first edition. Readers looking for a more detailed historical study of aging in the West, or for more material on fairy tales, poetry, fiction, art, storytelling, or late-life learning, should consult chapters on these topics in the first edition. We acknowledge, too, that we were not able to overcome a weakness of the first edition—our failure to provide coverage of aging in diverse populations in the United States and Europe or in the countries of Africa and Latin America. In pointing to these deficiencies, we can only encourage others to direct their scholarship in these directions.

INTERDISCIPLINARY CHALLENGES, MOTIVATIONS, INTENTIONS

This volume demonstrates the many ways that humanistic gerontology both necessitates and promotes interdisciplinary thinking. We have divided the chapters into four sections: 1) Disciplinary approaches; 2) Interdisciplinary perspectives; 3) Humanistic themes in the study of aging; and 4) Reflections. Fully one-third of our authors are trained in one of the social sciences. Even Part I, which reviews ideas and approaches from established humanistic disciplines, is permeated with boundary crossings. The history of aging (Thane, Haber), for example, cannot be surveyed without substantial understanding of demography and public policy as well as of traditional literary and visual representations of and by older people. Literary gerontology (Wyatt-Brown) is no longer confined to the studies of authors, texts, and images of aging/old age but is now shaped by cultural studies and its latest offspring, "age studies." Philosophical thought (Manheimer) about aging and old age encompasses more material written by authors trained in social science than by those trained in philosophy. The topic of bioethics and aging (McCullough) requires knowledge not only of the growing bioethics literature but also of clinical care and outcomes research in medicine and the helping professions. Religious perspectives (Isenberg, Kimble, Thursby) on aging bridge theology, literature, end-of-life care, and multiculturalism.

The disciplinary reviews in Part I surely invite an interdisciplinary reading as well. The authors raise questions of interest to scholars in their fields, but they write in a way that offers background information and insight that is relevant to other fields and interests. Scientists, social scientists, physicians, policy makers, and students will come to this section with their own questions (how is old age defined in humanistic fields? how is it studied? how can the work of humanists inform research in my own field?) and, we hope, leave asking new questions informed by their reading (what does it mean to grow old? who and what influences our interpretations of "old age"? what is the value of old age for individuals, for culture, for history?).

Parts II, III, and IV demonstrate sophisticated interdisciplinary readings on the part of each author. Three of the contributors to Part II focus on aspects of aging—filial relations (Thang), the aged body and its representations (Basting), the aged self and its representations (Berman)—that demand disciplinary crossing. The other two contributors (Gullette and Weiland) consider interdisciplinarity itself, arguing for its absolute necessity in the study of age. Part III is structured around broad themes of perennial interest in the humanities—generational relations, spirituality, death, human development, and creativity. Most of the authors in this section are gerontologists trained in the social sciences who have increasingly gravitated toward humanistic topics and methods. They are working in that hybrid area sometimes known as the "human sciences." Finally, the authors in Part IV survey the field of gerontology at large, analyzing how this handbook relates to other handbooks and considering its overall contribution to the interdisciplinary study of age.

Besides crossing *academic* borders, interdisciplinarity in gerontology functions critically and politically. Critically, interdisciplinary scholars respond to the intellectual limits of disciplinary thought; politically, they insist on social and intellectual change in order to move beyond these limits. As Julie Klein suggests in *Crossing Boundaries,* fields such as women's studies and cultural studies offer examples of the transformative potential of interdisciplinary scholarship. Women's studies, for example, deliberately challenges the ways knowledge is constructed in established disciplines. Because feminist questions, themes, and problems can not be adequately addressed by any single field, scholars in women's studies have had to stake out a more "innovative terrain" or "borderland" from which to do their research. These scholars not only cross but contest disciplinary boundaries and work to restructure prevailing modes of inquiry. We see this same transformative potential in the interdisciplinary crossings of gerontology. Indeed, several contributors to this edition of the *Handbook* are critically motivated in this way, most notably Margaret Gullette, who takes her cues from both feminist theory and cultural criticism to lay out the parameters of a new area she calls "age studies."

One of the best arguments for advancing interdisciplinarity in gerontology, however, is progress. Our colleagues in women's studies have argued convincingly that intellectual and social change is faster and more comprehensive through interdisciplinary exchange. This edition of the *Handbook of Humanities and Aging* offers a range of interdisciplinary accomplishments and possibilities, and it aspires to help transform gerontology into a more critical and intellectually self-conscious enterprise. The volume's final chapters by Katz and Achenbaum explicitly articulate these revisionist intentions.

CHAPTERS AND SECTIONS: A SUMMARY

We begin this forward-looking *Handbook,* appropriately, with a review of historical approaches to the study of age. The chapters by Pat Thane and Carole Haber demonstrate that historians are developing a more complex understanding of the experience of aging and old age in the past. As Thane points out, definitions of later life vary substantially according to time period, class, region, and the ethnic or religious composition of the populations being studied. While contemporary historical research on aging in the West fails to support any overarching theory or synthesis, Thane reminds readers of the profound changes since 1900, when longevity for the entire population grew dramatically and when welfare states enabled the mass of poorer people to approximate what the wealthy had always possessed—"a regular income for which they need not work or degrade themselves by begging for poor relief or charity."

Haber's chapter on the historiography of aging in America points out that large-scale social science theories (e.g., modernization theory) were substantially revised when historians undertook genuine empirical research beginning in the mid-1970s. Even since then, however, there has been a troubling tendency for historical research to omit the goals and values of the elderly themselves. Since older people are not and have never been a homogeneous group, the task of linking quantitative and qualitative research remains a challenging one. As she puts it: "In the search to understand aging in the past, scholars must rescue the old from aggregate statistics without assuming that the reminiscences of one individual or even a small group characterize all aged individuals."

While historians in the 1970s became the first group of professional humanists to devote serious attention to aging, they were joined in the mid-1980s by scholars and clinicians in the new field of bioethics. The 1990s, however, witnessed an explosion of scholarship and clinically relevant work in literary studies. A growing number of writers, literary critics, actors, storytellers, gerontology professors, and linguistic scholars saw that the search for more satisfying meanings and experiences in later life depends considerably on how aging is narrated, represented, figured, debated, and performed in various cultural and historical contexts.

Anne Wyatt-Brown and Teresa Mangum discuss central themes in the literary study of aging. Wyatt-Brown surveys the dramatic growth of literary studies in gerontology since she wrote a similar chapter for the first edition. Demonstrating the field's increased attention to the interplay of age, gender, race, class, and ethnicity, she addresses: 1) literary attitudes toward aging, which are primarily informed by a postmodern sociological perspective; 2) late style and creativity across the life course; 3) cultural studies of aging; 4) narrative studies of life review and autobiography; and 5) explorations of the emotions in later life. Discussing representations of older characters in children's literature and in the novels of Charles Dickens, Teresa Mangum exemplifies how "seemingly idiosyncratic and widely dispersed ideas about old age harden into a cultural formation" that influences how old age is defined and experienced. "I ask," she writes, "how meanings and associations [e.g., second childhood] that become attached to aging interact with representations of aging, the treatment of older people, and even the way an individual feels compelled to think and act in his or her late years."

In his survey of philosophical thought about aging and old age, Ronald Manheimer addresses four questions: 1) depictions of the possibilities and limitations of later life; 2) ethical questions of meaning and purpose in old age; 3) the study of wisdom as a case study for examining methods of research in gerontology; and 4) the current relationship of academic philosophy to the subject of aging. Manheimer notes two basic trends in the fate of philosophy in 20th century gerontology: 1) philosophical inquiry into positive meanings of old age and the contributions of older people has been overshadowed by behavioral and clinical criteria (e.g., social adaptation, life satisfaction, maximum physiological functioning); and 2) very few contemporary academic philosophers participate in critical discourse on aging, which means that traditional philosophical concerns about wisdom, self, time, memory, morality, and meaning now fall to scholars trained in the social sciences and various other fields of the humanities.

Laurence McCullough's chapter, "Bioethics and Aging," treats four basic areas: decision making in geriatric health care; the ethical dilemmas posed by managed care; health care policy; and challenges to orthodoxy in geriatrics and gerontology. Specifically, McCullough challenges the current wisdom that there are diseases associated with aging rather than diseases inherent in the process of aging. Drawing on neurological research, he discusses the troubling possibility that diseases of the aging brain commonly lead to impaired executive control functions in the oldest old, thereby disabling all three traditional components of autonomy: intentionality, understanding, and noncontrol (the ability to resist environmental cues detrimental to one's plans). McCullough's discussion has profound implications for our assumptions about the nature and possibilities of autonomy among the very old.

The last three chapters in Part I look at aging from the vantage points of religious studies and pastoral care. Sheldon Isenberg and Gene Thursby have updated their chapters from the first edition—respectively, on Judaism and on Eastern Religious Traditions—from their perspectives as scholars of religious studies. Mel Kimble writes on aging in Christianity from his perspective as a practicising Christian and Professor of Pastoral Care.

Each of the three authors provides insight into how we might interpret the meaning of old age and how we might move beyond the aging body in our thinking. Isenberg combs through four thousand years of Jewish literature, highlighting two main themes: the idea of old age as a blessing, a reward for fulfilling the covenant; and the idea of aging as a source of physical, emotional, and mental suffering, especially toward the very end of life. Isenberg also touches on Judaism's skeptical wisdom theme which scoffs at the idea of a morally responsive universe and at the idea that we can understand God's moral calculus or will. Mel Kimble shares his "conviction that the Christian religion . . . sets forth affirmations and principles that help individuals and the community confront the human aging process in all its bewildering ambiguity." Drawing on authors from Augustine to Niebuhr to John Paul II, Kimble lays out views of the redemptive pattern in Christian life as a response to the crisis of meaning in contemporary secular culture. Gene Thursby argues that religion needs to be viewed in the context of cross-cultural or multicultural gerontology. As he points out, the religions of Buddhism, Hinduism, and Islam are no longer "foreign" to North American and European societies, given the vast wave of Asian migration that has taken place since 1965. Buddhist notions of selflessness, the Hindu unchanging Self, and the Muslim conception of a personal self are all essential to gerontological inquiry, since, quoting Shrinivas Tilak, "what aging is . . . depends upon what is understood by the notion of human beings and their embodiment . . . It must be . . . determined just what it is that ages."

Part II exemplifies the kind of "border crossings" between the humanities and social science that are required by scholars pursuing difficult questions about the aging experience. Anthropologist Leng Leng Thang considers what aging means in East Asian cultures. She offers a rich description of the cultural *ideal* of filial piety compared to its actual *practice* in contemporary families and communities. Through an impressive review of literature in the humanities and social sciences, she explains modernization and the changing status of the elderly in Japan, China, and Korea, ultimately redefining filial piety in a way that acknowledges diversity and older adults' own understandings of "a good old age" in the face of rapid social change. Similarly, psychologist Harry Berman questions the nature of the older self by looking to philosophy, literature, and literary criticism. He takes an interpretive turn away from the authentic or essential self of traditional psychology and moves toward the interpreted self, arguing that scholars who study the writings of older adults must distinguish between the "self" and textual representations of the self. He encourages gerontologists to study self-*representation* (in the forms of autobiography, memoir, letter) for greater insight into the experience of aging and late-life development.

The other three chapters in Part II address the topic of interdisciplinarity itself, explaining what is gained in merging and blurring disciplinary boundaries. Anne Basting and Margaret Gullette write as interdisciplinary scholars who contribute to interdisciplinary fields that have just begun to take up the subject of age. Basting, a playwright and theatre scholar, describes the hybrid field of performance studies and its offshoot—performative studies of age. The latter is a critical and revisionist enterprise demanding that "we acknowledge individual, physical and psychological experiences of age as well as the possibility of transformation and social change through role-playing." Basting's chapter encompasses many disciplines in describing how age is "staged" and how insights arise when we consider aging as "drama."

Gullette, a literary scholar and cultural critic, describes another hybrid field—cultural studies—in terms of the opportunities it provides for rethinking age. Gullette challenges us to interrogate age categories, narratives of aging, and "age ideologies" that socialize us into certain beliefs and ways of speaking, while suppressing alternative ways of conceptualizing age. She asserts the need for a new hybrid field she calls "age studies," a combination of critical gerontology and cultural studies. Gullette argues that theorists across disciplines must deconstruct their own gerontophobia and examine age as rigorously as they examine race, class, gender, sexuality, and other forms of difference.

The chapter written by Steven Weiland identifies gerontology as a field which is ripe for scholarly hybridization; he describes "humanistically oriented social science" studies which are based on theories of interpretation, rhetoric, and narrative borrowed from the humanities. Weiland considers these studies exemplars of a new gerontology which more accurately reflects intellectual moves in the academy toward postmodern theories, cultural criticism, and an emphasis on diversity and multiculturalism over the past 20 years. Weiland argues that gerontologists may best learn the "meaning" of age from the "messy texts" of human interactions and not from careful adherence to scientific procedures or strict disciplinary paradigms.

In Part III, contributors explore humanistic themes—broad topics which center around the nature of a meaningful old age. Robert Yahnke, for example, analyzes the themes of intergeneration (relationships between generations) and regeneration (emotional and psychological change in older adults) in films and videos produced within the past 30 years. Yahnke's chapter provides a valuable gloss on some 47 American and foreign films which deal with aging issues, including life in nursing homes, illness and disability, active aging, aging in place, the multiple meanings of home and community, memory and reminiscence, love and intimacy, family and friendship, interracial relations, role reversals, caregiving, and death. Yahnke's aim is to remind us that the media and the visual image have had a major impact on our interpretations of age, as well as our cultural expectations for a "good" old age. Robert Atchley attempts to define that most nebulous of terms—spirituality—and to explain the relationship between aging and spiritual development. Drawing on several mystical traditions, he identifies two qualities of spiritual growth on the part of the individual: maintaining an intense presence in the world without preoccupation or judgement and developing an awareness of the self as part of all things and "permeated by the ground of all being." Spiritual development, then, is a process of transcendence that entails an ever-broadening sense of one's self in the universe. Although aging does not necessarily bring spiritual development, it does alter life conditions in ways that can heighten the need for spiritual awareness. Sharon Kaufman, in an equally ambitious chapter, takes on the subject of death and argues for the importance of narrative approaches and a focus on the social and historical constructions of meaning in the study of death. As an analytic strategy and a mode of thinking, narrative is the kind of "expansive tool" which assists scholars in articulating the "native's point of view" and revealing an "open, richer field of cultural understanding than objectivist perspectives allow." Kaufman describes her own research on hospitalization and death, illustrating the multiple meanings of death as represented in the narratives of medical staff, family members, and medical charts.

In looking at meaning through the lenses of developmental theory, Gisela Labouvie-Vief and Robert Kastenbaum, both psychologists, offer new insights into the changes that occur in individuals over time. Informed by the humanistic and spiritual psychology of Carl Jung, Labouvie-Vief reviews the strengths that can be associated with advancing age. She does not romanticize late life, but offers a more nuanced view of "positive aging" which encompasses a range of experience and feeling from the positive to the negative. She argues that positive aging involves the integration of thinking and feeling and the development of strategies for optimizing a sense of well-being, even in the face of illness, disability, and death. Robert Kastenbaum approaches the subject of artistic creativity and its various expressions over the course of a long life. Kastenbaum reviews quantitative, narrative, and interpretive research in the social sciences and the humanities in moving toward his conclusion that artistic creativity does seem to decline with age, although the type and level of decline differ across domain, sociocultural context, and personal situation. Kastenbaum notes, however, that the world does not have a coherent theory of creativity, much less a theory of aging and creativity, so the collected research is far from conclusive. Kastenbaum recommends new directions which address the limitations of current research: longitudinal studies of creativity along with more indepth retrospective studies; a combination of qualitative and quantitative methods; studies of gender-related creativity across the life course (many classic studies are based on "great men"); and analyses of antecedents and consequences of thwarted creativity over a life time. Most importantly, research on aging should put creativity at the center, rather than the periphery, of a meaningful life.

In Part IV, Stephen Katz and W. Andrew Achenbaum look broadly at the humanities and gerontology. Katz considers gerontological handbooks in general, locating their history as part of the wider cultural development of textual practices in western society. His chapter is premised on the classic humanist notion that facts are *made* (not *found*) and that the language and texts used to make facts are not neutral lenses but essential cultural and historical forms of composition which must be analyzed in their own right. He pursues two basic questions: 1) how have gerontological handbooks become authoritative, especially in the U.S.? and 2) what other textual activities (beyond the choice of chapters, themes, and topics) in handbooks define and configure the field of aging studies as a professional enterprise?

In his overview of humanities research in gerontology, Achenbaum emphasizes both the maturation of an earlier cohort of scholars and the extraordinary creativity of a newly emerging group of humanists. He examines the disciplinary make up of the well-known MacArthur Foundation study of "successful aging" and notes, with dismay, that none of "our stars" from the humanities were involved. The exclusion of humanists, he concludes, stems not from lack of excellence or mature scholarship, but from an apparent conviction that "real" knowledge in gerontology can only come from researchers working within disciplinary-specific modes of scientific inquiry. This is a pity, since historians, philosophers, literary and cultural critics, and religious scholars have a great deal to say *at precisely the point where positivist science falls silent:* e.g., where did the idea of successful aging come from in the first place? What are its conceptual limitations and ambiguities? What cultural values embedded in the concept remain unarticulated and therefore unavailable for discussion and critique? What moral assumptions does successful aging make? What existential issues does it mute? Achenbaum urges us to take a hard look at the gaps in gerontological knowledge-making.

HOW TO READ THIS BOOK

The *Handbook* may be read conventionally as an example of "humanities concerns" and "humanities approaches," but this would not be true to the spirit of the book, nor would it exercise the full potential of the book. The *Handbook* should really be read alongside of other texts in order to open up the possibilities of age inquiry, rather than to close them down around narrow disciplinary lines. Below we offer a few suggestions for reading that might prove more generative.

In an often quoted essay published in the academic journal *Profession,* Mary Louise Pratt coins the phrase "contact zone" to describe the space where diverse groups come into contact and negotiate meaning through interaction, conflict, and improvisation. She works on the premise that any community in the late 20th century (including a community of scholars) is far more diverse and heterogeneous than unified and homogenized. The contemporary challenge, then, is to make the "contact zone" a site for learning and social transformation that puts all "ideas and identities on the line." We see the field of gerontology as a "contact zone" and the gerontology classroom as a microcosm of the same, where conflicting disciplinary approaches, practices, policies, texts, voices, and visions of aging and age research converge. Ideally, the *Handbook* should be read as one of the many texts in this zone of negotiation, juxtaposed with books and articles from geriatric medicine, the sciences, the social sciences, and other humanistic texts, including films, poems, letters, narratives, and oral histories about aging and old age. The *Handbook,* which itself invites a heterogeneous reading, should be read in a spirit of textual and conceptual diversity.

There are unlimited possibilities for juxtaposing texts and ideas within the contact zone of gerontology. Readers could, for example, read chapters of the *Handbook* according to theme and look at texts from other disciplines and genres which address the same theme. One thematically organized reading of the *Handbook* might look something like this (many other categorizations are possible):

Cultural meanings of age—Thane, Haber, Thursby, Mangum, Gullette
Intergenerational relations—Gullette, Thang, Yahnke
Philosophical and ethical concerns—Manheimer, McCullough, Kaufman
Religiosity and spirituality—Kimble, Thursby, Atchley, Isenborg
Creativity and alternative representations of age—Wyatt Brown, Basting, Berman, Yahnke, Kastenbaum
Issues around death and dying—Manheimer, McCullough, Kimble, Kaufman

Life span development—Gullette, Atchley, Labouvie-Vief, Kastenbaum

Methodological readings of the *Handbook* are also possible. One example:

Discussion of narrative method—Wyatt Brown, Weiland, Berman, Kaufman
Use of narrative analysis—Haber, Wyatt Brown, Mangrum, Weiland Basting, Berman, Yahnke, Kaufman
Interdisciplinary reviews of literature—Thane, Haber, Thang, Kastenbaum
Cultural critique—Mangum, Gullette
Disciplinary critique—Weiland, Berman, Katz, Achenbaum

Our point in presenting these alternatives is to show how different groupings of chapters lead to different questions and point in the direction of additional texts. A reading of Gullette in terms of Thang and Yahnke, for example, invites an examination of the forces that sustain age divisions in western and eastern cultures, as well as those that might promote more fluid boundaries between the generations. Reading these chapters in this way would make us want to look further—to view some of the films Yahnke describes, for example, and to read works in other disciplines which examine filial relationships and responsibilities. Reading the chapters on disciplinary critique together encourages us to step back and look at the knowledge-making practices in gerontology, considering questions like these: What makes gerontology a "discipline"? In what ways is it and is it not interdisciplinary? How does the field of gerontology legitimize and authorize certain kinds of knowing and de-legitimize others? How are the humanistic disciplines and their ways of knowing regarded in the contact zone of gerontology? How is the category of old age established and maintained through the disciplinary practices of gerontology? How does gerontology classify and govern older people themselves through its theories, methods, and practices? Such questions lead us further into the terrain of critical interdisciplinarity.

However readers combine the chapters in the *Handbook of Humanities and Aging,* at the very least they should provoke new questions and generate more thinking about the meaning and purpose of age.

In his "Afterword," Andrew Achenbaum suggests that the future of humanistic gerontology is more uncertain than recent accomplishments would seem to warrant. He is pessimistic about "whether scholars in the humanities will ever secure a place at the gerontological table." Our view, however, is that the gerontological table will have to change: Modern science alone cannot accommodate the ever-growing needs of an aging society to make moral, spiritual, and aesthetic sense of the experiences, problems, and possibilities in late life.

Humanistic research and teaching in gerontology will become increasingly necessary. In using the word "humanistic," we are referring to knowledge and competence inspired by the ancient ideal of *humanitas*—whose original Latin meaning was "human feeling." Gradually, the word *humanitas* became associated with an educational ideal which blended knowledge, humane feeling, and compassionate action. This wonderful and elusive mix of knowledge, feeling, and action—what Lionel Trilling called the "humanistic educational ideal"—needs to be recaptured and reinfused into gerontological education and research today. To accomplish this, however, we academic humanists will have to cross more than disciplinary boundaries! We will need to join hands with our humanistic colleagues in the sciences and the helping professions. And we will need to circulate more widely in places where the meanings of age are negotiated: nursing homes, adult education centers, senior centers, hospitals and clinical care arenas, volunteer programs, and governmental agencies, just to name a few. We will also need to assist with end-of-life planning, and the education of health care professionals, and become vocal advocates in public policy debates.

We are grateful for the support and assistance of many individuals in the making of this book. Excellent chapter reviews were written by David Troyansky, Gene Thursby, Steve Weiland, Kathleen Woodward, Patrick McKee, Marshall Kapp, Dayle Friedman, Susan McFadden, Timothy Tsu, Jay Gubrium, Victor Marshall, Ron Manheimer, Anne Wyatt-Brown, and Dean Simonton. At the Institute for Medical Humanities, Denise Morris typed countless letters to authors and reviewers, and Rosemary Lindley did a superb job of organizing the entire production process—she kept track of (and often tracked down) essential details from authors, reviewers, and editors while managing the flow of information and communication with Springer Publishing. At Springer, we are grateful to Ursula Springer, Bill Tucker, Dora Summa, and Renata von Stoephasius.

REFERENCES

Allen, J. A., & Kitch, S. L. (1998). Disciplined by disciplines? The need for an interdisciplinary research mission in women's studies. *Feminist Studies, 24,* 275–300.

Klein, J. T. (1996). *Crossing boundaries: Knowledge, disciplinarities, and interdisciplinarities.* Charlottesville, VA: University Press of Virginia.

Pratt, M. L. (1991). Arts of the contact zone. *Profession 91.* New York: Modern Language, 33–40.

PART I
Disciplinary Approaches

The History of
Aging in the West

Pat Thane

The growing skepticism of historians about simplified grand narratives, combined with the use of a greater variety of sources to explore the past (literary, visual, and personal, for example, as well as statistical and official sources) has, in recent years, moved us toward a more complex understanding of the historical experience of old age. This is appropriate for the stage of life which encompasses greater variety than any other. It can be seen, in any time period, as including people aged from their 50s to past 100; those possessing the greatest wealth and power, and the least; those at a peak of physical fitness and the most frail. In consequence of this variety many different histories and fragments of histories of old age are emerging. This does not imply that there are no overarching narratives, that the history of old age is no more than an accumulation of small stories; rather it suggests that we are at an exciting, if incomplete, stage of assembling both small and large stories about different times and places in the search for a total history of old age.

This process is shaped and sometimes distorted by the different preoccupations of historians of different national and cultural backgrounds. Histories of old age in Britain have been relatively extensive and centrally preoccupied with demography and with material concerns: the numbers of old people, their geographical distribution, their living arrangements; with household structures and family relationships; with welfare arrangements, medical provisions, property transactions, work and retirement. Studies in France have not neglected these obviously important material matters, especially demographic studies, which in their modern form were invented in France, or the history of medicine, but more attention has been paid to representations of old age, to how the idea of old age has been constructed in the past. The relatively sparse, but fine, work on old age in Germany (Borscheid, 1987; Conrad, 1994; Von Kondratowitz, 1991) provides examples of both approaches, as do the more extensive studies of the United States and the growing body of work from, and about, Canada, Australia, and New Zealand. Histories of old age in other "western" countries are more fragmentary still.

In consequence it is difficult to assert with any certainty that the history of old age in the diverse regions of "the West" has unity, or to examine similarities and differences between different countries and regions as systematically as is, in principle, desirable. And there have been important absences in the histories of all countries. New approaches to historical writing in general are being drawn upon in the study of old age, though sometimes extremely gradually. For example, awareness of gender is hardly a novelty in historical scholarship, but it has been surprisingly slow to enter studies of old age. This is perhaps because historians share the mistaken view of Georges Minois that until the relatively recent past, the history of old age is largely a history of men, because few women survived the rigors of childbirth to reach old age (Minois, 1989); or that of the medievalist, Joel Rosenthal that "Matriarchy and the culture of old women, whether on their own or in extended family households, is mostly a lost topic, worth investigation, but hard to treat other than anecdotally" (Rosenthal, 1996). Historians of women have recently begun to prove them both wrong, through the imaginative use of a wide range of sources (Stavenuiter, Bjisterfeld, & Jansens, 1996; Botelho & Thane, 1999).

The ideal, total, history of old age must unite all of the approaches currently available to historians, and no doubt others of which we are not yet aware. We need to draw together historical knowledge of the demographic and material experience of old age in different times and places with cultural histories of representation and self-representation and of the varieties of experience of older people, since these approaches to history can never be wholly separate from one another. Image is not distinct from experience, nor cultural history from economic, social, and political history. Cultural representations of old age, whether drawn from philosophical or medical texts, literature, paintings, film, recorded expressions of everyday opinion or any other source, shape individual imaginings of the life course and hence individual and collective action. If people are culturally conditioned to expect to be dependent and helpless past a certain age, they are more likely to become so, with consequences for their own lives and those of others, which may include provision of formal or informal welfare services. Reciprocally what takes place in the political and economic spheres—for example, the provision of retirement pensions—helps shape private experiences and perceptions. Official sources such as those of poor relief administration or debates about pensions policy in representative assemblies tell us much about political and administrative history, but they are also texts which can reveal a great deal about the cultural construction of old age in past societies.

If we are still far from achieving the "total" history of old age, how far are we along the way? To begin with the basic demographic picture:

DID PEOPLE IN "THE PAST" GROW OLD?

Clearly they did, and in larger numbers than is often thought. However, the numbers surviving to what was defined as old age varied from time to time, from country to country, and from place to place within nation-states, in ways which illustrate the complexity of the experience of old age within "western" culture. English population figures have been studied over a long time period. Life expectancy at birth in England averaged around 35 years between the 1540s and 1800 (Wrigley & Schofield, 1981) and is unlikely to have been higher at any earlier time. But the high infant mortality rates at all times before the mid-19th century drastically pulled down such averages. Those who survived the hazardous first years of life had, even in the 16th century, a respectable chance of living at least into what would now be defined as middle age, and often longer (Wrigley et al., 1997). It is estimated that the proportion of the English population aged over 60 fluctuated between 6% and 8% through the 17th and 18th centuries. But the numbers varied from place to place. In the rapidly growing town of Manchester, full of young migrants at the end of the 18th century, during the industrial revolution, only 3.4% of the population was over 60, 1.9% over 70. In depressed rural Sussex, which young people were fleeing in search of work in the towns, 19% were over 60, 7% over 70. The national average fell to 6% in the 19th century, when high birth rates raised the percentage of the very young. Then from the late 19th century through to the late 20th, as birth rates and death rates in childhood, youth, and middle age fell, came the long climb in the proportion of the population living past 60: 6% in 1911, 14% in 1951, 18% in 1991. Most developed countries have experienced this climb in the 20th century.

France, by contrast, experienced falling rather than rising birth rates in the 19th century, which influenced the overall age structure. In the mid-18th century 7% to 8% of the population were aged 60 or above. By 1860 the proportion was 10%; by the early 20th century 12%, by 1946 14% (Bourdelais, 1998).

In Britain, women were a clear majority among those aged 60 and above from the time that vital statistics began to be officially and comprehensively recorded in 1837; and women appear to have had a longer life expectancy, on average, in Britain and elsewhere in Europe for long before. Medieval commentators noted that women seemed to have longer life expectancy and wondered how that could be, when it seemed natural that men were stronger and should live longer (Shahar, 1997). Physicians in 18th-century France were still puzzled by the consistency with which females "went against nature" and outlived men. It is sometimes thought that before at least the 19th century female life expectancy must have been sharply reduced by the ravages of death in childbirth (Minois, 1989). But though such deaths undoubtedly, and tragically, occurred more frequently than in the 20th century, childbirth was not a mass killer of women in western societies (Schofield, 1986). It was not comparable with the ravages of work, war, and everyday violence on the lives of men. In France in the mid-19th century there were more old men than old women, but by the time of the First World War women had gained the advantage in life expectancy, which they have never since relinquished (Bourdelais, 1998).

If there were divergent demographic experiences within the "Old World" of Europe, the "New World" of outposts of western culture, far from Europe, was different again. Migrant countries disproportionately attracted males. Hence in Australia and New Zealand by the later 19th century, most older people were male. In Ontario, Canada, the balance shifted from a majority of older men in 1851, to a female majority in 1901 (Montigny, 1997). In the United States the picture must have varied from place to place, according to length of settlement. Women in America are estimated, on average, to have had a lower life expectancy than men from the mid-17th century to the 1890s (Haber & Gratton, 1994). The proportion of the U.S. White population aged 60 and above rose steadily from 4% in 1830 to 6.4% in 1900 to 12.2% in 1950. The survival rates of African Americans were somewhat lower (Achenbaum, 1976); and those of Native Americans (as of Australian aboriginals) one assumes, considerably so. Another absence in historical work on aging concerns such excluded and persecuted groups. The population of Ontario aged as the colony made the transition from migration to long-established settlement. Three percent of the population was aged over 60 in 1851, 4.6% in 1871, 8.4% in 1901 (Montigny, 1997). Different "western" societies indeed "aged" at different paces and with different gender balances. It took France 140 years to double its population of people over 60 from 9% to 18% (from 1836–1976), Sweden, 86 years (1876–1962), the United Kingdom, 45 years (1920–65); the proportion over 60 had not reached 18% in the United States by the late 1990s. Such varying paces of demographic change had probable cultural effects, but they have barely been explored.

The growing proportions of older people in western societies over the 20th century have, periodically, caused panics which are revealing about attitudes to old age in at least some sectors of society. This panic first became acute in the 1920s at least in France and Britain, the only countries for which it has been studied (Bourdelais, 1993, 1998; Thane, 1990). The combination of rapidly falling birthrates and lengthening life expectancy in a period when there was a perceived military threat from apparently "younger" countries, in particular Germany, and a perceived cultural threat from the growth of non-White populations outside the "West," produced in France and Britain countries doomladen predictions from demographers and social scientists about the social conservatism and economic and military decline which was anticipated, as these nations lost their youthful vitality. In France, according to Bourdelais, such fears reinforced negative views of old age. In Britain, however, Thane points out that the initial negative assessment of an "aging society" led to demonstrations of the positive capabilities of older people (at work, for example) and to government-led attempts to improve both their social conditions and their cultural value, though with only partial success.

The panic about aging in the mid-20th century, which was replicated in the 1980s and 1990s, suggests a close link between demographic change and cultural change: that changing proportions of old people in a society may influence attitudes toward them and affect their own behavior. But the different responses in Britain and France to similar demographic situations in the 20th century suggest that the relationship between demography and culture is complex, variable and, as yet, little understood. A similar contrast can be found in interpretations of the 18th century, for much of which both the proportions of older people and average expectancy of living to later ages in the two countries were comparable, in both cases rising. In France this has been seen—through the use of a great variety of sources—as a period in which older people came into favor and acquired a positive image, in contrast to previous denigration. "This major [demographic] change in humanity's history was accompanied by a mutation in sensitivities, in perceptions of life and its different ages that transformed the conception of the older generation's role and position in society" (Bourdelais, 1998, p. 111). Old people in France "began to be actively esteemed." One sign of this esteem was the establishment of pensions for public servants for the first time. No parallel change in esteem has been detected in Britain. Rather, by the end of the century impoverished old people were less rather than more likely to receive poor relief. The 18th century in Britain also saw the introduction of systematic pensions for public servants, but, rather than signs of esteem, these were outcomes of the professionalization of government: pensions explicitly

provided an acceptable means to rid the public service of those thought
to have aged past their usefulness (Raphael, 1964). Similar demographic
regimes may have different cultural outcomes in different social, economic, and political contexts.

What is "Old Age"?

But historians have begun to ask whether age-based statistics tell us
everything about the age-structure of a society; or about how old age
has been defined in the past. Conventionally gerontologists and demographers choose 60 or 65 as the lower limit of "old age." It is essential to
choose a fixed age threshold if statistical comparisons of age structure
are to be made over time. But have these ages always had the same
meanings? Sixty and 65 are the ages at which state or private pensions
are most frequently paid in present-day western societies and they
have become common ages of retirement from paid work. These ages
were generally fixed earlier in the 20th century when both pensions
and retirement gradually became normal features of aging in most
western countries (nowhere were they universal before the 1940s). At
that time they were thought to approximate the ages at which most
people were no longer fit for full-time work. Standards of physical
fitness of people in their 60s rose in most western countries over the
course of the 20th century. In some countries, ages of retirement were
raised or abolished at the end of the 20th century, though in others
they fell for reasons connected with the state of the national and international economy, or with personal preference, rather than with physical
aptitude (Kohli et al., 1991). In the late 20th century physical condition
was detached from social and bureaucratic markers of "old age" and
recently established age boundaries were destabilized. Were they more
stable in the more distant past? Did people become "old" at earlier ages
in previous centuries, when living standards were lower?

The concept of old age was firmly present in all known past cultures
and it had multiple meanings and uses. Significantly, the ages of 60 and
70 have been used to signify the onset of old age in formal institutions
in Europe at least since medieval times. Sixty was long the age at which
law or custom permitted withdrawal from public activities on grounds
of old age (Shahar, 1997). Even in ancient Greece the formal obligation
to perform military service did not end until age 60 and men in their
50s were indeed conscripted (Finley, 1984). In ancient Roman writings
people were defined as old at ages varying from the early 40s to 70
(Parkin, 1998). In medieval England, in a succession of enactments
from the Ordinance of Laborers of 1349 onwards, men and women
ceased at 60 to be liable for compulsory service under the labor laws,
to prosecution for vagrancy, or to perform military service. From the

13th century, 70 was set as the upper limit for jury service. Similar regulations held elsewhere in Europe (Shahar, 1997). It can be argued that governments generally had an incentive to set such ages as high as possible, especially when they might exact taxation in lieu of service. However, it is unlikely that such ages could be set at levels far removed from popular perceptions of the threshold of old age. Furthermore, there was in medieval and early modern Europe, (and is in many societies in the 20th century) no fixed retirement age for many elite positions, and appointments could be made at advanced ages. In England the average age at death of the nine 17th-century Archbishops of Canterbury was 73 and the average age of appointment was 60.

On the other hand, it was long assumed that most manual workers could not remain fully active at their trades much past age 50, especially when performance depended upon such physical attributes as good eyesight. Literary evidence from the 16th century suggests that the 50s were regarded as the declining side of working maturity, the beginning of old age, as is still popularly assumed at the end of the 20th century. For women old age was often thought to start earlier, in the late 40s or around 50, when the physical concomitants of menopause became visible (Botelho, 1999); for men the defining characteristic was capacity for full-time work. For both men and women in preindustrial Europe old age was defined by appearance and capacities rather than by age-defined rules about pensions and retirement; hence people could be defined as "old" at variable ages. English poor relief records in the 18th century first describe some people as "old" in their 50s, others not until their 70s. Supplicants for public service pensions in 18th-century France ranged in age from 54 to 80 years (Troyansky, 1993).

This suggests that over many centuries old age has been defined in different ways in different contexts and for different social groups. Three of the commonest ways of framing old age are: chronological, functional, and cultural. A fixed threshold of "chronological" old age has long been a bureaucratic convenience, suitable for establishing age limits to rights and duties, such as access to pensions or eligibility for public service. It has become more pervasive in the 20th century, when societies have become more rigidly stratified by chronology, as increasing numbers of people experience fixed ages for retirement and receipt of pensions. "Functional" old age is reached when an individual cannot perform the tasks expected of him or her, such as paid work. "Cultural" old age occurs when an individual "looks old," according to the norms of the community, and is treated as old. It combines aspects of the other modes of definition; it is an expression of the value system of the community and may define individuals as old according to codes of dress or other commonly accepted signifiers. Despite impressive continuities over long time periods in both official and popular definitions of the onset of old age, undoubtedly a high proportion of survivors in medieval and early modern society felt and looked "old" at earlier ages than has become the norm in the second half of the 20th century. In consequence, the numbers of people who appeared to be "old" in past communities might have been greater, and would therefore have been a more visible cultural presence, than is revealed simply by calculation of the numbers past the age of 60.

Also, it has long been recognized that there is immense variety in the pace and timing of human aging, that people do not age at the same pace or in the same ways. In consequence, since antiquity (Parkin, 1998) old age has long been divided into stages. Some of these were elaborate, such as medieval "ages of man" schema, which divided life into 3, 4, 7, or 12 ages (Burrow, 1986; Sears, 1986). These stylized age divisions often had didactic or metaphorical purposes. More commonly, in everyday descriptive discourse, old age has been divided into what in early modern England was called "green" old age, a time of fitness and activity, with perhaps some failing powers, and the later, last phase of decrepitude; a division which in the 20th century is less imaginatively labeled "young" and "old" old age, or in France the Third and Fourth ages. Texts referring to the decrepit final age cannot be taken to express attitudes to old age in general. Some mistaken comparisons over time arise from comparing accounts of different phases of life. The sad decline with which some, but not all, older lives end has never been represented positively, in any age or culture (Amoss & Harrell, 1981), with good reason.

Modes of Survival: Work

Historians have also discovered more about the ways older people supported themselves and were supported through time and consequently about how they lived and perceived their own lives. Such public documents as wills, legal documents, inventories, poor relief records, census statistics, records of pension funds and such private ones as diaries, letters, biographies, and autobiographies can be combined to provide a greater understanding of these processes. Again the picture is one of variety among social groups and across space and time (Botelho & Thane, 1999; Pelling & Smith, 1981; Troyansky, 1989).

Some older people, of course, have always possessed property, often in substantial amounts, with which they could support themselves to the end of life, employing others to care for them, if necessary, either in institutions or in their own households. From the earliest times in most western countries aging individuals could legally assign property to relatives or nonrelatives in return for guaranteed support until death, and they could invoke the protection of the law if the agreement was not honored. Old people determinedly sought to control their own lives and to retain their independence throughout much of western culture through time. For the propertyless and impoverished there was, through most of time, little choice but to work for pay for as long as possible, whereas the propertied could in all times afford to retire from work when they chose (Harvey, 1993; Shahar, 1997; Smith, 1991). As states and later business enterprises began to bureaucratize along modern lines, from the 18th century, and became concerned to maintain the efficiency of their officials, pensions were introduced to encourage retirement when aging was thought to impair performance (Raphael, 1964; Thuillier, 1994; Troyansky, 1998).

The poorest people expected, and were expected to, work to late ages, often excluded from, or refusing to accept, stigmatizing poor relief though living in pitiable conditions. For example, in a census of the poor taken in Norwich, England, in 1570, three widows, aged 74, 79, and 82, were described only as "*almost* past work" and they were still earning small sums at spinning (Pelling, 1991). This remained so in most western countries until the 20th century. Poor relief systems encouraged older people to work, supplementing but not replacing meager incomes. This was true of both men and women. In early modern Europe, most communities provided specified tasks for older people. Such activities as roadmending, caring for the churchyard, fetching, carrying, or caring for horses on market days were tasks for old men. It was often easier for women to support themselves at later ages. They could care for children, engage in casual domestic labor, such as cleaning or washing; commonly they earned an income by taking in lodgers, running small shops or alehouses (Jutte, 1994).

This unremitting lifetime toil was relieved for the poorest people with the emergence of retirement as a normal phase of life only in the mid-20th century. Census data can give the impression that mass retirement first emerged in the later 19th century, but this is an artifact of the construction of censuses, which recorded retired people according to their preretirement occupations. Deconstruction of the American and British censuses (there appear to be no equivalent studies of other countries) demonstrates that most of the apparent 19th-century decline in employment at older ages was due to the decline of agriculture. Retirement from white-collar occupations, combined with improved occupational pensions, was visible through the first half of the 20th century. Retirement from blue-collar occupations did not increase significantly until the 1940s and beyond (Johnson, 1994; Ransom & Sutch, 1986).

Why did retirement become a mass phenomenon at this time? Attempts to explain it as a feature of capitalist manipulation of a reserve army of labor (Macnicol, 1998; Phillipson, 1982) are unconvincing, since the most rapid spread of retirement coincided with the post-World War II labor shortage in most western countries, when older people were needed in the labor force rather than in reserve. Rather, retirement became a social norm along with the introduction of improved pensions, provided by the state, which promised at least tolerable incomes in later life. This coincided with increased capacity of relatives to help in a period of generally rising living standards and full employment. To some degree individuals chose at the end of life the leisure always previously denied them, though in the 1980s and 90s increasing numbers of people retired in their 50s, sometimes willingly, often under pressure from management engaged in "downsizing" their operations (Kohli, 1986). As retirement became a norm it perhaps reinforced the prevailing view of business management that older people were marginal workers, and the popular views of older people as redundant and dependent. Once again, cultural and material phenomena were mutually reinforcing.

Older People and Their Families

Older people who had little or no savings or property, and who could not earn a living from a single source of employment throughout time have been locked into what early modern historians term an "economy of makeshifts," and 20th century economists less picturesquely label "income packaging": pulling together a shifting variety of resources to achieve survival. There has been much debate among historians about the role of family support in these individual economies.

The family has a central place in the cultural histories of all western societies. It has long been clear that as far back in time as can be traced, it has not been the norm in all western societies for older people to share households with their married children. To do so was conventional in Mediterranean societies and in some north European peasant cultures, such as Ireland and parts of France, where land was the family's only asset and the heir shared land and household with the elders until their death (Kennedy, 1991; Troyansky, 1993). In much of North-western Europe, however, elders retained control of their own households for as long as they were able, rarely sharing them with adult married children, though they might move to the home of a relative when they were no longer capable of independence, perhaps for a short time before death. North European folklore, even in medieval times, expressed few illusions about intergenerational support, but long conveyed warnings of the danger to older people of placing themselves and their possessions under the control of their children. Such stories achieved their most sublime expression in William Shakespeare's *King Lear,* itself a reworking of a number of medieval folktales. In the

18th century the gates of some towns in Brandenburg were hung with large clubs bearing the inscription:

> He who made himself dependent on his children for bread and suffers from want, he shall be knocked dead by this club (Gaunt, 1983, p. 259).

Most countries incorporated into law some obligation upon adult children and sometimes other close relatives to support their elders, for example, the English Poor Law from the late 16th century; and this was the practice, if not the law, in parts of early modern Germany (Jutte, 1994). How frequently such practices were implemented was variable, not least because the kin of the aged poor were often very poor themselves and could not realistically be expected to give support from already inadequate resources (Montigny, 1997; Thane, 1996; Thomson, 1991). The customs and practice of the Old World were transported to the New, with adaptations to new circumstances. Settler societies gave even greater salience to the independence and self-help which was a necessity for survival in the early years, and such societies necessarily took time to build the communal, often religious-based institutions which supplemented self- and family support in much of Europe (Montigny, 1997; Thomson, 1998).

But the fact that older people did not conventionally share a home with close relatives, and determinedly retained their independence for as long as they were able, does not mean that there were not close emotional ties and exchanges of support between the generations. Recently even Peter Laslett has softened his belief in the universality of the nuclear family in preindustrial Europe and the slight obligations of younger to older generations, and has recognized the variability of family forms and relationships in European history (Laslett, 1995; Laslett & Wall, 1972). Parents and adult offspring might not share a household, but they often lived in close proximity, even in the highly mobile society that England was for centuries before industrialization. Generally in western societies "kinship did not stop at the front door" (Jutte, 1994). The Austrian sociologists Rosenmayr and Kockeis have described the North European family as characterized by "intimacy at a distance" (Rosenmayr & Kockeis, 1963, pp. 418–419), the intimacy being as important as the distance. "In early modern Europe old people could in general expect help from their children based on the sustenance and protection provided by parents during the childhood period" (Jutte, 1994, p. 85). Family members at all social levels have been found to have exchanged support and services from a mixture of material, calculative, and emotional motives. That it was often an *exchange* relationship should be emphasized. Older people in the past, as now, were rarely simply dependent upon others, unless they were in severe physical decline. They cared for grandchildren, for sick people, support-ed younger people financially when they could afford it and performed a myriad of other services for others. With lengthening life expectancy, over time the coexistence of three or more generations and hence the opportunity for exchange has become more frequent (Bourdelais, 1998). Although over the 20th century increasing numbers of old peo-ple have lived alone, they have relatively rarely been isolated or neglected by younger relatives (Rein & Salzman, 1995; Thane, 1998); rather greater numbers are able to seize the opportunity provided by greater affluence to preserve the independent control of their own lives to which older people have long aspired.

The importance of intergenerational exchange has been underesti-mated by historians because it often took the form of services or gifts in kind, which are difficult to trace historically because there was no reason for systematic records of such private, nonmonetary transac-tions to be taken or to survive. It was a taken-for-granted activity of everyday life of the kind that is most difficult to reconstruct in the dis-tant past. Even the participants took such transfers so for granted that they denied their significance, as when a 67-year-old retired mar-ket gardener gave evidence to a British Royal Commission of Enquiry into the Condition of the Aged Poor in 1895. He lived alone in a coun-try village. He had a cottage and a garden, rented an allotment, and kept a pig or two; both were useful sources of food and of earnings and/or exchange. He had occasional earnings from roadmending. When asked if his five surviving children gave him help, he replied: "No, I have had to help them when I can. They have got large families most of them. I do what I can in that sense. I do not get anything from them in any way. The daughter that I have lives the length of this room perhaps from me and she looks after my house." His daughter's house-work was a service which must have contributed greatly to his com-fort, but he so took it for granted that he did not define it as "help." In other respects this man's story exemplifies family relations and the survival strategies of older people, which were not peculiar to England or to the later 19th century. His children were too poor and too burdened with their own children to give him financial support; instead he gave support to them when he could. He was no longer in regular paid work but packaged together a living from the produce of his garden and from occasional earnings. It would be surprising if he did not sometimes share meals with his daughter's family and give them some produce from his garden, both common forms of intrafa-milial exchange among those too poor to offer cash, part of the net-work of exchange which held together poor communities through the ages, enabling survival in conditions of poverty (Jutte, 1994; Montigny, 1997; Thane, 1996).

Not all older people had families to support them through the centuries when high death rates meant that parents might outlive children. It has been estimated that up to one third of women living to 65 in 17th- and 18th-century England had no surviving children. By the mid-19th century perhaps two thirds of 65 year olds had surviving children (Pelling & Smith, 1991). In 18th-century France the average age at which a person became both fatherless and motherless was 29.5; in the 1970s it was 55 (Bourdelais, 1998). Geographical mobility in centuries when transport was slow and many people were illiterate might break contacts even with survivors. Migrants to far away "new" countries often lacked older relatives around them, hard though they strove to keep in touch with them at a distance.

Through the 20th century birthrates have fallen universally in the West, but so have death rates, and both marriage rates and levels of fertility have risen. In consequence in the late 20th century more people have children and they survive. Most older people who have surviving children are in close contact with some or all of them. At all times, recipients of welfare relief have been more likely to be people without surviving children, which further suggests the historical importance of family support. Modern forms of communication facilitate contact even over long distances. Far from "crowding out" family support, as social scientists once feared, modern welfare states facilitate it, enabling intergenerational relationships to be easier and less tension ridden by removing some of the costs from the family. The relationships between older people and their close relatives show striking long-run continuity and closeness in western culture even when they do not share a household.

Even those who had no families could create them. Older men would marry younger women able to look after them; rich older women might marry younger men; widowers with children might marry older women to care for them. Orphan children were adopted by older people, gaining a home in return for giving service. Unrelated poor people shared households for mutual support. Examples can be found as far apart as Norwich, England, in the 16th century and Ontario, Canada, in the mid-19th century and throughout early modern continental Europe (Jutte, 1994).

Aging and Welfare

But when families have not been able, willing, or available to help, many older people have needed the support of publicly financed welfare. Not all older people are, or ever have been, poor but in most past, and present, societies they have been more likely than younger people to be very poor, especially if they were female. In consequence, the study of poor relief systems and welfare states can tell us much about the histories of the older people with whom these systems so often dealt. Such studies are numerous, but they cannot tell us everything and we should be cautious about giving this theme too much weight. A focus on the relief of the aged poor runs the risk of conveying the message that most old people in the past were dependent as well as poor, when many were not, and it diverts attention from the remainder who were independent and sometimes wealthy. Also there is a danger of overestimating the importance of poor relief in the lives of older people because poor relief systems leave records behind whereas other, perhaps equally important sources of support, such as that within families, do not.

Nevertheless, poor relief and welfare have been important in the lives of many impoverished old people. All modern states have to some degree become "welfare states," though the meaning of this term varies from place to place and over time. In Europe, modern welfare states are profoundly marked by each country's long tradition of poor relief. These traditions were transported and transformed by migrants to "new" countries. All European countries for many centuries before the 20th century had some system of provision for the aged and other poor, who could not help themselves and had no family or other source of support. This was financed to varying degrees through public taxation (probably most extensively in England, through the mechanism of the national Poor Law which was in place from 1597 to 1948, though it had still earlier antecedents) (Slack, 1990), or by voluntary charity, often religious in motivation and institutionalization; most often by a combination of the two. "Relief" could take the form of payments in cash or kind (food, clothing, medical care) or shelter in a hospital or workhouse. Provision was of variable quality, within each country as well as over time, and it was guided by varied principles: supportive, rehabilitative, or punitive. Everywhere old people were numerous among recipients of relief, along with widows and children, but nowhere did reaching a defined age automatically qualify anyone for relief. The essential qualification was destitution, access to insufficient resources for survival, though poor relief could supplement partial incomes (Jutte, 1994). Even where the poor relief system was relatively generous, relief could be refused even to the very old if they were judged capable of earning some income. This is an important contrast with modern pension systems, which, whatever their inadequacies, normally provide for most of the population on attaining a certain age.

Countries of the New World tended to reject publicly funded welfare systems because initially they lacked both an established, substantial wealthy class capable of funding them and the mass of miserable poverty which required them. Also 19th-century migrants were often fleeing from punitive relief systems in Europe and had no desire to replicate them. Ideologically, too, they placed a premium upon independence and self-help. Australia and New Zealand never introduced publicly funded poor relief systems, relying instead upon voluntary charity, sometimes (and increasingly over time) subsidized from public funds (Dickey, 1980; Thomson, 1998). The picture was similar in 19th-century Canada (Montigny, 1997). In parts of the United States the extent of unmet need necessitated the introduction of poor relief, but "welfare" early acquired and retained more stigmatizing associations than elsewhere in the West. Most nation-states, at least by the 18th century and commonly in the 19th and 20th, provided publicly funded pensions for public servants and for the disabled veterans of war and sometimes for their families. Public service pensions rarely provided for the severely deprived.

Old people were in most countries the first to benefit from the transition from residual and often punitive poor relief systems to theoretically, and generally actually, more comprehensive and generous state welfare systems. This was because, being mostly marginal to the labor and capital markets, they were generally the last substantial social group to gain from the general improvement in living standards which took place in the West over the course of the 19th century. Also the "deservingness" and respectability of older people were more readily apparent to reluctant taxpayers than was the case with other impoverished groups such as the unemployed.

Old age pensions have been introduced throughout the West since the 1880s, but on different principles and for different reasons in the various countries. Where the motivation was mass deprivation among older people due to the absence or the deterrent and stigmatizing effects of a poor relief system, pensions were noncontributory and targeted upon the very poor, often especially providing for women, as in Denmark in 1891, New Zealand in 1898, most of the Australian states by the time of Federation in 1910, and in Britain in 1908. Where the main motivation was pressure from, and/or the desire of politicians to undermine, a growing labor movement, as in Germany in 1889, they tended to be insurance based and to target primarily the securely employed, generally male worker (Baldwin, 1990). Again, different cultural and political contexts produced different outcomes both in the origins and subsequent development of pension systems through the 20th century (World Bank, 1994).

Old people have also gained from increasing medical knowledge over time. Knowledge of the history of geriatric medicine is sparse but growing. Interest in the physical condition of aging people has been continuously present among medical specialists since ancient times, though always as a minority medical interest. It was for centuries uncertain whether old age should itself be defined as a disease and for centuries little could be done to alleviate the diseases accompanying old, or indeed younger, age other than to enjoin temperance, good diet, exercise, as specialists still do in the late 20th century. Investigation and understanding of the pathology of physical deterioration with aging developed especially in 19th-century France, spurred partly by the increasing numbers of older people in the French population (Bourdelais, 1993, 1998). Only in the 20th century did medicine acquire the capacity to diagnose and cure extensively, and only in the mid-20th century were medical services sufficiently democratized in most western countries to allow most old people access to medical treatment. Even so, they tended to be at the back of the queue for such treatment, their lives deemed less valuable than those of younger people. The specialty of geriatrics throughout the West from the early 20th century, though most strongly from the 1930s, sought primarily to protect older people against such discrimination and also to keep fit the aging populations of most western countries. It has had only partial success. Older people have gained most from medical techniques designed for all age groups, such as coronary bypass surgery, joint, especially hip replacements, but geriatrics remains at the end of the century in most countries a low status medical specialty and older people without personal power still suffer from exclusion from treatment in favor of the young, though not to any greater degree than in the past (Thane, 1993).

Has the Status of Older People Declined?

Social scientists sometimes argue that the spread of pensions and retirement in the 20th century has increased the dependence and marginalization of older people, that they have come to be less valued in modern society. The belief that the status of older people is always declining has a very long history. It is discussed, and dismissed, even in the opening pages of Plato's *Republic* and in a long succession of texts through the centuries. The longevity of this narrative trope in the discussion of old age suggests that it expresses persistent cultural fears of aging and neglect, and real divergences in experience in most times and places, rather than representing transparent, dominant, reality.

Early historical enquiry into old age tended to echo this narrative of decline. Georges Minois's history of old age in western culture from antiquity to the Renaissance acknowledged variations and complexities in experiences and perceptions of old age over this long time-span: "not so much a continuous decline as a switchback evolution." But he still concluded that "the general tendency however is towards degradation." And he had no doubt that the degradation was still greater in modern society (Minois, 1989, pp. 6–7). An extensive body of work on old age in the United States since the 18th century finds the status of old people to be in decline over a variety of time scales: from the late 18th century to the early 19th (Fischer, 1978), in the mid-19th (Cole, 1992), between the late 19th and 20th centuries (Achenbaum, 1976; Haber, 1983). Historians have reconstructed the different experiences of the political elite of New England in the late 18th century (Fischer, 1978), attitudes to East Coast Protestant clergy in the late 18th century (Cole, 1992), studies of labor force participation and the antecedents of social security legislation (Achenbaum, 1976), of the emergence of geriatrics and the attitudes of social welfare professionals in the late 19th and 20th centuries (Haber, 1983). They are mostly studies of White males. They have tended to represent the (scrupulously researched) experience of specific groups as representative of broader, even hegemonic values, rather as microstudies, valuable in themselves, contributing part, rather than representing the whole, of a complex total picture. The fact that some older men exerted power at a particular time is important, but it does not necessarily suggest that all old people at that time and place were highly regarded. In all times in western culture older people (female and male) who retained economic or any other form of power, along with their faculties, could command, or enforce, respect. At all times also powerless older people have, though not universally, been marginalized and denigrated.

More recent studies of old age in ancient (Parkin, 1998) and medieval (Rosenthal, 1996; Shahar, 1997) Europe and in France (Bourdelais, 1993, 1998; Troyansky, 1989, 1998), Germany (Borscheid, 1987; Conrad, 1994; Von Kondratowitz, 1991), and the United States (Haber & Gratton, 1994) in more recent times, acknowledge the variety of experience in old age and abandon the pessimistic framework. In consequence, a richly textured history is emerging which is making clearer differences between social groups, and between times and places, including between national cultures. For example, Troyansky describes the new confidence with which public servants requested pensions from the state in postrevolutionary France, asserting a sense of right to such a reward and in the process coming self-consciously to review their lives and to imagine a model of the life-course which incorporated a period of retirement at its end. All of this appears to have been new in early 19th-century France. In England, by contrast, aging small landowners, male and female, can be found in the law courts even in medieval times, vigorously ensuring for themselves a period of retirement on their own preferred terms, as they negotiated and defended contracts in which they transferred their lands to others in return for care and material support (Clark, 1990; Smith, 1991). English men and women at all social levels from an early date wheedled pensions from monarchs, bishops, and other influential patrons, stressing the characteristics of their past lives that merited support for a dignified old age. Even poor old people, in the 19th century and long before asserted their right to poor relief in similar terms (Sokoll, 1993). The difference between the two countries may lie in the fact that formal equality before the law was long established in England, carrying with it a sense of equal rights which were strongly held even among poor people, however imperfect the reality; whereas in France such equality was the outcome, indeed the central objective, of the great Revolution. Such profound legal and political differences shaped different cultural experiences of old age. Such experiences produced texts from which these differences can be reconstructed.

The greatly enriched histories of old age of recent years have alerted us to the complexity of attitudes to and experiences of older age in all times and over time, and to the rich range of sources and methods through which historians can seek to reconstruct them. It can be tempting, for example, to conclude, as Minois does (Minois, 1989), that Shakespeare's dismal conclusion to the "seven ages of man" described by Jaques in *As You Like It:* "second childishness and mere oblivion; sans teeth, sans eyes, sans taste, sans everything," is representative of 16th-century English perceptions of old age; if, that is, you fail to note that Jaques is a relatively young man but is given the conventional literary attributes of an old man, such as melancholy; and that the dismal description of the "seventh age" is followed by the transgressive entrance on stage of an octogenarian, Adam, who has earlier represented himself and been represented as "strong and lusty." The pervasiveness in English popular drama and literature (for example, in the work of Chaucer) of such dialogue between conflicting representations of old age, and its evident familiarity to medieval and early modern audiences, suggests its deep roots in English culture and perhaps in that of other countries.

Emerging from the cultural history of old age at the end of the millennium is a strong awareness of the plurality of representations and experiences of old age over time and in any one time and place. It is more difficult to assess, rather than to assert, whether certain values concerning old age are more dominant at certain times and places than others. At present we know enough to be wary of overarching schema of cultural decline, but the historical picture is too fragmentary to allow us to be certain that any one approach was ever hegemonic.

Conclusion

The history of old age became somewhat less pluralistic in the West in the 20th century, as the experience of later life became more uniform across national, cultural, and social boundaries, but, as pointed out at the beginning of this chapter, experience must always be far from uniform throughout so large and varied an age group—if indeed it makes any sense to regard people of 60 as more properly belonging to the same age group as those aged 100 than to that of those aged 40. But it is in the 20th century that experiences historically the privileges of a minority, generally a wealthy minority, were democratized and universalized.

Only for the first time in the mid-20th century did it become normal and predictable in western societies for almost complete birth cohorts to grow old. For the first time in history it became possible for everyone to imagine, and to plan realistically for, a long life. Imaginings of the life course, philosophical, imaginative, or visual representations of The Stages of Life or The Journey of Life had a long history, with roots in medieval and even ancient Europe, but these learned, often didactic usages of the life course to impart a moral message (responsible, temperate behavior could increase one's chance of a long life) were quite different from the everyday practical expectation of long life which emerged in the later 20th century (Cole, 1992). The cultural implications of this change are profound. The characteristics of this later phase of life were also democratized to some degree. Only from the mid-20th century did the mass of poorer people begin to share what the better off had always had available to them: a regular income for which they need not work or degrade themselves by begging for poor relief or charity, a period of leisured retirement between cessation of paid work and the onset of physical decrepitude, if they indeed experienced this, as was by no means always the case.

REFERENCES

Achenbaum, W. A. (1998). *Old age in the new land. The American experience since 1978.* Baltimore: Johns Hopkins University Press.

Amoss, P., & Harrell, S. (1981). *Other ways of growing old: Anthropological perspectives.* Stanford: Stanford University Press.

Baldwin, P. (1990). *The politics of social solidarity. Class bases of the European welfare states 1875–1975.* Cambridge: Cambridge University Press.

Borscheid, P. (1987). *Geschichte des Alters 16–18. Jabrhundert.* Münster: Deutscher Taschenbuch Verlag.

Botelho, L., & Thane, P. (1999). *Women and ageing in Britain since 1500.* London: Routledge.

Bourdelais, P. (1993). *Le nouvel age de la vieillesse: histoire du vieillissement de la population.* Paris.

Bourdelais, P. (1998). The ageing of the population: Relevant question or obsolete notion? In P. Johnson & P. Thane (Eds.), *Old age from antiquity to postmodernity* (pp. 110–131). London: Routledge.

Bulder, E. (1993). *The social economics of old age: Strategies to maintain income in later life in the Netherlands, 1880–1940.* Tinbergen: Tinbergen Institute.

Burrow, J. A. (1986). *The ages of man: A study in medieval writing and thought.* Oxford: Oxford University Press.

Clark, E. (1990). The quest for security in medieval England. In M. M. Sheehan (Ed.), *Aging and the aged in medieval Europe.* Toronto: Pontifical Institute of Toronto.

Cole, T. R. (1992). *The journey of life. A cultural history of aging in America.* Cambridge: Cambridge University Press.

Conrad, C. (1994). *Vom Greis zum Rentner: Der Strukturwandel des Alters in Deutschland zwischen 1830 und 1930.* Göttingen: Vandenhoeck and Ruprecht.

Conrad, C., & von Kondratowitz, H. J. (Eds.) (1993). *Zur Kulturgeschichte des Alterns/Towards a cultural history of aging.* Berlin:

Dickey, B. (1980). *No charity there: A short history of social welfare in Australia.* Melbourne: Thomas Nelson.

Finley, M. (1983). Old age in ancient Rome. *Aging and Society, 3,* 391–408.

Fischer, D. H. (1978). *Growing old in America.* New York: Oxford University Press.

Gaunt, D. (1983). The property and kin relationships of retired farmers in northern and central Europe. In R. Wall et al. (Eds.), *Family forms in historic Europe* (pp. 249–280). Cambridge: Cambridge University Press.

Haber, C. (1983). *Beyond sixty-five: The dilemma of old age in America's past.* New York: Cambridge University Press.

Haber, C., & Gratton, B. (1994). *Old age and the search for security: An American social history.* Bloomington: Indiana University Press.

Harvey, B. (1993). *Living and dying in England, 1100–1540.* Oxford: Oxford University Press.

Johnson, P. (1994). The employment and retirement of older men in England and Wales, 1881–1981. *Economic History Review, 47,* 106–128.

Johnson, P., & Thane, P. (Eds.). (1998). *Old age from antiquity to post-modernity.* London: Routledge.

Jutte, R. (1994). *Poverty and deviance in early modern Europe.* Cambridge: Cambridge University Press.

Kennedy, L. (1991). Farm succession in modern Ireland: Elements of a theory of inheritance. *Economic History Review, 3,* 478–496.

Kohli, M., Rein, M., Guillemard, A. M., & van Gunsteren, H. (Eds.). (1991). *Time for retirement: Comparative studies of the labor force.* Cambridge: Cambridge University Press.

Laslett, P. (1995). Necessary knowledge: Age and aging in the societies of the past. In D. I. Kertzner & P. Laslett (Eds.), *Aging in the past: Demography, society, and old age.* Berkeley and London: University of California Press.

Laslett, P., & Wall, R. (Eds.). (1972). *Household and family in past time.* Cambridge: Cambridge University Press.

Macnicol, J. (1998). *The politics of retirement in Britain, 1878–1948.* Cambridge: Cambridge University Press.

Minois, G. (1989). *History of old age: From antiquity to the renaissance.* trans. S. Hanbury Tenison. Oxford: Polity.

Montigny, E. A. (1997). *Foisted upon the government: State responsibilities, family obligations and the care of the dependent aged in late nineteenth century Ontario.* Montreal: McGill-Queens University Press.

Parkin, T. (1998). Aging in antiquity: Status and participation. In P. Johnson & P. Thane (Eds.), *Old age from antiquity to post-modernity* (pp. 1–18). London: Routledge.

Pelling, M., & Smith, R. M. (Eds.) (1991). *Life, death, and the elderly: Historical perspectives on aging.* London: Routledge.

Pelling, M. (1991). Old age, poverty, and disability in Norwich. In M. Pelling & R. M. Smith (Eds.), *Life, death, and the elderly: Historical perspectives on aging* (pp. 74–101). London: Routledge.

Phillipson, C. (1982). *Capitalism and the construction of old age.* London: Macmillan.

Ransom, R. L., & Sutch, R. (1986). The labor of older Americans: Retirement of men on and off the job, 1870–1937. *Journal of Economic History, 46,* 1–30.

Raphael, M. (1964). *Pensions and public servants: A study of the origins of the British system.* Paris: Mouton.

Rein, M., & Salzman, H. (1995). Social integration, participation, and exchange in five industrial countries. In Scott A. Bass (Ed.), *Older and active: How Americans over 55 contribute to society* (pp. 237–262). New Haven, CT: Yale University Press.

Rosenmayr, L., & Kockeis, E. (1963). Proposition for a sociological theory of aging and the family. *International Social Science Journal, 3,* 418–419.

Rosenthal, J. T. (1996). *Old age in late medieval England.* Philadelphia: Temple University Press.

Sears, E. (1986). *The ages of man: Medieval interpretations of the life cycle.* Princeton, NJ: Princeton University Press.

Schofield, R. S. (1986). Did the mothers really die? Three centuries of maternal mortality in "The World We Have Lost." In L. Bonfield et al. (Eds.), *The world we have gained* (pp. 231–260). Oxford: Blackwell.

Shahar, S. (1997). *Growing old in the middle ages.* London: Routledge.

Slack, P. (1990). *The English Poor Law 1531–1782.* Cambridge: Cambridge University Press.

Smith, R. M. (1991). The manorial court and the elderly tenant in late medieval England. In M. Pelling & R. M. Smith (Eds.), *Life, death, and the elderly: Historical perspectives on aging* (pp. 39–61). London: Routledge.

Sokoll, T. (1997). Old age in poverty: The record of Essex Pauper letters 1780–1834. In T. Hitchcock et al. (Eds.), *Chronicling poverty: The voices and strategies of the English poor 1640–1840* (pp. 127–154). London: Macmillan.

Stavenuiter, M., Bjisterveld, K., & Jansens, S. (1996). *Lange Levens, stille getuigen. Oudere Vrowen in het verladen.* Zutpen: Walburg.

Thane, P. (1990). The debate on the declining birthrate in Britain: The "menace" of an aging population, 1920s–1950s. *Continuity and Change, 5*(2), 283–305.

Thane, P. (1996). Old people and their families in the English past. In M. Daunton (Ed.), *Charity, self-interest, and welfare in the English past* (pp. 113–138). London: UCL Press.

Thane, P. (1993). Geriatrics. In W. F. Bynum & R. Porter (Eds.), *Companion encyclopedia to the history of medicine* (pp. 1092–1118). London: Routledge.

Thomson, D. (1991). The welfare of the elderly in the past: A family or community responsibility? In M. Pelling & R. M. Smith, *Life, death, and the elderly: Historical perspectives on aging* (pp. 194–221). London: Routledge.

Thomson, D. (1998). Old age in the new world: New Zealand's colonial welfare experiment. In P. Johnson & P. Thane, *Old age from antiquity to post-modernity* (pp. 146–179). London: Routledge.

Thuillier, G. (1994). *Les pensions de retraite des fonctionnaires au XIXème siècle.* Paris.

Troyansky, D.G. (1989). *Old age in the Old Regime: Image and experience in eighteenth century France.* Ithaca, NY: Cornell University Press.

Troyansky, D. G. (1993). Old age, retirement, and the social contract in 18th and 19th century France. In C. Conrad & H. J. von Kondratowitz, *Zur Kulturgeschichte des Alterns* (pp. 77–95). Berlin: Deutsches Zentrum for Alterstragen E. V.

Troyansky, D. G. (1998). Balancing social and cultural approaches to the history of old age and aging in Europe: A review and an example from post-Revolutionary France. In P. Johnson & P. Thane, *Old age from antiquity to post-modernity* (pp. 96–109). London: Routledge.

von Kondratowitz, H. J. (1991). The medicalization of old age: Continuity and change in Germany from the 18th to the early 19th century. In M. Pelling & R. M. Smith (Eds.), *Life, death, and the elderly: Historical perspectives on aging* (pp. 143–164). London: Routledge.

World Bank. (1994). *Averting the old age crisis.* Washington: World Bank.

Wrigley, E. A., & Schofield, R. S. (1981). *The population history of England, 1541–1871: A reconstruction.* London: Edward Arnold.

Wrigley, E. A., Davies, R. S., Oeppen, J. E., & Schofield, R. S. (1997). *English population history from family reconstitutions, 1580–1837.* Cambridge: Cambridge University Press.

2

Historians' Approach to Aging in America

Carole Haber

Before the 1970s, sociologists and anthropologists had briefly and succinctly written the history of old age in America. Often adopting large-scale models of societal change, such as modernization, they depicted a past in which urban and industrial growth transformed the lives of the old. According to this interpretation, the elderly had once been powerful and respected members of society. In communities in which experience and accumulated knowledge brought authority and respect, they wielded great and unchallenged power. Exerting control over extended kin, and dictating economic and social rituals, their age was a great predictor of their high status. Then, with the rise of the city and the growth of factories, the old found their lives remade. Torn from their families by migration patterns and a new mode of work, they ended their days in extreme isolation and poverty (Burgess, 1960; Clark & Anderson, 1967; Cowgill, 1972; Rosow, 1974; Simmons, 1945, 1960).

Beginning in the 1970s, however, American historians, along with qualitative sociologists and anthropologists, began to explore the elderly's past and came to challenge many of the untested findings. Did we, they asked, really know that the elderly were once uniformly held in high esteem? Were we sure that they had suffered a dramatic decline in status? If so, when did this occur? Moreover, were we certain that the source of this change was urban and industrial transformation? How could we correlate a theory of decline with economic evidence that hinted that the elderly experienced increasing wealth and self-sufficiency over the period of their supposed debasement? What about cultural evidence that revealed higher levels of contentment among the elderly now than in the past?

In asking these questions, the limitations of a strictly quantitative, broad-scale approach became clear. Although rarely discussed, the prevailing models looked for generalization; they did not explore individual differences or values. Moreover, they tended to be based on unquestioned assumptions about the direction and basis for changing attitudes toward the old. Assuming that the elderly's continued employment and coresidence with the young guaranteed their status, while the withdrawal of the aged from the labor market and the creation of solitary households were a clear sign of growing antagonism, models such as modernization directly tied the "negative" signs of ageism to the rise of the urban and industrial world. But did the old actually feel this way? What part did they have in shaping their own history? What, in fact, comprised a "good old age" in different historical periods?

In addition, the prevailing broad-scale theories paid little real attention to the issue of change over time. Pointing to some ill-defined era in which industrialization took hold, they postulated that all factors of the elderly's past were dramatically and permanently transformed at a single moment, or at the very least, during some ill-defined historical period. The argument had been simple: with industrialization, the once loved and respected old had suddenly become displaced and despised; they faced a world that bore little relationship to their previous beliefs and behaviors. Yet did all aspects of the elderly's life change simultaneously? Did they suddenly find themselves outcasts in their work and family simply because the means of production had changed? What specific factors caused the lives of the old to be transformed? And did all old people, regardless of economic status, education, gender, or family relationships, suffer the same negative experiences?

The challenge historians and humanistic social scientists had before them, therefore, was great. They had to rescue the old from some ill-defined past that treated them as the passive subjects of broad economic and demographic trends, without ignoring the importance of these forces. Examining the great variation in the lives of the old, they had to consider both individual differences among the old and the shared impact of their advanced stage of existence. Moreover, they had to separate the historical behavior of the old from contemporary assumptions about what comprised a satisfactory old age or the proper goals to achieve it.

While using the statistics and broad-scale paradigms of social science, historians brought a new approach to the study of old age. In trying to understand the past and the transformation to the present, they began to explore the motivations and beliefs of individuals and group of actors. Whether their subjects were old age home residents, retiring industrialists, aging widows, or advocates for social welfare, the values and motivations of such historic actors could not be determined through statistical analysis alone, and were often hidden under present-day assumptions about ideal behavior. Rather, historians were faced with tying sentiments, beliefs and actions to statistics. Not satisfied to cite the increasing rate of retirement among the old or the growth of independent households as an indication of their entire history, scholars needed to find out how people behaved, and why that behavior changed over time.

To accomplish these goals, historians and qualitative social scientists relied upon a variety of sources and methods not traditionally explored through quantitative analysis alone. While not ignoring census data or wealth surveys (and indeed, correlating them to individual motivations), they also explored the diaries, letters, and publications of the old and those who advocated for their needs and beliefs. In looking for evidence of how the lives of the elderly changed over time, some historians stressed the importance of institutional records; others looked at the elderly's interactions in their own families or employment; still others explored what advocates for the old had to say about aging. But behind these varied approaches was an attempt to place the beliefs, actions, and perceptions of individuals in the context of the eras in which they lived.

The resulting history of the old was far more complex than former narratives. As historians discovered, some attitudes and practices spanned the evolution of the factory; other beliefs and practices were transformed long before any industrial change. No longer could they simply accept the simplistic preindustrial/industrial periodization. And, by discovering that the pronunciations of aging advocates and the declarations of pension planners often contradicted the actual social experience of the old, they began to question the origins of crucial programs and policies.

In this essay, I will look at the questions, approaches, and conclusions of historians who have explored three central issues in the history of old age: family, work, and attitudes. Each of these issues has allowed scholars to trace important changes over time that challenge traditional assumptions about the role of the old in the past and their treatment by the culture. Moreover, in exploring family, work, and attitudes, scholars have been able to use the important statistical findings of many social scientists and link them to the actual beliefs of individual historical actors. While not all historians agree on the resulting historical interpretation, by tying sentiment to statistics they have begun to change our understanding of the experience of the old in America's past.

One of the first issues explored by historians was the role of the elderly in the family. How did the old live? What were their relationships to their kin? How did changing economic circumstances and mortality patterns affect their household structure? What influence did these changes have on the elderly's status? Previously, several untested assumptions had shaped the work of social scientists. Advocates of modernization had argued that before industrialization, the old served as powerful patriarchs dictating family decisions and controlling valued resources. They viewed the combined household as a longstanding ideal that awarded the old comfort and prestige. Then, according to this perspective, industrialization deprived the aged of this power and left them neglected and alone. As proof of the modern-day abandonment of the old, they pointed to the rise of the household composed only of a single elderly individual or aged couple. Nowhere was the hatred of old age assumed to be better depicted than in their newly formed isolated household.

Yet when scholars subjected this interpretation to historical investigation, the role of the elderly in the family appeared to be significantly different. Combining census and household data with the attitudes of the old themselves, historians found that the isolated household had a very different meaning. First, by exploring census data, community structure, and family records, scholars such as Philip Greven, John Demos, and Daniel Scott Smith argued that even in colonial America, kinship networks rarely encompassed three complete generations or contained a powerful patriarch ruling over extended kin (Demos, 1978; Greven, 1970; Smith, 1978; Waters, 1976). It was the exceptional old couple, rather than the norm, who lived in a complex three-generational home, complete with their married children and grandchildren. Given the late age of marriage and the long period of childbirth, most aging couples lived in a nuclear family, still responsible for the upbringing of adolescent children. Only incapacitation or the death of one of the couple led the old to seek residence with their grown children and offspring. Such individuals, though, hardly exerted broad, patriarchal power. Their control came from their role as parents rather than aging grandparents; their power came from their continued supervision of valued resources rather than their advanced chronological age. According to Philip Greven, the first generations of elders held on to their estates until death in order to insure the continued respect and care of their kin (Greven, 1970). Moreover, as the wills of the old revealed, they often guaranteed the continued respect of the widow through detailed restrictions, while limiting her control to specific rooms in the house and domestic articles. Although prescription dictated that children "honor thy father and thy mother," legal arrangements and court orders, rather than the ideal of patriarchy, insured the continued status of the old.

And, while historians discovered that industrialization did have an impact on this arrangement, it was in direct contrast to the assumed model. Surprisingly, as Steven Ruggles has shown, in the late 19th century, census data revealed that the old were *more* likely to live in three-generational households than their counterparts a century earlier (Ruggles, 1987). Due to changes in mortality and childbirth patterns, a greater number survived to see the adulthood and marriage of all their children. Moreover, demand for housing in the urban environment meant that the old often possessed a highly valued resource that allowed them to control the family resources while they shared their residences (Modell & Hareven, 1978).

Historians found, however, that by the first decades of the 20th century, the wealthiest of the old began to form a new pattern of household structure: they established homes apart from their children. Their turn to independent households arose, however, not out of abandonment, but as a result of increasing wealth and security. While the working class came to combine their homes out of necessity for shared resources, the upper and rising middle class sought the goal of "intimacy at a distance." As industrialization enriched the population as a whole, it came to support the autonomy of the old.

Using diaries, letters, and published stories, historians then uncovered a significant finding hidden beneath social statistics. The desire for separate households was a value shared by young and old rather than a symbol of ageism and debasement. Before Social Security, elderly individuals and their families repeatedly bemoaned the status of the mother-in-law in the home; they desired to live independently. Even in preindustrial households, old individuals often dreaded coresidence with the young. The extended household often was not, as social science theorists predicted, a foundation of power for the aging patriarch, but often a source of conflict and despair (Abel, 1992; Haber & Gratton, 1993; Ryan, 1981).

Given such sentiments, some elderly individuals attempted to remain outside the homes of their children, and expressed unhappiness when forced to take their place as the dependent grandparent in the household. Even in the early republic—well before the often-cited industrial transformation—the elderly's diaries and letters reflected their desire to live apart from their kin. In 1828, widow Hannah Carter Smith voiced the hope that despite the death of her husband, she would not have to enter her children's household. "It is important," she wrote her daughter, "that I should have a house of my own on moderate terms" (Smith, cited by Premo, 1990, p. 36). Many found their status within the home troubling. Living with her son in 1804, Alice Izard wrote that she was careful "to interfere as little as possible with the management of the family, and would never take the head of the table" (Izard, cited by Premo, 1990, p. 36). Others complained when their children and grandchildren moved in with them against their wishes. Martha Ballard, a 70-year-old midwife, was outraged when her son and daughter-in-law took possession of her house and relegated her to a room. Her daughter-in-law, she noted was "an inconsiderate or very imprudent woman to treat me as she does." Such behavior led Ballard to remark bitterly that her children ought to "Consider they may be old and receiv (*sic*) like Treatment" (Ballard, cited by Ulrich, 1921, pp. 281, 263).

In the early 20th century, decreased mortality and smaller families meant that even more middle-aged individuals faced the likelihood that they would coreside with the elderly. As in the early republic, the prospect was often not greeted happily or with the assurance of gerontocratic power. "When I was a child," wrote an anonymous magazine writer in the 1930s:

> I took it for granted that a grandmother or grandfather should live in the house of nearly every one of my playmates. Soon I came to take it for granted, also, that these houses should be full of friction. The association of grandparents with friction took such a hold in my mind that I called myself lucky because my own were dead!

When faced with housing her own mother, the writer longed for a source of income that would allow both generations to live independently. Ultimately, that revenue came in the form of federal assistance (Anonymous, 1931, p. 715).

These sources revealed a far different old age from the one presented by broad, quantitative analysts. The sentiments of the old rescued them from statistics that simply illustrated their singular lifestyle. For many, their new family relationship was the result of their own hopes rather than abandonment. By utilizing their words, historians found that the nuclear household structure—described by social science in terms of census data—was a goal shared by the elderly that preceded industrialization and came to fruition only when economic conditions supported its existence. Rather than a sign of decline of power in old age, the elderly's separate household reflected a long-desired ideal of kinship relations finally based on increased financial security.

The importance of this economic support for the old then informed a second issue explored by some historians—the meaning of work and retirement in old age. Scholars had long assumed that the high employment rates of the old in preindustrial America were a sign of their status and prestige. Possessing valued knowledge and skills, and often in control of desired resources, the old were assumed to be the wealthiest and most honored members of society. As their contributions were essential to the proper working of society, no mandatory retirement laws or societal pressures dictated their withdrawal. Then, according to social science research based on labor force statistics, industrialization forced the old into retirement and increasing impoverishment

(Markides & Cooper, 1987). Yet, like the belief in the combined household, this interpretation rested on untested value assumptions about the nature of work and the causes of retirement that failed to place the desires of the old within the context of their own histories.

By examining the lives of the old, historians first questioned the nature of preindustrial work. Although social scientists argued that continued labor was an indication of the elderly's high status, scholars discovered that many of the preindustrial old remained employed simply because they needed to work. Only the wealthiest had enough funds to allow the complete withdrawal from labor; even the middle class needed to work to support themselves. And, while land ownership often insured the continued activity of the old and made a segment of them wealthy, not all aged persons possessed such resources. Landless men worked intermittently as laborers; others wandered from town to town in search of employment. The fact that they could not retire was hardly a sign of their enduring high status.

Moreover, diaries and letters revealed that the young of the colonial society did not always value the continued labor of the old or respect them for their skills and experience. Able to hold on to their positions, and in need of economic support, the old often remained employed long after they were judged to be significant members of the community. In his advice to the old, the Puritan minister Cotton Mather, for example, admonished his elderly parishioners to withdraw from active employment. "Old folks," he wrote in 1726:

> often can't endure to be judged less able than ever they were for public appearances, or to be put out of offices. But good, sir, be so wise as to disappear of your own accord, as soon as you lawfully may. Be glad of a dismission from any post that would have called for your activities (Mather, 1726).

For those who followed Mather's advice, however, colonial society offered few supports. If they withdrew from labor, they had to rely upon their own savings, the contributions of their children, or the town's benevolence.

As historians uncovered a different view of preindustrial work and wealth, they also came to challenge the idea that industrialization caused the skills of the old to be degraded, leading the elderly directly into poverty and unemployment. Social scientists had argued that labor patterns of old men ran in direct inverse proportion to the rate of industrialization. The more industrial and urbanized an area, they contended, the less likely the old were to be employed; the more impoverished they became. This conclusion was easily supported by the writings of early 20th-century aging advocates. With industrialization, these experts had argued, the old were relegated to the "industrial scrap heap" (Todd, 1915; see also Devine, 1898, 1904, 1909; Epstein, 1922, 1929; Rubinow, 1913, 1934; Squier, 1912). Companies established arbitrary age-restrictions that rejected qualified workers simply because they were of advanced age.

According to these early experts no institution better symbolized the dire plight of the aged worker in industrializing society than the almshouse. Once home to a wide variety of inmates, it sheltered increasing numbers of aged individuals who had little chance of prospering in modern society. Espousing an argument that would be supported by both pension planners and social scientists decades later, the early advocates for the old contended that the almshouse proved that the elderly could only be rescued from the impoverishment of modern industrial society by a broadly based plan of national assistance. Eventually, they contended, all elderly individuals would require federal assistance (Pennsylvania Commission on Old Age Pensions, 1919).

Using a wide variety of sources from personal reminisces to labor force statistics, historians came to question the direct relationship between industrial growth and retirement, as well as the impact of age bias in the creation of retirement. Ironically, as Brian Gratton and others have pointed out, industrialized areas were not alone in reflecting high rates of retirement. In rich farm areas where older farmers sold their land and withdrew to small towns, rates of retirement actually were higher than in industrial states (Gratton, 1987; Moen, 1987). Moreover, several historians questioned the notion that the retirement of the old increased steadily from 1860 to 1930. According to Brian Gratton as well as Roger Ransom and Richard Sutch, retirement may have remained remarkably flat throughout that period. Ransom and Sutch argued, in fact, that in some areas the rate of retirement might actually have declined (Ransom & Sutch, 1986, 1989). Only with Social Security did the proportion of aged workers significantly and steadily increase.

Historians also came to question whether industrialization led directly to old-age impoverishment. While some aged craftsmen lost control of their work, other laborers found their income significantly increased. Using early 20th-century bank, home, and labor force records, scholars uncovered a seemingly remarkable reality: a large proportion of wage-earning elders were far more economically secure than their counterparts decades earlier. Where previous generations of aged workers had little savings or material goods, the old of the early 20th century were more likely to accumulate a small, though significant, amount of wealth (Haber & Gratton, 1993).

But what of the statistics from the almshouse that had become so much a part of the argument proving aged impoverishment? The idea that industrialization caused great dependency among the old seemed an easy explanation for the creation of the welfare state and the passage of Social Security. Yet in arguing that industrialization did not impoverish the majority of the old, historians also came to question the validity of almshouse statistics. Turning from a simple reporting of the data, scholars began to explore both the context of these figures and motivations behind their formation. Advocates for the old, it appeared, had purposefully excluded the successful old in their analyses of old-age poverty and focused upon those who suffered impoverishment as they aged. And while a significant proportion of the old did (as the aging advocates contended) experience distress and poverty in old age, other elders did not fit this characterization. They were neither unemployed nor displaced from their families. The rhetoric of advocates for the old clearly exaggerated the extent of impoverishment among the elderly. Most aged individuals simply did not end their lives in the almshouse. In fact, throughout the late 19th and early 20th centuries, the institutionalized proportion of the old remained rather stable at 2%. The increasing percentage of aged individuals within almshouses resulted from removing younger inmates to other institutions (Haber, 1993). Nor were the overwhelming majority of aged individuals dependent on relief. Industrialization, in fact, had served to enrich a significant proportion of the old who came to believe that retirement and separate households were attainable goals. When the Great Depression threatened these ideals, they (and their children) eagerly supported the formation of the welfare state.

These historical findings challenged traditional assumptions about the history of aging. At least in the United States, mass retirement appeared to be an aspiration of those elderly who had attained financial security. The more economically comfortable—rather than the most despised—voluntarily withdrew from work. In the late 19th and early 20th century, the diaries and letters of the old reveal that, for many, their aim was not to remain employed, but to spend their last years with decreased responsibilities or in relative leisure (Haber & Gratton, 1993). Given this perspective, historians came to view retirement as a symbol of its security, rather than an indication of the debasement of age. Withdrawal from work had finally become a goal not only for the very rich, but also for the majority of aged workers. Beneath the statistics of retirement lay a positive value for old age far different from the dire situation theorists had once proposed.

Finally, historians applied the same humanistic approach to understanding the changing attitudes toward the old. Previously, models such as modernization had argued that preindustrial societies honored the old for their wisdom and experience. In these gerontocracies, the old exerted unchallenged political and social power. Then, industrialization robbed the old of their skills and prestige. Categorized as useless and outdated, the elderly became the most despised members of society (Simmons, 1945, 1960).

In studying the actual status of the old in colonial America, however, historians first discovered the limitations of social science theories. Neither the words of the old themselves nor the timing of perceived changes neatly fit the predicted "gerontocracy." Instead, scholars uncovered an array of ambiguities that lay beneath the assumptions of prestige and power. Although social scientists had presupposed that the elderly in the colonial era were uniformly esteemed, the actual words and treatment of the elderly often challenged this assumption. Few colonial elders actually thought of themselves as powerful or in command; even the most respected lamented their loss of power and deference. In the early 18th century, for example, Increase Mather, once the pillar of colonial society, spent his old age complaining of his declining status. "My aged father," wrote his son Cotton, "too much lays to Heart; the withdrawal of a vain, proud foolish people from him his Age (Mather, 1912, p. 617). The elder Mather lamented that it was his work and activity, rather than his age, that had once granted him prestige. His new status was simply another test from God to show his power of resignation. "If God will have it so," he wrote, "his holy will must be humbly and patiently submitted to" (Mather, 1716). According to the preindustrial model, the last decades of Mather and others of his generation should have been most powerful. In reality, however, their own words revealed that they were often filled with doubt and dissatisfaction. George Washington, Benjamin Franklin, Thomas Jefferson, and John Adams all expressed complaints about the physical and social changes that accompanied their old age (Fischer, 1977).

As colonial society did not uniformly esteem the wealthy old, communities awarded even less prestige to the aged poor. Although the impoverished old lived in a world that repeatedly argued that individuals of advanced age should receive respect, their destitute state clearly precluded any deference. Those who were poor were rarely addressed by both their first and last names; they were simply called "old Moore, or "old Hammond"; others were characterized as "touchy, peevish, angry, and forward" (Bridge, 1679; Demos, 1978). While their rich counterparts were given honored positions in the meetinghouse, the poor sat in the rear, away from all symbols of power (Demos, 1978; Stone, 1977). The most impoverished of the old, in fact, were often escorted out of town, admonished to return to their original towns of settlement (Record Commissioners of the City of Boston, 1701–1715, 1884, p. 57; 1716–1736, 1885, p. 76).

Colonial diaries further confirmed that the ideal view of aging propounded by leaders often differed from actual treatment. Although sermons and speeches often glorified the old, these verbal images were largely prescriptive in nature. The minister who admonished his congregation to respect the old, or the laws that dictated continued support, may have been more prescriptive than real. Time and again, aged parents actually complained of their treatment at the hands of the young. In their own eyes, their advanced age proved to be more of a burden than a benefit (Record Commissioners of the City of Boston, 1884; Willard, 1726, p. 608). Failing to receive the respect they assumed was theirs, they even resorted to legal contract and civil law for their protection. The assumption that old age equaled great power in preindustrial society was then further complicated by historians who studied issues of gender (Gratton & Haber, 1993). Advocates of the existence of a colonial gerontocracy based their assumptions on the power of men; they hardly considered the roles of aged women. Yet historians found that elderly women in colonial America did not exert the control or wield the power that was linked to their male counterparts. Upon the death of their husbands, aged women were often restricted in wills to a specific room in the house or command of limited resources. While some exerted unusual control over their offspring and their estates, many ended their lives submissive to their adult children or dependent on the relief of the community. In colonial America, the term "aged widow" implied neither authority nor control, but simply sympathy and benevolence. "A state of widowhood," Cotton Mather decreed, "is a state of affliction . . ." (Mather, quoted by Keyssar, 1974, p. 99). And, in the early republic, as Terri Premo has shown, a good old age for women did not necessarily mean one filled with power and control but with strong ties to family and religion (Premo, 1990).

As cultural evidence questioned the notion of colonial power, it also challenged the idea that a dramatic change in attitudes occurred with modernization. Theorists had argued that as long as America was an agricultural, rural society, the old were respected; their displacement came with the urban and industrial transformation. When examining the colonial and early republic artistic images of old age, however, David Hackett Fischer concluded that pivotal changes in belief and depiction occurred well *before* urban and industrial change. By 1820, he argued, family portraits no longer placed the aged man as the superior figure in the family group; he took his place below the middle aged. Moreover, the accepted clothes, and the venerable white periwig that had once complemented the figure of the old, were replaced by styles that gave public display to their frailties. Even the new words and phrases that began to fill the language spoke of old age in less than positive tones. Old people became *fogies, crones,* and *gaffers,* increasingly pejorative terms to describe individuals of great age (Fischer, 1977).

These cultural symbols led Fischer to challenge the prevailing theory that a change in attitudes arose with the development of urban and industrial growth. By placing the transformation before 1840, he found little tie to the burgeoning American cities or rapidly expanding industrial work force. Rather, he located the source of the elders' displacement in culture. In America, after the Revolution, youth and vitality replaced age and experience as desirable qualities. To be young was to be part of a new and important generation, to be old was to be nothing more than outdated.

While disagreeing with Fischer's timing, W. Andrew Achenbaum also challenged the social science model. Achenbaum concluded that this transformation could not be linked to industrialization but to cultural ideals. He argued that perceptions of aging were altered well before the elderly's economic displacement or their demographic transformation. "Ideas about the worth and functions of the elderly," Achenbaum wrote, "have a life of their own: the unprecedented denigration of older Americans arose independently of the most observable change in their actual status" (Achenbaum, 1978, p. 86).

From a humanistic perspective, then, the broad model of gerontocratic society destroyed by urban and industrial growth seemed questionable. Not only had cultural investigations of early America raised questions about the very existence of a colonial gerontocracy, but they also allowed historians to distinguish between prescription and reality. While the culture gave voice to ideals of respect, the actual behavior of individuals appeared far more equivocal. Regardless of the era, old age was never a time that gained unquestioned respect or adoration.

Yet this investigation also led to a new and important finding in aging history, previously hidden by broad generalizations about social change. Although historians disagreed over when attitudes altered in America, and whether there was a "revolution" in beliefs, it seemed clear that an important cultural transformation had occurred. While colonial scholars had uncovered negative attitudes toward old age, the expression of these beliefs, ultimately, was not culturally acceptable. The lectures of ministers and the laws passed by magistrates made clear that society still gave support to the notion of respect and deference—even if people failed to behave correctly. What had changed in American society over time, then, was not the existence of these beliefs, but their *acceptance* by the culture as legitimate expressions. In the 17th century, those who openly voiced disdain for the weakness and debility of the old, were admonished for their behavior; by the 19th century these expressions were no longer inappropriate but had come to seem completely legitimate. Why, then, did a society that had once at least verbally applauded age later come to see it as a hindrance?

These again were not questions that could be answered by qualitative analysis or broad-scale social models. They relied upon the exploration of literature, religion, and popular culture. In *The Journey of Life,*

Thomas Cole argued that the key to this verbal alteration was the religious movement known as the Second Great Awakening and its inherent middle-class values (Cole, 1992). In the early 19th century, according to Cole, the exhortation of ministers clearly changed. Rather than admonishing their congregations to respect age, they praised the vitality and energy of the young. While the adolescent could be saved and perfected, society could offer the old little except consolation and relief. Cole disagreed with Fischer that the American Revolution held the key to the new image of old age. "If old age in America had only suffered the usual misfortune of being identified with an order," Cole wrote, "the impact might have been short-lived. But old age not only symbolized the 18th century world of patriarchy and hierarchical authority, it also represented an embarrassment to the new morality of self control" (Cole, 1986, p. 61). The value inherent in old age had disappeared, to be replaced by an adoration of youth.

In *Beyond Sixty-Five,* Carole Haber also explained the 19th-century cultural acceptance of ageism, but linked it instead to the rise of a variety of scientifically based professions. Based on the medical model of aging, she argued, social workers, statisticians, doctors, and businessmen increasingly came to see and speak of the old as debilitated and disabled (Haber, 1983). Haber disagreed with Achenbaum, however, that these ideas were disconnected entirely from social and economic trends. The key figures in creating the new images of the old were those who dealt directly with the old in a variety of urban and industrial settings. Excluding the old who were successful or settled, they focused on hospital wards, almshouses, and relief roles in which they discovered an isolated, ailing, and destitute elderly. This population and its extreme needs led to the conviction that all aged persons were impoverished and in need of professional intervention.

Studies of attitudes toward the old also revealed the limitations of splitting the history of the old into broad categories of pre- and postindustrial society. According to Carole Haber and Brian Gratton, not only had family and work patterns changed significantly after the enactment of Social Security, but these trends were accompanied by a new set of attitudes about the behavior of the old (Haber & Gratton, 1993). Gone were notions that the old could not escape disease and dependence. Recent publications to and by the old argued that the best and easily attainable old age fostered independence and autonomy. Commentators sang the praises of financially secure old people who climbed mountains, won triathlons or (most recently) journeyed into space. While this new paradigm of proper aging had little room for those who suffered from illness or weakness, it stressed the unlimited possibilities open to individuals entering the "third age" (Fahey & Holstein, 1993). There seemed little doubt that the old could now "successfully age" and live meaningfully for years after retirement and the departure of their kin (see, for example, Avert, 1987; Bellak, 1975; Belsky, 1988; Linkletter, 1988).

The findings of historians have clearly challenged long-standing social science theories. By incorporating an understanding of the *goals* and *values* of the elderly and their families, historians retrieved them from the onslaught of irreversible economic trends. Central to this interpretation, as we have seen, was a consideration of the elderly's own definition of how they wished to live. This approach, of course, was not completely divorced from the tools of social science or the insights of its scholars. The discovery that the old were not uniformly impoverished nor abandoned by their families depended on analysis of census reports, residence patterns, property listings, savings records, and a host of other data. The challenge historians have then faced was to formulate an interpretation of the past that correlated this statistical evidence with the beliefs expressed by the elderly and their families.

This, of course, has not been, nor is it an easy task. At times, the rhetoric of the old and their advocates has clearly contradicted their actual condition. Moreover, the elderly themselves never were a homogeneous group with uniform desires and experiences. These complexities, then, underscore the task for the next generation of historians. They must explain the difference between the varied realities of aging and the rhetoric that has surrounded it. They need to understand the values behind the data, whether they are issues of work, family structure, wealth or residence. And, most important, in the search to understand aging in the past, scholars must rescue the old from aggregate statistics without assuming that the reminiscences of one individual or even a small group characterize all aged individuals. Obviously, old age does not have a single meaning to all individuals, but reflects a variety of values, ideas, and experiences. Yet, as studies have shown, such findings have true implications for understanding both the experiences of the old and their status. The work of historians, therefore, promises to turn a once unchallenged and rather irrelevant past into a far more complex and meaningful narrative.

REFERENCES

Abel, E. K. (1992). Parental dependence and filial responsibility. *Gerontologist, 32*(4), 519–536.

Achenbaum, W. A. (1978). *Old age in the new land.* Baltimore: The Johns Hopkins Press.

Anonymous. (1931). Old age intestate. *Harper's.* May, pp. 712–715.

Atchley, R. C. (1994). *Social forces and aging,* 7th edition. Belmont, CA: Wadsworth Publishing Co.

Avert, A. C. (1987). *Successful aging.* New York: Ballantine Books.

Bellak, L. (1975). *The best years of your life.* New York: Atheneum.

Belsky, J. K. (1988). *Here tomorrow.* Baltimore: The Johns Hopkins Press.

Bridge, W. (1679). *A word to the aged.* Boston: John Foster.

Burgess, E. W. (1960). *Aging in western society.* Chicago: University of Chicago Press.

Clark, M., & Anderson, B. G. (1967). *Culture and aging.* Springfield, MA: C. C. Thomas.

Cole, T. (1986). Putting off the old. In D. Van Tassal & P. Stearns (Eds.), *Old age in a bureaucratic society.* New York: Greenwood Press.

Cole, T. (1992). *The journey of life.* New York: Cambridge University Press.

Cowgill, D. O. (1972). *Aging and modernization.* New York: Appleton-Century Crofts.

Crandall, Richard C. (1980). *Gerontology.* Reading, MA: Addison-Wesley.

Demos, J. (1978). Old age in early New England. In M. Gordon (Ed.), *The American family in socio-historical perspective* (2nd ed.). New York: St. Martin's Press.

Devine, E. T. (1898). *Economics.* New York: Macmillan Company.

Devine, E. T. (1904). *The principles of relief.* New York: Macmillan Company.

Devine, E. T. (1909). *Misery and its causes.* New York: Macmillan Company.

Epstein, A. (1922). *Facing old age.* New York: Alfred Knopf.

Epstein, A. (1929). *The problem of old age pensions in industry.* Harrisburg, PA: Pennsylvania Old Age Commission.

Fahey, C. J., & Holstein, M. (1993). Toward a philosophy of the third age. In T. Cole, W. A. Achenbaum, P. L. Jacobi, & R. Kastenbaum (Eds.), *Voices and visions of aging.* New York: Springer Publishing Co.

Fischer, D. H. (1977). *Growing old in America.* New York: Oxford University Press.

Gratton, B. (1987). The labor force participation of older men. *Journal of Social History, 20,* 689–710.

Gratton, B., & Haber, C. (1993). In search of intimacy at a distance. *Journal of Aging Studies, 49,* 183–194.

Greven, P. J. (1970). *Four generations.* Ithaca, NY and London: Cornell University Press.

Haber, C. (1983). *Beyond sixty-five.* New York: Cambridge University Press.

Haber, C. (1993). Over the hill to the poorhouse. In K. W. Schaie & W. A. Achenbaum (Eds.), *Societal impact on aging.* New York: Springer Publishing Co.

Haber, C., & Gratton, B. (1993). *Old age and the search for security.* Bloomington: Indiana University Press.

Keyssar, A. (1974). Widowhood in Eighteenth-Century Massachusetts. *Perspectives in American History, 8,* 83–119.

Linkletter, A. (1988). *Old age is not for sissies.* New York: Viking Press.

Markides, K. S., & Cooper, C. L. (1987). Industrialization and retirement. In Markides & Cooper (Eds.), *Retirement in industrialized societies.* New York: John Wiley and Sons.

Mather, C. (1726). *A brief essay on the glory of aged piety.* Boston: S. Kneeland and T. Freen.

Mather, C. (1912). *Diary of Cotton Mather, Vol. 2.* Boston: Massachusetts Historical Society.

Mather, I. (1716). *Two discourses.* Boston: B. Green.

Modell, J., & Hareven, T. (1978). Urbanization and the malleable household. In M. Gordon (Ed.), *The American family in socio-historical perspective* (2nd ed.). New York: St. Martin's Press.

Moen, J. (1987). The labor of older men. *Journal of Economic History, 47*(3), 761–767.

Pennsylvania Commission on Old Age Pensions. (1919). *Report.* Harrisburg, PA: Kuhn Publishing.

Premo, T. (1990). *Winter friends.* Urbana: University of Illinois Press.

Ransom, R., & Sutch, R. (1986). The labor of older Americans. *The Journal of Economic History, 46*(1), 1–30.

Ransom, R., & Sutch, R. (1989). The trend in the rate of labor force participation of older men, 1870–1930. *The Journal of Economic History, 49.*

Record Commissioners of the City of Boston. (1884). *Report containing the records of the Boston selectmen, 1701–1715.* Boston: Rockwell & Churchill.

Record Commissioners of the City of Boston. (1885). *Report containing the records of the Boston selectmen, 1716–1736.* Boston: Rockwell & Churchill.

Rosow, I. (1974). *Socialization to old age.* Berkeley: University of California Press.

Rubinow, I. M. (1913). *Social insurance.* New York: Henry Holt & Co.

Rubinow, I. M. (1934). *The quest for security.* New York: Henry Holt & Co.

Ruggles, S. (1987). *Prolonged connections.* Madison: University of Wisconsin Press.

Ryan, M. (1981). *Cradle of the middle class.* New York: Cambridge University Press.

Simmons, L. W. (1945). *The role of the aged in primitive society.* New Haven, CT: Yale University Press.

Simmons, L. W. (1960). Aging in preindustrial societies. In C. Tibbits (Ed.), *Handbook of social gerontology.* Chicago: University of Chicago Press.

Smith, D. S. (1978). Old age and the "great transformation." In S. F. Spicker, K. M. Woodward, & D. D. Van Tassel (Eds.), *Aging and the elderly.* Atlantic Highlands, NJ: Humanities Press.

Squier, L. W. (1912). *Old age dependency in the United States.* New York: Macmillan.

Stone, L. (1977). Walking over Grandma. *New York Review of Books, 24*(8), 10–16.

Todd, A. J. (1915). Old age and the industrial scrap heap. *American Statistical Association 14*(3), 550–557.

Ulrich, L. T. (1991). *A midwife's tale.* New York: Random House.

Waters, J. J. (1976). Patrimony, succession, and social stability. *Perspectives in American History, 10,* 131–160.

Willard, S. (1726). *A complete (sic) body of divinity* (Sermon 180). Boston: B. Eliot and D. Henchman.

3

The Future of Literary Gerontology

Anne M. Wyatt-Brown *

Literary studies in gerontology have expanded dramatically since the publication of the first edition of the *Handbook of the Humanities and Aging* (Cole, Tassel, & Kastenbaum, 1992). A number of recent books—most notably Kathleen Woodward's *Aging and Its Discontents* (1991) and Margaret Morganroth Gullette's *Declining to Decline* (1997)— have moved literary gerontology from its position as a relative newcomer in Humanities and Aging to a higher stage of scholarly maturity. Growth has occurred in ancillary areas. For example, in 1993 a new book series, Age Studies, began at the University Press of Virginia. Another positive sign was the emergence in March 1996 of the *Journal of Aging and Identity.* A periodical devoted exclusively to humanities and aging, it welcomes essays on literature. Moreover, in 1996 Kathleen Woodward began administering a 3-year Rockefeller grant for Age Studies for the Center for Twentieth Century Studies at the University of Wisconsin, Milwaukee. At the end of the first year she organized a conference at the center, "Women and Aging: Bodies, Cultures, Generations." Revised versions of many of the papers have appeared in *Figuring Age: Women, Bodies, Generations* (Woodward, 1999). The question remains how to take advantage of the public interest that has been stirred up by such innovations, without losing the ability to serve our original audience, clinicians in gerontology for whom literature has been an important resource for many years.

* Many thanks to Steve Weiland and Margaret Morganroth Gullette who suggested additional material to include.

Since the *Handbook's* first review of literary gerontology (Wyatt-Brown, 1992b), cultural studies have broadened our interests. Considerably more attention is now being paid to issues of diversity, the interplay of age, gender, race, class, and ethnicity. Of course, humanistic gerontologists share many of our interests, but few of their practitioners analyze literary texts or employ theories of reading and writing. As a result of the shift, some of the sections of the first review have been either altered beyond easy recognition or dropped for the time being. At this point five categories dominate: (1) literary attitudes toward aging, largely examined from a postmodern sociological perspective; (2) late style and creativity across the life course, using psychoanalytic and biographical perspectives; (3) cultural studies of aging, in particular those that analyze the politics of decline and progress discourses; (4) narrative studies of life review and guided autobiography; and (5) explorations of emotions.

POSTMODERNISM AND
ATTITUDES TOWARD AGING

Early scholars in literary gerontology devoted their energies to countering the negative stereotyping of the elderly that they found in literature and the popular culture. Far more sophisticated versions of that activity have appeared in recent years. British sociologists Mike Featherstone and Mike Hepworth have contributed their knowledge of postmodern theory to literature with good results. For example, Hepworth (1996) has written an amusing and insightful study of Richmal Crompton's stories about William and his friends, the Outlaws. In these English children's stories, which appeared between 1919 and 1970, elders and children outwit members of "the sandwich generation," their rather stodgy keepers, and reassert their independence even if only for a short time. Although infantilization is unpleasant when imposed upon anyone, in these stories the children, together with members of their grandparents' generation, deliberately regress as a means of resistance. They create an alliance which, as Bertram Wyatt-Brown (1993) tells us, southern short-story writer Peter Taylor examines from a more ironic perspective in "In the Miro District." Identifying with childhood can at moments be a means of "recovering or sustaining an essential sense of enduring personal identity" (Hepworth, 1996, p. 427), a point which Gloria Fromm (1993) also made in her moving essay on Dorothy Richardson's "Excursion" and "Visitor."

Another stimulating and lively essay is Hannah Zeilig's "The Uses of Literature in the Study of Older People" (1997). Like most sociologists, she assumes "literature can be used as a means of interpreting society"

(p. 40). Fortunately her sophisticated analyses do not ignore the literary quality of what she discusses. As a result her balanced reading of *King Lear* enhances an understanding of the play. Moreover, she sensibly warns against using literature to make "grandiose claims for the historical, psychological or other insights which may be gained by reading a certain novel" (p. 47). On the other hand, some might temper her stricture against treating literary characters as if they had inner lives. E. M. Forster was asked if his novels ever took a surprising turn and replied diffidently, "Of course, that wonderful thing, a character running away with you—which happens to everyone—that's happened to me, I'm afraid" (Furbank & Haskell, 1958, p. 28). Likewise literary critic Bernard Paris (1997, p. xi) argues forcefully that one can analyze an "imagined human being," provided the theory is appropriate. In some cases writers deliberately erase the boundaries between fiction and autobiography. Regardless of these caveats, Zeilig has offered a provocative argument that encourages useful debate.

One especially fruitful idea that sociologists Featherstone and Hepworth (1991) have contributed to literary studies is the concept of the "mask of ageing." Drawing on Gubrium's study of Alzheimer's disease, they find that elders unconsciously develop a mask that separates their youthful inner selves from their decaying bodies. Featherstone and Hepworth assume that most elders prefer their young mind to their frail bodies. Subjects interviewed by Sharon Kaufman in *The Ageless Self* (1986) provide evidence for their conviction. Most elders may share this preference, but one's feelings depend upon the emotional hardiness of the internal self.

Many of the essays in Kathleen Woodward's (1999) book build upon a combination of postmodernism and feminism, thereby expanding the horizons of literary gerontology. For instance, Nancy Miller (1999), in an elegant essay discusses the need for older women to take up cultural space. Teresa Mangum's (1999) chapter on Lewis Carroll suggests that his negative depiction of the Duchess and the Red Queen, along with Tenniel's line drawings, affects children's developing ideas about older women. The King is attractive and mild-mannered while the two older women are ugly and frightening. No wonder young people regard older women as dragons, who must be conquered, as Gullette (1988) has observed.

LATE STYLE AND CREATIVITY IN THE LIFE COURSE

Simone de Beauvoir's *The Coming of Age* (1970) was the first comprehensive study of late style and creativity in old age. She offered mixed evidence in her account of famous male artists, writers, and musicians. In deep old age, she related, "some aged men continue the struggle with a passionate heroism . . . delighting in a progress that must soon be cut short by death, the carrying on the attempt to outdo oneself in full knowledge and acceptance of one's finitude" (pp. 409–410). More commonly, however, the aging writer "often has nothing left to say" (*Ibid.,* p. 406). Largely because of its negative findings, *The Coming of Age* has been ignored by literary gerontologists, but Beauvoir's breadth of scholarship could provide a model for our work. Happy exceptions are Kathleen Woodward (1991), who has written about the disparity between Beauvoir's theories and her productive old age, and Margaret Morganroth Gullette (in press). Gullette criticizes Beauvoir's findings but praises her argument that our attitudes toward aging are social not biological in origin. In fact, she uses Beauvoir's idea of social construction to attack the very decline theory of aging that Beauvoir endorsed. Stephen Katz in *Disciplining Old Age* (1996) has pondered Beauvoir's failure to influence gerontologists. He comments upon her unfamiliar mixing of philosophical, artistic, literary, and autobiographical sources with sociological and economic ones. . . ." According to Katz, her negative assessments of old age and her unconventional tactics put "her work outside of gerontology and perhaps dangerously close to exposing its borders" (1996, p. 108).

Timing also hurt the reception of her book. Not only was Beauvoir 20 years ahead of the trend of genre crossing, but she also had no way of anticipating the dramatic change in publishing that occurred in the 1970s after her book was launched. Ever mindful of changing demographics, editors and publishers began to encourage the publication of works with old-age themes and heroes in response to the increase of elderly members of the population. No longer would middle-aged writers have to worry, as E. M. Forster did in 1927 after the success of *A Passage to India,* "a *middle-aged* novel, i.e., by myself as an M.A., does attract [me]. Would anyone want to read it though? . . . I must get nearer myself, but how? how get out my wit and wisdom without this pretense that it is through the young and on behalf of the young. Puberty-sauce—hiding the true flavor of M.A. dishes" (Gardner, 1985, p. 29).

In contemporary fiction, according to Constance Rooke (1992) "old people . . . are considerably more likely to be granted their fair share of the author's gaze and the available print" (p. 241). Even fiction that centers on young or middle aged characters, such as Anne Tyler's *A Patchwork Planet* (1998) and Alison Lurie's *The Last Resort* (1998), pays close attention to the elderly ones. Their fate engages the attention of the young protagonist and readers alike. Partly in response to this marketplace change, Dean Simonton (1990) has introduced the idea of "career age" (p. 105). He suggests that those who enter their professions late, including women, may have their creative fulfillment much later than those who have been laboring since their 20s. Daycare for children and modern medicine, he notes, can ameliorate the conditions for creative women and older people. A good example is British novelist Penelope Fitzgerald who began writing fiction in her 60s as her husband lay dying. Now in her 80s she still publishes.

The first comprehensive study of the work of famous male artists in old age since Beauvoir's *The Coming of Age* (1970) is Amir Cohen-Shalev's "Both Worlds at Once: Art in Old Age" (in progress). It promises to be of great interest. His study of old age style in art, music, and writing will challenge Beauvoir's negative assessment of elderly artists. Articles which contain earlier versions of his chapters, including one on Ibsen (1992) and another on Beckett (Cohen-Shalev & Rapoport, 1993), have appeared in the *Journal of Aging Studies* and the *International Journal of Aging and Human Development.*

Biographical studies of aging make an important contribution to our understanding of late-life creativity. Kathleen Woodward's *Aging and Its Discontents* (1991) provides a successful psychoanalytic interpretation of Freud's view of aging. Her work contributes to literary theory, psychoanalysis, and gerontology. She examines the roots of Freud's ageist assumptions but resists demeaning Freud in the process. Woodward argues persuasively that Freud's phobic attitudes toward aging resulted from his ambivalent affection for his father and most of the women in his life, especially his mother, mother-in-law, and his wife. Instead of criticizing Freud for not sharing the views of humanistic gerontologists of our generation and younger, she refuses to exaggerate the claims for old-age wisdom. Her book, widely cited, makes an enduring contribution to the field. Biographical essays examining creativity in old age have also appeared in recent years. Some scholars challenge the proposition that poetry is a young man's game by examining the lives of female poets. Marcia Aldrich (1993) argues that Louise Bogan derailed her career at the menopause because she associated poetry with sexual allure. In contrast, Diana Hume George's (1993) moving essay on Maxine Kumin's elegies to Anne Sexton demonstrates that late midlife can be an extraordinarily productive time in the life of a poet. The two essays together demonstrate that to remain productive in later life a poet needs a broad conception of appropriate topics.

Trauma—severe illness, tragedy, and impending death—has also been the source of creativity for some writers. The poet Josephine Miles wrote very little about the difficulties of living with degenerative arthritis when she was young, but, according to Carolyn Smith (1993), in her later poems she speaks "as an aging woman about the concerns such a woman has regarding bodily pain, disintegration, role loss, and dying" (p. 291). Poet Virginia Hamilton Adair was blind and in her eighties when she finally agreed to publish a collection of poems, *Ants on the Melon* (Adair, 1996). She had written poetry throughout her long life and at midlife published a few in literary magazines. Her husband, Douglass, however, taught her "about the corrosive effects of ambition" by his excessive striving for recognition and his suicide after 35 years of marriage (Alvarez, 1996, p. 5). As a result, she made no effort to publish a collection until the poet Robert Mezey (Mezey, 1996) helped her organize a book and find a publisher. My study (Wyatt-Brown, 1992a) of British novelist Barbara Pym demonstrates that *Quartet in Autumn* (1977),[1] her novel of retirement, grew out of her own struggles with breast cancer and a stroke. Surprisingly, the beleaguered writer was able to revive her moribund career when she realized that serious illnesses and retirement could provide new topics for her novels. Moreover, Pym's last novel, *A Few Green Leaves* (1980), written while she was dying from yet another cancer, this time of the stomach, contains a farewell to life and art in which her characteristic comic sensibility remains undiminished.

Impending death can also accelerate the experience of aging in relatively young people. A friend of mine, Claire Philip (1995), began keeping a journal and writing poetry in her forties when the encroachments of cancer made it impossible for her to maintain her career as a psychiatric social worker. Besides her newfound creativity, she wrote articles in social work journals on the ethics of disclosure when therapists know they are dying (Wyatt-Brown, 1995). We organized a panel on her work at the 1994 Gerontological Society of America and later published the essays in the *Journal of Aging Studies* (Vol. 9, 4). As Carolyn Smith (1995) points out, Philip's poems contributed to a genre known as the "art of dying." Rather than writing about "how we die," Philip explores "how we live when we realize we will die" (p. 347). More recently, Edward Said (1998), a prominent literary critic at Columbia University, began writing a memoir about childhood in Palestine, when he began chemotherapy treatment for leukemia. Only recently did he realize the conjunction of the dates (Scott, 1998).

CULTURAL STUDIES OF AGING

Cultural studies of aging have been a particularly productive area in recent years. One of the most important to humanities and aging is Thomas Cole's *The Journey of Life* (1992). He combines prodigious historical research on the development of ideas of aging in the United States with a strong sense of personal commitment. His *Journey of Life* includes literature and art, as well as brief descriptions of the lives of famous men. An important text for Cole is John Bunyan's *Pilgrim's*

Progress. Not only does he discuss at length the well-known journey of Christian, but he includes the section about Christiana, Christian's wife, which few other than specialists will know. Cole's participation in a medical humanities department greatly enhances the breadth and profundity of his study. Working in a hospital with dying patients makes him specially sensitive to the ethical issues that trouble practitioners.

Lois Banner's (1992) *In Full Flower* provides a useful and compendious historical study of attitudes of history throughout western history. Unlike Cole, she concentrates on the lives of women. For example, when discussing medical breakthroughs and aging attitudes in the late 19th century, she argues that Cole's (1992) "otherwise admirable study of life-cycle thought" has paid "insufficient attention to women's experience" (p. 279). Her commitment is partly personal. As she points out, she began to explore aging issues after she fell in love with a younger man. A feminist historian, she quickly turned to cultural studies to examine the history of relationships between aging women and younger men, but her project expanded into the development of attitudes toward aging women in western culture. The book, readable and well researched, explores the interconnection of films and literature. Of particular interest is her reconstruction of Chaucer's Wife of Bath "as historical prototype" (Banner, 1992, p. 129).

Some works written for an extensive audience have ignored literary gerontology. One is Betty Friedan's *The Fountain of Age* (1993). She writes as an advocate to encourage elders, particularly women, to celebrate their strengths rather than bemoan their weaknesses, to refuse to play the role of victim accurately described by Achenbaum (1998). In the early 1980s she attended several literature panels at the Gerontological Society of America but makes no reference to our studies of creativity in older writers. Two studies of the rise of gerontology as a discipline by Achenbaum *Crossing Frontiers* (1995), and Katz *Disciplining Old Age* (1996), examine the development of gerontology as a scientific enterprise. Neither pays much attention to any area of humanities and aging. Achenbaum briefly compliments a few researchers in humanities, while Katz mentions Simone de Beauvoir, *The Coming of Age,* but little else.

Finally, one of the most lively and argumentative works to appear recently is Margaret Morganroth Gullette's *Declining to Decline* (1997). She intends her study of "cultural combat" to be "a survival manual and guide to resistance" (p. 18), but it transcends the genre. She creates a new kind of nonfiction by combining passionate commitment, personal accounts which theory allows her to universalize, and sensitive and insightful discussions of literature. Her purpose is to remove life writing from the area of "secret history." Instead she encourages her readers to consider other factors which have influenced their lives:

history, cohort, generation, social movements and other social change, structural/economic pressures, biosocial forces, media, and literary influences. If we do, then we will be more likely to produce "freer narrative, narrative not forced into decline models by the culture or progress narratives by the positive aging forces" (Gullette, e-mail, September 24, 1998). Gullette's activist view of Jane Eyre encouraged her to devote herself to resisting decline stories of the midlife. Her chapter on female midlife progress heroes also contributes to humanistic gerontology. She writes about characters who repudiate sex after many unsuccessful relationships without adapting the somewhat depressed tone that occasionally creeps into Carolyn Heilbrun's account of the failure of the romantic myth to sustain older women in *The Last Gift of Time* (1997).

Gullette's energetic championing of midlife progress is extremely welcome. Yet as a group we should not overlook the strengths of the very old whose situation is more problematic. Each of us experiences episodes of frailty, and we need to remember Ronald Blythe's (1979) sustaining conviction that those who are no longer energetic still have the capacity to make "something from the ashes." An excellent example of that buoyance is British literary critic John Bayley's (1998) cheerful account of life with his wife, the late novelist Iris Murdoch. During the years that she suffered from Alzheimer's disease, he was her sole caretaker. Yet, according to his "Elegy for Iris," there were moments when he still has "the illusion, which fortunate Alzheimer's partners must feel at such times, that life is just the same, has never changed" (*Ibid.,* p. 61). Even more than the middle-aged men and women to whom culture has given negative messages, the frail elderly need champions, those who can encourage them to create something out of "one's frailty and slightness, the knowing how short a distance one can go—and then going it" (Blythe, 1979, p. 18).

NARRATIVE STUDIES AND GUIDED AUTOBIOGRAPHY

Narrative studies and guided autobiography have also been a fertile field in recent years. It has allowed scholars from many disciplines to contribute their expertise and expand their repertoire. An acknowledged leader in this research is Jaber Gubrium. His work pertains to literary studies, furnishing a perspective from which we can better understand biographies and autobiographies. His prize-winning *Speaking of Life* (1993) provides an impressive model for writing about the lives of nursing home residents, who otherwise would remain "faces in the hall, without any stories" (p. 11). Gubrium's empathic interviewing technique encouraged his subjects to speak their minds, and subsequent interviews reveal that they had actively constructed their roles, even though physical problems limited their autonomy. He concludes that the questionnaire was "biographically active" (*Ibid.*, p. 182). The interviews, he notes, stirred the emotions of both the respondents and the interviewers. "The life narrative," he concludes, "is the subjectively constructed life" (p. 178), no more literal truth than autobiography or biography. That being the case, he sensibly suggests that we had best consider life stories as reflecting stories in the here and now, an insight that can also be applied to autobiographical novels and memoirs. As a result of his fieldwork, Gubrium also suggests that the contingency of the stories he heard casts doubt on Robert Butler's (1963) definition of the life review. Butler regarded the phenomenon as an ideal type, "a time of final reckoning or stocktaking" undertaken primarily by the elderly and the dying (Gubrium, 1993, p. 188). Using Kathleen Woodward's (1997) careful classification, we can distinguish the stories Gubrium hears as reminiscences, not life review. These memories are more fragmentary and less unitary than a life review.

Gubrium's observations, as well as other autobiographical research, encourage us to reformulate Butler's (1963) notion that in old age impending death allows individuals to construct a coherent and complete narrative, even though such perfection has escaped them earlier. Sharan Merriam's (1995) recent study of life review finds that many of the people in her sample, regardless of age, claimed not to review their lives. Even psychoanalytic patients, who inevitably reconstruct the story of their life, rarely construct a tidy story. Aware of that fact, many years ago Woodward (1986) contrasted Butler's "Aristotelian" notion of plot with "a Freudian theory of narrative" (p. 146). Therapy, as psychoanalyst Roy Schafer had pointed out in *The Analytic Attitude* (1983), does not produce a complete and final version of patients' lives. Instead, analysts, Schafer argues, learn to appreciate their patients for their ability to deal with contingency and change, for "living out all of this adversity and achievement during the analytic process itself and reflecting upon it with benefit" (p. 65). Schafer declared that narratives are "constructed by two people under highly specialized dialogic circumstances" (p. 52). In the process of analysis the therapist learns to "[taste] the experience of the other through vicarious introspection" (Fliess & Kohut, cited in Cohler & Cole, 1996, p. 70). These psychoanalytic ideas have recently been echoed by several gerontologists. Gubrium and Holstein (1998) note that storytellers adjust their account depending upon the listeners and the environment. Moreover, Gary Kenyon (1996b) asserts, "we are not one story, but stories" (p. 26). When people are asked to talk about their lives, he observes, accounts emerge "as a function of a specific interpersonal context"(p. 27).[2] It seems that Butler has conflated the human desire that "things need to make sense" (Carr, 1986, quoted in Kenyon, 1996b, p. 35), with the construction of some sort of personal "grand narrative" (Kenyon, 1996b, p. 35), a task which few of us can ever accomplish.

To return to Gubrium, he has been a leader in other ways as well. Repeatedly throughout his career, he has discussed the ethics of using the personal narratives of one's subjects directly and is consistently careful to protect their identity. His concern about story ownership (Gubrium & Holstein, 1998) and about what Kenyon calls the "practical ethics" of protecting one's subjects from harm (1996a, p. 660) apparently did not trouble Tracy Kidder (1993) when writing his novelistic *Old Friends*. Kidder did not raise the question of whether he had the right to the stories he recounted. Nonetheless we must ask what obligations do researchers and writers have to protect those whose lives they transform in their texts.

Of course, *Old Friends* (Kidder, 1993) is a sanguine account of two roommates in a nursing home. He demonstrates that this old-age friendship is life-enhancing for both old men. Yet the conversations Kidder reports are so detailed and extensive that they must involve invented narrative. Recent historical works have also used reconstructed or fictionalized conversations. The historians who employ these techniques, however, usually acknowledge that fact explicitly. Kidder tells nothing about his subjects or the nursing home. We simply plunge into the story without any guidance. For the casual reader these are matters of little import, for Kidder's account is vivid and benign. Many of Kidder's observations about nursing home life reveal his concern for the denizens of Linda Manor and their families. He creates a telling aphorism, "the trouble with visitors is that they have to be thanked for coming, and forgiven for going away" (1993, p. 345). Certain deathbed scenes are touching. The reader, though, might wish to know if these "spots of time" actually occurred or are products of the author's vivid imagination.

Other literary gerontologists have also made good use of people's lives in writing about aging. For example, Harry Berman's *Interpreting the Aging Self* (1994) reminds us that journals provide an emic (insider) perspective on aging. Unlike those researchers who seem determined to hold up examples of successful aging for our adulation, Berman prefers to emphasize that one diarist, May Sarton, "forces herself to be open to negative feelings because of her faith that 'the courage to despair' . . . is essential to creativity" (p. 80). Moreover, creative people are not model citizens, as Anthony Storr points out in *Solitude* (cited in Berman, 1994). As Sarton reiterates countless times in her journals, she needed solitude but she also longed for acolytes. As a result, she would encourage young women to serve her and then grow weary of their company. Despite her ambivalence she never wanted for caretakers, most of whom were eager to minister to her needs. Berman comments that she could not resolve this "conflict between attachment and separateness. . . . But she does articulate the dilemma in ways that are beyond most people's capabilities." As a result, Berman continues, Sarton's journals, which indicate that age brought no surcease, may yet "help us to comprehend" our own conflicts better (p. 93), as well as the ambivalent behavior of elders whom we love. Berman's thoroughly professional writers have the ability to transform the story of their later lives into absorbing and helpful accounts.

Another remarkable study of literary autobiographies of aging, Barbara Frey Waxman's *To Live in the Center of the Moment* (1997), also takes us directly into the heart of what May Sarton in *As We Are Now* called the "foreign country" of old age (quoted in Waxman, 1997, p. 2). Waxman expertly offers us her reader response to autobiographies of aging, acting as a guide and explicator of these personal narratives. Besides May Sarton, she discusses Madeleine L'Engle's *The Summer of the Great-Grandmother* (1974), Philip Roth's *Patrimony* (1991), and Doris Grumbach's *Coming into the Endzone* (1991), among other remarkable examples of writing about life. Both L'Engle and Roth describe the effect of a dying patriarch and matriarch on themselves, and in L'Engle's case, on her children. Writing about parental loss helps them stave off the depression that otherwise might have engulfed them. Life review may not be a universal phenomenon in old age, yet when thinking about the loss of someone one loves or one's impending death, it can be very helpful. Waxman suggests that L'Engle "*needs* to do some romanticizing of her mother" (1997, p. 23) in order to survive intact. Her reconstruction of her mother's past, like Philip Roth's recollections of his vigorous father, allows us to see these frail elders in the round. They are not merely objects of pity or disgust, despite the two writers' "unflinching descriptions of the aged body's deterioration and pains" (Waxman, p. 41).

In contrast to L'Engle and Roth's wrenching narratives of impending death, Doris Grumbach (1991) wrote a midlife progress memoir at the age of 70. Life in the District of Columbia was beginning to frighten the aging Grumbach, who began to think of retirement and escape. Like Barbara Pym, who resisted the notion of retirement but enjoyed life when ill-health forced her to stop working (Wyatt-Brown, 1992a), she found the idea of retirement worse than the reality. As Waxman says, Grumbach starts off the book by regarding this transition as "beginning of the end" (p. 78). Writing her memoir, however, gave her the courage to revise her view and to begin to see her life as entering a new phase, one which she could enjoy. Borrowing Gullette's terms, Grumbach learned to recast her story of decline as one of progress. By the end of the account she is no longer unhappy. Instead she has started out on a new adventure, life in Sargentville, Maine.

Waxman takes seriously Cole's warning to avoid "a dualistic construction of a 'good' versus a 'bad' old age" lest such oversimplification lead to "spiritual vacancy in old age" (1997, p. 3). Her analysis illuminates the narratives she discusses. Her comments are appropriate and helpful for those who may not be familiar with autobiographical and reader response theories. Waxman's postmodern analysis of the effect of gender, class, and ethnicity on the writers' narratives is subtle and unjudgmental. She acknowledges that many of her writers were privileged people without assuming that good fortune vitiated their view of the human condition. Finally, her personal observations avoid the banality and self-indulgence of some scholars who mine the personal vein in talk-show fashion. A recent *New Yorker* cartoon (Ziegler, 1998) makes fun of our predilection for personal writing and Oprah-like disclosures. The scene takes place in a hospital where an old man lies gravely ill. A boy, who is writing in a notebook near the bed, asks cheerfully, "Hey, Gramps, is 'deathbed' one word or two?"

Writing about one's life has also emerged in gerontological circles in a less literary vein, namely, as courses in guided autobiography. Coordinated by James Birren this project emerged, according to Ruth and Kenyon, as an attempt to "integrate the philosophical base for biography" with empirical methods and clinical insights (1996, p. 654). One particularly fascinating study (Ruth, Birren, & Polkinghorne, 1996) identifies five life scripts: "living is achieving, living is being social, living is loving, living is family life, living is struggling" (p. 677). These life stories, some of which are heavily gendered, can shed light on writers' lives and on their characters. Although the purpose of the project is to explore "the subjective experiences of ageing" (p. 678), clearly writing about one's life has consequences for the authors themselves. As Kenyon (1996b) mentions, exploring the story of one's life outside of therapy reveals an "existential dimension. . . . What becomes visible is the process by which the I, today, continues to create the person that I was, and am, yesterday" (p. 27).

This existential aspect is something that Ruth Ray (in press) is exploring in *Writing a Life,* a remarkable account of life-writing groups which she organized. She gives such rich accounts of the interactions during the reading sessions that one can see the individual group members reinforcing or challenging the ideas of their friends. Her vivid descriptions illustrate McAdams' (1996) contention that life writing "ideally . . . *produce[s] new beginnings* (p. 143, italics McAdams's). Repeatedly her participants make it clear that their life stories "will," in McAdams's words, "continue to generate, create, nurture, or develop a *gift* of the self, to be offered to subsequent generations" (p. 143). Arlene, a mere youngster at 58 in this group of older women, reports that her children interrupt her stories with "Yeah, right, we know you grazed with the dinosaurs," but having her 85-year-old mother develop Alzheimer's taught her to hunger for stories of her mother's early life (Ray, in press).

One can exaggerate the wisdom of aging, but learning that children's interest in the family history may emerge at midlife is surely one of the great lessons of surviving one's youth. As Carolyn Heilbrun (1997) wisely tells us, "it is our very presence that is important to the young. . . . We assure them that life continues. . . ." Surviving into old age represents "the unstated assurance that most disasters pass, it is the survival of deprivation and death and rejection that renders our sympathy of value" (p. 163). Heilbrun's insight also helps us understand why young people are inclined to develop obsessions about the early death or suicide of a poet such as Sylvia Plath. They lack the certitude that they will be able to stay the course. Fortunately we have stories of survival to pass on to the next generation, such as Elinor Fuchs's (1999) wrenching account of her mother's Alzheimer's disease. We can celebrate the fact Fuchs survived 10 years of caring for her demented mother with her sense of humor and lively writing style intact.

This section on personal reflections would be incomplete without mentioning Cole's innovative autobiography of Eldrewey Stearns (Cole, 1997), which creates a new kind of literary genre. Stearns was an African American civil rights leader in Houston who fell upon hard times when manic depression began to dominate his life. Cole met him in 1984 when the old activist was a patient in a hospital at the University of Texas Medical Branch. Struck by Stearns's eloquent but incoherent account of his life, he decided to help him write his life history. That decision turned out to be far more difficult than he had anticipated. Stearns's mental condition did not lend itself to constructing a readable narrative, even with Cole's expert guidance. Ultimately, Cole solved the problem by creating a hybrid discourse. From newspapers and interviews he reconstructs the Houston civil rights era of the 1960s, the highpoint of Stearns's leadership. He also adds a poignant account of their troubled coauthorship, the process by which both men came to understand each other better. Another section recapitulates Stearns's troubled childhood to determine the roots of his strengths as leader and the life events that exacerbated his mental difficulties. Finally Cole outlines the literature on manic depression and comments upon the cultural implications of the coconstructed story.

For our purposes Cole's comments on the "politics of identity" are most apposite. He remarks that many scholars in recent years have "tended to locate individuals exclusively within one or another protected ethnic or racial group." That strategy, Cole asserts, is "crazy-making and impossible." His struggle to understand even imperfectly Stearns's life story taught him to separate individual lives from "group identities, whether singular or plural." Rather we should, Cole continues, accept "our separate and related selves, maintaining relationships, sharing responsibilities, and negotiating differences" (p. 200). Few scholars would have Cole's patience. Many times he had to bail Stearns out of jail or endure his hostile ranting. His understanding of manic depression and his determination to complete the account, however, sustained him even when he lost the grant that had made the project possible. Cole's endurance teaches us that we need to grow into our projects, especially ones as innovative as attempting to write the life history of conflicted, uncooperative, but gifted individuals. A cartoon by Lynn Johnston (1995) humorously dramatizes what working with Stearns might have been like. In this episode of "For Better or For Worse," college student Michael complains that he lacks the temperament of a writer, "Maybe I'm too emotional for this! I'm full of self-doubt, I'm sarcastic and compulsive and analytical—and half the time, I live in a fantasy world!! . . . I don't have any of the creative elements that make someone a *WRITER!*" Stearns has the volatility of Michael, but his mental disorder overwhelmed his talent.

THE EMOTIONS OF AGING

A new field, the history and reconstruction of feeling, represents another attempt on the part of scholars to recreate an insider's view of Sarton's "foreign country of old age" (Waxman, 1997, p. 2). Several of the studies already discussed, particularly those by postmodern sociologists like Hepworth (1996) and Featherstone and Hepworth (1991, 1995), explicitly discuss the emotions of those in "deep old age." They describe the efforts of elders to free themselves from the domination of the middle aged and their displeasure with their aging bodies. In another essay Hepworth (1998) challenges the assumptions that the elderly are necessarily nostalgic or emotionally rooted in the past, although younger people often assume that they are. Drawing upon the work of literary gerontologists who have studied the creative imagination, he explores the sometimes unruly emotions that emerge in later life.

On the whole, sociologists and historians (Stearns & Lewis, 1998) view the emotions as something to be reported and recreated. For example, Achenbaum describes G. Stanley Hall's wrestling with depression, his honesty and bravery in facing his own prejudice against aging when writing his innovative study, *Senescence* (Achenbaum, 1998). In contrast, Kathleen Woodward explicitly seeks to influence future feelings. In recent years she has broadened her focus from mourning, the subject which permeates *Aging and Its Discontents* (1991), to recollections of her grandmother (Woodward, 1994), who, like my own (see later, Note 2), provided a positive view of "the figure of the older woman." Woodward remarks that if we survive, we women will all become older ourselves, "time willing" (p. 103).

Another positive reading of the older woman as an important figure in our lives appears in Ann Romines's (1995) empathic account of Willa Cather's later fiction. With some difficulty she resists the strong temptation to view the Nebraska writer "as a female elder" to whom she can look for guidance. Fearing, perhaps unnecessarily, to "infantilize" herself and to "erase" Cather she recommends reading Cather's later fiction as "a passionate, measured, and shifting response to personal, cultural, and historical issues concerning the processes of aging" (Barbara MacDonald's words, quoted in Romines, 1995, p. 398). Fortunately, unlike those critics who emphasize their own response so much that their subjects nearly disappear in their effusions, Romines handles her reactions tactfully. According to her, thoughts of gender differences dominate even Cather's most positive view of aging, found in *Death Comes for the Archbishop* (1927). The powerful and insightful Archbishop Latour is able to arrange many aspects of his death to his satisfaction. In contrast, age diminishes the power of Doña Isabella Olivares, who must choose between inheriting her husband's property and maintaining "the fiction of her perpetual youth." The "discordant" account of Doña Isabella's later life suggests, Romines argues, that Cather was well aware that women had little chance to create a "Golden Legend" of their own (1995, p. 401–402).

More optimistic about aging women than Cather, Mildred Hill-Lubin (1991) analyzes the role of grandmothers in African American culture. Ever since crack cocaine has become a public health problem, many African American grandmothers have been forced to rear their grandchildren, often by default. Many of these aging grandmothers lack the physical and emotional strength for the task, especially when the children exhibit symptoms of prenatal exposure to drugs themselves. The grandmothers whom Hill-Lubin discusses were more fortunate. They were not the sole support of their grandchildren. Hence they could provide positive models "of action, involvement, hope, and dignity." Using literary autobiography as her source, Hill-Lubin asserts that African American grandmothers have historically preserved their families, passed on the family history and "Black lore" (p. 174). They have also, as she reminds us, communicated spiritual values by exemplifying them in their lives. Naturally not all grandmothers, Black or White, want to become culture-bearers, but Hill-Lubin's optimistic readings remind us of happier times.

Intergenerational connections are also explored in Carolyn Smith's (1991) study of Adrienne Rich and Ruth Whitman. Like Hill-Lubin's and Woodward's recent work, Smith's essay examines the importance of grandparents as a potentially sustaining force in a young poet's life. Smith finds that some of Rich's anger arose from her family's failure to maintain contact with their roots. Her Jewish father preferred to suppress his "rich, thousand-year-old Ashkenazic culture of Eastern Europe" (Rich, quoted in Smith, 1991, p. 204). In contrast, Ruth Whitman's family reconciled their Chassidic heritage with their American customs so that she grew up with a positive view of their family and culture. Both of them produced poetry which can be characterized as "a long conversation with the elders and with the future" (Rich, quoted in Smith, 1991, p. 208), but clearly Whitman's was the happier conversation. Emotionology, the study of emotions, being a new field, we can look forward to more investigations that will illuminate and broaden our understanding of aging, and with luck offer us strategies of resistance and hope for the future.

CONCLUSION

The last 6 years have produced a remarkable number of important articles and books, almost as many in 6 years as in the 20 years preceding the first edition of this *Handbook*. Complacency should not be a consequence. Even a superficial glance at the reference pages demonstrates that much of this work has been done by a few people. If they should tire of strain, we would need newcomers to take up their burden. At present few graduate programs are producing the next generation of literary gerontologists. It is up to us to attract the culture theorists and encourage them to broaden their scope so that they can be read with pleasure by clinicians, social workers, and others whose literary education may be scanty.

Moreover, at present the research of literary gerontology has had little effect on the public's view of aging and creativity. For example, in a recent *New Yorker* article (1998) on musical taste, Robert Sapolsky raises serious questions about creativity and aging. He asserts that in creativity research, "age has emerged as a leading factor." Drawing upon quantitative studies, he notes that if one counts the number of melodies a composer produces, one discovers a pattern of decline after a "relatively youthful peak" (p. 71). At this point he mentions Dean Simonton's discovery that age itself is less significant than the length of time one works in a profession. Sapolsky consoles himself for being on the wrong side of 40 and thus less adaptable in musical taste than the young by recalling Tracy Kidder's (1993) notion that repetition can be comforting as we grow older.

Regrettably, Sapolsky makes no mention of research on late style and the innovations that older artists often make in their swan songs.

As scholars in this field, we need to publicize our ideas more broadly and reach a nonspecialist audience. By such means general readers and scholars from different fields will develop a more complex view of how aging affects every aspect of our lives. To that end the Henry A. Murray Research Center at Radcliffe is studying psychological development at midlife. In an attempt to stir up public interest, the *Radcliffe Quarterly* devoted much of its Fall 1996 issue to reporting some of its findings. The issue also included short reflections from some middle-aged graduates, such as Margaret Morganroth Gullette (1996). Gullette has consciously placed her essays in a variety of journals, scholarly and mass market alike. There is no simple path to popularity. Surely the first step, though, is to write as accessibly as we can in as many venues as possible without oversimplifying or distorting our arguments. If we do, literary gerontology will continue to play an essential role in the expanding field of gerontology.

NOTES

[1] Extensive abstracts of most of the novels and memoirs mentioned in this essay can be found in a brief bibliography (Wyatt-Brown & Waxman, 1999) published by the Association for Gerontology in Higher Education.

[2] Talking to two friends, April 1, 1998, I was discussing the influence of parents and grandparents upon my ideas of self and career. I began by mentioning parental constraints, but a chance question reminded me that my maternal grandmother had provided a model of independence. Thanks to my friends' energetic listening and questioning, my story changed dramatically from one of complaint to one of celebration.

REFERENCES

Achenbaum, W. A. (1995). *Crossing frontiers: Gerontology emerges as a science.* Cambridge: Cambridge University Press.

Achenbaum, W. A. (1998). Toward a psychohistory of late-life emotionality. In P. N. Stearns & J. Lewis (Eds.), *An emotional history of the United States,* (pp. 417–430). New York: New York University Press.

Adair, V. H. (1996). *Ants on the melon: A collection of poems.* New York: Random House.

Aldrich, M. (1993). Lethal brevity: Louise Bogan's lyric career. In A. M. Wyatt-Brown & L. Rossen (Eds.), *Aging and gender in literature: Studies in creativity* (pp. 105–120). Charlottesville: University Press of Virginia.

Alvarez, A. (1996). New poet in town: A review of *Ants on the Melon* by Virginia Hamilton Adair. *New York Review of Books,* May 23, pp. 4–6.

Banner, L. W. (1992). *In full flower: Aging women, power, and sexuality. A history.* New York: Alfred A. Knopf.

Bayley, J. (1992). Elegy for Iris: Scenes from an indomitable marriage. *The New Yorker,* July 27, pp. 44–61.

Beauvoir, S. (1970). *The coming of age.* Translated by Patrick O'Brian. New York: W. W. Norton & Company, 1996.

Berman, H. J. (1994). *Interpreting the aging self: Personal journals of later life.* New York: Springer Publishing Company.

Blythe, R. (1979). *The view in winter: Reflections on old age.* New York: Harcourt Brace Jovanovich.

Butler, R. N. (1963). The life review: An interpretation of reminiscence in the aged. *Psychiatry: Journal for the Study of Interpersonal Processes, 26,* 65–76.

Cohen-Shalev, A. (1992). Self and Style: The development of artistic expression from youth through midlife to old age in the works of Henrik Ibsen. *Journal of Aging Studies, 6*(3), 289–299.

Cohen-Shalev, A. (in press). *Both worlds at once: Art in old age.*

Cohen-Shalev, A., & Rapoport, A. (1993). The play's the thing: Samuel Beckett's midlife transition and the theatre of the absurd. *International Journal of Aging and Human Development 37*(2), 81–90.

Cohler, B. J., & Cole, T. R. (1996). Studying older lives: Reciprocal acts of telling and listening. In J. E. Birren, G. Kenyan, J. Roth, J. J. F. Schroots, & T. Svensson (Eds.), *Aging and biography: Explorations in adult development* (pp. 61–76). New York: Springer Publishing Company.

Cole, T. R. (1992). *The journey of life: A cultural history of aging in America.* Cambridge: Cambridge University Press.

Cole, T. R. (1997). *No color is my kind: The life of Eldrewey Stearns and the integration of Houston.* Austin: University of Texas Press.

Cole, T. R., Tassel, D. D. Van, & Kastenbaum, R. (Eds.). (1992). *Handbook of the humanities and aging.* New York: Springer Publishing Company.

Featherstone, M., & Hepworth, M. (1991). The mask of ageing and the postmodern life course. In M. Featherstone, M. Hepworth, & B. S. Turner (Eds.), *The body: Social process and cultural theory* (pp. 371–389). London: Sage Publications.

Featherstone, M., & Wernick, A. (1995). *Images of aging: Cultural representations of later life.* London: Routledge.

Friedan, B. (1993). *The fountain of age.* New York: Simon & Schuster.

Fromm, G. G. Being old: The example of Dorothy Richardson. In A. M. Wyatt-Brown & J. Rossen (Eds.), *Aging and gender in literature: Studies in creativity* (pp. 258–270). Charlottesville: University Press of Virginia.

Fuchs, E. (1999). Making an exit. In K. Woodward (Ed.), *Figuring age: Women, bodies, generations* (pp. 340–348). Bloomington: Indiana University Press.

Furbank, P. N., & Haskell, F. J. H. (1958). E. M. Forster. In M. Cowley (Ed.), *Writers at work: The Paris Review interviews* (pp. 23–35). New York: The Viking Press.

Gardner, P. (Ed.). (1985). *E. M. Forster's commonplace book.* Stanford, CA: Stanford University Press.

George, D. H. (1993). Keeping our working distance: Maxine Kumin's poetry of loss and survival. In A. M. Wyatt-Brown & J. Rossen (Eds.), *Aging and gender in literature: Studies in creativity* (pp. 314–338). Charlottesville: University Press of Virginia.

Grumbach, D. (1991). *Coming into the endzone: A Memoir.* New York: W. W. Norton & Company, 1993.

Gubrium, J. F. (1993). *Speaking of life: Horizons of meaning for nursing home residents.* New York: Aldine de Gruyter.

Gubrium, J. F., & Holstein, J. A. (1998). Narrative practice and the coherence of personal stories. *The Sociological Quarterly 39,* 163–187.

Gullette, M. M. (1988). *Safe at last in the middle years: The invention of the midlife progress novel: Saul Bellow, Margaret Drabble, Anne Tyler, and John Updike.* Berkeley: University of California Press.

Gullette, M. M. (1996). Middle-ageism in the postmodern economy. *Radcliffe Quarterly,* Fall, p. 26.

Gullette, M. M. (1997). *Declining to decline: Cultural combat and the politics of the midlife.* Charlottesville: University Press of Virginia.

Gullette, M. M. (in press). Age studies, and gender. In L. Code (Ed.), *Feminist literary theories,* London: Routledge.

Heilbrun, C. G. (1997). *The last gift of time: Life beyond sixty.* New York: The Dial Press.

Hepworth, M. (1996). William and the old folks: Notes on infantilisation. *Society, 16,* 423–441.

Hepworth, M. (1998). Aging and the emotions. In G. Bendelow & S. J. Williams (Eds.), *Emotions in social life: Critical themes and contemporary issues* (pp. 173–189). London: Routledge.

Hill-Lubin, M. A. (1991). The African-American grandmother in autobiographical works by Frederick Douglass, Langston Hughes, and Maya Angelou. *International Journal of Aging and Human Development, 33,* 173–185.

Johnston, L. (1995). "For Better or For Worse." *Gainesville Sun,* D4

Katz, S. (1996). *Disciplining old age: The formation of gerontological knowledge.* Charlottesville: University Press of Virginia.

Kaufman, S. R. (1986). *The ageless self: Sources of meaning in late life.* New York: New American Library, 1987.

Kenyon, G. M. (1996a). Ethical issues in ageing and biography. *Ageing and Society, 16,* 659–675.

Kenyon, G. M. (1996b). The meaning/value of personal storytelling. In J. E. Birren, G. M. Kenyon, J. E. Ruth, J. J. F. Schroots, & T. Svensson (Eds.), *Aging and biography: Explorations in adult development* (pp. 21–38). New York: Springer Publishing Co.

Kidder, T. (1993). *Old friends.* Boston: Houghton Mifflin Company.

Lurie, A. (1998). *The last resort.* New York: Henry Holt and Company.

L'Engle, M. (1974). *The summer of the great-grandmother.* San Francisco: Perennial Library, Harper & Row Publishers.

Mangum, T. (1999). Little women: The aging female character in nineteenth-century British children's literature. In L. Woodward (Ed.), *Figuring age: Women, bodies, generations* (pp. 59–87). Bloomington: University of Indiana Press.

McAdams, D. P. (1996). Narrating the self in adulthood. In J. E. Birren, G. M. Kenyon, J. E. Ruth, J. J. F. Schroots, & T. Svensson (Eds.), *Aging and biography: Explorations in adult development* (pp. 131–148). New York: Springer Publishing Co.

Merriam, S. B. (1995). Butler's life review: How universal is it? In J. Hendricks (Ed.), *The meaning of reminiscence and life review* (pp. 7–19). Amityville, NY: Baywood Publishing Company, Inc.

Mezey, R. (1996). Afterword. In V. H. Adair (Ed.), *Ants on the melon: A collection of poems* (pp. 151–158). New York: Random House.

Miller, N. K. (1999). The marks of time. In K. Woodward (Ed.), *Figuring age: Women, bodies, generations*. Bloomington: Indiana University Press.

Paris, B. J. (1997). *Imagined human beings: A psychological approach to character and conflict in literature*. New York: New York University Press.

Philip, C. E. (1995). Lifelines: A journal and poems. *Journal of Aging Studies 9*, 265–322.

Pym, B. (1980). *A few green leaves*. New York: E. P. Dutton.

Pym, B. (1972, 1977). *Quartet in Autumn*. New York: E. P. Dutton.

Ray, R. E. (in press). *Beyond nostalgia: Aging and life story writing*. Charlottesville: University Press of Virginia.

Romines, A. (1995). Willa Cather and the coming of old age. *Texas Studies in Literature and Language, 37*, 394–413.

Rooke, C. (1992). Old age in contemporary fiction: A new paradigm of hope. In T. R. Cole, D. D. Van Tassel, & R. Kastenbaum (Eds.), *Handbook of the humanities and aging* (pp. 241–257). New York: Springer Publishing Co.

Roth, P. (1991). *Patrimony: A true story*. New York: Vintage International, Vintage Books, Random House, Inc., 1996.

Ruth, J. E., Birren, J. E., & Polkinghorne, D. E. (1996). The projects of life reflected in autobiographies of old age. *Ageing and Society, 16*, 677–699.

Ruth, J. E., & Kenyon, G. M. (1996). Introduction: Special issue on ageing, biography and practice. *Ageing and Society, 16*, 653–657.

Said, E. (1998). Between worlds: Edward Said makes sense of his life. *London Review of Books*, May 7, pp. 3–7.

Sapolsky, R. M. (1998). Open season: Why do we lose our taste for the new? *The New Yorker*, March 30, 57–72.

Schafer, R. (1983). *The analytic attitude*. New York: Basic Books.

Scott, J. (1998). A Palestinian confronts time: For Columbia literary critic, cancer is a spur to memory. *New York Times (National Edition)*, September 19, pp. A17, A19.

Simonton, D. K. (1990). Does creativity decline in the later years? Definition, data, and theory. In M. Perlmutter (Ed.), *Late life potential* (pp. 83–112). Washington, DC: The Gerontological Society of America.

Smith, C. H. (1991). Adrienne Rich, Ruth Whitman, and their Jewish elders. *International Journal of Aging and Human Development, 33*(3), 203–209.

Smith, C. H. (1993). Old-age freedom in Josephine Miles's late poems, 1974–79. In A. M. Wyatt-Brown & Janice Rossen (Eds.), *Aging and Gender in Literature: Studies in Creativity* (pp. 271–295). Charlottesville: University Press of Virginia.

Smith, C. H. (1995). Claire Philip's poems and the art of dying. *Journal of Aging Studies, 9*, 343–347.

Stearns, P. N., & Lewis, J. (1998). *An emotional history of the United States*. New York: New York University Press.

Tyler, A. (1998). *A patchwork planet*. New York: Alfred A. Knopf.

Waxman, B. F. (1997). *To live in the center of the moment: Literary autobiographies of aging.* Charlottesville: University Press of Virginia.

Woodward, K. (1986). Reminiscence and the life review: Prospects and retrospects. In T. R. Cole & S. A. Gadow. (Eds.), *What Does It Mean to Grow Old? Reflections from the Humanities* (pp. 135–161). Durham, NC: Duke University Press.

Woodward, K. (1991). *Aging and its discontents: Freud and other fictions.* Bloomington: Indiana University Press.

Woodward, K. (1994). Tribute to the older woman: Psychoanalytic geometry, gender, and the emotions. In J. H. Smith & A. M. Mahfouz (Eds.), *Psychoanalysis, feminism, and the future of gender* (pp. 91–108). Baltimore: Johns Hopkins University Press.

Woodward, K. (1997). Telling stories: Aging, reminiscence, and the life review. *Journal of Aging and Identity, 2,* 149–163.

Woodward, K. (Ed.). (1999). *Figuring age: Women, bodies, generations.* Bloomington: Indiana University Press.

Wyatt-Brown, A. M. (1992a). *Barbara Pym: A critical biography.* Columbia: University of Missouri Press.

Wyatt-Brown, A. M. (1992b). Literary gerontology comes of age. In T. R. Cole, D. D. Van Tassel, & R. Kastenbaum (Eds.), *Handbook of the humanities and aging* (pp. 331–351). New York: Springer Publishing Company.

Wyatt-Brown, A. M. (1995). Creativity as a defense against death: Maintaining one's professional identity. *Journal of Aging Studies, 9*(4), 349–354.

Wyatt-Brown, A. M., & Waxman, B. F. (1999). *Aging in literature Brief Bibliography: A selected bibliography for gerontological instruction.* Washington, DC: Association for Gerontology in Higher Education.

Wyatt-Brown, B. (1993). Aging, gender, and the deterioration of southern family values in the stories of Peter Taylor. In A. M. Wyatt-Brown & J. Rossen (Eds.), *Aging and gender in literature: Studies in creativity* (pp. 296–313). Charlottesville: University Press of Virginia.

Zeilig, H. (1997). The uses of literature in the studies of older people. In A. Jamieson, S. Harper, & C. Victor (Eds.), *Critical approaches to ageing and later life* (pp. 39–48). Buckingham, England: Open University Press.

Ziegler, J. (1992). "Cartoon." *The New Yorker.* p. 71.

4

Literary History as a Tool of Gerontology

Teresa Mangum

If you are not familiar with Southern style and you are driving in the South, mentally prepare yourself before asking directions. "How do I get to the Bolivia County Courthouse?" you innocently ask a local. "Now, you know that red house on the corner?" your informant queries, ignoring protests that you are a stranger. "That's where my sister-in-law used to live. Don't turn down that road. Take the second left. If you see a burned out barn? Miz Pearl owned that barn and the whole neighborhood turned out for the fire. Ignore that and look for a barbecue sign." Stemming the tide of information is impossible. Instead, consider the speaker's narrative motivation. He wants to get you where you want to go, but he believes that you need the lay of the land—its historical as well as geographical parameters—in order to reach your final destination. Implicitly, he assumes that a fact can only be rendered meaningful within a dense contextualizing body of detail. Though superhighways hasten a journey, all landscapes look the same. Drivers who choose the back roads, like humanities scholars, value a different kind of excursion. They want to understand how people live and think, what desires motivate choices and actions, and when differences among communities spur cooperation versus conflict. Those who choose the back roads not only go home with good stories (most Southerners' idea of a real souvenir), but also with a complex understanding of a place and its inhabitants and, therefore, with a context for interpreting their experiences.

In this essay, I want to make a case for the conviction that understanding the human condition in a meaningful way requires attention to the relationship between the present and the past. More particularly, I hope to convince readers from outside my own discipline that the literary past can provide insight into the current experience of aging, of being old, and of interacting with an older person positioned as an object of study, a client, or a patient. Advocating the need for "critical gerontology," historian Martha Holstein proposes that incorporating literature and literary theory into the study of aging "can enlarge understanding of the self-determining and meaning-making aspects of old age within particular sociopolitical and cultural contexts . . . , can help develop a critical sensitivity to theory . . . , [and] can expand the researcher's self-awareness and insight, thereby facilitating empathetic understanding and encouraging a more open recognition of one's own values and prejudices and how those influence—and also contribute to—the work that we do" (Holstein, 1994, p. 822).

The following itinerant directions demonstrate how literary history furthers these objectives by providing significant insights into our own cultural perceptions of aging. I offer two clusters of examples from Victorian Britain. In the first, we see changes in representations of older characters in children's literature—arguably, the narratives which have the greatest influence on the formation of our understanding of age and aging. Even a quick comparison of past and present children's literature challenges the general assumption that our own attitudes toward aging are inevitably more progressive than those of the past. The novels of Charles Dickens form a second cluster of examples. Should Dickens's representations of old age be treated as past or present narratives? His characters inhabit our literary landscape—from annual television and community theatre resuscitations of the miserly Ebenezer Scrooge of *A Christmas Carol* (1843) to the many films, plays, and musicals featuring the demonic Fagin of *Oliver Twist* (1837–1839). Whether comparing past and present representations of aging in popular literary forms or tracing the mutations of a plot or character that maintains its hold on a culture for decades, even centuries, we gain powerful insights into our own ideological assumptions about aging through the study of old age as figured in literature of the past (Cole, 1992; Mangum, 1998).

Throughout this essay I address readers as fellow teachers. Ideally, some of these readers teach in literature departments. The push for programs in age studies, a term coined by Margaret Gullette (1997), asks researchers in the humanities to contemplate age with the same thoughtfulness that marks studies of other aspects of identity, such as race and gender, and the increasing number of anthologies will make this task easier (Booth, 1992; Cole & Winkler, 1994; Kohn, Donley, & Wear, 1993). However, another of my objectives is to persuade readers from the social sciences, the applied sciences, and the health care system to take literary history seriously. Doing so would change the questions, the practices, and the training of researchers from the various fields that comprise gerontology. Taking the more expedient highway might lead a researcher to a list of the difficulties an older person faces in our culture and a list of services an agency can provide in response. But the byways of literary history teach us the evolving values, beliefs, practices, and images that converge into an often gerontophobic culture. Consequently, we can work for fundamental changes in the ideology of aging even as we solve immediate problems for individuals.

PART I: BYWAYS—LOOKING TO THE PAST

Although scholars of literature and culture committed to age studies have begun to produce ground-breaking studies of age as a category affecting 20th-century representational practices (Basting, 1998; Cole, 1992; Featherstone & Wernick, 1995; Gullette, 1998, 1997; Pearsall, 1997; Ragland-Sullivan, 1991; Riggs, 1998; Woodward, 1991, 1998; Woodward & Schwartz, 1986; Wyatt-Brown & Rossen, 1993), the majority of studies focused on past attitudes toward aging have been undertaken by demographers, sociologists, and historians rather than by literary scholars (Achenbaum, 1995; Haber, 1982, 1996; Hareven, 1982; Hazan, 1994; Katz, 1996; Kertzer & Laslett, 1995; Laslett, 1977; Pelling & Smith, 1991; Quadagno, 1982; and others). Similarly, only a few studies exist of representations of aging in the visual arts (Covey, 1991; Frueh, 1997; McKee & Kauppinen, 1989).

Like many literary historians, when I become interested in a current problem—for example, why is old age so frequently portrayed as childlike?—my impulse is to track backward (Brown, 1995; Hamilton, 1996; Perkins, 1992; Veeser, 1989). Current practices seem more open to question and analysis if I follow their paths into the past. We experience these practices as normal, commonsensical, and unalterable. To interrogate the meaning and effects of these practices, which Gullette calls "age ideology," requires critical distance (Gullette, 1988, 1997). Often this occurs painfully, as when we find ourselves thrust to a perceptual distance by some rupture—by a shocking incident that discloses the limits of "normal" as a category, for instance, or a jarringly contradictory juxtaposition of events, or by the dislocation felt by many people who live in a precarious balance between their dominant culture and subculture. Such experiences are likely to provoke a questioning or resistant stance to "commonsense" and generally accepted rules governing people's behavior to one another. The past provides at least one kind of perceptual distance.

In addition, historical distance can act as a temporary buffer against the powerful emotions or fears that inevitably surface when one explores a vexed current problem, such as euthanasia. Anthony Trollope's satiric novel, *The Fixed Period* (1882), presents a "futuristic" colonial society of 1979 which advocates voluntary euthanasia for each citizen who reaches 67 years of age. The action hinges on the fact that this policy was established when the oldest colonist was 30, but the novel opens as the first citizen approaches 67. When I teach this novel, we consider it in the context of late-Victorian debates over both colonialism and parliamentary reports urging the state to assume greater responsibility for the care of older citizens. However, my students use this literary past as a means to make sense of their own feelings about aging and their obligations to older people.

This brings me to an important limitation faced by any scholar interested in history: we can never actually recover the past. We can never fully grasp what life was, what people felt and believed in the past, or how individuals absorbed literary or other forms of their culture. We can, however, use empathy, curiosity, and imagination to conjecture about the past and to juxtapose our beliefs and practices to those of the past in an attempt to come at the present from a comparativist's position. The past cannot provide a direct linear progression to the present nor even a clear originary cause for present-day effects. Juxtaposing the past to present representations and practices, however, demonstrates repetition and differences that shift us to a new point of view, a telling synthesis, or unsuspected alternatives to heretofore unquestioned assumptions. The energy, interest, and commitment that students bring to the study of the literary past (after their first horrified realization that Victorians wrote very, very long books) convince me that the past can still perform what Jane Tompkins calls "cultural work" in the always-turning-into-the-past we call the present (Tompkins, 1985).

PART II: DESTINATIONS—VICTORIAN REPRESENTATIONS OF AGE

My book project, "The Victorian Invention of Old Age," explores conceptions of aging and old age in the literature of 19th- and early 20th-century Britain. This was a time and place in which many current perceptions of childhood, middle age, old age—in short, age—germinated. As a literary historian I investigate wide-ranging literary and visual representations not just of older people, but also of aging as a process; of places, activities, and assumptions which come to be associated with old age; and of the intersections between age and other categories of identity such as gender, race, class, and nationality. From early in the 19th century, Victorians debated how best to care for the poor, many of whom were elderly. Changes in the Poor Laws established workhouses where paupers were forced to "earn" relief payments, shelter, and food through demeaning labor. The public's ambivalence, even hostility, to these policies circulated in popular forms such as Charles Dickens's *Oliver Twist* or Hubert Von Herkomer's 1870s magazine illustrations and paintings, both of which detail sufferings of the elderly poor (McLerran, 1993). Sentiments against mistreatment escalated in the 1890s when Charles Booth's study of urban poverty revealed that a startling percentage of the poor were over 65 (Booth, 1894). Late in the century, Parliament debated the merits of mandatory retirement and pension plans, in part as an alternative to the welfare system legislated by the Poor Laws. The pension plan, passed in 1908, provided some social support to retirees. It also forced Parliament to agree upon an age at which a person became eligible to receive a pension and thus, in effect, became old. Menopause had long been the most prominent biological marker of a woman's transition to old age, but neither women nor men were described in the most negative age-related adjectives—dependent, unproductive, feeble, or senile—until they ceased to work. After 1908, health, activity, and employment would no longer define old age (Covey, 1992; Roebuck, 1979). Thus, seemingly progressive rhetoric and legislation paradoxically imposed a new rigidity on the aging process.

Less obviously, public debates about responsibilities to the elderly turned Victorian legislators and taxpayers' attention to the human life span, a popular topic throughout the century. This interest heightened as the public contemplated paying for pensions. At the same time, largely because paupers were the chief subjects of medical study, clinical medicine built itself on the unwell bodies and cadavers of the elderly poor, especially in European hospitals. Hence, sociologically, economically, medically, and politically, the older body, especially of the poor, quietly assumed increasing cultural significance (Achenbaum, 1995; Freeman, 1979; Katz, 1996; Thane, 1993).

In public rhetoric, this elderly presence blurred into a curious abstraction as older individuals dissolved into a faceless collective often referred to as "the aged" or "the poor," a dependent, helpless group for whom the state assumed responsibility. Paintings, novels, poetry, and other forms of popular media, however, countered vague generalizations with vivid (if often stereotypical) faces, bodies, actions, and feelings. These representations suggest how various and vexed Victorian feelings were about being old, about the so-called aged, and about the contrasts between any one person's knowledge of individual older people ("my grandmother") versus the vague collective "they" of stereotypes and public rhetoric.

I tether the interpretive strategies of the literary critic with the social and political questions that drive cultural studies. Thus, my approach has the historicist objective of juxtaposing representations of aging in popular culture and the arts with discourses about aging that emerge from "official" channels such as the government and the medical community and with firsthand accounts of aging and old age recorded in diaries and personal writing. Thereby, I consider how seemingly idiosyncratic and widely dispersed ideas about old age harden into a cultural formation that then determines how old age will be defined and experienced. In other words, I ask how the meanings and associations that became attached to aging and old age interact with representations of aging, the treatment of actual older people, and even the way an individual feels compelled to think and act in his or her late years. Considering that most Victorians found it impossible to believe that normal elderly people could feel something as fundamental to human experience as sexual desire and therefore ruthlessly ridiculed any signs of sensuality, I believe we want to interrogate the representational choices of the past that shape our present. Studying literary history, we recover perspectives on aging and being old that have been unfairly dismissed as unnatural or implausible.

One of the enduring clusters of images associated with old age that is especially damaging to older people is encapsulated in the phrase "second childhood" (Covey, 1992–1993; Hockey & James, 1995). Victorian children's literature is a particularly fruitful field for understanding the appeal as well as the dangers of this analogy. Although this formulation was not new to the Victorians, its repeated representation in children's books in tandem with the parliamentary accounts of frail, dependent elderly who were assumed to require not just financial support, but also supervision and even benevolent incarceration provides one explanation for the long life of this conception of old age. Moreover, children's literature is an especially rich source for a scholar interested in aging because this book market depends upon unique relationships among readers of different ages for its circulation. Written by adults about characters of all ages, children's literature is ostensibly addressed to child readers. However, these texts are inevitably constructed of adult fantasies about childhood; they are selected by adults for children; and successful sales depend more heavily on adults' memories than on actual children's tastes. Such nostalgia explains the continuing popularity of Lewis Carroll's Alice books, James Barry's Peter Pan plays and books, and innumerable earlier fairy tales, now circulating in videos rather than print.

In the 18th century, when a book market addressed to children emerged, reading of fairy tales was discouraged as frivolous, even corrupting. Today many fairy tales are revised to eliminate violence as well as potentially offensive messages about women, people of color, and the elderly. However, between these two centuries, in what is often called the golden age of children's literature, elderly nursery rhyme characters like Old Mother Hubbard were joined by a host of Victorian figurations of old age. Kings, queens, widows, grandmothers, old maids, sorcerers, dwarves, crones, witches, and fairy godmothers populate the fairy tales of writers like Charles Dickens, George MacDonald, Harriet Louisa Childe-Pemberton, and Frances Browne (Honig, 1988; Mangum, 1998; Temke, 1978).

Victorian children's stories often treat the metaphor of second childhood as literal truth by representing older characters and child characters as strikingly similar. These texts pictured older male and female characters as tiny, frail, and peevish rather than malevolent. Moreover, young and old alike are represented as requiring the care of middle-aged adult characters. Both are also often shown acting with comparable defiance as they rebel against middle-aged characters who try to dominate children and grandparents (or witches or ancient fairies). In addition, elderly figures are likely to be depicted as subject to the needs and desires of the child protagonist. For instance, fairy tales often pit protective and generous elderly fairy godmothers who live only to serve children against an evil fairy or witch who would destroy the young, as in George MacDonald's "Little Daylight" (1864). In other stories, the "evils" of old age are magically cured through a child's kindness, as in several of the framed tales included in Frances Browne's *Granny's Wonderful Chair* (1857).

Careful readings of fantasy can thus be used to raise important issues for the study of intergenerational relations. We can see that descriptions as well as illustrations depend upon the principle of incongruity to create comedy when an older character is depicted in terms only appropriate for a child. John Tenniel's illustrations of the queen's puerile tyranny in Lewis Carroll's *Adventures of Alice in Wonderland* (1865) serve as a dramatic example. The incongruities at once create and expose the distorted logic that shores up images of second childhood. While the comedy of the image is seductive, the incongruities on which the comedy depends provide a means to dismantle the false analogy. This approach is an effective teaching tool because readers can grasp the conventions of comedy and learn to perform the analysis themselves, thereby carrying this "unlearning" strategy into situations outside the classroom. Various late 20th-century television advertisements deploy a similar incongruity, but now "wild and crazy" seniors—complete with skateboards, funky fashions, and boom boxes—imitate adolescents (an age category that only emerged late in the 19th century) rather than children. While we tend to see "our" comic representations as harmless, a comparison between today's images and figures of second childhood in Victorian children's literature uncovers striking similarities. Neither cultural form seems to address elderly audiences, though older people presumably are encouraged to share the humor by distancing themselves from "those" (i.e., absurd) old characters. Because both past and present representations depict old and young as oppositions and simultaneously limit pleasures of fashion, leisure, and libido to youth, viewers are left with few ways to imagine vitality in old age that will not provoke incredulity or ridicule. This juxtaposition helps us to see how standards of "appropriate" age behavior are enforced through the narratives that we encounter in popular culture. Historical recognition thereby enables both resistance and revision.

The many variations of the second childhood trope in Victorian children's literature also help us to perceive the interplay of age identities within texts. Reading with the theoretical premises of deconstruction in mind, we see that many children's texts focused on either children or older characters are also preoccupied with middle-aged adults, the very people who wrote and read most of this literature. In Charles Dickens's *The Magic Fishbone* (1868) and Mary de Morgan's *A Toy Princess* (1877), for instance, young princesses and their diminutive elderly godmothers collaborate against middle-aged kings. Peter Pan's great obsession is avoiding adulthood because as an adult he would have to work and care for others. In innumerable renditions of Cinderella and Snow White stories, the chief antagonists are midlife stepmothers. In this respect the trope of second childhood functions as a commentary on the power, but also the burdensome responsibility of generations between the ends of the spectrum of first and second childhood. While sociologists Jenny Hockey and Allison James have convincingly demonstrated that second childhood consolidates the status of the middle-aged, fantasy versions of these midlife victims and tyrants may also have powerful imaginative appeal for the adult reader in ways quite different from the pleasure a child would take from correspondingly tiny fairy godmothers or dangerously wicked childlike witches. Bruno Bettelheim drew upon the insights of psychoanalysis to suggest that children use these fantasies as a safe way to explore forbidden feelings, such as fears of death or the pleasures of revenge upon authority figures. Perhaps these tales engage middle-aged readers by appealing to their socially forbidden frustration with dependents. I have not encountered studies of elderly readers' responses, but studies like Bettelheim's work with children and literary critic Janice Radway's ethnography of a group of adult women romance readers suggest that the ways we use texts change over the course of a life. Further research in readers' reception could offer important insights into the imaginative lives of older readers (Altick, 1957; Riggs, 1998; Tompkins, 1980).

One particularly suggestive way of tracing the shifting status a culture permits elderly figures is to compare versions of the same character types over several centuries. The figure of the grandmother undergoes significant changes through the multiple versions that have been conveniently collected in Jack Zipes's anthology *The Trials and Tribulations of Little Red Riding Hood: Versions of the Tale in Sociocultural Perspective*

(1983). In earlier versions, she is sometimes the victim of the wolf and even the agent of Little Red Riding Hood's destruction. One Victorian revision, Harriet Louisa Childe-Pemberton's *All My Doing; or Red Riding-Hood Over Again* (1882), shifts the blame to the grandchild, who naively grants a con artist access to her grandmother's estate. This wolf assaults and robs the grandmother. Two recent versions completely rewrite the narrative, attempting to jettison the correspondences implied by second childhood. In Lisa Campbell Ernst's *Little Red Riding Hood: A Newfangled Prairie Tale* (1995), the grandmother is a successful farmer and entrepreneur who curbs the wolf's appetites with her muffins and then puts him to work in her bakery. Susan Lowell's witty *Little Red Cowboy Hat* (1997) features a pistol-packin' cowgirl grandmother who terrorizes the wolf and makes sure her granddaughter learns that "a girl's gotta stand up for herself."

Contemplating these updated versions might lead to the conclusion that we are making progress toward "positive images" of old age. However, in the act of revising the grandmother, these updated versions summon Little Red Riding Hood's lineage of helpless grandmothers. In fact, the comic effect of the cowgirl counterpart depends upon adult readers' memories of previous grandmothers. By considering the present in juxtaposition with the past rather than along a simple trajectory that presumes "progress," we can also ask whether past images have been abandoned or merely repressed and seek the consequences these seemingly progressive images might have. This approach reveals the limitations of any simplistic representation, even a supposedly "positive" one (Cole, 1992). While metaphors of second childhood encourage children (and adults) to interpret the behavior of older people in trivializing ways, the all-powerful images of these new grandmothers may impose an impossibly high standard of competence, assertiveness, and independence. Seen from a distance, then, the diversity of attitudes toward aging in earlier children's literature functions not so much as a yardstick to measure progress but as a starting point for discussions of the work of representation.

To move from children's literature to that written explicitly for adults, another Victorian writer whose work is valuable to age studies is the novelist Charles Dickens. Dickens possessed a rare capacity to recall the language and feelings of childhood while simultaneously capturing an adult narrator's poignant sense of distance from and loss of that childhood. Thus, in *A Christmas Carol* (1843) Scrooge pathetically attempts to comfort his childhood self when the Ghost of Christmas Past reveals young Scrooge alone in a schoolroom. The adult Pip of *Great Expectations* (1860–1861) bemoans his younger self's snobbery to his adoring, uneducated uncle, Joe. While Dickens's novels sometimes rely on the trope of second childhood, they often thoughtfully connect the stages that mark the history of a life by reading childhood and middle age through the pleasures and longings of later life.

Dickens's novels also provide a rich field for studying the ways in which an abstract concept like old age accrues social meanings that come to be accepted as fixed, even natural. Despite the proliferation of old-age stereotypes, Dickens's older figures are flawed in ways that are likely to highlight rather than parody the complexities of late life. For example, Little Nell's grandfather in *The Old Curiosity Shop* (1840–1841) becomes addicted to gambling when all his other attempts to make a living fail. His character is an unusual and sympathetic portrayal of the economic, domestic, and psychological difficulties attendant upon the elderly poor. Similarly, the elderly flighty spinster, Lady Volumnia Dedlock of *Bleak House* (1852–1853), reminds readers of the fearful fate that awaited even aristocratic older women who lacked husbands and property.

But Dickens also includes elderly characters among his famous cast of eccentrics, such as the rapacious elderly dwarf Quilp in *The Old Curiosity Shop* or Krook, the mad purveyor of the Rag and Bone Shop in *Bleak House,* or, in contrast, the saintly schoolmaster of *The Old Curiosity Shop* or gentle Solomon Gills in *Dombey and Son* (1846–1848). The exaggerated portrayal of these eccentrics trains the reader's eye on the targeted qualities tweaked through eccentricity, as in the case of the wizened, ruthless, money-lending Smallweed grandparents of *Bleak House,* whose sheer querulousness and greed keep them alive.

Dickens's most intriguing elderly characters are distinguished by violent acts of "improper" aging which contrast sharply with Victorian philosophical treatises on old age or advice in conduct literature. Often these representations of dangerous, desirous, or destructive aging are heightened when old age combines with another social identity that "typical" Victorians found troubling. For example, descriptions of characters' bodies may forge illogical connections between old age and other cultural stereotypes. As audiences grow familiar with these linked characteristics, they begin to define old age in terms of pejorative characteristics that do not actually depend on one's age. In *Oliver Twist,* for instance, Victorian stereotypes of "the Jew," denoted by adjectives like greedy, thieving, and conniving, are imported into a lexicon of stereotypical features of certain images of old age, such as "the miser." Ageism fuses with antisemitism to explain the evil influence of the elderly gang leader, Fagin: he lures children into a pickpocketing ring, entraps girls in prostitution, and even trumps middle-aged thieves through cunning learned from long experience. Comparing the many film versions of the novel reveals how directors and actors have struggled to rationalize Fagin's unlikely powers, alternately playing the Jewishness of Fagin broadly or subtly, a change which, in turn, affects the age of the character.

As suggested in Fagin's case, characters in Dickens's novels who are portrayed as possessing two or more socially devalued identities are especially likely to become villains or victims. Physical deformity unites with signs of age to magnify the dwarf Quilp's rapacity and lechery in *The Old Curiosity Shop.* Scrooge is redeemed when he realizes he is a victim of the poisoning effects of being simultaneously a miser and a tyrannical old man. Perhaps the most dangerous combination of all in Dickens's work is the character who refuses to accept old age and so, in effect, inhabits two problematic categories—adolescence and senescence. Such characters are depicted as particularly absurd when their performance of youth is expressed through sexual desire as in the lascivious game of courtship and control between the leering Major Bagstock and the grotesque Mrs. Skewton of *Dombey and Son.* The very qualities which give these elderly characters energy and interest flout Victorian social expectations, desires, and behaviors tolerated in people deemed old.

Dickens's novels also raise questions about our too easy reliance on biology or chronology as the determinants of age. Extreme experience or feeling, especially of a violent or overwhelming nature, is especially likely to induce preternatural aging in Dickens's imagined universe. Accelerated old age registers a fictional protest against the evils of poverty in the case of Tiny Tim of *A Christmas Carol.* The 20-something Smallweed twins, Bart and Judy, are aged by greed. They become appalling doubles of their grasping grandparents in *Bleak House.* The extreme sensitivity of the child Paul Dombey renders him unable to survive the cruelties of a long life: he becomes wizened and dies from excessive goodness. Even the comic character, the Artful Dodger of *Oliver Twist,* who looks and behaves more like a shrunken, thieving, tough-talking man of the streets than the child he is, is remarkable for the unnatural aging that comes of losing his childhood.

Dickens's tendency to invest details of age-related description with moral significance also reveals the illogical yet powerful symbolic meanings a culture attaches to simple physiological signs. In Dickens's novels, then, the qualities, characteristics, and behavior attributed to human beings as "natural" signs of aging, in fact, have a symbolic life quite apart from real bodies and beings. In fact, in *The Old Curiosity Shop* as in *Great Expectations,* even buildings and streets take on features of old age as the narrators seek to communicate in one case the grandfather's psychological state and in the other Miss Havisham's by comparing collapsing houses to old faces and bodies (Walsh, 1993). When we read literature from an earlier period, the temporal distance helps us to see how difficult it is to resist representing characters as comic tenants of second childhood, harmless nonentities, or dangerous, mad age-overreachers.

As my examples suggest, Dickens uses the resources of literary language to draw readers' attention to the biases which mark characters as social insiders or outsiders. As we learn from these novels, comic exaggeration encourages readers to maintain distance and make judgments. Exaggeration can also take the form of melodrama, horror, or bathos—all literary effects. These forms of exaggeration engage readers' emotions very differently. Fagin's sensational crimes and the atmosphere of horror that surrounds his death left little room for analysis or sympathy while the melodrama of Little Nell's death in *The Old Curiosity Shop* overwhelmed Victorian readers in bathos and tears rather than encouraging social analysis. The passing of time, however, gives us a privileged vantage point. The mixture of social realism and sentimental or sensational extravagance transforms Dickens's novels into a dramatic stage upon which readers watch the spectacle of 19th-century attitudes toward aging. Ideally, learning how the properties, costumes, and language in Dickens's novels clothe the abstraction of *old age* enables us to approach our own culture's representations of aging as a set of material effects that we too have dressed up in assumptions and emotions—an important step toward imagining alternative ways to be old, to react to older people, and to plan for late life.

BACK TO THE FUTURE

Though the 19th century became increasingly prone to the specialization and compartmentalization of knowledge that separate many of us at work in age studies, Victorians fortunate enough to be well educated lived in a far more fluid world of ideas than academics do at present. The greater permeability of boundaries between scientific discourse, philosophical essays, and imaginative literature invited the kind of collaboration that we try to build under the flag of interdisciplinarity. Scholars in literature departments who want to make age a serious category of analysis have much to learn from historians, sociologists, psychologists, and others whose work focuses on the material realities and practical problems faced by older people. However, I hope that my contribution to this volume successfully argues that theoretically informed studies of the literary past can also help researchers from the social and applied sciences and the health care system to see how deeply their projects, patients, disciplines, and perspectives are affected by the complex forces of representation that shape our culture and its social as well as literary narratives. We are just as embedded in our narratives of aging and our constructions of age identities as the Victorians were in theirs. Exploring our assumptions through the comparative fusion of their literary and cultural narratives can guide us to unsuspected destinations in age research and help us build the roads to reach them. By developing interdisciplinary research resources—

from standardized search terms to bibliographies to web sites (with syllabi and other materials) to joint conferences to research centers to cotaught courses for students in literature, age studies, and critical gerontology to creative joint community projects—we will discover the directions (and follow the byways) toward that future together.

ACKNOWLEDGMENTS

I am grateful to Corey Creekmur, Fred Mangum, Margaret Morganroth Gullette, Stephen Katz, and especially Kathleen Woodward for their thoughtful responses to an earlier draft of this essay.

REFERENCES

Achenbaum, W. A. (1995). *Crossing frontiers: Gerontology emerges as a science.* New York: Cambridge University Press.

Altick, R. (1957). *The English common reader: A social history of the reading public, 1800–1900.* Chicago: University of Chicago Press.

Basting, A. D. (1998). *The stages of age: Performing age in contemporary American culture.* Ann Arbor: University of Michigan Press.

Bettelheim, B. (1976). *The uses of enchantment: The meaning and importance of fairy tales.* New York: Knopf.

Booth, C. (1980). *The aged poor in England and Wales.* 1894; Reprinted. New York: Garland.

Booth, W. (1992). *The art of growing older: Writers on living and aging.* New York: Poseidon Press.

Brown, M. (Ed.). (1995). *The uses of literary history.* Durham, NC: Duke University Press.

Browne, F. (1995). *Granny's wonderful chair.* 1857; Reprinted. Hertfordshire: Wordsworth's Eds. Ltd.

Carroll, L. (1982). *Alice's adventures in wonderland.* 1865; Reprinted as *Alice's Adventures in Wonderland and Through the Looking Glass.* New York: Oxford University Press.

Childe-Pemberton, H. L. (1987). All My Doing; or Red Riding-Hood Over Again. 1812; Reprinted in J. Zipes (Ed.), *Victorian fairy tales: The revolt of the fairies and elves.* New York: Routledge.

Cole, T. R. (1992). *The journey of life: A cultural history of aging.* New York: Cambridge University Press.

Cole, T. R., & Winkler, M. G. (Eds.). (1994). *The Oxford book of aging.* New York: Oxford University Press.

Covey, H. C. (1991). *Images of older people in western art and society.* New York: Praeger Publishers.

Covey, H. C. (1992). The definitions of the beginning of old age in history. *International Journal of Aging and Human Development, 34,* 325–337.

Covey, H. C. (1992–1993). A return to infancy: Old age and the second childhood in history. *International Journal of Aging and Human Development, 36,* 81–90.

DeMorgan, M. (1987). A Toy Princess, 1877; Reprinted in J. Zipes (Ed.), *Victorian fairy tales: The revolt of the fairies and the elves* (pp. 165–174). New York: Routledge.

Ernst, L. C. (1995). *Little Red Riding Hood: A newfangled prairie tale.* New York: Simon and Schuster.

Featherstone, M., & Wernick, A. (Eds.). (1995). *Images of aging: Cultural representations of late life.* New York: Routledge.

Freeman, J. (1979). *Aging: Its history and literature.* New York: Human Sciences.

Frueh, J. (1997). Visible difference: Women artists and aging. In M. Pearsall (Ed.), *The other within us: Feminist explorations of women and aging* (pp. 197–219). Boulder, CO: Westview Press.

Gullette, M. M. (1988). *Safe at last in the middle years.* Berkeley: University of California Press.

Gullette, M. M. (1997). *Declining to decline: Cultural combat and the politics of midlife.* Charlottesville: University Press of Virginia.

Haber, C. (1982). *Beyond sixty-five: The dilemma of old age in America's past.* Cambridge: Cambridge University Press.

Hamilton, P. (1996). *Historicism.* New York: Routledge.

Hareven, T. K. (Ed.). (1996). *Aging and generational relations over the life course: A historical and cross-cultural perspective.* New York: W. de Gryter.

Hareven, T. K. (1982). *Family time and industrial time.* Cambridge: Cambridge University Press.

Hazan, H. (1994). *Old age: Constructions and deconstructions.* Cambridge: Cambridge University Press.

Hockey, J., & James, A. (1995). Back to our futures: Imagining second childhood. In M. Featherstone & A. Wernick (Eds.), *Images of aging: Cultural representations of late life* (pp. 135–148). New York: Routledge.

Holstein, M. (1994). Taking next steps: Gerontological education, research, and the literary imagination. *The Gerontologist, 34,* 822.

Honig, E. L. (1988). *Breaking the angelic image: Woman power in Victorian children's fantasy.* New York: Greenwood Press.

Katz, S. (1996). *Disciplining old age: The formation of gerontological knowledge.* Charlottesville: University Press of Virginia.

Kertzer, D. I., & Laslett, P. (Eds.). (1995). *Aging in the past: Demography, society, and old age.* Berkeley: University of California Press.

Kohn, M., Donley, C., & Wear, W. (Eds.). (1993). *Literature and aging: An anthology.* Ohio: Kent State University Press.

Laslett, P. (1977). *Family life and illicit love in earlier generations.* Cambridge: Cambridge University Press.

Lowell, S. (1997). *Little red cowboy hat.* Illustrated by Cecil Reid. Ontario: Henry Holt and Co.

MacDonald, G. (1994). "Little Daylight." 1864; reprinted in Jan Marks (Ed.), *The Oxford Book of Children's Stories* (pp. 102–117). New York: Oxford University Press.

Mangum, T. (1999). Passages of life: Growing old. In H. Tucker (Ed.), *Blackwell guide to Victorian literature and culture.* London: Blackwell Press.

Mangum, T. (1998). Little women: The aging female character in nineteenth-century British children's literature. In K. Woodward (Ed.), *Figuring age, women, bodies, and generations.* Bloomington: Indiana University Press.

McKee, P., & Kauppinen, H. (1989). *The art of aging: A celebration of old age in Western art.* New York: Human Sciences Press.

McLerran, J. (1993). Saved by the hand that is not stretched out: The aged poor in Hubert von Herkomer's "Eventide: A scene in the Westminster Union." *The Gerontologist, 33,* 762–771.

Pearsall, M. (Ed.) (1997). *The other within us: Feminist explorations of women and aging.* Boulder, CO: Westview Press.

Pelling, M., & Smith, R. M. (Eds.) (1991). *Life, death, and the elderly: Historical perspectives.* London: Routledge.

Perkins, D. (1992). *Is literary history possible?* Baltimore: Johns Hopkins University Press.

Quadagno, J. (1982). *Aging in early industrial society: Work, family and social policy in nineteenth-century England.* New York: Academic Press.

Radway, J. (1924). *Reading the romance: Women, patriarchy, and popular literature.* Chapel Hill: University of North Carolina Press.

Ragland-Sullivan, E. The phenomenon of aging in Oscar Wilde's *Picture of Dorian Gray:* A lacanian view. In K. Woodward & M. Schwartz (Eds.), *Memory and desire: Aging/literature/psychoanalysis* (pp. 14–33). Bloomington: Indiana University Press.

Riggs, K. (1998). *Mature audiences: Television in the lives of elders.* New Brunswick, NJ: Rutgers University Press.

Roebuck, J. (1979). When does "old age" begin? The evolution of the English definition. *Journal of Social History, 12,* 416–428.

Temke, S. (1978). Human values and aging: The perspective of the Victorian nursery. In S. F. Spicker, K. M. Woodward, & D. D. Van Tassel (Eds.), *Aging and the elderly: Humanistic perspectives on gerontology* (pp. 63–81). New Jersey: Humanities Press.

Thane, P. (1993). Geriatrics. In W. F. Bynum & R. Porter (Eds.), *Companion encyclopedia of the history of medicine,* 2 vols. (pp. 1092–1115). New York: Routledge.

Tompkins, J. (Ed.). (1980). *Reader-response criticism: From formalism to post-structuralism.* Baltimore: Johns Hopkins University Press.

Tompkins, J. (1985). *Sensational designs: The cultural work of American fiction, 1790–1860.* New York: Oxford University Press.

Trollope, A. (1993). *The fixed period.* 1882; Reprinted. New York: Oxford University Press.

Veeser, H. A. (1989). *The new historicism.* New York: Routledge.

Walsh, S. (1993). Bodies of capital: *Great Expectations* and the climacteric economy. *Victorian Studies, 37,* 73–98.

Woodward, K. (1997). *Aging and its discontents: Freud and other fictions.* Bloomington: Indiana University Press.

Woodward, K. (Ed.). (1998). *Figuring age: Women, bodies, and generations.* Bloomington: Indiana University Press.

Woodward, K., & Schwartz, M. (Eds.). (1986). *Memory and desire: Aging/literature/psychoanalysis.* Bloomington: Indiana University Press.

Wyatt-Brown, A., & Rossen, J. (Eds.). (1993). *Aging and gender in literature: Studies in creativity.* Charlottesville: University Press of Virginia.

Zipes, J. (Ed.) (1983). *The trials and tribulations of Little Red Riding Hood: Versions of the tale in sociocultural perspective.* South Hadley, MA: Bergin Publishers.

5

Aging in the Mirror of Philosophy

Ronald J. Manheimer

How have philosophers and their methods of analysis, explanation and description contributed to our understanding of aging and later life? In his unique anthology, *Philosophical Foundations of Gerontology,* Patrick McKee (1982) identifies three ways in which philosophers, ancient and modern, have applied their craft to the subject of aging: by identifying the strengths, weaknesses, and appropriate social roles elders may play; by analyzing ethical dilemmas intensified by old age; and by evaluating epistemological claims about older persons' achievement of knowledge and wisdom (McKee, 1982, p. ix). McKee also points to a fourth area of inquiry into presuppositions underlying gerontological research and scholarship. Modifying McKee's approach, in this chapter we explore: (1) philosophers' depictions of the possibilities and limitations of later life, (2) ethical questions of meaning and purpose in old age, (3) the study of wisdom as a case in point for examining methods researchers bring to gerontology, and (4) the current relationship of academic philosophy to the subject of aging.

Our premise is that as gerontology emerges in the 20th century as a full-fledged discipline for research, scholarship, and practice, two trends become apparent: (1) philosophical inquiry into the positive meanings of old age and older persons' societal contributions—"successful aging"—get overshadowed by such behavioral and clinical criteria as social adaptation, life satisfaction, and maximum physiological functioning (Rowe & Kahn, 1987); and (2) traditional philosophical concerns about wisdom, the self, time, memory, mortality, and meaning—as they pertain to old age—now fall to scholars and researchers trained in the social sciences and fields of the humanities. Apart from those engaged in bioethics (the subject of another chapter in this volume), relatively few contemporary academic philosophers participate in critical discourse on aging and later life, while a number of gerontologists adopt methods of analysis and interpretation drawn from philosophical schools of phenomenology, critical theory, and hermeneutics. These shifts, reflecting broad trends in the social sciences and humanities, make the field of aging a battle ground for contesting the value and meaning of later life.

PHILOSOPHIES OF AGING

Gaining familiarity with classical frameworks through which old age is apprehended prepares us to identify variants as they appear in the 20th century. Indeed, ancient philosophers are sometimes cited to affirm a contemporary view of aging. For example, in *Aging and Old Age* (1995) legal scholar and economic theorist Richard Posner claims that a passage in Aristotle's treatise on rhetoric concerning the cognitive orientation of youth toward hope and expectation, and the elderly toward memory and the past, leads him to the view that each of us possesses, successively, a younger and then older self. This helps Posner account for the different abilities, interests, and behaviors of older and younger persons and helps him to justify society's continued investment in older persons' well-being. In his study of *Reminiscence and the Self in Old Age* (1991), researcher Edmund Sherman claims that Plato's doctrine of *anamnesis,* the theory that *a priori* knowledge can be gleaned through a deductive process that resembles remembering, provides an analogy to the value of reminiscence in old age. Reviewing one's life may enable an older person to extract permanent truths from those more transitory. These and other commentators presume the continued relevance of thinkers who lived and wrote about aging prior to the 20th century's remarkable extension of life expectancy and vastly improved conditions of old age. What enduring truths do these philosophers proclaim?

We may classify philosophers into four groups, each answering the question: "What is the best response to the changing conditions of life we experience in old age?" A transformed outlook and unique contributive role is suggested by Plato in *The Republic,* where he shows that old age holds the promise of unique insights and perspectives deriving from continued study and contemplation. A second response, withdrawal from society and resignation in the face of loss, is recommended by Aristotle and the first-century (C.E.) Hindu prophet, Manu. A third, less pessimistic, response is represented in writings of the first-century Roman orator Cicero and 17th-century French philosopher

Montaigne, who advocate remaining actively involved in community life while striving against decrements and losses associated with aging. And a fourth, apparently unprecedented view (which McKee does not include), that attitudes about growing old are nothing more than culturally imposed narratives, a "master plot" of "decline" (Gullette, 1997), based on falsehoods about physical aging from which we can eventually free ourselves. We will call this the liberated/deconstructed philosophy of later life.

These paradigmatic viewpoints about old age—the transformed/contributive, resigned/disengaged, and active/engaged—can be found in various combinations throughout the narrated history of aging. The liberated/deconstructed view is a species of postmodernism and may be compared to aspects of feminist theory. It is not surprising that French novelist and existential philosopher Simone de Beauvoir followed her epoch-making study of gender, *The Second Sex* (1950) with her highly influential *The Coming of Age* (1972).

The transformed life perspective is suggested in a famous scene in Plato's *Republic* (trans. 1941). Socrates, honoring the retired merchant Cephalus, tells a gathering of younger men that only those who are at life's "threshold"—close to death—have the wisdom to say whether the path of life is "rough or smooth." Cephalus agrees, explaining that while his older male friends lament their loss of sexual prowess, familial respect, and political power, he feels no such deprivation. He is grateful to be freed from the passions and desires which earlier in life troubled his soul, enabling him to turn his attention to the pleasures of the mind. A key to his tranquility, Cephalus explains, is his prior encounter with frightening dreams about death that produced pangs of conscience: had he led an honorable life? Now, he has made sure he owes no debts and has fulfilled his religious obligations. His message is that good men, conditioned by a virtuous life, may enjoy happiness in old age.

This classic portrait of contented aging and freedom from desire, echoed several centuries later in Cicero's famous treatise, *De Senectute,* is challenged by Socrates. Perhaps Cephalus's contentment is derived less from virtue than from accumulated wealth and power. Many have wealth, counters Cephalus, who lack contentment. Solid character and the qualities of temperance and piety make a person's life worthwhile whether old or young, he insists. Asked by Socrates to define what makes a person righteous, Cephalus, caught in contradiction, departs to attend a religious event without resolving whether, besides virtuous habits, wisdom requires the critical intellectual ability to conceptualize abstract universals.

Plato's student, Aristotle, seems to hold a different viewpoint. His treatise on the powers of argument and persuasion, the *Rhetoric* (1954), includes a compelling distinction between young and old that has influenced commentators of aging down through the centuries. Describing types of human character, Aristotle contrasts the qualities of youth and "elderly men." While young people dwell in expectations about the future, the old "live by memory rather than by hope; for what is left to them of life is but little as compared with the long past; and hope is of the future, memory of the past" (Aristotle, 1390a). Moreover, while youth is gullible, old age is cynical, and so on down the line of moral qualities. Aristotle reserves to "men in their prime" (between the ages of 35 and 49) an ideal character between young and old, "free from the extremes of either," for these midlife males are neither too confident nor too timid, too trusting nor too distrusting. Instead men in their prime combine qualities like bravery and temperance, whereas these attributes are unevenly distributed among the old and the young.

Though seeming to advocate disengagement and withdrawal from society, Aristotle does suggest something positive older people have to offer. In his *Nichomachean Ethics* (Aristotle, 1962) Aristotle distinguishes between *phronesis,* "wisdom in action," and *sophia,* "theoretical wisdom." Aristotle argues that applied or "practical" wisdom involves our ability to exercise good judgment in matters of commerce, profession, friendship, family, and civic life. Underscoring the difference between the two types of wisdom, Aristotle observes that while young people can attain theoretical wisdom in such matters as mathematics and geometry, they do not possess practical wisdom gleaned through concrete experience requiring "a quantity of time" (Aristotle, p. 160). We should listen to older people, says Aristotle, "for since experience has given them an eye, they see correctly (p. 167)." So time and age turn out to be advantages.

We find another position showing advantages from disengagement in the writings of the ancient Hindu sage Manu, who divides the life course into four traditional stages and roles. The period of "studenthood" is devoted to study and development of self-control, followed by the "householder's" involvement in marriage, career, and family responsibility. Next comes the "hermit" stage of early old age that brings a gradual liberation from preoccupation with practical affairs and diminishing attachments to worldly pleasures. Finally, in late old age, the "ascetic" follows a life of simplicity and withdrawal from public participation. For Manu, it is the ascetic, freed from the cycle of birth and death, who achieves "true insight into the nature of the world," gaining spiritual rather than, as in Plato and Aristotle, intellectual insight

By contrast, the activist role of Cicero's older citizen is far afield from spiritual disengagement. Reflection, strength of character, and refined judgment make the wise elder an ideal statesman. Cicero (1994) likens the city-state to a ship with its youthful and middle-aged citizens a busy crew doing the hard physical or practical work of seamanship. Although the older person may lack the physical stamina to operate the ship of state, he finds a vitally important place at the helm. Cicero is careful to distinguish maturity from frailty, chronological age from debilitating illness. It is the latter that incapacitates people and prevents their continued participation in society. He argues that good physical and mental health practices can help prevent premature decline, thereby increasing our chances for a robust and productive old age. Cicero thus favors continued engagement drawing upon experience-strengthened insight.

Like Cicero, Montaigne believes older citizens have special leadership roles to play in society. But Montaigne also believes that too long a delay prevents younger people from making their contribution at an earlier age. By 20, says Montaigne, our abilities are already fully realized "and give the promise of all they ever can do." Therefore, the young should be encouraged early to play responsible roles in society.

The prominent thinkers we have selected represent the range of viewpoints found throughout the centuries and influential into the modern period. For example, like Cicero, Simone de Beauvoir advocates continued social engagement and resistance to the stereotyping tendencies of society as she calls for older persons to refrain from excessive reminiscing (social disengagement through dwelling in the past) and to press on with their life projects (de Beauvoir, 1972). While Beauvoir's philosophy contains elements of engagement, she rejects notions of intrinsic purposes of later life and is aligned with the postmodern deconstructionist approach, of which she was an influential forerunner.

We find strikingly similar notions to Manu in Arthur Schopenhauer's frequently cited essay, "The Ages of Life" (1890), in which he argues that in old age we realize that striving for happiness is a chimera, pain alone is real. Compensation for abandoning the quest for the "rainbow of happiness" is "seeing the whole of life." While disillusionment is the chief characteristic of old age, as compensation, we get a clear, undiluted picture of life as it really is, not the phantom projections of our earlier years.

To this catalogue of philosophies of aging stretching from antiquity to modern times, we add the contemporary American philosopher David Norton, whose approach in *Personal Destinies* (1974) aligns the stages of life with the process of ethical attainment and understanding. Combining Aristotle's notion of "potential" and humanistic psychologist Abraham Maslow's theory of self-actualization, Norton presents development as the forward-directed process through which each person strives toward his or her unique destiny. Norton faults Aristotle's hypothesizing a "plateau" stage of ages 35 to 49, arguing that Aristotle's own concept of "right living" requires "progressive actualization of one's innate potentiality." Thus, moral development must be ongoing, a continuing "ascent" without which a person would be spiritually dead (Norton, p. 163).

Characterizing the incommensurableness of life stage transitions as the result of "surprises" to consciousness, Norton argues that self-perceived old age is recognizing we no longer have a future to provide further opportunities for self-actualization. The driving motive of life, fulfilling one's potential, simply ceases in old age. Gaining a clear real-ization of the finality of life, the individual finds a special task of recov-ering the "eternal past," the past of many generations, of humankind, "the world, the past of historical being." The older person becomes a beacon of generational consciousness. The very presence of older peo-ple is a sign both of life's impermanence and continuity.

If we detect ambiguity and inconsistency in the various philoso-phers we have surveyed, we have to remember they are often using aging and later life to support broader assertions about human nature and the social good (Minois, 1989). For example, Plato believes in the unreliability of emotions and perceptions of the transitory world of sensuous experience. He redirects us to the invisible world of durable truths in the form of ideas arrived at through reason. So, it is not sur-prising that he both applauds Cephalus's piety and orientation to the life of the mind, yet criticizes his limited capacity for abstract thinking. And Aristotle's praise of midlife men is a direct byproduct of his famous doctrine of the mean—an achieved balance point between the extremes of deficiency and excess in matters of character that yield the higher virtues. Repeatedly, we will find that not only do philoso-phers present us with reflected images of aging, but the subject of aging also functions as a mirror onto which philosophers project their cherished ideals, especially as a symbol of temporality.

Old age bears witness to the problematic quest for permanence, cer-tainty, immortality, and wisdom in the face not only of change but peri-odic chaos, social upheaval, personal disappointment, reversal of fortune, physical decline, injustice, and the flaw of excessive pride. The challenge aging and old age place before the philosopher is whether the search for ultimate truths must always founder on the reef of fini-tude and the shoals of mortality or whether something enduring may be retained or won back from time.

In summary, the history of philosophy does not present one best way to achieve a satisfying and fruitful old age nor a consensus on the roles older citizens should play in society. Most philosophers are mindful of the harsh conditions often accompanying later life and keep that in mind as they champion ideals of aging. The philosophical tradition helps us see that such goals as contentment, contemplation, statesmanship, ethical discernment, social engagement, and humility are interwoven with theories about nature, society, the universe, human purpose, and the good life. Philosophies of aging, such as the resigned/ disengaged, active/engaged, transformed/contributive, liberated/deconstructed, serve as reflective mirrors illuminating contemporary claims about old age, and helping us discern inherent values and beliefs sometimes obscured by complex scientific or metaphysical arguments. Thus, we now turn to evaluations of purpose in later life—meaning as an aspect of ethics.

ETHICS AND MEANING

Ethics refers to character, to what and how a good and wise person would choose and, by implication, the manner in which a collection of such individuals would constitute a just society. Good character suggests qualities or virtues possessed by the individual. The status of these qualities in old age provides an index to the overall sense of coherence, direction, purpose, in short, meaning of later life, without which the ethical debate about old age rings hollow. Ideals of fulfilled or appropriate aging, and the individual and social purposes of later life, help define the significance of old age. And here is where problems arise.

Old age has lost its societal meaning since we no longer share commonly held expectations, values, or understanding of its place in the life course (Cole, 1985). Though liberated from social and cultural stereotypes of the predestined and immutable character of old age as a time of inevitable decline, the new old age is besieged by theorists, marketeers, and the media, who advocate an ethos of boundless activity— social participation, education, volunteerism or recreation. This, in turn, has contributed to new normative stereotypes also conveying impoverished social meanings of aging and old age. These can be traced historically to post-Victorian theological and hygienic moralisms (Cole, 1992), the ideology of consumer capitalism (Moody, 1986), and the denial that frailty and death could have any positive significance (Gadow, 1983).

Others argue that the elderly suffer from personal meaninglessness because society deems their past experiences obsolete. Developmentally, the old have run out of growth potential. At best, they may accomplish life adjustments which gerontologists, perhaps reflecting the work ethic, call "tasks" (Havighurst, 1952). Inward meaninglessness takes the form of despair over the sense of one's having led an irrelevant and incomplete life (Erikson, 1975) which, in the face of impending death, produces anguishing loss of self-esteem (Butler, 1963), leaving the psyche prey to dominating unconscious forces, such as narcissism (Downing, 1981; Jung, 1933; Woodward, 1986).

Those who have articulated these problems also have set out to redeem the meaning of aging. Taking the cognitive transformation view that regards later life as a time when unique metamorphoses of self and society are possible, Cole and Moody, inspired by virtue ethicist Alasdair MacIntyre's (1989) notion of a "narrative quest," encourage older people to find their voices to demonstrate through stories and artistic expression, the significant moral and intellectual contributions which the old can make in the larger schema of the generations. Cole (1983) is dubious of the narrow, scientifically "enlightened" view of aging that emphasizes ameliorating the illnesses and weaknesses of old age through medical manipulation and rational social policies. He believes old age is not simply a set of problems to be managed and controlled, rather that by overcoming the fragmentary treatment of later life and studying the unity and interdependence of life stages, a meaningful, holistic, understanding will be possible.

Moody, writing about the value of continued learning on the part of older people (Moody, 1976), regarded "self-actualization" a key to releasing personal potential leading to ego integrity. Later, drawing on the Frankfurter School of "critical theory," Moody (1988) critiqued his own existential-humanistic approach in favor of a sociopolitical philosophy aimed at "emancipation" of the elderly through intergenerational cooperation, group initiative (such as self-help groups), mentoring roles the old can play for the young (especially the disenfranchised poor and minority), and release from the dominating ideologies found in public policies that preempt the initiative of the elderly, or which pit the old as a special interest group against the needs of other age groups.

Cole and Moody's transformational views of later life contrast with a more modest, sometimes conservative, position that later life is primarily a time for adapting to personal and social limitations. Elsewhere, we have called these "transformational" versus "adaptational" perspectives (Manheimer, 1992, 1989) on later life. Those, like Moody and Cole, who argue for developmentally appropriate roles guided by cultural traditions and classical virtues (Moody, 1997) stand on the side of the spiritual tradition, especially when compared to postmodernist students of aging who reject notions of age-appropriate roles as social stereotyping. For them, aging is an unwritten history yet to be evolved by each person, limited only by imagination and pressures of society to conform. A postmodern view of the purpose of old age holds that "age does not represent a place on a temporal trajectory or historical time line" but is simply an "existential construct" people use in fashioning their personal and social possibilities (Murphy & Longino, 1997, p. 90).

The postmodernist attitude places greater emphasis on the act of choice itself than on the thing chosen. Self and social construction—à la the "multiple realities" social phenomenology of Alfred Schutz (1962)—are the results of deliberate acts, not acceptance of or surrender to a superordinate reality. The ultimate transformational modernist view is that of unconstrained choice indifferent to age restraints, and contributing to an "age-irrelevant" society (Neugarten & Neugarten, 1986) in which the older person is simply that, a person, free to actualize his or her own individual potential (Gruman, 1979).

The philosophical difficulty we encounter in arguments about what constitutes a meaningful and purposeful later life is in finding adequate criteria for determining their validity and evaluating their explanatory power. It is not always clear when these descriptions of later life are to be understood as empirical statements, normative declarations, advocative utterances, or hypothetical ideals. A large body of literature, drawing from empirical, quantifiable studies as well as from oral histories and personal documents, has convincingly shown that, for a variety of reasons such as identity loss from retirement or absence of a sense of productivity, old age can bring about a crisis of meaning in one's life that is, at the same time, a social malaise amplified by certain values and social arrangements. But the cure for the crisis of meaning is harder to observe, measure or logically deduce.

Is the role of philosophy in gerontology to produce ideals, to advocate for change, to posit values—in short, to liberate older adults? Care must be taken to avoid a new form of paternalism by asserting norms for old people (McCullough, 1993).

Concerning the issue of meaning, philosophy adds to gerontology by offering critical analysis along historical, political, ethical, and epistemological lines, while striving for a synthesis of ideas making up an evaluative-normative construction of later life's purpose and meaning (Manheimer, 1999). But the discomfort of humanistic endeavors in a field dominated by clinical and behavioral science reveals itself even more clearly in the corresponding critique of investigative methodologies and their reporting narratives—especially those dealing with asserted strengths of aging. Research methodologies in the study of aging and later life do not stand outside the debate over meaning.

THE METHODS OF GERONTOLOGY

To redeem the meaning of aging against age stereotypes and reductivist tendencies that view old age as decline and dependency, a number of theorists have championed qualitative research and narrative approaches that seek to understand older persons through techniques of participant observation (Myerhoff, 1978), phenomenologically identified themes of continuity (Kaufman, 1984), and hermeneutic sensitivity to

the first-person accounts found in diaries, novels, poems, and autobiographies (Berman, 1996) written in old age. These interrelated
approaches seek to highlight the multiple dimensions of growing old as
influenced by personal history, gender, age cohort, ethnicity, geography (i.e., urban, rural, suburban), religiosity, and social class. As such,
these theorists draw on perspectives of social phenomenology (Schutz,
1962), studying subjective accounts of how individuals describe and
construct their own experiences, rather than categories and measures
imposed by the researcher. They risk generalizing from selective
research populations and interpreting qualitative data through the
lenses of their own midlife concerns. But what of scientific investigators who adhere to empirical, usually quantitative methods, yet seek
to study aspects of later life that traditionally belonged to the humanistic realm? Wisdom is a case in point.

The ancient and debated idea that wisdom might be the reward of
advancing age has taken on new significance in the 20th century. A
seminal article by social scientists Clayton and Birren (1980) reviews
the history of wisdom in ancient western and eastern traditions, draws
on quantified interview research data, and inquires whether wisdom is
a unique quality of later life. Significantly, Clayton and Birren are interested not only in wisdom as the capacity to make thoughtful, informed
decisions or to contemplate eternal truths, but as a set of behavioral
attributes that enhance individual adaptation, and even evolution-
favoring, species survival in old age which Birren, elsewhere, has
termed "strategic adaptability" (Birren, 1988). They conclude that wisdom represents "the integration of general cognitive, affective, and
reflective qualities."

In related works, psychologist Labouvie-Vief (1980, 1990) looks
developmentally at the culminating stages of life in old age arguing
against unilinear theories of development that presuppose a single trajectory, the familiar life curve of growth and decline. For Labouvie-Vief
growth and regression are interwoven throughout the life span. She
(1990) reads the entire history of discourse on cognitive development
as a clash between the tradition that favors *"mythos,"* intuitive, narrative
ways of knowing and experiencing, and *"logos,"* conceptual, rational
orientations. Rather than favoring one over the other, she believes in
the "balanced dialogue" between these two modes of knowledge that
defines wisdom (1990, p. 53). Labouvie-Vief cites the research findings
of Basseches (1984), Kramer (1983) and Sinnott (1984), among others,
as producing evidence supporting "transformation, dynamic, and dialectical thought" (p. 68) among middle-aged and old adults who display
cognitive abilities that surpass "single abstract systems" of thought—
the level of postformal attainment considered the apex of cognitive
development by Piaget and his followers. Still, she adheres to the

evolutionary biological premise that cognitive attainment should yield adaptive advantage and, hence, serve as a coping mechanism for species survival. She remains faithful to the biological foundations of psychology, as do Clayton and Birren, who place the purposiveness of wisdom outside the domain of wisdom itself. Their positions underscore just how interwoven is the search for understanding wisdom with the method of that search.

The debate over methods of studying aging could be summarized as a face-off between *mythos* and *logos*. On the *logos* side is what Moody (1993, pp. xv–xvi) calls "the conventional positivism and empiricism so prevalent in social gerontology," that links a presumed value-free or objective science with the aims of mainstream medical research in exercising "instrumental reason" to improve the lives of older people. Moody argues that beneath the surface of this seemingly benevolent approach lurks an unselfconscious commitment to problem solving that seeks to conquer old age in a battle against decline and death without paying attention to the personal and social meanings of growing old, the spiritual importance of aging, the relationship of older persons to other generations, and the larger purpose of keeping people alive only to place them further into dependency and irrelevance. We need the *logos* contribution, Moody would agree, but not without the integration of the *mythos* approach that seeks to investigate the subjective dimensions of old age and the unity of the life course. We need wisdom to study wisdom.

Perhaps Swedish sociologist Lars Tornstam satisfies Moody's criteria in his qualitative and quantitative studies of "gerotranscendence," a concept akin to wisdom. According to Tornstam (1997), gerotranscendence is a natural and universal process that accompanies aging, which he characterizes as a shift from "a materialistic and pragmatic view of the world to a more cosmic and transcendent one" (Tornstam, 1997, p. 17). Tornstam uses a variety of research tools, ranging from the open-ended interview to self-administered, Likert-scale type questionnaires that are analyzed using generally accepted methods of statistical analysis. Remarkably, he finds older Danish and Swedish subjects embracing attitudes about space, time, identity, life, and death that correspond more closely to the views of nondualistic Zen Buddhism (Tornstam, 1996) than the conventional dualistic views of a midlife western European or American. His subjects experience an intermingling of the historical past with the personal present, a blurring of sharp distinctions between self and others, identity and community.

Unlike Birren and Labouvie-Vief, and other social scientists, Tornstam refuses to attribute social, psychological or biological advantages to wisdom, except to say that gerotranscendence can bring about a higher degree of life satisfaction. He takes the radical (for a social scientist) view that wisdom, or gerotranscendence, in this case, is not a means but an end in itself. What makes gerotranscendence in the elderly difficult to study, Tornstam suggests, is similar to the problem posed by cultural anthropologists: the world view of the subjects (older people) may be impervious to the research paradigm of the investigator.

The field of gerontology seems divided between scientific empiricists pursuing research to improve the lives of older persons, and those who argue that empiricism based on a biomedical paradigm of later life restricts researchers to too narrow an appreciation for the lived experience of growing old, an appreciation better served by inclusion of personal accounts of old age in written, spoken, and visual forms. Those who rally around the banner of "critical gerontology" call for self-awareness among researchers, policy makers, teachers, and service providers who may be perpetuating old and new stereotypes of old age, and ideological entanglements with political agendas that do not adequately support older persons' dignity and resourcefulness. If Labouvie-Vief is correct about wisdom as balance between the two ways of knowing, *mythos* and *logos,* perhaps her formulation also holds for the gerontologists' quest for wisdom: integrating quantitative and qualitative research, behavioral empiricism and narrative, and showing their complementarity.

GERONTOLOGY AND PHILOSOPHY TODAY

Apart from the field of biomedical ethics, the topics of aging and later life have attracted few academic philosophers. Dutch philosopher Jan Baars (1997) attributes this indifference to contemporary philosophy's rejection of subjectivity as a realm deemed worthy of study. For the academic philosopher, says Baars, "aging does not fit well into the vision of the human condition" (p. 260). He may be referring to certain Anglo-American schools of philosophy that dominated the field through much of the 20th century. To reject subjectivity is to dismiss self-reported experiences that are difficult to observe and confirm and that, hence, challenge attempts to align philosophy with the methods of the natural sciences. Baars embraces those schools of thought that explore subjectivity as traceable through narrative and open to descriptions of what phenomenologists call "lived experience." With its emphasis on subjective states of inner-time consciousness (temporality), phenomenology may provide a corrective to scientific approaches that regard the process of aging as a march through chronological time. Following Ricoeur (1984), Baars argues that inner-time consciousness, communicated through narratives, is the mode of discourse through which temporal being is brought to language. When people write or tell their life stories, they "emplot" events and feeling into a coherent, if "fragile integration of a profound discordance" (p. 291).

Another explanation for philosophers' reluctance to engage in the discourse on aging comes from German philosopher Thomas Rentsch (1997), who argues that ever since the enlightenment when Kantian metaphysics proclaimed that necessity and universality were the twin-criteria of logical truths, philosophy has "ignored the content of the conditions and relative nature of human life" (p. 263). Unlike the ancient ethicists, such as Aristotle, who asked what a good life might be in relation to a person's stage of life, enlightenment and modern ethicists have assumed that certain general rules should hold independent of age. Rentsch, too, finds aging fertile ground for framing ethical theory.

Rentsch argues that old age "intensifies the experience of finitude," disclosing the true mirror of human existence—"our inability to repeat the past, the irreversibility of life's direction, the unavoidability of passage through stages of development, the irrevocability of the past in memories of unattained meaningfulness, and unpredictability of the future"(p. 267). "Only a calm look backward," says Rentsch, who echoes Schopenhauer, "can help us achieve an emancipated clarification of life" (p. 271).

Philosophers' seeming indifference to the subject of aging and later life and gerontologists' growing interest in ethical and epistemological aspects of aging reflect a major paradigm shift in the social sciences and humanities. The subject of aging and old age may strike many philosophers as belonging to the purview of biological research and clinical medicine or a scientific gerontology that has as its core a biological (genetic or evolutionary) paradigm into which new knowledge can be integrated. What role could philosophers play? Meanwhile, a small set of gerontological social scientists seeks to venture where philosophers fear to tread—incorporating traditional philosophical questions and methods into a scientifically oriented scholarship.

Contemporary philosophy encounters the same problems as other disciplines of the humanities; it has few commonly agreed upon methods and no central paradigm for integrating knowledge—as the human genome project functions in the biological sciences. Sociobiologist Edward Wilson may be correct in arguing that while the natural sciences and the humanities will continue as the "two great branches of learning in the twenty-first century," the social sciences will split, "with one part folding into or becoming continuous with biology, and the other fusing with the humanities" (Wilson, 1998). Currently, that split shows up in gerontology, with the majority of social scientists leaning toward biology and a minority toward the humanities.

Aging and later life will continue to be an intellectual battleground between those who regard later life as a time of unique understanding leading to a transformed consciousness and those who regard it as a period of adaptive accommodation to physical and mental decline. Old age is also the battleground between those who see senior adults as representatives of enduring values and permanent truths and those who champion liberating old age from imposed norms and decline to attribute any set of virtues or insights to the elderly, leaving each person free to reinvent him- or herself.

Are the views about aging espoused by philosophers from the time of Plato to that of Norton simply a fun house of distorting mirrors? There are no unfiltered perceptions of aging and old age and every theory is colored by the prejudices, preoccupations, hopes and fears of its time. What philosophic investigations of aging have to offer us is heightened awareness of the possible meanings of old age both for the aged person and for society as a whole. Later life, we believe, is a mirror reflecting the profound significance of human temporality and its relationship to how we think about human purpose, the aims of development, justice between generation, continuity and change, and the prospects for transcendence of the finite.

REFERENCES

Aristotle. (1954). *Rhetoric.* Book 2, chapter 12, translated by W. R. Roberts. New York: Modern Library.

Aristotle. (1962). *Nichomachean Ethics,* Book 6, translated by M. Ostwald. New York: The Library of Liberal Arts.

Baars, J. (1997). Concepts of time and narrative temporality in the study of aging. *Journal of Aging Studies, 11,* 283–295.

Beauvoir, S. de. (1972). *The coming of age.* Translated by P. O'Brian. New York: Putnam.

Berman, H. J. (1994). *Interpreting the aging self: Personal journals of later life.* New York: Springer Publishing Co.

Birren, J. E., & Fisher, L. M. (1990). The elements of wisdom: Overview and integration. In R. J. Sternberg (Ed.), *Wisdom, its nature, origins, and development* (pp. 317–332). Cambridge: Cambridge University Press.

Butler, R. N. (1963). The life review: An interpretation of reminiscence in the aged. *Psychiatry, 26,* 65–75.

Cicero. (1994). *De Senectute* (On Aging). Excerpt in T. R. Cole & M. G. Winkler, *The Oxford Book of Aging* (pp. 48–53). New York: Oxford University Press.

Clayton, V. P., & Birren, J. E. (1980). The development of wisdom across the life span: A reexamination of an ancient topic. In P. B. Baltes & O. G. Brim, Jr., (Eds.), *Life-span development and behavior* (Vol. 3, pp. 103–135). New York: Academic Press.

Cole, T. R. (1983). The enlightened view of aging: Victorian morality in a new key. *Hastings Center Report, 13,* 34–40.

Cole, T. R. (1985). Aging and meaning: Our culture provides no compelling answers. *Generations, 10,* 49–52.

Cole, T. R. (1992). *The journey of life: A cultural history of aging in America.* Cambridge: Cambridge University Press.

Downing, C. (1981). Your old men shall dream dreams. In J. R. Staude (Ed.), *Wisdom and age.* Berkeley, CA: Ross Books.

Erikson, E. (1975). *Life history and the historical moment.* New York: W. W. Norton.

Gadow, S. (1983). Frailty and strength: The dialectic of aging. *Gerontologist, 23,* 144–147.

Gruman, G. J. (1978). Cultural origins of present day "ageism": The moderniza-tion of life cycle. In S. F. Spicker, K. M Woodward, & D. Van Tassel (Eds.), *Aging and the elderly.* Atlantic Highlands, NJ: Humanities Press.

Gullette, M. M. (1997). *Declining to decline.* Charlottesville: University Press of Virginia.

Havighurst, R. J. (1952). *Developmental tasks and education.* New York: McKay.

Jung, C. G. (1933). *Modern man in search of a soul.* New York: Harcourt, Brace and World.

Kaufman, S. R. (1986). *The ageless self: Sources of meaning in later life.* Madison, WI: University of Wisconsin Press.

Labourvie-Vief, G. (1980). Adaptive dimensions of adult cognition. In N. Datan & N. Lohman (Eds.), *Transitions of aging.* New York: Academic Press.

Labouvie-Vief, G. (1990). Adaptive dimensions of adult cognition. In N. Datan & N. Lohman (Eds.), *Transitions of aging* (pp. 3–26). New York: Academic Press.

MacIntyre, A. (1989). *After virtue: A study in moral theory.* Notre Dame, IN: University of Notre Dame Press.

Manheimer, R. (1999). *A map to the end of time: Wayfarings with friends and philosophers.* New York: W. W. Norton & Co.

Manheimer, R. J. (1989). The narrative quest in qualitative gerontology. *Journal of aging studies, 3, 5,* 231–252.

Manheimer, R. J. (1992). Wisdom and method: Philosophical contributions to gerontology. In T. R. Cole, D. D. Van Tassel, & R. Kastenbaum (Eds.), *The handbook of the humanities and aging* (pp. 426–440). New York: Springer Publishing Co.

McCullough, L. B. (1993). Arrested aging: The power of the past to make us aged and old. In T. R. Cole, et al. (Eds.), *Voices and vision of aging* (pp. 184–204). New York: Springer Publishing Co.

McKee, P. L. (1982). *Philosophical foundations of gerontology.* New York: Human Sciences Press.

Minois, G. (1989). *History of old age.* Trans. by S. H. Tenison. Chicago: University of Chicago Press.

Moody, H. R. (1976). Philosophical presuppositions of education for older adults. *Educational Gerontology, 1,* 1–16.

Moody, H. R. (1986). The meaning of life and the meaning of old age. In T. R. Cole & S. A. Gadow (Eds.), *What does it mean to grow old?* (pp. 11–40). Durham, NC: Duke University Press.

Moody, H. R. (1988). *Abundance of life, human development policies for an aging society.* New York: Columbia University Press.

Moody, H. R. (1993). Overview: What is critical gerontology and why it is it important? In T. R. Cole (Ed.), *Voices and vision of aging* (pp. xv–xli). New York: Springer Publishing Co.

Moody, H. R., & Carroll, D. (1997). *The five stages of the soul.* New York: Doubleday.

Moody, H. R., & Kapp, M. B. (1995). Ethics. In G. Maddox, et al. (Eds.), *Encyclopedia of aging.* New York: Springer Publishing Co.

Murphy, J. W., & Longino, C. F., Jr. (1997). Toward a postmodern understanding of aging and identity, *Journal of Aging and Identity, 2,* 81–91.

Myerhoff, B. G. (1978). *Number our days.* New York: E. P. Dutton.

Neugarten, B. L., & Neugarten, D. A. (1983). Age in the aging society. *Daelalus, 115*(1), 31–49.

Norton, D. L. (1976). *Personal destinies: A philosophy of ethical individualism.* Princeton, NJ: Princeton University Press.

Plato. (1941). *Republic,* trans. F. MacDonald Cornford. New York: Oxford University Press.

Posner, R. A. (1995). *Aging and old age.* Chicago: University of Chicago Press.

Rentsch, T. (1997). Aging as becoming oneself: A philosophical ethics of late life. *Journal of Aging Studies, 11,* 263–271.

Ricoeur, P. (1984). *Time and narrative, vol. 1.* Translated by K. McLaughlin and D. Pellauer. Chicago: University of Chicago Press.

Rowe, J. W., & Kahn, R. L. (1987). Human aging: Usual and successful. *Science, 237,* 143–149.

Schopenhauer, A. (1890). The ages of life, from *Counsels and Maxims,* translated by T. B. Saunders. London: Swan Sonnenschein.

Schutz, A. (1967). *The phenomenology of the social world.* Translated by George Walsh and Frederick Lehnert. Evanston, IL: Northwestern University Press.

Sherman, E. (1991). *Reminiscence and the self in old age.* New York: Springer Publishing.

Tornstam, L. (1996). Gerotranscendence: A theory about maturing into old age. *Journal of Aging and Identity, 1,* 37–50.

Tornstam, L. (1997). Gerotranscendence in a broad cross-sectional perspective. *Journal of Aging and Identity, 2,* 17–36.

Woodward, K. (1998). The mirror stage of old age. In K. Woodward & M. M. Schwartz (Eds.), *Memory and desire.* Bloomington: Indiana University Press.

Wilson, E. O. (1998). Back from chaos. *Atlantic Monthly, 281, No. 3,* 41–62.

6

Bioethics and Aging

Laurence B. McCullough

T his chapter concerns the issues that arise in the complex intersection of bioethics and aging. Bioethics and aging is properly
understood to be a subfield of the larger field of bioethics.
This chapter therefore begins with a brief introduction to the field of
bioethics. Subsequent sections then address major current topics in
bioethics and aging: decision making in geriatric health care, at the
end of life and in long-term care; managed care, a topic of increasing
importance as Medicare and Medicaid experiment with enrolling their
beneficiaries in the new forms of health and medical care gathered
under this rubric; health policy issues concerning health care for the
elderly; and challenging orthodoxy in geriatrics and gerontology.

BIOETHICS: A BRIEF INTRODUCTION

The term "bioethics" was first coined in the early 1970s (Reich, 1994).
Bioethics is defined as the intellectually disciplined study of the morality of the health care professions, of patients, of health care institutions, and of health care policy (Jonsen, 1998; Reich, 1995). Morality
concerns both right and wrong behavior and good and bad character.
As a subdiscipline of ethics, bioethics concerns what morality *ought* to
be for health care professionals, as well as for patients, health care
institutions, and public policy. Asking what morality ought to be involves
identifying the grounds, nature, and limits of the obligations of health
care professionals, patients, and health care institutions in clinical
practice in both the outpatient and inpatient settings, and of society
regarding the development and implementation of health policy that
makes health care professionals, patients, and health care institutions
accountable to society through the institutions of self-government.

The grounds of these obligations are found variously in ethical principles such as respect for autonomy, beneficence, and justice (Beauchamp & Childress, 1994); in theories of care based on affiliative psychology and ethical analyses of human relationships (Jecker & Reich, 1995); in narratives of peoples and nations (Hunter, 1995); and in accounts of the virtues (habits or dispositions of character that routinely help us to discern our obligations and to discharge them) (Hauerwas, 1995) relevant to health care professionals, patients, institutional managers, and citizens.

Bioethics is a field of intellectual endeavor marked by a striking methodologic diversity, with healthy competition among various methods of ethical inquiry. Bioethics is therefore a markedly interdisciplinary field, drawing on the disciplines of philosophy, religious studies, law, qualitative social sciences, and the basic and clinical sciences of the health care professions. This disciplinary diversity contributes to and synergizes the methodologic diversity of the field (Moody, 1992a).

Bioethics and aging, as a subfield of bioethics, undertakes the disciplined study of what morality ought to be for health care professionals responsible for the care of elderly patients and clients, for family members who participate in the care of elders and decisions about that care, for health care institutions (broadly understood) responsible for the care of elderly patients and clients, and for society regarding health care services for the elderly and their families. Bioethics and aging is, like bioethics, a strikingly interdisciplinary field (Cole & Holstein, 1996; Moody, 1992a). This chapter reflects that interdisciplinarity and draws particularly on philosophy.

Bioethics had its beginnings in issues that surround death and dying, as well as those at the beginning of life. In Paul Ramsey's phrase bioethics began at the "edges of life" (Ramsey, 1984). The current concern and debate about the relevance and effectiveness of advance directives—the living will and the durable power of attorney for health care—continue this limited focus on bioethics and aging. The law also continues to be preoccupied with issues surrounding death and dying, most recently in the pair of United States Supreme Court rulings on physician-assisted suicide and the legalization of this practice in the state of Oregon (Annas, 1994; *Vacco v. Quill,* 1997; *Washington v. Glucksberg,* 1997).

Bioethics and aging, however, has made significant progress in breaking out of this narrow—and unrealistic—equation of ethics and aging with the ethics of death and dying. This has mainly been the result of the properly broadening influence of gerontologists and geriatricians coming to the field with their clinical experience and sciences. Geriatricians and gerontologists know that most of their patients and clients are not gravely ill and dying and so, as these individuals brought their clinical experience and disciplines to the field of bioethics, the scope of ethics and aging has expanded to include more than simply death and dying. The topics addressed in the sections that follow reflect this broadening scope of bioethics and aging.

DECISION MAKING IN GERIATRIC HEALTH CARE

Much recent work on bioethics and aging has focused on decision making in health care by patients and clients and the need to respect and implement their decisions by health care professionals, by health care institutions, and by family members who care for them and become involved in decisions about their care. This should come as no surprise, given the considerable emphasis in recent bioethics on the ethical principle of respect for individual autonomy. This principle requires health care professionals and institutions, along with family members, to acknowledge the values and beliefs of elders, elicit their health care preferences that support and express these values and beliefs, and, unless there is an ethically compelling reason to the contrary, implement their health care preferences.

Understood in these terms, the ethical principle of respect for autonomy obligates health care professionals to protect and promote the interests of their geriatric patients and clients as those individuals understand their own interests and not as health care professionals, from their perspective, or family members, from their sometimes different perspective, claim to understand elders' interests. Elders, like other individuals, can reach understanding and adoption of their values and preferences through many routes, including moral traditions of families, communities (especially religious communities), peoples and societies, and nations. The concept of autonomy in bioethics does *not* require that elders generate their values and preferences *de novo,* only that they embrace those values and preferences as substantially their own (Faden & Beauchamp, 1986).

The ethical principle of respect for autonomy came to prominence in bioethics as a counterbalance to a principle with an ancient pedigree in the history of medical ethics, "beneficence." Beneficence is an ethical principle that obligates us to protect and promote the interests of others as those interests are understood from a perspective that is both external to that individual and that is intellectually and morally authoritative. For centuries in the West, beginning with the Hippocratic oath and the texts that accompany it, the health care professions have claimed such a perspective, but only with respect to the health-related interests of those who become patients or clients.

Bioethics has for decades opposed paternalistic exercise of benefi-cence, the health care professional acting unilaterally on clinical judg-ment about patients' interests and interfering with their autonomy in doing so. Whether and how beneficence-based obligations should limit autonomy-based obligations has become a central topic in bio-ethics and aging, particularly concerning elders' decision making about health care.

Two areas of decision making have received considerable attention. The first is end-of-life decision making, especially the use and imple-mentation in the clinical setting of advance directives. The second con-cerns the most common health problems among the elderly, affecting millions every day and bringing them to the attention and care of health care professionals and institutions and raising significant policy issues (e.g., the rapid rise in home healthcare costs for Medicare in recent years), namely, chronic diseases and the progressive disability that they can often cause. The nature and meaning of chronic illness, especially its implications for how the central bioethical concept of autonomy should be understood, has now become a prominent topic in the bioethics literature (Toombs, 1992; Toombs et al., 1995). In addition, the increasing disability of progressive chronic disease often reduces an elderly individual's capacity for self-care, resulting in increased dependence on others to supplement this loss (Kane & Kane, 1982, 1987). Ethical issues in long-term care have therefore come to the fore (Agich, 1993; Dunkle & Wykle, 1988; Jecker, 1991; Kane & Caplan, 1990, 1993; Lidz et al., 1993; McCullough & Wilson, 1995; Moody, 1992a), in no small measure as a result of the initiative to promote research on ethics and long-term care supported by the Retirement Research Foundation in the 1980s (Hofland, 1988).

End-of-Life Decision Making

Over the past two decades informed consent has become one of the most well understood aspects of bioethics. The ethical principle upon which informed consent is based is respect for the autonomy of the patient (Faden & Beauchamp, 1986). In the informed consent process the health care professional remains *an authority* (Engelhardt, 1995)—someone who is expected to be able to form and explain expert clini-cal judgments about the patient's diagnosis or condition, the reason-able alternatives for managing that diagnosis or condition (i.e., those accepted in clinical judgment and practice of the relevant health care profession) including the alternative of nonintervention, and the bene-fits and risks of these alternatives.

However, the health care professional is not *in authority;* the health care professional lacks the legal power to act on his or her clinical judgment and recommendations independently of explicit authorization for doing so by the patient, except in emergencies. Instead, the patient is *in authority*, i.e., has the final say about what clinical management, if any, will be implemented. Being *in authority* creates the basis for what is now accepted clinical practice, namely, the right of an elderly patient to accept proffered clinical management or to refuse it. For example, when the patient refuses such intervention for end-stage or life-threatening disease or injury, i.e., elects to be allowed to die, then his or her right to do should be respected. Neither health care professionals, institutions, family members, friends, nor the courts have the legal power to override such refusal by adult, competent patients. The patient can refuse any and all clinical management, including critical care, resuscitation, antibiotics, pressor drugs, fluid, nutrition, or any other medical or nursing intervention that would prolong the dying process. The patient's refusal should be implemented in all cases by a physician's order, usually known as a "Do not resuscitate" order. "Do-not-resuscitate" order forms (they should really be called "nonaggressive management of life-threatening events" protocols) reflect the wide range of interventions that patients can refuse as a result of being in authority over the outcome of the informed consent process.

It should go without saying that, when a patient refuses life-preserving interventions, his or her pain, distress, and suffering should be appropriately managed. Such management, however, is not routinely provided in a disturbing percentage of cases (The SUPPORT Investigators, 1995). In response, many medical schools and residency training programs have made pain control a central component of their basic science and clinical curricula.

It often occurs that, in the end-stages of disease or injury, elderly patients lose the capacity to make decisions about the clinical management of life-threatening events. These cases are governed by the law of advance directives. These are legal instruments by which the patient makes his or her wishes known in advance. The Living Will does so in advance of *both* terminal illness (as defined in the applicable statute or, in the case of Veterans Affairs facilities, VA policy) and loss of decision-making capacity and is usually used to refuse intervention for life-threatening events. In some jurisdictions the Living Will can be either written or oral. Relevant statutes (sometimes known as a "Natural Death Act") and policies also provide for surrogate decision makers when the patient has left no Living Will. The typical list is a spouse, majority of reasonably available adult children, parents, or siblings. The Durable Power of Attorney applies in advance *only* if there is loss of decision-making capacity and names someone to act as his or her surrogate or "agent." William Reichel and David Doukas (1993) have recently produced an excellent resource for elders considering advance directives, a guide also addressed to family members, health care professionals, and others who may be involved in the elder's decision-making process about end-of-life care.

Both the Living Will and Durable Power of Attorney for health care are grounded in the ethical principle of respect for autonomy. This autonomy-based justification has led to philosophical puzzles about whether the decisions made by a patient when mentally competent should be authoritative when the patient has lost such competence, e.g., as a result of advanced Alzheimer's disease (Post, 1995). Questions have therefore been raised about the validity of projected decision making that is at the heart of advance directives (Dresser & Robertson, 1989). The concepts of personal identity that form the basis for such questions appear to require a metaphysics of personal *unity*. In my judgment, such a philosophical concept of personal identity demands too much because it is not consistent with lived experience and the instruction of philosophy by contemporary basic and clinical science of brain physiology. These teach that the coherence of an individual's cognitive and affective life is variable and that individuals can get along well enough even when that coherence is low. Moreover, the brain does not function as a single organ, but rather as a more or less well associated collection of quasi-organs that have evolved in sufficient association—but not unity—over time. This concept of personal identity as personal unity also demands too much in that it violates the presumption of autonomy that advance directives are designed to protect. The concept of personal identity proposed by such critics of projected decision making as Dresser and Robertson (1989) sets those thresholds for autonomy at the time of executing an advance directive very high (one must display a very highly developed stage of personal identity), thus denying autonomy to many and therefore subtly but powerfully undermining the presumption of autonomy that is supposed to govern the ethics of advance directives. What seems, at first, to be an abstract philosophical preoccupation turns out to have major clinical and policy implications, which continue to be explored in the bioethics literature. Stephen Post (1995) has recently argued that there is sufficient continuity of identity through the stages of Alzheimer's disease. He bases his argument on a concept of radical human equality that has the advantage of avoiding the problem of a too demanding concept of personal identity.

Advance directives are also understood to be powerful tools to protect patients from the paternalism of health care professionals, physicians in particular, who might override the autonomy of patients out of the beneficence-based concern to prevent death. The antipaternalistic dimension of advance directives, however, becomes effective only when physicians routinely turn advance directives into "Do-Not-Resuscitate" orders. The SUPPORT Study suggests that this remains a serious problem. SUPPORT involved a large clinical study of end-of-life decision making, the goals of which included attempts to increase the completion and utilization of advance directives by patients who would need them, those thought reliably to be within 6 months of death—a population dominated by geriatric patients in hospitals and nursing homes. Their strategy was to train nurses to gather information about the preferences of patients regarding end-of-life clinical management of life-threatening events and to communicate this information to physicians. The SUPPORT Investigators tested the hypothesis that this intervention would increase neither the rate at which advance directives were completed nor the rate at which physicians implemented existing advance directives. Indeed, the SUPPORT Investigators found that physicians often failed to implement patients' directives, thus extending their dying process beyond that which they had apparently preferred (The SUPPORT Investigators 1995). This comprehensive, multicenter study indicates that respect for autonomy as expressed in advance directives may sometimes be more a matter of rhetoric than the standard of clinical practice for geriatric patients. The conclusion of the SUPPORT Investigators in this respect is striking:

> Advance directives had no clinically important effect on decision making concerning resuscitation among seriously ill patients in SUPPORT . . . These findings fail to support the widespread public and professional enthusiasm for advance directives (The SUPPORT Investigators, 1994, p. 27).

The SUPPORT Study began before the implementation of the Patient Self-Determination Act, federal legislation designed to increase at least the completion rate of advance directives that took effect in 1991 (OBRA, 1990). This legislation points in the direction of the need for institutional approaches to increasing the completion and utilization of advance directives. In an important commentary on the SUPPORT Study, Bernard Lo underscores the need for an approach that attempts to change the culture of hospitals and nursing homes as the key to achieving the antipaternalistic, autonomy-supporting goal of advance directives.

> Improving the quality of care generally requires changes in the organization and culture of the hospital and active support of hospital leaders . . . Such changes might include conferences on decisions near the end of life, case management meetings regarding individual patients, individual feedback to physicians on their performance, and recognition of clinicians who provide outstanding care at the end of life. To improve pain management, clinical services might hold conferences on pain management,

establish a pain consultation team, or record assessments on the
patient's vital signs sheet (Lo, 1995, p. 1636).

In the author's experience, some institutions have begun to make
such changes. For example, "Do-Not-Resuscitate" order forms have been
changed to include orders for pain control, antiseizure medications,
and measures to protect the dignity of the dying patient. The completion and implementation of such orders can be encouraged by having
such physician-order forms regularly reviewed as part of the total quality management process of a hospital or nursing home. Peter Singer
and his colleagues have also developed disease-specific advance directives that could contribute to such institutional change (Berry & Singer,
1998; Singer et al., 1994, 1995, 1997).

Lo (1995) also identifies a major conceptual change that needs to
occur: viewing admission to the critical care unit as a trial of intervention rather than an intervention that either runs without limit or is not
initiated in the first place. The concept of a trial of intervention means
that, first, there must be a reasonable expectation of benefit outweighing iatrogenic harm from admission to the critical care unit and, second, there must be reasonable expectation of benefit outweighing
iatrogenic harm from continued admission to the critical care unit.
Although the first clinical judgment is sometimes difficult to make, the
second can be made with increasing reliability. In this way, patients can
be given a reasonable chance to benefit from critical-care intervention
but to be protected from ultimately futile and iatrogenically harmful
intervention from unnecessarily prolonged critical care management.

Physician-assisted suicide has come to greater prominence recently
in end-of-life decision making (Battin et al., 1998). Physician-assisted
suicide is usually understood to mean that the physician provides to
the autonomous patient, at the explicit request of that patient, the
means to cause death and that the patient then self-administers these
means with the intent of causing death. It should come as no surprise
that this remains a matter of deep disagreement in the bioethics literature. The U.S. Supreme Court has ruled that, while there is no constitu-
tionally protected right to physician-assisted suicide, there is also no
constitutional bar to it (Annas, 1997; *Vacco v. Quill,* 1997; *Washington v.
Glucksberg,* 1997). Oregon allows physician-assisted suicide by referen-
dum, in a paradigm example of the "laboratory of the states" for the
development of public policy that is a hallmark of the American federal
approach to self-government (Annas, 1994). The Oregon approach
assumes that physician-assisted suicide is not inconsistent with professional integrity of physicians, but may violate individual conscience. Thus, there is no legal mandate that physicians participate at
the request of patients.

Long-Term-Care Decision Making

The distorting effect on bioethics and aging of the strong emphasis on end-of-life decisions has in the past decade received a powerful and welcome corrective, by the expansion of the scope of bioethics and aging to other areas of improving decision making. Sustained attention to long-term-care decision making has led this change.

Long-term care has been defined as "a set of health, personal care and social services delivered over a sustained period of time to persons who have lost or never acquired some degree of functional capacity" (Kane & Kane, 1987, p. 4). Long-term-care needs trigger responses within the elder's family to meet those needs. The typical pattern of response is that the female members of the family provide so-called "informal" long-term-care services. In contemporary American society, women tend increasingly to be in the work place and so, when a woman makes the decision to meet the long-term-care needs of an elderly family member, she does so either by adding hours of "informal" work at the end of her workday (thus imposing psychosocial costs on her family as well as opportunity costs on herself) or at the expense to herself and her family of lost income from fewer hours at work, sometimes including no hours at work. Reducing one's work hours, taking an extended leave (as now permitted under federal law), or quitting paid work altogether impose psychosocial costs on women who make these difficult decisions as well as opportunity costs.

Through such heroic efforts and nontrivial financial, opportunity-cost, and psychosocial sacrifice the long-term-care needs of millions of older Americans are met every day. Some states have experimented with ways to help families cope with these caregiving burdens, while others have done little—for the simple, and correct, reason that doing so is probably not cost-beneficial. These expenditures will probably not save that public source any significant amount of money. Any costs that do occur show up, as it were, on someone else's books. Payers, private and public alike, have an incentive only to avoid cost-nonbeneficial strategies when they themselves incur the unnecessary added cost. The nonsystem of American health care—with a mix of private and public payers and private and public providers with no comprehensive, central management or guiding policies—perpetuates the shifting of care burdens onto families and the direct and indirect costs of various kinds of doing so, in good measure, because there is no consistent economic incentive for a more rational alternative.

Medicare has been exploiting the nonsystem of health care in the United States for more than a decade with its prospective payment system under Diagnostic Related Groups (DRGs). DRGs-based payment provides hospitals—for-profit and not-for-profit alike—with an incentive to shorten length of stay as a major means to control costs and thus continue to profit from Medicare. Medicare has benefited by being able to slow the rate of inflation for its hospital expenditures, thus postponing a financial and political crisis for the Medicare Trust Fund. In addition, more and more geriatric medical care is being shifted to the outpatient setting, following the general trend in medical care of the past decade. As a consequence, also, patients admitted to hospitals tend to be sicker and frailer than they were in the past. As a consequence also, geriatric patients are frequently discharged from the hospital with new or increased long-term-care needs, with the hospital in some cases "coming home" (Arras, 1995). The Veterans Affairs health system is now rapidly following suit, e.g., in profiling of physicians that focuses intensely on hospitalization as a measure of quality.

In this environment it seems plain that there is an implicit policy assumption in Medicare's DRGs-based payment system and in the VA shift to controlling utilization of hospital admissions and days: families will pick up where hospital admissions used to continue. Put in a more unfriendly way, it seems to be Medicare's and the VA's policy to systematically exploit the sense of moral obligation on which so many American families act to meet the long-term-care needs of their loved ones. Medicaid and private insurance, in my experience teaching in a major children's hospital, have adopted the same implicit policy for meeting the long-term-care needs of disabled and seriously ill children—an experience from which geriatrics and gerontology need to learn.

This exploitation of families has occurred without any explicit public policy debate about whether such policies are consistent with social justice. We know that most of the "informal" long-term care is provided by women, raising the justice-based issue of whether the exploitation of these women unfairly builds on and sustains gender bias in our society. Men in the household, and children, need to work more hours to replace needed, lost income. It does not take much reflection to appreciate that Americans—through our elected representatives in the Congress—have decided that it is politically acceptable to impose these burdens on families and to do so with little or no public debate about the justice of such policies.

As a consequence, we put families between the rock of doing everything and the hard place of doing less than everything or sometimes nothing and often judging themselves selfish or morally inadequate for doing the latter. There is a middle ground: setting reasonable limits on one's caregiving obligations. Identifying this middle ground can be undertaken within the larger context of identifying the values and preferences of elders and involved family members and negotiating caregiving obligations, shares, burdens, and limits in a values-rich discourse (McCullough & Wilson, 1995). The health policy challenge will be how to adjust policy constraints to accommodate families that, on careful and informed reflection, reach the well-reasoned judgment that they can no longer provide "informal" long-term care at their current levels.

Now, accommodating such families will almost certainly mean an increase in taxes, both state and federal. We live in an America in which the old concept of citizenship, built around virtues of self-sacrifice and compassion for the unfortunate, has become attenuated, perhaps destroyed (Holstein & Cole, 1995). This language needs to be revived, although without the special pleading that advocates for the elderly sometimes employ in our public discourse.

Inquiry into long-term care has, in important ways, enriched bioethics and aging conceptually (Moody, 1992b). This is especially the case for the concept of autonomy in bioethics. It now seems plain that the ethical principle of respect for autonomy and the concept of autonomy of patients was developed in and for the acute-care setting. The decision-making group in this setting was understood to be the physician and health care team with the patient, with the patient's family regarded as third parties to the decision-making process (Beauchamp & McCullough, 1984). Ethical issues concerned decisions made in the hospital about hospital-based care, especially admission to and discharge from the critical care unit. Patient autonomy was understood to involve the exercise of rights by the patient about hospital-based clinical management of the patient's problems. Discharge planning did not get much attention in the bioethics literature; this setting of decision making, where families are vitally involved, is still largely ignored in the bioethics literature.

Recent work on ethics and aging has called this narrow focus of decision making and narrow concept of autonomy into question. George Agich has forcefully argued that long-term care requires us to rethink the eviscerated concept of autonomy that developed in the acute-care setting, a setting that ignores the life-world of the elderly, a concept that Agich takes from the phenomenologist Alfred Schütz (Agich, 1993). Based on such a phenomenological analysis of the life-world of the elderly, Agich draws a useful and very powerful distinction between nodal and interstitial autonomy in autonomous decision making. Nodal decisions involve the "either/or" choices, such as to continue to live at home or to move to congregate housing or even a nursing home. Interstitial autonomy concerns the everyday decisions we all make about people with whom we want to spend time, having some quiet time, the objects of art or decoration with which we want to be surrounded, and the like. Agich notes that there are indeed powerful policy constraints on nodal decisions in long-term care, for example, those created by income eligibility for various publicly funded services. These constraints can and do restrict the exercise of autonomy in nodal long-term-care decisions. Once nodal decisions have been made, however, many opportunities for the exercise of interstitial autonomy remain and the ethics of long-term-care decision making is incomplete if it omits this varied and large domain of decision making and meaning for elders.

Agich's innovative and original analysis of autonomy in long-term care expands the agenda of ethics in long-term-care to include both nodal and interstitial decision making. Because the latter is not so restricted by policy constraints, it should receive greater attention and emphasis, especially in long-term-care institutions. These, therefore, need not be "total" institutions (Lidz et al., 1993). On this account, too, we can see that acute-care, hospital-based bioethics has been impoverished by failing to acknowledge the importance of interstitial autonomy, which is exercised chiefly in the discharge planning process.

Nodal decisions in long-term care frequently involve trade-offs between safety and independence. Bart Collopy (1995) has recently provided a provocative analysis about these trade-offs, arguing that they invoke a false dichotomy. Safety, Collopy argues, has been construed narrowly to mean physical safety only, e.g., from falls or wandering off grounds onto a busy thoroughfare. If safety is rethought, Collopy argues, in biopsychosocial terms, then personal and psychological and social safety become just as important as physical safety. Independence, on this account, involves psychosocial safety, which is now seen as one end of the continuum of biopsychosocial safety, with the other end concerning physical safety. Within this biopsychosocial concept of safety physical safety does not automatically receive priority, as it often, in fact, does, especially in the judgments of health care professionals and concerned family members. Instead, Collopy persuasively argues, it may be obligatory to respect the elder's person and autonomy, to risk physical safety in order to preserve a larger, more meaningful, and therefore more morally compelling, domain of psychosocial safety.

Long-term-care decision making needs to take account of these remarkable conceptual advances. Family members may place a priority on physical safety of an elderly loved one partly to avoid or reduce caregiving burdens on themselves, including the psychosocial burden of worry or the disruption of phone calls from parents' neighbors about dad wandering yet again in the neighborhood in the wee hours of the morning. Indeed, family members may place such a priority on physical safety that they describe the elder's circumstances in ways that differ markedly from the description the elder offers, itself shaped by psychosocial safety. A small fire in the kitchen from an untended pot on the stove thus becomes an unacceptable emergency for family members but a minor nuisance to the elder who cannot countenance leaving home and sustaining her sense of personal identity—a core concern of biopsychosocial safety.

This problem has been termed "contested reality" in the recent literature (McCullough et al., 1995). The contest does not arise from some value-neutral account of the facts but from value-laden accounts of the elder's life world. An emphasis on physical safety links to a concern with nodal decisions—dad just cannot be left at home alone any longer, according to an exhausted and concerned daughter—to reach one description. An emphasis on psychosocial safety links to a concern with interstitial decisions—what's the fuss about; it wasn't a big fire and was out as soon as the fire department put water on it, dad says. Long-term-care decision making that ignores the problem and challenges of value-laden contested reality will probably only make interpersonal and intrapsychic conflicts among elders and family members worse in an already stressful decision-making process.

In long-term care, the stage has been set to build on these innovative conceptual analyses and ethical arguments. It is time to undertake clinical investigation of experimental long-term care decision-making processes developed in response to this original and important work. This reflects a broad trend in clinical bioethics: In many areas the conceptual groundwork has been undertaken successfully and has stabilized and this conceptual groundwork needs to be transformed into innovative and proven clinical practice. In such work is to be found the future of ethics and aging.

MANAGED CARE

Medicare, Medicaid, the Veterans Affairs Department, and TRICARE (the new federal program for military dependents and retirees) constitute major health care delivery systems for the millions of elders in the United States. They are rapidly being transformed by the adoption of the techniques of managed care.

The changes in the public payment systems that pay for health care for the elderly, especially those that pay for medical care, are like all social experiments that Americans undertake. These changes are usually not carefully thought through and are therefore poorly planned and often implemented in an uncoordinated, if not chaotic, fashion, inducing both stress resulting from poorly managed change and skepticism that the changes are real and lasting. These outcomes reflect the fact that the United States has no system for health care, i.e., no centrally organized, paid for, and managed mechanism of paying for, organizing, and providing medical care for elders, much less the entire population.

Managed care utilizes two business tools to change the clinical decision making, judgment, and behavior of physicians. The first involves paying physicians in ways that provide economic incentives for the prudent, reduced utilization of resources—e.g., referral services, imaging, expensive medications, hospitalization. Such payment schemes— withholds, discounted fee-for-service, capitation—impose economic conflicts of interest on physicians, i.e., a conflict between their moral fiduciary obligation to provide patients with appropriate clinical management of their problems and self-interest in income and job security (Khushf, 1998). In the old, now passing, era of fee-for-service there also existed economic conflicts of interest, as built-in features of that payment scheme. Patients had to rely on the integrity of their physicians not to overuse resources and thus earn more income, a reliance that was not always well placed, given the excessive rates of cesarean delivery, hysterectomies, tonsillectomies, heart catheterizations, and bypass procedures that were not—and too often still are not—medically indicated. In the managed practice of medicine patients still must rely on the integrity of their physicians—and also managed care organizations and hospitals—to manage economic conflicts of interest well. Integrity is a virtue that obligates physicians and institutions to practice medicine according to the highest intellectual and moral standards. It is undoubtedly the case that integrity of clinical judgment, decision making, and practice is consistent with lower levels of utilization of health care resources and therefore better controlled costs—to exactly what levels we do not know, and therein lies the heart of the great social experiment called the managed practice of medicine.

The second business tool of managed care is to regulate the clinical judgment, decision making, and practice of physicians by bringing them to a more rigorous scientific and clinical standard of excellence. This standard requires that the variation in utilization of medical services should reflect only (a) the biologic variability of disease, injury, and handicap, and (b) the biological variability of the response of disease, injury, and handicap to clinical management. Geography should never be *destiny* (Wennberg, 1998; Wennberg et al., 1973); it should not even be relevant except insofar as geography affects the variability of disease, injury, and handicap in our species. Medicine, in other words, needs to be made *more* scientific, not less, and the way to do this is to regularize medical practice in ways that bring greater scientific and clinical discipline to patient care and to do so on population-based grounds. The result should be healthier patients and perhaps considerable reduction in the rate of growth of health care costs.

As managed care continues to become dominant in the delivery of medical services to geriatric patients, geriatrics and clinical gerontology will need to expand their ethical agenda to include identifying, understanding, and managing well the ethical challenges of the managed care. The goal of this new and rapidly developing agenda in the bioethics (and law) of aging will be to identify and sustain forms of the economically disciplined, fiduciary practice and professions of medicine, nursing, psychology, social work, and the other health care professions serving geriatric patients and clients (McCullough, 1999). An economically disciplined fiduciary profession is inherently unstable because it involves an inherent and inescapable potential for conflict between meeting the clinical needs of patients and the legitimate self-interest of health care professionals in adequate income and job security. One thing seems plain: continued economic self-sacrifice on the part of health care professions and institutions will be required to manage this moral instability well. How many clinicians and institutions will be willing to accept the logic of the core fiduciary professional virtue of self-sacrifice will determine—more than any other factor, in my judgment—the outcome of the experiment called the managed practice of medicine. Health care professionals, as they always have been, will remain responsible for their integrity. They can give it up, but they cannot have it taken from them—a simple piece of wisdom that has been clear in world intellectual traditions for millennia.

HEALTH CARE POLICY

Health care policy concerns the obligations of society, exercised through the institutions of self-government, in paying for, delivering, and regulating health care. Elders enjoy considerable health care entitlements in the United States at the present time. Any adequate ethical analysis of health care policy regarding the elderly must begin by acknowledging that the elderly constituted a politically advantaged population for health care policy (Feder, 1990; Kapp, 1989). Such ethical analysis must also acknowledge that, with the projected growth in the percentage of elders in the United States, the many advantages of elders vis-à-vis health care policy are likely to be called into question in the political process and public discourse.

Justice arises as an ethical concern when demand for resources outstrips supply. Demand for health care, among elders in particular (given the incidence of chronic, expensive diseases among the elderly vis-à-vis younger populations) threatens to outstrip supply, a problem that will become worse as the American population continues to age. In addition, there are problems of access to health care for elders, given the high out-of-pocket costs for medical care for Medicare beneficiaries (less of a problem for elderly veterans, especially those who meet the VA economic criteria for mandatory status). Justice is thus the ethical principle most pertinent to health care policy.

Justice, Aristotle teaches us, requires that we render to each what is due to him or her and that like cases of what is due to individuals be treated alike (Aristotle, 1984). Over the centuries, there have emerged competing concepts of what is due to individuals in conditions of scarcity. This competition among diverse concepts of justice, each with different implications for the allocation of scarce resources, appears to be permanent. No single concept of justice has emerged to canonical authority, i.e., able to show all other concepts of justice to be disabled by irreversible inadequacy and able to show itself to be the only intellectually defensible concept of justice.

In the bioethics literature there have emerged at least four main competitive concepts of justice. An egalitarian concept of justice requires that each should receive health care services in proportion to his or her needs. Robert Veatch has put this concept in terms of an obligation to meet the needs of patients equally, with the goal of producing an equality of health status insofar as possible. Elders with greater than normal needs, e.g., those with congestive heart failure, would receive preferential health care, to maintain their functional status. Daniel Callahan has argued for a variant of this concept, taking the view that each elder has a basic need to reach a normal life span and not to have death fought at all costs (Callahan, 1987). This proposal defines equal health care at the end of life as palliative, not critical care. This provocative proposal has met with important criticism (Barry & Bradley, 1991). A basic decent minimum concept of justice requires that each have his or her basic health care needs met, but beyond that he or she should receive health care services according to ability to pay. This concept of justice was adopted by the President's Commission for the Study of Ethical Problems in Medicine and in Biomedical and Behavioral Research (1983). This would result in publicly funded basic health care plans for everyone, the elderly included, but could require significant out-of-pocket payment for medical care above the basic, decent minimum. The third concept is a libertarian concept that takes private property seriously and also claims that differences in health status are primarily a result of natural and social lotteries. Thus, that someone experiences poor health is regarded as unfortunate, but not unfair. The libertarian concept of justice requires that each should receive health care services according to what he or she has paid for, e.g., in the form of insurance or the accumulation of personal savings. Libertarian justice would let markets resolve the allocation of scarce medical resources for the elderly. The fourth concept of justice in health care is the maximin principle that comes to bioethics from the work in ethics and political philosophy of the distinguished

Harvard philosopher, John Rawls (1971). This view holds that there should be equality of opportunity of access to health care as a basic social good and that allocation of resources should favor those who are least well off in terms of health, income, and other forms of social status. Norman Daniels (1988) has championed this concept of justice for geriatric health care.

All of these concepts of justice agree that scarcity must be managed in a fair fashion. Fairness means, at least, that not every elderly patient will receive all health care that he or she *wants*. That is, autonomy is not an adequate principle to address the allocation of scarce health care resources. Indeed, justice in its various concepts is designed to *constrain* individual autonomy.

CHALLENGING ORTHODOXY IN GERIATRICS AND GERONTOLOGY

Geriatrics and gerontology hold that there are diseases *associated with* aging, but not diseases *of* aging. This distinction was developed to counter intellectually, scientifically, and clinically unfounded prejudices against the elderly in the many forms that ageism once took. This distinction has done important intellectual, moral, clinical, educational, and political work, to be sure.

In keeping with the traditional role of the humanities, philosophy especially, to challenge orthodoxy, I want to challenge this orthodoxy by considering impaired executive control functions. These can lead to impairments of all three components of autonomy—intentionality, understanding, and noncontrol—identified in the now classic (in the field of bioethics) work of Faden and Beauchamp (1986) on informed consent. These patients experience deficits especially in intentionality— the ability to make and adapt plans—and in noncontrol—the ability to resist environmental cues that are detrimental to their plans. As a consequence, they experience significantly impaired autonomy, requiring surrogate decision making about their care subsequent to hospitalization for health problems that themselves are the sequelae of impaired intentionality and noncontrol. The ethical issue concerns whether the substituted judgment standard, i.e., decision making based on the patient's prior values such as independence, or the best interest standard, i.e., decision making based on prudent judgments about how best to protect the patient's health, functional status, and remaining independence and autonomy, should guide surrogate decision making for these patients.

Royall and his colleagues (1997) have suggested that there is a strong correlation between an autonomy-disabling pathology, frontal lobe disorders, and aging. Given this correlation, which appears to increase with age among the elderly, such disorders may well indeed be diseases *of* the aging brain, not diseases *associated with but not caused by aging.* This is, to be sure, a gerontologically heterodox—even heretical—view, but this does not make the view scientifically unsound.

This gerontological heterodoxy has important implications for the ethics and law of aging. There may be diseases of aging that significantly impair the autonomy of elders and may do so with increasing frequency in the oldest old. If this is the case, should there be routine screening of elders for these deficits of autonomy? If such deficits are discovered and if there is also no way presently to treat them, should we discount the autonomy of affected elders? If so, to what degree?

Consider, for example, the impact answers to these questions could have on interstitial decisions such as driving or nodal decisions to complete an advance directive or to undertake value-rich long-term-care decision making in which both nodal and interstitial autonomy is at risk. As a stable matter of both ethics and law, both advance directive and long-term-care decision making involve and therefore presume intact autonomy. On the Faden-Beauchamp analysis, autonomy includes intentionality, the ability to make and adapt plans. Executive dysfunctions impair this ability, frequently significantly. Moreover, autonomy on the Faden-Beauchamp analysis includes noncontrol, the freedom from substantially controlling influences. Executive dysfunctions can impair impulse control, making the elder more susceptible to substantially controlling environmental cues, such as the strongly stated and directive recommendations of involved family members and health care professionals.

In most jurisdictions witnesses to the Durable Power of Attorney attest to soundness of mind. Should witnesses do so in the absence of evaluation of executive control functions? Most statutes governing Living Wills require witnesses only to attest that the patient did indeed make the decision orally or in writing, but not to attest to competence. Should this policy be changed, given the apparent prevalence of executive dysfunctions with increasing age? Long-term-care decision making, if it involves any assessment at all, usually involves only cognitive assessment via such clinical tools as the Mini-Mental Status Examination. But this tool evaluates only cognitive functions that Faden and Beauchamp call understanding; this examination does not evaluate intentionality and noncontrol. Given the stakes for elders and involved family members, and the importance of at once respecting the elder's nodal and interstitial exercises of autonomy and the reasonable limits of family members on the direct and indirect burdens of "informal" long-term care, should the evaluation of decision-making capacity for long-term-care decision making be more thorough?

Is even raising these questions an unwarranted moral, social, and legal threat to elders? I think that raising these questions is indeed a threat to their autonomy, but it may be warranted scientifically, clinically, and ethically. It is not unreasonable to be disturbed by this judgment, creating an important and compelling item for the future agenda of bioethics and aging.

REFERENCES

Agich, G. J. (1993). *Autonomy and long-term care*. New York: Oxford University Press.

Annas, G. J. (1994). Death by prescription—the Oregon initiative. *New England Journal of Medicine, 331,* 1240–1243.

Arras, J. Conflicting interests in long-term-care decision making: Acknowledging, dissolving, and resolving conflicts. In L. B. McCullough & N. L. Wilson (Eds.), *Long-term-care decisions: Ethical and conceptual dimensions* (pp. 197–217). Baltimore: Johns Hopkins University Press.

Aristotle. (1984). *Nichomachean Ethics*. In J. Barnes (Ed.), *The complete works of Aristotle* (pp. 1729–1867). Princeton: Princeton University Press.

Barry, R. L., & Bradley, G. V. (Eds.). (1991) *Set no limits: A rebuttal to Daniel Callahan's proposal to limit health care for the elderly*. Urbana: University of Illinois Press.

Battin, M. P., Rhodes, R., & Silvers, A. (1998). *Physician assisted suicide: Expanding the debate*. New York: Routledge.

Beauchamp, T. L., & Childress, J. F. (1994). *Principles of biomedical ethics* (4th ed.). New York: Oxford University Press.

Beauchamp, T. L., & McCullough, L. B. (1984). *Medical ethics: The moral responsibilities of physicians*. Englewood Cliffs, NJ: Prentice-Hall, Inc.

Berry, S. R., & Singer, P. A. (1998). The cancer specific advance directive. *Cancer, 82,* 1570–1577.

Callahan, D. (1987). *Setting limits: Medical goals in an aging society*. New York: Simon and Schuster.

Cole, T. R., & Holstein, M. (1996). Ethics and aging. In R. H. Binstock & L. K. George (Eds.), *Handbook of aging and the social sciences* (pp. 480–493). San Diego: Academic Press, Inc.

Collopy, B. (1995). Safety and independence: Rethinking some basic concepts in long-term care. In L. B. McCullough & N. L. Wilson (Eds.), *Long-term-care decisions: Ethical and conceptual dimensions* (pp. 137–152). Baltimore: Johns Hopkins University Press.

Daniels, N. (1988). *Am I my parents' keeper?: An essay on justice between the young and the old*. New York: Oxford University Press.

Dresser, R., & Robertson, J. (1989). Quality of life and treatment decisions for incompetent patients: A critique of the Orthodox approach. *Law, Medicine, and Health Care, 17,* 234–268.

Dunkle, R. E., & Wykle, M. L. (Eds.). (1988). *Decision making in long-term care: Factors in planning*. New York: Springer Publishing Co.

Engelhardt, H. T., Jr. (1995). *Foundations of bioethics,* 2nd ed. New York: Oxford University Press.

Faden, R. R., & Beauchamp, T. L. (1986). *A history and theory of informed consent.* New York: Oxford University Press.

Feder, J. (1990). Health care and the disadvantaged: The elderly. *Journal of Health Politics, Policy, and Law, 15,* 259–269.

Hauerwas, S. (1995). Virtue and character. In W. T. Reich (Ed.), *Encyclopedia of bioethics* (2nd ed., pp. 2525–2532). New York: Macmillan.

Hofland, B. F. (1988). Autonomy and long-term care: Background issues and a programmatic response. *Gerontologist, 28,* 3–9.

Holstein, M., & Cole, T. (1995). Long-term care: A historical reflection. In L. B. McCullough & N. L. Wilson (Eds.), *Long-term-care decisions: Ethical and conceptual dimensions* (pp. 15–34). Baltimore: Johns Hopkins University Press.

Hunter, K. (1995). Narrative. In W. T. Reich (Ed.), *Encyclopedia of bioethics* (2nd ed., pp. 1789–1794). New York: Macmillan.

Jecker, N. S. (Ed.). (1991). *Aging and ethics.* Clifton, NJ: Humana Press.

Jecker, N. S., & Reich, W. T. (1995). Contemporary ethics of care. In W. T. Reich (Ed.), *Encyclopedia of bioethics* (2nd ed., pp. 336–344). New York: Macmillan.

Jonsen, A. (1998). *The birth of bioethics.* New York: Oxford University Press.

Kane, R. A., & Caplan, A. L. (Eds.). (1990). *Ethical issues in the everyday life of nursing home residents.* New York: Springer Publishing Co.

Kane, R. A., & Caplan, A. L. (Eds.). (1993). *Ethical conflicts in the management of home care: The case manager's dilemma.* New York: Springer Publishing Co.

Kane, R. A., & Kane, R. L. (1982). *Values and long-term-care.* Lexington, MA: Lexington Books.

Kane, R. A., & Kane, R. L. (1987). *Long-term-care: Principles, programs, and policies.* New York: Springer Publishing Co.

Kapp, M. (1989). Rationing health care: Will it be necessary? Can it be done without age or disability discrimination? *Issues in Law and Medicine, 5,* 337–366.

Khushf, G. (1998). Understanding, assessing, and managing conflicts of interest. In L. B. McCullough, J. W. Jones, & B. A. Brody (Eds.), *Surgical ethics* (pp. 342–366). New York: Oxford University Press.

Lidz, C. W., Fischer, L., & Arnold, R. M. (1993). *The erosion of autonomy in long-term care.* New York: Oxford University Press.

Lo, B. (1995). Improving care near the end of life: Why is it so hard? *JAMA, 274,* 1634–1636.

McCullough, L. B. (1999). A basic concept in the clinical ethics of managed care: Physicians and institutions as economically disciplined moral co-fiduciaries of populations of patients. *Journal of Medicine and Philosophy, 24,* 77–97.

McCullough, L. B., & Wilson, N. L. (1995). *Long-term care decisions: Ethical and conceptual dimensions.* Baltimore: Johns Hopkins University Press.

McCullough, L. B., Wilson, N. L., Rhymes, J. A., & Teasdale, T. A. (1995). Managing the conceptual and ethical dimensions of long-term care decision making: A preventive ethics approach. In L. B. McCullough & N. L. Wilson (Eds.), *Long-term-care decisions: Ethical and conceptual dimensions* (pp. 221–240). Baltimore: Johns Hopkins University Press.

Moody, H. R. (1992a). Bioethics and aging. In T. R. Cole, D. D. van Tassel, & R. Kastenbaum (Eds.), *Handbook of the humanities and aging* (pp. 395–425). New York: Springer Publishing Co.

Moody, H. R. (1992b). *Ethics and aging.* Baltimore: Johns Hopkins University Press.

OBRA (Omnibus Budget Reconciliation Act) of 1990, P. L. 101-508, secs. 4206, 4751.

Post, S. G. (1995). *The moral challenge of Alzheimer disease.* Baltimore: Johns Hopkins University Press.

President's Commission for the Study of Ethical Problems in Medicine and in Biomedical and Behavioral Research. (1983). *Securing access to health care.* Washington, DC: U.S. Government Printing Office.

Ramsey, P. (1984). *Ethics at the edges of life.* New Haven, CT: Yale University Press.

Rawls, J. (1971). *A theory of justice.* New York: Basic Books.

Reich, W. T. (1994). The word Bioethics: Its birth and the legacies of those who shaped its meaning. *Kennedy Institute of Ethics Journal, 4,* 319–336.

Reich, W. T. (1995). Introduction. In W. T. Reich (Ed.), *Encyclopedia of bioethics* (pp. xix–xxxii). New York: Macmillan.

Reichel, W., & Doukas, D. (1993). *Planning for uncertainty: A guide to living wills and other advance directives for health care.* Baltimore: Johns Hopkins University Press.

Royall, D. R., Cordes, J., & Polk, M. (1997). Executive control and the comprehension of medical information by elderly retirees. *Experimental Aging Research, 23* 301–313.

Singer, P. (1994). Disease-specific advance directives. *Lancet, 344,* 594–596.

Singer, P. A., Thiel, E. C., Naylor, D., Richardson, R. M. A., & Llewellyn-Thomas, H. (1995). Life-sustaining treatment preferences of hemodialysis patients: Implications for advance directives. *Journal of the American Society of Nephrology, 6* 1410–1417.

Singer, P. A., Thiel, E. C., Salit, I., Flanagan, W., & Naylor, C. D. (1977). The HIV-specific advance directive. *Journal of General Internal Medicine, 12,* 729–735.

SUPPORT Investigators. (1994). Do formal advance directives affect resuscitation decisions and the use of resources for seriously ill patients? *Journal of Clinical Ethics, 5,* 23–30.

The SUPPORT Investigators. (1995). A controlled trial to improve care for seriously ill hospitalized patients. *Journal of the American Medical Association, 274,* 1591–1598.

Toombs, S. K. (1992). *The meaning of illness: A phenomenological account of the different perspectives of physician and patient.* Dordrecht, The Netherlands: Kluwer Academic Publishers.

Toombs, S. K., Barnard, D., & Carson, R. A. (1995). *Chronic disease: From experience to policy.* Bloomington: Indiana University Press.

Vacco v. Quill. 117 S. Ct. 2293 (1997).

Washington v. Glucksberg, 117 S. Ct. 2302 (1997).

Wennberg, D. E. (1998). Variation in the delivery of care: The stakes are high. *Annals of Internal Medicine, 128,* 866–868.

Wennberg, J., & Gittelsohn, A. (1973). Small Area Variations in Health Care delivery. *Science, 182,* 1102–1108.

7

Aging in Judaism: "Crown of Glory" and "Days of Sorrow"

Sheldon Isenberg

How has Jewish civilization in its varied, related manifestations expressed itself on the ending of life's trajectory? Jewish history covers nearly four millennia, and the literature produced during that time, given the modest numbers of people involved, is immense and varied. We shall consider the literature of three overlapping periods. First, the literature of the Bible covers more than a millennium, from the patriarchal period through the 2nd century B.C.E. Second, the literature of traditional, or classical, Judaism includes the legal (*halakhic*) and nonlegal (*aggadic*) rabbinic collections as well as philosophical and mystical texts that cover the long stretch from Pharisaic-Rabbinic Judaism to contemporary orthodoxy, from the 2nd century B.C.E. through today. Third, western European Jews moved into modernity early in the 19th century, with some earlier encounters, whereas the mass of eastern European Jews entered the posttraditional world toward the beginning of the 20th century, most of them as American immigrants. We shall look at both continuities and radical transformations in modern Jewish conceptions of aging.

This study focuses on Jewish voices transmitted in writing, although for centuries much had been preserved in oral forms. Of course, in Jewish literature, as in virtually all literature of all traditions, male voices and perspectives are heard nearly exclusively until the modern period. We are usually told specifically about aging males and beliefs about and attitudes toward their process, so we must continually remind ourselves that we are woefully ignorant of what at least half of the Jews were feeling and saying. Only in the modern period, from the moment that it was possible for women's voices to be heard, can we begin to consider a more complete range of Jewish perspectives, including diverging images of Jewish men and women in the aging process.

Relatively little appears to indicate that problems of aging were singled out until the modern period.[1] In premodern texts the elderly are not listed with the poor, orphans, or widows, those groups requiring public care. Because traditional sources assume that the extended family is the setting for caring for aging parents, it is likely that care for the elderly was not specifically an extrafamilial issue. Perhaps the elders for whom families could not provide were thought of as poor or widowed.

But in the late 17th century care for the aging emerged as a Jewish communal concern. In the mid-18th century the first Jewish home for the aged was built in Amsterdam. By the end of the 19th century most of the major European Jewish communities had established similar institutions. In contrast to traditional sources, contemporary Jewish fiction expresses explicit concerns for problems of aging, reflecting developments in modern society such as extended life spans, the nuclearization and atomization of the modern family, and the proliferation of segregated living arrangements for the aged (Herr & Olitzky, 1989).

POSITIVE AND NEGATIVE STRANDS

In each of the major strata of traditional Jewish literary reflection we find positive and negative valuations that persist as diachronic strands weaving through the generations of texts. As we shall see, the worldviews through which these strands weave shift over time, with a radical break in the modern period. We should not expect univocity of such a long tradition, especially one that, although very prescriptive of behavior, has encouraged creative speculation and theorizing about living— and dying—Jewishly.

The opening verses of the Bible assert that life per se is good; there is no serious contradiction of that primordial evaluation of God's creation in the thousands of years that follow. The positive strands value long life as a divine blessing, often romanticizing the process by ignoring the suffering associated with aging. The reference in Proverbs (16:31) to gray hair as "a crown of glory" is typical. Even when the negative strand warns of old age as "days of darkness" (Qohelet 11:8), it never calls into question the ultimate value of life.[2]

Long life is valued for different reasons. Aging enables the ripening of what had been seeded, a time of continued growth and harvest, a time for sharing the wisdom of experience (Prov. 22:6). In biblical and classical Judaism, a happy old age is seen specifically as an opportunity and reward for fulfilling current cultural values, a view that tends to play a socially conservative role. In Deuteronomy, for instance, long life is a reward for keeping the covenant requirements specified in that layer of tradition, whereas a short life signifies faithlessness to that covenantal understanding. Because Jewish tradition as a whole often focuses on the mental and spiritual dimensions in which aging presents opportunities for the accumulation and integration of the wisdom of experience, an extended life implies an increase in wisdom and Torah as well as in political authority. Fulfilling the core values associated with attaining a happy extended life and even immortality, is often viewed as protection against a difficult aging.

Such promises address the universal vulnerability to the physical, emotional, and mental disintegration that so often precede dying. The negative strand speaks of aging as the side of death we know about: dissipated power; loss of autonomy, respect, and self-worth; alienation from family and society; and the intimate loss of the capacity to enjoy living. In a late Midrash an old man is described as "apelike . . . and childlike . . . his children and household mocking at him, disregarding him and loathing him."[3]

Negative aspects of aging are also justified in various ways. Suffering in old age is often seen as a punishment for not living in accord with God's will, the correlate of the belief in old age as a reward. A contrasting voice, heard in all ages, and a central theme of skeptical wisdom literature questions the implied belief in a morally responsive universe. This negative wisdom strand scoffs at our presumption to comprehend God's moral calculus or will.

THE HEBREW BIBLE

Although biblical literature gives us insight into the values and concerns of biblical Jews, just as significant is its authority for Jews and Christians throughout the ages. In Jacob Neusner's (1988b) terminology, traditional Judaism is "Torah-centric" (pp. 81–85). Torah is a central term that has several interrelated meanings. In the Bible, *torah* does not refer to a body of literature but means, generally, "teaching" or "way." For Judaism, the Bible or *Tanakh*, after its canonization, is "written Torah."[4] The Bible is the basis of nearly two millennia of rabbinic commentary, whether narrative, nonlegal *(aggadic)*, or legal *(halakhic)*. Claiming the authority of revelation, the rabbis called the results of their holy hermeneutics "oral Torah." Only in the 20th century, with the decline of traditional education, can we no longer take for granted the authority of and familiarity with the Bible for the average Jew.

The references to old age in the Hebrew Bible, although limited, are spread out through a literature that accumulated in oral and written forms over the course of a millennium or so (Reuben, 1987). The positive and negative voices heard at the beginning of the biblical tradition are continuations of themes found in earlier cultures that formed the historical-cultural matrix of the Israelite tradition.

Biblical Ages and Origins

Traditions tend to gild their origins in myth and legend. Myths about beginnings are often cast heroically (Eliade, 1963). The early chapters of Genesis tell the story of the universe, stretching from its creation to the beginnings of the Jewish people. Narratives about creation, the flood, and the Tower of Babel are connected by genealogies of fathers and sons—the names of no mothers or daughters are listed—that link Adam, the first father, to Abraham, the first Jewish father. Primordial time is different: a universe is created in a week, and lifetimes cover centuries. Adam's life spanned 930 years, and Methuselah was said to have died at 969 years. In these genealogies quantity of years indicates quality of life.

The first biblical genealogies record not only monumental life spans but also the ages, ranging from 60 to more than 800 years, at which men were still virile and fertile (Genesis 5). Methusaleh, for instance, "begat" Lamech at 187 years and continued to beget for nearly another 800 years. The focus on engendering children corresponds to God's directive to all Creation and specifically to humanity: "Be fruitful and multiply."

The numbers taper as they approach the legendary patriarchal-matriarchal history that occupies the rest of Genesis, marking a transition from the narratives about creation of the world to those about the sacred national history of the Israelites. The theme of infertility adds suspense to the story of the transmission of Abraham's covenant, in which God promises the continuation and proliferation of his progeny. In the story of the conception of Isaac, the "right" inheritor of the covenant, that tension is heightened by the advanced ages of his parents: Sarah is 90; Abraham, 100. Until that moment the fulfillment of the covenant is in question.

The lives of the founding couple are of legendary length, although the numbers are less exaggerated than those found for earlier genealogies. It is significant that in these legends of long-lived women and men, there is only one story that tells of interaction between grandparent and grandchildren (Genesis 48). The first biblical figure described as aged *(zagen)*, Abraham died still vigorous at 175; Sarah, at 127.[5] According to the priestly narrator, Abraham was 75 when he entered into the covenant, initiating Israelite history, still without heirs. Even Abraham's servant Eliezer, also called *zagen,* was spry enough to cross the great desert to find a wife for Isaac.

But the patriarchal history provides sharp contrast in the story of Isaac, who, in his old age, feeble and blind, was manipulated by his wife and children. Even with the propensity to mythologize the founding fathers and mothers, a strain of realism about the infirmities attendant on aging emerges. In a narrative about a later period, an 80-year-old ally of King David, invited to join the royal household, responds grimly: "Your servant is far too old . . . I cannot tell good from bad, I cannot taste what I eat or drink; I cannot hear the voices of men and women singing. Why should I be a burden any longer to your majesty?" (2nd Sam. 19:32f.). David himself, after a long life of unrelenting activity and royal accomplishment, spends his last days sick and surrounded by intrigue, so lonely and cold that a young woman had to be found to help warm his body at night (1 Kings 1: 1–4).

Blessings and Curses

Long life, then, may be a blessing or a curse. In those strata where a happy, vigorous old age is experienced as a reward for fulfilling God's will, each layer of tradition adds its own understanding of God's will to the accumulating tradition.

In all of Jewish history, there is no more significant figure than Moses, the leader of the Exodus who receives God's Torah on Mount Sinai on behalf of the people. The Bible's own narrative framework presents much of Torah as God's speech to Moses, to be transmitted to the people. More than a millennium later, the rabbis began to cloak their own legislation with the authority of Moses' Torah (Urbach, 1987). According to the biblical tradition, when he died at the age of 120, "his eye had not dimmed, nor had his life force [moisture] fled" (Deut. 34:7). Yet he died short of completion of his life's dream, for God did not permit him to lead the people into the promised land. The ending of Moses' life thus connects positive and negative strands: his vigorous old age as leader of the people and transmitter of Torah and commandments is framed by a life divinely shortened as punishment for his disobedience of a divine directive.

Priesthood, monarchy, and prophecy emerge during the First Temple period (10th through 6th centuries B.C.E.). The prophetic understanding of the Israelite covenant relationship with God informs the final book of the Pentateuch, Deuteronomy, and gives shape to a major portion of the historical narrative that follows. The prophets understood the historical fate of the nation to be dependent upon the Children of Israel's fulfillment of their covenant obligations: great empires won and battles lost, all in relation to the Israelite performance of their duties. This prophetic view of history has continued as a major Jewish hermeneutical principle across the ages.

In this view the people's fate and the individual's quality of life are tied to ethical fulfillment of the covenant demands. Thus, long life was valued as a reward for fulfillment of the *mitzvot* of God's Torah, and a short life indicated punishment. At the core of Deuteronomy's covenantal vision is the choice given by God to adhere to Torah or not. Obedience brings blessing, including "length of days"; disobedience brings disaster (Deut. 38:19f.). The covenant not only protects the continuation of the people through time; it also protects against the dangers of daily living that might prematurely end a life.

Elders and Elders

The Deuteronomic narrator presents the story, distasteful to him, of the disintegration of David and Solomon's kingdom as the result of the refusal of Solomon's son, Rehoboam, to accept the wisdom of the elders; "the elders" *(z'genim)* were described as a political force to be considered in an unsettled monarchy. The same Deuteronomic tradition records the following advice: "Remember the days of old, consider the years of many generations; ask your father and he will show you; your elders, and they will tell you. (Deut. 32:7)

In various Biblical narratives the elders play important governing roles, representing the interests of their extended families or tribes. In the desert, the elders were commanded to stand with Moses at the "Tent of Meeting," where they would also be official recipients of the divinely revealed laws. For that voice, the Torah of Moses is really the Torah of Moses and the elders. The text and readers know that, at the time of reading, Moses is dead—but there are still elders.

Elders play a variety of roles through the First Temple period (ending ca. 586 B.C.E.), including appointing kings and declaring war. They constituted an institution with analogues throughout the ancient Near East.[6] However, there is no specific age requirement for being counted as an official *zagen*. Although chronological age provides no guarantee of mature judgment, the symbolization of the experience and wisdom to serve the community by advanced age is compelling and universal in the ancient Near East. The metaphor remains, as we shall see.

More directly relevant, of course, is the generic use of "elder." In the biblical law codes, the automatic respect due to the aged is part of what makes the Children of Israel a "holy nation," according to the priestly tradition. One of the Ten Commandments (Exod. 20:12) connects the instruction to honor mother and father with the promise of a long life in the land. Respect for the preceding generation that gave life and sustenance is a life-and-death matter. In the priestly Holiness Code we find "Rise before the aged and show deference to the old" (Lev. 19:32), a commandment that reverberates throughout Jewish history. No matter how the biblical tradition evaluates a long life from the perspective of the one living it—positive, negative, or mixed—the attitude that others should hold is clear: respect.

This attitude converges with the notion that long life brings with it a wisdom born of experience. Respect for all elders—particularly parents—is so strong a principle in the Bible that the punishment for disobedience of the covenant, according to Deuteronomy, is that "the Lord will raise against you a nation that does not revere the old or pity the young" (28.49f.)

The prophetic tradition teaches that mistreatment of the elderly by any human community is a sign of being outside God's will, devoid of any morality. A symptom of the deepest evil, it reveals complete alienation from God's demands of humanity. Isaiah declares that a sign of God's punishment is precisely a disorderly and sinful society, characterized by infighting, a society in which "the young shall bully the old and the despised, the honored" (3:5).[7]

ESCHATOLOGICAL REWARDS OF OLD AGE

The development of eschatological and apocalyptic perspectives, after the destruction of the First Temple, marks a significant shift in the Jewish experience of time. For some biblical voices the prophetic relation of action to immediate reward and punishment seemed too mechanical and failed to match common experience. Eschatological and apocalyptic literature project reward and punishment into an end time when all the struggles of human existence have been completed. A characteristic expectation of the end time is that "the just" will live to ripe old ages, if not forever. Psalm 92, an eschatological song, looks forward to the time when "the righteous . . . shall still bring forth fruit in old age; they shall be full of sap and richness" (92:15). This promise is to be fulfilled alter the Lord's enemies have been destroyed. With the end of all that is evil in the world, all of the causes for suffering and untimely deaths will also come to an end.

Zechariah promises that at the end of time "old men and old women shall again sit in the streets of Jerusalem, each with staff in hand for very age" (8:4). The presence of the aged is a sign of the transformation of the world into what it should be. When a new heaven and new earth shall have been created, "there shall be no elder who will not complete his days" (Isa. 65:20). This theme extends into an infinite prolongation of life in other eschatological speculations—an end to death (25.8).[8]

Wisdom and Old Age

Proverbs, Job, and Qohelet (Ecclesiastes) attest to the participation of
Israelite thought in and contributions to the widespread wisdom tradition of the ancient Near East. Collections of aphorisms, proverbs, alle-
gories, and scholarly lists may have served as materials for "wisdom
schools" to train governing elites and/or may simply reflect non-
institutionalized popular wisdom. Here too we find the strands of contrasting attitudes: the positive view in the socially conservative book
of Proverbs that old age is a ripening and opposing views in Job's outraged questioning and Qohelet's skeptical fatalism.

Proverbs focuses on that part of the tradition that saw old age as
wisdom, beauty, and strength, warning both about the dangers of ignoring the wisdom of the elders and about despising the aged mother
(23.22). The whole book is framed as the advice of an experienced parent or teacher to an already adult son or student about to set out in
the world (Prov. 1:8). Heeding this wise instruction will result in
"length of days, and years in life, and peace" (Prov. 3:2). The correla-
tive warning is clear: "the upright shall live on in the world . . . but the
wicked's life on earth will be cut short" (Prov. 2:21–22). The general
perspective on aging throughout the book is that old age is a blessing
for the righteous, who please God, for true wisdom is rooted in fear of
God: "The *savya,* the grey hair, is a crown of glory, it shall be found in
the way of righteousness" (Prov. 16:31). A good aging, however,
depends on early training in wisdom: "Train the young man according
to its way, so that even in his old age it shall not depart from him"
(Prov. 22.6).[9]

A very different picture emerges in the less trusting wisdom of Job,
who questions the power or honor due to mere quantity of years. Most
of the Book of Job is a forceful refutation of the prophetic view of a
moral universe, including the equation of long life with wisdom and
virtue. Life is not just, says the poet, for the connection between one's
fate and actions is mysterious. When his conservative advisors claim
the wisdom of age as they argue against Job's questioning of God's justice (15:7–10) Job dismisses this conventional wisdom, asking sarcasti-
cally, "Does wisdom come with age, and understanding in length of
days?" (12:12).

Thus, the negative strand as it manifests in the wisdom literature
denies the automatic connections between age and wisdom. Indeed, the
central message of Job is that what happens to us is beyond our ken.
Ironically, when Job accepts the limitations of his wisdom, his suffering
ceases, and he is rewarded by God with another 140 years of life: "So
Job died, old and sated with days." Many scholars regard this return to
the prophetic view of long life as a reward as a later, pious addendum.

The latest of the canonical wisdom books, Qohelet, or Ecclesiastes, begins with a theme to be repeated throughout: "Utter futility! says Qohelet, utter futility! Everything is futile!" (1:2).[10] The passage of time has no meaning; no accomplishments will be remembered by coming generations. Wisdom gives no special insights (8:16f.), for death ultimately reclaims all. In this context Qohelet contrasts youth and old age:

> Indeed, let anyone who lives many years rejoice in all of them, but remember the days of darkness, for they will be many; everything that comes is absurd. Rejoice young man, in your youth and let your heart be glad during the days of your prime . . . for youth and black hair are fleeting, And remember your wife in the days of your youth, before the evil days come and the years approach of which you will say, "I have no pleasure in them . . ." Absurdity of absurdities, says the Qohelet, everything is absurd. (11:7–12:8)

Thus ends Qohelet's words. The meaninglessness and vulnerability of old age evoke the cry of futility. Nevertheless, in contrast to comparable texts from Egypt and Mesopotamia, Qohelet does not draw the conclusion that life is not worth living, that one might just as well end life at will. The fundamental biblical impulse toward life persists in the darkest speculations: "Yes, sweet is the light, and it is good for the eyes to behold the sun."

Elsewhere, we find the negative perspective of a wisdom psalm (Ps. 90:10) somewhat less severe: "The days of our years are threescore and ten, and if by reason of strength, they be fourscore years, yet is their strength labor and sorrow." But in another wisdom psalm, we read an elder's plea: "Do not cast me off in old age; when my strength fails me, do not forsake me . . . and now that I am old and my hairs are gray, forsake me not, O God" (71:9, 18). Here again, the suffering of old age is neither reward nor punishment but cause for fear if one is "cast off," so we can only appeal to God.

TORAH AS THE SOURCE OF VALUE

Positive voices often value long life, not for itself but for the enlargement of life's container of virtue and meaning: the more life, the more Torah. For instance, the stanza chosen to open the Book of Psalms celebrates the one who takes pleasure in God's *Torah.* The desire to fulfill God's will brings the promise of a happy, vigorous old age ("his leaf does not wither" [1:3]). This strand makes not only obedience to but also study of divine instruction the criterion of value, for the wisdom gained from Torah exceeds that gleaned from the experiences of a long life (Ps 119.99f.).

This theme continues into the Hellenistic Jewish wisdom literature Ecclesiasticus, the Wisdom of Ben Sira (25:4–6), from Hellenistic Palestine (ca. 180 B.C.E.), has deep appreciation for the generic wisdom that comes from the experience of a full life, reminding us of some passages from Proverbs: "Much experience is the crown of old men, their enhancement is reverence for the Lord" (Olitzky, 1989, p. 340)[11] In contrast, the apocryphal Wisdom of Solomon, written in Egypt perhaps a century later, affirms that "it is not length of life that makes for an honorable old age . . . but rather is it wisdom which constitutes a man's silvery brow, and a spotless life the true ripeness of age" (4:8–9).

Indeed, God may snatch the life of a good person in youth to protect him from the influence of the wicked and godless (4:7ff.), for "swiftly perfected youth I shall condemn the old age of the unrighteous rich in years" (4:16). The truth that scoundrels too may enjoy old age disintegrates the belief in a tie between length of life and virtue. At the same time, the prophetic notion that length of days is a reward for virtue in this life is transformed by the belief that righteousness leads to immortality—the death of the righteous is only apparent. Nonetheless, sin brings death (2.21–3.9) (Nickelsburg, 1981).

AGING IN RABBINIC JUDAISM

The rabbinic tradition is collected in the Talmud and Midrash. The literature deals with a period that includes the Maccabean period (second century B.C.E.), the destruction of the Second Temple in 70 C.E., the codification of early rabbinic law and lore collected in the Mishnah and Tosefta in Palestine around 200 C.E., and the formation of the two great commentaries on the Mishnah. the Palestinian and Babylonian Talmuds, which were completed by the end of the 5th century C.E. The other great rabbinic collections are the *midrashim,* legal and nonlegal materials arranged as commentaries on the biblical text. The rabbis rooted their writings in the Bible, usually by creatively interpolating their beliefs and values into their readings of the text. Rabbinic Judaism is not only intrinsically important but also serves as the matrix of many forms of post traditional Judaism.

References to aging and its problems in the immense rabbinic literature are relatively rare, although still more than we shall be able to consider. Given all of the complaints one might have heard about old age—such as those expressed by Qohelet—the only specific regret in the sayings of the early Palestinian rabbis collected in the Mishnah is the loss of intellectual potency for the study of Torah. There is no mention of physical and emotional disintegration, on the one hand, and no claims for prolongation of life as a result of study, on the other. The rabbinic belief in an afterlife in which rewards and punishments were measured out relieved the pressure to view an extended life as a reward.

Several references to old age are found in the fourth chapter of the tractate *Avot,* which contains collections of wisdom-like sayings of the early rabbis. This totally *aggadic* (nonlegal) tractate has become the most widely read part of the Talmud. Included in the Siddur, the prayer book, these sayings were often studied on the Sabbath afternoon, a custom that continues in some communities. One rabbi says: "He who learns when a child—what is he like? Ink put down on a clean piece of paper. And he who learns when an old man-what is he like? Ink put down on a paper full of erasures." Another says: "He who learns from children—what is he likes One who eats sour grapes and drinks fresh wine. And he who learns from old men—what is he like? He who eats ripe grapes and drinks vintage wine." Judah ha-Nasi, the compiler and editor of the Mishnah, says: "Do not look at the bottle but at what is in it. You can have a new bottle full of old wine, and an old bottle which has not got even new wine" (4:20) (Neusner, 1988a).

For the rabbis, study is the major purpose of the male life; not to study is not to live. But when age diminishes one's capacity to absorb and learn, study is futile. In this first view, then, youth is an advantage in studying. The next view, not wholly incompatible, argues that learning from the young is far inferior to learning from the old, the experienced. Judah ha-Nasi rejects the generalizations of both, noting, in consonance with a negative strand of the wisdom tradition, that age is irrelevant to the wisdom of Torah. Youth can absorb old wisdom and old people can be ignorant fools. Nevertheless, although the age of the container is not important, the age of the contents is![12]

The Tosefta, a collection of materials contemporaneous with and overlapping the Mishnah, records the following saying that identifies wisdom with age (Tos. Avodah Zara 1.19): "If young people advise you to build the Temple, and old men say destroy it, give ear to the latter; for the building of the young is destruction; and the tearing down of the old is construction" (Neusner, 1981). The young are profoundly distrusted when it comes to public religious policy. If old men, whom we might expect to conserve the past, advise to destroy, then listen! The passage, referring to Rehoboam's refusal to consider the advice of the elders, is a continuation of the biblical strand that enjoins deference to elders. The Palestinian rabbis may be recalling the destructive and internally divisive wars against Rome that culminated in the destruction of the Second Temple and enormous suffering.

The use of *zagen* as metaphor for the highest values of the tradition continues through the Mishnah and into the Talmudic literature. In the Mishnah, *zagen* is used to designate a *hakam,* a sage or scholar steeped in Torah, and especially members of the Sanhedrin, who were said to have advised the priestly temple hierarchy on ritual matters (Yoma 1:3, 5). The use of "elder" to designate a man distinguished in Torah study continues in Talmud and Midrash (Ben-Sasson).

TALMUD AND MIDRASH

Torah as Good Medicine

Rabbinic tradition amplifies the virtues and failings of biblical figures in Midrash. A story is told that at the circumcision party for Isaac, Sarah—more than 90 years old—nursed a hundred babies to counter the suspicion that Isaac was not really her child but a foundling (Ginzberg, 1961). In contrast, Barzilai the Gileadite's description of his decrepitude in old age (2nd Sam. 19:32f.) drew a wide range of rabbinic comments preserved in the Babylonian Talmud. Rab called him a liar because he knew someone older than Barzilai's 80 years whose taste buds were still functioning; Raba, however, accepted the accuracy of Barzilai's self observation but imagined that his problems arose from his dissolute life. In either case, the validity of Rabbi Ishmael's view is sustained: wisdom comes with age—if you are a scholar (Shabbat 152a). This continues the thread in which longevity is taken to be more valuable for someone who is occupied with study of Torah than for an ignoramus. But there is also an implicit threat that a difficult old age awaits the nonscholar (i.e., the nonrabbi).

It is not just that study keeps the mental dimension of aging at bay but also that filling one's mind with Torah is per se an antidote to senility. This motif appears in the Mishnah:

> When someone falls into sickness or old age or troubles and cannot engage in his work. he dies of hunger. But with Torah this is not so; for it guards him from all evil while he is young, and in old age it grants him a future and a hope. Of his old age what does it say? They shall still bring forth fruit in old age" (Ps. 92.14; Kiddushin 4:14).

This corresponds to the *aggadic* identification of Torah study as the "elixir of life" (*Ta'anit* 7a).[13]

Even the mind that has begun to disintegrate with age, if it once held words of holy Torah, is to be valued: "Be careful [to respect] an old man who has forgotten his knowledge through no fault of his own, for it was said: 'Both the whole tables and the fragments of the tables were placed in the Ark'" (*Berachot* 8b).[14] The container of Torah is sanctified by its contents, even when those contents are no longer accessible. In the same vein: "Respect even the old man who has lost his learning"

(Kiddushin 32a). No wonder that in this Torah-centric community, the text inscribed by those to whom Torah was life was known as the Tree of Life *(etz hayyim)!* Torah may not always bring long life as its reward, but to be occupied with Torah makes any length of life worth living.[15]

Honoring the Carriers of Torah

In the Babylonian Talmud, tractate *Kiddushin* 32–33, there is an extended discussion that attempts to establish a calculus to relate the biblically mandated honor due an elder to that required by the rabbis for a scholar. To authenticate the principle of honoring the learned, some rabbis read biblical passages that require respect to the aged as referring only to scholars, making the Mishnaic practice into a hermeneutical principle. Surely, says one rabbi, Torah would not mandate honor to an "axed sinner"—or, by implication, to an ignoramus.

But the alternative reading, that "elder" refers to chronological age, is discussed in the same passage. In this characteristic spectrum of views, Rabbi Issi commands respect for any "hoary head." Rabbi Johanan goes further, maintaining that the value of life experience even transcends the boundary between Jew and non-Jew. On the other hand, for Rabbi Nahman, Raba, and Abaye, the respect due to a scholar was greater than that due even an elder nonscholar. Rabbi Issi's view that age per se is worthy of respect reflects the simple reading of the biblical command to rise up before the aged and is echoed in the Midrash: "Concerning he who welcomes an old man, it is as if he has welcomed the Shekhinah *(Genesis Rabbah,* Toledot 43.6).[16] Respect for the aged is equivalent to respect for God.

The Negative Strand

The negative strand, reminding us of the organic sufferings of old age, continues to spin through Talmud and Midrash. There are some passages that give specific warnings: "[One must pray in the later years that] his eyes may see, his mouth eat, his legs walk, for in old age all powers fail" (Herr, p. 345). In other passages we find references to stages of life. One vehicle was the midrashic adaptation of a Greek counting of seven stages of life.

A comparison of the treatment of the final stage of life in two texts, one found in the Midrash Tanhuma and the other in the Midrash Rabbah to Qohelet, is illuminating. The account of the stages is the same, but each version adds a different comment about the final stage, that is, the apelike countenance of the old (a literary image apparently originating with the Greek savant Solon). Midrash Tanhuma gives a graphic description of the seventh and final stage as impotent senility, when elders are at the mercy of their hostile families. When the elder complains that he did not ask to be born, the angel of death admonishes him: "And have I not already told thee, that against thy will thou art created, against thy will thou art born, against thy will thou lives, and against thy will thou must render account for thy actions before the Supreme King of Kings, blessed be He" (translation in Kohut, p. 234).

Although the description of old age sounds like an exception to the universal valuation of life, the context emphasizes that this pathetic figure nevertheless resists his ending. The passage expresses appreciation of the energy and freedom of youth but acknowledges the increasingly heavy cares of supporting a family and the indignities of old age, including loss of function and respect in the extended family. The angel of death's stern speech is reminiscent of the divine response to Job's complaints. Life and the indignities of its ending come without easy explanations, as mystery.

Another version of the stages-of-life motif is found as a comment in the Midrash Rabbah to Qohelet 1:2 on the keystone passage, "Futility! Futility! All is futility!" The presentation of the same stages is unelaborated until the final one: "When he is grown old he is like an ape. What has just been said holds good only of the ignorant; but of those versed in the Torah it is written, 'Now King David was old' (I Kings 1.1)—although he was 'old,' he was still a 'king.'" Qohelet's despair is midrashically laundered by exempting the learned one, the rabbi, from the ravages of age. The inevitable pathos of the ending is undercut by the revisionist affirmation of the aging- and death-defying powers of Torah study. The 11th-century Midrash Rabbah on Song of Songs 1:10, in contrast, gives a compact, astringent summary of the stages of life of the negative wisdom type—with no promises of amelioration: "When a man is young, he quotes poetry; when he matures, he quotes proverbs; when he grows old he speaks of futilities."

Finally, it is clear that rabbinic law understands the biblical injunction to honor one's parents as the requirement that children care for their aging parents. No matter what virtues an extended life might bring, that the aging require special care is never denied. But that care is almost always seen as a family issue, especially as women's responsibility. Talmud, Midrash and medieval writings deal extensively with the dimensions of the requirements of Torah having to do with aging parents.[17] This source material has been thoroughly treated by Gerald Blidstein (1975) and, in a more concentrated way, by Elliot Dorf (1987). There is relatively little said about the responsibility of the larger Jewish community for the aging who are without means, as Immanuel Jacobovitz (1988) has noted, reflecting that elders were not viewed collectively as a category of people requiring special aid until nearly the modern period (Ben-Sasson).[18]

THE CAIRO GENIZA DOCUMENTS

Talmud and Midrash give us limited and indirect evidence for reconstructing Jewish attitudes toward aging in Palestine and Babylonia from the Roman period through the 10th or 11th century C.E. A very different kind of literature was recovered early in this century from the Cairo Genizah, which provides extraordinary insight into the social and economic history of lower- and middle-class Jews who lived in Muslim territories, including Palestine, Sicily, and Spain, from the 10th through 13th centuries.

Letters tell stories of parents abandoned as well as parents well cared for or able to care for themselves. S. D. Goitein (1988), who reconstructed this major segment of Jewish civilization in a remarkable five-volume work, theorizes that only 5% of the population reached the age of 70. He cites the 12th-century poets Judah ha-Levi and Abraham Ibn Ezra, who pinpoint 50 as close to the endpoint of life. Judah ha-Levi at one point mocks the elder who tries to ignore his age: "Chasing after youth at fifty/when your days are about to vanish?"[19] Yet those who survived to 70 and beyond were very likely healthy and vital. Many documents indicate that men and women at that age retained control over their own affairs and felt themselves blessed with children and grandchildren. Elderly men were acknowledged for a lifetime of charitable deeds, public service, and learning. Goitein concludes: "In the Bible-oriented society of the Geniza, good old age was the natural reward for (and, therefore, proof of) a virtuous life" (p. 125). Even though the Cairo Geniza documents are far more concerned with business dealings than with pious scholarship, the values represented seem to extend naturally those of Talmudic society, both in positive and negative evaluations.

SABA' IN KABBALAH

Besides the well-known Talmudic injunction against involving oneself with mysticism, Kabbalah, before the age of 40—perhaps implying the last decade of life to many—we can follow the metaphorical use of "elder" into the mystical tradition. The *Zohar,* a 13th-century mystical Midrash, is the central text of Kabbalah. Its fragmentary narrative framework has almost a novelistic flavor, with names of mystics constructed as sources of various teachings. One of the most illustrious characters is called *saba',* the "old man" ("grandfather" in Aramaic). In several passages he mysteriously appears as a donkey driver and surprises the learned rabbis with his marvelous mystical teachings (Matt, *Wisdom of the Zohar,* I: 169–197).

A Kabbalist from the Zoharic period. Moshe de Leon, whom many believe to have authored the Zohar; explicitly disconnects chronological age from the spiritual maturity that comes from mystical wisdom:

> . . . a man who engaged in Mishnah and Talmud all his days . . . began shouting at everyone, "I do not know my own self! . . . All my days I have toiled in Torah until I was eighty years old. But in the final year I attained no more wisdom or essence than I attained in those first years when I began studying. . . . See now how my eyes shine, for I have tasted a bit of this [mystical] honey!" (Matt, p. 7)

The *Saba'* of the Zohar earned the title, not merely by study of Talmud but by his capacity to interpret Torah mystically.

AGING AND THE ALIENATION OF GENERATIONS IN MODERNITY

The entry of Jews into the modern world in the 19th and 20th centuries brought new forms of literary expression, new contributors, and an ever accelerating rate of publication. As the proportion of elder Jews who survived well into grandparenthood increased, their presence in literature also increased, a theme yet to be thoroughly studied. The older generation came to symbolize something radically different from what it had. The presumption of traditional literature is that the world would remain relatively stable from generation to generation. As far as the rabbis were concerned, Abraham and Moses lived like rabbis and the "world to come" was imagined as an idealization of their world. A long-lived person in such a world might experience personal change but not epochal transitions.

Premodern, traditional literature was concerned with the problem of being a good person—an observer of Torah, a scholar, a moral person in God's creation. Modern Jewish writers have been more focused on boundaries: the problems of remaining a Jew in the face of a secularizing modernity, the conflicted relationships with the past in a world of exciting and frightening change. To be a Jew in traditional society was to be part of an extended family, the usual context for aging. The abrupt entry of Jews into a modernity that had begun without them focused attention on generational differences and the transformation of family structures. The freedom that children sought was experienced by many parents as an abandonment, which often occurred after the most radical dislocation of their lives.

In a perceptive essay, Harry Moody (1986) relates our ability to give meaning to our lives as a whole, to our evaluations of old age. Traditional societies, he notes,

> contain dual, even contradictory images of the movement of aging: a
> downward movement toward debility and death and an upward movement
> toward unifying knowledge . . . The sufferings of old age, in the traditional
> view, are seen against the wider background of the cosmos. (p. 31)

Modernity is characterized by the loss of that "wider background."
The positive images are more difficult to construct and less convinc-
ing, no longer rooted in the myths, theologies, and philosophies of
traditional culture. The recognition of "the downward movement"
remains as a continuation of the negative wisdom strand that insists
that we should make no attempt to rationalize or justify the sufferings
endured by the aged.

The universal modern nuclearization of the family, combined with
increased length of life, has resulted in increasing age segregation,
especially in the United States. One consequence has been a growing
number of "adult living" communities, homes for the aged, nursing
homes, and the like. Modern Jewish literature interprets age segregation as a matter of separating out not only bodies but also minds and
spirits. A spiritual rift is disclosed that precedes, and certainly accompanies, the crossing of the ocean from Europe. For many that passage
was also a crossing of a psychic divide between traditional and posttraditional.

In Jewish fiction and poetry, figures of old men and women or of
aging parents often represent the passing of the traditional way of life.[20]
Positive or sympathetic presentation of the elderly may signify regret
or nostalgia for the loss of the old ways. Presenting youthful impatience
with the aging becomes a way to express a desire to be rid of those elements of premodern life that were hindrances to full participation in
and enjoyment of the benefits of modern living, benefits that were not
only material. In American Jewish and Israeli literature, all of the ambivalence and ambiguities about the Old World, often idealized as the
shtetl (Yiddish for "town"), became embodied in the figure of the elder.

Modern Jewish literature is immense, so any selection is more or
less arbitrary. Stories that feature elderly characters often imaginatively
represent and work with the conflicts of old and young, Such themes
abound in Yiddish fiction, which bridges Eastern European Jewry to
the New World: in Hebrew fiction in which Israelis struggle to relate
their political and cultural independence to their Eastern European
roots and in American Jewish fiction, which deals with unprecedented
identity crises for Jews and Jewish communities, The one nonfiction
work that I use to frame this account is anthropologist Barbara
Meyerhoff's (1978) superbly sensitive, empathetic, and intensely personal study of a community of elderly Jews living in Southern California
in the early 1970s.

The "Yiddishe Velt"

For most American Jews, the Judaism of the Eastern European *shtetl* represents their ancestral past. Until recently the same could be said for Israeli Jews, although the rapid influx of Jews from Northern Africa, Arab countries of the Middle East, and now the Soviet Union is changing even the demographics of memory. Meyerhoff (1978) looked to the life of the *shtetl* in order to understand why women as a group dominated the aging immigrant Jewish community she was studying—a dominance co-existing with occasional lip service to male superiority. She found her answers in the prevailing roles and stereotypes of the *shtetl* that could not be transplanted but were remembered. Those answers give us insight into the radical transformation of values about aging expressed in Yiddish literature of transition, as well as in Israeli and Jewish American literature.

The values of the *shtetl* continued the traditional emphasis on male scholarship and piety, removed from affairs of the world and the nitty-gritty of physical survival. The female stereotype included modesty, submission, and service to men and children. The common goals of the society were to maximize study of Torah and piety and to have as many children as possible to walk the same path. In the *shtetl* these women had the responsibility for the basic survival of their families. Men avoided hard labor, yearning for study. The women, Meyerhoff (1978) reasoned, had embodied characteristics that stood them in better stead for aging in the New World than their men had.

Yiddish was the language of the Eastern European *shtetl* and of the first-generation immigrant communities. Its literature included religious voices, but it also provided the first major outlet for secular Jewish voices. European *yiddishkeit* was largely destroyed by the Holocaust. After a brief flowering in America, today it struggles to survive. The ability to understand Yiddish came to designate a generational divide in America and Israel. Yiddish was the language of the old.

Isaac Bashevis Singer, prolific Nobel laureate, and widely translated, writes of the European *shtetl* world and the consequences of the relocation of that consciousness into the New World. "The Little Shoemakers," a seemingly sentimental fable, tells the story of Abba, the "papa." (Howe & Greenberg, 1973, pp. 523–544). In the old country, he was a fine shoemaker, pious, happy, successful, and appreciated in his *shtetl,* and he trained his sons in his craft. After his sons emigrate and open a successful, modern shoe factory, they bring their parents to the New World. Abba feels alien and uprooted until one day he finds his old cobbler tools and sets to work mending the shoes of the household. His sons build him a replica of his old workshop in the backyard and soon find themselves working alongside him, singing along as they had in the old country. But it was on their day off and in the backyard that they worked. Abba's work did not fit in the world of youth and mechanical productivity, but nevertheless it represented to the sons something valuable that was in danger of being lost.

Anzia Yezierska (197S) wrote in English about the Yiddish-speaking worlds of Eastern Europe and of American immigrants. Without sentimentality she tells of the squalor, the crushing poverty, and the struggles between the sexes and generations. Her 1925 novel, *Bread Givers,* presents the struggle for power between father and daughter. The father wants to transport to the New World the oppressive old patterns in which women—wife and daughters—served the patriarchal scholar of Torah, who was incapable of supporting himself, to say nothing of a family. The daughter tries to free herself from her aging father's demands, pulling away to study and acquire a profession:

> I almost hated him again as I felt his tyranny—the tyranny with which he tried to crush me as a child. Then suddenly the pathos of this lonely old man pierced me. In a world where all is changed, he alone remained unchanged—as tragically isolate as the rocks. All that he had left of life was his fanatical adherence to his traditions. (p. 296)

At the end, the issue still undecided, she observes, "It wasn't just my father, but the generations who made my father whose weight was still upon me" (p. 297). She sympathizes with his need to cling desperately and futilely to his traditions, even in her anger at how destructive they had been for her and her family. The old ways that her father represented, the traditional female duties to care for the elder sage, are perceived as oppressive traps.

The story also illuminates how, in the New World, caring for old parents became a question with hard choices to be made, not an automatically assumed duty. Perhaps no other reality of modern life illustrates so clearly the radical transformation of Jewish communal structures and reconfiguring of Jewish identity. Abba in the Singer story and the father in Yezierska's story are both viewed in relation to a non-Jewish scale of social values. The criteria of the negative and positive strands have lost their clarity and can bc perceived only through a double vision.

In Cynthia Ozick's (1971) "Envy, or Yiddish in America," we follow how an intellectually and emotionally incestuous community of aging Yiddish writers, publishers and translators. Edelshtein, poor, jealous, and envious of the successful Ostrover, chases after a young woman who, he believes, has the power to restore his life and virility by translating his poetry into English. The world of Yiddish writers, says Ozick, is fading away, for there are too few readers. Even the young woman, a phenomenon because she can read but not write Yiddish, is taken only with the famous Ostrover, who can be read in English. Yiddish, for her, is a route to literature—a tool, not a cause. The old, except for the famous Ostrover, are impotent, helpless, and resentful. The question is left undecided—is Edelshtein's poetry good even in Yiddish? Is there automatic virtue in the elder who is ignored? In any case, even the posttraditional secular Yiddish world, with its aging denizens, has no power, no juice, no capacity to reproduce itself. For Edelshtein, it has lost the Darwinian battle for survival.

Israel

S. Y. Agnon bridged the Old World to the new Israel. One of his legendary-style Hebrew stories, "Tehilah," presents the title character "as comely an old woman as you have seen in your days . . . Righteous she was, and wise she was, and gracious and humble: for kindness and pity were the light of her eyes, and every wrinkle in her face told of blessing and peace" (Blocker, 1965, p. 23). She is the angelic essence of all that was good and sacred about life in the Old City of Jerusalem among the pious. Devout, always performing *mitzvot* of service, Tehilah is filled only with blessings for others—and she is more than a century old. Her counterpoint in the story is the old, cranky *rabbanit,* the rabbi's widow who is sick, bitter, and utterly cynical about the changes approaching. From two different perspectives, the same message comes from the old women. The sacred world, built on the values of scholarship, piety, and *mitzvot,* is ended. Her commitment to the values of the old has filled Tehilah's inner life with pain; she has outlived her life but cannot leave until she finds a way to right a wrong committed long ago by her father against someone already dead. The end of the story is Tehilah's end and is the end of that kind of Judaism, in Agnon's view. The traditional positive images, no longer supported by a traditional community, also age.

Aharon Megged's "The Name," the work of a Polish-born Israeli author, also focuses on new and old in the Holy Land (Blocker, 1965). To the postindependence, native-born Sabra, the ghetto-ish, Yiddish-speaking, religious Jew represents passivity, weakness, cowardice—and being old. Grandfather Zisskind was about to become a great-grandfather. He asks his granddaughter and her husband to name their child Mendele in remembrance of the grandchild who did not survive Hitler. They refuse the memories, the ties, the name. He cracks, and when they bring the great-grandchild to visit, the aged father did not recognize the great-grandchild whose life would be no memorial" (p. 105). Zisskind's daughter, the new grandmother, seems to represent Megged's viewpoint, "I don't know . . . at times it seems to me that it's not Grandfather who's suffering from loss of memory, but ourselves, all of us."

Hugh Nissenson, an American writer, gives another picture of the old, pious European Jew transplanted to Israel. "The Crazy Old Man" is set in Jerusalem during the 1967 war (Chapman, 1974). The narrator is an intelligence officer who is trying to pry information out of two Arab soldiers. When he aims to kill one to loosen the tongue of the other, his neighbor, an elderly Hasid, tries to convince him that such a murder will defile the holy city. Concerned only with the current battle, the officer takes aim again. The old man grabs the gun, kills the Arab himself, and walks away. The other prisoner talked.

The next time the officer sees the Hasid: "His eyes were blue and slightly glazed with the madness that had made him take my crime upon himself because I had been born in the country into which his God had returned the Jews to give them their last chance" (p. 136). The old man acted with decisiveness and strength, even ruthlessness, but he acted to fulfill the values of the tradition.

Contemporary American Portraits

Jewish-American fiction presents strong elders and pathetic elders. Their weakness is presented as the result of the normal failings of age—the familiar negative strand—and of the dislocation of the culture—a distinctly modern negative feature. They are admired now for what others perceive as atypical strengths, rather than for their fulfillment of widely accepted roles as traditional Jewish elders.

Bruno Lessing's "The Americanization of Shadrach Cohen" presents a counterpoint to Singer's story about Abba and his sons (Olitzky, 1989). This father too was a pious Russian Jew whose two sons emigrated and, having established a business, sent for him, expecting him to retire and give them his money. They had become "Americanized" and were ashamed of his traditional clothing and ways. In contrast to Abba, the father asserts his economic power over them, takes charge of the store, and teaches them both how to run a business American-style while retaining his patriarchal position and religious practice. He gained their respect because he had proved himself in their world. Lessing gives us an active, aggressive elder who was able to outstrip his sons in the public world of commerce without sacrificing his religion. But in modern style, his Judaism had become his personal way of being.

A number of portraits recall the gloomy picture of old age in Qohelet Rabbah: being mocked, infantilized, and even ignored by one's own family. Such images are mostly of old men and correlate with Meyerhoff's (1978) description of a typical divergence of men and women in the aging process, which must be connected somehow with women normally outliving their partners. She tells of her grandmother Sofie, who, after the death of her husband, lost her home and became a "perpetual visitor in her grown children's households." Toward the end of their life together, Jacob, her husband, "appeared to shrivel while his wife, Sofie, expanded. There was the suggestion of a similar reversal taking place among the old men and women in the Center community" (p. 241).

Eugene Ziller's "Terrible Mistakes" tells the story of a widower who refused to live with his children or spend his time in clubs or sitting on park benches (Olitzky, 1989). He decides to go back to work. There is no job for him in the garment trade where he had worked his whole life. Eventually, he takes a job as a newsstand operator in a subway station, where he is exploited by the manager. Trying to protect his merchandise and job, he is seriously beaten-perhaps killed. An active desire to continue functioning doesn't mean that there will be an appropriate place—or a safe place.

Seymour Epstein's Mr. Isaacs, far more passive externally, sits daily almost immobile on a chair outside the apartment house where he lives with his complaining daughter and her husband (Olitzky, 1989). His inner world is filled with memories of a past full of acts of loyalty and courage but without rewards. Each day as he goes to bed, the same scene repeats itself:

> Now he composes his body for sleep, or death—he knows not which. Often it is for death he decides. but in the moment of choice a figure springs up . . . a shabby figure, pathetic, neither old nor young, but one whose story is so unique, so full of failures close to Mr. Isaacs' heart, so devoid of triumphs, that Mr. Isaacs feels toward it a great compassion— and would linger one more day in a world that contains its presence. (p. 173)

He lives out of pity for an unfulfilled self, as if he were a *dybbuk* occupying his own body.

Yet there are small triumphs when a measure of choice is left. Edna Ferber tells the story of "Old Man Minick," who, after his retirement, his wife's death, and financial disaster, is taken in by his dutiful son and daughter-in-law (Olitzky, 1989). There is not enough room, his daughter-in-law watches carefully what and how much he eats, and he is deprived of the second pillow he loves to fall asleep with. He finds community in political discussions with other old men on park benches; but when winter comes, that too ceases. When he overhears his daughter-in-law telling friends that the reason she doesn't get pregnant is that there is no room for a baby, he takes his life back into his own hands and signs into a "home" where some of his park friends live. In the final scene of the story, he is at the home happily engaged with his park cronies, and he breaks off the discussion to tell an attendant to inform the housekeeper that he wants two pillows on his bed. Meaning and a certain measure of freedom require separation from his family in a world where living arrangements are not designed to include grandparents.

Women's Voices

As women's voices are heard, the experience of the daughter with aging parents emerges, as we see in Yezierska's (1975) work. In 1983, Kim Chernin published a memoir of four generations of mothers and daughters—her family story. The immigrant great-grandmother of the story suffered and broke under the oppression of an unhappy, frustrated, brutal husband; her story differs little from that told by Yezierska. The grandmother escaped that oppression by her own initiative, working hard for the education that was now available to her. She became radicalized in the process—a Communist organizer who fought for human liberation. Her daughter, a writer, agrees to write her story, and her daughter's daughter's path is still unknown.

Although the loving connection between the generations of women is strong, each ages differently. The patterns of aging for each gender now change from generation to generation with astonishing rapidity. When patterns change, meanings change, and there is less confidence that one can discover some already existing, ageless meaning in any stage of life.

> Old age no longer represents an anchor in the past, a reward for fulfillment of ageless values. A stage of life without personal function or social function is a prospect at least as terrifying as physical decomposition.

Jewish women have pioneered in creating new initiatory rituals to affirm the beauty and wisdom of their aging and to acknowledge the completion of their childbearing years (Adelman, 1986; Spiegel 1988/5749).

POSTMODERN ELDERING

There are no convenient summaries that can embrace traditional modern and postmodern worlds. Problems and interpretations of aging among contemporary Jews are likened to the problems of aging in contemporary western society. Remarkable advances in life expectancy are accompanied by widespread uncertainty and confusion about what it means to live many years beyond child-rearing and full-time employment. Rabbi Zalman Schachter-Shalomi, founder of the Spiritual Eldering Institute, asks, "Are we living longer or dying longer?" As we have seen, even during the Biblical period, Jewish voices questioned the tight connection between virtue and longevity. What was a minority opinion then is certainly a majority opinion today. As Olitzky and Borowitz write, "while there are those . . . who would still hold that there is a necessary relationship between righteous living and old age as a blessing by God, most Jews would argue that righteous living is important but not the primary cause for old age" (Olitzky & Borowitz, 1995).

So Jews continue the age-old search for new theological understandings and for new wisdom to bear the knowledge that aging involves both a "crown of glory" and "days of sorrow." Addressing the 1961 White House Conference on Aging, Rabbi Abraham Joshua Heschel spoke from an understanding of time rooted in the Jewish mystical tradition. He called on individuals of all religious denominations to sanctify time by renewing their relation to the living God. "The aged thinks of himself as belonging to the past. But it is precisely the openness to the present that he must strive for. . . . All it takes to sanctify time is *God, a soul, and a moment. And the three are always here.*" Heschel called on Americans to overcome their traumatized fear of aging that results in prejudice and discrimination against older people. "The effort to restore the dignity of old age will depend on our ability to revive the equation of old age and wisdom. Wisdom is the substance upon which the inner security of the old will forever depend. But the attainment of wisdom is the work of a lifetime" (Heschel, 1966, 84).

More recently, Rabbi Zalman Schachter-Shalomi—former professor of Jewish mysticism at Temple University, known as the "Zaide," the grandfather, of Jewish Renewal and now at Naropa University—has developed a vision of "spiritual eldering." He has designed a training program to aid elders in doing the necessary inner work to turn their life experience into wisdom so that they may take on the needed role of mentors to generations following. In this way elders are empowered to transcend the isolation of age segregation that is as much a matter of consciousness as of living arrangements. This transdenominational training program is housed at the Spiritual Eldering Institute of Philadelphia which has begun to develop "Sage-ing Centers" to train health professionals to understand and to help realize the potential for spiritual development among elders.

Although Jewish textual and theological study of aging remains largely undeveloped, Susan Berrin's (1997) recently published collection, *A Heart of Wisdom: Making the Jewish Journey from Midlife through the Elder Years,* reveals a fresh outpouring of scholarly, rabbinic, personal, literary and practical concerns about aging, caring for the frail elderly, and being old. Jews continue to bring their four thousand year old tradition to bear in their search for ways to renew their ancient covenant while living longer. As has always been the case, the results are unpredictable. However, if the past is any guide at all, they will serve far beyond Jewish communities. In the coming years, humanistic scholarship and gerontological practice will both assist and benefit from this search.

NOTES

[1] The study of aging in Jewish literature and history is rudimentary. There is one modest article in *The Jewish Encyclopedia* (Philipson) and another more recent one in the *Encyclopedia Judaica* (Ben-Sasson, Herr). Both collect the traditional sources; the limited space devoted reflects the relative scarcity of materials for comment. A useful resource is Leopold Loew's (1875) late-19th-century treatment of stages of life In Jewish literature. Sheldon Blank has a very useful article on aging in the Hebrew Bible in the *Interpreter's Dictionary of the Bible*. Recent interest in the topic is a response to an ever-increasing proportion of elderly in the population. Several years ago, *The Journal for Aging and Judaism* began publication under the editorship of Professor Kerry M. Olitzky of Hebrew Union College. Some articles have examined traditional sources.

[2] Even when Job is in his deepest suffering and spiritual disillusionment, he rejects his wife's suggestion that he "curse God and die," a prescription for a peculiar form of suicide. An early rabbinic tradition tells of a dispute about whether it would have been better for God not to have created humanity, given the resulting aggravation. But the question is asked from the Divine point of view, never questioning the value of life to the human (Urbach, 1987).

[3] See below, p. 160.

[4] *Tanakh* is a common acronym for *Torah*, the *Chumash* (Pentateuch), or the Five Books of Moses; *Nevi'im*, "prophets," including historical narratives and the prophetic books; and *Ketuvim*, "writings" of various kinds, including Psalms, Proverbs, Job, and Qohelet. Torah in this sense is the most specific use of the term.

[5] Sarah is the only woman in the Bible whose age at death is recorded.

[6] H. H. Ben-Sasson, "Elders" in *Encyclopedia Judaica*, 6:578–581. See also Reviv. Accounts of the powers of elders stretching beyond tribal boundaries probably reflect later attempts to read early Israelite institutional history nationally rather than tribally.

[7] See also Isaiah 47:6 and Lamentations 5:11ff.

[8] This theme appears also in an apocalyptic Talmudic dictum (Sotah 49b) which takes "the lack of respect and courtesy shown by the young toward elders" as a sign of the approaching time of troubles that precedes the coming of the Messiah.

[9] These views continue later, e.g., in the apocryphal *Wisdom of Jesus the Son of Sirach*, later called Ecclesiasticus, which is preserved in Greek, although originally written in Hebrew in Palestine during the early second century C.E. Its general perspective is very similar to that of Proverbs:

> If you have not gathered wisdom in your youth, how will you find it when you are old? Sound judgment sits well on grey hairs and wise council

comes well from older men. . . . Long experience is the old man's crown and his pride is the fear of the lord. (25:3–6)

[10] Quotations From Qohelet are from James L. Crenshaw's (1987) judicious commentary.

[11] Olitzky points to this passage as one of several, beginning with the biblical command to rise before the aged (Lev. 19:32) and continuing with Genesis Rabbah (Toledot 43.6), that directly relate respect for elders with reverence for God.

[12] In a *halakhic* Midrash, Sifra Kedoshim 7:12, we find this parallel, which totally disconnects scholarly attainment from age: "The rabbis held that even a young scholar is called *zaken* and should be honored, while no honor is due the ignorant or sinful, although old."

[13] For the world- and humanity-sustaining powers of Torah study, which sometimes seem theurgic, see Urbach (1987, chap. 12).

[14] Translations of the Babylonian Talmud are from the Soncino edition.

[15] However, in a 15th-century midrash a story is told of a woman whose life had become artificially prolonged by her continuing performance of a *mitzvah* that was not required of her. One can live too long; she was compassionately advised to let go of the *mitzvah* (Patai, 1980).

[16] Olitzky (1989) cites this as another passage that connects deference to elders with respect for God.

[17] Dorf (1987) brings together texts on honoring and caring for parents from traditional sources with a view to illuminating current issues. He finds in tradition both the obligation to care for aging parents and the need to live one's own life, to care for one's own family.

[18] The first Jewish "home for the aged," an institution specifically for caring for the aged, was founded in Amsterdam in the mid-18th century. The need increased with the loss of traditional communal settings (Ben-Sasson).

[19] Goitein (1988) discusses aging as reflected in the Geniza documents in volume 5, pp. 116–128. Judah ha-Levi, translated by Nina Salaman, is cited on p. 119.

[20] As Howe and Greenberg (1973) note, Yiddish fiction tended toward symbolic or "representative" figures. See their introduction, p. 33.

[21] Information about Spiritual Eldering seminars and Sageing Centers is available from the Spiritual Eldering Institute, 7318 Germantown Ave., Philadelphia, PA 19119.

REFERENCES

Adelman, P. V. (1986). *Miriam's well: Rituals for Jewish women around the year.* Fresh Meadows, NY: Biblio Press.

Babylonian Talmud, Hebrew-English Edition of (1990). (H. Freedmen, Trans.; I. Epstein, Ed.). London: Soncino Press.

Bellow, S. (1970). *Mr. Sammler's planet.* New York: Fawcett.

Ben-Sasson, H. H. Ageanel the aged. *Encyclopedia Judaica, 2,* 343–348. "Elders," *Encyclopedia Judaica, 6,* 578–581.

Berrin, S. (Ed.). (1997). *A heart of wisdom: Making the Jewish journey from midlife through the elder years.* Woodstock, VT: Jewish Lights Publishing.

Blank, S. H. (1962). Age, old. In *The interpreter's dictionary of the bible,* Vol. 1. (pp. 54–55). New York: Abingdon Press.

Blidstein, G. (1975). *Honor thy father and mother: Filial responsibility in Jewish law and ethics.* New York: KTAV.

Blocker, J. (Ed.). (1965). *Israeli stories.* New York: Schocken.

Chapman, A. (Ed.). (1974). *Jewish-American literature: An anthology.* New York: New American Library.

Chernin, K. (1983). *In my mother's house: A daughter's story.* New York: Harper Colophon Books.

Crenshaw, J. L. (1987). *Ecclesiastes: A commentary (The Old Testament Library).* Philadelphia: Westminster Press.

Dorf, E. N. (1987). Honoring aged fathers and mothers. *The Reconstructionist,* 5314–5320.

Eliade, M. (1963). *Myth and reality* (W. R. Trask, Trans.). New York: Harper Torch Books.

Ginzberg, L. (1961). *The legends of the Jews.* Philadelphia: Jewish Publication Society.

Goitein, S. D. (1988). *A Mediterranean society: The Jewish communities of the Arab world as portrayed in the documents of the Cairo Geniza: Vol. 5. The individual.* Berkeley: University of California Press.

Herr, M. D. Age and the aged. *Encyclopedia Judaica, 2,* 344–346.

Heschel, A. J. (1966). To grow in wisdom. *The insecurity of freedom: Essays on human existence.* New York: Schocken Books.

Hillers, D. (1969). *Covenant: The history of an idea.* Baltimore: Johns Hopkins University Press.

Howe, I., & Greenberg, E. (1973). *A treasury of Yiddish stories.* New York: Schocken.

Jacobowitz, I. (1988). Ethical guidelines for an aging Jewish world. *Journal for Aging and Judaism, 2*(3), 145–157.

Kohut, G. A. Ages of man, the seven. *The Jewish Encyclopedia, 1,* 233–235.

Loew, I. (1875). *Die Lebensalter in der Juedischen Literatur.* Szegedin, Hungary: Sigmund Berger.

Meyerhoff, B. (1978). *Number our days.* New York: E. P. Dutton.

Matt, D. C. (Transl.). (1983). *Zohar, the book of enlightenment.* New York: Parlist Press.

Moody, H. R. (1986). The meaning of life and the meaning of old age. In T. R. Cole & S. A. Gadow (Eds.), *What does it mean to grow old?* (pp. 9–40). Durham, NC: Duke University Press.

Neusner, J. (1981). *The Tosefta.* New York: Ktav Publishing.

Neusner, J. (1988a). *The Mishnah: A new translation.* New Haven, CT: Yale University Press.

Neusner, J. (1988b). *The way of Torah: An introduction to Judaism* (4th ed.). Belmont, CA: Wadsworth.

Nickelsburg, G. (1981). *Jewish literature between the Bible and the Mishnah.* Philadelphia: Fortress.

Olitzky, K., & Borowitz, E. B. (1995). A Jewish Perspective. In Kimble, M., et al.

(Eds.), *Aging, spirituality and religion: A handbook.* Minneapolis: Fortress Press.

Olitzky, K. M. (Ed.). (1989). *"The safe deposit" and other stories about grandparents, old lovers, and crazy old men.* New York: Markus Wiener.

Ozick, C. (1971). *The pagan rabbi and other stories.* New York: Alfred A. Knopf.

Patai, R. (1980). *Gates to the old city: A book of Jewish legends.* New York: Avon Books.

Philipson, D. Age, old. *The Jewish Encyclopedia, 1,* 230–232.

Reuben, S. (1987). Old age: Appearance and reality. *Journal of Aging and Judaism, 2*(2), 117–122.

Reviv, H. (1989). *The elders of ancient Israel: A study of a biblical institution.* Jerusalem: Magnes Press.

Schachter-Shalomi, Z. (1995). *From age-ing to sage-ing: A profound new vision of growing older.* New York: Warner Books.

Schachter-Shalomi, Z. (1991/5751)). The practice of spiritual eldering. *New Menorah: The P'nai or Journal of Jewish Renewal* (2nd ser.) *22,* 9ff.

Spiegel, M. C. (1988/5749). Becoming a crone: Ceremony at 60. *Lilith, 21,* 18f.

Urbach, E. E. (1987). *The world and wisdom of the rabbis of the Talmud* (I. Abrahams, Trans.). Cambridge, MA: Harvard University Press.

The Wisdom of the Zohar: An anthology of texts (F. Lachower & I. Tishby, Trans. [into Hebrew]; D. Goldsmith, Trans. [into English]. (1989). New York: Oxford University Press.

Yezierska, A. (1975). *Bread givers.* New York: Persea Books.

8

Aging in the Christian Tradition

Melvin A. Kimble

The historic Christian faith has no doctrine of theology of aging, per se. As with each stage of the life cycle, the basic Christian theological affirmations are to be applied to the challenges of older adulthood. This lack of specificity raises the question: Is the historic Christian religion a friend or foe of the last stage of the human life cycle? Does it make any substantive difference to the older person whose last stage in the human life cycle is unfolding?

There is a growing recognition that a wider frame of reference is required to explore more fully the multifaceted and complex questions about older adulthood and its meaning. The natural sciences with their positivistic empirical approach are too narrow and unidimensional in their definition and understanding of aging. The most deeply human is not a subject that is amenable to digital reduction. There is an imperative need for the inclusion of the spiritual dimension in the study of aging and its meaning.

I write with the conviction that the Christian religion with its historic perspective on the cumulative resources of the spirit sets forth affirmations and principles that help individuals and the community of faith confront the human aging process in all of its bewildering ambiguity. The heartiness of any religious tradition lies in its capacity to offer images and understandings and metaphors and insights that provide a sense of the transcendent meaning of life conveyed by an Ultimate Being. The Christian tradition nurtures a transcendent perspective on life that is neither escapist or evasive.

UNPACKING THE CHRISTIAN TRADITION

A traditional Christian image of aging is that of a spiritual journey. My purpose in this essay is to explore the insights concerning this journey of aging and becoming old that comes through the Christian tradition. What does it mean, for example, to grow old under the promises of the love of God? What does the Christian God have in mind for persons at the last stage of their life cycle? What are the resources within the Christian tradition to make the later years of life's journey a new adventure of grace?

In responding to such questions, I glean from the congregated affirmations of a selected assortment of representative Christian theologians down through the centuries who have formulated responses to such questions. Church fathers such as St. Paul, Augustine, Tertulian, Gregory of Nyssa, Ireneaus and Aquinas, and later theologians, such as Luther, Calvin and Schleiermacher, and more contemporary theologians, such as Paul Tillich and Reinhold Niebuhr, have all provided insightful perspectives concerning old age and its meaning.

Although this assignment does not afford the luxury of exploring in depth the contribution of each of the aforementioned, it is possible to tease out several of the main tenets from the Christian tradition which have been set forth and are relevant to any discussion on aging.

Imago Dei

Central to the Christian tradition is the belief that human life is created in the image of God. This means that aging, although not part of God's nature, is included in God's intended plan for human beings. The acceptance of aging as part of the creative order means that individuals are to be valued as they age. Biblical authors suggest that it was part of God's intention that we grow old and mature to old age. Augustine, for example, views aging as a natural process to be expected as persons move through the life cycle, although he believed that humanity's beginnings were a pinnacle of perfection without suffering or death.

Ultimately, the person will be understood only when seen to be created in the image of God. There is no other way for a human being to understand himself or herself other than in terms of transcendence. The Christian tradition, as Reinhold Niebuhr (1953) notes:

> ... emphasizes the height of self-transcendence in man's spiritual stature in its doctrine of the "image of God" ...
>
> ... In its purest form the Christian view of man is a unity of God-likeness and creatureliness in which he remains a creature even in the highest spiritual dimensions of his existence and may reveal elements of the image of God even in the lowest aspects of his natural life (p. 15).

The first principle of Christian anthropology is that humankind, like the animals, are God's creatures but, unlike the animals, they are more than a natural creature. From a theological perspective Niebuhr (1953) has described this crucial distinction as follows:

> Man is a child of nature, subject to its vicissitudes, compelled by its necessities, driven by its impulses, and confined within the brevity of the years which nature permits its varied organic forms, allowing them some, but not too much, latitude. The other less obvious fact is that man is a spirit who stands outside of nature, life, himself, his reason and the world (p. 3).

The revelation that we are made in God's image is an indispensable truth about humankind. Human life is God's gift. Life and dignity are bestowed by God. We are meant to become a center of freedom and love and have a special part to play in God's creation. We are named and blessed to this destiny by God. This responsible awareness which God created in us (*Ansprechbarkeit,* as Emil Brunner puts it) is our uniqueness and fatal temptation. This answerability or responsibility, however, is not a task but a gift.

Our imaging of God, as Walter Burghardt (1991) argues, has two facets: it is dynamic and ontological. To be like God is not only to be gifted as a center of freedom and love, but we are to be "a new creation" (2 Corinthians 5:17), God's "workmanship" (Ephesians 2:10). We have put on "a new nature, created after the likeness of God in true right-eousness and holiness" (Ephesians 4:24). Such divine resemblance, utterly unmerited, demands of us a living likeness.

Augustine understood this well and pleads:

> Our whole business, therefore, in this life is to restore to health the eye of the heart whereby God may be seen . . . to this end is directed the whole aim of the divine and holy scriptures, that that interior eye may be purged of anything which hinders us from the sight of God . . . but God made thee, O man, after His own image. Would He give thee wherewithal to see the sun which He made, and not give thee the wherewithal to see Him who made thee, when He made thee after His own image? (Przywara, 1958, p. 494)

The image of God is not, therefore, static reality, but as Gregory of Nyssa affirms, ". . . continual growth; and far from being an object of clear vision, it keeps sinking deeper into God's unknown" (Burghardt, 1991, p. 13). We can add even more; namely, that a human person is a person only to the extent that he or she understands himself or herself *sub specie aeternitas,* under the aspect of eternity. Aging is a singular way to see ourselves in the image of God.

The Human Condition and God's Redemptive Response

In our spiritual journey of aging through the life cycle we become aware of ourselves as an indissoluble amalgam of shadow and light, angelic and demonic, *simul justis et peccator,* saint and sinner, in the paradoxical unity of contraries that constitute our essential humanness. This taffy pull of good and evil in human life and history constitutes the moral puzzle and dilemma in the mystery of human existence. Long before psychoanalysis, Christian doctrine had unmasked much that passes for righteousness and high moral principle. Great Christian writers like Blaise Pascal have exposed the human heart and told the truth about its strengths and weaknesses, its goodness and its evil.

> What a chimera then is man! What a novelty! What a monster, what a chaos, what a contradiction, what a prodigy! Judge of all things, imbecile worm of the earth; depository of truth, a sink of uncertainty and error; the pride and refuse of the universe! (Eliot, 1958, p. 121)

Such probing confirmed the radical realism of the biblical view of man, namely, the congenital weakness of human nature.

Every aspect of the historic Christian tradition suggests the impossibility of persons fulfilling the true meaning of their lives, and discloses how God meets us in our sinful human condition and how he has revealed himself in Jesus Christ. This revelation of the Gospel concerning the good news of Jesus Christ's incarnation, proclaims our deliverance not only from our sinfulness, but from death itself.

The incarnation and the act of reconciliation of Christ gives us the *leitmotif,* or basic redemptive pattern, to the Christian life. God's reconciling activity heals the disorders of existence and redresses our sinful alienation from God. This redemptive activity is inseparable from God's creating activity. "When the time had fully come, Jesus sent forth his son" (Galatians 4:4). For Christianity this is the primordial revelation on which the community of faith is founded and provides the way of understanding God. Jesus Christ then is the focus where the very mystery of Being is disclosed. He reveals the essential mystery of human life and is himself the *unum necessarium.*

Time: A Shaping Force in Life

Over 1500 years ago St. Augustine struggled with his understanding of time:

> For what is time? Who is able easily and briefly to explain that? Who is able so much as in thought to comprehend it, so as to express himself

concerning it? . . . Boldly for all this, dare I affirm myself to know thus much; that if nothing were passing, there would be no past time: and if nothing were coming, there should be no time to come: and if nothing were, there should be no present time. (Oates, 1948, p. 191)

The mystery of time and its passing continues to be a concern to humankind. A cartoon suggests that God invented time to keep everything from happening at once. Christianity takes time seriously. For the Christian, time is God's creation and a workshop of his holy purposes. Human history is the arena where he expresses himself in action. God uses history to make his eternal and holy purposes of redemptive action manifest.

From the furthest reaches of space to the deepest recesses of the human heart time is a shaping force in life. Longevity and older adulthood bring with them a special appreciation of time and its passing. Memory implies time lapsed. In remembering, persons take responsibility for values actualized and values denied. An individual must bear the pain of remembering himself or herself as one who denied values closely identified with one's self-image or with the doing of God's will.

Unlike western existentialism, which eclipses every past and future with the "now" of existential decision, the Christian tradition sets forth an understanding of an absolute future that confesses God's love to be the guarantor of our time—its fulfilling horizon and final consummation. This love exposes the transcendence which calls us forward into the future. Our spirituality is an opening out from space and time—a window which discloses a destiny inextricably tied to mystery. In Christianity the resurrection of Jesus Christ and the promise of the resurrection transform the ultimate shape of time.

As Mary Knutsen (1995) contends:

Humanity need not work toward an endlessly deferred future; rather, an astonishingly gracious future comes toward humanity in the risen Jesus. For Christianity, in short, the center of gravity for shared human life in time is not an eternalized past or timeless now, but the promise and power of an astonishingly gracious new future already coming toward humanity and all creation in the risen Jesus (p. 475).

The future comes to human beings as a gift. An ever unfolding new future spares us from frantically grasping an eternalized past.

As Paul Tillich maintains "eternity transcends and contains temporality, but temporality which is not subject to the law of finite transitoriness and temporality in which past and future are united . . . though not negated in the eternal present (Tillich, 1955, p. 78).

REFLECTIONS ON THE CHRISTIAN TRADITION: THREE PROBLEMATIC CRISIS AREAS OF THE AGING EXPERIENCE

We live in a society where aging is an embarrassment, suffering and dying a meaningless experience and death a medical failure. The following sections are an examination of what the historic Christian tradition has to say to these challenging crises.

Aging and the Crisis of Meaning

Albert Camus (1955) once stated, "There is but one truly serious problem, and that is . . . judging whether life is or is not worth living." That basic, fundamental "problem" emerges with considerable urgency as persons become aged. Such questions as, Is growing old worth one's whole life to attain? What is the meaning of life when one is elderly? Can the meaning of who I have become be sustained in this last stage of my life? To respond to these questions requires more than a biomedical paradigm, for such a model is powerless to reveal to us the meaning of our lives.

There is an increasing body of evidence to suggest that the crisis of aging and being old is a crisis of meaning. It has been observed that the enormous gains in longevity as the result of medical and technological progress have been accompanied ". . . by widespread spiritual malaise . . . and confusion over the meaning and purpose of life . . . particularly in old age" (Cole, 1984). Increasingly more people today have the means to live, but no meaning for which to live. An individual throughout her or his lifespan is motivated to seek and to find personal meaning in human existence.

A central activity of the species Human Being is meaning formation. The supply of meanings is essential in maintaining the vitality of a person's life. This is especially true in the second half of life and constitutes a major emphasis in ministering and serving older persons.

Contributing to the pervasive grimness about aging and growing old is this lacuna of symbols and appropriate rituals to mark and give positive meaning to the passing of lifetime. Rituals are the entrée to the hidden meanings of life. Symbols provide guideposts for us as we move into the future, even into death. A true symbol moves beyond itself, not only denoting something but also suggesting that which is hidden. The hiddenness is not just buried in the past, but also contains a promise of the future. It captures the undiscovered "more" to which symbols always point. It never simply escapes into the past, but always opens to the future.

Devoid of transcendent symbols that facilitate confrontation and acceptance of the natural process of aging and dying, persons frantically search for deliverance in the latest medical messiah or technology. They await the discovery of an "immortality enzyme" that delays and reverses the aging process and dangles the prospect of some temporal immortality before them. The present crisis of meaning calls for relevant symbols that sustain meaning as individuals live out their longer life expectancies.

A symbol system that is impoverished results in expressions of guilt without absolution, of isolation and alienation which have forgotten God's covenant of promise and relationship as well as its expression in the household of faith, and of suffering that is void of meaning and only devalues and debases the sufferer. Responsible and creative ministry using the healing and salvific symbols of the Christian tradition incorporate understanding of guilt, suffering and death. The cross, cup, wine, bread—these and other Christian symbols speak to the deepest substrata of our being. They involve all of our nature—the senses, feelings, memory, mind, subconscious, etc. In this encounter with the symbolic, our fragmented selves may be healed and reconstructed. The introduction of such symbols of meaning in the midst of suffering, however, does not deny the inevitable reality of suffering, but rather transcends it.

An examination of aging from the perspective of the Christian tradition explores the human dimensions and contours of the aging experience. It probes the interior as well as the exterior dynamics of the aging process. The goal is to examine the unique personal experiences of aging with its increasingly narrowing boundaries and the cascade of changes and losses that mark one's passage through lifetime. It includes those occasions in which God's love most poignantly interfaces with a person's life and when a sense of life's ultimate meaning is introduced. The Christian faith has an extraordinary opportunity to claim a primary role as an affirmer of the value and worth of all persons at every stage of life and to become a generator of personal and social meanings.

As a covenant community of believers, the church has the source and center of the ultimate meaning of life in the proclamation of the Gospel, the Good News about aging. In a society that measures the value of life in ways that often devalue and dehumanize, the Gospel with its recreative power confronts Christians at whatever stage with a destiny and a purpose. The Christian faith tradition seeks to find ways to assist older adults who struggle with issues of integrity and meaning and provide them with ready access to the rich heritage of images and symbols through which persons understand their relationship to God, the source of ultimate meaning. Eschatology is a symbolic way of expressing the reality of God's purpose within history. Theologian David Tracy

(1975) asserts that the Christian symbols of eschatology can orient us positively for the process of aging:

> What is fundamentally at stake . . . is but a reverence for ourselves as part of nature and a respect for the diversity of that temporal, aging self in such a manner that the integrity or dignity of every human being is affirmed without qualification. The Judeo-Christian symbol-system, I believe, can disclose precisely that reverence and illuminate that dignity. Theological reflection, therefore, may provide something like a horizon of meaningfulness, an orientation to the value of aging that may serve to clarify and strengthen the specific analysis found by the sciences (p. 133).

The Challenge of the Crisis of Suffering

Suffering is present at every stage of the life cycle, an integral part of human life and destiny. The historic Christian tradition regards suffering as inseparable from humankind's earthly existence. To become human, it would seem, always entails suffering.

In our present culture, however, an insidious view of pain and suffering has appeared. Some current theories of pop psychology and mechanistic psychotherapy tend to deny the concept that suffering, however it is manifested—as a sense of loss, grief, loneliness, guilt, or anxiety—is inevitable. In addition, often there is an outright rejection of any positive interpretation of the experience of such suffering.

Suffering inexplicably is part of human life, though only a certain part is inevitably necessary. For example, suffering from war and torture, hunger and homelessness and the many other human injustices that cause pain and suffering often can and should be eliminated. But the Christian understanding that unavoidable suffering is part of the normal human condition is disappearing. Even more troubling is the rejection of the idea that unavoidable suffering can potentially be a redemptive experience that enriches the sufferer and may even result in some discovery of truth or value or meaning. A rather odd and oppressive judgment has also fallen upon the person who is suffering. His or her suffering is viewed as avoidable, the result of a defective personality structure, a lack of enlightenment, or even irresponsibility.

Much of the contemporary popular therapeutic philosophy which has its roots in the human potential movement of the 1960s is opposed by the Christian tradition on two counts. First, this Christian tradition accepts the reality of suffering. That an individual's destiny, the circumstances in which events place us, sometimes imposes experiences of pain and suffering is affirmed as a basic truth of life. This painful imposition of the outer world cannot be negated by any solipsism. Suffering belongs to the human condition and is inescapable. Second, and more important, the Christian perspective holds to the conviction that suffering and dying are potentially meaningful. Such a viewpoint challenges the pervasive thinking that the existence of a debilitating disorder in a frail older person, for example, diminishes and devalues the individual. Persons who suffer from some incurable disease are not morally or spiritually inferior. One can be plagued by life's diminishments and still maintain human worth and dignity. Even in a comatose condition, a person does not cease to be fashioned in the image of God.

The question concerning God's suffering and its meaning is answered by a "theology of the cross," as Martin Luther labeled it, with its understanding of God's vulnerability to shame, defeat, and death in the person of Jesus. For Christians, the cross is a powerful symbol of meaning, fashioned out of suffering and bears witness to the one who took upon himself the rejections of this world in order to reveal the gift of God's restorative and healing love. God's love may heal and restore. In the theology of the cross, even when finding oneself caught up in the harsh and relentless losses of aging, one at the same point discovers hope. Hope is not real hope if it is attached only to polished techniques of positive thinking and to exercises that promise health. As Leland Elhard (1979) states, "Authentic trust and hope are attached to the invisible, waiting upon an uncontrollable intervention of grace."

As set forth in the Apostolic Letter by John Paul II *On the Christian Meaning of Human Suffering,* the witnesses of the cross and resurrection "have handed to the Church and to humankind, a specific gospel of suffering, that Christ has raised human suffering to the level of redemption." It has been observed in various Christian documents that in suffering a power draws a person "interiorly close to Christ;" the person discovers a new dimension of his or her life and vocation, the call to "faithful endurance" (Hebrews 12:2). This observation appears to confirm Pope John Paul's contention that "when the body is gravely ill, totally incapacitated, and the person almost incapable of living and acting, all the more do interior maturity and spiritual greatness become evident . . . constituting a touching lesson to those who are healthy and normal" (John Paul II, 1984).

The Christian faith is also a friend of the aged as it calls persons to become a singular neighbor to the suffering one. A Christian understanding, for example, views persons within the context of a broader faith community rather than as isolated individuals. Institutions, health care professionals, community volunteers, and family are called upon to respond to human suffering with compassion and care. The church as well as the synagogue through the centuries have taken the lead in encouraging sensitive and supportive responses to suffering throughout the life cycle.

Old and New Testament texts as well as other sacred writings of the Christian tradition speak of the meaning of life and the meaning of death, of the mysteries of pain and suffering, as well as the mysteries of love and healing. But it is, perhaps, the apostle Paul who speaks most plainly about suffering with its potential for meaning in the Epistle to the Romans. "We rejoice in our suffering, knowing that suffering produces endurance, and endurance produces character, and character produces hope, and hope does not disappoint us because God's love has been poured into our hearts . . ." (Romans 5:3–5).

The Crisis of Death

The belief system with which any religion views the process of dying and death is crucial in examining the framework out of which one's faith is lived. Jaroslav Pelikan (1961) suggests that "the biography of a crucified Jew," which is the central message of the Christian faith, "cannot avoid speaking about death whether it be about his death or ours" (Pelikan, 1961, p. 5).

Death is the greatest trial of human life. It is the supreme external manifestation of temporality. Death infiltrates our being progressively as we experience the abrasion of time, finitude and physical diminution. At no stage of life does it impact us more threateningly than in the stage of older adulthood. Aging with its narrowing boundaries reminds us that we are death-bound creatures. Indeed, to live in time is to live toward death. Augustine underscored this by stating:

> For no sooner do we begin to live in this dying body, than we begin to move ceaselessly towards death. For in the whole course of this life (if life we must call it) its mutability tends toward death. Certainly there is no one who is not nearer it this year than last year, and to-morrow than to-day, and to-day than yesterday, and a short while hence than now, and now than a short while ago. For whatever time we live is deducted from our whole term of life, and that which remains is daily becoming less and less; so that our whole life is nothing but a race towards death, in which no one is allowed to stand still for a little space, or to go somewhat more slowly, but all are driven forwards with an impartial movement, and with equal rapidity. (Oates, 1948, p. 217)

Facing one's own death is the final developmental stage of life. Although we must be careful about equating aging and growing old with death, death for most persons these days comes during the stage of older adulthood. In our society, with the real possibility of longer life expectancy, more persons get a chance at frailty and death when they are elderly. About three quarters of all deaths today occur among those over 65 years of age (Bronte & Pifer, 1986). In addition, the longer an older person lives, the more members of his or her family and friends are lost in death.

Human life has a limit. It moves inexorably toward death. The Christian tradition serves as a friend if it helps persons to view death as a natural part of the created order of life. Like all other creatures, human beings have a limited life span (Psalm 90:10). Biological death is intrinsically connected with our organic existence. The historic Christian faith affirms that both living and dying are part of the dynamic processes of the created order.

Our society, however, as Ernest Becker (1973) has observed, conspires to disguise the fact that death occurs and to deny its reality. Behind that façade, we live with great fear of death, and death, when it occurs, is frequently perceived as a medical failure, not a natural event. But we are all going to die. The question is under what circumstances and at which stage of our life cycle. Medicine's proper job is to make sure that people don't die prematurely or for the wrong reasons. Modern medicine has introduced this question: Are people living for the wrong reasons? That is, have their lives been extended as an exercise in medical technology, but with no promise of quality of life in their final days? Medical technology now allows that. Getting out of life has become more complicated than getting in. But what is technically possible should not set the moral boundaries for what should be done medically to preserve or extend life. However, both in the realms of medicine and the military, technical possibilities unfortunately often define and determine the situation.

As we face the avalanche of premortem questions that have been introduced in present day health care, the shared wisdom of the historic Christian tradition offers guidance. Human life is God's gift to be received with thanksgiving. Life, however, is not absolute. It is not for itself; it is given for the purpose of glorifying God and serving one's neighbor. This means that we should neither end life prematurely nor attempt to prolong life and the dying process endlessly. Property and autonomy should not become the primary metaphors in withholding, withdrawing, or refusing medical treatment or engaging in euthanasia. From a Christian perspective, the sacrament of baptism breaks down the metaphor of property. When parents bring their child for baptism or a service of dedication, for example, they acknowledge that they don't own their child. In the symbolic mystery of that sacrament, they acknowledge that child's new identity and life and relationship with God. Baptism points parents and child to their dependence on the creator and author of life.

We are never called upon to determine whether life is worth living. Over that question God remains the sole arbiter. There is always the danger that we make decisions regarding termination of life because we infer that a person's life has no meaning or value. Meanings, however, are personal and unique, and thus it is impossible for one to evaluate or measure the worth of another person's life. There is an increasing danger in our society that human life will be evaluated in terms of its productivity and utility. To be created in the image of God is to be significant and valuable, irrespective of a productive capability, physiological limitations, or any of the other ordinary standards of value and worth that we arbitrarily apply to persons. The historic Christian tradition emphasizes the imperative of upholding the inviolable worth of the frail aged and acts in compassion and acceptance of them and their rights as human beings.

Even as we can err in undervaluing life, so we can err in overvaluing it. As suggested, life has a limit and time leans forward. Dying is not an occasion, it is a process, even as life is a process. Being prepares for nonbeing. This is what it means to be finite. The constitutive construction of life begins to crumble interiorly so that death can become acceptance, a *Gelassenheit* (a letting go). To live is to be utterly dependent on what Tillich calls the "ground of being." It is in the face of death that such absoluteness of dependency is clear. Such trust is central to the Gospel of Matthew: "Do not be anxious about your life . . . about your body . . ." (Matthew 6:25). This has been witnessed to in the Christian tradition through the centuries by many, including St. Augustine, St. Thomas Aquinas, and Martin Luther. From the Watch Night Service John Wesley sets forth the same theme: "I am no longer my own, but thine. Put me to what thou wilt, rank me with whom thou wilt; put me to doing, put me to suffering; let me be employed for thee or laid aside for thee, exalted for thee or brought low for thee . . ." (Davies, 1972, p. 155).

These testimonies do not represent simply fatalistic resignation but rather surrender to the mystery of God's love that envelops life. As the Roman Catholic theologian Karl Rahner confessed shortly before his death at the age of 80:

> The real high point of my life is still to come. I mean the abyss of the mystery of God, into which one lets oneself fall in complete confidence of being caught up by God's love and mercy forever (p. 38).

CONCLUSION

In the foreseeable future the number of older adults in our global society will continue to grow. Because a large percentage of these are members of the Christian faith community and participate in congregational life, the religious community has a unique opportunity to share with them in the exploration of their new world of longer life expectancy. A life of deeper meaning and hope is made possible by an approach which takes the human experience of aging seriously, and creatively links that experience to salvific symbols. Reinhold Niebuhr (1953) captures this challenge as he writes:

> All structures of meaning and realms of coherence which human reason constructs, face the chasm of meaninglessness when men discover that the tangents of meaning transcend the limits of existence. Only faith has an answer for this problem. The Christian answer is faith in the God who is revealed in Christ and from whose love neither life nor death can separate us (p. 295).

In the quest of older adults for a fuller understanding of aging and its limits and meanings the historic Christian faith tradition can be a critical guide as well as a supportive resource.

REFERENCES

Becker, E. (1973). *The denial of death.* New York: Free Press.

Bronte, D. L. &, Pifer, A. (Eds.). (1986). *Our aging society: Paradox and promise.* New York: W. W. Norton & Co. Inc.

Burghardt, W. J. (1991). Reflections on aging: Personal and theological. *New Theology Review, 4*(1), 11–13.

Camus, A. (1955). *The myth of Sisyphus.* New York: Vintage Books.

Cole, T. R. (1984). Aging, meaning and well-being: Musings of a cultural historian. *International Journal of Aging and Human Development, 19,* 329–336.

Davies, J. G. (1972). *The Westminister dictionary of worship.* Philadelphia: Westminister Press.

Elhard, L. E. (1979). The theology of the cross and the realities of aging. Paper delivered at the National Interfaith Conference on Aging, Indianapolis, IN.

Eliot, T. S. (1958). *Pascal's pensées.* New York: E. P. Dutton & Co., Inc.

John Paul II. (1984). Apostolic Letter *On the Christian Meaning of Human Suffering (Salvifici Doloris).* Washington, DC: U.S. Catholic Conference.

Knutsen, M. (1995). A feminist theology of aging. In M. Kimble et al. (Ed.), *Aging, spirituality and religion: A handbook.* Minneapolis: Augsburg Fortress.

Niebuhr, R. (1953). *The nature and destiny of man.* New York: Charles Scribner and Sons.

Oates, W. J. (1948). *Basic writings of St. Augustine.* New York: Random House.

Pelikan, J. (1961). *The shape of death.* Nashville, TN: Abingdon Press.

Przywara, E. (1958). *An Augustine synthesis.* New York: Harper Torchbooks.

Rahner, K. (1990). *Faith in a wintry season: Conversations and interviews with Karl Rahner in the last years of his life.* Edited by P. Imhof and H. Bullowans. Trans. and edited by H. D. Egan. New York: Crossroad.

Tillich, P. (1955). *Biblical religion and the search for ultimate reality.* London: James Nisbet & Co.

Tracy, D. (1975). Eschatological perspectives on aging. In S. Hiltner (Ed.), *Toward a theology of aging.* New York: Human Sciences Press.

9

Aging in Eastern Religious Traditions

Gene R. Thursby

E astern traditions are a newly emerging field in the study of aging from the standpoint of the humanities in North America. An increasing interest in these traditions is one result of changes in patterns of immigration to the New World during the last third of the 20th century. In consequence of the 1965 Immigration Act in the United States, there is now a significant and still growing number of followers of religious traditions that previously were little represented here. The rapidly changing religious landscape is being mirrored by the production of innovative scholarly models of American religious history, and this major shift in academic perspective is particularly well marked by the ongoing work of the Pluralism Project (http://www.fas.harvard. edu/~pluralsm/), a large cooperative study funded by the Lilly Endowment and directed by Diana Eck at Harvard University. This growing attention to diversity in American religious history, and the matching impulse to tell the story in a more inclusive way (Conser & Twiss, 1997; Tweed, 1997), is just beginning to influence humanistic gerontology. Many recent and otherwise helpful studies of aging and religion (e.g., Kimble, McFadden, Ellor, & Seeber, 1995) tend to perpetuate by omission the unquestioned assumptions of an earlier era that only Judaism and Christianity are religiously significant. However, the present *Handbook* reflects the contemporary reality of a religiously diverse and multicultural North America.

In fact the Americas have been entangled with eastern traditions since the first voyage of Columbus to the so-called New World, which was itself confused by European explorers and their patrons with India and the East (Thursby, 1995). Hence its native inhabitants came to be called Indians, too. North Americans descended from Europeans, although they restricted the entry of Asian emigrants until the late

20th century (Chan, 1990), remained fascinated with spiritualized images of a mysterious Orient or a mystic East. Ralph Waldo Emerson and the New England Transcendentalists, for instance, were deeply influenced by the Hindu sources of an Oriental Renaissance (Schwab, 1984). There was an equally notable influence from Buddhism on North Americans in the 19th century, which continued in a variety of forms throughout the 20th as well (Tweed, 1992). Indeed there has been a long period of two-way traffic of people and ideas between East and West. For example, Henry Steel Olcott went to South Asia after the U.S. Civil War and became a major contributor to the modern revival of Buddhism in its ancient homelands (Prothero, 1996). The Hindu monk Swami Vivekananda and other representatives of Asian traditions came to the New World to speak at the first World Parliament of Religions when it met in Chicago during the 1893 Columbian Exposition, and stayed on for a time in response to the demand for lecture tours. Such displays of enthusiasm among some North Americans were enough to spread worry among the more Eurocentric (Thomas, 1930). Yet, despite these early and ongoing connections with the East, until quite recently its traditions have been misunderstood by most North Americans, largely due to images in the popular media and political propaganda that intermix the alien with the sinister (Isaacs, 1958; Said, 1997).

At century's end, we live in a world of rapidly shifting imaginary boundaries (Rushdie, 1991) generated by processes that are also producing a "dehomogenizing" of religious formations as people move across fading states (Rudolph & Piscatori, 1997). In the last two decades of the 20th century, the boundaries of nations have been redrawn in such rapid succession that atlas makers have been plunged into despair. Civil wars, ethnic cleansings, and major population movements have prevented the establishment of the stable post-Cold War patterns anticipated in the optimistic label of New World Order. Some results of this ferment are at once strange yet familiar: people of exotic appearance, dress, and beliefs now regularly appear in locales no more exotic than the local mini-mall. Already there are estimated to be more Muslims than Methodists in the U.S. population. Current projections suggest that these shifts in world population will continue into the 21st century, which will make the values preserved and transmitted by formerly foreign traditions increasingly relevant to the lives of all residents of previously Eurocentric societies. The present chapter will introduce ideas and ideals concerning aging in Islam, Hinduism, and Buddhism— three traditions from West and South Asia that no longer should be considered foreign to North America (Metcalf, 1996; Williams, 1988). For ideas and ideals of aging derived primarily from the traditions of East Asia and the Pacific Rim, the reader is referred to the research reported in chapter 10 of this book.

If we take a planetary point of view, then Islam, Hinduism, and Buddhism are three of the world's largest religious traditions. According to conservative estimates, together the three represent about two billion followers or nearly 40% of all human beings now living. Hinduism (about 700 million) is the oldest among them and, like Judaism, is a religion of the ethnic or national type. As the cumulative tradition of a distinctive people and place, over the centuries most of its participants have entered the religion by birth to Hindu parents or by membership in groups that underwent slow acculturation rather than by individual conversion from other great faiths. However, Hinduism also traveled along with the general cultural influence of India into Southeast Asia (Indochina, Indonesia, etc.) and along with the emigration of Hindus from their traditional homeland in the subcontinent of India to other parts of the world. Islam (approaching a billion members) and Buddhism (about 300 million) are traditions of the missionary or universal type which admit individuals from other faiths, although the latter originated in India and emerged from Hinduism. Especially in earlier centuries, both engaged in proselytizing and conversion to recruit followers from many of the world's inhabited regions and religions. Current projections into the 21st century foresee the combination of emigration and proselytization bringing these and other eastern traditions into major numerical importance, if not dominance, in North America, too (Eck, 1997; Neusner, 1994).

These three great traditions differ from one another in the concepts and prescriptions by which they give shape to their respective visions of life. Islam, in its general attitude toward the world, has discouraged ascetic and monastic styles of life, and has celebrated the family. Hinduism has sought ways to balance ascetic with family values. And Buddhism, from the beginning, made its monastic community the model for right living. Moreover, each of the three is a cumulative, complex, and internally differentiated tradition whose followers have come to include inhabitants of diverse cultures (e.g., Geertz, 1968; Lapidus, 1988) who have represented in various ways their understanding of religious truth. In each tradition, therefore, support can be found for a range of alternative ways to define the stages of human life and to interpret the significance of aging (Geertz, 1973; Ostor, 1984). To treat the three together and to call them religious traditions is not to claim that they are simply like one another nor even singular in their own outlook.

ISLAMIC OR MUSLIM TRADITION

Contemporary followers of Islam understand it to be the most recent and complete version of the revealed religions of the Abrahamic or

Semitic family. Along with Judaism and Christianity, Islam (Peters, 1982) incorporates the biblical heritage that links current Muslim believers with prophets and patriarchs, and back through Abraham and Adam to the one divine Creator. Muslims also trace a line of descent from Ibrahim (Abraham) and Hagar through Ismail (Ishmael) and on down to the first Muslims at Mecca in Arabia in the 7th century of the current era. Most Muslims (Combs-Schilling, 1989) believe that Ismail, not Isaac (as in Genesis 22:2), was the son whom Abraham was called by God to sacrifice. They believe that Hagar and Ismail eventually reached Mecca after Sarah had them cast out of Abraham's household (Genesis 21:9–21). And that when Abraham later visited them, he and Ismail built the Ka'ba at Mecca to replace a temple to God that Adam himself had first placed there. These beliefs encourage Muslims, the followers of Islam, to see themselves as rightful heirs of the biblical heritage. To group them among eastern traditions is neither to deny a place to their tradition among the Abrahamic faiths nor to fall prey to falsifying Orientalist images (Said, 1978), but rather it is a way to acknowledge the extent of its following and the predominance of its influence throughout much of Asia.

The language of scripture and divine revelation in Islam is Arabic, and nearly all of the key terms and concepts of Muslim religious life derive from that language, which is used in scripture in ways that Muslims regard as "extraordinary beyond emulation" (Bogle, 1998, p. 37). The word "Islam" is the name given this religion in scripture (Qur'an 5:5). It means reconciliation or surrender, and it is closely related to the word 'salam' meaning peace or salvation. The derivative term "Muslim" refers to the follower of the religion, literally one who has been reconciled or who has surrendered to God. The way of reconciliation and the appropriate attitude to God are the same—submission to the divine will as revealed by the various prophets down through the last great divine messenger, the Prophet Muhammad (570–632 C.E.).

Allah is the Arabic name of God. This revered name refers to the sole divine Creator (Williams, 1963), of incomparable majesty, who is to be supremely praised and respected. As "the center and foundation of Islam" (Esposito, 1988, p. 25), Allah is believed to have revealed perfectly in the Qur'an, the holy scripture that was transmitted through Muhammad over a period of some 22 years from 610 to 632 C.E., how he intends for people to live. The divine message in the Qur'an was extended and elaborated (Denny, 1985) by exemplary teachings and practices of the Prophet who, as the final messenger of God, also was considered the most authentic interpreter of the Qur'an. Muhammad's exemplary words and deeds are known as Sunna and were recorded in collections called Hadith. Together with the Qur'an which they complement, they formed the core of traditional Muslim law, the Sharia.

Although the Sharia has been enlarged and extended over time by analogical extrapolation from this core, by learned opinion, and by consensus of the community, Muslims still maintain that Allah alone is the ultimate source of Islamic law and of its authority. Therefore, the teachings of the Qur'an, the precedents preserved in the Sharia, and the practices traditionally prescribed for ritual performance continue to provide the basic framework for Muslim religious life and Islamic values.

The Qur'an contains only about a dozen passages that make significant reference to elders, old age, and the aging process. Yet, few as they are, they clearly and forcefully express the most characteristic features of the Islamic vision (Watt, 1968) of human life that informs the Qur'an, Sunna, and Sharia as a whole. The key Arabic terms in the passages that make reference to old age in the Qur'an (Kassis, 1983) are "shaykh" (an old man, elder, aged), "kabira" (to grow, old age, to be aged, to be an old person), and "qadim" (aged, old, ancient).

Most of the Qur'an's teachings about elders are set in the context of biblical narratives. Prominent among them is the theme of the great patriarch Abraham and his wife receiving the good news that in old age, when it should be humanly impossible, they are to have a son (11:72; 14:39; 15:54). The tales of other patriarchs and faithful followers of the one God are recounted, too. These include the story of Joseph and his brothers in Egypt (12:78). As related in the Qur'an, it assumes that their aged father should be thought to be above them but below God in authority. And Moses (28:23), as he begins his exile from Egypt, performs the good deed of watering the flocks of an elder father in Midian who lacks sons of his own, and he is thereby drawn into that family's life. Finally, the motif of the aged Abraham is repeated in references to Zachariah (3:40; 19:8), who learns in his declining old age that he is to have a son named John.

The attitude toward old age suggested by these and other passages in the Qur'an takes for granted the relatively weak and limited character of human life in contrast to the absolute power and majesty of Allah. Hence the Qur'an tends to regard the loss of capacities that typically are suffered in old age to be only the most obvious evidence of the universal frailty and dependence that is the inevitable condition of all human creatures. The Qur'an affirms that it is the nature of ordinary human life, as established by divine will, to be limited and to undergo eventual destruction. Old age, according to an extraordinarily intense image in the Qur'an (2:266), will overtake and destroy a person in the same way that even a flourishing and well-watered orchard will be burned up by a scorching whirlwind. In this vision of life, aging and the human being who suffers it are considered to be neither more nor less than one more sign and reminder (36:68) of the overwhelming mercy, justice, and power of Allah.

Therefore, the true Muslim—the properly responsive and faithful type of human being who is the effective beneficiary of the Qur'an's clear vision of the nature of life—is called upon to turn away from all individual, private, and personal consolations, and to conform to the rules of obedience to the divine will that are revealed in the Qur'an and subsequent tradition. From an Islamic perspective, only one response to the awareness of human limitation is appropriate when it is beheld in relation to the awesome majesty of Allah; and that is to submit to Him and to fulfill the requirements for living as a Muslim. According to Qur'an 40:67-68 (Ali, 1988):

It is He who created you from dust,
then a drop of semen, then the embryo;
afterwards He brings you forth as a child;
then you attain the age of manhood,
and then reach old age.
But some of you die before you reach the appointed term
that you may haply understand.
It is He who gives you life and death.

Ethical standards derived from the Qur'an assume that those who have been blessed by sufficient resources should take a familial stance toward the less fortunate, less able, and weaker members of society—in particular, the orphaned, the aged, and women. The Qur'an (4:2-6) requires mature adults to hold in trust the property of orphans until they attain the age at which they can manage for themselves, and it directs (17:23-25) mature adult children to show kindness and respect to aged parents. The Sunna of the Prophet (Suhrawardy, 1941) reinforces the second command by connecting respect shown the elderly with honor offered to Allah. But the unstated premise is that obedience and honor to Allah always take first place in Muslim life; idolaters, whatever their age or station, can neither be respected nor tolerated. An incident concerning the great patriarch Abraham in the Qur'an (26:69-104) reports his response to an encounter with men whose culture was based on the worship of idols. When they tried to justify themselves by saying that they were only continuing a practice that had been passed down to them by their elders, the patriarch nevertheless pronounced a severe judgment on them. In Islam, the unreserved reliance on Allah that is represented by Abraham as a prototype of the true Muslim must take precedence over, and thereby qualify, all other responsibilities and relationships, including respect for elders.

In traditional Islamic societies the norms applying to women have been similar to those in most of the traditional cultures that closely interacted with the other major religions. Their proper place was defined as complementary (Nasr, 1975), rather than equal in status, to men.

Since the primary roles of females were identified with their childbearing function in the family (Ati, 1982), until recent times Muslim women tended to be excluded from most public religious, political, and social activities. Since midcentury (Beck, 1980) there have been considerable variations in the status accorded to women and the lifestyle required of them in the diverse cultures with which Islam interacts (Weekes, 1984), but the most characteristic traditional pattern was to subordinate women to men and to value them mainly for bearing sons.

In countries in which Muslims have undertaken experiments in social reform during the colonial era or after national independence was attained, the position of women has been a major point of discussion. In South Asia, for example, where the practice of seclusion of women (*purdah*) in the inner household (*zanana*) has been widespread (Vreede-De Stuers, 1968), Muslim reformers have sought ways to enhance the status of women (Metcalf, 1984) by asserting their moral and religious capacities, their right to receive support in case of divorce, their right to inherit property, their right to education, and in some cases their right to participate in public life so that they no longer would be invisible to society (Minault, 1986). But Muslim sectors of South Asian culture continue to evidence the pattern found in a study of rural Bangladesh (Ellickson, 1988, p.53) where "the woman, even in old age, remains subdued, withdrawn at least from the public realm and, sometimes, even forgotten." In that kind of cultural setting, there is hardly any convergence of female and male roles in old age. Gender-based status differentiation, in which the wife's standing derives from the husband's, tends to be supported by a patriarchal, patrilocal, and patrilineal family structure throughout the course of life. The eldest male in the household, for example, will retain an age-based seniority in status until death, but his wife will lose her position as female head of the house should she survive him. And, as a widow, she is likely to find herself reduced to the position of an inconvenient and apparently anomalous dependent.

Although traditional Islamic law and ethics currently provide some measure of real protection to the less powerful (Esposito, 1982), in the ordinary circumstances of life in Muslim societies, many elderly persons, orphans, and women simply lack the means to secure equitable treatment for themselves (Pathak & Rajan, 1989). A modernist strategy, encouraged by some Muslim jurists who hope for the gradual improvement of this situation (Weeramantry, 1988), has been to frame and propose for general adoption a Universal Islamic Declaration of Human Rights. However, it is an open question whether or not such a strategy ever would reduce the circulation of negative images of older people (Peters, 1986), preserved in folk and popular aspects of culture neither derived from nor supporting Qur'anic values, that additionally victimize the elderly.

The most certain consolation available to a Muslim in difficult straits during the upward years may be the confidence that Allah knows the plight of every creature and will reward the faithful on the Day of Judgment. In the Qur'an, the whole of human life is considered to be a trial (Mir, 1987). While a Muslim lives, even a difficult old age is regarded by the devout as an opportunity to strive to perform good action and to remain faithful to God. Then, at precisely the time He determines (O'Shaughnessy, 1969), death will bring the trial to a close. In the hereafter Allah will judge, and punish or reward, each soul. Right through to the end of life and beyond (Smith & Haddad, 1981), the one Creator who alone transcends all earthly joys and woes is trusted to bring about an entirely appropriate deliverance.

HINDU TRADITION

Among Hindus today, whether they live somewhere in the subcontinent of India or have emigrated elsewhere abroad, there is so great a diversity of religious convictions and practices that inevitably this feature invites special notice (Flood, 1996, p. 8). There are two general reasons for the extraordinary diversity that characterizes Hinduism. One of them is implicit in the term "Hindu" itself, which was first used by the Persians as a general label to refer to everything that involved India, and so (Zaehner, 1966) "Hinduism is thus the '-ism' of the Indian people." What may be called "Hindu," therefore, derives from various human groups, languages, and cultures that have been indigenous to the subcontinent of India over more than 4,000 years. A second reason is that neither a single authority nor a uniform creed, dogma, or statement of doctrine unifies Hinduism (Weightman, 1998). No single founder, savior, or scripture is acknowledged by all who are given or who actively accept the label "Hindu."

Because of the difficulty of establishing a clear and comprehensive definition of Hinduism, colonial administrators in British India (Jones, 1981) treated "Hindu" as a residual category to denote the great majority of the population that remained after Muslims, Christians, Jews, and members of other clearly identifiable religious groups had been counted; and in contemporary independent India, leading intellectuals (Thapar, 1989) continue to puzzle over the theoretical assumptions and practical implications of Hindu identity. But, for our purpose here, a sufficiently close approximation to a set of defining features of the Hindu "great tradition" (Singer, 1972) can be derived from the following: the enduring influence of the early Aryan people, the high respect accorded the Vedic teachings that the Aryans preserved and transmitted, the Sanskrit language in which those teachings have been preserved and passed on, and the hereditary class of people known as Brahmans who have functioned as the chief mediators of religious authority (B. Smith, 1989).

The religious life of the Aryans, at around 1500 B.C.E. when they became culturally dominant on the alluvial plains of northern India, was polytheistic. Aryan ritual specialists, acting on behalf of their people, made sacrificial offerings to various divine beings who they believed could control particular features of the operation of the natural world. But, while most of the divine beings to whom the ancient Aryans sacrificed eventually fell from prominence, the ritual specialists who were the mediators between the divine and the human—called Brahmans— became increasingly important. Along with their sacrificial functions, the Brahmans knew and could teach other qualified pupils how to chant the Veda. The Veda was a secret oral tradition transmitted in an early version of the Sanskrit language, and Vedic chants were thought to have a sacred power (also known as *brahman*) that could confer great benefits when properly recited. For that reason, the Veda, the Sanskrit language, and the Brahman specialists who knew how to use them continued to be held in highest esteem.

In the religion of early Indo-Aryan culture, sacrifice served as the principal ritual technique to satisfy divine beings so that in turn they might provide help for human beings. Three of the four oldest sections of the Veda—the Rig, the Sama, and the Yajur—were recited at sacrificial ceremonies. The chants recorded in them contain many general references to goods sought for the patrons of the sacrificial rituals. A similar emphasis is found in the fourth section—the Atharva Veda— which contains charms and spells that were used to bring about more specific remedies. The Brahmans presided at sacrifices in order to obtain for their patrons the divine blessings that would maintain good health, provide protection from natural and human enemies, give healing from afflictions, bring progeny and prosperity, and assure a long life. An expansive affirmation of these aims appears in an invocation in Rig Veda 1.116 (O'Flaherty, 1981, p. 184): "Let me be lord over this world, with good cattle and good sons; let me see and win a long lifespan and enter old age as if going home."

The technique-oriented religion of the Aryans in India placed a strong emphasis on life-enhancement and life-extension. Although it took for granted that there was some kind of survival beyond this life, the notion of the afterlife in early Vedic as in early Greek tradition was a limited one that held little appeal (Basham, 1989). Early Aryans assumed that life is good, that more life would be better, and that the procedures performed by the Brahmans could produce it. An enthusiastic expression of this confidence in sacrificial ritual as a means of securing a ripe old age is found in Atharva Veda 19.67 (Panikkar, 1977, 303):

For a hundred autumns may we see,

for a hundred autumns may we live,
for a hundred autumns may we know,
for a hundred autumns may we rise,
for a hundred autumns may we flourish,
for a hundred autumns may we be,
for a hundred autumns may we become,
—and even more than a hundred autumns!

The practical optimism of the early Aryans who sought to be the beneficiaries of Vedic sacrificial rites may seem familiar, and indeed it is quite similar to that of the old man in a modern American novel (Updike, 1968, p. 37) who "felt that he would persist, on this earth, forever; that all the countless others, his daughter and son among them, who had vanished, had done so out of carelessness; that if like him they had taken each day of life as the day impossible to die on, and treated it carefully, they too would have lived without end and have grown to have behind them an endless past, like a full bolt of cloth unravelled in the sun and faded there, under the brilliance of unrelenting faith."

But, by about 600 B.C.E., the unrelenting faith in long life as good in itself was failing due to a radical shift away from the idea of the cosmos advocated by early Vedic tradition. The later Vedic view assumed that there is nothing new under the sun, that no event is unique. Every worldly occurrence is instead part of a pattern that recurs in endlessly repeating cycles throughout vast periods of time. The Upanishads, the last section of the Vedic teachings, exemplify the adaptation of Aryan religion to the revised cosmology. They do not argue the shift in the significance of time and change but take it for granted while continuing to employ the language of sacrificial ritual. In the Upanishads, however, sacrifice becomes a metaphor for the personal striving that is required if one is to engage successfully in ascetic discipline and meditation. Moreover, these practices are considered to be effective means that are crucial to the attainment of an experience of the only dimension of oneself that is unchanging and imperishable *(atman)*. Within the context of this world picture, simple life-extension lost its appeal.

The later Vedic vision of the cosmos awakened a sorrowful sense that worldly life is part of an oppressive cycle that subjects a person to pain and suffering *(duhkha)* again and again, without cease. Although that ancient evaluation of the plight of the ordinary or unrealized person who is pulled along by time and change might seem far from contemporary attitudes, it has affinities with the modern "theater of the absurd." In the play *Waiting for Godot,* for example, while the other characters sleep, one of them reflects on the human predicament. Part of his soliloquy so closely links together images of coming to life and of departing from it that the two become interchangeably identified with one another (Beckett, 1954, pp. 58–59): "Astride of a grave and a difficult birth. Down in the hole, lingeringly, the grave-digger puts on the forceps. We have time to grow old. The air is full of our cries. . . . But habit is a great deadener." This convergence of images denies any discernable difference between the birth canal and the burial ground or crematory. The two signify the same thing—a single circle of pain and suffering. The sense of "the absurd" in the later Vedic vision, however, was enlarged by the expectation of a surfeit of lifetimes to be spent in a Hindu version of a "No Exit" (Sartre, 1958) setting in which every soul is subjected to a seemingly endless series of lives in innumerable bodies—including diverse human ones—until all desires and their consequences have been completely extinguished. This idea of *karma* and reincarnation, of a law of action that operates to carry one through countless rebirths, is central to the later Vedic and classical Hindu view of the human dilemma (Keyes & Daniel, 1983; Neufeldt, 1986; O'Flaherty, 1980).

The Hindu vision of the cosmos as a place marked by painful recurrence *(samsara)* had the power to motivate a person to undertake rigorous methods *(yoga)* to attain release *(moksha)*. Although the old sacrificial rituals performed by the Brahmans had declined in prestige by 500 B.C.E., partly because their effectiveness was believed to be limited to providing boons within this world of suffering, individual techniques of sense control taught by masters of yoga and meditation were thought to meet the need of the new situation. But they required ascetic withdrawal from the world of sensuous pleasures, material interests, and family responsibilities. Sparsely inhabited forests and hills, therefore, became places for retreat from the world where people of all ages sought spiritual realization to effect a route of escape from the otherwise endless cycles of rebirth. The joy of the perfected soul or *atman* that has succeeded in "shaking off" the body in order to pass into the "uncreated" reality of *brahman* is recorded in a prayer in the Chandogya Upanishad (8.13). Immediately following it, a pupil on the path to perfection is represented by a prayer (Chandogya 8.14; cf. Hume, 1949 or Olivelle, 1996) that includes this petition: "May I, who am the glory of the glories, not go to hoary and toothless, yea to toothless and driveling [old age]! Yea, may I not go to driveling [old age]!" In sharp contrast to the longing that the aging process attracted in early Aryan culture, here the prospect only prompts disgust.

The search for an ageless, unsullied self within the individual that was so characteristic of the Upanishads remained a minority pursuit within Hindu tradition. Even so, it continued to be an influential one, and representatives of the mainstream of classical Hinduism repeatedly challenged the assumption that withdrawal from the world was the only sure way to attain release from rebirth. The most successful of these mainstream efforts is embodied in the Bhagavad Gita. It is a brief scripture, some 650 Sanskrit verses, that calls itself an Upanishad but is not in fact part of the Veda. Nevertheless, it is widely acknowledged to be "the most important and influential religious text of India" and "also the best-known Hindu text in the West" (Basham, 1989, p. 82). The Gita, dating from about 200 B.C.E., is set within a great epic that concerns a feud between two warrior clans. The Gita's portion of the great epic is a dialogue between a warrior, Arjuna, and his charioteer and spiritual master, Krishna, that takes place just before the decisive battle begins. The dialogue opens with Arjuna's initial shock in antici-pation of the bloody battle in which his friends and family members are sure to be killed; it passes through a discussion of the nature of time, change, selfhood, and duty; it considers the value of the old Vedic sacrificial rituals; and then it takes a surprising turn by displaying the hidden identity of Krishna as the presiding personal spirit and con-tinuous Creator of the universe, thereby backing the Gita's teachings by the highest authority.

The guidance that is given Arjuna more than once in the Gita is that he should maintain his proper position within the world and learn how to perform all of his rightful duties *(dharma)* without fear, regret, or any attempt to anticipate what might be their outcome. In the Gita, as in the Upanishads, the first step toward mastering this skill derives from the distinction between the apparent individual—the observable psycho-physical entity that is subject to time and change—and the unchanging and unborn real self (2:22; Deutsch, 1968): "Just as a man casts off worn-out clothes and takes on others that are new, so the embodied soul casts off worn-out bodies and takes on others that are new." The essential self, not the evident one, establishes the ground for fearless ethical action in the ordinary world. Further support fol-lows from the Gita's reinterpretation of the Vedic concept of *sacrifice* and of the Upanishadic concept of *renunciation* of the world. The two serve as metaphors for diligent performance of right "action . . . done without concern for its fruits" (6:1). The final warrant for the inner-worldly asceticism commended by the Gita is Krishna, when revealed to be the supreme personal spirit. He is at once the tireless source of the cosmos who must act ceaselessly and disinterestedly in order to maintain it in existence, and the blessing-bestowing heart of reality who cares equally for everyone who is devoted to Him. These com-bined strands of "secret knowledge" mediated by the Bhagavad Gita made it seem possible for a Hindu to experience spiritual freedom without departing from the ordinary responsibilities of human life in the world. And the Gita's influence in tilting the balance toward mas-tering the responsibilities of worldly life and away from withdrawing from the world in order to seek spiritual fulfillment also lent considerable support to the structure of social values that became the most distinguishing features of classical to modern Hinduism.

The distinctive social norms of Hinduism are based on a theory of classification known as caste *(varna* or *jati)* that establishes a closed hierarchy in which one's position is determined by birth (McGilvray, 1982). The Brahman has the highest status, next is the Kshatriya or warrior, then the Vaishya or merchant. All three are termed "twice-born" because their males are eligible to experience the "second birth" of initiation into learning the Veda. Below these three are the Shudra or laborer, and then anyone else not born into one of the four principal classes. The traditional Hindu social ideal is one in which caste organizes people into separate categories for marriage and other close contacts, justifies a hereditary division of labor, and ranks the various categories of people and their occupations as relatively superior or inferior in relation to one another (Dumont, 1980).

For members of the "twice-born" castes, the standard pattern for the life cycle is defined by a sequence of four stages *(ashrama)* that are supposed to make possible harmonious and complete human development. The first stage is initiation by a Brahman master into Vedic learning. It is open only to the unmarried twice-born male and is marked by his investiture with a sacred cord. He will wear it, until the last stage of life, over his left shoulder. This *brahmacharya ashrama,* or student stage, may last anywhere from a few hours to several years. The second stage, *grihastha ashrama,* mutually involves both sexes in the sanctification of marriage and in the active responsibility for family life. This householder stage is essential to the ongoing support of the Hindu social order. The third stage, *vanaprastha ashrama,* may be entered following the birth of grandsons who assure the perpetuation of the family line. At this stage the senior couple make a transition from household duties to a more retiring and contemplative mode of life together. If they pass through this stage to the last one, *sannyasa ashrama,* they must undergo a ceremony that will strip them of their familial and social identity. In this fourth stage, the ideal type of human being is a solitary homeless wanderer who is dedicated solely to spiritual realization.

The framework of the caste hierarchy and the four stages generate a structure within which status and age are correlated with specific ethical and behavioral expectations. Hence the Bhagavad Gita admonishes (18:47; Deutsch, 1968): "Better one's own *dharma,* though imperfect, than the *dharma* of another, well performed." Although everyone is subject to duty *(dharma),* its particular requirements are relative to one's position in the structure. For example, the *dharma* of the student initiate requires temporary withdrawal from worldly responsibilities, obedience to a preceptor, and celibacy. In contrast, the *dharma* of the householder requires dedication to the things of the world *(artha)* and a sexual relationship *(kama)* that is fertile and adds to the family. And these earlier stages are prerequisite to the later and the last. The Hindu tradition assumes that every twice-born male incurs three debts by virtue of being born, and is required to repay them before the final stage of life. As *The Laws of Manu,* which dates from sometime after 200 B.C.E. and is the most influential text on Hindu *dharma,* allows (6:37; cf. Buhler, 1964 or Doniger & Smith, 1991): "Having studied the Vedas in accordance with the rule, having begat sons according to the sacred law, and having offered sacrifices according to his ability, he may direct his mind to final liberation."

The traditional ideology of caste and the stages of life remain a significant influence on Hindu cultural values despite the contemporary decrease in exacting penalties for breaking caste rules. Even the great 20th-century Hindu social reformer Mahatma Gandhi's eldest sister (Zinkin, 1962, pp. 49–50) "exploded into toothless anger and tears: Gandhi's insistence on mixing with unclean people, on being his own sweeper, and his trips over the sea, had led to the excommunication of his whole family. For Ralihat Behen this had meant a lifetime of ostracism and humiliation by the people about whom she minded: the orthodox of her own sub-caste and neighborhood. Far from feeling proud of her brother, she stood there, doubled up by rheumatism, calling him a man so selfish that he had not cared what harm he had done to his family." Since India became a constitutional republic, most caste rules have lost their legal basis and are rarely enforced (D. E. Smith, 1963), but caste ideals persist because they are suffused with the traditional concern for spiritual liberation and diffused throughout the extended family system. And two studies (Hiebert, 1981; Vatuk, 1990) suggest that these traditional ideals continue to serve useful functions among the aging peasantry in South Asian society. Hiebert (1981, p. 211) observes that the ideal of caste and stages of life in Hinduism "provides its followers with explicit and detailed plans for living, in which age is charted as a series of progressively higher stages of human activity."

Because the most obvious beneficiaries of the traditional values of caste are twice-born Hindu males, there remains the question of the relative status of aging and elderly women. In the polytheistic pattern of traditional Hinduism, goddesses have a prominent place, and so the feminine is certainly honored at the level of worship and religious myth (Kinsley, 1988). But unless supported at the social level, this could be an instance (Sinclair, 1986, p. 112) of the "apparent paradox between symbolic ascendancy and the social denigration of women." Evidence on this question is not conclusive (Robinson, 1985), but there are some data which suggest that elderly Hindu women in upper caste urban settings may be more likely than men to seek new sources of support for their sense of identity in old age. Roland (1988, p. 217) claims that "the overt hierarchical structure of male dominance which is so evident in any number of ways in the family and other social structures is balanced by the enormous, covert structural powers of the women." But Roy (1975) found that in their later years high caste women from Bengal tended to shift toward an identity increasingly based on a relationship with a spiritual master or *guru* and away from a family nexus in which support for their status was declining with the onset of old age. As in some Muslim cultures, there is evidence that elderly women in Hindu culture may be more likely than men to be marginalized within the family by the aging process and so to be more motivated than elderly men to seek solace in spiritual activities and associations.

BUDDHIST TRADITION

Islam promotes family life. Hinduism reveres the renouncer but seeks to protect family values by establishing a balance between the claims of worldly responsibilities and the call of spiritual pursuits that may require their renunciation. The Hindu ethos nonetheless favors the family. "Hindus themselves acknowledge the fascination with renunciation," sociologist T. N. Madan (1989, pp. 119–120) notes, "and yet postpone it to the very end of a person's life as its fourth stage, after the stages of study, householdership, and retirement. In fact, only a microscopic minority actually renounce the world." But while mainstream Islam and Hinduism tip the scale of values toward the home and world, the early and determining orientation of Buddhism was toward the celibate, homeless, wandering world-renouncer.

The orientation was not unique to Buddhism. It was shared by the later Vedic tradition, as represented in the Upanishads, and by Jainism— another Indian ascetic movement that eventually came to be regarded as a separate religion, too. The attitudes and aims of these faiths were deeply influenced by the ancient Shramans (Johnson, 1980), wandering ascetics who were antiworldly counterparts to the Vedic Brahmans. Accordingly, they share a cosmology in which the fate of all beings, as determined by their own *karma* or modes of action over successive lifetimes, is to suffer a ceaseless round of rebirths *(samsara)* into various bodies until they are able to discover and dedicate themselves to an effective method for attaining release.

When Gautama the Buddha (about 560–480 B.C.E.) made a monastic community central to his religious movement, it indicated that status distinctions determined by birth are spiritually irrelevant and that freedom from worldly values is required for release from *samsara*. Although

a large lay following later became associated with the Buddhist movement, the monk remained a presiding ideal type. And a characteristic
emphasis in Buddhist literature continued to be withdrawal from the
world (Rangdrol, 1989, p. 21): "One who does not abandon worldly
pleasures squanders this life. Therefore, completely sever attachments
and ties and remain in secluded mountain dwellings. Yet unlike the
birds, deer, and other animals in such secluded places, exert body,
speech, and mind in what is virtuous."

In Buddhism, and in Jainism and Hinduism as well, the subject of old
age serves as a source of object lessons to motivate people to cultivate
the attitude of detachment that eventually turns toward a renunciation
of worldly values. Therefore, in the spiritual literature of all three traditions there are incisive images of old age in terms of its most painful
prospects (O'Flaherty, 1988, pp. 100–101): "When old age shatters the
body, gradually the limbs become loose; the old person's teeth decay
and fall out; he becomes covered with wrinkles and sinews and veins;
he can't see far, and the pupils of his eyes are fixed in space; tufts of hair
appear in his nostrils, and his body trembles. All his bones become
prominent; his back and joints are bent; and since his digestive fire has
gone out, he eats little and moves little. It is only with pain and difficulty that he walks, rises, lies down, sits, and moves, and his hearing
and sight become sluggish; his mouth is smeared with oozing saliva.
As he looks toward death, all of his senses are no longer controlled;
and he cannot remember even important things that he had experienced at that very moment."

According to Buddhist tradition (Pye, 1979; Schumann, 1989),
Gautama is said to have set out on the search for realization that led
him to become the Buddha, the Enlightened One, after seeing four disturbing sights. The first of them was an old man in about the same
decrepit condition as just described. That sight, which revealed to the
innocent Gautama the consequences of aging, was crucial. The next
two, of a sick man and a dead man, further developed the awareness of
suffering that had been awakened by the first sight. Then the fourth
sight was of a monk whose appearance represented to the receptive
Gautama an alternative way to engage the limited resources and possibilities of a human lifetime.

Traditional versions of the life of the Buddha tell that after his comfortable worldly existence had been interrupted by the preliminary
realization conferred by the four sights, he left his home and family
in order to find spiritual teachers and to take up the austere life of a
Shraman. After some years of study and self-denial, he adopted a more
moderate way of living and then experienced a deep realization of the
human predicament. During a long night of quiet sitting, he was able to
see the roots of suffering *(duhkha)* in ignorant craving and the means

of release from it through the "middle way" of an ordered life that would facilitate meditation and make possible the cultivation of disinterested compassion. From that decisive enlightenment experience (Robinson & Johnson, 1997), the Buddha went out to teach his new Dharma and to enlist disciples into a new monastic community, the Sangha, that was open to all who would follow its rules of discipline (Dutt, 1957).

The Buddha taught a method for attaining release that assumed (Little & Twiss, 1978, p. 211) "the dissolution of suffering depends on the dissolution of the concept of the self." Buddhist meditation became the laboratory for work on the project of dissolving the sense of separate selfhood—which the Buddha had defined as rooted in ignorance and had identified as a link in the chain of desire, craving, and *karma* that distorts reality into repetitive cycles of suffering that give shape to *samsara*. By adopting meditation as his principal technique (Collins, 1982, p. 235), the Buddha replaced the procedures of physical mortification required by the Shramans and the Jains with "the mental mortification of the contemplation of universal suffering." The Buddhist aim was similar to theirs, release from ceaseless becoming. But the point of departure was different from theirs. What set the Buddhists apart (Loy, 1988, p. 209) was the "claim that the ontological self is a delusion, and that this delusive sense of self is the fundamental duhkha (frustration) which distorts our experience and disturbs our lives. Contrary to all schools of ego psychology, such a self can never become secure because its very nature is to be insecure. . . . [T]he sense of self is not a thing but a lack, which can conceal its own emptiness only by keeping ahead of itself—that is, by projecting itself into the next thought, action, and so on—which process is craving or desire."

In the Buddhist analysis of existence, impermanence is the actual condition of life in the world, and the sense of separate selfhood is inevitably a failing, false refuge from it. Any effort to deny the certainty of the aging and death of the embodied self, for instance, merely intensifies (Huntington, 1989, p. 87) "pervasive anxiety that is held at bay only through the strength of forgetting or refusing to look more closely." Rather than denial, the Buddhist method of meditation or mindfulness opens with a preparatory level of practice in which one is required to look closely and repeatedly at all conditions of embodied life until no longer perturbed by them. Then, at a second level of practice, the goal is to settle into calm, clear insight. As support for practice, Buddhism recommends a triple refuge comprised of the method and teaching of the Buddha and the life of the monastic order. Together they constitute a path of spiritual development that is directed toward the cessation of a desire-driven separate identity, toward release, toward *nirvana*.

Paradox is prominent in Buddhist teaching at all levels and in all cultures in which Buddhism has been practiced. After the four sights that prompted his searching and Shramanic self-denial, at last sitting quietly the Buddha arrived at decisive clarity and commitment to a middle path. An old Buddhist text presumes to preserve his insight (Beyer, 1974, p. 200): "For the attached there is wandering, but for the unattached there is no wandering: without wandering there is serenity; when there is serenity there is no lust; without lust there is neither coming nor going; without coming or going there is neither passing away nor being reborn; without passing away or being reborn there is neither this life nor the next, nor anything between them. It is the end of suffering." And it is the end of aging as a problem. But most people, even those who find Buddhist truth clear and bracing, find that it is difficult to give up their attachment to the seemingly enduring personal identity that is created by interaction with family, friends, and institutions. Consequently, South and Southeast Asian elite or monastic Buddhism differs greatly from popular or lay Buddhism (e.g., Gombrich & Obeyesekere, 1988; Spiro, 1970; Tambiah, 1970) even though the status of women in Buddhist tradition (Barnes, 1987; Willis, 1985) probably differs less from that of men than in Islam or Hinduism. "Canonically," Spiro observes (1970, p. 232) in reference to Southeast Asian monastic religion, "Buddhism is not at all involved in the changes of status that sociologically mark the individual's passage through the life cycle. Although contemporary Buddhism pays greater attention to these points of transition, it too has less involvement in them than is characteristic of other religions." And since it tends not to be involved in these conventional concerns, the practices of its laity tend not to be limited exclusively to Buddhism. Lay Buddhists, especially in South and Southeast Asia, are likely to consult local charismatic figures, participate in spirit cults, or rely upon other religious traditions for help in crisis situations and for rituals that support transitions through the life cycle. In East Asian Buddhism, monks are more likely to provide ritual services at times of major life transitions and particularly at death. A contemporary Japanese Buddhist reformer, in fact, laments the widespread presence of "luxurious and ostentatious rituals" long ago developed for royalty and more recently preformed for commoners (Akizuki, 1990, p. 14).

Buddhist selflessness *(anatman* or *anatta)* and the Hindu unchanging Self *(atman)* that is its polar complement are assumed by their respective traditions to be "autochthonous" (Bharati, 1985, p. 203). Therefore, both of those images of human identity differ radically from the Muslim conception of a personal self whose continuity through old age, death, and beyond is dependent upon a Creator to whom it remains ever responsible. Because of such basic conceptual differences, Shrinivas

Tilak (1989, p. 148) concludes that "what aging is . . . depends upon what is understood by the notion of human beings and their embodiment. It must . . . be determined just what it is that ages." Responses to this question of "what it is that ages," from Buddhist perspectives are represented in recent books by Harding (1988), Kapleau (1989), and Sogyal Rinpoche (1993). They aim to calm anxiety and awaken an "ageless" presence.

RELIGION IN THE CONTEXT OF CROSS-CULTURAL OR MULTICULTURAL GERONTOLOGY

The humanities long have taken as their main tasks to discern the perennial meanings and at the same time to find new insights in ancient texts and traditions. The introduction to aging and eastern traditions offered above is compatible with those time-honored tasks of the humanities. But as the 20th century draws to a close, the conventional distinctions between academic disciplines with their respective tasks are difficult to maintain, and in any case it is evident that combined resources from the humanities and social sciences are required in order to continue to develop the kind of cultural gerontology—and more specifically, the cross-cultural and multicultural gerontology—most needed at the turn of the century. Happily, several recent publications help to contextualize and provide content for an interdisciplinary and multicultural gerontology that allows for the diverse ways in which religious traditions structure contemporary human expectations about the elder years and the significance they might have in a larger scheme of things.

Key images or root metaphors tend to provide the basic point of departure and organizing center for any newly developing field of study as well as for ancient texts and traditions. Kenyon, Birren, and Schroots (1991) organized a series of contributions to the study of aging from that perspective, Olds (1992) applied it in an exemplary way in her proposals for new directions in psychology, and Cole, Achenbaum, Jakobi, and Kastenbaum (1993) supported a similar mode of inquiry into theoretical and epistemological bases for what they called a critical gerontology. The combination of theory and case study offered in those works was complemented by the analyses of cultural representations of later life that were offered in a collaborative volume edited by Featherstone and Wernick (1995).

Among relevant introductions, surveys, and handbooks, the introduction to cultural gerontology by Ellen and Lowell Holmes (1983, 2nd ed., 1995) merits special mention as do the studies edited by Kertzer and Schaie (1989) on age structuring in various cultures, edited by

Thomas and Eisenhandler (1994) on aging and the religious dimension, and on aging and empowerment edited by Thursz, Nusberg, and Prather (1995). A reference shelf for this emerging field also should include The International Handbook on Aging Research edited by Palmore (1993) and the remarkable interpretive study undertaken by Inglehart (1997) of recent changes in more than 40 societies.

A key variable across cultures as well as within and among religious traditions is the root metaphor by means of which organizing images of identity or selfhood are constructed and maintained over the various stages of life and beyond. In this regard, work in the emerging fields of comparative- or ethno-psychology and comparative philosophy are particularly relevant to the topics treated in this chapter. See, for instance, the collaborative volumes edited by Paranjpe, Ho, and Rieber (1988), Leroy S. Rouner (1992), and Pandey, Sinha, and Bhawuk (1996). And, while beyond the main focus of this chapter, several brilliant works authored or edited by David L. Hall and Roger T. Ames on traditional Chinese ways of construing human selfhood and society have rich potential for application to issues in cultural gerontology. Most recently the two have made clear the relevance to contemporary problems of learning to think and act in ways exemplified by ancient Chinese models(Hall & Ames, 1998). Their work provides an eloquent counterpoint to many currently reigning social constructionist assumptions, such as are prominent in Michael Harris Bond's (1997) collaborative volume and the at times insightful discourse analysis that Bryan S. Green (1993) applies to the study of the construction of old age.

Traditional patterns of gender relations are one more dimension of aging experience that requires particularly close study in a cross-cultural gerontology attentive to the influences of religious traditions. The extensive literature in religious studies is introduced and critiqued effectively by Jordan Paper (1997), and several chapters in the handbook on aging in international perspective edited by Minichiello, Chappell, Kendig, and Walker (1996) deal with this topic. A useful starting point for West Asian cultures and Islam is Valentine M. Moghadam's (1993) study of social change and gender roles. For South Asian cultures and Hinduism, the collections edited by Alice W. Clark (1993) and the insightful Nita Kumar (1994) provide a helpful orientation, while Steve Derne's (1995) study of urban family life in north India is instructive about tensions not only between people but also between religious ideals and ordinary human actions. The studies of widowhood collected by Helena Znaniecka Lopata (1987) and of inequality in the aging experience by Stoller and Gibson (1994) underline the point, too.

Aging, when examined cross-culturally or multiculturally and in relation to traditional religious institutions and ideas, is at the center of an emerging interdisciplinary field in which one's assumptions and agendas should be made as explicit as possible. Whether or not these reflect a conventional school or ideology, it is likely they will to tend toward either a modernizing (and emancipating or liberating) or an archaizing (and nostalgic or romantic) perspective. Each of these kinds of preferences gets challenged, for the most part tacitly, by Humphrey and Onon (1996) in their intriguing account of a contemporary Mongolian shaman, a field report that raises profound questions about what may be the most fitting assumptions for a creative practitioner of cultural gerontology.

REFERENCES

Akizuki, R. (1990). *New Mahayana: Buddhism for a post-modern world.* Trans. by J. W. Heisig & P. L. Swanson. Berkeley, CA: Asian Humanities Press.

Ali, A. (1982). *Al-Qur'an: A contemporary translation.* Princeton, NJ: Princeton University Press.

Ati, H. (1982). *The family structure in Islam.* Lagos, Nigeria: Islamic Publications Bureau.

Barnes, N. S. (1987). Buddhism. In A. Sharma (Ed.), *Women in world religions* (pp. 105–133). Albany: State University of New York Press.

Basham, A. L. (1989). *The origins and development of classical Hinduism.* K. G. Zysk (Ed.). Boston: Beacon Press.

Beck, L. (1980). The religious lives of Muslim women. In J. I. Smith (Ed.), *Women in contemporary Muslim societies* (pp. 27–60). Lewisburg, PA: Bucknell University Press.

Beckett, S. (1954). *Waiting for Godot.* New York: Grove Press.

Beyer, S. (Ed. & Trans.). (1974). *The Buddhist experience: Sources and interpretations.* Encino, CA: Dickenson Publishing Company, Inc.

Bharati, A. (1985). The self in Hindu thought and action. In A. J. Marsella, G. DeVos, & F. L. K. Hsu (Eds.), *Culture and self: Asian and Western perspectives* (pp. 185–230). New York and London: Tavistock Publications.

Bogle, E. C. (1998). *Islam: Origin and belief.* Austin: University of Texas Press.

Bond, M. H. (Ed.). (1997). *Working at the interface of cultures: Eighteen lives in social science.* London: Routledge.

Buhler, G. (Trans.). (1964). *The laws of Manu.* Delhi: Motilal Banarsidass.

Chan, S. (1990). European and Asian immigration into the United States in comparative perspective, 1820s to 1920s. In V. Yans-McLaughlin (Ed.), *Immigration reconsidered: History, sociology, and politics* (pp. 37–75). New York: Oxford University Press.

Clark, A. W. (Ed.). (1993). *Gender and political economy: Explorations of South Asian systems.* Delhi: Oxford University Press.

Cole, T. R., Achenbaum, A. W., Jakobi, P. L., & Kastenbaum, R. (Eds.). (1993). *Voices and visions of aging: Toward a critical gerontology.* New York: Springer Publishing Co.

Collins, S. (1982). *Selfless persons: Imagery and thought in Theravada Buddhism.* Cambridge: Cambridge University Press.

Combs-Schilling, M. E. (1989). *Sacred performances: Islam, sexuality, and sacrifice.* New York: Columbia University Press.

Conser, Jr., W. H., & Twiss, S. B. (Eds.). (1997). *Religious diversity and American religious history: Studies in traditions and cultures.* Athens: University of Georgia Press.

Denny, F. M. (1985). *An Introduction to Islam.* New York: Macmillan Publishing Company.

Derne, S. (1995). *Culture in action: Family life, emotion, and male dominance in Banaras, India.* Albany: State University of New York Press.

Deutsch, E. (Trans.). (1968). *The Bhagavad Gita.* New York: Holt, Rinehart and Winston.

Doniger, W., & Smith, B. (Trans.). (1991). *The laws of Manu.* London: Penguin Books.

Dumont, L. (1980). *Homo hierarchicus: The caste system and its implications.* Rev. ed. Trans. M. Sainsbury, L. Dumont, & B. Gulati. Chicago: University of Chicago Press.

Dutt, S. (1957). *The Buddha and five after-centuries.* London: Luzac & Company Limited.

Eck, D. L. (1997). *On common ground: World religions in America.* CD-ROM. New York: Columbia University Press.

Ellickson, J. (1988). Never the twain shall meet: Aging men and women in Bangladesh. *Journal of Cross-Cultural Gerontology, 3,* 53–70.

Esposito, J. L. (1982). *Women in Muslim family law.* Syracuse: Syracuse University Press.

Esposito, J. L. (1988). *Islam: The straight path.* New York: Oxford University Press.

Featherstone, M., & Wernick, A. (Eds.). (1995). *Images of aging: Cultural representations of later life.* London: Routledge.

Flood, G. (1996). *An introduction to Hinduism.* Cambridge: Cambridge University Press.

Geertz, C. (1968). *Islam observed: Religious development in Morocco and Indonesia.* New Haven, CT: Yale University Press.

Geertz, C. (1973). Religion as a cultural system. In C. Geertz (Ed.), *The interpretation of cultures: Selected essays* (pp. 87–125). New York: Basic Books.

Gombrich, R., & Obeyesekere, G. (1988). *Buddhism transformed: Religious change in Sri Lanka.* Princeton, NJ: Princeton University Press.

Green, B. S. (1993). *Gerontology and the construction of old age: A study in discourse analysis.* New York: Aldine de Gruyter.

Hall, D. L., & Ames, R. T. (1998). *Thinking from the Han: Self, truth, and transcendence in Chinese and Western Culture.* Albany: State University of New York Press.

Harding, D. E. (1988). *The little book of life and death.* London and New York: Arkana.

Hiebert, P. G. (1981). Old age in a South Indian village. In P. T. Amoss & S. Harrell (Eds.), *Other ways of growing old: Anthropological perspectives* (pp. 211–226). Stanford, CA: Stanford University Press.

Holmes, E. R., & Holmes, L. D. (1995). *Other cultures, elder years.* Thousand Oaks, CA: Sage Publications.

Hume, R. E. (Trans.). (1949). *The thirteen principal Upanishads* (2nd ed.). Madras: Oxford University Press.

Humphrey, C., & Onon, U. (1996). *Shamans and elders: Experience, knowledge, and power among the Daur Mongols.* Oxford: Clarendon Press.

Huntington, C. W., Jr., & Wangchen, G. N. (1989). *The emptiness of emptiness: An introduction to early Indian Madhyamika.* Honolulu: University of Hawaii Press.

Inglehart, R. (1997). *Modernization and postmodernization: Cultural, economic, and political change in 43 societies.* Princeton, NJ: Princeton University Press.

Isaacs, H. R. (1958). *Scratches on our minds: American images of China and India.* New York: The John Day Company.

Johnson, W. (1980). *Poetry and speculation of the Rig Veda.* Berkeley: University of California Press.

Jones, K. W. (1981). Religious identity and the Indian census. In N. G. Barrier (Ed.), *The census in British India: New perspectives* (pp. 73–101). New Delhi: Manohar.

Kapleau, P. (1989). *The wheel of life and death: A practical and spiritual guide.* New York: Doubleday.

Kassis, H. E. (1983). *A concordance of the Qur'an.* Berkeley: University of California Press.

Kenyon, G. M., Birren, J. E., & Schroots, J. J. F. (Eds.). (1991). *Metaphors of aging in science and the humanities.* New York: Springer Publishing Company.

Kertzer, D. I., & Schaie, K. W. (Eds.). (1989). *Age structuring in comparative perspective.* Hillsdale, NJ: Lawrence Erlbaum Associates.

Keyes, C. F., & Valentine, D. E. (Eds.). (1983). *Karma: An anthropological inquiry.* Berkeley: University of California Press.

Kimble, M. A., McFadden, S. H., Ellor, J. W., & Seeber, J. J. (Eds.). (1995). *Aging, spirituality, and religion: A handbook.* Minneapolis: Fortress Press.

Kinsley, D. (1988). *Hindu goddesses: Visions of the divine feminine in the Hindu tradition.* Berkeley: University of California Press.

Kumar, N. (Ed.). (1994). *Women as subjects: South Asian histories.* Charlottesville: University Press of Virginia.

Lapidus, I. (1988). *A history of Islamic societies.* Cambridge: Cambridge University Press.

Little, D., & Twiss, S. B. (1978). *Comparative religious ethics.* San Francisco: Harper & Row, Publishers.

Lopata, H. Z. (Ed.). (1987). *Widows Vol. 1: The Middle East, Asia and the Pacific.* Durham, NC: Duke University Press.

Loy, D. (1988). *Nonduality: A study in comparative philosophy.* New Haven, CT: Yale University Press.

Madan, T. N. (1989). Religion in India. *Daedalus, 118*(4), 115–146.

McGilvray, D. B. (Ed.). (1982). *Caste ideology and interaction.* (Cambridge Studies in Social Anthropology, No. 9.). Cambridge: Cambridge University Press.

Metcalf, B. D. (1984). Islamic reform and Islamic women: Maulana Thanawi's *Jewelry of Paradise.* In B. D. Metcalf (Ed.), *Moral conduct and authority: The place of Adab in South Asian Islam* (pp. 184–195). Berkeley: University of California Press.

Metcalf, B. D. (Ed.). (1996). *Making Muslim space in North America and Europe.* Berkeley: University of California Press.

Minault, G. (1986). Making invisible women visible: Studying the history of Muslim women in South Asia. *South Asia, 9,* 1–13.

Minichiello, V., Chappell, N., Kendig, H., & Walker, A. (Eds.). (1996). *Sociology of aging: International perspectives.* Melbourne: International Sociological Association, Research Committee on Aging.

Mir, M. (1987). *Dictionary of Qur'anic terms and concepts.* New York: Garland Publishing, Inc.

Moghadam, V. M. (1993). *Modernizing women: Gender and social change in the Middle East.* Boulder, CO: Lynne Rienner Publishers.

Nasr, S. H. (1975). *Ideals and realities of Islam.* Boston: Beacon Press.

Neufeldt, R. W. (Ed.). (1986). *Karma and rebirth: Post classical developments.* Albany: State University of New York Press.

Neusner, J. (Ed.). (1994). *World religions in America: An introduction.* Louisville, KY: Westminster John Knox.

O'Flaherty, W. D. (Ed.). (1980). *Karma and rebirth in classical Indian traditions.* Berkeley: University of California Press.

O'Flaherty, W. D. (Ed. & Trans.). (1981). *The Rig Veda: An anthology.* Harmondsworth, England: Penguin Books.

O'Flaherty, W. D. (Ed. & Trans.). (1988). *Textual sources for the study of Hinduism.* Totowa, NJ: Barnes & Noble Books.

Olds, L. E. (1992). *Metaphors of interrelatedness: Toward a systems theory of psychology.* Albany: State University of New York Press.

Olivelle, P. (Trans.). (1996). *The Upanishads.* New York: Oxford University Press.

O'Shaughnessy, T. (1969). *Muhammad's thoughts on death: A thematic study of the Qur'anic data.* Leiden, Netherlands: E. J. Brill.

Ostor, A. (1984). Chronology, category, and ritual. In D. I. Kertzer & J. Keith (Eds.), *Age and anthropological theory* (pp. 281–304). Ithaca, NY: Cornell University Press.

Palmore, E. B. (Ed.). (1993). *Developments and research on aging: An international handbook.* Westport, CT: Greenwood Press.

Pandey, J., Sinha, D., & Bhawuk, D. P. S. (Eds.). (1996). *Asian contributions to cross-cultural psychology.* New Delhi: Sage Publications.

Panikkar, R. (Ed. & Trans.). (1977). *The Vedic experience.* Berkeley: University of California Press.

Paper, J. (1997). *Through the earth darkly: Female spirituality in comparative perspective.* New York: Continuum.

Paranjpe, A. C., Ho, D. Y. F., & Rieber, R. W. (Eds.). (1988). *Asian contributions to psychology.* New York: Praeger.

Pathak, Z., & Rajan, R. S. (1989). Shabano. *Signs, 14,* 558–582.

Peters, F. E. (1982). *Children of Abraham: Judaism/Christianity/Islam.* Princeton, NJ: Princeton University Press.

Peters, I. (1986). The attitude toward the elderly as reflected in Egyptian and Lebanese proverbs. *The Muslim World, 76,* 80–85.

Prothero, S. R. (1996). *The white Buddhist: The Asian odyssey of Henry Steel Olcott.* Bloomington: Indiana University Press.

Pye, M. (1979). *The Buddha.* London: Duckworth.

Rangadrol, T. N. (1989). *The mirror of mindfulness: The cycle of the four Bardos.* Trans. E. P. Kunsang. Boston: Shambhala.

Robinson, R. H., & Johnson, W. L. (1997). *The Buddhist religion: A historical introduction* (4th ed.). Belmont, CA: Wadsworth Publishing Company.

Robinson, S. P. (1985). Hindu paradigms of women: Images and values. In Y. Y. Haddad & E. B. Findly (Eds.), *Women, religion, and social change* (pp. 181–215). Albany: State University of New York Press.

Roland, A. (1988). *In search of self in India and Japan: Toward a cross-cultural psychology*. Princeton, NJ: Princeton University Press.

Rouner, L. S. (Ed.). (1992). *Selves, people, and persons: What does it mean to be a self?* Notre Dame, IN: University of Notre Dame Press.

Roy, M. (1975). *Bengali women*. Chicago: The University of Chicago Press.

Rudolph, S. H., & Piscatori, J. (Eds.). (1997). *Transnational religion and fading states*. Boulder, CO: Westview Press.

Rushdie, S. (1991). *Imaginary homelands: Essays and criticism, 1981–1991*. London: Granta Books.

Said, E. W. (1978). *Orientalism*. New York: Pantheon Books.

Said, E. W. (1997). *Covering Islam: How the media and the experts determine how we see the rest of the world* (rev. ed.). New York: Vintage Books.

Sartre, J. P. (1958). *No exit: A play in one act*. Adapted from the French by Paul Bowles. New York: French.

Schumann, H. W. (1989). *The historical Buddha: The times, life and teachings of the founder of Buddhism*. Trans. M. O'C. Walshe. London: Arkana.

Schwab, R. (1984). *The oriental renaissance: Europe's rediscovery of India and the East, 1680–1880*. Trans. G. Patterson-Black & V. Reinking. New York: Columbia University Press.

Sinclair, K. (1986). Women and religion. In M. I. Duley & M. I. Edwards (Eds.), *The cross-cultural study of women: A comprehensive guide* (pp. 107–124). New York: The Feminist Press.

Singer, M. (1972). *When a great tradition modernizes: An anthropological approach to Indian civilization*. New York: Praeger Publishers.

Smith, B. K. (1989). *Reflections on resemblance, ritual, and religion*. New York: Oxford University Press.

Smith, D. E. (1963). *India as a secular state*. Princeton, NJ: Princeton University Press.

Smith, J. I., & Haddad, Y. Y. (1981). *The Islamic understanding of death and resurrection*. Albany: State University of New York Press.

Sogyal, R. (1993). *The Tibetan book of living and dying*. P. Gaffney & A. Harvey (Eds.). San Francisco: Harper San Francisco.

Spiro, M. E. (1970). *Buddhism and society: A great tradition and its Burmese vicissitudes*. New York: Harper & Row, Publishers.

Stoller, E. P., & Gibson, R. C. (Eds.). (1994). *Worlds of difference: Inequality in the aging experience*. Thousand Oaks, CA: Pine Forge Press.

Suhranardy, A. (1941). *The sayings of Muhammad*. London: John Murray.

Tambiah, S. J. (1970). *Buddhism and the spirit cults in North-East Thailand*. Cambridge: Cambridge University Press.

Thapar, R. (1989). Imagined religious communities? Ancient history and the modern search for a Hindu identity. *Modern Asian Studies, 23,* 209–231.

Thomas, L. E., & Eisenhandler, S. A. (Eds.). (1994). *Aging and the religious dimension*. Westport, CT: Auburn House.

Thomas, W. (1930). *Hinduism invades America.* New York: The Beacon Press.

Thursby, G. R. (1995). Hindu movements since midcentury: Yogis in the states. In T. Miller (Ed.), *America's alternative religions* (pp. 191–213). Albany: State University of New York Press.

Thursz, D., Nusberg, C., & Prather, J. (Eds.). (1995). *Empowering older people: An international approach.* Westport, CT: Auburn House.

Tilak, S. (1989). *Religion and aging in the Indian tradition.* Albany: State University of New York Press.

Tweed, T. A. (1992). *The American encounter with Buddhism, 1844–1912: Victorian culture and the limits of dissent.* Bloomington: Indiana University Press.

Tweed, T. A. (Ed.). (1997). *Retelling U.S. religious history.* Berkeley: University of California Press.

Updike, J. (1968). *The poorhouse fair.* Harmondsworth, England: Penguin Books.

Vatuk, S. (1990). To be a burden on others: Dependency anxiety among the elderly in India. In O. Lynch (Ed.), *Divine passions: The social construction of emotion in India* (pp. 64–88). Berkeley: University of California Press.

Vreede-De Stuers, C. (1968). *Parda: A study of Muslim women's life in Northern India.* Assen: Van Gorcum & Co.

Watt, W. M. (1968). *What is Islam?* London: Longmans, Green and Co. Ltd.

Weekes, R. V. (Ed.). (1984). *Muslim peoples: A world ethnographic survey* (2nd ed.). Westport, CT: Greenwood Press.

Weeramantry, C. G. (1988). *Islamic jurisprudence: An international perspective.* London: Macmillan Press.

Weightman, S. (1998). Hinduism. In J. R. Hinnells (Ed.), *A new handbook of living religions* (pp. 261–309). London: Penguin Books.

Williams, J. A. (Ed.). (1963). *Islam.* New York: Washington Square Press.

Williams, R. B. (1988). *Religions of immigrants from India and Pakistan: New threads in the American tapestry.* Cambridge: Cambridge University Press.

Willis, J. D. (1985). Nuns and benefactresses: The role of women in the development of Buddhism. In Y. Y. Haddad & E. B. Findly (Eds.), *Women, religion, and social change* (pp. 59–85). Albany: State University of New York Press.

Zaehner, R. C. (1966). *Hinduism.* New York: Oxford University Press.

Zinkin, T. (1962). *Caste today.* London: Oxford University Press.

PART II
Interdisciplinary Approaches

10

Aging in the East: Comparative and Historical Reflections

Leng Leng Thang

In commenting on eastern and western attitudes toward age in the 1930s, the essayist, Lin Yutang (1983), argues for an exactly opposite point of view between the two. People in the West, he observes, fear growing old, while in the East, people look forward to becoming old:

> It is to be assumed that if man were to live this life like a poem, he would be able to look upon the sunset of his life as the happiest period, and instead of trying to postpone the much feared old age, be able to look forward to it, and gradually build up to it as the best and happiest period of his existence (p. 95).

His comment on the "sunset of life" depicts the common conception of the East as a culture where a person ages with respect, dignity, authority and love. Such perceptions of the eastern cultures as a "paradise for the old" and the debates arising from the related themes surrounding the roles and statutes of the elderly have dominated cross-cultural research on aging. This chapter will begin with a discussion of the emergence and recent development of research in this area. This is followed by a focus on the concept of filial piety, widely regarded as the key of aging well in East Asian cultures. The chapter will conclude with a glimpse into future directions on aging research in this area. Although the materials referred to here are far from exhaustive, I hope this chapter will benefit readers intending to have a grasp of the knowledge and development on aging in the East.

To begin with, a definition of the East is necessary. The scope of the East could be conceptually broad, encompassing whatever belongs to the non-West. Within this broader frame, I have confined the scope to the Asian societies in the Pacific Rim, mainly Japan, Korea, China, Taiwan, and to some extent Singapore[1] and Hong Kong (now part of PRC). These societies are traditionally connected by the common cultural heritage of Confucianism. They are also characterized by unprecedented transformation. In the span of a generation, this part of the world has made headline news in its economics and more recently, in leading the pace of aging in the world. The elderly in East Asian societies are people caught in the middle of the changing map of what a "good life" should be (Amoss, 1981, p. 21). These transitions have contributed to make the East an increasingly interesting and exciting site to understand changing experiences and expectations of aging.

DEVELOPMENT

Earlier discussions on aging and the elderly in East Asian societies were commonly embedded in the study of family and community life (Embree, 1939; Wolf, 1968). This is inevitable, given the pivotal position of the elderly in the traditional family system.

Research on aging in the East, however, is generally developed from the 1960s, a period where cross-cultural concerns began to emerge in the field of aging. Smith's article on old age and the concept of time in Japan (1961) could be considered a pioneer in this sense. His presentation of the elderly in Japan as a population accorded great respect and indulgence is largely taken to affirm earlier writings, such as those by Benedict (1946) who contributed significantly to the image of Japan as a gerontocratic society. At the same time, Smith's article suggests a new scope of research in what we could refer to now as "humanistic gerontology," as he urges the study of aging from both the perspective of history and time, and aging as a subjective experience. "We need to know how compelling the requirements of fixed life cycle stages really are. Adherence to these in terms of style of dress and ornamentation is easy enough to determine, but in the realm of attitudes and ideas we have virtually no information. What does the older person think about himself and his lot? In what frame of mind does the older person approach death?" (p. 110). His questions continue to be of relevance to research on aging today.

Increasing concerns on aging in the East came about with expanded interest on aging in nonwestern societies by anthropologists.[2] Beginning with Amoss and Harrell's (1981) volume, *Other Ways of Growing Old: Anthropological Perspectives,* which included in its collection an article on growing old in rural Taiwan by Harrell, the numerous publications on cross-cultural aspects of aging that followed have at least one article concerning aging in the eastern cultures (e.g., Fry, 1981; Keith et al., 1994; Rubinstein, 1990; Skolovsky, 1990, 1997). Since the 1980s, monographs devoted to aging in specific Asian societies have also increased in number. The rich ethnographic data presented in these writings have contributed to more diversified and realistic views of aging.

Modernization and the Status of the Elderly

Questions focusing on the treatment and status of the elderly have dominated research in Asian cultures. The most common framework used to explain the relations between modernization and aging is represented by Cowgill and Holmes (1972), first proposed in *Modernization and Aging.* They propose an inverse relationship between modernization and the status of the elderly. With a tradition emphasizing the veneration of the old, there seems to be little doubt that East Asian societies are an exception to Cowgill and Holmes's thesis. It is not uncommon for researchers doing fieldwork in East Asian societies to encounter adamant feelings expressed by informants who pride themselves on their respectful treatment of the elderly, while pinpointing the West as a different culture which abandons the old in old folk's homes and forgets its ancestors (Thompson, 1990).

Such a view, however, is questioned by Plath (1972) when he writes about the case of Japan in *Aging and Modernization.* Plath has painted a somewhat gloomy picture of the Japanese elderly, concluding that the modern society "has equipped them only with medieval maps, full of freaks and monsters and imaginary harbors" (p. 150). This is a surprising contrast to the popular image of Japan as the "paradise for the elderly" and quickly led to rebuttals by Palmore (1975, 1985). He draws support from government surveys and controversial works such as Benedict's *The Chrysanthemum and the Sword* to maintain that the elderly in Japan still enjoy high status and integration despite modernization, even urging that America and the West learn from the Japanese practices.

Palmore's position draws controversial responses. Writings that support him claim that modernization has indeed generated resources to improve the position of the elderly in Japan. In his discussion of welfare in Japan, Nakagawa (1979) proposes that Japan has become a "super welfare power" since 1968 with economic development, citing the 30% rise of Japanese pensions over those in the U.S., with upward revaluation of the yen as evidence. He further claims the tremendous improvement in life expectancy as an indicator for the comprehensive level of welfare in Japan. On the other hand, Palmore's stand has been criticized. Tobin (1987), for example, counters Palmore's rosy picture, pointing to it as an American idealization of old age in Japan. Koyano (1989) suggests that Palmore's examples, such as the "silver seats" which exist on every train, the Respect of Elders Day held every September 15, and the Law for the Welfare of the Elderly (enacted in 1963), represent only the ideal perceptions of old age in Japan. The reality is characterized by "ageist" images of elders as silly, senile, weak, and stubborn. Kiefer (1990) challenges both the modernization theory and Palmore's conception of old age in Japan by comparing aging in Japan and America with the three indices of prestige, power, and security— regarded as "the tripod which supports benign old age"(p. 185). He concludes that Japanese elderly enjoy higher prestige but relative deprivation in power and security when compared with their American counterparts, and proposes a pluralist model of modernization which recognizes the elderly as one of many subcultures.

Modernization, too, cannot adequately explain the changes in the status of the elderly in the case of China. Detailed studies on how political changes affected the Chinese elderly during and after the Mao regime in communist China show factors, such as government policies and one's class background, as prominent in affecting the status and experience of the elderly (see, for example, writings by Davis-Friedmann, 1983; Cherry & Magnuson-Martinson, 1981). Parallel to Kiefer's view above, Yin and Lai (1983) differentiate between status and respect for the elderly, claiming that although the communist government deliberately diminished the status of the aged by rejecting filial piety as feudalistic, respect of the elderly was still emphasized unless it conflicted with the demands of the state.

The positive perception of the elderly in the East as claimed by Palmore is associated with the golden age model, a widespread American belief that "in more labor-intensive cultures old people play more significant roles, that older people are always better valued in stable, preliterate or primitive societies, and that only in westernized or modernized cultures are they poorly treated. (Eisdorfer, 1981, p. xv). Such perception has since been under review. Kiefer criticizes the golden age ideal as "really brass and was quickly turning green in the corrosive atmosphere of the Enlightenment" (p. 182), questioning the homogeneous treatment of elderly through historical evidence, showing both positive and negative attitudes toward the elderly. Rather, a theme on the ambiguities of aging seems to be a more realistic view. Minois (1987, p. 18) finds ambiguity "throughout the whole of history" and sees it as "a phenomenological universal of old age, a time both of maximal experience and of maximal debility, simultaneously vaunted and evaded (Cohen, 1994, p. 143).

Ambiguities of Aging

Such a trajectory in the study of aging in the West is also experienced by the East as the image of the "golden age" in both the preindustrial and modern East gives way to a more ambivalent image of old age. Literary and philosophical evidence from research on social and cultural history of old age in East Asian cultures have contributed largely to the conflicting views of old age. One commonly cited example is the folklore on abandonment of the elderly in the Japanese legend *obasuteyama,* which literally means "granny-abandoning-mountain" (Plath, 1972). It also has an equivalent in the Korean legend called *koryŏjang* (Soh, 1997). Although there are debates on whether such a practice actually existed, the idea that elderly parents may be deserted to die in the mountains or buried alive to lessen the burden of the young reveals that at least such negative thoughts were present in the past.

The research on social history of the elderly in Japan shows ample evidence of the negative "traditional views" of old age (Formanek, 1997; Skord, 1989). However, when examined against gender, the ambiguities in the images of elderly women seem more prominent. Formanek's (1997) study of the views of crones in pre-Meiji Japan concludes that a certain demonic quality is associated with old women, and the demonization is greater for elderly women who did not succeed in securing a son to provide for her old age. This is supported by Yamaori (1997a) who examines the ambivalent image of *rōjo* (elderly women) in Japanese legend through an analysis of three different types of *rōjo* in Noh plays of medieval Japan. Two of these plays, *Yamamba* and *Yamasute,* portray the isolated elderly women as demons and objects of fear and dread while the last one, *Takasago,* has a positive depiction of an elderly woman who is partnered with an elderly man. The double pine in *Takasago* highlights the union of the elderly couple and represents the nobility of their old age. The plays present a dichotomized image of *rōjo:* on the one hand, she is both an object of fear and dread when isolated and abandoned; on the other hand, she is one who has approached maturity with dignity and elevation, enjoying the love and affection from the accompanying elderly man. The negative image of an isolated elderly women suggests the problematic status of being old, widowed and childless in a traditional culture that provides little for such deviation.

Compared to elderly women, elderly men are found to draw more positive perceptions in Japanese legends and history. Yamaori (1997b) observes that religious sculptures in ancient Japan are mostly in the image of the *okina,* or elderly man for the male God, but of youthful women in the prime of maturity for female statues. Moreover, in contrast with the elderly woman's image of a demon, the *okina* dance in the Noh play presents the mask of a man with a gentle, kindly, and smiling face (Yamaori, 1997b, p. 87). From this evidence, the author interprets *okina* and its positive portrayal as a manifestation of the fundamentally positive attitudes toward men's aging as a maturation process.

Yamaori's thesis assuming the final stage of human life as the climax of maturation is similar to Rohlen's (1978) approach on adulthood in Japan. But instead of proposing that any adult will attain maturation and fulfillment in old age, Rohlen suggests that elderly who have practiced their traditional art pursuits (such as tea ceremony, flower arrangement, and calligraphy) long enough, will naturally be venerated as "living testimonies of their art" (Formanek & Linhart, 1997, p. 19).

The conditions for dignity in old age are further restricted in Scheid's (1997) analysis of the figure of the elderly in Zeami's Noh theater and the aging actor. If we follow Rohlen's proposal, all old actors who have spent long years in Noh performance will be well respected. But Zeami's concept of the actor's process of aging shows that in reality, an actor begins to lose attractiveness at about age 40, and it is only in very exceptional cases that an old actor achieves the picture of "an old tree in bloom" (pp. 104–105).

Many of the studies on ambiguities of aging are derived from humanistic points of view in the research on aging, including philosophy, literature and history. Compared with the development of historical studies of old age in the West, which has witnessed a promising rise since the 1980s,[3] information on the history of old age in the East remains relatively scant. In the introduction of a recent volume including historical perspectives on aging in Asia, Formanek and Linhart, after a discussion of Confucianism and other Asian traditions, lament the lack of knowledge in the field of social history of aging: "In many instances, however, we have to admit that we do not know how these philosophical systems or overall spiritual values in fact influenced the view of aging and the elderly at different stages of history, nor what were the actual living conditions of the aged in the past" (Formanek & Linhart, 1997, p. 13). The humanistic field of aging reveals much potential for future development. Much of the focus on aging in the East since the 1970s, however, has been on contemporary situations of aging from the perspective of old age as social, economic and demographic "problems."

Aging as a Social Problem

Following the western industrial societies, aging has become increasingly defined as a social problem in East Asian societies as they experience an increase in life expectancy and changing demography. This is made more problematic with the decline in multigenerational house-holds. Sensing the urgency for measures to cope with a rapidly aging population, the resolution of the United Nations General Assembly requires each of its member nations to set up a committee to deal with issues related to aging (Hsia, 1993). These committees have a similar goal of identifying and solving the "problems" of aging scientifically— which departs from the idea that Asians had not so long ago thought of aging as a problem which only bothers the West; even "if and when aging became an issue in their countries, the family would take care of its respected elderly members, not abandon them as the West is per-ceived to have done" (Martin, 1988, p. 99).

Today, the issue of social support is one of the recurring themes in social gerontological studies of aging in East Asia. In these studies, the family is frequently mentioned as the most significant source of social support, and it is usually measured in terms of a intergenerational coresidence rate. It is common for these studies to equate the concept of social support with caregiving, given the background of the focus on coresidence in studying social relationships of the elderly in East Asian societies. Recently, Koyano et al. (1994) have criticized this approach by arguing that since caregiving is usually required only in the final stage of a life-long history of social relationships, it is thus not an essential part but merely a small portion of social support provided by others.

Despite their argument to look beyond caregiving and the family in discussing social support, most studies on similar issues still focus on coresidence and reveal fear that with the eroding effect of moderniza-tion, the family will no longer be adequate (or even functional) as a safety net for the elderly. The support persons that are diminishing in numbers are the caregivers, predominantly women who were once taken as a given in a family system where the daughter-in-law was expected to marry into the same household. This change has led to various works focusing on the caregivers and their dilemmas in an aging society.

In Japan, awareness of the caregiving dilemma in the age of increas-ing life expectancy begins with literary works such as Niwa's *The Hateful Age* (1962) and particularly Ariyoshi's *The Twilight Years* (1972). Descriptive research on the issue has also increased in sociological and anthropological studies, especially in the 1990s (for example, Anbacken, 1997; Elliot & Campbell, 1993; Jenike, 1997). These studies generally show the Japanese middle-age women as "sandwiched in the middle" in many situations. On the one hand, although they would prefer to engage professional care for their elderly, they fear receiving social disapproval for failing to provide care at home. On the other hand, while they are obliged to fulfil their caregiving duties as daughters-in-laws (or sometimes daughters), with a changing social welfare system and attitudes, they can neither expect nor want to receive care from the next generation. Moreover, with a smaller family size and the growing acceptance of daughters (instead of daughters-in-law) as caregivers, these middle-aged Japanese women will increasingly be forced to decide whether they should care for their own parents or their parents-in-law.

Korea is similarly disturbed by a gradual erosion of traditional home-based care. In writing on the family and the aged in Korea, Choi (1996) claims that "aging has never been experienced as a social problem before. It is a new challenge to the family and the state, in that it requires the state to take responsibility for supporting elderly people and strengthening the family's care function by allowing it to utilize services provided by non-familial persons" (p. 2).

In China, where family care is also expected, policy changes seem to have more influence on the availability of women as caregivers at home. Ikels's (1997) study of long-term care and the disabled elderly shows that in urban China, although the availability of family caregivers was once guaranteed through a workplace policy which required women to retire at either 50 (for factory workers) or 55 (for technicians, professionals, or cadres) with full benefits, recent developments, such as postretirement opportunities, a one-child family policy, and a rise in the retirement age for women, are threatening the availability of women caregivers at home.

In Taiwan, the fast pace of division of farm families and rural-urban migration have changed the traditional patterns of coresidence. In cases where circumstances do not allow the elderly to stay permanently with one child, or to stay alone, they may be rotated from the home of one child to another on a regular basis, spreading the burden of care among the children. However, Wolf (1972) notes how difficult such a "meal-rotation" system can be for the elderly, especially when the relationship between the mother-in-law and daughter-in-law is a difficult one.

Although the family context still dominates in the research on aging in the East, increasingly in the late 1980s and 1990s we see a rising interest in research that looks beyond the family in providing care for the elderly. These works address the reality of the demand for extra-familial care as a result of the rapid social and demographic transitions in contemporary East Asian society. I shall introduce now three such ethnographic studies of elderly institutions in Japan, each a pioneer in its respective institutional form. The first, an ethnographic study of a private retirement community for middle-class Japanese retirees by Kinoshita and Kiefer (1992), marks the first detailed study ever done on a planned retirement community in a non-western culture. *Refuge of the Honored* concludes that social integration has been relatively poor in the retirement community because the Japanese framework of interpersonal relationship lacks a preexisting structure for regulating interaction between individuals without ascribed roles in an age-homogeneous setting.

While Kinoshita and Kiefer's western-style and peer-group oriented residential setting was novel and experimental in the 1980s, the home for the elderly in Bethel's (1992) work, *From abandonment to community: Life in a Japanese institution for the elderly,* is regarded as the earliest form of a welfare institution for destitute elderly, present since the 1890s in Meiji Japan. Compared to the residents in Kinoshita and Kiefer's work, the elderly in Bethel's study seem successfully integrated, adapting to institutionalization by constructing their own social universe from familiar cultural concepts. Here, the hierarchical relations characterizing the family are highlighted as a symbol in "unifying and bridging the social distance between individuals unrelated by blood" (p. 291). Bethel's emphasis on the family as the "most powerful image and tool for constructing the social organization of the institution" (p. 290) also resonates in Thang's (1997b) research on the meaning of intergenerational interaction between the old and young in an age-integrated welfare center combining a nursing home, a care home for the elderly, and a child care center in a Tokyo neighborhood. The ethnographic case study reveals the significance of the image of *daikazoku*—a multigenerational big family—in providing meaning to the elderly residents as they play the role of grandparents to the children living under the same roof.

These studies show that the idealized image of a multigenerational family pattern remains a salient topic to institutions and the elderly themselves, reflecting the Japanese concept of defining one's personhood and sense of well-being in relation to the biological family (Plath, 1964). With the expectation of intergenerational reciprocity espoused through the ideology of filial piety from the Confucian ethic, the elderly often find it difficult to address old age outside the familial context. Entering an institution, even if it is one which provides professional care, includes the social stigma of being cast out of the family. Bethel illustrates this with a statement from one 79-year-old resident who professed, "To live happily with a good daughter-in-law, good son, and good grandchildren, and to hear them call you 'grandma, grandma' is a human being's greatest happiness. It is our greatest hope. There is nothing more fulfilling as a human being, than living with one's family [in old age]" (p. 100).

Gender and Family Centrality

From the 1980s on, along with an increase in gerontological research, writings which emphasize subjective experience and meaning related to aging have emerged. We are now fully aware that the era of *mass longevity* has arrived, but how do individuals view and experience longevity and aging amid these changes? Taking the life-cycle approach, Plath—who coined the term *mass longevity*—provides an in-depth understanding of how Japanese experience maturity and aging through four engaging case studies of middle-aged Japanese (Plath, 1980).

The 1980s, too, saw a development in research on the experience of aging among women. Lebra (1984), also using the life-cycle approach in her study of a sample of Japanese women ranging from age 28 to 80, brings the issue of gender and aging into focus. She argues that the later years are the most paradoxical period for a woman because "on the one hand, this is a stage when a woman, freed from the burden of childrearing, can enjoy autonomy, obtain power and leadership in and out of the household, begin to have her past hardship and energy investment repaid, taste a sense of accomplishment and *ikigai* (purpose and meaning in life), and develop a retrospective insight and wisdom on life. On the other hand, she must confront her role atrophy and eventually the inevitable tragedy of aging, possible invalidism, and death." She also shows how older women come to "transcend their gender or assume male prerogatives" (p. 253) when discussing sex polarity.

While Lebra juxtaposes social structure and culture with life histories, Lock (1993), in *Encounters with Aging,* examines the interplay of culture and the aging body as she discusses the process of growing old among Japanese women through a focus on menopause. Although menopause has largely become a medical category in the West, Lock discovers that it remains a social category in Japan. She predicts that if Japanese women were to start taking hormone therapy on a long-term basis like women in the West, "they will usually think of it not as a bid to exchange aging bodies for younger ones but rather as a tool to help maintain indirectly the old order, in which women preserve their health for the sake of others, so that society may depend on women's nurturance as the pillar of the family" (p. 380).

The family remains a central theme in the study of aging and life course among Japanese women. In Lebra's comparison of American women with their Japanese counterparts, she discovers that while American women tend to recollect by positioning themselves at the center in all phases of their life, Japanese women always frame themselves within a group or interpersonal relationships—particularly relating to the family in their life histories.

Greater emotional "investment" in the family by women seems to affect their experiences in old age. Harrell's study (1981) of a rural community in Taiwan shows that although women are known to have a lower status in a traditional Chinese family, they actually enjoy more respect and affection from their children than the men in old age. The

fundamental difference is that although older men are provided security and respect by the younger generation based on the concept of filial piety, they may be supported more out of fear and duty than love.

Meaning of Old Age

The East Asian societies have experienced a phenomenal rise in life
expectancies since the end of World War II. Japan, in particular, has the
highest life expectancy in the world today, where a man could expect
to live up to 78 and a woman to 83 in 1995, compared to 50 and 53,
respectively, in 1947. The higher life expectancy is one reason contributing to the compelling concern for the meaning of growing old.
The Japanese concept of meaning or purpose in life is *ikigai*. *Ikigai* has
become a popular discourse in Japan since the 1970s, when the search
for meaning emerged as the standard of living rose with rapid economic expansion. Rising life expectancy further contributes to its becoming an integral part of the welfare policy for the elderly. However, few
English materials on aging in Japan have directly addressed this issue,
although the works I have discussed above do provide insights on *ikigai* for the elderly. One recent study examines the sources of *ikigai* and
longevity among the elderly in Okinawa, the prefecture in Japan which
boasts the highest life expectancy and highest proportion of centenar-
ians in the population (Thang, 1997a). The study concludes that
besides work, organized activities and interpersonal relationships,
one's perception of the past and future, as well as the desire to challenge long-lived kin, also provide *ikigai* to the elderly. A more comprehensive study on *ikigai* is provided by Mathews in his work, *What
Makes Life Worth Living?*, where he provides a comparison of *ikigai*
between Japanese and Americans. Although not restricted to old age,
Mathews offers a significant glimpse of aging and meaning in later life.

In Mathews' study, the Japanese mothers are found to be practic-
ing ancestor worship. Although his 68-year-old female informant has
expressed skepticism about it, Mathews concludes that since she still
practices ancestor worship and thinks of the familial ancestors, "the
disjuncture between this world and the next isn't absolute" (Mathews,
1996, p. 143). The desire to protect their family seems the main reason
for their faith and practice. Older women are a familiar sight in the
Buddhist and Taoist temples in the East, praying for the safety and
prosperity of their spouse and children. Their motives again show family as a source of significance in later life.

Mathews also questions to what extent religion is one's *ikigai*. In a
time of rapid social change, religion seems increasingly important as
the "imaginary harbor" which shelters us from apprehension. Young
and Ikeuchi (1997) refer to pokkuri temples as such a harbor for many

Japanese elderly.[4] Their study, the first in western research literature to provide historical and contemporary details of the institutions, sees the development of the *pokkuri* phenomenon from a "preoccupation with geriatric illnesses such as enuresis toward a more pronounced concern about senile dementia" (p. 252).

One of the developments in extreme aging is the rising experience of senile dementia among the elderly. In Japan, senile dementia—commonly referred to as *boke*—has become an emerging concern in gerontological research as the number of elderly suffering from senile dementia is expected to increase more than threefold between 1990 to 2025. Besides receiving medical attention, senile dementia as an issue has also received historical, religious, and anthropological attention. Early and medieval Japanese literature portrays a mystical view of senile elderly as liminal figures belonging fully neither to this world nor the next. Perceived as closer to the ancestors and gods, they are thus tolerated with fear and admiration (Young & Ikeuchi, 1997). Contemporary views of senile dementia, however, are related more closely to the issue of care. The fear of becoming a burden to those around them and the apprehension of inadequate care for the demented have sometimes made dementia prevention itself an *ikigai* to the elderly. Trapagen's (1997) anthropological research on group activities and old age in a town in northeastern Japan discovers the elderly's participation in social activities such as hobbies and sports as a health management strategy to prevent or delay the onset of dementia. He also concludes that Japanese society attaches social and moral values to senility and sees it as a reflection of one's irresponsibility of oneself. This makes senility a condition viewed as a fate worse than death.

This review so far has focused overwhelmingly on studies related to aging in Japan. Japan has developed research somewhat more rapidly in this area partly because its developed status has attracted much comparative research with the West. Since the 1980s, we also observe a gradual increase in cross-societal research in aging on Asia, reflecting a growing emphasis on cross-cultural variations among the Asian societies (Martin, 1988; Phillips, 1992).

In viewing research in East Asian cultures as a whole, a developmental sequence seems to have emerged in the studies of aging, with Japan developing most rapidly, followed by Mainland China,[5] including Hong Kong, Taiwan, then Korea and Singapore. Population aging experienced in this region will nevertheless enhance research efforts begun in the 1970s. Although there is still a paucity of attention given to various aspects of aging research (such as historical studies of old age), we can look forward to a gradual bridging of the gap between aging research in the East and the West, partly facilitated by the increasing presence of western-trained native scholars.[6]

The following section will focus the discussion more specifically on the theme of filial piety, which, along with subthemes such as Confucianism, ancestor worship, and the family, has long been a recurring subject of inquiry pivotal in understanding the cross-cultural context of aging and old age in the East.

FILIAL PIETY—IDEALS AND REALITIES

Confucianism

Confucianism, a dominant doctrine in East Asia, is a keyword commonly used to explain social, cultural, economic, political and philosophical differences between East Asia and the West. Confucianism is undeniably a dominant ideology regulating the civil order and moral conduct in East Asia. Confucian tradition has its root in traditional China more than 2,000 years ago, and has represented the mainstream of Chinese thought, cultural and intellectual development in Chinese society. Throughout the centuries, however, Confucianism has had to compete with other emerging schools of thoughts and religions, such as Taoism and Legalism (during the Han dynasty), as well as Buddhism (in the Sui Tang period 581–907 A.D.).

Confucianism was introduced to Korea in the 4th century A.D. through higher learning, where a "university" was set up to teach Confucian classes in Koguryo, one of the three kingdoms in Korea at that time. Korea was instrumental in introducing Confucianism to Japan in the 5th century, where it became popular by the 7th century. Although Korea and Japan are profoundly influenced by the Sinic civilizations, Confucianism in these societies has over the centuries developed with different emphases distinguishing one from the other. Japan shows the most divergence from the Confucius origin. The divergence appeared as early as the 7th century, for instance, in the use of *ren* (benevolence) as a central focus. Confucianism in Japan relied on *ren* from the beginning when it was used by Prince Shotoku in 604 as a guidance for officials at all levels to consciously emphasize *chu* (loyalty). It is thus important to bear in mind that distinguishing characteristics exist even though East Asian cultures and practices may seem generally similar when compared with the West.

The three cultures, however, do share a similar basis. One basis of Confucianism commonly shared is the emphasis of harmony and social relations. Confucianism regulates social behavior through the emphasis of appropriate behavior or "propeity" (*li*) in five cardinal relationships: relations between ruler and subjects, husband and wife, parent and child, elderly and young siblings, and between friends. Except for the last one, the other four relations preach benevolence on the part of a senior and willing obedience on the part of a junior. Of the five relations, the parent-child relation is most emphasized as the root of all virtue and the model for all human propriety. The assumption is that those who honor their parents will also respect and accept authorities; thus filial piety is useful as the foundation of peace and harmony in the state and empire.

Laws regulating filial piety have been imposed since historical times, thus morally and legally obliging the children to support their elderly in the family. For example, in Japan, the Civil Code was revised in 1899 to require families to care for their aged members. More recently, the 1980 Article of Marriage Law in the People's Republic of China states that the children have the duty to support and assist their parents. China's criminal law also punishes those who fail to support their parents (Tsai, 1997). In Singapore, the Maintenance of Parents Act was passed in 1995, and a tribunal court was set up under the Act for neglected parents to claim maintenance from their children. In the East Asian societies, filial piety has always been a part of a moral education curriculum showing the Confucian emphasis, although curricular content is sometimes appropriated to serve the shifting needs of the state (see, for example, Yamashita, 1996).

Filial Piety—The Traditional Ideal

The practice of filial piety requires that children devote themselves without reservation to the welfare of their parents. The son's wife is expected to share in this complete devotion to her husband's parents (Tsai, 1997, p. 274). To be filial also means producing grandsons to carry on the patriline and performing the rites of ancestor worship for them after they have departed (Harell, 1981).

The concept of filial piety in China can be traced to various writings of Confucian teaching. Tsai refers to three major sources when examining the features of traditional Chinese filial piety: *The Analects (Lun Yu)*, the *Book of Filial Piety (Xiao Jing)*, and the *Twenty-Four Examples of Filial Piety (Er Shi Si Xiao)*. The messages in these writings represent Confucius' definition of a "good son" as a "filial son." *The Analects* shows a good son as one who treats his parents with respect, follows his father's footsteps, serves and supports his parents with love, does not let his parents worry about his whereabouts, and shows gratitude to his parents (cf. Tsai, 1997, p. 276). Model examples on filial piety are further shown in the *Twenty-Four Examples of Filial Piety,* which mainly feature government officials as the filial sons serving their parents. Using the government officials as role models implies that officials who serve their parents well will be equally good officials to their subjects.

The relationship between filial piety and political leadership is emphasized in the *Book of Filial Piety,* which urges the political leaders to act like fathers to their subjects, so that they may in return get respect from their subjects in the same way as do their fathers. Such political implications in the *Book of Filial Piety* was welcomed by the rulers. The ideology was also introduced to Japan, and the *Book of Filial Piety* and it was said to have become required reading for members of the Japanese imperial court. It also contributed to the enactment of the first Japanese law concerning care of the elderly in 718 A.D. (Tsai, 1997).

Besides filial piety, the Confucian ideal of human maturity also contributes to a positive image of aging in the East by linking aging with moral development and wisdom, where one finally reaches the ideal of maturity as a harmonious inner life develops with age (Ikels, 1980, p. 112). In addition, the various spiritual and psychological traditions in East Asian cultures also influenced the perception of old age positively. Buddhism, for example, encourages an active, focused redemption in old age to overcome all earthly worries and return to the true self (Formanek & Linhart, 1997, p. 12). Taoism, too, promotes old age as a highly rewarding stage of life with its emphasis on longevity and happiness. It accepts decline as inevitable, and advocates for ways to lead meaningful and fulfilling later years (Munro, 1988). Tsuji (1997) notes that the concept of *amae* (dependency) in Japanese mentality encourages dependency in old age. Coupled with filial piety, it helps to give the elderly a right to be provided for by the young.

Filial Piety and the Family

Family is the root of stability in Confucianism. Traditionally, the family is defined as an ethical entity that has meaning far beyond economic and biological relations. It is the basic entity of life, which shows the position and identity of one person. A family is also a lineage where an individual is but a member of the lineage, which stretches into the past and continues into the future.

Family systems in Chinese, Korean, and Japanese societies show great similarities. All three societies traditionally regard the elderly as the most authoritative and respected figure in the family. In the patriarchal and patrilineal family and kinship system, the most senior male in the family and lineage is given the highest authority and respect. The family expresses one cultural form of honor for old age in the elaborate celebrations of the 60th, 70th, 80th, 88th, and 100th birthdays. In the past when most people did not live beyond 60, to have completed the 60-year cycle (based on the association of the 12 Animal Years with the Five Phases in ancient Chinese philosophy) is considered a personal achievement in a society which honors longevity. From the cyclical view of the life cycle, a perspective different from the western notion of a linear life cycle, completion of the cycle marks the beginning of one's second childhood, which symbolizes the regaining of leisure and freedom (Smith, 1961). Soh (1997) notes that in Korea, with mass longevity now, the 60th birthday as a rite of passage no longer holds the social significance it used to. The new trend seems to be for elderly to celebrate their 70th birthday (called the age of "old and rarity") as a rite of passage in longevity. This also seems to be an emerging trend in Chinese and Japanese societies where reaching 60 years is now more a norm than an exception.

The three family systems also show differences. While the ideal extended family arrangement in Chinese families expects adult married brothers and their families to stay together in the same household, in Korea and Japan only the eldest son is expected to stay with the parents. What we now know as the traditional *ie* system—the Japanese ideal of the stem family which practices the norm of the elderly couple staying with the eldest son and his family while other siblings are expected to move out upon marriage—was only consolidated in late 19th century under the Meiji government. China and Korea show greater similarities compared with Japan. Although lineage plays a more important part in the Chinese and Korean family systems, in the Japanese system, family is a kind of "corporation" or "collective," where the continuation of the *ie* is more important than ensuring the purity of blood (Watanabe, 1996).

Such different emphasis in filial piety shows the likelihood of a pre-Confucian past influencing the social and ethical cultures of Japan.[7] In the same line of argument, the widely held characteristics of Japan as a vertical society with harmonious relations, very much in tune with the Confucian concern with hierarchical relationships and its emphasis on family and state harmony, may just as likely have been present in the pre-Confucian period. Confucian teaching in Japan might have been selected simply because it complements these ideas and serves to strengthen these characteristics (Smith, 1996).

Despite differences in conceptualizations, family traditions, along with filial piety, remain important and effective in ensuring security for the elderly. Among the three cultures, Korea, said to be the last Confucian society in the world (Linhart, 1997, p. 326), seems the most fundamental to the extent that it unabashedly practices ageism, slighting the young and esteeming the old (Soh, 1997).

While the daughter-in-law caring for a Japanese elder may have assumed responsibility for the sake of collective interest in a corporate-oriented traditional Japanese life, in China, filial piety has been viewed as more of an obligation on the grounds of gratitude, since the debts of one's parents are beyond number. Lin (1983) claims that the desire to have the privilege of serving their parents in their old age actually became a consuming passion for the Chinese. And for the elderly, "there is no shame attached to the circumstances of depending on his children in old age. Rather it is considered good luck to have children who can take care of one. One lives for nothing else in China" (p. 100). Ideally, the practice of filial piety in the family ensures the status of elders in the family.

Ancestor Worship

The practice and belief of ancestor worship is another feature viewed as instrumental in maintaining the status of the elderly in East Asia, since the elderly themselves are the closest to the ancestors and will in due course join them. Defined widely as a household religion which "emphasizes the influence of the deceased kindred on the living" (Spier, 1957), ancestor worship is closely related to Confucian teachings of filial piety, respect for senior authority, and family continuity.[8] It is centered on the family, expressing a concept of continuum and mutually dependent relationships among the living, the yet unborn and the dead members (Smith, 1974). In writing of ancestor worship in Taiwan, Wolf (1968) notes that this concept is "one link in an awesomely long chain, unimportant in [itself] yet essential to the continuation of the chain, [which] gives meaning to what might be an unkind world of hard work and hunger" (p. 26). It is perhaps most comforting for the elderly and helps them to face death with little fear to know that they are ensured of continuing veneration when they join the ancestors whom they have already worshiped for decades. Having offspring, especially sons and grandchildren, thus becomes all the more important to the elderly to be ensured of care not only in this life, but also the next.

Although there are variations in practices of ancestor worship among the East Asian societies as well as within them, the ideas are quite similar. Filial piety is expressed through keeping the memories of the departed elders alive. They are worshiped in rituals observing their birthdays, death anniversaries as well as other family celebrations such as the New Year and winter solstice. During the rituals, their favorite food and flowers are presented before the altar to show special remembrance and filial respect. Among the Chinese in Singapore it is becoming increasingly more common to place ancestral tablets in Mahayana Buddhist temples than to set up an altar at home. But as temples may have restrictions, such as allowing only vegetarian food to be offered, family members during the rituals sometimes feel compelled to explain to their ancestors through prayers why they were not served their favorite meat dish. With busy urban living in Singapore, there are instances where family members leave the preparation for and the performance of the ancestral rituals in the hands of their foreign domestic home help (usually from the Philippines or Indonesia), reducing the veneration of their ancestors to merely a form to be observed.

Giving offerings to the ancestors represents a legitimate extension of the obligation of filial piety. But ancestor worship also includes an element of fear, where a neglect of the rites is regarded as undesirable because it will anger the ancestors and may bring severe supernatural retribution upon the descendants' families. In general, though, the ancestors are regarded as friendly and supportive. With the power they now have in the supernatural world, they are believed to be overseeing the welfare of their descendants at all times, reciprocating the offerings received with blessings and favors desired by the descendants.

FILIAL PIETY—REALITIES

The concept of filial piety has traditionally placed old age at a premium in the East Asian cultures. It is no wonder that Lin Yutang (1983) cannot stop counting the advantages of being old in China:

> In China, the first question a person asks the other on an official call, after asking about his name and surname is "What is your glorious age?" . . . And if the person is anywhere over fifty, the inquirer immediately drops his voice in humility and respect. That is why all old people, if they can, should go and live in China, where even a beggar with a white beard is treated with extra kindness. (p. 96)

The extremely positive images of aging as portrayed by Lin, however, are increasingly shown to be an idealization. As discussion in the earlier section has shown, there can be considerable differences in the experience of aging with class and gender differences, complicated by social, economic and political changes. Yin and Lai's (1983) study of social stratification in China shows that only the upper socioeconomic class had the resources to support large extended households, practice ceremonies associated with ancestor worship, and consolidate power in the senior family heads. Experiences in Korea, too, differ with social classes (Soh, 1997). Kiefer (1992) has noted that although distinct class division of the landed gentry, *yanban,* and peasants exist in Korea, the distinction is only perceived as important because there is still little sociological study along class stratification. Gender differences in aging have been discussed in the "ambiguities of aging" section earlier, highlighting the tragedy among women of being old and without family support.

Filial Piety From the Exchange Perspective

Instead of the cultural perception of filial piety as a "consumed passion," writings on filial piety also consider it from the perspective of exchange and reciprocity theories. The mutual obligations governing family relations in East Asian cultures require the older members to care for the younger ones until they can care for themselves. This can be interpreted as a form of investment that will hopefully yield good returns in the form of future support.

The issue of reciprocity in family care in Japan has been explored in various sociological and anthropological studies. Lebra (1974) points to compensative transference through generational succession as a mechanism to validate reciprocity, in which parents have the right to demand care from their children as compensation for their caring for their own parents. But norms are changing in contemporary society, and women caregivers can only hope that instead of the right to demand care in exchange, their caregiving roles at home will inspire the younger generation to do the same in the future. This is expressed by one informant in Elliot and Campbell's (1993) study of changing ideas of family care in Japan, who revealed that "If you are nice to old people, the children will see this and when you grow old, they will be nice to you. This is teaching through your own action" (p. 131).

Hashimoto (1996) contends that the Japanese elderly could retain a sense of self-worth while depending on their family, not merely from the normative structure of filial obligation based on tradition, but also because of the attitude that they have accumulated credit (by bringing up the children and enduring hardship for the family) and therefore deserve to be helped. Akiyama et al. (1990) distinguish between symmetric and asymmetric rules of reciprocity in their study of relations between older mothers and their middle-aged daughters and daughters-in-law in Japan and America. They conclude that Japanese elders maintain reciprocity in exchange through many forms, not necessarily in kind. This includes "repaying to the grandchildren for the kindness of their daughters-in-law" (p. 133). On the other hand, Elliot and Campbell (1993) discover that more Japanese are seeing the idea of exchanging elderly care with inheritance as a fair deal.

It is not uncommon for children to quarrel over who should take responsibility for their parents, even when it is traditionally the duty expected of the eldest son. Ikels (1993) shows how some provincial governments in China resolve this by requiring written contracts of support between parents and their children. The age-old mother-in-law and daughter-in-law conflicts may further make multigenerational living less desirable. Yamanoi (1995), an advocate of the Swedish welfare state model, has cited cases of "silver harassment"—family abuse of the elderly—and the high suicide rate among elders living with their families in Japan to advance his argument. Similar reports on the abuse and neglect of elderly in China are also noted by Ikels (1993).

From the exchange perspective, the practice of ancestor worship can be explained as linking the living and the departed in reciprocal flows of assistance and dependence. This is clearly shown in an analysis of Chinese death rituals in Singapore by Tong (1993). Chinese death rituals are known for their elaborateness and the huge amount of money usually spent to ensure the proper enactment of rituals. An elaborate death ritual is desirable from the perspective of both the elderly and their descendants. To the elderly, the ritual is an announcement to others that he had lived a good life and had produced filial and successful children who are both willing and rich enough to spend on the ritual. From the descendants' perspective, besides an expression of filial piety, it is a manifestation of the family's status and social connections. Moreover, it also creates a reciprocal relationship where filial descendants will in turn be blessed by the power of the deceased. One example of exchange is the ritual of burning the sacrifices to the deceased to ensure that they are luxuriously provided for in the "otherworld." This practice shows the perception of Chinese ancestors as anthropomorphic, having the same needs and desires in the otherworld as the living (Wee, 1977). Because of this perception, sacrifices transferred to them through burning often demonstrate this-worldly needs, such as a large quantity of paper money symbolizing gold and silver money, huge houses, cars, clothes, daily needs, even credit cards and servants, all made from paper. This practice continues to be observed in ancestor worship rituals although only paper money is burned, symbolizing the need to replenish the ancestors with "cash" for their otherworld living. By providing the ancestors in another world with riches, the living place the dead in their debt, where they are expected to reciprocate with even greater benefits to the descendants (Tong, 1993, p. 147). The exchange perspective helps explain why these death rituals continue to remain in practice as the society modernizes. In fact, in recent years, these rituals have sometimes become even more elaborate and traditional as growing affluence allows the descendants more resources to spend "lavishly" on their ancestors.

In trying to hypothesize the cultural variations observed in the status of the elderly, anthropologists Amoss and Harrell argue that generally "the position of the aged in a given society can be expressed in terms of how much old people contribute to the resources of the group, balanced by the cost they exact, and compounded by the degree of control they have over valuable resources" (Amoss & Harrell, 1981, p. 6). Their hypothesis complements the modernization theory and exchange perspective, which would assume that with technological change, the elderly today have a lower position in the society, as they have fewer resources and roles deemed valuable. With this assumption, the departed will seem to command a better position as their transition into ancestorhood increases their influence on descendants through the supernatural powers they are now perceived to possess.

Re-Defining Filial Piety

Modernization also plays a part in influencing the developments of "filial piety" in East Asian societies. Nobushige Hozumi, a famous law scholar in Japan concluded in his work, *Inkyo ron* ("On Retirement"), written in 1915, that "it is the eastern way to take refuge in the family, and the western way to take refuge in the state" (Hozumi, 1978, pp. 688–689; Linhart, 1997, p. 298). More than half a century later, however, writings on aging in the East are beginning to argue for a change. Despite consistent emphasis on family care for the elderly in public discourse, there is nevertheless an inclination toward extra-familial support, not necessarily a complete shift from one to another, but a re-definition of filial piety by a juxtaposition of the two.

When arguing for the development of social welfare to solve the problem of aging in Korea, Choi (1996) claims that the traditional value of filial piety is hampering the development of social welfare for the elderly. Instead he suggests that filial piety be preserved by "developing and transforming it so that it may fit a modernizing Korean society." (Choi, 1996, p. 20):

> Filial piety, according to its original meaning, can be dealt with at both the familial level and the societal level. What filial piety requires at the familial level is to provide economic support and direct care services to parents in order to repay them for their affection and care, whereas what it requires at the societal level is the state's welfare provision for the elderly in order to repay them for their contributions to society. Traditional Korean society has emphasized the familial level, but not the societal level. (p. 20)

A "transformed filial piety" thus calls for a development of domiciliary-care programs provided by home-health-care persons and home helpers to support family responsibility in elderly care. Choi is careful to argue that this should not be the only justification for filial piety at the societal level, adding other advantages such as "it can slow down the diminishing of elderly people's status within the family, the pace of family disorganization and the disruption of the community" (p. 21).

Noting that a rapidly industrializing Taiwan has made traditional filial piety impossible to fulfil, Tsai (1997) has also proposed for a re-definition of filial piety he called "extended filial piety," involving the family, philanthropic foundations[9] and the government in providing care for the elderly. The model is similar to that of a "transformed filial piety" suggested by Choi, except for more details such as including the role of voluntary organizations to supplement the government and family by providing financial and organizational support. The extended filial piety model echoes the Singapore government's position on elderly, which states that "The aged are an integral part of our society. Their problems, needs and aspirations are the responsibility of everyone: the family, the community (voluntary organizations), the government and the aged themselves" (Report of the Advisory Council on the Aged, 1989, p. 3). The inclusion of the elderly as part of the responsibility implies the expectation for the elderly to be self-reliant, a departure from the idea of dependency in traditional filial piety.

Anbacken's (1997) study of elderly care in Japan coins the term "kinstitution" to encompass the idea of both family and social filial piety (*shakaiteki oyakōkō*). Parallel to Choi's and Tsai's re-definition of filial piety, Anbacken's concept refers to the "family as a base, but not having to shoulder the ultimate responsibility but with enough support and help so that women can continue working outside the family, while supporting their elderly parents (in-law) either at home or living nearby." With the recent expansion of elderly services under the New Gold Plan (1994),[10] she questions the possibility of "kinstitution" as making up a new "Japanese-style social welfare" (Anbacken, 1997, p. 282).

Studies on elderly in China show a more uncertain outlook for the future, although they are evaluated to have fared quite well even under "market socialism" today (Davis, 1997).[11] The one-child family policy, unprecedented in history, has been the focus of much discussion. Cheung (1988) argues that families will face additional burdens with a future scenario of one couple supporting four parents and eight grandparents. He proposes a comprehensive social welfare policy developed by the government as pertinent in solving the problem.

It should be noted here that East Asian societies do provide social welfare for the elderly, usually in a limited form such as public assistance and old folks homes, exclusively focusing on the poor or low-income elderly group. In China the system of providing for the elderly has existed since antiquity (Hsia, 1993). The practice of offering pensions to retired officials, similar to the retiree pension today, began as early as the Han dynasty (206 B.C. to 189 A.D.). During the reign of Emperor Ping (1–6 A.D.), elderly officials retired from their posts might receive one-third of their original salary until death. The practice of permitting officers to retire at the age of 70 with half of their salary granted until death, started by Emperor Xiaoming of the Northern Wei Dynasty (409–424 A.D.) was followed until the beginning of the Qing dynasty (1644–1911 A.D.). To help people carry out their filial duties to their parents, there was exemption of taxes and labor services for families with elderly relatives. It was also stipulated that officials who had senile parents were allowed to be transferred to wherever their parents lived, so that they could take good care of them (Hsia, 1993).

A comparison of the state support of filial piety in older China with the "transformed filial piety," "extended filial piety," and "kinstitution" suggested by Choi, Tsai, and Anbacken, respectively, seems to suggest an interesting development in the conceptualization of filial piety, from the traditional ideal of filial piety as personal care and love provided by the *children* to the contemporary re-definition of a separation of filial piety into two distinctions, physical care and emotional care, where the former has evolved to permit help from outsiders.

This emerging characteristic of elderly care in East Asian cultures draws contradictory responses. On the one hand, advocates for a welfare state suspect it as an intention of the state to revive traditional ideals of filial piety so as to limit government expenditure on aged welfare. The Japanese government's Gold Plan to increase services and facilities to help maintain the elderly within the family is objected to by some as a case of *obasuteyama*—abandonment and neglect initiated by the government (Bethel, 1995, p. 301). On the other hand, gerontologists and welfare specialists in the West, who are beginning to doubt the effectiveness of the welfare state system, are turning to see what the East can offer. Hermalin (1995) sees the possibility of Asia developing new solutions in policies and institutions that could influence western approaches to issues of aging.

Anbacken compares Sweden and Japan only to realize that they are drawing closer to each other in the practice of elderly care. The prevailing view in Sweden claims that "The State takes care of you, it is the civil right of every Swedish citizen." However, the system and ideology has shifted with economic downturns in the 1980s and 1990s. Anbacken notes that in Sweden in the 1990s, "suddenly other parts of the 'package' of welfare are focused on, such as the importance of the family, the neighborhood, volunteer spirits, etc." (Anbacken, 1997, p. 280). On the other hand, the 1990s also brought an increase in Japanese groups arriving in Sweden to learn the Swedish model of elderly care. If Japan works toward an increase in nonkin measures while Sweden moves in the direction of family care, Anbacken reckons that Japan will eventually be on more equal terms with Sweden, where the emphasis will be on learning from each other.

A re-defined filial piety, located midway between traditional family cares and state welfarism, thus provide grounds for debate. The concept stresses public involvement (of both the state and voluntary organizations) to *strengthen* the family responsibility instead of *replacing* the family as welfare policies in most welfare states do. Developments

in filial piety in East Asian cultures show the renegotiation of traditional ideals as social demands and attitudes change. But how does the
dichotomization of filial piety affect the experience of aging? To what
extent is it considered a distinct development of its own? Studies from
the U.S. show that indeed, family care and concerns have always been
practiced (Monk, 1992). Can we consider frequent phone calls and holiday get-togethers with the elderly in the western family also a form of
re-defined filial piety? What are the implications of the West learning
from the East, or the two coming closer in terms of aging issues? Are
we moving toward some form of integration in a cross-cultural
approach, along with the interdisciplinary approach already emerging
in the study of aging?

FUTURE DIRECTIONS

Scholars studying aging in the East will certainly agree that we are in
for an exciting challenge. The East in transition provides new opportunities for research as changing norms bring into question our normative understanding of aging and the life course in the region. How
do cultural traditions adapt to change? How do the elderly themselves
perceive change? How do they define a "good old age" in the face of
change? How has the definition of old age shifted among the elderly
themselves? In recent years, more films in the East have been made
with the elderly as protagonists. How do these films portray the
meaning of life in old age? Even though Smith (1961) called for it more
than 30 years ago, humanistic gerontology in the East is still a relatively new venture which offers much potential. One future direction
of aging research in the East would be to gain more insights into the
cultural and time-specific issues of aging, and expand our knowledge
through an understanding of the diversities of the aging experience in
the East.

The second direction I envision will only be possible if researchers
are able to recognize the fact that first, the East and West are not
antipodal and that developments in the West can also be concurrently
happening in the East. And second, the East is in itself a great diversity
not only in terms of regional, historical, religious and cultural differences, but also in terms of societal development. If we posit a linear
view of development from traditional to modern to postmodern, then
we will find eastern societies represented in all three stages. Thus, the
gerontological research agenda in the West could also apply to the East.[12]
Compared to studies in the West, studies on eastern societies more
often than not focus on intergenerational relationships between the
elderly and the family. However, we are witnessing an emerging cohort

of elderly—often the more affluent and highly educated urban elderly—who wish to remain independent in old age.

This is reflected in the boom of the "silver business" of retirement housing in Japan since the 1980s. Even in a society like Singapore, which has consistently emphasized coresidence, the recent launching of studio apartments for the elderly as part of public housing reflects the state's coming to terms with the changing needs of today's elderly. Soh (1997) discovers that compared to the elderly in Korea, those who have migrated to the U.S. have a higher tendency to live apart from their children who were instrumental in their emigration. Ironically, they consider their new homeland a 'paradise of the elderly' compared to the situations in their native country.

With this emerging trend toward elderly staying alone or as couples only, we need to expand beyond the family as a unit of analysis to dyadic relations between individuals. To what extent do conjugal relations between elderly couples provide support and meaning? What is the role of friendship among the elderly?

Related to the shift to dyadic relations in social support analysis is the question of loneliness. Yet little has been done on the issue of loneliness in the East, compared to the West. Perhaps the focus on family gives the impression that elderly in eastern societies have little time to feel lonely. Kinoshita and Kiefer (1992) have addressed this issue in the study of elderly in a retirement community in Japan. But the issue should not be limited to elderly who are staying alone or those who are institutionalized. I think it is equally important to understand the issue of loneliness among elderly within the family. What do the elderly associate loneliness with? Staying alone but occupied with activities? Or staying with the children but left alone at home during much of the day? What is the role of religion or spiritual activities in coping with loneliness? Relating it to a humanistic perspective, how was loneliness addressed by elderly in the past, through literary works and journals? What is its relationship to human maturity? I find the standpoint of critical gerontology useful in trying to answer these questions. Moody (1993) defines critical gerontology as "concerned with the problems of emancipation of older people from all forms of domination" (p. xv). Perhaps the East must first be "emancipated" from the value-laden East-West dichotomy before we can really hope to understand old age and aging in the East.

The boundaries between East and West, as represented in Lin Yutang's view, are blurring. What Moody (1993) termed as a "postmodern life course" in the West, characterized by "fluid movement and multiplicity of life-styles" and "based not on productivity but on consumerism" (p. xx) is not a development only evident in the West. A shift away from the modernized life course—with rigid boundaries and concentrated productivity in the middle years—is happening particularly in the postindustrialized parts of the East. The search for an ideal life style in old age among elderly in East Asia is in the process: there are people opting for early retirement on one extreme, and there are people becoming entrepreneurs and embarking upon their dream career after age 60 on the other extreme. Already in the late 1980s and increasingly in the 1990s, there is a trend toward "retirement migration" to the West, especially among the emerging group of affluent elderly. This signifies a shift in the conceptualization of "paradise for the old," from depending on children to provide a "good old age" toward the emphasis of freedom and self-fulfillment in later life.

Developing a critical perspective on the "sunset of life" in the East has just begun.

NOTES

[1] Vast majority of the population in Singapore is of Chinese ancestry. In 1996, Chinese comprises 77.3%, Malays 14.1%, Indians 7.3%, and Others 1.3% (Depart-ment of Statistics, 1997).

[2] See Cohen (1994) for a review of the study of aging in anthropology.

[3] Some of the recent works include Kertzer and Leslett, "Aging in the Past: Demography, Society and Old Age" (1995), and Cole, "The Journey of Life: A Cultural History of Aging in America" (1992).

[4] Pokkuri temples are where the "elderly undergo proleptic rituals to achieve equanimity in the face of aging and to avoid chronic illnesses prior to a timely departure into the world of gods, buddhas, and ancestors" (Young & Ikeuchi, 1997, p. 230).

[5] There were little developments in research on China in the 1960s and 1970s because the country was relatively closed to foreign scholars during the Mao era.

[6] Research on aging in Korea, for example, was almost non-existent before the 1990s (except for Korean elderly in America) and the limited number of papers in English language which appears since 1990 are mainly the efforts of Korean scholars who are trained in America (for example, Soh, 1997; Choi, 1996).

[7] Befu (1962) calls this emphasis on collectivity over individuality evident in Japanese social structure as "corporate emphasis." Such characteristics have appeared in the pre-Confucian period where middle-size territorial units held together by bonds of kinship and fictive kinship were already present to ensure efficient collective work (Kiefer, 1992).

[8] It is however arguable whether ancestor worship is purely influenced by Confucianism, for the practices and rites have shown an amalgam of indigenous, Confucian, and Buddhist elements (Smith, 1996, p. 174).

[9] A philanthropic foundation for the elderly is a voluntary organization financed by large business corporations and/or a group of wealthy individuals with the primary goal of serving the elderly. Many contributors see their

participation as an extension of traditional filial piety beyond the limit of a single family (Tsai, 1997, p. 288).

[10] The 1994 New Gold Plan is a revised version of the 1990 Gold Plan for the development of health and welfare service for the elderly promulgated by the Japanese National government. It emphasizes the increase of services and facilities to enable elderly to stay at home as much as possible (Maeda, 1996).

[11] The old age pensions given to city workers ranges from 60% to 100%. Retirement pay in the rural areas is much lower, only about a quarter of that in the city. However, many rural retirees continue to participate in agricultural production, and receive support from their co-residing children. China also implement the "five guarantees" system providing guaranteed food, clothing, medical care, housing, and burial expenses to childless elderly.

[12] Koyano et al. (1994)'s sociological studies of social support and living arrangement of the elderly provides an example.

REFERENCES

Akiyama, H., Antonucci, T., & Campbell, R. (1990). Exchange and reciprocity among two generations of Japanese and American women. In J. Sokolovsky (Ed.), *The cultural context of aging: Worldwide perspectives.* New York: Bergin and Garvey.

Amoss, P., & Harrell, S. (Eds.). (1981). *Other ways of growing old.* Stanford, CA: Stanford University Press.

Anbacken, E. (1997). *Who cares? Culture, structure, and agency in caring for the elderly in Japan.* Stockholm: The Institute of Oriental Languages.

Ariyoshi, S. (1972). *Kokutsu no hito* (The Twilight Years). Tokyo: Kodansha.

Befu, H. (1962). Corporate emphasis and patterns of descent in the Japanese family. In R. J. Smith & R. K. Beardsley (Eds.), *Japanese culture: Its development and characteristics.* New York: Viking Publications.

Benedict R. (1946). *The chrysanthemum and the sword.* Boston: Houghton Mifflin.

Bethel, D. (1992). *From abandonment to community: Life in a Japanese institution for the elderly.* Ph.D. diss., University of Hawaii.

Cherry, R., & Magnuson-Martinson, S. (1981). Modernization and the status of the aged in China: Decline or equalization? *The Sociological Quarterly, 2,* 253–261.

Cheung, F. C. H. (1988). Implications of the one-child family policy on the development of the welfare state in the People's Republic of China. *Journal of Sociology and Social Welfare, 15,* 5–25.

Choi, S. (1996). The family and ageing in Korea: A new concern and challenge. *Aging and Society, 16,* 1–25.

Cohen, L. (1994). Old age: Cultural and critical perspectives. *Annual Review of Anthropology, 23,* 137–158.

Cole, T. R. (1992). *The journey of life: A cultural history of aging in America.* Cambridge: Cambridge University Press.

Cowgill, D. O., & Holmes, L. D. (1972). *Aging and modernization.* New York: Appleton-Century-Crofts.

Davis-Friedmann, D. (1983). *Long lives: Chinese elderly and the communist revolution.* Cambridge, MA: Harvard University Press.

Davis, D. (1997). Inequality and insecurity among elderly in contemporary China. In S. Formanek & S. Linhart (Eds.), *Aging: Asian concepts and experiences past and present.* Vienna: Velag der Osterreichischen der Wissenschaften.

Eisdorfer, C. (1981). Forward. In P. Amoss & S. Harrell (Eds.), *Other ways of growing old.* Stanford, CA: Stanford University Press.

Elliot, K. S., & Campbell, R. (1993). Changing ideas about family care for the elderly in Japan. *Journal of Cross-cultural Gerontology, 8,* 119–135.

Embree, J. (1939). *Suye Mura: A Japanese village.* Chicago: University of Chicago Press.

Fry, C. L. (1981). *Dimensions: Aging, culture and health.* Brooklyn, NY: J. F. Bergin.

Formanek, S. (1997). Views of the crone in pre-Meiji Japan. In S. Formanek & S. Linhart (Eds.), *Aging: Asian concepts and experiences: Past and present.* Vienna: Verlag der Osterreichischen Akademie der Wissenschaften.

Formanek, S., & Linhart, S. (1997). Problems and opportunities of the study of old age in Asian cultures. In S. Formanek & S. Linhart (Eds.), *Aging: Asian concepts and experiences past and present.* Vienna: Verlag der Osterreichischen Akademie der Wissenschaften.

Harrell, S. (1981). Growing old in rural Taiwan. In P. Amoss & S. Harrell (Eds.), *Other ways of growing old.* Stanford, CA: Stanford University Press.

Hashimoto, A. (1996). *The gift of generations: Japanese and American perspectives on aging and the social context.* Cambridge: Cambridge University Press.

Hermalin, A. I. (1995). Aging in Asia: Setting the research foundation. Asia-pacific Population Research Reports #4. East-West Center.

Hozumi, N. (1978). *Inkyo ron* (On Retirement). Reprint of 2nd ed. from 1915. Tokyo: Nihon Keizai Hyōronsha.

Hsia, L B. (1993). China. In E. B. Palmore (Ed.), *Developments and research on aging: An international handbook.* Westport, CT: Greenwood Press.

Ikels, C. (1980). Coming of age in Chinese society. In C. L. Fry (Ed.), *Aging in culture and society.* New York: Columbia University.

Ikels, C. (1993). Settling accounts: The intergenerational contract in an age of reform. In D. Davis & S. Harrell (Eds.), *Chinese families in the post-Mao era.* Berkeley: University of California Press.

Ikels, C. (1997). Long-term care and the disabled elderly in urban China. In J. Sokolovsky (Ed.), *The cultural context of aging* (2nd ed.). New York: Bergin & Garvey.

Jenike, B. (1997). Home-based health care for the elderly in Japan: A silent system of gender and duty. In S. Formanek & S. Linhart (Eds.), *Aging: Asian concepts and experiences past and present.* Vienna: Verlag der Osterreichischen Akademie der Wissenschaften.

Keith, J. et al. (1994). *The aging experience: Diversity and commonality across cultures.* Thousand Oaks, CA: Sage Publications.

Kerlzer, D., & Leslett, P. (1995). *Aging in the past: Demography, society and old age.* Berkeley: University of California Press.

Kiefer, C. W. (1990). The elderly in modern Japan: Elite, victims, or plural players? In J. Sokolovsky (Ed.), *The cultural context of aging.* New York: Bergin & Garvey.

Kiefer, C. W. (1992). Aging in eastern cultures: A historical overview. In T. R. Cole, D. Van Tassel, & R. Kastenbaum (Eds.), *Handbook of the humanities and aging.* New York: Springer.

Kinoshita, Y., & Kiefer, C. W. (1992). *Refuge of the honored: Social organization in a Japanese retirement community.* Berkeley: University of California Press.

Koyano, W. (1989). Japanese attitudes towards the elderly: A review of research findings. *Journal of Cross-cultural Gerontology, 4,* 335–345.

Koyano, W., et al. (1994). The social support system of the Japanese elderly. *Journal of Cross-Cultural Gerontology, 9,* 323–333.

Lebra, T. S. (1974). Reciprocity and the asymmetric principle: An analytical appraisal of the Japanese concept of *On.* In T. S. Lebra & W. Lebra (Eds.), *Japanese culture and behavior: Selected readings.* Honolulu: University of Hawaii Press.

Lebra, T. S. (1984). *Japanese women: Constraint and fulfillment.* Honolulu: University of Hawaii Press.

Lin, Y. T. (1983). On growing old gracefully. In P. L. McKee (Ed.), *Philosophical foundations of gerontology.* New York: Human Sciences Press.

Linhart, S. (1997). Does *Oyakoko* still exist in present-day Japan? In S. Formanek & S. Linhart (Eds.), *Aging: Asian concepts and experiences past and present.* Vienna: Verlag der Osterreichischen Akademie der Wissenschaften.

Lock, M. (1993). *Encounters with aging: Menopause in Japan and North America.* Berkeley: University of California Press.

Martin, L. (1988). The aging of Asia. *Journal of Gerontology, 43,* S99–113.

Mathews, G. (1996). *What makes life worth living? How Japanese and Americans make sense of their worlds.* Berkeley: University of California Press.

Minois, G. (1987). *History of old age: From antiquity to the Renaissance.* Trans. S. H. Tensiun. Chicago: University of Chicago Press.

Monk, A. (1992). Aging, generational continuity, and filial support. In H. Cox (Ed.), *Aging.* Guilford, CT: Dushkin.

Moody, H. R. (1993). Overview: What is critical gerontology and why is it important? In T. R. Cole et al. (Ed.), *Voices and visions of aging: Toward a critical gerontology.* New York: Springer Publishing Co.

Munro, D. J. (1985). The family network, the stream of water, the plant, picturing persons in Sung Confucianism. In D. J. Munro (Ed.), *Individualism and holism: The Confucian and Taoist philosophical perspectives.* Michigan: Michigan State University Press.

Nakagawa, Y. (1979). Japan, the welfare super-power. *Journal of Japanese Studies, 5,* 5–51.

Niwa, F. (1962). The hateful age. In I. Morris (Ed.), *Modern Japanese stories: An anthology.* Rutland, VT: Tuttle.

Palmore, E. B. (1975). *The honourable elders.* Durham, NC: Duke University Press.

Palmore, E. B., & Maeda, D. (1985). *The honourable elders revisited.* Durham, NC: Duke University Press.

Phillips, D. (Ed.). (1992). *Ageing in East and Southeast Asia.* London: Edward Arnold.

Plath, D. W. (1964). Maintaining social ties after death of kin in Japan. In K. Geiger (Ed.), *Comparative perspectives on marriage and the family.* Boston: Little, Brown & Co.

Plath, D. W. (1972). Japan the after years. In D. Cowgill & L. Holmes (Eds.), *Aging and modernization.* New York: Appleton-Century-Crofts.

Plath, D. W. (1980). *Long engagements.* Stanford, CA: Stanford University Press.

Report of the Advisory Council of the Aged. Singapore 1989.

Rohlen, T. (1978). The promise of adulthood in Japanese spiritualism. In E. Erikson (Ed.), *Adulthood.* New York: W. W. Norton and Co.

Rubinstein, R. L. (Ed.). (1990). *Anthropology and aging: Comprehensive reviews.* Dortrecht, Netherlands: Kluwer.

Scheid, B. (1997). An old tree in bloom: Zeami and the ambivalent perspectives on old age. In S. Formanek & S. Linhart (Ed.), *Aging: Asian concepts and experiences past and present.* Vienna: Verlag der Osterreichischen Akademie der Wissenschaften.

Skord, V. (1989). Withered blossoms: Aging in Japanese literature. In P. von Dorotka Bagnell & P. Soper (Eds.), *Perceptions of aging in literature: A cross-cultural study.* New York: Greenwood Press.

Skolovsky, J. (Ed.). (1990). *The cultural context of aging: Worldwide perspectives.* Westport, CT: Bergin and Garvey.

Skolovsky, J. (1997). (Ed.). The cultural context of aging: Worldwide perspectives (2nd ed.). Westport, CT: Bergin and Garvey.

Smith, R. J. (1961). *Japan: The later years of life and the concept of time.* In R. W. Kleemeier (Ed.), *Aging and Leisure.* New York: Oxford University Press.

Smith, R. J. (1974). *Ancestor worship in contemporary Japan.* Stanford, CA: Stanford University Press.

Smith, R. J. (1996). The Japanese (Confucian) family: The tradition from the bottom up. In W. Tu (Ed.), *Confucian traditions in East Asian modernity.* Cambridge, MA: Harvard University Press.

Soh, C. S. (1997). The status of the elderly in Korean society. In S. Formanek & S. Linhart (Eds.), *Aging: Asian concepts and experiences past and present.* Vienna: Verlag der Osterreichischen Akademie der Wissenschaften.

Spier, L. (1957). Ancestor worship. In Encyclopedia Americana I:651–652.

Thang, L. L. (1997a). *Ikigai* and longevity among the elderly in Okinawa. In S. Formanek & S. Linhart (Eds.), *Aging: Asian concepts and experiences past and present.* Vienna: Verlag der Osterreichischen Akademie der Wissenschaften.

Thang, L. L. (1997b). Generations in touch: Linking the old and young in a Tokyo neighborhood. Ph.D. diss., University of Illinois at Urbana-Champaign.

Thompson, S. (1990). Metaphors the Chinese age by. In P. Spencer (Ed.), *Anthropology and the riddle of the Sphinx.* London: Routledge.

Tobin, J. (1987). The American idealization of old age in Japan. *Gerontologist, 25,* 53–58.

Tong, C. K. (1993). The Inheritance of the dead: Mortuary rituals among the Chinese in Singapore. *Southeast Asian Journal of Social Science, 21,* 130–158.

Trapagen, J. (1997). In the shadow of Obasuteyama: Old age and the disembodiment of social values in a Japanese town. Ph.D. diss., University of Pittsburgh.

Tsai, W. (1997). Oriental filial piety and modern Chinese society in Taiwan. In

S. Formanek & S. Linhart (Eds.), *Aging: Asian concepts and experiences past and present*. Vienna: Verlag der Osterreichischen Akademie der Wissenschaften.

Tsuji, Y. (1997). Continuities and changes in the conceptions of old age in Japan. In S. Formanek & S. Linhart (Eds.), *Aging: Asian concepts and experiences past and present*. Vienna: Verlag der Osterreichischen Akademie der Wissenschaften.

Watanabe, H. (1996). They are almost the same as the ancient three dynasties: The West as seen through Confucian eyes in nineteenth-century Japan. In W. Tu (Ed.), *Confucian traditions in East Asian modernity*. Cambridge, MA: Harvard University Press.

Wee, V. (1977). Religion and ritual among the Chinese of Singapore: An ethnographic study. M.A. thesis, University of Singapore.

Wolf, M. (1968). *The House of Lim*. New York: Appleton Century.

Wolf, M. (1972). *Women and the family in rural Taiwan*. Stanford, CA: Stanford University Press.

Yamanoi, K. (1995). *Kazoku o shiawaer ni suru oikata*. (The ways of aging for the happiness of the family). Tokyo: Kodansha.

Yamaori, T. (1997a). The image of *Rojo* or elderly women in Japanese legend. *Japan Review, 9,* 29–40.

Yamaori, T. (1997b). Buddha and Okina ("aged man"): The expression of dying and maturity. In S. Formanek & S. Linhart (Eds.), *Aging: Asian concepts and experiences past and present*. Vienna: Verlag der Osterreichischen Akademie der Wissenschaften.

Yamashita, S. H. (1996). Confucian and the Japanese state, 1904–1945. In W. Tu (Ed.), *Confucian traditions in East Asian modernity*. Cambridge, MA: Harvard University Press.

Yin, P., & Lai, K. H. (1983). A reconceptualization of age stratification in China. *Journal of Gerontology, 38,* 608–613.

Young, R., & Ikeuchi, F. (1997). Religion in the "Hateful Age": Reflections on *Pokkuri* and other geriatric rituals in Japan's aging society. In S. Formanek & S. Linhard (Eds.), *Aging: Asian concepts and experiences past and present*. Vienna: Verlag der Osterreichischen Akademie der Wissenschaften.

11

Age Studies as Cultural Studies

Margaret Morganroth Gullette

"but the human mind no the human mind has nothing to do with age.
As I say so, tears come into my eyes."
—Gertrude Stein, 1936 (aged 62)

I

Age Foregrounded

Over the past century in the United States, "age" has become increasingly dominant as a social classifying device and a determinant of subjectivities (Kohli, 1996). In the 1990s, age provides ever more expectable and subtle ways of fragmenting the life course, the work force, and the citizenry. Social gerontology and, now, age studies have tried to counter this secular force by emphasizing the discursively constructed, historically contingent aspects of age and aging. Yet despite our efforts, common sense considers age ahistorical, another "body-based" fact of life like "gender" and "race." Indeed, the habit of naturalizing age becomes more deeply entrenched.

Begin with the imperious trend toward sundering the continuous life course into imaginary parts, reified by naming. The West long managed to make do with fewer categories and vaguer boundaries between "youth" and "old age." "Childhood" only gradually became differentiated. Looking back to the turn of the last century, however, age historians witness in rapid succession stricter age grading in schools, rewriting old age as a medical problem, the inventions of "retirement," pediatrics, gerontology, geriatrics, "adolescence," "the middle years," a male climacteric relocated to the midlife, "flapper," "empty nest," and "postgraduate mother"—all by about 1935; "teenager" in the 1940s; the naming of cohorts, "Baby Boomers" in the 1980s and "Generation X" in the 1990s.[1] The parts of the life course (called "stages" by those who refuse to regard them as inventions of culture) might now more usefully be called *age classes* (Gullette, 1997b, pp. 4–5).

Now one's age class, "generational identity," or named "cohort" can in certain contexts trump other identities. Being "old" probably was the first age category to suffer that de-individualizing power (Cole, 1992, p. xix; see also Gruman). By now, being "an X-er" or an "aging" boomer can seem more significant than being, say, a woman, Chinese-American, or gay, to the person in question. Belonging to an age class is now supposed to predict attributes, styles (or even more sharply, "cultures"), group interests, values, even feelings. Homogenization by age can not only subordinate differences like gender, race, class, etc., it can also strip away other personal, idiosyncratic identities.[2] To be sure, age attributions change, and there's even some give within each age class; but age as a system gets more rigid. Age is becoming a Superfact at all ages.

Difference marked by age can thus now be used to create public consensus that certain age classes are hostile to each other. Between the two currently dominant segments, young adulthood and the middle years, the advantages of power are increasingly said to be in contest—over who deserves to get employment, Social Security, a future. "Youth" and "childhood" are wielded against the elderly as well. The latter—many still the poorest of the poor—are often represented as "greedy geezers" possessed of world-historical riches.

In the century in which old-age-before-mortality[3] has become a norm, miracles of public health and pharmacology do not prevent longevity from being rendered problematic. Media pundits, labeling ours "an aging society," pronounce it a problem of mounting expense (read: money wasted on old women). Meanwhile, utopian claims about "cracking the code" of bodily aging distract attention from the many ways life chances remain linked to income.

Once primarily a euphemism for "old age" (and still used in that way), "aging" has come implicitly to signify decline. The trope circulates in discourses about everything from biotechnology to pop music, from *young* cities to *sunset* industries, from the *old* Cold War to the *new* globalized economy.[4] Aging-discourse slides into dying-discourse without critique, although a concept like "thanatology" could usefully separate them. Even though health and wealth burnish the stereotype of the wealthy as they age, the decline narrative has in fact been backing down the life course to become a midlife phenomenon. The rise in the commerce in midlife aging—from Viagra-as-recreational-drug to "preventive" plastic surgery for women nearing 40—suggests that the state of being Not-Young can be dreaded earlier, and by men as well as women. "Positive-aging" rhetoric, once reserved for the elderly, is now defensively applied to those in their middle years. Ageism may be an ancient prejudice, but *middle-ageism* is our own postmodern toxin (Gullette, 1997b, 1998a, 1998b). Like Chernobyl's fumes, it is spreading globally to "cosmopolitan elites" (Shweder, 1998, p. vii).

Although "youth" is the object of a cult, it too is viewed as a set of crises (drugs, crime, suicide, unemployment) for some young people. Youth is still a "dangerous age" (Spacks, 1981; Hareven, 1995, p. 123), as 1950's "bad boys" (Medevoi, 1997a) and Beats are succeeded by '68ers, '70s' Yuppies, '80s' rappers, and '90s' slackers, lifers, and "teen mothers." Childhood too is being seen as at risk, although whether from loss of innocence or loss of autonomy is undecided.

In short, the negatives linked to having an age have spread. *Every* age (after the pre-oedipal) has been problematized. Although only the midlife has the term "crisis" regularly attached to it, the century's reconstructions have effectively posed every marked age of life as a crisis.

Even in summary, these constitute vast modern and postmodern shifts in all aspects of "age": more age classes and emphasis on divisions between them, more age grading and stereotyping, earlier age-related decline. We don't yet know the full range of effects. But Gertrude Stein's tears responded, I believe, to the first barbs of change (Gullette, 1993). For Stein's peers, decline narrative caused pain by asserting that creativity helplessly wanes with the body. Today, no individual exposed to dominant acculturations can be entirely unaffected by current age lore—in their intimate self-assessments, judgments of others, narrative practices—plausible expectations, inevitable nostalgias.[5] If we mean by ideology a system that socializes us into certain beliefs and ways of speaking about what it means to be "human," while suppressing alternatives, it is now necessary to speak of *age ideology* (Gullette, 1997b). Potentially, all persons—whatever their chronological age—might recognize that they have a stake in *age studies,* now developing as a movement of thought in the human and social studies. Its goal cannot be to make age irrelevant—it's long been too late for that—but to understand first of all how and why age is being insistently foregrounded.

II

Toward Age Studies

The picture of age that is emerging suggests immense ideological forces at work. The magnitude of these shifts is not fully understood; their interactions are only beginning to be studied; in the academy the urgency of the study has not yet been argued. In mainstream culture, the entire subject of "age" is mystified, as the media drop increasingly under the sway of market capitalism and niche marketing. Most people even in the academy understand "age" and interpret their own aging partly through mainstream discourses.

Age studies believes that the need to understand "age" *across the life course* is great, and that this examination must be multidisciplinary and concerted, reaching into theory, research, social policy, self-understanding, discourse, and praxis. The social constructionist approach has explained gendering and race-ing as (in part) the outcome of powerful forces interpreting *difference* to the advantage of certain groups. Theorists have to expand their imaginations to encompass all the situations where the key axis of difference is the one never mentioned—"being aged by culture" (Gullette, 1997b). We must teach ourselves to read all texts and relationships "for" age as the human studies have learned to read for gender, race, sexuality, class, etc.

This reconceptualization demands changes in the approaches that already focus on "age" or the life course, such as gerontology, auto/biography, anthropology, social history, developmental psychology, sociology, feminist theory, and women's studies (see Gullette, 1997a). Even in many of those fields, obstacles exist to moving "age" into a more prominent position conceptually.

Here, as another way of strengthening age studies, I want to argue for the necessity of a convergence between critical gerontology and cultural studies. The two share ideas and values that fit them to understand age ideology and they supply complementary tools for confronting it. Influenced by feminist, poststructuralist, multicultural, and left theories, both share a commitment to examining cultural practices, economic conditions, and public policy from the point of view of their involvements with power. History-minded though both are, their involvement in the fluctuating contemporary world makes both alertly, not to say nervously, presentist. Both are committed to enabling people to become and remain active—*agents*. Harry Moody describes critical gerontology as focused on "problems of social justice . . . interpreting the meaning of human experience . . . understanding cultural tendencies" (1993, p. xv). Stuart Hall, the charismatic director of the original Centre for Contemporary Cultural Studies in Birmingham, England, would use similar language (Hall, 1992, p. 278; also Bennett, 1992). Both approaches know that culture deals out life or death, literally—the rationing of health care illustrates this (see Bell, 1989, p. 158) as does the production of famines.

Finally, some gerontologists could be considered "organic intellectuals" in ways that age critics—who know the term comes from Antonio

Gramsci—might emulate. These public intellectuals, many of them feminists, speak about, on behalf of, to, and *from* the group they study. I am thinking of Barbara MacDonald, Baba Copper, Maggie Kuhn, Bernice Neugarten, Betty Friedan, the Rileys, among others. Their efforts have enrolled members of this age class within a self-conscious antisexist and anti-ageist movement, beating a drum for progressive public policy. People who do not themselves know the meaning of "age grading" call their congressional representatives when the rights of the elderly are threatened. They make it harder for the media to spin these threats into nothing. Age studies too needs to create a constituency of the concerned. No easy feat. Who speaks for the life course? How would we learn to do it?

To converge, critical gerontologists would have to expand beyond their subjects of expertise, old age and the elderly. Cultural critics, whose relation to age is buried in unconsciousness, would have to become as open to "age" as they have to gender, race, class, ethnicity, sexuality, place, and nation. A joint transfusion of keywords could be one means and measure of interchange. *Key Words in Sociocultural Gerontology* is the title that Andrew Achenbaum, Steven Weiland, and Carole Haber borrowed, as they declare in their preface, from one of the founders of cultural studies, Raymond Williams *(Keywords,* 1976). Deciding exactly what concepts should be joint could be—I'd like it to be—a chewy philosophical issue. Here I propose only a short list, to try to provoke fuller inventories without making premature trouble. Age studies should be as comfortable utilizing "representation" as "age stratification," "historical conjuncture" as "ageism," "hegemony" as "age consciousness."[6] Age studies should be as comfortable dealing with "the midlife" as with "youth" or "old age."Age studies should be like the other "socially-informed humanities" in being neohistorical, materialist as well as textually skillful.[7]

An ideal field. A "field" that scarcely exists; that was named only in 1993;[8] that lacks "an intensified collective consciousness" or "self-conscious debates" (to borrow terms from Achenbaum, 1995b, p. 11, and Woodward, 1991, p. 21). True, but not necessarily discouraging. Cultural studies itself, dating only from the 1960s and called by some of its practitioners "impossible," has provoked immense cognitive reorientations.

For some readers, rapprochement may not be stressless. Age studies makes an offer that critical gerontology—with some notable exceptions from its humanist/feminist wing—has rather consistently refused: to wit, to study narratives, because they coauthor the life course. Age and aging as we evolve is a personal residue—of stories we have heard, received or rejected, renegotiated and retold. In age studies, conjunctural analysis needs to be sensitive to the ways "troubles and issues" permeate life stories (Mills, 1959, p. 226). Cultural critics are notoriously sensitive to the stories inherent in mass culture (texts like newspaper polls, interviews, cable TV, book clubs, pop music, and practices like fashion, bodybuilding, and karaoke), putting them on a par with such other signs and instruments of consciousness as diaries, poetry, fiction, film, the psychotherapeutic case, the sermon. Age analysis ties all these ideological vehicles, where possible, to their rhetorics and politics of age and aging. Speculation is the tensile strength—power and risk—of all cultural studies. Like a bridge linking an archipelago, whose piers must be set on many islands, age studies must reach in all directions for explanatory breadth.

It is impossible in an essay and premature to try to survey the "field" on which these two bulky players approach each other. Instead, three "cases" follow, involving recent studies of ageism, middle-ageism, and a crisis of youth. They were chosen *as* cases, to enable me to note the likeliest directions age studies might go in, name certain problems that might hinder its effectiveness, and prove that working toward this new intersection is already exciting and productive. Indeed, its challenges make it *the* place to do the next work.

III

Case #1 Against Ageism and Gerontophobia

In the critique of "the fundamentally ageist ideology of twentieth-century western culture" Kathleen Woodward's landmark book, *Aging and Its Discontents* (1991, p. 17), focuses on Freudian psychoanalysis and canonical modern literature. With her subtle readings of photographs, correspondence, fiction, theory; her mix of challenge and respect for her influential sources; her sense of the stubborn refusal of many persons in old or sick bodies to be rewritten positively, and her own mostly positive experiential writing, Woodward made age textually *interesting.* Although she does not accept the idea of old age as "an empty signifier" (p. 17), she hollows out many a gerontophobic panic and ageist representation.[9] The book gave impetus to interrogating ageism (and by extension, middle-ageism, the cult of youth, etc.) in the highest places of culture.

One heart of her argument is that the ageism within Freudian psychoanalysis (which she rightly calls "preeminently a theory of childhood" [p. 26]) arises from Freud's own autobiography. He was 40 when his father died; in the son's opinion, after "his life had [long] been over" (quoted, p. 35). "It is the middle-aged who . . . are apprehensive about old age" (p. 82), Woodward observes later. Freud was also aged by his culture in interpreting his own experience. Influenced by the same babble about hormonal decline that caused Gertrude Stein's tears, he believed he experienced a climacteric at 50. Once having crusted midlife with decline associations, he noted his declines into older age more minutely. "Freud found aging more threatening than death itself"; "he displaced his fear of old age onto death" (p. 38). Because he had based transference on sexualized cathexis, he concluded that the very foundation of analysis was denied to him when old because, as he said in frustration to the poet H. D., "You do not think it worth your while to love me" (quoted, p. 51). He constructed a "theory" of male psychical rigidity advancing with age. Teresa Brennan comments, "Later analysts will take him seriously, and advise against analysis for those over forty, on the grounds that the psyche is too set in its paths" (Brennan, 1999, p. 134).

Woodward builds anti-ageist theory in ways that invite development. Her Freud chapter led Brennan to meditate on the causes of "rigidity" that are *not* linked to old age, exemplified by "Iris Murdoch's 'mother of a very large family' . . . often worn out before her time" or people who are "too rigid" at 40 (pp. 138, 134). In an essay in the collection *Figuring Age,* Brennan provides a theory of ego development that makes learning lessons, establishing "fixed points" for selfhood, and following "pathways" interactively necessary starting in infancy. In the process, the ego must "bind" "freely mobile energy that was so abundant in its youth" (p. 138). The downside (in Freud energy is finite) is that this reduces energy for other projects. In the longer run, she asserts, "The more we see things from our own fixed point, the stronger the ego; . . . the more *sedimented* [our pathways] . . . *the more we age, and the closer we come to death"* (p. 137; emphasis added).

Unwilling to see this psychic journey as a historical, ungendered, uniform or irreversible, Brennan adds social causes. It is because a stronger "masculine party" seeks to "stave off aging" and reduce anxiety from threats of change that he draws parasitically on the nurturing energies of another and projects "that which is anxiety-ridden and confusing" (p. 140) onto "the feminine party," who absorbs them. Likewise, as we age, men and women alike must deal not only with our own sedimentation, but with "the refuse" flung off by the strivings of powerful younger others, enforced economically (p. 140). Images, in Brennan's theory of permeable selves, have "energetic" effects. When negative, they mount up on vulnerable subalterns as a kind of anaerobic waste.

Yet Brennan finds many practices that counter rigidity: viewing a play, meditating, lucking into a "sunny retirement" (pp.138–139). Presumably also divorce, or joining the Gray Panthers. Many practices "cathect to that refreshing consciousness which is free of the self" (p. 38).

I read Brennan's essay as drawing ego psychology toward cultural politics. In her theory, although ego-supportive rigidity begins very early in life and is cumulative, it can be accelerated or ameliorated at any age. It may be possible to unlink psycho-cognitive rigidity even further from the earthy metaphors of "sedimentation," "refuse," and "crusting" that are so age-graded. We might note that even in an ego-centered time of life like adolescence, the crust can be broken when a person falls in love or encounters the intensities of higher education. If anxiety binds energy and escalates interpersonal cruelty, age theorists could produce an inventory of socially constructed sources of anxiety: capitalism's obsessive profit-motivated need for change, the exhaustion of child care and overwork. Answers to the syndrome formed by anxiety/projection/parasitism/bound pathways would then come from politics: shorter work weeks and more worker control over conditions of employment, for example, national daycare, healthcare, and long-term-care, gender and race equality.

More fundamentally, we might query the link between "free mobile energy" and infant beings that cannot crawl or speak. The *use* of creative energy, as opposed to the potential, comes (to those with class freedom) only with adult agency, and that freedom may last even after disease weakens the organism: one thinks of Flannery O'Connor writing despite lupus. In optimal circumstances, inertia might not be a correlate of increasing experience. Even in the here and now, since energy can be added by reciprocal love or engaging work, we could reconceive the pathways we have "lovingly crafted" as identity landmarks, recognizing that we have also built stimulating paths elsewhere. Who is to say that "sedimentation" is the human default? As multiple selves, can we not experience good fixedness, unnecessary fixedness, and mobility simultaneously at any age?

Perhaps the deconstruction of gerontophobia requires severing many sutures between metaphors of generic aging-into-old-age (like borrowed energy and unmitigated decline), and "the drive toward death" that Freud posited. Woodward says, "to completely rewrite the ideology of the aging body in the West, we would have to rewrite the meaning of death. And this we are not likely to do easily" (1991, p. 19). Yet she herself begins the severing in many ways. Freud's own stoic despair in fact had little to do with old age per se: as Woodward points out, over 16 years he had many surgeries for cancer.

If we start not from psychoanalysis but from critical sociology, history, or anti-ageist memoir, "death" becomes rather more easily distinguished from old age. As David Sudnow argued years ago, after having witnessed 250 deaths in hospitals, "procedural definitions" (that, say, conceal the moment of a person's death from other patients) treat "dying" as disjunct even from severe illness. Helping care for my terminally ill father years ago, I was shocked when, suddenly comatose, he was treated by a doctor as "essentially a corpse." With tremendous energy, my father had fought his terminal illness even past the point of paralysis. Those who watched him resist could never again associate dying with inertia. Stricken at 68, he died before he had a chance to grow old. In an anti-ageist culture, confusing being ill or being old with dying would be condemned as the premature imposition of "social death" (Sudnow, p. 65)[10] and confusing being ill with being old would be frowned upon as a cruel category error.

Case # 2 Against Middle-Ageism

The invention of "the middle years" is proof positive of the drastic secular change in "age" and "aging." Before 1900 people in "the long midlife" were the unlabeled norm against which other age classes were implicitly measured (Gullette, 1994, 1998b). Now the midlife is being degraded into just another special interest, like childhood, youth, old age, except that it lacks a lobby. Now that so many fight over its meaning, it would be preposterous for anyone raised within mainstream culture to deny its existence. Understanding this contested invention has been my project since about 1984. I think of the books in it under the portmanteau title *Midlife Fictions.* (I have been asked to use my own work as one of my cases.) The problem I first posed in the work that became *Declining to Decline. Cultural Combat and the Politics of the Midlife* (1997b) was to explain how, in recent decades in the U.S., the cultural category "middle years" gained a firmer ontological status as part of being human (see Benson and Hepworth on Britain). The book took a major step in disaggregating the cacophony of discourseland by marshaling evidence about the social construction of *male* aging. Antimale cartoons, anecdotes about "entering"midlife from novels and experts, articles about male plastic surgery in "Living" sections of newspapers—all worked to suggest that midlife men, a group previously protected by the double standard of aging, were being exposed to a "culture of feeling" rather new to them: decline.[11] Women, on the other hand, were absorbing from the feminist movement and fiction a complex sense of "progress" at midlife. Yet they too continued to be targeted by a pervasive, devious, interlocking system promoting midlife decline.

It is the addition of men that has most naturalized the age class. This naturalization undoes the work of "positive aging" even as proponents work tirelessly to strengthen intrapsychic resistance. Aging is becoming a unisex complaint with a childhood or adolescent exposure and a midlife onset. I redefined my task as explaining the increasing power of *middle-ageism.*

While this problematic expanded, age remained an impoverished concept in most of the theorizing that was keeping American intellectual life exciting. Yet certain developments in theory (critical, feminist, poststructuralist, and left) could be useful in age studies if reconceived with sufficient single-mindedness. I pick here only a few instances. Profeminist men's studies encouraged me to examine the supposedly privileged gender in its supposedly supreme moment, the middle years; while the feminist left nerved me to reread patriarchy as being slowly humbled by capitalism. Antipositivism meant that I didn't have to answer the question, "When do the middle years begin?" with a chronological number, as many interlocutors expected. I could ask instead, "In what context? For what subject? At what level of employment or consumption?" Foucault led me to Sandra Bartky's analysis of power's construction of emotions like feminine shame, and that eventually enabled me to write about the construction of *midlife* emotions: especially, the scene of age anxiety with which *Declining to Decline* begins (Bartky, chapters 4–7).

With midlife contexts so heterogeneous, I had to move rapidly beyond thinking of my objects as solely literary or "high," to thinking broadly about culture. How does a *midlife imaginary* get constructed, in which most listeners know what "The big 5-Oh" means, know what tones are possible in response and what rebuttals are not? How do ideas circulate from a cartoon to conversation, or change from data into fiction? How do circumstances outside text also press human subjects toward new beliefs and feelings about aging into another age of life?

Feminist political economy urged me not to ignore economic data: I found a few economists who disaggregated unemployment statistics in order to discover serious midlife job loss after around 50. As I was writing, corporate and governmental downsizing was axing once secure middle-class people. The pieces that an age critic ideally needs—discourses, practices, and material conditions—came together. I had what felt like a book, a story with historical salience and psychological urgency. The story already had a name—midlife crisis—but that name is misleading: it implies that what is happening is only personal, intrapsychic, trivial, and occasional. I believe this given name hides one of the historic shifts I noted earlier—that it obscures a potential danger for the nation and the life course. The missing piece was to imagine resistance: a political agenda, a plausible collective to realize it, a more resistant self to join the collective.

To encourage that self in my self, I developed a new mixed genre. *Age autobiography* is life-writing acutely aware of how we are aged by culture. "The narrative turn" that had profound effects on the social studies had always been the beat of the humanities. I started from *age identity*, adding temporality to static postmodern identity theory by arguing that we can discover how aging has affected any one of our multiple identities. I know, for example, that "girl" or "woman" doesn't mean what it meant at 20 in 1960 to the same female person in 1998. Much of this knowledge is only semi-conscious, but writing it out could give us access to the basic idea that "aging" is a thread constitutive of all identities.

To conceptualize *age autobiography,* I had to add that a person could figure out how to do conjunctural analysis on her own ways of being-aged-by-culture, by applying insights from literary criticism, sociology, history, life-course development, age theory. I wrote about being socialized into decline lore from childhood on, and being resocialized into applying midlife decline narrative to myself, about having my son injected into X-er discourse and my mother subjected to matrophobia. I wrote about being dragged along by history: learning how to tell my own tiny hopeful progress narrative as a child reading under the cold drenching of the Cold War. Aware that culture compels us toward what Ulrich Beck calls "standard biographies" (1992, p. 134)—decline or progress narratives—I tried to figure out how writing *through* this material might slowly free us, enabling us to create our own secret stories. I found writing age autobiography quite difficult, partly because my fine theories had worked themselves into my practice quite unevenly. But if many people tried the genre, we would come closer to understanding the psyche-in-culture over time, a goal the disciplines dream of.

What difference could it make when the midlife becomes an object of study on a par with "old age" or "youth"? I hope cultural critics will no longer treat it simply as a solid background of power: e.g., the "parent culture," rich "Boomers." People in their middle years have never been homogeneous in privilege. Before 1900, when a "gerontocratic economy" ruled (Gullette, 1994), what good did age hierarchy do middle-aged men who were slaves or factory-workers, or women past child-bearing age? Those who study "fathers" and "mothers" historically or in film and fiction should be aware that parenting babies or middle-aged children are quite different matters. The very fact that people in the midlife age class can be objectified and named—as "Boomers" or "the middle-aged"—should warn us that the 20th century is an era in which "power" at midlife is waning even among those on whom it had been conferred. Fortunately, subcultural midlife narratives are beginning to appear (see Katherine Newman and Thomas Weisner in Shweder, 1998). It will become harder to ignore the vast range of midlife experiences.

Gerontologists—even feminists writing about women—often treat the midlife implicitly as a time that blends into old age prospectively, so that "aging" is a process that collapses 40 or 50 years of living and being represented. Gerontology thus inadvertently converges with the narrative of decline in using "later life" vaguely as the Other to youth. Age studies' focus on the midlife could help explode what Christoph

Conrad has called "this artificial unity" on which gerontology's "self-defined competence" was based (1992, p. 66).

Above all, adding the midlife means that we are aged by culture from birth through death. Age critics suddenly have an entire *life-course imaginary* to reckon with, instead of disjunct parts. This changes the object of study. I return to the new problematic this constructs after my third case.

Case #3 Against Youth in Crisis

Youth "is present only when its presence is a problem, or is regarded as a problem," according to Dick Hebdige, who helped found subcultural studies of youth in Britain (quoted in Acland, 1995, p. 28). Cultural critic Lawrence Grossberg considers youth too "an empty signifier" (1992, pp. 175–177). Charles Acland's *Youth, Murder, Spectacle* demonstrates how one figure of youth—"youth gone wild" (1995, p. 10)—can be utilized to create a sense of crisis in the U. S. Deviant youth—"and this is doubly true of African-American and Hispanic-American youth—is increasingly symbolically central, [. . .] defined as a threat to the stability of the social order" (p. 41). "This book is not about 'real' youth," he warns. It's about "a discursive construct" that often imagines a "white upwardly mobile youth standing in for the U.S. as a whole." He too believes that such fictions have "profound effects upon the imaginary formation of youth as well as the real lives of the young" (p. 20).

Acland's subject is the representation of youth crime in the 1980s, and the debates constructed around it. He singles out one White male-on-female murder in the upper-middle class (Robert Chambers's 1986 strangling of Jennifer Levin in New York, the so-called Preppie Murder), and follows its textual permutations through news reports, criminal confession, photos, editorials, TV movies, talk shows. With each medium he shows how the discourse about the crime worked: first, how the two main characters were narrated and how the legal system participated in the narration, so that the discourse worked to maintain traditional sex and gender relations and racial stereotypes; second, how the "crisis" was transposed as a "youth" crisis.

His details are riveting. The press picked Levin's murder instead of a simultaneous rape and murder that was witnessed by police officers who did nothing to stop it (p. 48). The dead woman was framed as a kinky seducer, as if she had the "male role of rapist," while the male murderer was given the part of the "not-too-bright bimbo" who went along as she ordered until things got out of control (p. 73; see also Benedict). Chambers's confession appeared to speak "the truth of female adolescent sexuality" rather than the truth of his misogyny or male sexual hysteria (p. 83). "As the initial crime is being left far behind," Acland argues, "a general crisis of youth is being established" through "the intractable activity of sounding alarms" (pp. 14, 112).

How could all this happen? Acland gives clues: "The next generation as a rhetorical concept has carried the impression of vision and hope," yet now, the young "cannot expect even the same quality of life as their parents" (p. 4). Age studies urges critics to try to determine the exact economics and politics of using age-classes for crises. In the mid-80s, did too many parents and adult children already anticipate a declining future for "the young"? In my own current work on the contrived war between the "Baby Boomers" and "Generation X" in the 1990s (Gullette, in press), the Bush recession that left young people without jobs led immediately to the construction of the "slacker" stereotype. The media took on the responsibility of muting sympathy and resistance by hinting that the victims didn't want to work hard enough; this also disciplined those who had jobs. A little later the growth of jobs led the media to spend years recharacterizing the X-ers as valuable members of society and then blaming all-powerful, selfish, envious, *"aging* Boomers" for having attacked helpless kids. What was hidden was the decline in good and secure jobs for people in their middle years as well as the young. Economic history was disguised as generational rivalry. In the 1990s, the press invented "juvenile superpredators," even though most violent crime is committed by adults; this label is eroding juridical distinctions between juveniles and adults (Templeton, 1998).

Age studies must also propose that a close look at a single age class be accompanied by an inquiry into how other age classes are affected. Acland notes that the rhetoric of youth in crisis points an accusing finger at "negligent parents," especially working mothers, and that all the debates have a conservative bias. "'Generation' has no fundamental essence except as a problem," he says early on (1995, p. 24). Generation "gaps" blind critics to "intra-cohort differences"; Audre Lorde adds that they construct "historical amnesia" (1984, p.117). Any construction of difference could be a problem for two or all generations. Yet Acland constructs his own generational difference when he invents "the disciplinary gaze of the adult" in film and decides it has a "patriarchal function as it attempts to replicate the qualities of the economic social" (1995, p. 118). Presumably this "adult gaze" is modeled on the "male gaze," a concept of film theorist Laura Mulvey that brought film criticism out of its universalizing fog by gendering it.

"The disciplinary gaze of the adult" could serve to analyze some movies. But Acland's term constructs a monolith of homogeneously censorious "adults." "Patriarchal gaze" might be a more fruitful term; at least it admits that power is unevenly distributed among adults. He ignores the gender of film-makers—still mostly male—and their chronological ages and psychological motives. Many turn their backs on their notion of "adult" perspectives, because the viewers they envision are mainly 12–28, or they themselves are young men, or because even though older they continue to identify with a particular junior self.

The tendency to homogenize "older" age groups arises from a deep problem in cultural studies: its "long love affair with masculinist youth culture, romanticizing the tough rebelliousness of working-class boys" (Medevoi, 1997b, p. 165, paraphrasing Angela McRobbie, 1991). Adding (young) women, as McRobbie herself did, still left only the young endowed with intra-cohort variability and compelling individuality. (Indeed, adding the once-neglected gendered or racial other often has the effect of fortifying the age class.) On the left, it can still be asserted that the young are—or once were—a naturally oppositional class. It would be considered condescending to suggest that their values or point of view might improve as they "mature." "Youth culture contains all the appeal of that contentious time *outside* the adult," Acland says oddly (1995, p. 137, my emphasis). He misconceives development as "the easy flow toward the adult" (p. 121). Nor does it occur to him that actors playing parents could and sometimes do model something other than the "economically productive" or the utterly failed. In youth studies, aging-into-adulthood seems to be an unimagined process; adulthood a flawed fall from grace; intergenerational relations primarily adversarial. There's no sense that this imaginary supports the cult of youth, or that the cult of youth reinforces middle-ageism, and that middle-ageism hardens gerontophobia. Surely, age studies can be class-conscious and antipatriarchal without being a priori hostile to development and adulthood.

IV

Conclusion

It is time to point out that each of the three cases I've analyzed foregrounds its own chosen age class and scales down others. For worthy reasons: resistance to ageism, middle-ageism, youth-as-crisis. But age fragmentation jams us onto the tiny separate terrains it has constructed. The fact is, we don't have much in the way of age studies yet. On the whole, we have sophisticated, fascinating, and revelatory *slice-of-life studies.* And we're likely to have more.

To undertake age studies properly, however, at least some critics and theorists need to study and relate all parts of the life-course imaginary, so that all of us may work with a sense of the problematics of the whole. Clearly, representations of crises of old age, midlife, and youth operate simultaneously, in their curious antagonistic ways, on American culture. There should be speculation about whether and how the "three" crises interrelate. (And, as I observed earlier, there are far more than three.) Do these crises get sequenced in popular imagination, so that people unconsciously believe in one or another life-course imaginary of their time? Violence and sexuality at the start of adulthood; rigid pathways and rigor mortis at the other end; in the middle, premature superannuation across the board? Or perhaps, for a higher class, beauty, flexibility, and promise in youth; lavish consumption and boughten friends at the end; in the middle, a contest between the "too-late" syndrome and a high age-wage curve, healthy positive aging, no retirement, and long life.

Let's ask whether people in different cohorts "read" the same sequence at all. If you're 30, do you misread or skip the chapters that 45-year-olds are supposed to attend to? It's no good snapping, "This is all unreal." Age fictions have effects. And a final question. Is it possible phenomenologically if not in logic that the social status of all age classes *qua* age classes is declining together?

A political scientist predicts that more public policy debates will be cast in young-versus-old terms. "Age will likely be to the next millennium what race [and, I would add, gender and sexual orientation, have] been to the last half of the twentieth century—a high-profile, highly divisive problem for which it will be extremely difficult to devise solutions that work" (MacManus, 1996, p. 252).[12] Once the wrong terms for a problem are locked in place, solutions often exacerbate the problem. Age ideology will be manipulated as we have seen: to construct standard biographies that end in later-life sorrow, to force groups into combat for allegedly scarce goods, to divide the citizenry and the workforce (and promote slice-of-life studies), to explain History and preclude intergenerational solidarity. For postindustrial economic forces around the globe, age is opportune.

Age theory is getting under way in the nick of time, I hope. It needs to prioritize what it wants to resist. In advance of anticipated debate, I single out *fragmentation of the life course* as one giant-sized enemy. Slice-of-life studies are scarcely the main obstacle. They will remain necessary within any theory of the whole. Among other things, they discover the circumstances under which age can be made so salient, and have so many ideological functions. The difficulties for theorists of the whole are practical, conceptual, psychological, disciplinary. To begin with, we lack terminology (Gullette, 1997b, chap. 10).While race and gender slowly come to be understood as socially constructed, age may turn out to be the most resistant to erosion, perhaps because of its undertheorized relation to "the body": the last biological given, the only essential, the one and only *real*. Even a mature age critic writes at any given moment out of only one age location, one generation, one historical experience of aging, calmed by the illusion of generational solidarity that comes from having moved from one age to the next.

Age studies must start with a deep suspicion of all age divisions and attributions, especially those we inherit. Yet what principles follow after? Objectivity? From the standpoint of what age? Equality? "Age equality"would be a treacherous goal. We must be willing to consider, and I would argue, maintain, the proposition that in current historical circumstances a hierarchy by age is the only fair and universal one, and that a modest, democratized age hierarchy must remain one foundation of a decent society. In an era when aging-into-the-middle-years is being devalued by global capitalism to reduce seniority systems and wage curves that rise with age, no one should blindly let age hierarchy slide out of historical memory. The costs are too high (Gullette, 1997b, pp. 226–240; 1998b). Were those in the middle years to find themselves "equal" competitors with the young in the workforce, the wage race to the bottom would indeed have hit bottom. Gerontologists, aware of the cultural devaluation that can afflict even the prosperous young-old, should lend their moral authority to shoring up and expanding the midlife age-wage peak. If we lose the midlife as a time of respect, aside from every other loss that entails, we lose all hope of fighting ageism and gerontophobia.

The generations must unite to survive. Deconstructing difference, age studies could emphasize a variety of continuities. Likenesses and reciprocity between familial generations, mutual influences, links between the fictive life-slices, and whole-life approaches—they need to be explicitly promoted as resistances to fragmentation and age war. Kathleen Woodward (1999) writes about loving bonds between herself and her grandmother, I about those with my mother and son. Historian Tamara Hareven shows how "one generation transmits to the next the ripple effects of the historical circumstances that shaped its life history" (1996, p. xiv); psychologists, how adolescent individuation affects midlife parents; memoirist Alix Kates Shulman, how much a midlife caretaker can enjoy her frail mother although she is suffering from Alzheimer's (1999). Cultural critics Jenny Hockey and Alison James find that tropes of dependency constructed for controlling children are used to marginalize the elderly (1993). Sociologist Doris Ingrisch (1995) interviewed Austrian women born early in the century about their growing unease with gender conformity, a hindrance that consciously pained them only later in life.

Age autobiography is premised on a basic continuity: that despite imposed and willed changes in selfhood, something called "I" always tells the stories about my many successive, lost, and parallel identities.

Some feminists critique continuous narrative because it can be modeled on men's lives or middle-class careers (Long, 1989; Walker in Walker, 1999). Perhaps women's continuity—if we still want binary life-course models—could be envisioned as based on overlapping or evolving traits, values, relationships, and work. In any case, stressing continuity in acceptable ways is going to matter more in the next millennium, as age theorists position themselves to answer the question, "What life-course imaginary can *we* develop to replace the divisive sequential-crisis model?"

The final challenge is to devise countermovements. Teachers can formulate appropriate training to heighten age-consciousness at every educational level, from Head Start to Elderhostel. We can monitor the media, treat "age" as a specialty for which expertise is required, make all divisive allegations of age difference seem suspect. We can develop legislative programs that will restore seniority to working life. The subtitle of a famous early longevity text was *Studies in Optimistic Philosophy* (1903).[13] At the beginning of the 21st century, age studies cannot be optimistic until, with strengths joined, we learn to name the current enemies of the life course, even within our selves and our disciplines; accurately describe the methods they deploy; and institute resistances that have some chance of success.

NOTES

The epigraph comes from Stein's *Geographical History of America. The Relation of Human Nature to the Human Mind.* 1973. New York, Vintage, p. 63. Thanks to Agnes Dunogue for bringing this passage to my attention. Thanks for editing help go to Kathleen Woodward, Teresa Mangum, Ruth Ray, and Tom Cole.

Some sections of this chapter are taken verbatim from other works of mine.

[1] On age-grading, see Chudacoff. On the transformation of old age, see Cole (1992). On retirement, Graebner. On gerontology, Katz. On adolescence, Spacks. On "the postgraduate mother" or what I call the "postmaternal woman," see Gullette (1995). On the middle years, I rely on research done for my work in progress *Midlife Fictions.* Work on the generation gap comes from "The Contrived War Between 'the Xers' and 'the Boomers.'" (Gullette, forthcoming)

[2] For the term "identity stripping," see Gullette (1997b), pp. 6, 8, 197, 169–170, 215–216.

[3] In fact, most of the 20th-century increase in longevity derives from decreases in infant mortality. Even in times and places where average age at death was, say, 35–45, royalty and the rich—including women who survived childbirth—lived long lives.

[4] On ageism in biotechnology discourse, see Woodward (1994); on youth in cold war rhetoric, see Medevoi (1997a).

[5] The question of who could be relatively immune to the concept of midlife decline is of immense potential interest. Gerontologists and age critics, people in subcultures or religions that maintain traditional values; feminists; people with instinctual narcissistic resistance to derogatory forces, the top 10% of the income curve—members of these groups might have some immunity.

[6] Curiously, the terms "conjuncture" and "representation" are also missing from *A Dictionary of Cultural and Critical Theory,* edited by Michael Payne.

[7] "Socially-informed humanities" comes from the self-description of the *South Atlantic Quarterly,* edited by Frederic Jameson.

[8] The name "age studies" was suggested by Gullette (1993); see also Wyatt-Brown, p. 5. The Age Studies book series at the University Press of Virginia started in 1993. The Rockefeller Fellowships in Age Studies began at Kathleen Woodward's Center for Twentieth Century Studies, at the University of Wisconsin (Milwaukee) in 1995.

[9] On the difference between ageism and gerontophobia, see Woodward, 1992.

[10] See also Gullette (1997b), calling for the sick and the elderly to write their own memoirs rather than letting their midlife children expropriate their experience for "filial illness-and dying accounts" (pp. 208–211). Woodward explains the midlife desire to see the old parent as weakened or humiliated as a "reverse Oedipal complex" in which the children enjoy taking the place of the parent in the power seat (1991, pp. 34, 37, 43).

[11] The term "culture of feeling" is Raymond Williams's (1966, p. 100).

[12] For a review of factors that might make for more or less conflict between age groups between now and 2020, see Bengtson, pp. 3–23.

[13] The author was Elie Metchnikov: *The Nature of Man. Studies in Optimistic Philosophy.*

REFERENCES

Achenbaum, W. A. (1992). Afterword: Integrating the humanities into gerontologic research, training, and practice. In T. R. Cole, D. B. Van Tassel, & R. Kastenbaum (Eds.), *Handbook of the humanities and aging* (pp. 458–472). New York: Springer Publishing Co.

Achenbaum, W. A. (1995). *Crossing frontiers. Gerontology emerges as a science.* Cambridge: Cambridge University Press.

Achenbaum, W. A., Weiland, S., & Haber, C. (Eds.). (1996). *Key words in sociocultural gerontology.* New York: Springer Publishing Co.

Acland, C. R. (1995). *Youth, murder, spectacle. The cultural politics of "Youth in Crisis."* Boulder, CO: Westview.

Bartky, S. L. (1990). *Femininity and domination: Studies in the phenomenology of oppression.* New York: Routledge.

Beck, U. (1992). *Risk society. Towards a new modernity.* Trans. Mark Ritter. London. Newbury Park, CA: Sage.

Bell, N. (1989). What setting limits may mean: A feminist critique of Daniel Callahan's setting limits. In M. Pearsall (Ed.) (1997), *The other within us.*

Feminist explorations of women and aging (pp. 151–159). Boulder, CO: Westview.

Benedict, H. (1992). *Virgin or vamp. How the press covers sex crimes.* New York: Oxford University Press.

Bengtson, V. L. (1993). Is the "contract across generations" changing? In Bengston & W. A. Achenbaum (Eds.), *The changing contract across generations* (pp. 3–23). New York: Aldine de Gruyter.

Bennett, T. (1992). Putting policy into cultural studies. In L. Grossberg, C. Nelson, & P. A. Treichler (Eds.), *Cultural studies* (pp. 23–50). New York: Routledge.

Benson, J. (1997). *Prime time. A history of the middle aged in twentieth century Britain.* London and New York: Longman.

Brennan, T. (1999). Social physics: Inertia, energy, and aging. In K. Woodward (Ed.), *Figuring age: Women, bodies, generations* (pp. 131–148). Bloomington: Indiana University Press.

Chudacoff, H. (1989). *How old are you? Age consciousness in American culture.* Princeton, NJ: Princeton University Press.

Cole, T. R. (1992). *Journey of life. A cultural history of aging in America.* Cambridge: Cambridge University Press.

Cole, T. R., Van Tassel, D. D., & Kastenbaum, R. (Eds.). (1992). *Handbook of the humanities and aging.* New York: Springer Publishing Co.

Conrad, C. (1992). Old age in the modern and postmodern Western world. In T. R. Cole, D. D. Van Tassel, & R. Kastenbaum (Eds.), *Handbook of the humanities and aging* (pp. 62–95). New York: Springer Publishing Co.

Graebner, W. (1980). *A history of retirement: The meaning and function of an American institution* 1885–1978. New Haven, CT: Yale University Press.

Grossberg, L. (1992). *We gotta get out of this place. Popular conservatism and postmodern culture.* New York: Routledge.

Gruman, G. J. (1978). Cultural origins of present-day "Ageism": The modernization of the life cycle. In S. F. Spicker, K. M. Woodward, & D. D. Van Tassel (Eds.), *Aging and the elderly: Humanistic perspectives in gerontology.* Atlantic Highlands, NJ: Humanities Press.

Gullette, M. M. (1988). *Safe at last in the middle years: The invention of the midlife progress novel.* Berkeley: University of California Press.

Gullette, M. M. (1993). Creativity, gender, and aging. A study of their intersections, 1910–1935. In A. M. Wyatt-Brown & J. Rossen (Eds.), *Aging and gender in literature: Studies in creativity* (pp. 19–48). Charlottesville: University Press of Virginia.

Gullette, M. M. (1994). Male midlife sexuality in a gerontocratic economy: The privileged stage of the long midlife in nineteenth-century age ideology. *Journal of the History of Sexuality, 5,* 58–89.

Gullette, M. M. (1995). Inventing the "postmaternal" woman 1898–1927: Idle, unwanted, and out of a job. *Feminist Studies, 21,* 221–254.

Gullette, M. M. (1997a). Age/Aging. In E. Kowaleski-Wallace (Ed.), *Encyclopedia of feminist literary theory.* New York: Garland.

Gullette, M. M. (1997b). *Declining to decline. Cultural combat and the politics of the midlife.* Charlottesville: University Press of Virginia.

Gullette, M. M. (1998a.). Midlife discourse in the twentieth-century United States: An essay on the sexuality, ideology, and politics of "Middle Ageism."

In R. Shweder (Ed.), *Welcome to middle age! (And other cultural fictions)* (pp. 3–44). Chicago: University of Chicago Press.

Gullette, M. M. (1998b). Politics of middle ageism. *New Political Science, 20,* 263–282.

Gullette, M. M. (in press) Age studies, and gender. In L. Code (Ed.), *Encyclopedia of feminist theories.* London: Routledge.

Gullette, M. M. (in press). The contrived war between 'the Xers' and 'the boomers.' *American Scholar.*

Hall, S. (1992). Cultural studies and its legacies. In L. Grossberg (Ed.), *We gotta get out of this place. Popular conservatism and postmodern culture* (pp. 277–294). New York: Routledge.

Hareven, T. (1995). Changing images of aging and the social construction of the life course. In M. Featherstone & A. Wernick (Eds.), *Images of aging. Cultural representations of later life* (pp. 119–134). London: Routledge.

Hareven, T. (1996). Introduction to *Aging and generational relations: Life-course and cross-cultural perspectives.* New York: Aldine de Gruyter.

Hepworth, M. (1987). The mid life phase. In G. Cohen (Ed.), *Social change and the life course* (pp. 134–155). London: Tavistock.

Hockey, J., & James, A. (1993). *Growing up and growing old. Ageing and dependency in the life course.* London: SAGE Publications.

Ingrisch, D. (1995). Conformity and resistance as women age. In S. Arber & J. Ginn (Eds.), *Connecting gender and ageing. A sociological approach.* Buckingham: Open University Press.

Katz, S. (1996). *Disciplining old age: The formation of gerontological knowledge.* Charlottesville: Univ. Press of Virginia.

Kohli, M. (1986). Social organization and subjective construction of the life course. In A. B. Sorensen, F. E. Weinert, L. R. Sherrod (Eds.), *Human development and the life course. Multidisciplinary perspectives.* Hillsdale, NJ: Lawrence Erlbaum.

Long, J. (1989). Telling women's lives: 'Slant,' 'straight' and 'messy.' In D. Unruh, & G. S. Livings (Eds.), *Current perspectives on aging and the life cycle. Vol. 3. Personal History Through the Life Course.* Greenwich, CT: JAI Press.

Lorde, A. (1984). *Sister outsider.* Trumansberg, NY: Crossing Press

MacManus, S. A., with P. A. Turner (1996). *Young v. Old: Generational combat in the 21st* century. Boulder: Westview.

McRobbie, A. (1991) *Feminism and youth culture. From 'Jackie' to 'Just Seventeen.'* Boston: Unwin Hyman.

Medevoi, L. (1997a). Democracy, capitalism, and American literature: The Cold War construction of J. D. Salinger's paperback hero. In J. Foreman (Ed.), *The other fifties.* [See original]. Urbana: University of Illinois Press.

Medevoi, L. (1997b). Reading the blackboard. Youth, masculinity, and racial cross-identification. In H. Stecopoulos, & M. Uebel (Eds.), *Race and the subject of masculinities* (pp. 138–169). Durham, NC: Duke University Press.

Mills, C. W. (1959). *The sociological imagination.* New York: Oxford.

Moody, H. R. (1993). Overview: What is critical gerontology and why is it important? In T. R. Cole, W. A. Achenbaum, P. L. Jakobi, & R. Kastenbaum (Eds.), *Voices and visions of aging: Toward a critical gerontology* (pp. xv–xli). New York: Springer Publishing Co.

Newman, K. (1998). Midlife experience in Harlem. In R. A. Shweder (Ed.), *Welcome to middle age! (And other cultural fictions)* (pp. 259–293). Chicago: University of Chicago Press.

Payne, M. (1996). *A dictionary of cultural and critical theory.* Oxford and Cambridge, MA: Blackwell.

Shulman, A. K. (1999). *A good enough daughter.* New York: Schocken.

Shweder, R. A. (1998). Preface. In R. A. Shweder (Ed.), *Welcome to middle age! (And other cultural fictions)* (pp. vii–viii). Chicago: University of Chicago press.

Spacks, P. M. (1981). *The adolescent idea. Myths of youth and the adult imagination.* New York: Basic Books.

Sudnow, D. (1967). *Passing on.* Englewood Cliffs, NJ: Prentice-Hall.

Templeton, R. (1998). Superscapegoating. Teen "superpredators" hype sets stage for draconian legislation. *Extra!* (January/February), pp. 13–14.

Walker, M. U. (1999). Getting out of line: Alternatives to life as a career. In M. U. Walker (Ed.), *Mother time. Women, aging, and ethics* (pp. 87–111). New York: Rowman and Littlefield.

Walker, M. U. (Ed.). (1999). *Mother time. Women, aging, and ethics.* New York: Rowman and Littlefield.

Weisner, T. S., & Bernheimer, L. P. (1998). Children of the 1960s at midlife: Generational identity and the family adaptive project. In R. A. Shweder (Ed.), *Welcome to middle age! (And other cultural fictions)*, (pp. 211–258). Chicago: University of Chicago Press.

Williams, R. (1966). *Modern tragedy.* Stanford, CA: Stanford University Press.

Williams, R. (1976). *Keywords: A vocabulary of culture and society.* New York: Oxford Univ. Press.

Woodward, K. (1991). *Aging and its discontents: Freud and other fictions.* Bloomington: Indiana University Press.

Woodward, K. (1992). Gerontophobia. In E. Wright (Ed.), *Feminism and psychoanalysis.* Cambridge: Basil Blackwell.

Woodward, K. (1994). From virtual cyborgs to biological time bombs. In G. Bender & T. Druckrey (Eds.), *Culture on the brink. Ideologies of technology.* Seattle: Bay Press.

Woodward, K. (1999). (Ed.). *Figuring age. Women, bodies, generations.* Bloomington: Indiana Univ. Press.

Wyatt-Brown, A. M. (1993). Introduction: Aging, gender, and creativity. In A. M. Wyatt-Brown & J. Rossen (Eds.), *Aging and gender in literature: Studies in creativity* (pp. 1–15). Charlottesville: University Press of Virginia.

Wyatt-Brown, A. M., & Rossen, J. (Eds.). (1993). *Aging and gender in literature: Studies in creativity.* Charlottesville: University Press of Virginia. Age Studies Series.

12

Social Science Toward the Humanities: Speaking of Lives in the Study of Aging

Steven Weiland

"I am not a good 'discipline' man and do not like boundaries," the famed cognitive psychologist Jerome Bruner (1983, p. 8) said a few years before he began working in a scholarly vein bringing him closer to the humanities. When he named "acts of meaning" as the primary focus of inquiry, and as the most desirable products of it, he challenged psychologists and other social scientists to remake their work with a fresh configuration of methods (Bruner, 1990). For most scholars loyalty to a discipline is essential to intellectual identity. But in young fields they can discover how scholarly habits fare when there are opportunities to adapt them to new problems. Any discipline will show in its history a record of give and take about methods. Our own time, with its debates about the sources and uses of knowledge, has been a demanding if fruitful one, with many opportunities for scholarly invention.

Thus, even as gerontology was making a role for itself in American academic life there were signs that its scientific ("positivist" or "objectivist" in the common shorthand) methods were going to have the skeptical attention not only of scholars in the humanities, but of social scientists. Historian W. Andrew Achenbaum (1987) and psychologist Nancy Datan (1987) agreed that gerontologists should question research conventions, there being the need to find forms suited for illuminating aging and its complexities. Achenbaum, reflecting on the dilemmas of the young field, cautioned against unnecessary parochialism in science and scholarship, and urged colleagues not to "lose sight of the larger forces and underappreciated anomalies that cumulatively might make one's findings mere artifacts" (p. 11). Datan proposed that "methodological heresies" be incorporated into the study of aging if it was to supply images of adult life in keeping with the deepest and most durable meanings of human experience at the border of science and myth.

In the years since these statements, scholars in the humanities working in gerontology, and their allies in other fields, have argued for "humanistic," "critical," or "imaginative" approaches to the study of adulthood and aging (Cole, Achenbaum, Jacobi, & Kastenbaum, 1993; Cole, Van Tassel, & Kastenbaum, 1992; Estes et al., 1992; Moody, 1988). Such work seeks to prompt empirical projects carried out from these perspectives, though without prescribing what texts might look like that meet the new criteria. The goal of this chapter is to identify work in the social sciences on adulthood and aging affiliated with the humanities.

The alternative (so to speak) gerontologies are part of the process by which the field, in its brief history, has come to recognize the great variety of problems it can investigate. In his account of the status of gerontology as a discipline, Stephen Katz (1996) identified the range of knowledge of aging, situated it among similar contemporary enterprises, and asserted its capacity for remaking itself in accord with allied scholarly activities. "Old age has become a significant, epiphenomenal resource for the production of knowledge because its sites of problematization are boundless, its disciplinary affiliations are multiple, and its universality is constantly recontextualized" (p. 119). Thus is the impact of humanistic perspectives on gerontological inquiry in the social sciences less a case of application and adaptation than of the unfolding of gerontology as a subject. Gerontology is one of those scholarly enterprises whose "marginality" reflects porous boundaries, a site for many kinds of scholarly "hybridization" which presumably can fill in gaps in knowledge beyond the capacities of routine disciplinary discourses (Dogan & Pahre, 1990). Even so, there are traditions of humanistic social science represented by, for example, Florian Znaniecki in sociology, Henry Murray in psychology, and Margaret Mead in anthropology, whose work preceded the hardening of disciplinary boundaries in the second half of this century.

In what follows there are first brief statements of the situation of the humanities and the general intention of humanistically oriented social science. There is then a review of developments in scholarship focusing on three primary groupings of ideas and methods associated both with the humanities and the social sciences: Interpretation, Rhetoric, and Narrative. After a brief comment on "critical gerontology" there is an account of humanistically oriented studies of aging in sociology, anthropology, and psychology. In a brief conclusion I suggest how humanistic social science in the study of adulthood and aging can be understood as a theoretical and empirical activity.

THE HUMANITIES AFTER THE CULTURE WARS

As is well known, disagreements about their meanings and uses have been part of the recent academic history of the humanities (e.g., Bérubé & Nelson, 1993; Bloom, 1987; Kernan, 1998; Levine, 1997). The turmoil in what are generally taken to be their core fields—literary studies, history, and philosophy—has centered on these issues: (1) The nature of knowledge or scholarly epistemologies, including the impact of "postmodern" ideas, and the uses of "theory" across the disciplines; (2) scholarly and scientific methods, including favored genres and the fate of the conventional voice of the scholar and scientist in the representation of behavior or experience; (3) the impact of demography, primarily the role of "diversity" or "multiculuralism" in the organization and representation of knowledge; and (4) the public responsibilities of the humanities, particularly with regard to the implications of theoretical and empirical work that focuses on race, class, and gender. As is evident in the latter two categories, age has been a less demanding element of inquiry but humanistic social science may help to make attention to late life more visible in the humanities.

The results of the debates over these issues have been inconclusive. That is because the work is in the humanities, where the combined epistemological, linguistic, demographic, social, and political challenges that produced the "culture wars"—the phrase used to refer to the institutional and public impact of the matters named above—will not yield anything but the best knowledge we can have of what divides us, and then perhaps strategies for teaching and writing from that conflicted position (Graff, 1992; Readings, 1996). If the scholarly and educational disputes are intractable, or even if they only appear to be so, there are still cultural consequences and the need for "making sense of how incommensurable moral disputes actually play out in the larger social world" (Hunter, 1996, p. 249). Policies and practices in aging are sites for such disputes and for a "reoriented" social science because of the potential for "rethinking knowledge" on fundamental questions of "method, values, mind, and self" (Goodman & Fisher, 1995). In these circumstances, the new category of scholarship called "cultural studies," as well as interdisciplinary projects in women's studies, may be called signs of the humanities "toward" the social sciences.

Still, in a paradox humanists can relish, there is little uncertainty or conflict in the humanities about their uses in revealing the limits of objectivist inquiry, and for guidance in reforming the social sciences. Thus, the "toward" in my title reflects two related meanings but also differences in the scholarly future that humanistic inquiry projects. "Toward" can suggest "in the direction of," as in the statement "I am leaning toward that position in the matter," and thus the adoption of a humanistic orientation even as any social science maintains its historical trajectory and essential commitments. But "toward" is also used with more durable directional force, when we say, for example, that we are "on the way to" a destination. Thus, the social sciences not only borrow from the humanities in an adaptive spirit but can be transformed by them, accepting new methods for new purposes.

In the view of many "critical" thinkers in gerontology, humanistic versions of sociology, anthropology, or psychology are not merely forms of these fields but their future, once recognition of the limits of objectivism and artificial disciplinary distinctions are enacted in the work of sufficient scholars. "Social science toward the humanities" names a way of working in gerontology and a program of disciplinary evolution in which traditional differences matter less than how individual scholars find opportunities in particular projects. The work exploits the freedom associated with uncertainty about the epistemology and meanings of aging, and with today's methodological pluralism, genre innovation, and reflexive habits of expression across the disciplines (Cole, 1992; Rosenau, 1992).

IN SEARCH OF LIFE AS A WHOLE

While social scientists speak with confidence about the necessity of quantitative methods they can no longer do so in the tones William Ogburn employed in his 1929 Presidential Address to the American Sociological Association. He predicted then that "In the future . . . everyone will be a statistician, that is nearly everyone. . . . Statistics will be identified with the subject matter of each social science rather than set apart as a special discipline" (cited in Maines, 1993, pp. 19–20). Ironically, Ogburn himself is the subject of an essay on qualitative methods in sociology, particularly biographical ones (Laslett, 1991). His case demonstrates the relations between personal and professional life, and the need for what another sociologist—in a suggestive metaphor—has called "Whole Life Social Theory" (Lemert, 1986).

There are influential statements by scholars in the humanities who have returned to the history of ideas in order to persuade scientifically minded colleagues in other fields of the traditions of inquiry concealed by today's disciplinary parochialism (Toulmin, 1990). But so too do the social sciences themselves house resistance to scientific or positivist conventions, now in abundance as accomplished scholars register their skepticism (e.g., McCloskey, 1995) and "qualitative methods" proliferate throughout the disciplines (e.g., the publishing success of a recent handbook on such methods [Denzin & Lincoln, 1994]).

In a representative recent statement, the sociologist of aging, Jaber Gubrium (1993), has challenged the methodological habits of his field, particularly the positivists' neglect of the subjective experience of their subjects, and one might add, of the person who is studying and representing them in scholarship. "As researchers, we diversely construct, deliberate over, debate, and periodically reformulate our own ideas about the lives we study. Why should we suppose that those studied don't do likewise also? (p. 6). Gubrium favors the metaphor of "surface" and "depth" to express the differences between statistical research and its opposite, often called "qualitative" rather than humanistic inquiry because of the implied symmetry and competition with "quantitative" research. Work in this format now generally carries abundant signs of the author's role in its making (see Behar, 1993, for a frequently cited example) but that, it should be noted, is increasingly seen as problematic of a popular element of text either because of its unacknowledged complexities (Marcus, 1994) or its unsuitability to the scholar's vocation, at least in social inquiry (Patai, 1994).

An equally popular way of characterizing the difference in methods can be observed in the choice of qualitative researchers in mainly quantitative fields to have as their distinguishing aim the "whole" subject, whether that is a social phenomenon or problem, a group, or an individual. As his work has changed over the years Gubrium—like those who share his stance—has made its goals, in particular representation of the intentions of his subjects, "take account of the meaning [of any experience] in relation to life as a whole" (p. 7). The "whole" here refers to the total experience of living for individuals *themselves,* as opposed to the areas of life of interest to gerontologists and other researchers who unnecessarily narrow their inquiries and focus attention on *their* understanding of what experience means to research participants. Scholars and scientists specialize but however they draw the limits of their work should not be mistaken for the way their subjects understand the significance of the phenomena of aging under study.

The "whole" can also refer to a stance toward inquiry some social scientists find missing from the work of colleagues: "Politicians and our academic experts find it easier to talk about the standard of living than about what a society might be living for. In social technocracy as in scientism, analytic reason has cut itself off from *the human whole* that could give some sense to its formal operations" (Rabinow & Sullivan,

1987, p. 16; emphasis added). Paradoxically, those dedicated to the whole will make the strongest effort to understand individual and subjective experience as concretely as possible, precisely the forms of knowing conventional social science rejects as irrelevant to "rational" discourse and policy making.

ACTORS AND THEIR STORIES

It is the rare social scientist—Bruner in psychology or Clifford Geertz in anthropology—whose experience in literature, history, and other fields shows up in his or her work. Instead, key humanistic themes can be observed in social science in the form of a related group of beliefs about problems of knowing and the uses of language and genre. It has been leading social scientists themselves who have come forward to redefine the meanings for their fields of ideas associated with the humanities: anthropologists and sociologists proposing the uses of *interpretation* (Clifford & Marcus, 1986; Geertz, 1973; Rabinow & Sullivan, 1987), political scientists, economists, and communications theorists insisting on the centrality of *rhetoric* (McCloskey, 1985; Nelson, Megill, & McCloskey, 1987; Simons, 1990), and psychologists and scholars in education naming *narrative* as the essential form for seeking and representing knowledge (Bruner, 1990; Casey, 1995; McAdams, 1993; Polkinghorne, 1988; Rosenwald & Ochberg, 1992).

This collective stance toward inquiry—with its independent manifestations in all three domains—includes features of "postmodernism" but it should not be taken as representing that large and often obscure category of ideas and practices, and its impact on social science (Rosenau [1992] offers a useful account). Each proposal for a new way to understand and to do scholarship has been described as a "turn" in the history of inquiry, providing a way of revealing the limits of previous forms of research and of suggesting how current and future work can better represent experience in aging and other domains.

Interpretation: In a pathmaking anthology of the 1970s (revised in the 1980s) anthropologist Paul Rabinow and sociologist William Sullivan traced the genealogy of the "interpretive turn" and offered examples of it in the work of figures like Habermas, Foucault, Geertz, Charles Taylor, and others (for a related effort see Hiley, Bohman, & Shusterman, 1991). In general, the goal of interpretive inquiry is primarily to reveal the meanings of human experience from the perspective of individuals, groups, institutions, and organizations being studied, with a prominent role also for the point of view of the researcher. Geertz (1973) names the chief criterion for an interpretive study to be that it is "actor oriented." But as his own ethnographies show, scholars themselves are now more clearly seen to be "actors" in their work though influential examples of humanistic social science exhibit varying ratios of attention to the author's part. Still, it is not position alone that defines interpretation, but intention, however deep, inaccessible, and even obscure the target of inquiry might be. So Geertz adds, risking a necessary but inevitable metaphor in a statement that characterizes inquiry across the social sciences and humanities, that "a good interpretation of anything—a poem, a person, a history, a ritual, an institution, a society— takes us into the heart of that of which it is the interpretation" (p. 18).

In an important essay by one of contemporary gerontology's founders, Bernice Neugarten (1985) relied on Rabinow and Sullivan to assert her own emerging differences with "rational empiricism" and to name the key features of the "interpretive framework":

> [T]here are no immutable laws; no reductionist models that are securely based in logical self-evidence; no "received" truths; and surely no value-free social science. Change is fundamental; change is dialectical; meanings are multiple and inexhaustible. The aim is understanding, within the limits of our cultural and historical present.

Neugarten names interpretation the cornerstone of "a more open world for social scientists," who can now practice diverse forms of inquiry, borrow from other fields, choose subject matter with greater freedom, and represent more self-consciously their own role in research.

Interpretation has gained many advocates in social science, too quickly and perhaps even too many from the perspective of Rabinow and Sullivan, who worry about it becoming simply another method. "Understanding the human world from within a specific situation" (p. 20) is what makes interpretation necessary and distinctive, as well as historical and moral. With newly defined vocations, interpretive social scientists need to know and express more about their subjects' lives, including what relations between subjects and scholars mean for any study.

Rhetoric: The "Rhetorical Turn" (e.g., Campbell & Benson, 1996) incorporates what has been called the "Linguistic Turn" in philosophy. But Richard Rorty (1992) is happy to assimilate that scholarly formation with the now widespread activity known as "Rhetoric of Inquiry." In identifying, as a young scholar, a new direction in inquiry, he wished to explore how it is that language ("marks and noises") is used by human beings in "the development and pursuit of social practices— practices which enable people to achieve their ends" (p. 373). To practice "Rhetoric of Inquiry"—I am paraphrasing Geertz (1988) in a similar vein on ethnographic writing—is to pay "attention to how [any disciplinary discourse] gets it effects and what those are" (p. 149).

Rhetoric of Inquiry has ancient roots in Greek and Roman oratory but it also reflects the postmodern position in intellectual and (less often) scientific and professional life that there are no eternal or fixed criteria of method or reasoning. Thus, as forms of prof ssional practice in old and new domains, texts reveal habits and possibilities of argument, narrative, metaphor and figurative expression, and other strategies of persuasion. According to Herbert Simons (1990) today's interest in rhetoric directs us to how scholarly genres are "instruments of discovery and sound judgment" (p. 15; see Nelson, Megill, & McCloskey [1987] for a second text that initiated in the late 1980s new attention to rhetoric across the disciplines).

In its broadest form, Rhetoric of Inquiry focuses on science, scholarship, and the professions as social institutions with distinctive habits of communication. In so far as knowledge depends on writing, part at least of the longstanding interest of scholars in the "sociology of knowledge" can be seen as the wish to understand the role of texts and of expressive practices as they differ by field in the history of ideas. By studying the forms of communication in a discipline or profession we can understand its epistemology, traditions, goals, claims, and relations with adjacent and sometimes remote fields of study and practice. As has been demonstrated for gerontology, the history of a discipline's rhetorical practices is also an account of how its authority is made, maintained, and changed (Green, 1993; Katz, 1996).

But to working scholars, and particularly those in new fields which represent competing disciplinary interests, rhetoric is a practical as well as a critical and historical matter. It is a format for understanding and producing individual texts, the classics that make up any discipline or professional tradition, and the work of scholars, scientists, and practitioners as it appears in recent and current books and periodicals. Scholars incorporate rhetorical interests into their work, reflecting both forms of activity, that is, a sense of their place in and resistance to discursive conventions and a wish to use the resources of expressive self-consciousness to make their writing persuasive and useful. They often do so without recognizing any affiliation with the "Rhetorical Turn" but with considerable care for how language and discourse operate in a text, particularly with regard to disciplinary genres, representing participants' perspectives, registering their own presence or "voice" in the text, and other matters.

Rhetoric of Inquiry is positioned at the border of the modern and postmodern. Thus, scholarly rhetoric in gerontology and other fields is "unstable, self-questioning and reflexive—always in the process of reconstituting itself" but it need not leave us adrift in relativism and uncertainty. "If it cannot lay claim to fixed and immutable standards of judgment, or to formal devices by which to compel assent, it can nevertheless provide ways of engaging one's hearers, of clarifying ideas and also of rendering them plausible or probable" (Simons, 1990, pp. 16–17). As a new field makes its way, seeking legitimacy and impact, it relies on both rhetorical tradition and innovation.

Narrative: According to proponents of the "narrative turn," we live "storied lives" where narrative guides experience as well as describing and explaining it (McAdams, 1993; Rosenwald & Ochberg, 1992). Thus, narrative is a form of knowing that supplies a temporally organized and ordered "self-concept." When made part of the "script" or "plot" of our lives, experience gains meaning. "We come to know ourselves by discerning a plot that unifies the actions and events of our past with future actions and the events we anticipate. Self-concept is a storied concept, and our identity is the drama we are unfolding" (Polkinghorne, 1988, p. 149).

In *Acts of Meaning* Bruner traces the genesis of recent scholarly interest in narrative. According to him the cognitive revolution—with its beneficial focus on the formative role of language—has finally recognized the work of the mind in culture, its habits of interpretation and situated meaning making. "It was probably the rising revolt against verificationist epistemology that freed social scientists to explore other ways of conceiving of Self aside from looking at it as a reckoning agent governed by logical rules" (p. 111). Bruner's own, and now well-known, contribution to these ways of thinking about thinking (and the behavior reflecting it) is a distinction between two forms of cognitive functioning—"paradigmatic" and "narrative"—and the kinds of inquiry deriving from them. The social sciences have favored paradigmatic or rule-seeking approaches over narrative ones, the latter aimed at revealing meaning in experience rather than rules for generalizing about it. But the difference has consequences not only for personal cognitive habits. It defines the worlds of science and scholarship, particularly the study of human development.

To be sure, Bruner grants that the "imaginative" application of the paradigmatic mode can lead to suggestive theorizing, sound arguments, and valuable empirical discoveries guided by well-reasoned hypotheses. But the narrative mode is designed to yield understanding of the meanings of experience to individuals themselves. Favoring pluralistic styles of thought rather than interdisciplinary ones, Bruner does not think that progress in science and humanistic inquiry will yield an integrated conception of knowing and human behavior: "As with the stereoscope, depth is better achieved by looking from two points of view at once" (p. 10).

Partisans and skeptics have asked of narrative researchers more precision in their methods (Atkinson, 1997; Phillips, 1994). In response to increasing enthusiasm for the very perspective he sought to promote,

Donald Polkinghorne (1995) has asserted that there is too much variety in work calling itself "narrative." As a "special type of discourse production" a narrative must be seen as a form that is shaped (or even constrained) by particular interpretive intentions. In "narrative analysis" as opposed to the "analysis of narratives," it is the task of the researcher "to configure the data elements into a story that unites and gives meaning to the data as contributors to a goal or purpose" (p. 15). He knows that the appeal of narrative is in its resistance to the quest for rules and prediction. Thus, in the kind of inquiry he proposes on behalf of complementary disciplines, "the search is for data that will reveal uniqueness of the individual case or bounded system and provide an understanding of its idiosyncrasy and particular complexity" (p. 15). Some scholars working in narrative understand "reveal" to mean making their texts mainly the medium for subjects' storytelling with varying ratios of expert commentary. Others, and Polkinghorne urges more efforts of this kind, actually adopt narrative for the form of their work, using a story (of an individual, an institution, etc.) to interpret aging. As I suggest below, some texts attempt both.

In the abundant recent work in aging deriving from the "narrative turn" there are virtually always signs, even if unacknowledged, of the allied turns. It is, I think, because it joins together interpretation and rhetoric in its appealing conventions (rooted in the humanities) for representing subjects' experience, that narrative has become such a popular format among gerontologists and other scholars for representing also their own experience, the work in language of discovery and reflection.

THE STUDY OF AGING AFTER "CRITICAL GERONTOLOGY"

The expression "speaking of lives" is adapted for my title from Gubrium (see later). It expresses all three "turns" as they appear in the work of social science "toward" the humanities. Thus, interpretive studies are "actor oriented" (in Geertz's terms) in bringing us the perspectives of research participants in their actual speech. Such speech, and that of the scholars who talk to participants and then organize and represent what they say for readers, is always rhetorical by nature or design. And the speech (or data) of which we now see more than any other kind is autobiographical or biographical, narrative being the genre favoring representation of the lives of a text's speakers: participants and scholars alike (Birren et al., 1996). Altogether, "speaking of lives" is an apt way to summarize the general direction of humanistic social science in gerontology, with its focus on life stories told in inventive ways, or on the expressive authority individuals themselves bring to the interpretation of the experience of aging.

"Interpretation," "rhetoric," and "narrative" are categories in which to observe the stance and activities of the humanistic researcher in any gerontological field. Of course, researchers have produced texts that represent the categories—and the issues and problems they include—in different ways. Still, as stated by sociologist Jon Hendricks (1996) in his account of methods for the study of aging, "If there is a single principle to which all qualitative research subscribes, it is that meaning emerges from human interaction and not from methodological procedures or disciplinary perspectives" (p. 55).

All three "turns" are represented in the stance toward the study of aging called "critical gerontology" (Cole et al., 1992). But it would be a mistake to assume that phrase to be a synonym for the pattern of scholarly influence and adaptation under review in this chapter, just as the "turns" have different meanings for particular empirical efforts. They are part of the debate about "theory" in scholarship generally, or the challenge to empiricists in the disciplines—from historians to demographers—to search out the epistemological, linguistic, and political premises of their work and weave them back into fresh formulations of the subject and the conditions of inquiry.

The contributions of the "critical" gerontologists have been primarily and usefully foundational. They have been aimed, in the tradition of "criticism" in the humanities, at searching out principles and defining conditions of practice (e.g., social policy [Moody, 1988] and education [Weiland, 1995a]). The task ahead is to identify characteristics of texts in the category of "social science toward the humanities."

MESSY TEXTS AND EXPERIENCE AS EVIDENCE

When gerontological inquiry in the social sciences is positioned "toward" the humanities it has characteristics of what Geertz (1983) called "blurred genres" and George Marcus (1994) named "messy texts." Geertz meant to identify the ways that inventive writing often claims two or more forms of knowing and representation. Thus, specifying the distinction between what should be classified as the social sciences and what as the humanities matters less than observing how it is that texts at the border gain the effects and audiences they do, and what thinking about behavior and society will come to mean if genres no longer have the force they have always had, or are redefined to "blur" their disciplinary legacies.

"Messy texts" name a kind of work marked by "its resistance to [the] too-easy assimilation of the phenomenon of interest by any given analytic, ready-made concepts." Such texts are disorderly, Marcus claims, because rather than being "fixed" in their methods they seek out analytic frameworks in "indigenous discourses," or represent the scholar "moving and acting within [the landscape] rather than being drawn in from a transcendent and detached viewpoint." These features of texts at disciplinary borders are among the primary resources of the "turns" named above. But "blurred" and "messy" are subjective categories meant to describe a great variety of intentions and forms.

In offering accounts of three recent books displaying "social science toward the humanities" I do not claim that they are typical or exemplary, particularly because the criteria are only now emerging. In making arguments, the social sciences have sought evidence for purposes of demonstrating causes and generalizing across cases. Humanistic social science seeks the representation of experience as the evidence that counts most in illuminating the meanings of human thought, speech, and action. Accordingly, each of the texts described below focuses on the lives of individuals, in the manner of literature or history we might say, for a "science" reflecting new ratios of the analytic authority of scholars to the perspectives of research subjects (or participants as they are often called in humanistic social science).

Ordinary Talk of Aging: What is a sociologist to do when he comes to believe that his field, and the policy makers in long-term care it supports, must see beyond "formal criteria" or "cosmetic evidence" in understanding the experience of nursing home residents? Messages come from the aged in forms that are "indecipherable" to care givers, demanding new ways of listening. Indeed, the paradox of research among the elderly is that much that needs to be said about their lives and interests is beyond words. Only a social scientist committed to the exploration of radical change in methods (Gubrium & Holstein, 1997) would risk urging scholars, as Gubrium (1988) did in a study of "poetic documentation" in Alzheimer's disease, to pay less attention to what words plainly communicate than to what they do not, "yet admittedly do," somehow tell us. Thus, Gubrium (1989) asserts that "against the incommunicable, studies that model and measure the domestic meaning of institutionalization are experientially inauthentic" (p. 98). In the decision to place someone in a nursing home there is an "unspecifiable underlife" that comes through only by "attending descriptively to its native and practical character" (p. 105).

In *Speaking of Life* (1993) Gubrium presents the narratives of 22 nursing home residents, sometimes in the form of actual interview transcripts. Though the stories are "mundane" they reveal that "quality of life and quality of care, in residents' voices, are not so much rationally assessable conditions, as they are horizoned, ordinary, and biographically active renderings of lifelong experience" (p. xvi). These accounts are shaped jointly by the speakers and Gubrium, and by the metaphor of "horizon," a spatial concept made temporal. Thus, as the aged themselves "see" late life, a distant but defining boundary gives form to experience. A horizon is (literally) the boundary of that part of the earth's surface visible from a given viewpoint. But it is used by Gubrium to suggest the extent of any sphere of thought or action seen against distant antecedents or anticipated continuities. Thinking and feeling in terms of "horizons" allows individuals to situate their experiences in ways of living that have emerged over many years, and which continue to have meaning even in contexts offering (or demanding) redefinition according to institutional or medical criteria. Thus "disability" or "faith" or "marriage" are horizons providing meaning over time to those looking back on their lives for purposes of telling a unified and purposeful story of their experience needed in the present and the future.

The participants in Gubrium's study, being "biographically active" or eager to situate themselves in a long and ongoing narrative of living, resist taking on the fixed and narrow institutional role of nursing home resident that sociological studies of aging and health generally provide. So too does Gubrium himself reject, in his revised rhetoric of inquiry, the roles of conventional interviewer and sociological author with what they suggest about his analytic authority. Instead, he recognizes how it is that the participants construct and reconstruct their lives outside another generontological convention, the well known "life review." While there are occasional "terminal horizons," with their stock-taking and efforts at a final reckoning, participants speak of their lives with an active sense of the present and future. Gubrium supplies what Bryan Green (1993) calls gerontology's characteristic "narrative voice" as a mediator in the "plot" making the aged a challenge or even a threat to modern society (p. 145). He insists on the primacy of the talk of everyday life because it reflects an "ordinary" and practical rationality among the aged: "[T]heorists of the self should . . . attend to the descriptive organization of everyday situations and vocabularies that fuel the self's embodiments" (Gubrium & Holstein, 1994, p. 699).

Before interdisciplinariety became a scholarly and curricular trend, research innovations like ethnomethodology tested some limits of social science and generated forms of inquiry consistent with the orientation of the humanities (Gubrium & Holstein, 1997). Gubrium works in this vein, but with the burden (though he would not call it that) of reproducing in texts the "mundane" and the "ordinary" as forms of argument as well as representations of experience. This is especially the case when an author, like Gubrium here, wishes to constrain his interpretive habits in order to defer to research participants. In forgoing what is prized in the humanities—a vivid sense of authorship—Gubrium offers a timely lesson in how they can influence the social sciences in other ways. In this case, he believes it is in the art of the ordinary.

Aging and Professional Identity: Work and careers are topics of infrequent attention in the study of aging, particularly so if there is a focus on what is conventionally called the "post-retirement" years. But occupational or professional identity is a cornerstone of lifespan development. The study of careers has been the province of the social sciences but recent work demonstrates the interpretation (as above) of what work means, including its role in "storied" lives (Young & Collin, 1992).

In *The Healer's Tale* (1993) anthropologist Sharon Kaufman explores the careers of seven physicians whose lives span the period of the transformation of American medicine. Each was transformed as well as a professional (by new technologies for example) and as a person, with regard to the peculiar dilemmas and responsibilities of medical and scientific practice. Kaufman adopts an unusual rhetorical structure for her study, dividing and arranging the life stories as told to her by her subjects against the background of the history of American medicine from the 1920s to the 1980s. Thus, each "healer's tale" begins with education and training and ends with reflections from the perspective of late life on the meanings of experience in medicine over a long and productive career. All of the physicians were in their eighties when they were interviewed by Kaufman. As we hear their voices we get a part of each story contextualized by the predominant medical themes of a period, like the introduction of antibiotics after World War II.

Kaufman's approach is private in the manner of the anthropological life history, and it is public in the sense that each personal account is part of the history of medicine and of the social and economic processes that have brought it to its current state. Medicine changed dramatically as the doctors advanced in their careers. "Care was superseded by cure, and the long-held values of consolation and empathy came to be informed by the standardized and quantifiable methods of laboratory science" (p. 16). Thus, in their own way Kaufman's subjects themselves faced the dilemma of today's humanistically minded social scientist, that is, having methods deriving from strongly held values at odds with the professional conventions that supply mature career identity.

As an anthropologist Kaufman focuses on the "culture" of medicine, or the traditions and habits of practice (in thinking, feeling, relationships, etc.) making it to insiders and outsiders a distinctive form of work and, indeed, of living. As a partisan of the life history approach she presents intimate portraits of the participants in her study, largely in their own words. They speak of their lives, of course, in tones and on subjects generally very different from Gubrium's nursing home residents. And their long careers (though they are not without disappointments) are revealed to be, from the perspective of their late life and in Kaufman's own view, resources for a "good old age" (p. ix). Thus biography fulfills the normative obligations often associated with it in the humanities (Weiland, 1989).

But Kaufman not only offers "narrative analysis" via aggregate life history of the emergence of modern American medicine but, according to Polkinghorne's distinction, "analysis of narrative" as a way of having speech disclose more than it says (in the manner of Gubrium's poetic stance). As in other work (Kaufman, 1997), to carry out her interpretive project she must guide our readings of her subjects' stories even as their experiences and perspectives are represented as the rationale for the text. The familiar resource of the interview presents the social scientist with data for a text. The humanities show their influence on such material as scholars display abilities and judgments as readers, or as critics who must penetrate the text (as tape or transcript) to the same degree that they are devoted to bringing forward the voices of their subjects.

Kaufman believes that medicine today is in a "state of moral confusion" about the consequences of its transformation by science and technology. "The whole patient has been dismantled," she says in evoking that familiar figure, "and seemingly abandoned" (p. 302). But contrary to what we might expect in a study of elders, presumably wise enough to make themselves spokesmen for Kaufman's challenge to medicine, the doctors generally avoid talk of medicine's current moral dilemmas. True enough, they are aware of the "hurry of modern medicine" (p. 305), particularly as that is revealed in the demise of the house call and charity work, and the strains put on bedside manner by the routines of the hospital. And "with the wisdom of long experience" they regret the disappearance of what Kaufman calls the "generalist philosophy" they held. Thus they are often suitably ambivalent about the consequences of subspecialization and the near absolute reliance on medical technology.

What they are seemingly reluctant to address, however, indicates to Kaufman a critical absence in medicine. "Few elders, those individuals who are able to impart a sense of vision and overall purpose . . . are present in a manner sustained enough or authoritative enough to compete with the compelling, necessary, and all pervasive procedural and technological tasks of day-to-day hospital medicine" (p. 319). With so much at stake in medicine's well known moral dilemmas Kaufman speaks up herself on the meanings of the lives of her subjects. If they are now professionally "speechless," humanistic gerontology can give them a voice in medicine today and tomorrow. The "healer's tale" is thus a medium for understanding medicine's past but also what is missing from but still might be supplied to its present and future.

Unlike the work of mainstream academic humanists, Kaufman's work in narrative is decidedly practical. For her and other medical anthropologists, the "narrative turn" means that an ethnographic story-teller produces such texts as part of new roles in clinical intervention in people's lives, sometimes at the level of institutional policies as in *The Healer's Tale,* and sometimes very much more directly in clinical work itself (Kaufman, 1997). In the former, her moral tone reflects the lessons she herself has learned from her subjects, giving her interpretive stance plain subjective meaning and making her text humanistic to the degree that it is rhetorically activated by her preference for a genre experiment (a "messy text") that represents aging in professional life. We understand late life better—what is said, not said, and needs to be said of individual lives—because it is presented in a narrative well situated in experience and history.

Encountering Aging, Creating Conversations: Israeli psychologist Amia Lieblich's work has made her increasingly self-conscious about the nature of "psychological truth," and about its place in the methods most likely to gain access to and represent the life course. With the American psychologist Ruthellen Josselson (1996) she has challenged her colleagues to modify, if not abandon, the rhetorical structure of inquiry in their discipline. In *Conversations with Dvora* (1997) Lieblich offers a text as remote from the conventions of academic psychology as her subject—the reclusive writer Dvora Baron (b. 1887)—was from the intellectual mainstream. Turning more and more inward in midlife as she became preoccupied with her past and her unexpected and demanding fate as an Israeli pioneer in the first decades of the twentieth century, she established a pattern of living in which she never left her Tel Aviv apartment. Baron died in 1956. The text is organized into 24 imagined "encounters" Lieblich has with Baron in the last year of her life. Aging is at the center in this dialogical autobiography, particularly so as Lieblich brings into the encounters awareness of how the conditions and imperatives of her own life and career shape her text and the talk it represents.

Lieblich admires Dvora Baron as a writer and sensed that her unusual experience of adulthood and aging would yield insight into solitude and creativity. She was in midlife herself as she began work on her book and facing a personal and professional crisis, in part reflecting her deepening displeasure with the limits of academic psychology and its insistence on a suitable and objectifying distance between scholars and their research subjects. She was taught but now rejects the idea that it is "essential to distinguish between fact and interpretation, data and theory, as if the borders between them were etched in stone" (p. x). By ignoring such canons of research, Leiblich believed that Baron's unusual behavior might have something to teach her. She knew Baron's stories but not her whole personal "story," at least in the form that would yield to psychological inquiry. Baron had already been dead for more than three decades and there was no first hand account of her life that provided the psychological insight Lieblich thought it might hold. The scholar's solution was a radical one, representing one of the most inventive recent examples of humanistic social science.

For Gubrium, "speaking of life" means bringing forward the words of the participants in his study and using his own voice largely to reinforce and situate theirs in the search for a suitable vocabulary to evaluate long-term care. He is by no means a reluctant scholar but he believes that authority derives from what is communicated directly through the experience of research subjects, and that aging brings a revealing and highly functional form of "horizon"-based autobiographical speaking. Kaufman is equally committed to an interpretive stance focusing on the meanings made in her subjects' own talk. But she intervenes on their behalf when her policy related interests reveal the limits of what the doctors' narratives can say about what she believes it is necessary to address. Lieblich, wishing for the voice of a subject who cannot now actually "speak" at all, chooses to supply it herself by becoming Dvora Baron's "autobiographer." Such an effort would be dismissed as a narrative impossibility except in a time of "blurred genres" and "messy texts" which themselves express the epistemological anomalies of postmodern scholarship in the humanities. "Where can we find the definitive voice of experience?" she says, "Are not interpretations, expressions of meaning whatever their source, closer to the truth?"

Thus, Lieblich must abandon the empirical dogma of her discipline, and experiment in narrative, as she reconstructs Baron's life in her own voice (there are two "hers" in this text). She uses material from Baron's stories, and relies on interviews with people who knew the writer and her period to make her account as authentic as possible. In an explanation of how she gathered her data, sure to rouse academic colleagues in social science, Lieblich says: "I assumed that, just as imagined material provides important information to psychologists, Baron's creative works reflected her personal reality, and there was no point in questioning whether the stories she described ever occurred." Despite their differences, Lieblich came to identify strongly with Baron's personality, and "this empathy helped me construct her character until I saw her before my eyes as if she were alive, and heard her voice speaking to me" (p. x).

Whatever its rhetorical innovations, Lieblich intended her book to be about psychology and aging in a highly idiosyncratic life. The Dvora Baron of her imagination has many of the characteristics that psychologists now assign to late life, particularly her intense interiority and wish to make meaning from memory. But her resistance to any theory of aging—and ironically so because the format of the conversation puts her in the presence of a professional psychologist and student of the life cycle—are what make the text an example of the encounter between the social sciences and the humanities. Moreover, the unusual rhetorical structure of the text provides numerous instances of dialogue in which it is clear that the psychologist is using the form of the encounter to represent division and potential synthesis in her own thinking about aging. Thus at one point she says this after Baron (or Lieblich using Baron's voice) offers an account of her efforts to break away from village life and to become a university student: "You were an adolescent, the age when people construct their identities through the struggle between competing paths and values." Baron responds as she often does to Lieblich's textbook like analyses of her experience and memories: "Very nice she said with a touch of disdain, but even in my old age I am still left with these parts competing in me" (p. 80).

As her relationship with Dvora develops, Lieblich gradually gives up her professional vocabulary in favor of a more natural psychology expressed in a literary voice. In a particularly telling passage Lieblich has Baron urge her to make her academic psychology resemble fictional narratives.

> I try to shed some warmth and light on the sufferings of my characters by the very fact that I describe them. . . . One should not work one's material too much; explanation only further obscures things. One must learn to direct one's vision so things become visible in their own light. The intelligent reader can sense what is there in the darkened room, in the spaces around the page. (p. 206)

"I wish I could learn your art" is how Lieblich has herself reply in the text, a reminder of her decision to maintain enough detachment in her imagined encounters with Baron to allow her to react to them as a social scientist loyal to professional norms as they can serve innovations.

As the end—of Baron's life and the text—draws near, Lieblich's imagination joins with Baron's in a particularly intense way, their two voices seeming to merge (though it is prose from one of Baron's stories) in an evocation of life's seasons. "I could see her drawing deep into herself before my eyes; and along with it growing and expanding in perfect clarity, eyes radiant and wise" (p. 319). Lieblich evokes Baron's childhood memories, and states the terms of her reconciliation with the events of her personal and professional lives, in recognition of what will be required of her too in fortitude and consolation. Author and subject age together. In a gesture that simply but profoundly represents the reflexive structure of today's social science, Lieblich says simply, "I see the coming days" (p. 319).

CONCLUSION: WORLDS WE KNOW AND NAME

Dvora Baron tells Lieblich—an artist advising a psychologist—that "truth has many faces, according to when it is told" (p. 26). Indeed, such a sentiment—with its hint about aging and epistemology—might be claimed as a motto for the stance of humanistic social scientists. But a small minority, however independent, in the mainstream disciplines must recognize the firm structure of academic work. As Rosenau (1992) concluded in her account of conflicts in the aims and methods of scholarship, "post-modern social science is in its infancy, and thus, like many incipient paradigms, its overall shape and character is vague, its substantive contribution still shadowy and fragmentary, mixed and uneven" (p. 169).

Not so vague, I have sought to show here, because "speaking of lives" as a biographical orientation demonstrates, for the study of adulthood and aging at least, a convergence around a fruitful set of themes and methods shared with the humanities. In this form is represented too ambivalence about the uses of conceptual schema in social science texts, if not in the scholarly reflection that stands behind them. As Baron/Lieblich urges above, things must "become visible in their own light." In effect, as sectors of the humanities adopt a more abstract and "theoretical" posture, social scientists recover some of the humanist's animating particularism.

Gerontology is a young field, but no different in its fragmentation from the ones it relies on in the social sciences and the humanities. As Achenbaum's (1995) authoritative history of the study of aging shows, gerontologists have always been divided about aims and methods. And his proposals for the future of the field recognize its paradoxical if not conflicting needs and possibilities, spread across many disciplines and specialties. "There is still too little science in this multidisciplinary endeavor," and in some sectors of the field seemingly too much, as efforts in "critical" gerontology and other innovations are welcomed as resources for increasing the range of gerontology's meanings and uses. For, "investigators should consider a fuller repertoire of ideas about aging, including promising theories outside their specialties."

Neugarten (1985), though favoring "interpretation" and other revisions in method, did not wish to abandon all conventions of evidence and argument. What is needed are "theories of the middle range, even if theories are themselves interpretations." The humanities help us to moderate our intentions in the direction of human possibility. "We can attempt to represent the world that can be known to us, if not the 'true' world" (p. 293). Influential humanities scholars—some very traditional in their practices—are speaking in similar tones (Kernan, 1997). Presumably the "middle" is a resource for bringing together what is reconcilable among differing methods, although, as noted above, social and behavioral scientists like Bruner who are inclined toward the humanities, believe in the heuristic value of dichotomies.

One of Kaufman's doctors says of the ethical situation of medicine, "I don't think we are in a position to make judgments, we are only in a position to make observations" (p. 303). Many postmodern scholars in the social sciences and humanities would agree. But the question is open—for them if not always for physicians—about the forms for observing adulthood and aging. In representing the aging as story-tellers such "reciprocal acts" help us to resist categorical thinking because of the interpretive opportunities and choices in narrative, long a primary lesson in the humanities (Cohler & Cole, 1996).

A "blurred" or "messy" text signifies the possibilities of scholarship as well as its constraints. Innovative academic authors "struggle to pro-duce, within the given formats and practices of analytic writing, unex-pected connections and thus new descriptions of old realities and, in doing so, to critically displace sets of representations that no longer seem to account for the worlds we thought we knew, or at least could name" (Marcus, 1994, p. 391). In what spirit and in what forms gerontol-ogy's most inventive social scientists "know" and "name" their worlds of inquiry will depend not only on how they work within their own fields but in what ways they represent their alliance with the humanities.

REFERENCES

Achenbaum, W. A. (1987). Can gerontology be a science? *Journal of Aging Studies, 1,* 3–18.

Achenbaum, W. A. (1995). *Crossing frontiers: Gerontology emerges as a science.* New York: Cam-bridge University Press.

Atkinson, P. (1997). Narrative turn or blind alley? *Qualitative Health Research, 7*(3), 325–344.

Behar, R. (1993). *Translated woman: Crossing the border with Esperanza's story.* Boston: Beacon.

Bérubé, M., & Nelson, C. (Eds.). (1995). *Higher education under fire: Politics, eco-nomics, and the crisis of the humanities.* New York: Routledge.

Birren, J. E., Kenyon, G. M., Ruth, J., Schroots, J. J. F., & Svensson, T. (Eds.). (1996). *Aging and biography: Explorations in adult development.* New York: Springer Publishing.

Bloom, A. (1987). *The closing of the American mind: How higher education has failed democracy and impoverished the souls of today's students.* New York: Simon and Schuster.

Bruner, J. (1983). *In search of mind: Essays in autobiography.* New York: Harper and Row.

Bruner, J. (1990). *Acts of meaning.* Cambridge, MA: Harvard University Press.

Campbell, J. A., & Benson, K. R. (1996). The rhetorical turn in science studies. *Quarterly Journal of Speech, 82,* 74–109.

Casey, K. (1995). The new narrative research in education. *Review of Research in Education, 21,* 211–253.

Clifford, J., & Marcus, G. (Eds.). (1986). *Writing culture: The poetics and politics of ethnography.* Berkeley: University of California Press.

Cohler, B., & Cole, T. (1996). Studying older lives: Reciprocal acts of telling and listening. In Birren et al. (Ed.), *Biography and aging* (pp. 61–76).

Cole, T. R. (1992). *The journey of life. A cultural history of aging in America.* New York: Cambridge University Press.

Cole, T. R., Achenbaum, W. A., Jacobi, P., & Kastenbaum, R. (Eds.). (1992). *Voices and visions of aging: Toward a critical gerontology.* New York: Springer.

Cole, T. R., & Gadow, S. (Eds.), (1986). *What does it mean to grow old: Reflections from the humanities.* Durham, NC: Duke University Press.

Cole, T. R., Van Tassel, D., & Kasterbrum, R. (Eds.). (1992). *Handbook of the humanities and aging.* New York: Springer Publishing.

Datan, N., Rodeheaver, D., & Hughes, F. (1987). Adult development and aging. *Annual Review of Psychology, 38,* 153–180.

Denzin, N., & Lincoln, Y. (Eds.). (1994). *Handbook of qualitative research.* Thousand Oaks, CA: Sage.

Dogan, M., & Pahre, R. (1990). *Creative marginality: Innovation at the intersections of the social sciences.* Boulder, CO: Westview Press.

Estes, C. L., Binney, E. A., & Culbertson, R. A. (1992). The gerontological imagination: Social influences on the development of gerontology, 1945–present. *International Journal of Aging and Human Development, 35,* 29–45.

Geertz, C. (1973). Thick description: Toward an interpretive theory of culture. In C. Geertz (Ed.), *The interpretation of cultures.* New York: Basic Books.

Geertz, C. (1983). Blurred genres: The refiguration of social thought. In C. Geertz (Ed.), *Local knowledge: Further essays on interpretive anthropology.* New York: Basic Books.

Geertz, C. (1988). *Lives and works: The anthropologist as author.* Stanford, CA: Stanford University Press.

Goodman, R. F., & Fisher, W. R. (Eds.). (1995). *Rethinking knowledge: Reflections across the disciplines.* Albany: State University of New York Press.

Graff, G. (1992). *Beyond the culture wars: How teaching the conflicts can revitalize American education.* New York: Norton.

Green, B. S. (1993). *Gerontology and the construction of old age: A study in discourse analysis.* New York: Aldine De Gruyter.

Gubrium, J. (1988). Incommunicables and poetic documentation in the Alzheimer's disease experience. *Semiotica, 72,* 235–253.

Gubrium, J. (1989). The domestic meaning of institutionalization. In E. L. Thomas (Ed.), *Research on adulthood and aging: The human science approach.* Albany: State University of New York Press.

Gubrium, J. (1993). *Speaking of life: Horizons of meaning for nursing home residents.* Haw-thorne, NY: Aldine De Gruyter.

Gubrium, J., & Holstein, J. (1994). Grounding the postmodern self. *Sociological Quarterly, 35*(4), 685–703.

Gubrium, J., & Holstein, J. (1997). *The new language of qualitative methods*. New York: Oxford University Press.

Hendricks, J. (1996). Qualitative research: Contributions and advances. In R. Binstock & L. George (Eds.), *Handbook of aging and the social sciences*. San Diego: Academic Press.

Hiley, D. R., Bohman, J. F., & Shusterman, R. (Eds.). (1991). *The interpretive turn: Philosophy, science, culture*. Ithaca, NY: Cornell University Press.

Hunter, J. D. (1996). Reflections on the culture wars hypothesis. In J. L. Nolan (Ed.), *The American culture wars: Current contests and future prospects*. Charlottesville: University Press of Virginia.

Josselson, R., & Lieblich, A. (1996). Fettering the mind in the name of "science." *American Psychologist, 51*(6), 651–652.

Katz, S. (1996). *Disciplining old age: The formation of gerontological knowledge*. Charlottesville: University Press of Virginia.

Kaufman, S. (1986). *The ageless self: Sources of meaning in late life*. Madison: University of Wisconsin Press.

Kaufman, S. (1993). *The healer's tale: Transforming medicine and culture*. Madison: University of Wisconsin Press.

Kaufman, S. (1997). Construction and practice of medical responsibility: Dilemmas and narratives from geriatrics. *Culture, Medicine, and Psychiatry, 21,* 1–26.

Kernan, A. (Ed.). (1998). *What's happened to the humanities?* Princeton, NJ: Princeton University Press.

Laslett, B. (1991). Biography as historical sociology: The case of William Fielding Ogburn. *Theory and Society, 20*(4), 511–538.

Lemert, C. (1986). Whole life social theory. *Theory and Society, 15*(3), 431–442.

Levine, L. (1996). *The opening of the American mind: Canons, culture and history*. Boston: Beacon.

Lieblich, A. (1989). *Transitions to adulthood during military service: The Israeli case*. Albany: State University of New York Press.

Lieblich, A. (1997). *Conversations with Dvora: An experimental biography of the first modern Hebrew woman writer*. Trans. N. Seidman. Berkeley, CA: University of California Press.

McAdams, D. P. (1993). *The stories we live by: Personal myths and the making of the self*. New York: William Morrow.

McCloskey, D. (1985). *The rhetoric of economics*. Madison: University of Wisconsin Press.

McCloskey, D. (1995). Economics and the limits of scientific knowledge. In Goodman and Fisher (Eds.), *Rethinking knowledge: Reflections across the disciplines*. Albany: State University of New York Press.

Maines, D. R. (1993). Narrative's moment and sociology's phenomena: Toward a narrative sociology. *Sociological Quarterly, 34*(1), 17–38.

Marcus, G. (1994). On ideologies of reflexivity in contemporary efforts to remake the human sciences. *Poetics Today, 15,* 383–404.

Moody, H. R. (1988). *Abundance of life: Human development policies for an aging society*. New York: Columbia University Press.

Nelson, J., Megill, A., & McCloskey, D. (Eds.). (1987). *The rhetoric of the human sciences: Language and argument in scholarship and public affairs*. Madison: University of Wisconsin Press.

Neugarten, B. (1985). Interpretive social science and research on aging. In A. Rossi (Ed.), *Gender and the life course.* New York: Aldine de Gruyter.

Patai, D. (1994). Sick and tired of scholars' nouveau solipsism. *Chronicle of Higher Education, 23,* A52.

Phillips, D. C. (1994). Telling it straight: Issues in assessing narrative research. *Educational Psychologist, 29*(1), 13–21.

Polkinghorne, D. (1988). *Narrative knowing and the human sciences.* Albany: State University of New York Press.

Polkinghorne, D. (1995). Narrative configuration in qualitative analysis. *International Journal of Qualitative Studies in Education, 8*(1), 8–25.

Rabinow, P., & Sullivan, W. M. (Eds.). (1987). *Interpretive social science: A second look.* Berkeley: University of California Press.

Readings, B. (1996). *The university in ruins.* Cambridge, MA: Harvard University Press.

Rorty, R. (Ed.). (1992). *The linguistic turn: Essays in philosophical method. With two retrospective essays.* Chicago: University of Chicago Press.

Rosenau, P. (1992). *Postmodernism and the social sciences: Insights, inroads, and intrusions.* Princeton, NJ: Princeton University Press.

Rosenwald, G. C., & Ochberg, R. (Eds.). (1992). *Storied lives: The politics of self-understanding.* New Haven, CT: Yale University Press.

Simons, H. W. (Ed.). (1990). *The rhetorical turn: Invention and persuasion in the conduct of inquiry.* Chicago: University of Chicago Press.

Thomas, L. E. (Ed.). (1989). *Research on adulthood and aging: The human science approach.* Albany: State University of New York Press.

Toulmin, S. (1990). *Cosmopolis: The hidden agenda of modernity.* New York: The Free Press.

Weiland, S. (1989). Aging according to biography. *The Gerontologist, 29,* 191–194.

Weiland, S. (1995a). Critical gerontology and education for older adults. *Educational Gerontology, 21,* 593–611.

Weiland, S. (1995b). Interpretive social science and spirituality. In M. Kimble, S. McFadden, J. Ellor, & J. Seeber (Eds.), *Aging, spirituality, and religion.* Minneapolis, MN: Fortress.

Young, R., & Collin, A. (Eds.). (1992). *Interpreting career: Hermeneutical studies of lives in context.* Westport, CT: Praeger.

13

Performance Studies and Age

Anne Davis Basting

EXAMPLE ONE

In 1997, 1930s film star Gloria Stuart returned to the screen to play 101-year-old Rose DeWitt in James Cameron's *Titanic*. Her return was triumphant for more reasons than her Oscar nomination. That an 87-year-old woman appears in a major Hollywood epic, is depicted as a compelling and complicated character, and is revealed as beautiful in both her frailty and strength, is a hopeful sign that representation of the aged in this country might at long last be maturing.

But what contributes to the acceptance of this image? Can we recognize Stuart's beauty, as the camera slowly explores Rose's skin as she sleeps, because our memory of her youthful screen image has faded? Because, unlike Katherine Hepburn, whose young face is emblazoned in the minds of many Americans, audiences cannot readily compare Stuart to her youthful self?

EXAMPLE TWO

In a rehearsal room at the University of Wisconsin Oshkosh a 22-year-old woman explains her struggle to comprehend her grandmother's illness. "I know," says the man in his 60s standing next to her, "my mother disappeared before my eyes." This group of actors, ranging in age from 8 to 75, was gathered to develop and perform *Time Slips,* a play based on stories told by people with Alzheimer's disease. In the rehearsal room, it felt quite liberating to acknowledge that the disease concerns people of all ages by having the characters played by actors from four different generations. But how would this affect an audience, most of whom were drawn by the subject matter? Would having a 22-year-old play an 80-year-old be perceived as liberating, or as infantilizing the victims of the disease?

These two examples fall within the wide-reaching embrace of a relatively new mode of analysis within gerontology, *performative studies of age*. Here I blend two terms with tangled but distinct roots. First, *performance studies* is an interdisciplinary field that was formed in the 1970s from a series of alliances between anthropologists, social scientists, theatre specialists, and folklorists. Second, *performativity* is an aspect of performance theory that emerged within the development of postmodern theory in its journeys between Europe and the United States over the last three decades. These two terms, often indistinguishable in their contemporary use, present humanities scholars of age with tools to address the complexity of aging as a social construction, a physically and emotionally grounded experience, and a lifelong process of critical importance to people of all ages.

At heart, performative studies of age takes aging to be performed through social acts which occur at the junction of everyday life and theatrical illusion. This view demands that we acknowledge individual, physical, and psychological experiences of aging as well as the possibility of transformation and social change through role-playing. I have worked at this junction as both a creative artist and scholar, and believe it can offer a great deal to gerontologists invested in understanding and shifting contemporary, cultural constructions of aging. In this essay, I will trace the emergence of performative studies of age through (1) performance studies; (2) gerontology; and (3) theatre arts before giving an example of my own scholarly and creative work in this field.

PERFORMANCE STUDIES AND PERFORMATIVITY

Marvin Carlson's *Performance: A Critical Introduction* (1996) gives a thorough overview of the use of performance as a mode of social analysis in fields of anthropology, sociology, linguistics, and theater. My aim here is to trace where interests in *aging* and performance align, and to explore the as yet largely untapped potential of this mode of analysis within gerontology.

The roots of performative studies of age reach back to the rich interdisciplinary flowering in the 1970s in the work of people including Victor Turner, Richard Schechner, Barbara Myerhoff, and Marc Kaminsky. Turner laid the groundwork by developing ritual and "play" analysis within anthropology. Based on his own field work on Ndembu rituals and Arnold van Gennep's *Rites de Passage,* Turner advanced the concept of the "liminality" of ritual; that ritual provides a series of phases that allow for transformation and change. Richard Schechner organized conferences, catalyzed collaboration, and shared the fruits of these alliances by publishing his own writings on the subject as well as anthologies of essays from a wide variety of disciplines. In 1976, for example, Schechner and Mady Schuman edited *Ritual, Play, and Performance: Readings in the Social Sciences/Theatre,* which brought together essays as diverse as Johan Huizinga's "Nature and the Significance of Play as a Cultural Phenomenon," Irving Goffman's "Performance," and Jerzy Grotowski's "The Theatre's New Testament." In 1980, the Drama Department at New York University School of the Arts (founded in 1965 by Robert Corrigan), where Schechner still teaches, owned up to the fact that it was teaching more classes in ritual, shamanism, and performances of the self than traditional drama department fare of scenic design and Shakespeare, and officially changed its name to Performance Studies. Folklorist Barbara Kirshenblatt-Gimblett was brought in to administrate the department, which proceeded to develop in the direction of the varying interests of its diverse faculty and staff. Today NYU's program works in tandem with Northwestern University's Performance Studies program to lead the continued development of the field.

Meanwhile, in another alley of academia, performance theory was also developing in alliance with postmodern theory (Benamou, 1977; Fuchs, 1996). Major postmodern theorists settled on the metaphor of performance to describe the formation of culture and the expression of individual agency. For example, Jacques Derrida (1978) asserted that the repetition and revision of consciousness—in short its theatricality—is inescapable. Author of the germinal *The Postmodern Condition* (1984), Jean-François Lyotard described the basic element of the postmodernism as the dissolution of "master narratives," leaving the self to be expressed through individual performance in tension with cultural codes he calls "discourse." Over the last two decades, performance has become the ideal medium and model for a postmodern age in which the pervasiveness of media and information technologies heightens our awareness of which roles we play, as well as how and why we play them (George, 1989).

Feminist philosopher Judith Butler popularized the term *performativity* in her widely influential work on gender and sexuality including *Gender Trouble* (1990) and *Bodies that Matter* (1993). Performativity reinvests the present with the power to transform culturally coded behaviors by suggesting that in the moment a social act is performed, there is always a possibility of transformation—a moment in which social actors can revise their performances. Butler's writing has provoked considerable thought, the echo of which can be heard throughout the fields of queer theory, literary theory, and theatre studies in such works as *Cruising the Performative* (Case, 1995) and *Performativity and Performance* (Parker & Sedgwick, 1995).

But Butler and her followers' use of metaphors of performance in postmodern theory in general, and performativity in particular, have also come under fire for what some see as their fantastical yearnings to transform themselves right out of their material bodies, or for focusing on textual examples of bodies rather than their flesh and bone counterparts. I recognize and even launch such criticism myself.[1] But such criticism is also, at least in part, attributable to the negative connotations that have haunted performance since Plato, when role-playing was considered a form of dishonesty, a seamy distortion of "the real thing." Butler herself was quick to clarify what she saw as misinterpretations of her theory by asserting that performative choices range widely. They can be dangerous (threatening to social order), a reinforcement of existing social codes (playing it safe), or so small as to be undetectable.

Despite its critics, the term *performance* continues to spill over disciplinary boundaries. Today, as a flourishing field of its own with doctoral programs at New York University and Northwestern University, Performance Studies incorporates the interdisciplinary roots of performance theory, and addresses theatrical performance as well as performances of everyday life. Its focus has expanded to include considerations of the phenomenological experience of actors, and of *audiences,* both of which earlier metaphoric readings of the performative nature of postmodern culture commonly overlooked. In the past decade theatre theorists have insisted that performances cannot be read without interpreting their relationship to audiences who in turn shape their meaning (Bennett, 1990; Blau, 1990).

PERFORMANCE IN GERONTOLOGY

Within gerontology there are several interpretations and uses of performance: drama therapy, literary gerontology, and theoretical accounts of performance. Drama therapy, developed in the 1970s, has been used successfully to encourage older adults to adapt to the changing physical and emotional conditions and social roles that aging brings (Landy, 1986). Cattanach (1992) and Weisberg and Wilder (1986)

---

[1] See chapter 8 in *The Stages of Age* (1998) for my criticisms of postmodern theory's fantasies of bodilessness.

provide various therapeutic techniques for using dramatic exercises with older adults. As drama therapy, these exercises are designed solely for therapeutic effect with individuals and groups, and are not performed for outside audiences unless they are supportive audiences of caregivers.

Literary gerontology (Wyatt-Brown, 1992, 1995; Wyatt-Brown & Rosen, 1995) focuses on the interpretation of aging and creativity through close readings of literary texts. Scholars within this field have occasionally included plays in their studies, particularly those of Samuel Beckett (Woodward, 1986, 1991). Some scholars have created their own plays in order to express contemporary issues facing the aged (Cole et al., 1993; Kastenbaum, 1994), a tremendously powerful tool for raising ethical questions around the medical treatment of the aged, or challenging cultural perceptions of aging. Performative studies of age would expand the textual focus of literary gerontology to consider issues associated with the production of these plays. Such questions are far-reaching. How will the characters be depicted? Will they wear age makeup? Will they wear age-appropriate clothing? What *is* age-appropriate clothing after all? How will they move on stage? Will the characters be cast according to the actors' ages? Where will the performance take place and who, most likely, will make up the audience? The answers to all of these questions will have a significant impact on interpreting the meaning of the performance as a whole.

Barbara Myerhoff's writings and Marc Kaminsky's subsequent reexamination of her work (Kaminsky, 1993; Myerhoff, 1992) are among the early and scant explorations of aging and performance in theoretical terms. Both came to performance studies "dragging their histories behind them" (Kaminsky, 1998). Myerhoff was deeply influenced by anthropologist Victor Turner's work on social ritual. She came to view the older Jewish men and women whom she studied as creating their identities through "definitional ceremonies" (1992), her more individually focused adaptation of what she considered Turner's sociopolitical term "social drama" (Turner, 1974). As a writer and social worker, Kaminsky's early focus was on the creation of life stories through reminiscence and poetry. His later writings reveal the influence of his extensive readings in postmodern theory and its use of performance as metaphor for social action. For example, by 1992 Kaminsky describes narrative as "a performative activity" (1992, p. 314).

In addition to Myerhoff and Kaminsky, Robert Kastenbaum (1988, 1994) has also called for the study of aging as "drama." Without citing specific theorists, Kastenbaum intuitively adapts the terms of performance theory to gerontology, referring to gerontological sciences as a theater sorely missing a focus on the human, "natural" drama. Returning "drama" to gerontology, Kastenbaum believes, would encourage us to question tensions between scientific findings and "real life dramas," and to develop alternative scenarios for theorizing about aging and caregiving. In essence, Kastenbaum bends Myerhoff's "definitional ceremonies" into what he calls *defining acts:* fictional dramas that remind gerontology of its human subjects and its own human cast. His collection of dramatic texts use nontraditional forms of playwriting to express the pains and joys of the aging process. Brief "notebook" sections follow each text and offer interpretations of the worlds of the characters. But these "notebook sections" only occasionally address the merger of actor and role. *Defining Acts* and Kastenbaum's intriguing, creative interpretation of *and* sociohistorical look at the myth of Dorian Gray (*Dorian Graying,* 1995) provide foundational pieces to the development of performative studies of age. The next and natural step is to look more fully at the cultural context of the theatrical production—the plays' merger of actor, role, audience, and their potential to create social change.

Several theorists in age studies have approached performance as metaphor through postmodern theory. Kathleen Woodward (1991), Mike Featherstone and Mike Hepworth (1991), for example, refer to the performative aspects of aging as masquerade, capturing that haunting feeling that one's interior life is somehow masked by an outer, aging shell. These scholars, however, also caution against too radical a reading of performative possibilities of transformation, suggesting that there is a certain concrete material reality of aging from which the playfulness of performativity cannot release us.[2] No matter what role we play, for example, there is, as yet, no twisting free of mortality.

PERFORMANCE IN THEATER

In the 1970s, theatre artists were also exploring the relationship between social change and public performance. Theatre flourished as a tool for self-discovery, empowerment, and expression of identity, as well as a conduit for uniting people and shaping communities.[3] This could manifest itself in terms of (1) changing the shape of individual lives; or of (2) overt political action. Both are certainly "political" in today's use of the word, but in the 1970s, the distinction was still being theorized. An

---

[2] This note of caution about postmodern theory is also echoed by Harry Moody in his introduction to *Voices and Visions of Aging* (1993).

[3] Jerzy Grotowski's *Towards a Poor Theatre* (1968), and Augusto Boal's *Theatre of the Oppressed* (1979) were highly influential texts for those involved in "people's theatre," or theatre whose main emphasis was the quality of human relationships among the cast and audience. Artistic accomplishment was of secondary importance to many such groups.

example is Barbara Myerhoff's rejection of the large scale "political" aspects of Victor Turner's theory of social drama. Myerhoff turned the focus toward the individual lives of her subjects, transforming Turner's social dramas into "definitional ceremonies." Marc Kaminsky very astutely points out Myerhoff's rejection of the "political" (Myerhoff, 1992; Kaminsky, 1993). But we should also be sure to consider the varying uses of those terms (personal, political) evolving during this time period. For example, small, feminist theaters founded during this time commonly did both by emphasizing individual "consciousness raising" as well as pressing for larger-scale social change in roles and opportunities for women. Theatre techniques such as storytelling or role-playing became valuable tools to reenchant the daily lives of the displaced. Deanna Metzger, a playwright and former collaborator with the late Barbara Myerhoff, put it this way: "In the late 60s and 70s, we became interested in ritual. We recognized that we lived in a society in which the rituals had become empty. So there was an instinct to create rituals, to bring them back through everyday events."[4]

In 1981, theatre artists and academics with a common concern for social change met in St. Peter, Minnesota, for a theatre festival called simply The Gathering. Deanna Metzger, Naomi Newman, Arthur Strimling, Barbara Myerhoff, and Susan Perlstein were all present. For Perlstein, The Gathering "had the excitement of the beginning of a movement" in working with the aged through performance.[5] Strimling and Myerhoff, who met for the first time at The Gathering, collaborated over the next several years to create a series of workshops combining his theatrical expertise with her experience in oral history and storytelling at NYU and the Brookdale Center on Aging at Hunter College. Perlstein, a founding member of Elders Share the Arts (ESTA), developed the company into an intergenerational arts organization which continues to nurture storytellers among seniors and young people in the greater New York City area today. Strimling went on to found the intergenerational Roots & Branches Theater Company through the Jewish Association of Services for the Aged in 1990. Metzger continued her extensive solo career as well as her long collaboration with Myerhoff, and Newman continued her work as a founding member of San Francisco-based A Traveling Jewish Theatre which has produced works concerned with aging and relationships between generations.

Over the past two decades there has been an increasing interest in issues of aging among theatre artists. Senior theatre groups, once focused almost exclusively on the individual, therapeutic benefits of performance, have turned toward achieving professional, artistic status.

---

[4] Personal interview, 21 January 1998.
[5] Personal interview, 13 February 1998.

Their styles range from musical reviews to experimental plays based on oral histories of group members. Ann McDonough, a pioneer of "senior adult theatre," has established a training program for older actors at the University of Nevada Las-Vegas, the only actor training program to acknowledge the unique talents and needs of senior actors. Her book, *The Golden Stage* (1994), is one of the first manuals that addresses senior actors as artists rather than solely in therapeutic terms.

Established performing artists such as Rachel Rosenthal *(Zone),* Meredith Monk *(Volcano Songs),* and Kazuo Ohno *(Water Lilies)* have also turned their concerns toward aging. Their performances, as well as those of amateur senior performers, can help dismantle stereotypes of aging such as increasing rigidity and the lack of growth through the very act of acting—the taking on of new roles in older adulthood. They can also establish older adults as respected artists. In Myerhoff's terms, such performances create "definitional ceremonies" in which older adults can carve out their positions within culture at large.

Performances of this kind stand as scholarly offerings in their own right by providing models that can help us envision new ways to conceive of aging. A particularly exciting possibility within performative studies of age is the merger of creative and scholarly projects that combine the work of artists, historians, and cultural theorists. Suzanne Lacy's 1987 epic Whisper Minnesota project, a two-and-a-half-year-long effort to increase the role of older women as civic leaders in the state of Minnesota, is an inspirational model for the potential of multidisciplinary efforts of this kind.

Lacy orchestrated a complicated collaboration between public and private state-wide sponsors to launch older women's leadership workshops, a newsletter, a multimedia arts installation in Duluth, a traveling performance entitled *Ladies Who Lunch,* and a culminating performance featuring 430 older women from across the state. The performance took place in the atrium of a high-rise office building in downtown Minneapolis. The 430 older women, all dressed in black, sat 4 to a table in the atrium. The audience, gathered on the balconies above the women, watched and listened while the women made patterns through the simple movement of their hands, and while a soundtrack featuring interviews with the women echoed throughout the atrium. Set on Mother's Day, the performance encouraged audience members to see older women as an invaluable source of wisdom and leadership in their communities. Anthropologists and art critics were in on Whisper Minnesota from the ground floor, recording and analyzing the progress and scope of the project, and extending its reach from the local community to include scholars in a wide range of disciplines.[6]

---

[6] In 1988, a trio of essays appeared in *The Drama Review,* a journal of performance studies based at NYU. See Roth, Rothenberg, and Lippard.

PERFORMANCE: EXAMPLE

In 1997, I participated in *Time Slips,* a collaborative project at the University of Wisconsin Oshkosh that echoed Lacy's dual aims for immersion in the local community and artistic excellence. *Time Slips* exemplifies the multiple approaches possible in performative studies of age, and I describe it here in the hopes that it will spark interest in this growing and flexible field.

The project began in the spring of 1996 when I launched a storytelling project with a small group of people with Alzheimer's disease in a Milwaukee long-term-care center. Each week I brought an image clipped from a magazine, and copied down the group's answers to questions such as "Who is this? What does she do?" The Marlboro Man, for example, was transformed into Fred Astaire, a cowboy who lived in Oklahoma and whose horse was "big, but not so big he couldn't get on."

The stories were a remarkable blend of creativity, reminiscence, and illness that offered group members a chance to build social relationships and express themselves creatively. The stories were filled with songs and humor, as well as sometimes painful reminders of memories and words beyond their grasp. At the end of the workshop, I gathered the stories and shaped them into a play, hoping that the merger of joy and tragedy in these stories would increase awareness of the full dimension of the disease to the production crew as well as to audiences at large.

In December of 1996, a theatre designer, a multimedia specialist, and I joined forces to turn these stories into a collaborative production to be called *Time Slips.* The interactive nature of the storytelling workshops would now be echoed in the production process where students and faculty across generations would all contribute to shaping the play throughout rehearsal. With local grant support, particularly from the UW Oshkosh, we hired a professional director with whom I had collaborated several times, and went into rehearsal in May of 1997.[7] After sharing personal stories about Alzheimer's and dementia, and after a week of research on the topic, group members decided to depict the play solely from the perspective of the people with the disease themselves.

The world on stage was quite magical. In an effort to capture the fluidity of past and present in the world of Alzheimer's disease, characters entered and exited from three oversized pieces of furniture; crawling out of a three-drawered chest, an armoire, and a cupboard.

---

[7] *Time Slips's* collaborative team included Roy Hoglund (theatre designer) and Karla Berry (media specialist). The director, Ms. Gülgün Kayim, is based in Minneapolis and has considerable experience directing collaboratively created, experimental theatre.

Enormous piles of suitcases and chairs floated upward (some suspended from the ceiling) stage right and left, respectively. A doctor appeared (prerecorded) on a video monitor hidden in one of the suitcases and interacted with the characters. A nurse's aide crossed the stage rapidly, carrying odd objects, throughout the play. Five enormous screens filled the stage. Old family photos appeared on two side screens, while video clips of famous films cut with documentary footage and home videos appeared on three overlapping center screens.

The five main characters, Roberta, Fred, Millie, Audrey, and Sylvia, were based on a combination of the characters created in the Milwaukee workshop and the people with Alzheimer's themselves. *Time Slips* presented fragments of their stories that found their own "sense" through repetition. Each character had a moment in which the fragments of their memories "coalesced" in projected images, dialogue, movement, and music.

For example, Roberta's moment of "coalescence" occurred with projected, documentary footage of World War II as well as a home video of holiday meals, combined with the sound of Gene Autry's "Rudolph the Red-Nosed Reindeer." While these images and music played, Roberta tried desperately to hide in the cupboard and chest, finally coming to rest in a pool of light center stage where she faced her fears and quietly, simply took off her wig. By play's end, audiences could intuit a general sense of Roberta's joyful support of her fellow characters, as well as her fears lodged in her memories of WWII.

Time Slips succeeded in drawing an intergenerational audience and in encouraging discussion among cast, crew, and audience members. Each of the two performances was followed by a postshow discussion facilitated by specialists in the fields of theatre and of aging. Nearly a third of the audience stayed for each discussion. A community roundtable discussion, although lightly attended, generated heated debate about cultural myths surrounding Alzheimer's disease, quality of care, social-issue theatre, and intergenerational relationships. There was clearly a hunger to discuss the experience of caring for or about someone with Alzheimer's.

Additionally, as an intergenerational, collaboratively produced play, *Time Slips* created a space in which the actors could explore this world and exorcise their own fears by depicting the joys, humor, and tragedy of the disease. The youngest cast member, then 8, and the oldest at 76, shared their experiences with and awareness of the disease. Encouraging young and old to talk about fears together helps them plan, prepare, and act if they are faced with the difficult challenges that Alzheimer's disease presents.

This is not to say that there was not plenty of friction in the production process. Tensions arose when a young actress felt uneasy in the physical presence of one of the older men in the cast who had an awkward tendency, menacing or not, of staring at her. Another older actor resisted the use of cross-generational casting, and wrote a lengthy letter outlining his criticisms of this practice after the production closed. There were issues about authority between the generations that waxed and waned throughout the rehearsal process. Although these tensions raised hurdles for the production team, they mark steps that must be taken in order to begin the long process of working through generational divisions.

CONCLUSION

Performative studies of age have roots in multiple disciplines, including linguistics, anthropology, theatre studies, folklore, and sociology. I have found, however, that in spite of this wide range of disciplines, performative studies of age share several consistent characteristics:

1. Performative studies of age consider aging to be constructed through a series of social acts performed throughout one's life.

These social acts lie on a continuum between unconscious acts in everyday life, such as seemingly ingrained gestures, to more conscious acts of self-presentation, such as choices in clothing or the taking on of a theatrical persona. Social acts such as these are performed somewhere between individual resistance (agency) and the "big brother" quality of social structures, and reveal the potential for transformation—be it individual and/or cultural.

2. Transforming from one social act to another, from one moment to the next, in no way means that one can simply shed the skin of the past.

Our past roles remain with us, written in our memories and on our bodies. But it can mean that we as a culture can radically alter the way we conceive of aging, offsetting theories of rigidity and an inability to change with possibilities for continued growth.

3. Because any social act of aging is always done in concert with the past, present, and future, no single representation of age can be considered to be a stable identity.

The power of this point is perhaps most clear when applied to the young adult. In the light of performative studies of age, a woman of 19 cannot simply be seen as a young adult. She must be seen as a young adult in relationship to her own aging process, and eventually her own old age. A woman in her 80's, on the other hand, must also be seen as a woman of 19.

4. Performative studies of age look beyond textual "dramas" to include the phenomenological experience of the aging body.

Such an approach helps balance the playfulness of postmodern theory with a grounded acknowledgment of both the material body and individual accounts of the experience of aging. Within gerontology, such an approach would balance the "textbook" treatment of older adults with recognition of their spiritual, psychological, and everyday experiences.

5. To understand aging, we must look to the relationship between the social actor(s) and their audiences, including traditional audiences (audiences in the theater, for example) and culture at large.

This applies to everyday performances as well as more conscious theatrical roles. For example, if a man in his 90s living in a long-term-care facility cries out the name of a woman repeatedly, we might ask how the performance affects the audience. What kind of reaction does it cause? How might the social act be transformed? How might the community outside the long-term-care center contribute to his behavior?

6. Performative studies of age can help us contextualize the growing abundance of representations of the aged.

In film, for example, there are the powerful presences of Gloria Stuart in *Titanic* and Paul Newman in *Twilight.* In theatre, increasing numbers of mainstream plays are turning toward issues of aging, including the 1998 New York productions of Martin McDonagh's *The Beauty Queen of Lenane* and Jeff Baron's *Visiting Mr. Green.* There are also more community-based productions in which older adults are able to further their talents as actors, or begin the practice anew in late life. Questions that arise in each of these examples include: how does the image compare to the everyday appearance of the performer? To the experience of older adults in general? What does this tell us about the way aging is represented and valued?

The early alliances between performance studies and aging in the work of Barbara Myerhoff in particular held much promise for gerontology. Today, this much underexamined field has ripened in its promise, having become a powerful metaphor for life in our postmodern, aging society. It fuels my own scholarly and creative endeavors, which as of this writing, include a 3-year project that will share the creative efforts of people with Alzheimer's with their immediate and expanded communities. The project, funded in part by the Brookdale Foundation and the Helen Bader Foundation, has three phases. The first establishes creative storytelling workshops between high school and undergraduate students and people with Alzheimer's. The second phase translates these stories into a site on the World Wide Web. The third phase will see the production of a play, similar to *Time Slips.* Based in both Milwaukee and New York City, the project is poised to make precedent-setting, interdisciplinary steps, as it can potentially speak to audiences in fields of arts and humanities as well as gerontology and geriatrics. We will attempt to measure the shifts in perception (always a difficult task) through conducting a series of at least two, and ideally four qualitative, ethnographic interviews with the student storytelling facilitators, a member of the student's family, a family caregiver of the person with Alzheimer's, and a staff caregiver. Due to often high rates of turnover in staff and clients in Alzheimer's care facilities, as well as with students, the trick to a project of this kind is to remain flexible. We will also gather feedback from an interactive page on the project's web-site, as well as from postperformance discussions that will be facilitated by experts in the field of aging and the field of performance. It is my hope that by creating and expanding the social identity of people with Alzheimer's (as storytellers in this case), communities might improve the experience of the disease for those that suffer and those that give care. It is also my hope that the countless, intriguing possibilities that performative studies of age offer scholars in multiple disciplines and creative artists alike, inspire the further ripening of this field.

REFERENCES

Basting, A. D. (1998). *The stages of age: Performing age in contemporary American culture.* Ann Arbor: University of Michigan Press.

Benamou, M., & Caramello, C. (1977). *Performance in postmodern culture.* Milwaukee: Center for 20th Century Studies.

Bennett, S. (1990). *Theatre audiences.* New York: Routledge.

Blau, H. (1990). *The audience.* Baltimore: Johns Hopkins University Press.

Boal, A. (1979). *Theatre of the oppressed.* New York: Urizen Books.

Butler, J. (1990). *Gender trouble.* New York: Routledge.

Butler, J. (1993). *Bodies that matter.* New York: Routledge.

Carlson, M. (1996). *Performance: A critical introduction.* New York: Routledge.

Case, S. E. (Ed.). (1995). *Cruising the performative.* Bloomington: Indiana University Press.

Cattanach, A. (1992). *Drama for people with special needs.* New York: Drama Book Publishers.

Cole, T. R., Van Tassel, D., & Kastenbaum, R. (Eds.). (1992). *Handbook of the humanities and aging.* New York: Springer.

Cole, T. R., Achenbaum, W. A., & Jakobi, P. L. (Eds.). (1993). *Voices and visions of aging.* New York: Springer Publishing Co.

Derrida, J. (1978). *Writing and difference.* Chicago: University of Chicago Press.

Featherstone, M., & Hepworth, M. (1991). The mask of ageing and the postmodern life course. In M. Featherstone, M. Hepworth, & B. S. Turner. (Eds.), *The body: Social process and cultural theory* (pp. 371–389). London: Sage.

Fuchs, E. (1997). *The death of character.* Bloomington: Indiana University Press.

George, D. (1989). On ambiguity: Towards a post-modern performance theory. *Theatre Research International, 14.*

Grotowski, J. (1968). *Towards a poor theatre.* New York: Simon and Schuster.

Kaminsky, M. Personal interview. January 28, 1998.

Kaminsky, M. (1992). The story of the shoe box. In T. R. Cole, D. Van Tassel, & R. Kastenbaum (Eds.), *Handbook for the humanities and aging* (pp. 307–327). New York: Springer Publishing Co.

Kaminsky, M. (1993). Definitional ceremonies: Depoliticizing and reenchanting the culture of aging. In T. R. Cole, W. A. Achenbaum, & S. P. L. Jakobi (Eds.), *Voices and visions of aging* (pp. 257–274). New York: Springer Publishing Co.

Kastenbaum, R. (1995). *Dorian graying.* Amityville, NY: Baywood Publishing.

Kastenbaum, R. (1994). *Defining acts: Aging as drama.* Amityville, NY: Baywood Publishing.

Kastenbaum, R. (1988). Exit with thunder. In S. Reinharz & G. D. Rowles (Eds.), *Qualitative gerontology* (pp. 34–43). New York: Springer Publishing Co.

Lacy, S. (1995). *Mapping the terrain: New genre public art.* Seattle: Bay Press.

Landy, R. (1986). *Drama therapy.* Springfield, IL: Charles C. Thomas.

Lippard, L. (1988). Suzanne Lacy: Some of her own medicine. *The Drama Review, 32,* 71–81.

Lyotard, J. F. (1984). *The postmodern condition: A report on knowledge.* Minneapolis: University of Minnesota Press.

McDonough, A. (1994). *The golden stage.* Dubuque, IA: Kendall/Hunt Publishing Co.

Monroe, W., & Cole, T. R. (1993). Scenes from primary care: A drama in two acts. In T. R. Cole, W. A. Achenbaum, & P. L. Jackobi (Eds.), *Voices and visions of aging* (pp. 205–234). New York: Springer Publishing Co.

Moody, H. (1993). Introduction. In T. R. Cole, W. A. Achenbaum, & P. L. Jakobi (Eds.), *Voices and visions of aging.* New York: Springer Publishing Co.

Myerhoff, B. (1992). *Remembered lives: The work of ritual, storytelling and growing older.* M. Kaminsky (Ed.). Ann Arbor: University of Michigan Press.

Myerhoff, B. Personal interview. January 28, 1998.

Roth, M. (1988). Social reformer and witch. *The Drama Review, 32*(1), 42–60.

Rothenberg, D. (1988). Social art/social action. *The Drama Review, 32*(1), 61–70.

Schechner, R., & Schuman, M. (Eds.). (1976). *Ritual, play, and performance.* New York: The Seabury Press.

Sedgwick, E. K., & Parker, A. (Eds.). (1995). *Performativity and performance.* New York: Routledge.

Turner, V. (1974). *Dramas, fields, and metaphors.* Ithaca, NY: Cornell University Press.

Weisberg, N., & Wilder, R. (1986). *Drama therapy with older adults.* New Haven, CT: National Association for Drama Therapy.

Woodward, K. (1991). *Aging and its discontents.* Bloomington: Indiana University Press.

Woodward, K. (1986). Reminiscence and the life review: Prospects and retrospects. In T. R. Cole & S. Gadow (Eds.), *What does it mean to grow old?* (pp. 135–161). Durham, NC: Duke University Press.

Wyatt-Brown, A. (1995). Creativity as a defense against death: Maintaining one's professional identity. *Journal of Aging Studies, 9*(4), 349–355.

Wyatt-Brown, A., (1992). Literary gerontology comes of age. In T. R. Cole et al. (Eds.), *Handbook of the humanities and aging* (pp. 331–351). New York: Springer Publishing.

Wyatt-Brown, A., & Rosen, J. (Eds.). (1995). *Aging and gender in literature: Studies in creativity.* Charlottesville: University Press of Virginia.

14

Self-Representation and Aging: Philosophical, Psychological, and Literary Perspectives

Harry J. Berman

INTRODUCTION: THE HUMAN CONDITION

We are looking at a painting showing an easel with an oil painting standing in front of a window. Through the window we see sky, clouds, trees, and grass. But the oil painting itself shows the same sky, clouds, trees, and grass. A moment of disorientation. Is there really a painting— or just a glass window overlooking a pastoral scene? No, that can't be it. There *is* a painting. We see the white edge of the canvas on the right. Looking at the left side of the window, we see the way the left edge of the canvas blocks the curtain. There must be a painting after all. Then the view resolves itself. The disorientation is caused by the correspondence between what is represented on the painting and what lies beyond the window—so much so that the viewer must strain to distinguish between representation and that which is being represented.

And then the title: *La condition humaine.*

René Magritte's witty and profound visual comment on the human condition goes to the heart of the subject of self-representation and aging. In effect, Magritte is saying the essence of human being is meaning-making. The human condition is not simply to be, i.e., exist, in the world. Woven into human being in the world is the process of making sense of that world and of representing it to ourselves and to others. The process of representing the world includes not only the

FIGURE 14.1 *La condition humaine.* **Rene Magritte. 1933 Oil on canvas. 39 3/8 x 31 7/8 x 5/8". Gift of the Collectors Committee. National Gallery of Art, Washington.**

representation of the world outside of ourselves, but also the representation of ourselves as actors in that world.

Although self-representation may occur through visual media or in speech, this chapter addresses only the written form of self-representation, i.e., autobiographical writing. The chapter is written from the perspective of a psychologist who has studied published autobiographical works and examined them with the aid of ideas drawn not only from psychology but also from philosophy and literary criticism. It begins with comments on the self as treated in philosophy and psychology. The chapter then reviews forms of autobiographical writing and the significance of research on autobiographical writing and aging. It concludes with a discussion of the limitations of research in this area.

SELF-REPRESENTATION

Hermeneutics: Shifting Horizon of Self-Understanding

The observation that each characterization of the self is an interpretive effort means that the study of self-representation ought to be informed by what we know of the nature of interpretive activity. Hermeneutics is the branch of philosophy concerned with interpretation, and the work of a leading expositor of hermeneutics in the 20th century, Hans-Georg Gadamer, does indeed have great relevance to understanding self-reflection as interpretation. Already close to retirement in 1960, Gadamer brought a highly productive career not to a close but to a climax with the publication of *Truth and Method* (Gadamer, 1960/1992), a work that has left its mark everywhere in the human sciences—in sociology, literary theory, history, theology, law, and philosophy of science (Weinsheimer, 1985).

A key insight provided by Gadamer is to emphasize repeatedly that any interpretive act is a historically situated event. Understanding does not transcend time; it is *in* time. The understanding we have of, for example, a novel or a work of art is necessarily the understanding we have of it now, based on our current arsenal of interpretive constructs and our whole history of prior interpretations. Such constructs and prior interpretations serve as forestructures of understanding; any interpretation, in effect, amounts to an application of our current forestructures of understanding to a text. "This is what the text means" is really shorthand for the more accurate statement "This is what the text means to me now."

Gadamer's approach to the interpretation of texts is mirrored in one of the major contemporary lines of thinking in literary criticism, reader-response theory. Reader-response criticism is the term associated with the work of critics who argue that the literary work is realized only through a convergence of reader and text, rather than in any meaning located in the text itself. For reader-response critics, the reader is cocreator of the meaning of the text and critical activity involves exploration of the phenomenology of the reading process. Among the central expositions of reader-response theory are those of Rosenblatt (1964), Iser (1978), and Bleich (1978). Tompkins (1980) provides a critical over-view of the range of positions encompassed by the reader-response approach.

When people think back over their lives, it is as if the incidents of the past exist as a sort of text, which can be woven into a coherent account. But the account that is provided, as for example in life history interviews, is always and inescapably situated in the present. The descriptions people offer about the kind of people they are or about the meaning of incidents in their day-to-day lives do not hold for all time. Each enunciation of the meaning of an incident is an *event* of interpretation, not a timeless truth, but a creative act, a casting of lived experience into words.

In *Truth and Method* Gadamer offers a striking image for understanding interpretive events, including interpretations one offers of one's self. All understanding, he argues, is understanding from a vantage point. A given vantage point allows one to see, but only as far as the horizon. The horizon encompasses all that can be seen from a given location. Metaphorically, then, any given moment constitutes a vantage point in time and creates the opportunity for understanding within the limits of the time horizon of that moment. But because we're all always moving in time, accumulating experiences, aging, the horizon of understanding—and of self-understanding—is not a rigid boundary, but rather something into which we move and which moves with us. Meaning always stands in a horizontal context that stretches into the past and into the future. But that horizon is always in motion.

Self-Narratives

In recent years the study of the self in psychology has been strongly influenced by another metaphor, that of the self as story. In this view it is not only events which are narrated, but rather the self, itself, is a kind of story we tell ourselves about ourselves. The concept of self-narrative has been used productively by researchers in personality and social psychology (Bruner, 1990; Cohler & Galatzer-Levy, 1990; Freeman, 1993; Gergen & Gergen, 1983; Josselson & Lieblich, 1993; McAdams, 1993; Rosenwald & Ochberg, 1992; Sarbin, 1989), psychoanalysis (Schafer, 1992; Spence, 1982), clinical psychology (Hermans & Hermans-Jansen, 1995; Viney, 1993; White & Epston, 1990), and literary criticism (Benstock, 1988; Rorty, 1976; Spacks, 1976).

If selves are viewed as narratives, as stories we tell ourselves about ourselves, what can be learned from the general characteristics of narratives that might illuminate our understanding of the self? Here again, philosophical analysis in the hermeneutic tradition proves useful. The

French hermeneutic philosopher Paul Ricoeur has placed the study of narrative at the center of his life's work. In *Oneself as Another* (1992) he has pointed out that in all forms of narrative there are concordant and discordant events, roughly corresponding to the expected and the unexpected. The creation of narrative, what Ricoeur terms narrative configuration, involves reconciling the competition between the demands for concordance and the admission of discordance, a synthesis of the heterogeneous. Narrative plots have an instability that arises through movement between concordant and discordant events. Through the dialectical process of narrative configuration, unexpected events become transfigured into narratively necessary events—chance becomes fate.

When people are asked to tell the stories of their lives or when they write about their lives, they select events from the past and emplot them into narratives. The emplotment of life stories involves the reconciliation of concordant and discordant events so that the life as a whole constitutes a story.

Any given narrative configuration that a person provides of his or her own life is threatened by unforeseeable (discordant) events that punctuate it, such as accidents, illnesses, encounters with other people, winning the lottery, or large-scale historical events such as war or the AIDS epidemic. A discordant event may so alter one's life that what was formerly central to the life story becomes peripheral and what was formerly peripheral takes on central importance. A discordant event may thus force a reconfiguration of the life story, change a tragic self-narrative into a romantic one or vice versa.

Bringing together Gadamer's and Ricoeur's perspectives, we can say that when people tell the stories of their lives the account has to be given from the present horizon of self-understanding. We make sense of the present in terms of our working theory of the kind of story we are in the middle of. As the horizon of self-understanding shifts, it may become apparent that we were not in the middle of the story we thought we were in the middle of. Perhaps we thought our life was a tragedy and all along, unbeknownst to us, it was a romance. Or perhaps we thought our life was almost over, at least in terms of the future holding anything new, and it turned out, as May Sarton learned (Berman, 1994, pp. 180–194), that there was a lot more to it.

Memory

To the degree that the self as objectified in language can be understood to be a form of story, researchers interested in self-representation and aging will necessarily be led to consider the nature of autobiographical memory. This topic has received considerable attention in experimental psychology and gerontology. (For a review the experimental findings on autobiographical memory with special reference to the relevance of this research for psychotherapy, see Singer & Salovey, 1993.) In gerontology, the subject of autobiographical memory tends to be cast in terms of the concept of reminiscence. Sherman (1991) provides an especially thoughtful integration of the concepts of reminiscence and the self.

Blending phenomenological reflection and research findings, John Kotre (1995) offers an analysis of the relationship between memory and the self-as-story. Kotre notes that "the remembering self" has two very different aspects. "On the one hand it has the temperament of a librarian, a keeper of memory's most important archives . . . But memory's archivist by day has a secret passion by night: to fashion a story about itself . . . a personal myth. . . . As a maker of myth, the self leaves its handiwork everywhere in memory. With the passing of time, the good guys in our lives get a little better and the bad guys a little worse. The speeds get faster, the fish get bigger, and the Depression gets a little tougher . . ." (pp. 116–117).

Authors are quite aware that, when it comes to the remembering self, what passes as memory is more like storytelling in the sense of the creation of fiction. For example, the novelist and short story writer William Maxwell in his splendid short novel *So Long, See You Tomorrow* has the narrator comment that

> What we, or at any rate I, refer to confidently as memory—meaning a moment, a scene, a fact that has been subjected to a fixative and thereby rescued from oblivion—is really a form of storytelling that goes on continually in the mind and often changes with the telling. Too many conflicting emotional interests are involved for life ever to be wholly acceptable, and possibly it is the work of the storyteller to rearrange things so that they conform to this end (Maxwell, 1980, p. 28).

Doris Grumbach, a novelist, biographer, and critic who has written several self-reflective works exploring her own aging, has offered a striking image of what happens to memory in the course of creating a self-story: "At the moment of retrieval, in the process of recall, the initial observer-limited memory is there, incomplete and biased as it was when it was first stored in the mind. Then it is embroidered and encrusted over time . . . until it is like a barnacle-covered shell, with little of the original shape to be seen" (Grumbach, 1993, p. 14).

FORMS OF AUTOBIOGRAPHICAL WRITING

The study of autobiographical writing as related to aging can be viewed as an activity within the domain of the biographical method.

Denzin (1989) characterizes the biographical method as involving the studied use and collection of personal-life documents (p. 13). A family of terms combines to shape the biographical method. Among these terms are life, self, experience, autobiography, ethnography, biography, story, self-story, life story, fiction, history, life history, case history, case study, narrative, and writing. Drawing on Derrida's (1967/1978) notion of *différence,* Denzin argues that the meanings of these terms "spill over into each other" and the attempt to give a fixed meaning to each term is "doomed to failure" (p. 47). Every term carries traces of the other terms.

The recognition that terms related to the autobiographical method spill over into each other and cannot be unambiguously defined applies to discussions of literary forms in which the self is represented. For example, Waxman (1997), in an important recent contribution to humanities-oriented studies of aging, uses the term autobiography to include "a wide range of forms, such as the diary, the journal, the memoir, and the more conventional chronological narrative of the life history" (p. 10). Indeed, her book includes not only readings of works written in the preceding forms, but also analyses of several biographies on the argument that "biographers narrating others' lives subjectively choose their subjects, attracted to them out of their own needs, identifying with them as they construct their subjects' lives, and revealing their own personalities in what they construct" (p. 9).

Whether or not it is advisable to lump together biography and autobiography in the study of autobiographical writing, it is evident that particular examples of autobiographical writing are often difficult to classify. Nonetheless, pointing out the traditional forms in which the self can be inscribed helps reveal opportunities for future study.

Diaries

The diary[1] is a form of literary expression with a long history. The last four books of Augustine's *Confessions,* dating from the 4th century, provide an early example of diary-like writing. Famous books on English diaries (Matthews, 1950; Ponsonby, 1922) discuss texts that are cast in recognizable diary form from as early as the 15th century. The 17th century, notable for the landmark diary of Samuel Pepys, was a period of great proliferation of this form. By the beginning of the 19th century, diary writing began to be recognized as a literary activity open to both established and nonestablished writers. The writing in diaries came to be characterized by immediacy, self-reflection, and an effort toward authenticity. Some diaries of this period carried these characteristics to extremes, such as the 3,000-page diary of the 19th-century artist Benjamin Haydon and the French *journaux intimes,* in which the authors demonstrated their cultivated capacity for passionate responses to music and literature and their unusual sensitivity to all kinds of stimuli (Berman, 1994, p. 27).

In the Victorian era, diary writing as a conventional habit among persons of culture reached a peak. Victorian diaries, written by travelers, soldiers, politicians, and clergymen, present detailed pictures of contemporary life, attitudes, and values but tend to have little autobiographical energy or individual accent. In the United States, a different type of 19th-century diary has been the subject of recent critical attention: the substantial body of diary writing by pioneer women has created considerable interest among feminist literary critics (Schlissel, 1982).

Two trends in 20th-century diary writing are notable. The first is the preparation of a diary with the intention to have it published immediately. We have many published diaries from earlier centuries; however, the publication of such works is typically attributable to someone other than the author and almost always from a later historical period. The second is the institutionalization of the journal as a vehicle for self-understanding, self-guidance, psychological growth, and enhanced creativity. This trend is apparent in the numerous published guides to journal writing (e.g., Adams, 1990; Baldwin, 1991; Progoff, 1975); the workshops and classes on journaling available around the country; and the use of learning journals as an approach to student evaluation.

A technique related to such structured approaches to journal writing that has been developed in a gerontological context is Birren and Deutchman's (1991) guided autobiography. The guided autobiography technique involves exploring themes of human development in group sessions following which participants write their personal reflections on these themes and share them, in subsequent sessions, with other participants. The theoretical underpinnings of guided autobiography have been discussed by Kenyon and Randall (1997).

Examples of diaries likely to be of interest to gerontologists include those of Grumbach (1991; 1993), Horner (1982), Olmstead (1975), Scott-Maxwell (1979), and Sarton (1973; 1977; 1980; 1984; 1988; 1992; 1993b; 1996).

Autobiography

Formal autobiography is another literary form in which the self is inscribed.

Three characteristics of autobiographies are worth noting in order to clarify their relationship with diaries. First, in its contemporary form, autobiography involves an attempt to create a coherent narrative of a life. People account for their actions and explain their lives. Events are selected to accommodate the demand for creating a coherent narrative. Second, the author of an autobiography writes from the perspective of a completed sequence of events. The outcome is known and significant antecedent events—the ones worth telling—are those that are thought to bear on that outcome. Finally, in autobiographies, the *I* that is writing thinks back to and writes about a *Me* of an earlier time. The actor being described in autobiography is not identical to the actor doing the writing.

In keeping with the notion that the terms related to the biographical method "spill over into each other," we recognize that the differences between the diary form and autobiography are far from absolute. For example, as the autobiographer's story approaches the present, the gap in time between events and their inscription may approach that of a diary. Also, diarists clearly select events for inclusion in their works. Such selection is likely to be influenced by a self-narrative of the sort that could be set out in an autobiography.

The market for autobiography seems to be thriving. An on-line search in *Books in Print* of active English language works with the word autobiography in the title yielded 1,939 citations. However, the systematic examination of published autobiographies by gerontologists is in its infancy. Examples of recently published autobiographies likely to be of interest to gerontologists include those of the Delany sisters (Delany & Delany, 1993) and of Jessie Foveaux (Foveaux, 1997). In addition, an essay by Michael Korda (1997, October 6) about the writing of Ronald Reagan's autobiography (Reagan, 1990) highlights the way that, despite the expectations associated with this form of writing, some autobiographies can actually contain very little self-reflection.

Memoirs

Another type of text related to the diary and the autobiography is the memoir. The term is used very loosely and may be applied to works that appear to be either diaries or autobiographies. Still, it is possible to identify characteristics of the "ideal type" of memoir.

Like autobiographies and diaries, memoirs are concerned with the recording of experience. In both memoirs and autobiographies, the experiences written about tend to be separated from the act of writing by years, rather than by hours or days as would be the case with diaries.

Like autobiographies, memoirs are written from the perspective of a completed series of events; the outcomes are known. But whereas the aim of autobiography is to provide an account of the author's life as a whole, memoirs tend to be concerned with pivotal events in a life (as in memoirs of recovery from illness), with persons other than the author (as in memoirs of encounters with political figures), or with events to which the author was a witness (as in war memoirs). Nonetheless, authors of memoirs position themselves within situations they have experienced and about which they are bearing witness and may, in the process, use the persons and events described to "explain" themselves, as might be done in autobiography.

Recently published examples include the memoirs of Brown (1996), Lyden (1997), and McCourt (1996).

Letters

Letters may function as a form of self-representation. An exchange of letters resembles a conversation and may contain the questions, commands, requests, threats, and advice found in face-to-face conversation. The term "correspondence" captures in the idea of "co-responding" the dialogical feature that is unique to this textual form (Moffat, 1985).

But within the dialog of correspondence, the self may be inscribed. Because they are not together, letter writers must each in turn hold forth longer alone than in conversation. A correspondent must spin out a longer conversational turn without immediately knowing its effect on the partner in dialog. The recording and slowing down of dialog creates a space for self-representation. As is the case with diaries, published correspondences vary in the degree to which the writers attempt to represent themselves in their letters and, therefore, vary in their usefulness for understanding the experience of aging (see discussion of analyzability below).

The history of social science and psychology in the 20th century is marked by several notable uses of letter series as sources of data. The pioneering use of this form was in the monumental work *The Polish Peasant in Europe and America* by Thomas and Znaniecki (1958). *The Polish Peasant* was originally issued in five volumes and ran to 2,200 pages. One volume used 764 letters arranged into 50 series. *The Polish Peasant* gave birth to the important line of thinking in sociology known as symbolic interactionism. The most famous use of letters in psychology, and the one that best illustrates the potential of letters for illuminating issues of self-representation and aging, is Allport's *Letters from Jenny* (Allport, 1965). In the first part of this book Allport presents an edited version of 301 letters written to two young friends by Jenny Grove Masterson while she was between the ages of 58 and 70. The letters are followed by analyses of Jenny's personality from three theoretical perspectives: an existential (phenomenological) approach, a depth (psychoanalytic) approach, and a structural-dynamic (trait) approach. Contemporary published letters of potential value to the exploration of aging and self-representation include those of Sarton (1993a) and Margaret Laurence (Lennox & Panofsky, 1997).

Each of these four literary forms offers great potential for the study of aging; each has its strengths and limitations. For example, while autobiography's strength is presentation of the coherent self-narrative, diaries have the power to reveal the way that even in later life people—and their self-stories—can be transformed. For those who believe in the value of working with this material, the task is to recognize the type of insight into aging opened by each form.

SIGNIFICANCE OF RESEARCH ON AUTOBIOGRAPHICAL WRITING TO THE STUDY OF AGING

Once we acknowledge that descriptions of age-related experiences are part of what it means to understand the process of aging, the value of autobiographical writing in all its forms as a source of such descriptions becomes readily apparent.

The philosophical tradition of hermeneutics teaches us that the descriptions that people provide of themselves and their own aging are not theirs alone. The shared nature of the descriptions offered in autobiographical writing derives in part from the obvious fact that the interpretations offered in them are carried out linguistically. As individuals we do not have language. Rather we enter into language in our early years and for the rest of life are participants in linguistic traditions. We belong to language as much as language belongs to us.

Because of the shared nature of language, whenever a people express themselves linguistically there is a sense in which it is not solely their experiences being expressed. When people write about what they feel, what a particular incident in their lives—such as a hospitalization (Kleinman, 1988) or an encounter with a bag lady (Grumbach, 1991)—means to them, they draw on the means at hand, the available words and concepts to express themselves. As Palmer (1969) has put it, experience is linguistic through and through. We talk about being true to ourselves and the uniqueness of every person's experience, but we tend to overlook the way in which, because of the shared nature of language through which experience is constituted, no one's experience is unique. Self-representations are not created *ex nihilo.* What we usually refer to as the self is largely determined by the possibilities laid open to us by language and culture (Shotter & Gergen, 1989).

The process of aging is not just a matter of changes in the functioning of our bodies and concomitant changes in psychological functioning. The process of aging is in part a historical process involving not only the history of social customs toward the aged, but, equally, the history of older people's understandings of themselves. When people age they are necessarily involved in this historical process, the evolving history of the meaning of later life. The interpretations of aging offered in autobiographical writings should be studied because such interpretations are as much a part of the process of aging as the behavior of free radicals or changes in reaction time.

LIMITATIONS OF RESEARCH ON SELF-REPRESENTATION IN AUTOBIOGRAPHICAL WRITING

Validity

In empirical work in the natural and social sciences researchers are obliged to point out the limitations of their studies. The idea of *limitation* is bound up with the aim of generalizability. Questions of a study's limitations revolve around the extent to which the findings from a study can be generalized to other situations, with the ultimate goal being the development of "situationless," i.e., universal, laws of the behavior of persons and things. Limitations in social science typically relate to issues of sample characteristics, sample size, and the external validity of measurement instruments.

In the humanities, generalizability is not an aim of research; nor are universal laws the ultimate goal. Rather, the focus of humanities scholarship on interpretation of particular works leads to limitations of an entirely different order. The issue is not so much limitations on the generalizability of findings as the validity or adequacy of a particular interpretation. An extensive literature on validity in interpretation of qualitative data exists (see, for example, Bernstein (1983), Packer & Addison (1989), and Salner (1989)). It would be profitable for those who wish to relate autobiographical writing to the study of aging to become conversant with this literature.

Representativeness

All autobiographical writing emanates from a combination of historical circumstances and conceptual frameworks, "forestructures of understanding," available in cultures to writers. From this perspective any particular account of the self in later life is a "good" example, that is, an example reflecting the potentialities available to individuals in that place and time. In a sense it does not matter if Sarton's experience is representative of the experiences of others because no claim is being made for her texts other than that they represent a path of development made available in her culture.

That said, it is still worth recognizing that the preponderance of autobiographical writings that do get published are those of established writers or celebrities. Even without the aim of generalizing and the goal of discovering universal laws, researchers interested in examining published autobiographical works must exercise caution because of the narrow segment of the culture from which such works typically arise. Moreover, the idea that there is a single uniform culture in any given society is questionable. Therefore, published autobiographies could be more accurately characterized as reflecting developmental pathways available in a few subcultures than as reflections of *the* culture. The limited availability of autobiographical writing from diverse subcultures constitutes a limitation of this type of research. Having the opportunity to review and systematically reflect on autobiographical writing from a broader range of subcultures would be advantageous. As discussed below, technology may create that opportunity.

Authenticity

One of the most perplexing dilemmas facing those who study a work of autobiographical writing is whether the author is telling the truth. This seems like a simple question, but upon reflection it is found to open a metaphysical and epistemological Pandora's box. As the quotes cited above from William Maxwell and Doris Grumbach indicate, in the context of stories, including self-stories, events may have narrative truth independent of their historical truth (Spence, 1982). Such narrative truths can be likened to the "truths" expressed in fiction—or as Ricoeur (1981, p. 296) has put it, "By opening us to what is different, history opens us to the possible, whereas fiction, by opening us to the unreal, leads us to what is essential in reality."

Still, for purposes of investigating the experience of aging and the way the self develops in later adulthood, some assurance that an autobiographical work is a genuine reflection of the author's sentiments and not crafted merely to appeal to an audience would be comforting. Unfortunately, there is no way to be certain that the ideas and feelings expressed in autobiographical writing are, in fact, authentic. However, the case is no different with respect to empirical studies in social science using interviews or attitude questionnaires. Any given interview response may be as much a reflection of the interviewee's impression of what would appeal to the interviewer as an authentic rendition of the interviewee's "true" beliefs and feelings.

Literary critics have addressed the puzzles surrounding the "truth" of autobiographical accounts. Notable among such analyses is that of Gusdorf (1980) who reminds us that autobiography is art and, therefore, necessarily entails illusion:

> The illusion begins from the moment that the narrative confers a meaning on the event which when it occurred no doubt had several meanings

> or perhaps none . . . The failures, gaps, and deformities of memory are not due to purely physical cause or to chance, but are the result of the writer wanting to gain acceptance for this or that revised or corrected version of his past, his private reality (p. 42).

That private reality, Gusdorf argues, is ultimately all that is obtainable through autobiographical writing. More than anything autobiography should be viewed as an "avowal of values," rather than as an authoritative account of a life.

As Eakin (1989), cited in Waxman (1997), has noted, despite the impossibility of knowing with certainty the authenticity of an autobiographical account, one can think in terms of a truth compact existing between writers and readers. The argument is that authors, who themselves are readers, want to believe in the referentiality of the autobiographical text. Since autobiographers are motivated by their own desire to believe in the referentiality of autobiographical texts, they strive in their own writing for realistic correspondence between text and life. Both Gusdorf and Eakin offer helpful perspectives on authenticity, but their proposals do fully resolve the epistemological puzzles raised by considering autobiographical writing as a source of knowledge about aging.

For example, the issue is further complicated if one introduces the concept of self-deception. It might be possible for an autobiographical account to be an accurate reflection of the author's beliefs and feelings and, yet, to be so at variance with others' perceptions that the value of the author's rendition of events is thrown into question. The recent biography of Sarton (Peters, 1997) highlights just such tensions, for example, the disjunction between Sarton's accounts of her behavior and feelings toward Judith Matlack and her behavior as witnessed by others and described in the biography.

Yet another complication relating to authenticity is introduced in instances in which an editor stands between the author of the self-representation and the reader. For example, letter series are typically brought to publication by editors, not by the letters' authors. The self represented in such a case is, in a sense, the joint product of the author and the editor. Editors also have roles in shaping the presentation of self in the other forms of published autobiographical writings.

In sum, despite insights from literary critics and qualitative social science researchers, questions relating to the authenticity of autobiographical accounts persist and warrant further examination by those interested in using this material to illuminate the experience of aging.

Analyzability

In the practice of psychoanalysis it is recognized that not all people who seek analysis are analyzable. Originally, the determination of analyzability was based on age and diagnostic categories. Only individuals under age 50 and suffering from transference neuroses (hysteria, phobia, and obsessive-compulsive disorder) were deemed acceptable. As the practice of psychoanalysis evolved, the scope of indications for analysis widened, but the principle of analyzability remained: psychoanalysis is not for everyone.

Similarly, although a great mass of self-reflective writing exists, not all of it is analyzable in the sense of yielding potentially valuable information about aging and the self. A challenge for those who work in this area is to consider the characteristics of "good" self-reflective writing and to clarify the relationship between works that are valuable from a gerontological perspective and those that are valuable from other perspectives, e.g., literature or history. Analyzability, in this sense, refers to works that convey the day-to-day experience of later life, but which also trace the changes in the sense of self that accompany those day-to-day experiences.

Autobiographical works that meet such criteria include those cited earlier of Scott-Maxwell, Sarton, Horner, and Grumbach, as well as those of L'Engle (1974), Truitt (1982; 1986), and Vining (1978).

The full admission of the humanities into the field of gerontology should entail the recognition of some works such as these as being essential reading. The situation is analogous to the place held by some findings from the biological and social sciences. For example, gerontologists of all disciplinary persuasions need to be conversant with the Hayflick limit of cell division; with the confounding of age, period, and cohort in cross-sectional studies of intelligence; and with the myth that older people in the U.S. are neglected by their families. Similarly, future gerontologists of all disciplinary persuasions should be familiar with the essential works in which people have characterized their own aging. Judgments of what to include as essential autobiographical works for the study of aging would obviously differ. Nothing would be more beneficial to the field than a hotly contested debate at a meeting of the Gerontological Society of America about the autobiographies that should be required reading in a recognized program of gerontological education. The issue, of course, is not so much which autobiographies. Rather, the issue is the acknowledgment of the centrality of this form of literature to our understanding of aging.

When all is said and done, autobiographical works are valuable to gerontologists for how they make people think and feel about age. Feelings of camaraderie among readers of these texts arise because many of the published diaries and autobiographies are, in Waxman's (1997) terms, strong texts, that is, texts that change readers' assumptions, undermine stereotypes, and challenge myths. They are texts, in short, that help readers re-imagine their future selves and the range of experience available to them in later life. The sense of camaraderie, then, becomes a consequence of a shared experience, the experience of having one's sense of the possibilities of aging transformed by the self-reflections of older writers.

Thinking back to Magritte's painting, then, we might say that the effort to make sense of the world is not only part of what it means to be human, but also that people's efforts to represent themselves and their worlds—as found, for example, in autobiographical writing—have the power to transform the self-representations of others.

NOTES

[1] Literary critics—Fothergill (1974), Mallon (1984), and Nussbaum (1988)—who have written about the diary as a literary form agree that no consistent distinction can be made between the terms diary and journal. Some published texts labeled diaries are mere records of daily events with little reflection on the meaning of those events. Other published texts labeled diaries are full of personal reflection. Similarly, the term journal may be applied to books that concentrate on objective reporting of events, but may also be applied to books whose focus is on self-reflection.

Although no consistent distinction can be made between the terms journal and diary, it is worthwhile to distinguish between diaries/journals in which the life of the author is the prime subject and works in which the author is principally reporting on external events. The former which can be designated as personal diaries or personal journals, are likely to be of most interest to gerontologists (Berman, 1994).

REFERENCES

Adams, K. (1990). *Journal to the self: 22 paths to spiritual growth.* New York: Warner Books.

Allport, G. W. (1965). *Letters from Jenny.* New York: Harcourt, Brace & World.

Baldwin, C. (1991). *Life's companion: Journal writing as a spiritual quest.* New York: Bantam.

Benstock, S. (Ed.). (1988). *The private self: Theory and practice of women's autobiographical writings.* Chapel Hill: University of North Carolina Press.

Berman, H. J. (1994). *Interpreting the aging self: Personal journals of later life.* New York: Springer Publishing.

Bernstein, R. J. (1983). *Beyond objectivism and relativism: Science, hermeneutics and praxis.* Philadelphia: University of Pennsylvania.

Birren, J. E., & Deutchman, D. E. (1991). *Guiding autobiography groups for older adults: Exploring the fabric of life.* Baltimore: John Hopkins.

Bleich, D. (1978). *Subjective criticism.* Baltimore: Johns Hopkins.

Brown, R. (1996). *Against my better judgment: An intimate memoir of an eminent gay psychologist.* New York: Haworth.

Bruner, J. (1990). *Acts of meaning.* Cambridge, MA: Harvard University Press.

Cohler, B. J., & Galatzer-Levy, R. M. (1990). Self, meaning and morale across the second half of life. In R. A. Nemiroff & C. A. Colarusso (Eds.), *New dimensions in adult development* (pp. 214–263). New York: Basic Books.

Delany, S. L., & Delany, A. E. (1993). *Having our say.* New York: Dell.

Denzin, N. K. (1989). *Interpretive biography.* (Vol. 17). Newbury Park, CA: Sage.

Derrida, J. (1967/1978). *Writing and difference.* Chicago: University of Chicago Press.

Eakin, P. J. (1989). Foreword. In P. Lejeune (Ed.), *On autobiography* (pp. vii–xxvii). Minneapolis: University of Minnesota.

Fothergill, R. A. (1974). *Private chronicles: A study of English diaries.* London: Oxford University Press.

Foveaux, J. (1997). *Any given day: The life and times of Jessie Lee Brown Foveaux.* New York: Warner.

Freeman, M. (1993). *Rewriting the self: History, memory, narrative.* London: Routledge.

Gadamer, H.-G. (1960/1992). *Truth and method* (Weinsheimer, Joel). Marshall, D. G., Trans. (2nd, rev. ed.). New York: Crossroad.

Gergen, K. J., & Gergen, M. M. (1983). Narratives of the self. In T. R. Sarbin & K. E. Scheibe (Eds.), *Studies in social identity* (pp. 254–273). New York: Praeger.

Grumbach, D. (1991). *Coming into the end zone.* New York: Norton.

Grumbach, D. (1993). Conditions and limits of autobiography. In J. Olney (Ed.), *Autobiography: Essays theoretical and critical* (pp. 28–48). Princeton, NJ: Princeton University Press.

Gusdorf, G. (1980). Conditions and limits of autobiography. In J. Olney (Ed.), *Autobiography: Essays theoretical and critical* (pp. 28–48). Princeton, NJ: Princeton University Press.

Hermans, H. J. M., & Hermans-Jansen, E. (1995). *Self-narratives: The construction of meaning in psychotherapy.* New York: Guilford.

Horner, J. (1982). *That time of year.* Amherst: University of Massachusetts Press.

Iser, W. (1978). *The act of reading: A theory of aesthetic response.* Baltimore: Johns Hopkins.

Josselson, R., & Lieblich, A. (Eds.). (1993). *The narrative study of lives* (Vol. 1). Newbury Park, CA: Sage.

Kenyon, G. M., & Randall, W. L. (1997). *Restorying our lives: Personal growth through autobiographical reflection.* Westport, CT: Praeger.

Kleinman, A. (1988). *The illness narratives.* New York: Basic Books.

Korda, M. (1997, October 6). Prompting the president. *The New Yorker, 73,* 88–95.

Kotre, J. (1995). *White gloves: How we create ourselves through memory.* New York: Free Press.

L'Engle, M. (1974). *The summer of the great-grandmother.* San Francisco: Harper & Row.

Lennox, J., & Panofsky, R. (Eds.). (1997). *Selected letters of Margaret Laurence and Adele Wiseman.* Toronto: University of Toronto.

Lyden, J. (1997). *Daughter of the Queen of Sheba: A memoir.* Boston: Houghton Mifflin.

Mallon, T. (1984). *A book of one's own: People and their diaries.* New York: Ticknor and Fields.

Matthews, W. (1950). *British diaries: An annotated biography of British diaries written between 1442 & 1942.* Berkeley: University of California Press.

Maxwell, W. (1980). *So long, see you tomorrow.* New York: Ballantine.

McAdams, D. P. (1993). *The stories we live by.* New York: William Morrow.

McCourt, F. (1996). *Angela's ashes: A memoir.* New York: Scribner.

Moffat, J. (Ed.). (1985). *Points of departure: An anthology of nonfiction.* New York: New American Library.

Nussbaum, F. A. (1988). Toward conceptualizing diary. In J. Olney (Ed.), *Studies in autobiography* (pp. 128–140). New York: Oxford University Press.

Olmstead, A. H. (1975). *Threshold: The first days of retirement.* New York: Harper and Row.

Packer, M. J., & Addison, R. B. (1989). Evaluating an interpretive account. In M. J. Packer & R. B. Addison (Eds.), *Entering the circle: Hermeneutic investigation in psychology* (pp. 275–292). Albany: State University of New York.

Palmer, R. E . (1969). *Hermeneutics: Interpretation theory in Schleiermacher, Dilthey, Heidegger, and Gadamer.* Evanston, IL: Northwestern University Press.

Peters, M. (1997). *May Sarton: A biography.* New York: Knopf.

Ponsonby, A. (1922). *English diaries: A review of English diaries from the sixteenth to the twentieth century with an introduction on diary writing.* New York: George H. Doran.

Progoff, I. (1975). *At a journal workshop: The basic text and guide for using the intensive journal.* New York: Dialogue House Library.

Reagan, R. (1990). *An American life.* New York: Simon & Schuster.

Ricoeur, P. (1981). *Hermeneutics and the human sciences* (Thompson, J. B., Trans.). Cambridge: Cambridge University Press.

Ricoeur, P. (1992). *Oneself as another* (Blamey, K., Trans.). Chicago: University of Chicago Press.

Rorty, A. O. (1976). A literary postscript: Characters, persons, selves, individuals. In A. O. Rorty (Ed.), *The identity of persons.* Berkeley: University of California Press.

Rosenblatt, L. (1964). The poem as event. *College English, 26*(2), 126–128.

Rosenwald, G. C., & Ochberg, R. L. (1992). *Storied lives: The cultural politics of self-understanding.* New Haven: Yale University Press.

Salner, M. (1989). Validity in human science research. In S. Kvale (Ed.), *Issues of validity in qualitative research* (pp. 47–71). Lund, Sweden: Studentlitteratur.

Sarbin, R. R. (1989). Emotions as narrative emplotments. In M. J. Packer & R. B. Addison (Eds.), *Entering the circle: Hermeneutic investigation in psychology* (pp. 185–201). Albany, NY: SUNY Press.

Sarton, M. (1973). *Journal of a solitude.* New York: Norton.

Sarton, M. (1977). *The house by the sea: A journal.* New York: Norton.

Sarton, M. (1980). *Recovering: A journal.* New York: Norton

Sarton, M. (1984). *At seventy: A journal.* New York: Norton.

Sarton, M. (1988). *After the stroke: A journal.* New York: Norton.

Sarton, M. (1992). *Endgame: A journal of the seventy-ninth year.* New York: Norton.

Sarton, M. (1993a). *Among the usual days: A portrait.* New York: Norton.

Sarton, M. (1993b). *Encore: A journal of the eightieth year.* New York: Norton.

Sarton, M. (1996). *At eighty-two: A journal.* New York: Norton.

Schafer, R. (1992). *Retelling a life.* New York: Basic Books.

Schlissel, L. (1982). *Women's diaries of the westward journey.* New York: Schocken.

Scott-Maxwell, F. (1979). *The measure of my days.* New York: Penguin.

Sherman, E. (1991). *Reminiscence and the self in old age.* New York: Springer Publishing.

Shotter, J., & Gergen, K. (Eds.). (1989). *Texts of identify.* London: Sage.

Singer, J. A., & Salovey, P. (1993). *The remembered self: Emotion and memory in personality.*

Spacks, P. (1976). *Imagining a self: Autobiography and novel in eighteenth century England.* Cambridge, MA: Harvard University Press.

Spence, D. P. (1982). *Narrative truth and historical truth.* New York: Norton.

Thomas, W. I., & Znaniecki, F. (1958). *The Polish peasant in Europe and America.* New York: Dover.

Tompkins, J. P. (Ed.). (1980). *Reader-response criticism: From formalism to post-structuralism.* Baltimore, MD: Johns Hopkins.

Truitt, A. (1982). *Daybook: The journal of an artist.* New York: Penguin.

Truitt, A. (1986). *Turn: The journal of an artist.* New York: Viking.

Viney, L. L. (1993). *Life stories: Personal construct therapy with the elderly.* Chichester, UK: Wiley.

Vining, E. G. (1978). *Being seventy: The measure of a year.* New York: Viking.

Waxman, B. F. (1997). *To live in the center of the moment.* Charlottesville, VA: University Press of Virginia.

Weinsheimer, J. C. (1985). *Gadamer's hermeneutics: A reading of truth and method.* New Haven: Yale

White, M., & Epston, D. (1990). *Narrative means to therapeutic ends.* New York: W. W. Norton.

PART III
Humanistic Themes in the Study of Aging

15

Intergeneration and Regeneration: The Meaning of Old Age in Films and Videos

Robert E. Yahnke

T he aim of this chapter is to analyze two primary themes in the depiction of aging in films and videos—intergeneration and regeneration. Intergeneration refers to the basis of all relationships between the young and old. Particular attention will be given to two aspects of intergenerational relationships: the way the old serve as role models and mentors for the young, and the way middle-aged children face their parents' aging in the context of caregiving concerns. In the intergenerational world of films and videos the old are almost always portrayed as active, engaged role models that delight and inspire the young (Yahnke, 1985; 1988; 1989). In the context of specific intergenerational relationships, they are depicted as wise, nurturing mentors, and the fruits of intergeneration require that both the young and the old change dramatically and profoundly based on their interactions. When intergenerational relationships involve middle-aged children as caregivers for their parents, the middle-aged children gain insights into the process of their own aging, learn to accept new ground rules for their parents' independence and autonomy, and thus confront some of the limitations and boundaries of caregiving.

In other words, there is always a give-and-take basis in intergenerational relationships. The old serve the young as mentors and role models, but the young remind the old that there are unfinished tasks for them to complete. When they are the objects of caregiving, the old often rediscover latent strengths and untapped resources for adaptation as well. Regeneration is the key word in all of these interactions. Intergeneration almost always leads to regeneration (renewal, rejuvenation, and a restoration to wholeness of identity) for the old person. Regeneration signals an inward emotional and psychological change in the old person, manifested by a sense of closure, resolution, healing, acceptance, and clarity of purpose.

Regeneration can occur through intergeneration; or it can occur outside of a specific, focused intergenerational relationship. When combined with two related themes—aging in place and elders going home again—regeneration is revealed as a gradual ongoing process (in the former) or a sudden, cathartic response to stimuli (in the latter case). Aging in place grounds the old person in the traditions, values, and continuity of community and home. These qualities provide a context for an ongoing regeneration within the old person. Often elders who have aged in place are viewed metaphorically as the emotional "heart" of the community. People within the community are drawn to them as reconcilers and peacemakers. They possess an abiding wholeness of character that has sustained them, as well as their community, over time. When the old are compelled to make journeys back to their homes, for a variety of emotional and psychological reasons, then regeneration is characterized by a sudden, overwhelming sense of healing, restoration to wholeness, resolution of unfinished business from the past, redefinition of character and identity for the old person. Regeneration through such experiences reminds us that old age still is a time for new learning and new opportunities (Moss, 1976; Trojan, 1980).

Regeneration, finally, depends upon the variables of intimacy and love. Intergenerational relationships provide those qualities as an antidote to loneliness or unresolved conflicts. But some films and videos portray people in old age engaged in intimate and loving relationships with their peers. Just as intergenerational relationships break down barriers of ageism and age stereotyping by revealing the equality among the generations, intimacy and love between persons who are old affirm the reality of the deeply felt inner lives of the old, fully capable of friendship, devotion, and passion.

Of course, there are exceptions to the positive treatment of aging noted in the themes above. The old are not always wise and nurturing mentors or role models. They are not always capable of teaching their caregivers new insights about independence and autonomy. They are not always selfless and dedicated to their communities (Flynn, 1989). Going home again does not always ensure catharsis and resolution. The old are as capable of rejecting intimacy and love as are the young or the middle-aged. Several examples of such negative responses to intergeneration and regeneration appear in the analysis that follows. But the primary thrust of the portrayal of old age, in the context of films and videos, is to underscore the abiding resilience and forward-thinking attitudes of the old, especially as they relate to the young.

It should be no surprise that most films and videos about the experience of aging are generally upbeat and positive stories about elders who find some measure of fulfillment in their lives, either through intergenerational relationships, or meaningful connections with their communities, or intimate relationships with other elders. Since films and videos come in two forms—documentaries or fictional portrayals, it may help to examine how each format is related to these outcomes. Documentaries often are created by individuals who have had successful intergenerational relationships with the old or who have been embroiled in the human drama of aging themselves, perhaps as a caregiver to a parent. There are no documentaries about unregenerate elders who are unforgiving, unstable, and uncaring. There are many documentaries about elders who have overcome a number of conflicts or "low points" in their lives and regained their emotional and psychological balance. The person who conceived the documentary wants the film or video made in order to convey some idea of how a conflict was resolved, how a relationship was healed, how an old person was a mentor or a role model, or how an old person dealt with a difficult emotional and psychological crisis (Yahnke, 1988; 1989).

Fictional portrayals of aging diverge from documentaries slightly in terms of how they portray the experience of aging. Imagined characters replace real persons, and the inner workings of character and conflict can be explored more fully because of the flexibility of the screenplay. Characters can be alone in fictional films and reveal themselves in ways that they can not in documentaries. The language of fictional films, like drama, is about conflict and resolution. At the beginning of a film, an older character is not complete, appears unfulfilled, and his or her life is conflicted and unsatisfactory. The process of the film is a gradual unfolding of pathways to completeness or fulfillment—even if there is only a measure of resolution to be gained. These films, for the most part, are about persons who change and grow.

Films and videos, in the context of this chapter, refer to two types of media. The latter are educational films and videos and will be referred to hereafter as *educational videos.* Most videos are short in duration, often 28 minutes in length, and they are produced by independent filmmakers, not by large studios. A long video may be 45–55 minutes. Most videos are in the documentary mode, and thus are nonfiction portrayals of aging. A few are feature-length documentaries, again created by independent filmmakers. A lesser number of videos are fictional portrayals of aging. Films, in the context of this chapter, are feature-length films and will be referred to hereafter as *feature-length films*. Feature-length films are fictional portrayals of aging. They are approximately four to five times longer than the average educational video. Thus, they are able to employ much greater complexity of characterization, a higher number of subplots, and an increased level of subtlety and complexity in the interaction among characters. Feature-length films are to educational videos what novels are to short stories.

Educational videos are targeted for gerontological audiences. Titles are often marketed under specific categories, much like chapters in textbooks. For instance, distributors' catalogs list videos that relate to a variety of topics, including the following: Alzheimer's disease, caregiving, elder abuse, grandparenting, home care, hospice, long-term care, loss and bereavement, mid-life issues, nursing homes, rural aging, sexuality, widowhood, women's issues. Each educational video comes with a set number of applications. Sometimes a video may be relevant to two complementary topics, such as caregiving and family studies, or elder abuse and long-term care. But usually the application is made to one of the two topics. In other words, educational videos are an adjunct to print and lecture resources. Many instructors in introductory courses in psychology, social gerontology, or family studies relating to gerontology use videos as an integral part of their instruction (Yahnke, 1997). Feature-length films are more difficult to integrate into gerontological curricula than the shorter educational film and video.

For many years one fictional portrayal in the educational video medium was recognized as universally applicable to a number of gerontological topics (Yahnke, 1985). That video was *Peege* (1973), a portrayal of a family's Christmas visit to an old woman in a nursing home. The parents and their children visit the father's mother, Ethel, known affectionately by the family as Peege. Although she is blind, Peege is aware of her surroundings and receptive to the reminiscences that can tap her rich store of memories. But both parents and their younger sons are unable to interact meaningfully with Peege because they bring to this visit their own fears and insecurities about aging. The father is overwhelmed by his mother's disabilities, which make her a shadow of her former self. The mother feels threatened by fears and anxieties regarding the physical decline she associates with aging. Two younger brothers lack the intimate memories of a shared past with Peege.

Only the eldest son Greg, back for a visit from college, seems connected to his grandmother. The fullness of Peege's life is illustrated through numerous flashbacks, from her grandson's point of view, of the two interacting at different stages of their lives. As the scenes in flashback progress, viewers witness an active, high-spirited, and loving woman who was an able mentor for Greg throughout his childhood and adolescence. Only now—because of her blindness and a stroke—has she begun to exhibit signs of the stereotypically "old" person, the image of someone who sits in her chair all day and appears alienated and withdrawn. Although Greg is shocked at seeing her disabilities, he controls his fears and anxieties toward the losses implicit in aging and reclaims (through reminiscences) the memories he has of growing up with Peege.

Why was *Peege* such a pivotal educational video in gerontological education? It combines the two essential ingredients of all films and videos about aging—intergeneration and regeneration. The story is told from multiple points of view, including those representing the two younger generations, and thus provides insights into some of the barriers of intergeneration. Greg's point of view reveals his compassion for and devotion to his grandmother. His memories of happier times, and his later embrace of the old woman when he sits next to her and stimulates her reminiscences, teach younger viewers that viewing old age as necessarily unpleasant and abhorrent represents stereotypical thinking. Because Greg remains faithful to Peege, the viewer's attitude toward the old woman is revised. At the end of the video viewers see Peege as a whole person whose physical disability in no way detracts from her inner spiritual and intellectual qualities. Viewers see the world from Peege's point of view (this shift in point of view began during the scene where Greg reminisces with his Aunt Ethel). The last image in the video is that of the old woman, alone in her room, smiling broadly as she "remembers" those active days from the past with her loving grandson. In other words, through its revelation of a dynamic intergenerational relationship between a woman and her grandson, the video delivers us to the essence of how intergeneration (bonds between the young and the old) and regeneration (restoration to wholeness in one's old age) are the two poles of meaning in films and videos about aging.

INTERGENERATION: HOW THE OLD SERVE
THE YOUNG AS MENTORS AND ROLE MODELS

The young need mentors and role models. They need to understand that aging is a process of accrual and yet loss, of advancement as well as decline. But they also need to understand what it will be like someday to be alone with themselves in their old age—to face that aloneness and to find a measure of self-fulfillment as individuals. Films and videos teach us about both of these worlds—intergeneration and regeneration.

Educational Videos

These videos emphasize idiosyncratic, irrepressible characters that are models of positive aging. All examples of this theme are documentaries, and although specific intergenerational relationships are not depicted in these videos, the old are portrayed as role models because of their high energy, clearly defined values, and creativity—characteristics younger audiences can relate to easily. Old people in these documentaries become antidotes to ageism and age stereotyping, and the implicit message of such films is, "Don't be afraid of growing old."

Two documentaries from the 1970s offer compelling examples of how active aging is related to mentoring. *At 99: A Portrait of Louise Tandy Murch* (1974) portrays an avid exercise enthusiast, Louise Tandy Murch, whose enthusiasm for life is an inspiration to everyone around her. In one scene she plays her piano at an outdoor gathering for senior citizens, where her strong voice, good humor, and zest for life carry the day. When she gets tired or depressed, she says, "I lie down and have these happy memories." Louise Tandy Murch's philosophy is "accentuate the positive," and she projects a vision of old age that is upbeat, harmonious, and fulfilling.

Luther Metke at 94 (1978) is another example of a positive role model for younger viewers. A widower, he lives alone in a cabin in Oregon. Over the years he has constructed between 35–40 log cabins in the Northwest. In one scene he is shown working with a young couple who hopes to build their own cabin someday. Later, they invite him to their wedding, and he dances comfortably with the bride. Luther Metke projects a warmth and honesty that is genuine. Most important, he shares with viewers the conditions of a life lived alone in old age. Late in the film he says, "I've got to the point where I can live with myself." He is still engaged in the process of aging, even at 94, and that point is the greatest lesson in this video.

Later documentary videos that depict elders as active, engaged persons include *Steady As She Goes* (1981), an example of how retirement can become a separate and fulfilling stage in one's life; *Age is No Barrier* (1989), which provides a glimpse of Canadian elders who keep active and challenged through exercise and their participation in a special program called the "University of Age-rs"; and *Dorothy Molter: Living in the Boundary Waters* (1987), which profiles a fascinating woman who devoted her life to the service of people in the northern Minnesota wilderness. Another documentary, *The Stone Carvers* (1984), features a reunion of several Italian-American stone carvers, who reminisce about their halcyon days of stone carving on monuments in Washington, DC. Their creativity and lasting contributions to society and to the arts are celebrated through the whimsy of the visuals, the upbeat musical score, and the wonderful stories the old men share. None of these documentaries is an idealized or sentimentalized image of aging. All of these old people are aware of the loneliness, physical difficulties, and emotional toll of aging. But they are survivors who have a positive message for the younger generation.

Martha and Ethel (1995), directed by Jyl Johnstone and Barbara Ettinger, illustrates the ways in which the impact of intergeneration can have mixed results for different families. This feature-length documentary tells the story of the filmmaker's nannies—one a German immigrant and the other an African American woman from North Carolina. Martha and Ethel are remarkable opposites. Martha's strict upbringing as a child was manifested in her stern rearing of the Johnstone children. Martha was introverted, a loner, someone who viewed childrearing with inflexible ideas about discipline, cleanliness, and order. Ethel was from a warm and loving family, and she brought a similar model of family life to her work as a nanny. Ethel was an extrovert. She loved company and viewed childrearing as a series of opportunities for sharing, personal growth, and community.

The Johnstone children admit the many drawbacks of having Martha as their nanny. But later in the film, after Martha retires, several of the Johnstone children reenter her life and begin to relate to her on the basis of a more positive role. Now they learn new perspectives on her strength of character, and they come to know her as a grandmotherly friend of the family. They take Martha for a vacation back to the village in Germany where she grew up. The Town Council there arranges to have a parade in her honor, and Martha is carried in an old-fashioned carriage up and down the main street. In these scenes a softness and sensitivity in Martha's character is revealed. She relates to her former charges with humor and affection in ways she could not have imagined in her former limiting role as nanny.

Feature-Length Films

Three American films from the 1970s, *Harold and Maude* (1971), *Kotch* (1971), and *Harry and Tonto* (1974), explore specific intergenerational relationships between alienated troubled youth seeking transition to adulthood and idiosyncratic, irascible, fiercely independent older characters. The function of the older characters is to mentor, to listen, and to guide the youth through that passage. The middle generation (children of the older adults) typically is portrayed one-dimensionally as limited characters, trapped by the requirements of work and responsibilities, inept at resolving emotional dilemmas.

In the first film above, Maude rescues a young man who has withdrawn from life into a fantasy world of alienation and mock suicides.

Everything about Maude is creative and original. She embraces "change . . . all revolving . . . burials and rebirths . . . one linked to the other—the great circle of life!" Initially Maude is a surrogate grandmother to Harold. She initiates Harold into the joys of creative self-expression. She encourages him to take risks. Eventually, the basis of their relationship shifts to greater intimacy. Harold declares his love for Maude on the night of her 80th birthday and then is shocked to discover that Maude has taken an overdose of sleeping pills only hours earlier. Harold's world is turned upside down. How could Maude kill herself? The idiosyncrasies of *Harold and Maude* make it difficult to categorize it in any one gerontological theme. For the purposes of this theme, the film underscores—through its radical plot—the healing effects of Maude's actions, which culminate in her long-planned suicide. Harold is forced to confront the reality of her death—in contrast to his many pretend-suicides acted out earlier in the film—and thus learn the value of his own life. Harold overcomes his alienation and lack of emotional vitality. Maude experiences one last strong emotional bond before she dies.

Two other films from the early 1970s, *Kotch* (1971) and *Harry and Tonto* (1974), tell similar stories about old people whose roles within the family are either rejected or nonexistent. Like Maude, Kotch and Harry are willing to sacrifice for the younger generation. Joe Kotcher lives with his son and daughter-in-law, and he would love nothing more than to fulfill the role of kindly old grandfather. But his daughter-in-law is tired of accommodating herself to the old man's ways. Kotcher leaves them behind, befriends a pregnant teenager, and becomes a friend, listener, and surrogate grandfather. In this film both the old person and the teenager gain from the intergenerational relationship. The young woman sums up their relationship: "He was old and ending and kids and babies were new and beginning." Eventually she leaves and Kotch looks forward to a comfortable and family-centered old age—but on his own terms.

Harry and Tonto (1974) is another example of an irascible old man who is independent, free-spirited, opinionated, and rebellious. In this case the focus of the film is Harry's cross-country odyssey that leads to a series of intergenerational adventures. Evicted from his New York City apartment, Harry (with his orange tabby Tonto) tries to adapt to moving in with his son's family on Long Island. Although he is drawn to his kooky nephew, who is struggling with issues of identity and autonomy, Harry decides to leave and seek some answers for himself on the road.

Characters like Maude, Kotch, and Harry are to some extent stereotypical and even sentimentalized portraits of old age; that is, they are perfect, idealized images of old age, capable of rejuvenating the lost souls of adolescence, youth, and even middle age. They have financial independence, are not constrained by family systems, and offer an image of old age as a time of creativity and self-fulfillment. In many respects they are "younger" than their children or other middle-aged adults, who lead lives of quiet desperation. Their idiosyncratic behavior, sense of freedom, and prevailing optimism counter the negative stereotypes of old age that were prevalent in the early 1970s. Intergenerational relationships with characters like these are bound to be engaging and fulfilling.

On Golden Pond (1981), based on the Ernest Thompson play, portrays another example of mentoring between a troubled adolescent and an old man. But this relationship is secondary to a resolution of a strained relationship between the old man and his adult daughter. An old couple, Norman and Ethel, return to their Maine cabin for another summer. They know that each summer may be their last. Norman and Ethel are complementary opposites. She is active, ebullient, and energetic. Norman, a retired college professor, is acerbic, introverted, and becoming increasingly frail. He isn't afraid to "take on" irreverent youth. In one scene he scolds young people at the dock: "Do you think it's funny being old? My whole goddamn body's falling apart!" Ethel affectionately refers to Norman as "an old coot."

Their calm, self-contained world is invaded by their adult daughter, Chelsea, who comes with a new fiancé and the man's 13-year-old son from his first marriage. Chelsea's marriage also ended in divorce, and she brings with her an incompleteness and irresolution in her relationship with her father Norman. *On Golden Pond* is a lyrical, almost reverent film about reconciliation between generations. But the terms of the unresolved conflicts are arranged like a series of set pieces to be ticked off one by one. The adolescent boy is surly and uncooperative; but one fishing trip cures him of his emotional woes. Chelsea keeps insisting that something between father and daughter has left her wounded and lacking closure; so a climactic conversation between Chelsea and her father resolves her pain. In many respects the characterization of the elderly couple is more fascinating than the intergenerational relationships they resolve. Scenes between Norman and Ethel (played skillfully by Henry Fonda and Katherine Hepburn) are beautifully rendered. These two old actors light up the screen. Unfortunately, the requisite intergenerational conflicts overwhelm the fascinating give-and-take of the old couple's relationship.

Several international films provide more subtle and nonstereotypical portrayals of intergenerational relationships. *Cinema Paradiso* (1990), an Italian film, follows the experiences of its main character, Salvatore, across three stages of his life—childhood, adolescence, and late middle age. *Cinema Paradiso* incorporates themes of intergenerational relationships common to earlier films. The young Salvatore finds a mentor and guide in Alfredo, a weary, no-nonsense projectionist who works in the cinema—the heart and soul of the small Sicilian village. Like Maude or Kotch, this old man is a surrogate parent and grandparent. The film climaxes with the middle-aged Salvatore's return to his home of Giancaldo to attend Alfredo's funeral. Before long Salvatore becomes "trapped" in nostalgia. Everywhere he goes he finds evidence of the person he was 20, 30, even 40 years ago. The small town is seemingly unchanged from his youth. His mother has maintained her son's room as a shrine to his childhood.

Closure for Salvatore comes when he receives a final and liberating gift left behind by Alfredo—a short film that contains clips Alfredo spliced together of all the scenes of kissing he had to cut out of the films in the 1930s and 1940s (censored by the town priest when the cinema was owned by the church). When Salvatore views these clips, he finally grasps Alfredo's advice: "Get on with your life—move beyond the child self and the adolescent self you once were." *Cinema Paradiso* advances the theme of intergenerational relationships beyond the earlier examples of perfect mentors who neatly resolved the problems experienced by their youthful charges. Salvatore's emotionally charged return to his small Sicilian village (by the way, the director's own childhood home is near Palermo)—coupled with Salvatore's insight into Alfredo's final gift to him illustrate the ways one intergenerational relationship can impact a person's life across all stages of his life. Now the middle-aged Salvatore is free to rediscover the passion he experienced as a child and adolescent.

Two French films provide complex visions of intergeneration between a young woman and an older man. In *Nelly and Monsieur Arnauld* (1996), a beautiful young woman, troubled by the impending break-up of her marriage, the loss of her job, and serious debts, accepts a "loan" and part-time editorial work from Monsieur Arnauld, a friend of Nelly's mother. This relationship deepens as first Monsieur Arnauld, and then Nelly, reveals details about personal and familial conflicts. Both lives are changed by the dynamics of their intimacy and sharing. At the end of the film Nelly finalizes her divorce and finds a new job. Monsieur Arnauld's resolution is even more surprising. He decides to live with his wife again after years of separation, only weeks after another man, her long-time lover, dies. Through their intergenerational relationship both come to a clearer understanding of what is required of them to find emotional fulfillment at their respective stages of life.

A similar expression of intergeneration can be found in *Red* (1995), the third film in a trilogy (*Blue, White, Red*) by Krzysztof Kieslowski. *Red* explores *fraternity* (one of three symbols in the French tricolor) from the perspective of a compassionate young model, Valentine, someone who is all "heart." She meets and befriends a despondent and reclusive old man, a retired judge. Their relationship also fosters a regeneration of both of their lives. As in *Nelly and Monsieur Arnauld,* both young and old listen to each other and learn from each other. Their intimacy helps both to free themselves from unresolved issues from the past as well as present entanglements. Most important, their relationship enables the old man to restore his sense of honor and self-respect.

An unusual example of role reversal in intergenerational relationships is shown in *Pelle the Conqueror* (1988). Lasse Karlsson, an aging Swedish widower, emigrates to Denmark with his son Pelle to find work as a farm laborer. Pelle witnesses his father being repeatedly intimidated, cowed, and humiliated by the farm's owner, the young farm manager, and other female farm workers. The old man is unable to provide the expected mentoring and guidance for his young son. Lasse even fails to secure intimacy in his personal life and descends, temporarily, into alcoholism. But father and son survive because each supports the other. Finally, Pelle leaves the farm to "conquer" the world. His old father stays behind, admitting he is too old to travel: "There's no future for old men."

One feature-length film stands out as a negative example of intergeneration. *Lost in Yonkers* (1993) was written by Neil Simon, based on his 1991 play. The main character, Grandma Kurnitz, is mean-spirited and scarred by unresolved anger and unremitting hate. There is nothing sentimental about her. How can there be? She has squeezed out every bit of passion and sentiment in her life and become cold and hard and inflexible: she lives by the motto, "You don't survive in this world without being like steel." Grandma is proud to say, "I buried a husband and two children and I didn't cry." She believes that punishment, rejection, intimidation, and abuse all toughen the individual. She has had lots of practice. All of her children have been permanently scarred by her stern discipline.

The film takes place in the early years of World War II when two of her grandsons, Jay and Arty, are forced to spend a year with Grandma in her Yonkers apartment (above her candy store). The boys are "lost in Yonkers," and initially are terrified by this malevolent and unforgiving old woman—certainly not the stereotypical sweet grandmother who gives candy to little children. This grandma runs a candy store with an iron fist! But Jay and Arty are a match for Grandma's best attempts to alienate them. The two boys interact like a well-oiled comedy team. They perfectly complement each other—one the cautious, tactful straight man, the other the forthright and risk-taking punch-liner. They never lose sight of the values their father instilled in them. They have coping skills; they see Grandma's ruthlessness and yet her limits.

Intergeneration usually requires some emotional giving of ground by both the young and the old. When the older adult remains unyielding, resistant to change, then the burden falls entirely upon the young. It seems too much to ask of the child, young adult, or middle-aged person to carry the burden of intergeneration alone.

Bella, Grandma's youngest child, is the "emotional" heart of the family. She escapes Grandma's oppression because she admits her own loneliness and yearning for love. She is committed to relationships. She realizes that her mother is holding her back because the old woman thinks Bella is a child, one part innocent and one part stupid. Bella dreams of marrying someone and of having children. She tries to reach her mother, to reach some soft and gentle core of a giving, nurturing, loving person. Their final confrontation ends in a standoff. Bella storms out of the house and screams, "Thieves and sick little girls! That's what you've got! Only God did not make us that way! You did!" The director cuts to a shot of the old woman seated in her chair. She is on the verge of tears. But even as her eyes well up with tears she stuffs a handkerchief in her mouth and presses both of her hands over it to stifle her emotions. In the same way she wastes an opportunity for regeneration.

Lost in Yonkers reminds us that even when older adults are unable to change, or to admit their own vulnerability, they may be a stimulus for adaptation and personal growth on the part of the younger generation. Grandma developed impressive coping mechanisms in the face of a difficult and sometimes traumatic childhood. But her specific antidote to what was unfulfilled or unresolved in the past leads her to inflict severe emotional wounds on all of her children. Grandma doesn't respond positively to intergenerational relationships because it is too late for them, or because she is too old. She resists change because that is more comfortable, because that is her choice. *Lost in Yonkers* reflects all that is idiosyncratic and all that is unsentimental in intergenerational relationships.

INTERGENERATION AND CAREGIVING

The terms of intergeneration for those in middle age often require encounters with the stresses and burdens of caregiving. In three educational videos middle-aged daughters are faced with difficult judgments about their mother's emotional and physical needs. For these daughters, confronting the demands of caregiving leads to a number of concerns: persuading parents to accept some level of care, finding the right level of care, adapting to the reversal of roles in parent-child relationships, and—for themselves—adjusting to the changing perceptions of their own aging. Caregiving dilemmas also bring to the surface old hurts and unresolved conflicts between parents and children.

Educational Videos

Three documentaries offer compelling examples of intergeneration in the context of caregiving: *I Know a Song: A Journey With Alzheimer's Disease, Complaints of a Dutiful Daughter,* and *Curtain Call.* In each case, the documentary focuses on a daughter's attempts to reconcile herself to her mother's changing condition—in the first two cases the effects of Alzheimer's disease, and in the third video the effects of a stroke. In each case the daughter, who is intimately involved in the filmmaking process, also feels trapped by the pressures of caregiving. Thus, each video illustrates the daughters' decisions to document the process they went through to find a measure of resolution for their crises.

Brenda King's mother, featured in *I Know a Song: A Journey With Alzheimer's Disease* (1987), is in the last stage of the disease. Brenda visits her regularly at a nursing home, yet refuses to let her mother's identity slip away. Instead, Brenda affirms the unbroken bond between mother and daughter. Throughout the video Brenda touches her mother, holds her, kisses her, sings to her, and makes eye contact. The filmmaker incorporates images from the past, old photographs and home movies of her mother. In those images Brenda's mother is active, boisterous, playful. Several times the filmmaker employs an ingenious visual trick. Parts of old black and white photographs suddenly turn to vibrant colors—green, blue, red. This visual magic suggests that Brenda's reminiscences recover some of the color and life of the original experiences. Each glimmer of color is a brief reminder of the full and complete life that her mother was leading before she was struck with Alzheimer's disease. In some respects these scenes may suggest that there are corners of her mother's mind that are still in color, that is, alive and vivid with memory.

At the end of the video Brenda recalls that each time she ends a visit with her mother in the nursing home, the nurses ask if her mother recognized her. She always answers, "I felt she did." The last two images in the film reinforce Brenda's commitment to viewing her mother's identity as whole and untouched by the disease. The first is an image of Brenda looking up at her mother in the nursing home; the second is an old photograph that shows Brenda as a child. She is looking up into her mother's face. To Brenda, nothing has changed. Her mother is still her mother, and she is whole. In effect, Brenda restores her mother's identity just as Greg restored Ethel's through reminiscences that were visually displayed as flashbacks in *Peege*. Brenda's story triumphs because it communicates something permanent in her relationship to her mother that could not be destroyed even by a disease as relentless and devastating as Alzheimer's.

In *Complaints of a Dutiful Daughter* (1995) the filmmaker comes to a similar conclusion as she tells the story of her mother's severe decline because of Alzheimer's. Deborah is often distressed with her mother's compulsive, repetitive behaviors, and for some time she insists that her mother try to change those behaviors. In essence, Deborah is overwhelmed by how Alzheimer's has stolen her mother's identity and disrupted the basis of their relationship. Finally, Deborah gives up trying to control her mother's behaviors. She realizes it does not matter whether her mother knows her own identity or the identity of her daughter. Deborah admits that "It was a liberating moment" when she let go and began to interact with her mother "in the moment." Closure for Deborah comes when she acknowledges that her mother is a person with a new identity (based upon dementia) rather than a person who has lost her old identity.

A third video, *Curtain Call* (1995), is another example of a daughter having difficulty making her way through the unfamiliar territory of adult caregiving. Michel Jones returns home after her mother suffers a stroke because Michel wants to help her mother maintain herself in her own home and yet consider an eventual decision regarding her living circumstances. At the same time Michel seeks to resolve some personal conflicts with her mother and perhaps restore a diminished mother-daughter bond. She wants her mother to face openly some serious issues about her increasing frailty and what Michel views as her mother's resistance to her own aging. But Michel learns that her own wishes for her mother's well-being must be balanced by her mother's right to autonomy.

Michel allows her mother to speak on her own behalf throughout the video. At one point Edith complains, "Sometimes I'm a case history." She realizes that now her daughter is in some respects her "enemy"— Michel is plotting to take away her freedom. Although Michel views her mother as "an accident waiting to happen," she begins to realize that her own nagging reveals more about her needs than about her mother's frailty. The video ends without a specific resolution. Michel concludes, "In the end I go back to my life and she is left alone with hers." Michel makes the case that both her mother's and her own points of view have validity. Most important, despite her concerns as a daughter of a frail elder, she reaches a point where she can respect and affirm her mother's right to maintain her independence and autonomy. In all three videos the terms of intergeneration initially are characterized by loss: each daughter assumes that her mother's character and identity have been inextricably altered by the processes of disease or disability. But each daughter comes to redefine intergeneration so that it incorporates the restoration of the mother's identity and the rededication of mother-daughter bonds.

Two educational videos that are fictional portrayals of aging also illustrate the nuances of intergeneration and caregiving. *Weekend* (1971), a Yugoslavian film, tells the story of a three-generation family that goes on a picnic in the country, enjoys a last meal together, and then departs, after leaving the grandfather sitting in his favorite chair under a tree. After the family leaves, other old people can be seen sitting in chairs apart from each other at different points along the hillside. What are viewers to think? If the action of the video is viewed metaphorically, one can conclude that the old man has been "put out to pasture" by his family, just as the other old people seen at the end of the film have been left behind after similar "picnics." The video suggests that the family is acting out a ritual that has been set in motion some time in the past and now has become part of the fabric of this culture. Here the expected thing to do is to discard the oldest members of a family when they have outlived their usefulness. Unfortunately, the child in this video can not break the tragic circle that has been set in motion in ages past. The old man is abandoned, the family returns home, and someday this ritual of abandonment will be repeated with the son disposing of his father just as his father disposed of the old man.

An interesting companion piece to *Weekend* would be the Canadian video *The Elder* (1990). This short video is a haunting, symbolic treatment of a difficult passage in the life of a family—the day the elder leaves her home and moves into a long-term-care facility. Unlike *Peege,* the video is not a realistic presentation of the family's awkward visit to a nursing home. Instead, the video provides a symbolic setting, one populated by "elders," old persons who dress in long fur coats and wear large turbans and interact within a desert-like setting. The "elders" are seen for the first time through the eyes of the old woman's grandchildren, who accompany their parents to the institution. Only the "middle generation" fails to see the "elders" in their symbolic setting. The symbolic and the real settings are paralleled throughout the video until the moment when the old woman says a symbolic farewell to her grandchildren (who are also dressed like "elders") and then is alone in her room—and sitting on her bed in that remote desert setting. The video engages viewers at the level of visual metaphors. The "elders" are beautiful, seem fulfilled, but are isolated from the rest of the world. The images in this video will invite discussion of ways in which families may cope with the attendant separation from the elder in the family and ways in which our society fails to value its "elders."

Feature-Length Films

Young and middle-aged characters face challenges in caregiving in two films, *Tell Me a Riddle* (1980) and *Dad* (1989). The old couple in *Tell Me a Riddle,* based on the 1956 novella by Tillie Olsen, have become antagonists in their old age. Now David and Eva face the prospects of their old age with dissonance and disharmony. David wants to move into a union retirement home. But Eva clings to her revolutionary past in Russia and to memories of the woman who was her mentor when she was a teenager. She ignores David's ramblings. He tells his children, "She goes her way, I go mine."

Their intergenerational relationships with their granddaughter, Jeannie, offers closure for both old people. Jeannie is a modern woman, independent, self-reliant, committed to social action. Despite her advancing cancer, Eva is buoyed by her interactions with this young woman. At the same time Jeannie's caregiving for Eva and her ability to put Eva in touch again with her revolutionary past are precious gifts from a granddaughter. The film offers a fresh vision of intergenerational relationships that draws upon the strengths of both the young and the old.

Meanwhile, Jeannie succeeds in opening David to new possibilities in art and relationships. Near death, Eva is confined to a hospital bed in Jeannie's apartment. Closure for Jeannie occurs one night when she sees David lying next to Eva in the bed. Both are asleep and lie in each other's arms. She draws their picture, and later, after Eva dies, Jeannie encourages David to celebrate Eva's life by dancing with Jeannie at the bedside. *Tell Me a Riddle* shares the intergenerational linkage between the young and the old generations. As before, the middle generation is blocked from renewal and reconciliation. Only the very young and the very old share meaningful interactions.

In *Dad,* based on the 1981 novel by William Wharton, middle-aged executive John Tremont leaves his work to devote himself to full-time caregiving for his demented father. Early in the film his parents are characterized as complementary opposites of the couple in *Tell Me a Riddle.* In the case of *Dad* the father is the sensitive, nurturing type; the mother is the self-centered, narrow-minded type. She is a bossy woman, a slave of routines, who structures her husband's life to such an extent that she has made him into a kind of zombie. When she has a mild heart attack, John returns home to find his father apparently suffering from severe dementia.

John soon learns that his father's mental condition is the direct result of his mother's intimidation and control. He throws himself into the caregiving enterprise and single-handedly overcomes the negligence of doctors and nurses, figures out ways to help his father relearn simple tasks, and maintains vigils by his father's bedside at times of

crisis. Thanks to his heroic efforts, his father recovers from his dementia, begins to take charge of his own life, and turns into an energetic,
creative, engaging, dynamic old person—just the stereotype of positive
aging that was established by films like *Harold and Maude, Kotch,* and
Harry and Tonto. Even the mother is redeemed: before her husband
dies she grudgingly gives him approval for his fantasy life. Although
the intensity and dedication of the middle-aged son's caregiving is
impressive in this film, the negative stereotypes of the mother's character and the health-care system undermine its effect.

In *The Winter Guest* (1997), written by Sharman MacDonald and based
on his play, an old woman's anxieties are exposed in the context of a
complex intergenerational relationship with her middle-aged daughter,
who is "stuck" in the depths of her grieving after her husband's death.
The daughter lives in a small Scottish coastal town, and one cold gray
winter day her mother makes an unannounced visit. The mother often
ruminates negatively on the external changes based on her physical
aging. Once she complains, "I get a fright when I look in the mirror. I
hate my old face." What she will not do is reveal her greatest fear
explicitly to Frances: she is terrified that Frances and her son will
move to Australia and leave her behind.

The portrayal of the two women's intergenerational relationship is
complex and moving. Viewers are given an opportunity to sympathize
with both women, even the fussing and grumbling mother—even as
both characters perform an edgy and challenging dance as adver-
saries. In a key scene both women encounter by chance a young boy
who has skipped school and is emotionally adrift. Now three generations interact. The young boy's interest in Frances' newly cropped hair
impresses the mother, who had earlier viewed this act as a sign of
rebellion and a rejection of her values. She begins to appreciate her
daughter's need to assert her independence and individuality.
Eventually Frances gains insights into her mother's increasing frailty,
loneliness, regrets, and despair. At the end of the film mother and
daughter share an uneasy truce, and Frances admits that she is not
going to move to Australia after all. Both acknowledge the other's
needs as individuals, and both are regenerated, given a chance to
begin again. Caregiving issues will resurface in the future; but for now
both will acknowledge the other's needs and carry on.

An example of a middle-aged women confronting a horrifying existential moment in caregiving can be found in *Dolores Claiborne* (1995).
Kathy Bates plays an abused wife who ekes out a living for her alco-
holic husband and her daughter on the Maine coast as a housekeeper
and caregiver for Vera, a rich widow. Once an attractive, vibrant, and
elegant woman, the giver of gracious parties, now Vera has been reduced
to a caricature of her former self. She rages at her increasing frailty

and disabilities. Dolores is nearly overwhelmed by the responsibility of caring for a woman in the final throes of physical decline. The low point for Vera occurs after one of many episodes of incontinence. She faces her mortality head-on and declares, "I won't feel better. I never will." Later, Vera rolls out into the hall in her wheelchair and throws herself down the stairs, despite Dolores's attempts to restrain her. Vera hurtles down the winding stairway and lies in a heap on the landing. Dolores tries to comfort her and asks, "Why, Vera?" The old woman answers, "Because I hate the smell of being old. I'm tired, and I want it to be done." Afraid she will survive this fall, she pleads with Dolores to finish her off. Dolores grapples with the old woman's fearful request— and plot twists and a complicated narrative framework move the story forward and reveal multilayered meanings in the two women's inter-generational relationship.

REGENERATION: AGING IN PLACE AS A SOURCE FOR IDENTITY AND COMMUNITY

Older adults are valued as "elders" within their communities because they have aged in place, drawn people to them, functioned as mentors, and fought to maintain a sense of "community" within their rural areas, towns or villages. They have lived within the context of old traditions and unchanging ways. They have survived bad weather, poor crops, deaths, disasters, and wars. Aging in place is a central metaphor for a personal fulfillment in old age. The love of the land, and the commitment to continuing a way of life a family has known for generations, are the hallmarks of this theme.

Educational Videos

Three examples of rural individuals aging in place and facing the rigors of the natural world are a short video, *Last Stand Farmer* (1975), and two feature-length documentary videos, *Troublesome Creek: A Midwestern* (1995) and *Brother's Keeper* (1992). The first is a portrait of a Vermont farmer who has chosen to work the land as his ancestors did rather than to adapt to modern mechanization. Kenneth O'Donnell takes his "stand" on the values that are inherent in the relationship between a farmer and the land as well as the relationship between a man and his horses. He values the traditional means of farming even though his determination to adhere to the old ways makes him one of the last of a class of farmers that is passing from the landscape.

Two other videos develop the theme of aging in place in the context of farm life. The first, *Troublesome Creek: A Midwestern* (1995), is the compelling story of Ross and Mary Jane Jordan, farmers in southwestern Iowa, who at the end of the 1980s faced foreclosure because of the changing nature of the farm economy in America. The Jordans, whose family had farmed this land since 1867, came up with a novel idea. They would sell everything they own (except for the farmhouse and the land), invite one of their sons to operate the farm with his own equipment, and then rent a house in town. The subtitle of the documentary provides a clue to its special quality. The filmmakers use the myth of the American Western as an organizing motif. The Jordans are the good guys, and the big banks and their impersonal managers are the bad guys. In this case, the good guys win. Many emotional scenes portray the depth of their quiet strength and depth of resolve that always drives their response to crises. This documentary also reminds viewers that stressful transitions in old age may lead to positive change in character and outlook. For instance, Ross Jordan adjusts easily to retirement (much to the surprise of his daughter—one of the filmmakers). He becomes a more relaxed and optimistic man in his old age, eager to assist his son on the farm.

Brother's Keeper (1992) is an engaging view of the bucolic life of rural America, a reflection on stereotypical views of elderly rural citizens as country bumpkins, and an homage to close-knit farm communities that dot the landscape. Four bachelor farmers lived in close quarters on the old family farm in upstate New York. In fact, the brothers commonly slept together. Everyone in the area referred to them as the "Ward boys," even though the eldest was in his late 60s. Members of the community thought of them as illiterate and simpleminded. One night, the second-eldest brother died in his sleep. Or was he murdered by Delbert, one of his brothers? Although the climax of the video is footage from the trial (Delbert was found not guilty), the focus of the video is the way the filmmakers reveal the idiosyncrasies of the brothers' characters and the sympathetic response of their neighbors who rally to Delbert's defense.

Feature-Length Films

Several films illustrate the vital role played by an individual who is the "heart" of a community and whose aging in place inspires and sustains others in the community. For example, old Ninny Threadgood in *Fried Green Tomatoes* (1992) has her roots in the small rural community of Whistle Stop, Georgia. At 82 she resides in a nursing home and is visited by middle-aged Evelyn, a timid, overweight woman who is struggling to reawaken love in her marriage and striving to increase her self-esteem. Ninny's life review focuses on her friendship and love for her friend Ruth, their travails with the men in their lives, and their ownership of the Whistle Stop Cafe, the center of their small community. Ninny and Ruth were the unofficial "hearts" of this small community. The two young women join forces to defy an abusive husband and to resist racial discrimination and hatred. Ninny's life review closes with the death of Ruth and the demise of Whistle Stop. Ninny recalls, "When that cafe closed, the heart of the town just stopped beating."

Films from Holland and Denmark further this theme and suggest the way acts of compassion and mercy can restore a sense of community. *Antonia's Line* (1996) begins at the end of World War II when a middle-aged woman returns to her home in Holland after being away for 20 years. Soon she goes about restoring "community" to this morally bankrupt village and its embedded patriarchy. She resolves crises, roots out evil and moral decay, and draws people to her. Before long she becomes the matriarch of this community, and like Idgy and Ruth in *Fried Green Tomatoes,* she is not afraid to confront evil head-on in order to maintain her community. Meanwhile, Antonia finds solace in her family, in the affection of an old farmer, and in the cycle of seasons which provides a backdrop to the births and deaths, the comings and goings, of members of the community. Central to her story are the dinners she serves at long tables in her front yard, surrounded by her extended family. The sharing of a meal suggests the metaphor of communion and affirms the bonds of community.

Babette's Feast (1987), based on a story by Isak Dinesen, is a perfect complement to *Antonia's Line* because here the theme of food again is a central metaphor for community, celebration, and regeneration. Babette is an outsider when she appears in a bleak Danish coastal town in 1871; she becomes a servant to two women who live in a dwindling religious community founded by their late father. This community is filled with older individuals who have aged in place. After working 14 years as a servant, Babette wins the lottery and cooks a magnificent French dinner for the 2 women and 10 of their friends. The meal is practically a religious experience. The diners are changed by it. They respond with a newfound joy to the delicacies Babette serves them. The years seems to dissolve from their faces. After dessert they dance around the well in the yard. An old military officer, once one of the daughter's suitors, recalls a similar meal in Paris, and says the chef "made the dinner into a love affair that made no distinction between bodily appetite and spiritual appetite." Of course, Babette is that chef, and she has spent her entire winnings on the meal. For one night, and with one meal, a community of elders is affirmed and restored by her compassion, appreciation, and artistic skill.

Two other films offer additional perspectives on aging in place. *Madame Rosa* (1978) is a former prostitute, now in her 60s, who uses her Paris flat as a center for taking care of children of prostitutes and other homeless children. Her apartment building is a community of sorts, and Madame Rosa is respected as the heart and soul of that community. Now in failing health, she hangs on to the dwindling number of her charges and tries to find homes for them. In *Local Hero* (1983), a small Scottish community filled with engaging older characters is chosen as the site of a future oil refinery by a Texas company. At first the villagers are lured by dreams of sudden wealth. But when a reclusive old man who lives on the beach won't go along with the plan to sell the property, the young man's boss, the owner of the company, flies in to meet with the old man. The fate of the community is decided by these two old men, one a "local hero," and the other a jaded executive who is charmed by the simplicity and eccentricity of the community.

Three films represent negative outcomes associated with aging in place. The characters in these films reveal the dark side of old age, intergeneration, and aging in place. They have hardened their hearts through pride, greed, jealousy, and bitterness at serious personal losses. They fail to respond either to community values or to new emotional ties. All three films illustrate the pitfalls of irrational attachments to the land as a means of extending one's legacy into future generations. Thus, characters in these films have placed in front of themselves obstacles to personal growth, reconciliation, or the restoration of emotional wholeness. Even if these characters have aged in place, they have lost touch with their roots, with their community. They are rootless and alienated from important familial and community values. They have blinded themselves by a relentless and obsessive desire to control all external forces in their lives.

The Field (1990), by the Irish director Jim Sheridan, tells the story of an aging farmer who has rented a field from a widow for 10 years. But the widow refuses to sell. Frustrated by years of being terrorized by the man's son, she decides finally to leave her close-minded community after selling her field at public auction. The old man, Bull McCabe, is stunned. In his eyes he owns the land—after all, he has cared for it for 10 years and enriched it by long hours of labor. To Bull "the law of the land" is a higher law than common law. When it becomes clear that an American, visiting Ireland to rediscover his roots, will outbid Bull for the land, the full force of Bull's self-destructive rage is released upon his antagonist and, with an awful irony, even upon his own family. At the end of the film, after indirectly causing his son's death, Bull stands alone and apart from everyone in the community as he impotently rages at the sea.

A similar fate awaits an old bachelor, Cesar Soubeyran, the main character in Claude Berri's two-film epic, *Jean de Florette* (1986) and *Manon of the Spring* (1987). Soubeyran's greatest desire is to express his own legacy through his simple-minded nephew. Land provides income, and with land and money one can forge a legacy. The land he desires is owned by someone else, as it was in *The Field,* but in this case the land has value because of the presence of a spring on the property. Soubeyran's antagonist is a former city dweller and hunchback, Jean Cadoret, son of Florette, a woman old Soubeyran once loved. Through his nephew the old man destroys Jean Cadoret's ambitious plans and indirectly causes the young man's death. In the second film Soubeyran's plans for his legacy are derailed when his nephew falls madly in love with Manon, Jean's daughter, and then hangs himself when she rejects him. The irony of all of Soubeyran's malevolence is revealed when the old man learns that Florette, the woman he loved, was already pregnant with his child when she married another man. So Soubeyran, in pursuit of his legacy, destroyed his only son as well as his nephew—and all because of his lust for land and power.

REGENERATION: ELDERS GOING HOME AGAIN

The metaphor of "home" (Cole, 1991) offers significant insights into the experience of aging. In some contexts older characters view "home" as the primary locator of their character, values, and family ties (see above). But in some cases middle-aged or older characters need to find some form of emotional or psychological closure by "going home again." In this context the "journey" home becomes a psychological and spiritual pilgrimage that lays bare old hurts, yet invites resolution.

Feature-Length Films

Examples of metaphoric journeys home in films treated earlier include Ninny Threadgood's return to Whistle Stop in *Fried Green Tomatoes* (1992) and visits to childhood homes in America and Germany by two nannies in the documentary *Martha and Ethel* (1995). An old woman returns to her home on a remote lake in the Canadian wilderness in *Strangers in Good Company* (1990), a film that will be analyzed later under a different theme.

The Trip to Bountiful (1985), which tells the story of two generations in conflict, focuses on the closure an old woman experiences when she returns to her home after a long absence. This film reveals again the way intergenerational relationships can benefit both the younger and the older generations. But the focus of the film is the resolution sought by Mrs. Watts, an elderly widow, who finally realizes her dream of returning to the small town of Bountiful, Texas, where she lived when she was raising her family.

On her trip she befriends a young woman and shares deeply felt memories of a love lost, a loveless marriage, and the deaths of two of her children. The young woman offers Mrs. Watts companionship, solace, and a vision of what she missed herself: a woman who loves and is loved by her husband. The old woman's return to Bountiful, after 20 years, is charged with meaning. Only a few abandoned buildings remain, and her run-down house sits at the edge of an uncultivated field. In a haunting scene, the old woman enters her house and surveys the scene.

Most viewers remember her visit to her house as the climax of the film. But that scene sets up a crucial intergenerational encounter between Mrs. Watts and her son Ludie. Mrs. Watts begins to review her life in Bountiful. She remembers her own father, who farmed this land, and died when her son Ludie was only 10. Prompted by his mother's recollections, Ludie launches into reminiscence. He shares memories he had either denied having or had repressed for years. Mrs. Watts tries to pinpoint her emotional response to these memories, to this place: "The rivers will still be here, the field, the trees, the smell of the Gulf. I always got my strength from that—not from houses, not from people. . . . I had forgotten the peace." She realizes that they are bound to this place and to a former time by being part of the cycle of generations that planted cotton on this land, then left for the cities, then returned to farm again, and then left the land behind again. Mrs. Watts concludes, "One generation after the other. We're a part of all that. We left, but we'll never lose what it has given us." Ludie, who has been changed by this encounter, agrees. In this instance the intergenerational relationships are affirmed and resolved in an unexpected way. Now the purpose of the old woman's trip to Bountiful can be viewed in a larger context. The film ends with a family restored and with an acknowledgment of the role an old person can play in that reconciliation.

One of the most unusual examples of the theme of "going home again" is *Children of Nature* (1991), an Icelandic film about an old man, Thorgeir, who leaves his rural farm, moves to the city, and tries to adapt to life in a high-rise apartment in Reykjavik with his middle-aged daughter and her family. Soon he learns the futility of this move. The daughter tells him, "We hardly know each other." He checks into a retirement home and by chance is reunited with Stella, an old friend from his rural area. Stella repeatedly escapes from the home and then is returned. She dreams of someday being buried near her home. Soon they make a "great escape" (compare *The Trip to Bountiful)*, steal a vehicle, and drive out of the city and head inland. Eventually, they reach her remote homeland and spend part of an evening sitting in front of the fire in her old house. As Stella watches the fire, and later walks around the property, her life review is framed by a juxtaposition of her visions of her younger self, engaged in activities around the farm and of others from the community busily engaged in the tasks of daily living in the past. Now that she is home again, Stella's life is complete. The next morning Thorgeir finds her dead on the beach.

REGENERATION: INTIMACY AND LOVE

The terms of intimacy and love require two older adults who can respond to each other as equals and complement each other's shortcomings. Intimacy and love position the old also as equals to the young and to the middle-aged as persons who have access to a full range of emotions and who may fully express their passionate selves through friendships, loyalty, intimacy, sexuality, and love. In this case, old persons need each other to fulfill and complete themselves. Regeneration flows from the fruits of intimacy and sharing.

Educational Videos

Friendship and intimacy are the hallmarks of *Ernie and Rose* (1982), a fictional portrait of two older men, one White and one African American, who have lived together since Ernie's wife died, and who enjoy an unlikely and often comical set of bizarre adventures. Ernie is the boisterous and irascible one, not afraid to engage in petty thievery when necessary. Rose is the quiet and spiritual one, always reading about new religions, always working on his inner self. *Ernie and Rose* also pokes gentle fun at old age and mortality. Both men "go up in smoke" at the end of the video, but not before each has addressed the issue of mortality with wit and insight.

The Silver Maiden (1981) shows a lively, argumentative encounter between two strangers—a stately, attractive woman and an ill-tempered, irascible old man who share a park bench one morning. What appears to be a chance encounter actually is a profound reunion, for the two people sitting next to each other on this park bench are former lovers from Chile who have not seen each other in many years. The old woman was the beautiful "Silver Maiden," the governor's daughter, and the old man was her lover, a man from the lower classes. Only one of the two, in this case Laura, knows the truth behind their identities.

The audience is given the opportunity to watch the couple uncover the rich tapestry of their shared experiences from the past. As they recite the details of the failed love affair, long unresolved conflicts and repressed feelings surface and are communicated for the first time in a nonthreatening environment. Before their brief conversation ends, both explain some of the circumstances that dictated the course of their experiences and express some of the values which are an integral part of their characters. At the end of the video viewers are left with insights into the fragile nature of human relationships as well as a sense of perspective on the enduring quality of love as the basis of human relationships. Having resolved some long-unanswered questions about their past relationship, the old couple will work toward establishing a new relationship based on what they now have in common between them.

A Private Life (1980) is another psychologically complex story about friendship and intimacy. In this video the two main characters are German immigrants who share tragic pasts based on their experiences in World War II and now are faced with the ongoing need to reintegrate their lives. The video is told from Margot's point of view. Her attempts to move her relationship with Karl beyond friendship toward intimacy illustrate her personal strength and resilience just as they reveal his anxieties, an obsessive preoccupation with the past, and a strong need for security at all cost. As her relationship with Karl continues, she seeks to deepen their intimacy in order "to share what we have now." But Karl is unable to forge new bonds with another person. He leaves New York for a "retirement" community. Margot is stunned by his sudden departure, but she regains her sense of balance when she remembers that this city of immigrants "is a place to start over," and when she finds a way to draw upon the strength of her youthful innocence and will.

Young at Heart (1987) is a portrait of two older artists who share the story of their romance. That story is portrayed in the context of their life stories and their complementary artistic interests (one loves abstract art, the other loves representational art). They are both independent thinkers, committed to the expression of their art, and interested in life in the present. As the video progresses, we learn that the two live together in Reva's home. For some time they did not consider marriage. But eventually Reva suggests marriage as a natural next step. Louis's response: "There's no reason why we should not." The video ends with scenes from their wedding and honeymoon, and George Burns's rendition of *Young at Heart* is played through the credits.

Strangers in Good Company (1990), a feature-length video, tells the story of eight women, all but one are older adults, who are stranded for a few days in the Canadian wilderness when their small bus breaks down. The screenplay is organized around a series of intimate, subtle, and evocative encounters between two or three different women at different times and places each day. In that short time all of the women grow closer to each other and are able to expand their understanding of how to face the trials of old age. The video is a fictional portrayal of aging; but all of the women essentially play themselves and draw upon their own life stories as the basis for their interactions.

Feature-Length Films

Many of the films analyzed earlier contain subplots that emphasize the restorative qualities of intimacy between older adults. For example, David and Eva treasure their last moments of intimacy before Eva dies in *Tell Me a Riddle*. In *Antonia's Line,* the title character finds some comfort in her late middle age when she invites an old neighbor, who once had proposed to her, to share her bed on a regular basis. At the climactic dinner in *Babette's Feast* an old soldier, who once proposed to one of the minister's daughters, finds solace in his reunion with this woman in old age. Thorgeir's decision to help Stella return home in *Children of Nature* is based on his long-time affection for this woman. In fact, intimacy in this film is most clearly expressed through his response to her mortality. After she dies, he fashions her coffin from spare lumber around the property, drags the coffin down to the hillside near an old church, and buries her—as she had wished—in the earth of her childhood home. The quiet strength of Thorgeir is a testament to the intensity of purpose and the depth of intimacy still available to the individual in old age.

In *Mrs. Brown* (1997), old Queen Victoria withdraws emotionally from her duties and her people after the death of Prince Albert. Her relentless grieving threatens to topple the government. She is restored to her rightful place and regains her emotional strength through the efforts of Mr. Brown, an old family friend from Scotland. He deals with her grief in a forthright and unsentimental manner and both come to feel affection for each other that rivals the intimacy of lovers. *Mrs. Brown* reveals the powerful variable that class represents when it comes to setting up barriers to the development of intimate relationships.

When the variable of race is added to that of class, the barriers against the formation of friendship and intimacy in old age are nearly insurmountable. In this context, *Driving Miss Daisy* (1989), based on the play by Alfred Uhry, is a remarkable film because race and class are overcome, at least symbolically, in the relationship between Daisy Werthan and Hoke Colburn. Daisy, 72, is an upper-class Jewish widow who lives in Atlanta in the late 1940s. Hoke is in late middle age when he is hired by her son to be her chauffeur. Daisy is excitable, cantankerous, and petty. Hoke serves as an antidote to her fragile ego; he is calm, patient, and generous. Most of all, he is patient. But as the quarter-century of their relationship passes, Daisy makes progress and begins to yield to Hoke's gentle loyalty. Together they experience racial discrimination and intolerance, the Civil Rights movement, family celebrations, and finally a sudden onset of dementia that terrifies the old woman. In the climactic scene Hoke's comforting presence seems to shock her into lucidity. She sits in her nightgown, her thin hair down around her face, and acknowledges, "Hoke? You're my best friend." She takes his hand in hers. He lets her hold it but does not grasp hers in turn. All he can do is stand above her and nod his head to affirm the lifetime of friendship and affection that has led them to this intimate moment.

Further evidence of their intimacy occurs in the last scene of the film. Hoke and Daisy's son, Boolie, visit her in a nursing home. Boolie is nervous and awkward in the presence of his mother and tries to make pleasant conversation. But she responds to Hoke's gentle and affirming demeanor and abruptly sends Boolie away by saying, "Hoke came to see me—not you." Boolie leaves them sitting at a table across from one another. Hoke begins to feed Daisy small pieces of pumpkin pie, when she is not able to grasp the fork. His movements are restrained and loving, and she smiles at him with great affection. She tastes the sweetness of the pie, and viewers are reminded of an earlier scene, when on their trips she reminisced with Hoke about the time her father took the family to the ocean when she was 12. She told him then, "I'd never seen the ocean. I asked Poppa if it was all right for me to put my hand in the water. He laughed. I tasted salt water on my fingers. Mmmm." In the last scene the old woman tastes and appreciates the sweetness of life given to her by her longtime friend and companion, an old Black man who once was her chauffeur. The trust and love between the two is punctuated by the last image in the film: as the two sit across from one another, the image begins to dissolve to show the old Cadillac Hoke drove for Daisy, moving down a highway many years ago. Once again Hoke is driving Miss Daisy, and the permanence of their bond is made clearer by this visual metaphor.

CONCLUSION

Educational videos and feature-length films, like literary works, often defy easy categorizations. The analysis above is intended to suggest one way of synthesizing a number of works of art according to a complementary pair of themes: intergeneration and regeneration. The terms of this analysis suggest that films and videos about aging generally undermine negative stereotypes of aging by portraying original, idiosyncratic characters who are engaged in life, often more so than their middle-aged children. The old and the young, as they are realized in films and videos, have more in common with each other than the old and the middle-aged. Both groups are outsiders, often subject to control by the middle generation, and often invisible to that generation. Films and videos give persons who are old a voice and reinforce their claims of independence and autonomy.

FUTURE DIRECTIONS

The continuing video revolution requires an increasing willingness on the part of independent producers of audiovisuals to examine complex, emotionally charged subject matter. In recent years some of these issues have been addressed with surprising effectiveness, including death and dying, elder abuse, gay and lesbian issues, and sexuality and love. But still there are significant gaps in the subjects treated in audiovisuals. For example, more audiovisuals need to address health-care issues, such as stroke, disabilities, adult day care, chronic illness, and mental disorders. Furthermore, little coverage has been given to a variety of social issues as they relate to gerontology, including AIDS, autonomy, the ethics of extending life, ageism and age stereotyping, and rural aging. Finally, greater coverage is needed for issues that relate to the emotional and psychological reality of aging: suicide in old age, friendship and intimacy, the significance of oral history, grief and bereavement, the mutual benefits of intergenerational relationships, older couples, the place of religious belief and practice in old age, the satisfactions and frustrations of family life, widowhood and divorce, and the interior world of older men's lives. Many of these topics could be treated with dramatic portrayals, or audiovisual portraits, or documentaries that could incorporate interviews and scenes recording subjects engaged in their daily lives.

The cinema is one of America's enduring artistic forms, but the subject of aging has not been adequately and substantively treated in its feature-length films. The emphasis on the international cinema in the analysis above suggests that American culture can learn a great deal about the subtlety and diversity of old age by examining images of aging in international films. American audiences, and students at all levels of education, should be exposed to the most honest and sensitive renderings of old age that are available to them. For example, many of the feature-length films analyzed in the section above contain fascinating intergenerational relationships. Unfortunately, some of those films reflect a well-worn formula of the eccentric, dynamic elder who finds happiness by traveling across America with a misguided but warm-hearted adolescent. There are many more intergenerational relationships to explore beyond this and other formulas. In fact, intergeneration as a theme is crucial for helping young people reevaluate the aging process and gain a clearer understanding of the values and insights of the old—as well as the pitfalls of negative attitudes that persist in old age. Perhaps demographic trends that suggest a dramatic increase in the numbers of older adults in the next 10 to 20 years will redress such imbalances in subject matter. As more people discover that "old age" is a normal part of human development, their experiences may extend the range of complex, credible, and original images of older characters beyond the stereotypes from the past.

Additional perspectives on the complexity and ambiguity of the aging process may be found in films about the frail elderly, the disabled elderly, and the demented elderly—all of whom face particular conflicts that often diminish their humanity and sense of self-worth. More attention to the themes of friendship, intimacy, and sexuality in old age will provide insights into the significance of relationships in old age. Films about aging Latino Americans, Asian and Southeast Asian Americans, and immigrants from Europe, Russia, and Africa will expose a wide range of conflicts related to cultural adaptations. Gerontological education, as it relates to the visual medium, depends upon access to well-realized, credible, and diverse images of old age.

REFERENCES

Cole, T. (1991). Aging, home, and Hollywood in the 1980s. *The Gerontologist, 31,* 427–430.

Davis, R. H. (1979). Understanding media as instructional aids in gerontology. *Educational Gerontology, 4,* 57–65.

Flynn, B. L. (1989). Images of aging: 20 years of films about the elderly. *Sightlines,* 4–8.

Moss, W. G. (1976). *Humanistic perspectives on aging: An annotated bibliography and essay* (2nd ed.). Ann Arbor: Institute of Gerontology, Univ. of Michigan—Wayne State University.

Trojan, J. (1980). Film portraits of aging men. *Media and Methods, 20,* 42–44.

Yahnke, R. E. (1985). Classic educational films on aging. *Minnesota Journal of Gerontology, 1,* 31–35.

Yahnke, R. E. (1988). *The great circle of life: A resource guide to films on aging.* Baltimore, MD: Williams & Wilkins.

Yahnke, R. E. (1989). Films that recreate the experience of aging: A new direction for gerontological education. *Educational Gerontology, 15,* 53–63.

Yahnke, R. E. (1997). The art of audiovisuals and the "education" of gerontologists. *The Gerontologist, 37,* 1–3.

SELECTED FILMOGRAPHY OF EDUCATIONAL VIDEOS AND FEATURE-LENGTH FILMS

Intergeneration: Videos

Age is No Barrier, 1989. Dir: Francis Damberger.
At 99: A Portrait of Louise Tandy Murch, 1974. Dir: Deepa Mehta Saltzman.
Complaints of a Dutiful Daughter, 1995. Dir: Deborah Hoffman.
Curtain Call, 1995. Dir: Michel Jones.

Dorothy Molter: Living in the Boundary Waters, 1987. Dir: Judith Hadel and Wade Black.

Elder, The, 1990. Dir: Claude Palardy and Louise Marie Beauchamp.

I Know a Song: A Journey With Alzheimer's Disease, 1987. Dir: Peter Flood and Mary Beth Yarrow.

Luther Metke at 94, 1978. Dir: Jorge Preloran and Steve Raymen.

Martha and Ethel, 1995. Dir. Jyl Johnstone. Prod: Jyl Johnstone and Barbara Ettinger.

Peege, 1973. Dir: Randall Kleiser.

Steady as She Goes, 1981. Dir: Robert Fresco.

Stone Carvers, The, 1984. Dir and Prod: Marjorie Hunt and Paul Wagner.

Weekend, 1971. Dir: Ante Zaninovic.

Regeneration: Videos

Brother's Keeper, 1992. Dirs. Joe Berlinger and Bruce Sinofsky.

Ernie and Rose, 1982. Dir. John Huckert.

Last Stand Farmer, 1975. Dir: Richard Brick.

Private Life, A, 1980. Dir: Mikhail Bogin.

Silver Maiden, The, 1981. Dir: David Spiel.

Strangers in Good Company, 1990. Dir: Cynthia Scott. (This film is sometimes listed under the title *The Company of Strangers.*)

Troublesome Creek: A Midwestern, 1995. Dir: Steven Ascher and Jeanne Jordan.

Young at Heart, 1987. Dir: Sue Marx and Pamela Cohn.

Intergeneration: Feature-Length Films

Cinema Paradiso, 1990. Italy, Dir. Giuseppi Tornatore.

Dad, 1989. Dir. Gary David Goldberg.

Dolores Claiborne, 1995. Dir. Taylor Hackford.

Harold and Maude, 1971. Dir. Hal Ashby.

Harry and Tonto, 1974. Dir. Paul Mazursky.

Kotch, 1971. Dir. Jack Lemmon.

Lost in Yonkers, 1993. Dir. Martha Coolidge.

Nelly and Monsieur Arnauld, 1996. France, Dir. Claude Sautet.

On Golden Pond, 1981. Dir. Mark Rydell.

Pelle the Conqueror, 1988. Denmark, Dir. Bille August.

Red, 1995. France, Dir. Krzysztof Kieslowski.

Tell Me a Riddle, 1980. Dir. Lee Grant.

Winter Guest, The, 1997. Great Britain, Dir. Alan Rickman.

Regeneration: Feature-Length Films

Antonia's Line, 1996. Holland, Dir. Marleen Gorris.

Babette's Feast, 1987. Denmark, Dir. Gabriel Axel.

Children of Nature, 1995. Iceland, Dir. Fridrik Thor Fridriksson.

Driving Miss Daisy, 1989. Dir. Bruce Beresford.

Field, The, 1990, Ireland. Dir. Jim Sheridan.
Fried Green Tomatoes, 1992. Dir. Jon Avnet.
Jean de Florette, 1986. France, Dir. Claude Berri.
Local Hero, 1982. Scotland, Dir. Bill Forsyth.
Madame Rosa, 1978. Israel, Dir. Moshe Mizrahi.
Manon of the Spring, 1987. France, Dir. Claude Berri.
Mrs. Brown, 1997. England, Dir. John Madden.
Trip to Bountiful, The, 1985. Dir. Peter Masterson.

16

Spirituality

Robert C. Atchley

There is considerable evidence that spiritual concerns, experience, and development become increasingly important for many people in middle and later life. This evidence can be found in the narratives of individuals as well as in social science surveys. Beginning around age 35 or 40, a growing proportion of people become consciously involved in exploring the meaning of their existence and their relation to the universe. Such people are often engaged in spiritual practices that heighten the possibility of a noumenal, mystical experience. Those who experience transcendent, nonpersonal levels of consciousness often feel called to serve, and spiritually rooted service takes many forms.

But what is spirituality? As it is used here, spirituality refers to an inner, experiential region (including sensations, thoughts, and emotions arising out of a focusing on ultimate concerns) as well as to direct experiences of the ultimate that transcend the elements of conventional consciousness. It can also refer to actions arising from spiritual experiences. By ultimate concerns, I mean a region of awareness within which people *experience*—not just think about—a higher power: the Absolute, God, Allah, Nirvana, Yahweh, Cosmic Consciousness, Christ Consciousness, the Void or whatever label one uses to designate the undivided ground of all being (Huxley, 1944).

There are many spiritual traditions, each of which has its own language for articulating the path that must be followed to experience the ultimate, how spiritual realizations are confirmed, the nature of spiritual enlightenment, and the implications of spiritual understanding for ordinary human life. Although it would be a mistake to gloss over the importance of these differences, each major faith group—Christianity, Islam, Judaism, Buddhism, Taoism, and Hinduism—is rooted in the profound, direct, authentic mystical experiences of its founder(s). The contemporary surge in inner exploration is in many cases motivated by individuals striving to move beyond a second-hand spirituality that must be channeled by a clergy or other spiritual authority figures toward authentic, direct experiences of spirituality. In meditation and prayer, for example, learning to dwell in silence often helps create an inner opening for spiritual experience. Such explorations take place in the context of traditional religious groups and in alternative groups that take a more universalistic view of the spiritual journey. Some make their spiritual journey alone, following their inner light.

Any discussion of spirituality is contextual, rooted in a particular language, cultural milieu and historical era, and also in the specific spiritual journey and experiences of the writer. The ideas and observations in forming this chapter come from a variety of sources, but are always shaped by my own experiences of them.

In my college days in the early 1960s I was exposed to many writers with an existential perspective: novelists ranging from Jack Kerouac to James Joyce and philosophers ranging from Martin Heidegger to Allan Watts. In the mid-1960s, I encountered psychologist Abraham Maslow's work on self-actualization. These ideas were a great resource when, at age 35, I experienced a profound collapse of the "social success" I had relied on to provide life meaning. I was a full professor with tenure, had published several books and numerous articles, and had a wife and children I adored and who adored me. Yet I still felt that something was missing. It was as if I had run a very difficult maze only to find a large empty white room at the end. I embarked on a 25-year course of serious inquiry within a field that could be loosely described as spiritual studies, consisting of reading, meditation, and dialogues with sages.

My spiritual journey has been most deeply influenced by the Vedantic teachings of the Indian sage Sri Nisargadatta Maharaj, which have been published in Frydman (1973), Dunn (1982), Powell (1996), and Row (undated). These books consist of transcripts of taped dialogues between small numbers of visitors from all over the world and Maharaj, which took place between 1972 and 1982 in Maharaj's small dimly lighted loft, located in one of Bombay's oldest slums. I participated in these dialogues with Maharaj for extended periods of time in 1978 and 1979.

I also benefited from Alexander and his associates' (1990) description of the Vedic psychology of Maharishi Mahesh Yogi and from Ken Wilber's (1996) incisive discussions of Vedanta. Finally, I have learned a great deal from personal conversations with Ram Dass and from reading his excellent expositions of Vedantic Hinduism and Buddhism in language and concepts that could be understood in America (Ram Dass, 1971, 1978).

As a description of the nature of our relationship to the ground of all being, Advaita Vedanta can be considered a precursor of Buddhism (Radhakrishnan, 1989). So it is not surprising that my thinking has been heavily influenced by the Buddhist teachings of Allan Watts (1957), Chogyam Trungpa (1973), Thich Nhat Hanh (1987), Joko Beck (1989), Mark Epstein (1995), Jon Kabat-Zinn (1994), Pema Chodron (1994), and Surya Dass (1997).

I have also learned much from the autobiographical writings of contemplative Quakers contained in Brinton (1972) and from dialogues with many highly spiritual elders in the Religious Society of Friends (Quakers). Unprogrammed Meetings of the Religious Society of Friends rely heavily on existential, contemplative approaches to spirituality. Sacred texts are honored for the wisdom they contain and are used as sources of stimulation, reflection, and inspiration, but primary authority is given to mystical realizations that come from waiting upon and contemplating the ground of all being. I have learned much from the Friends about the power of collective silence in fostering spiritual growth.

I have also relied heavily on my own experiences of contemplative, mystical understanding. I have practiced mindfulness meditation and jnana yoga (based on contemplative understanding) for many years, and in that time I have directly experienced the states of consciousness and direct connection to the ground of all being that I describe later. But through participation in spiritual communities, I understand also that my experiences are only partly unique and that they have much in common with the mystical experiences of other people interested in contemplative spirituality.

Of course, part of my knowledge about the relationship between aging and spirituality comes from the fact that I am growing older—I will be 59 when this book is published; I have also increasingly turned my scholarly interests toward spirituality and aging, and in doing so have experienced first-hand that it requires many methods to understand how aging relates to spirituality. Since 1992, I have participated in over a dozen focus groups of elders in which participants shared the understandings they received from contemplative, mystical experiences. In addition, I have included questions about transcendent spirituality in surveys I have done (Atchley, 1999). I have reviewed scholarly literature on aging and spirituality (Bianchi, 1992; Koenig, 1994; Levin, 1994; McFadden & Levin, 1996; Payne & McFadden, 1994; Thomas, 1994; Thomas & Eisenhandler, 1994, 1999; and Tornstam, 1994) as well as recent books aimed at helping adults, including elders, meet their spiritual needs (Baldwin, 1990; Goldman & Mahler, 1995; Leder, 1997; Moody & Carroll, 1997; and Schacter-Shalomi & Miller, 1995).

I thus come well prepared to address the subject of aging and spirituality, but I am also quite humble in the face of such a complex and often contentious topic. What I have to say is simply a point of view that might have value. In the body of this chapter, I first define and differentiate terms that are necessary to the discussion and then look at the role of the humanities in the study of spirituality. Finally, I consider conceptions of spiritual development, and how age or life stage relates to the experience of spirituality and to spiritual development or deepening.

A LANGUAGE FOR DISCUSSING SPIRITUALITY

Spirituality has become a common buzzword in recent years. As a concept, spirituality has expanded to include such a large array of ideas and practices that its meaning has become blurred. Although recent literature on spirituality has grown rapidly, workshops and retreats with spiritual themes have proliferated, and the sales of self-help books on spirituality have been brisk, much of the discussion has used implicit rather than explicit definitions of spirituality. Perhaps such openness is unavoidable, but it has led to increased ambiguity concerning the essence of spirituality. Indeed, in his best-selling book on mindfulness meditation, Jon Kabat-Zinn preferred to avoid using the term spirituality, even though he admits that meditation practice is fundamentally a spiritual practice, because of all the "inaccurate, incomplete, and frequently misguided connotations of that word" (1994, p. 264).

At the same time, the "soft" nature of spirituality from a scientific point of view has caused the heightened interest in spirituality to be stereotyped by scientific gerontology as a suspect enterprise, because it deals with aspects of human life that cannot easily be measured by conventional scientific methods.

Nevertheless, millions of human beings have reported having spiritual experiences. Serious discussion of spirituality as an important aspect of human nature, the identification of pathways for spiritual growth and development, and reports of direct spiritual experiences have been part of the written cultural legacy of humanity for at least 5,000 years (Radhakrishnan, 1989). Part of our challenge is to retrieve language and knowledge that has been used in sacred traditions to discuss spirituality effectively. To minimize the potential for confusion, I offer brief definitions for spirituality, mysticism, transcendence, and religion, understanding that each of these terms can be defined in myriad ways.

In this paper, the term *spirituality* refers to an inner, experiential region of human awareness as opposed to experiences of a world "outside" the experience. Spiritual experience can occur at many levels:

physical, emotional, cognitive, and transcendent. Spirituality is a quality that can infuse experience in a wide variety of settings. Spiritual experience can be both transcendent and immanent (Wilber, 1996): It can be both an experience of transcending worldly concerns as well as an intense present-moment perception that the ground of all being permeates all things. Sri Nisargadatta Maharaj called this being "passionately dispassionate" (Frydman, 1973). Erik Erikson, Joan Erikson, and Helen Kivnick (1986) called it "truly involved disinvolvement." The essence of spirituality is an intense aliveness and deep sense of understanding that one intuitively comprehends as having come from a direct, internal link with that mysterious principle that connects all aspects of the universe. As awakened spiritual beings, we feel our interconnectedness with all things—past, present, and future (Tornstam, 1994).

In most spiritual traditions, mysticism lies at the heart of spirituality. *Mysticism* refers to transcendent, contemplative experiences that enhance spiritual understanding. Mystical experiences can occur during intentional practices designed to create conditions conducive to transcendent experiences, such as during Zen meditation or a Sufi dance, or mystical experiences can occur in the process of living a lifestyle that is conducive to transcendent experiences, as in contemplative gardening. In either case, contemplative or transcendent knowing is associated with spiritual experience.

Transcendence refers to contemplative knowing that occurs outside the boundaries of verbal thought (Wilber, 1996). Although transcendence can refer to increasingly abstract thought (Pascual-Leone, 1990), contemplative transcendence involves transcending thought itself. Mystical experiences of transcendence can be brought into thought, but they do not originate in thought or sensory perception.

Organized *religions* are social groups or social institutions that have both theological and behavioral doctrines, ministerial or clerical authority, and ritualized social worship. Of course, individual members can and do internalize both the theological beliefs and behavioral prescriptions and proscriptions associated with their organized religion. But individuals also often have their own unique interpretations of the tenets of their religion.

The relation of religion and spirituality is in the eye of the beholder. Many people use religion and spirituality as synonyms and see no difference between the two terms. Others use religion to refer to a sociocultural program for developing spirituality and for bringing spiritual realizations into everyday life, and they use spirituality to refer to the inner experiences that arise from trying to put such programs into practice. Most people see spirituality as a broader term that includes a greater variety of experiences than they would include under the term religion. Some people attach little or no importance to organized religion but at the same time see themselves as very spiritual persons.

THE IMPORTANCE OF THE HUMANITIES TO THE STUDY OF SPIRITUALITY AND AGING

The humanities offer vital perspectives for understanding both spirituality and aging. Among the traditional disciplines that make up the humanities, religious studies and theology have obvious and long-standing connections with our understandings of spirituality (Armstrong, 1993; Smith, 1991). For many centuries, philosophy has also grappled with questions concerning the fundamental nature of the human spirit (Mitchell, 1991). Classics examines and provides access to the writings of important philosophers and poets of antiquity, who discussed aspects of human life that existed outside thought and sensory perception (Mitchell, 1989). History traces the importance of changing sociocultural conceptions of spirituality and spiritual development (Cole, 1992). Literature and poetry include numerous verbal accounts through which the human spirit and our understandings about it find expression (Vardey, 1995). Recent anthologies have brought together resources on spirituality in various fields within the humanities (e.g., Hixon, 1978; Mitchell, 1989, 1991; Vardey, 1995; White, 1995).

Scholars in the humanities have also been active in helping us understand aging and the human spirit from a variety of points of view: religious studies and theology (Kimble et al., 1995), philosophy (McKee, 1982), classics (Falkner & de Luce, 1989), history (Cole, 1992; Fischer, 1978), and the humanities in general (Cole & Winkler, 1994). But so far the topics of spirituality and aging have remained largely isolated from one another in the mainstream literature in most areas of the humanities. The challenge now is to integrate what we know about spirituality with what we know about aging to achieve a better understanding of why growing old may in fact be a profound opportunity for spiritual growth and wisdom as so many cultures of the world have historically assumed.

The logical, interpretive, narrative, and experiential methods of the humanities address areas of the human experience that are not amenable to the methods of "hard science." Since 1980, a very modest literature examining the relation between age or life stage and spiritual development or spiritual maturity has also emerged (Ahmadi & Ahmadi, 1995; Atchley, 1997a; Moody & Carroll, 1997; Thibault, 1996; Thomas & Eisenhandler, 1994, 1999). Much of this integrative literature has come from humanistic social science, which has taken seriously Dilthey's (1977/1894) injunction that "sciences of spirit" are their own legitimate realm and must be studied with methods appropriate to human nature (Fischer, 1996).

If we can bring ourselves to allow the possibility that contemplative knowing raises us to a new level of understanding of rational thought (Wilber, 1996), then contemplative disciplines and contemplative knowledge become a new frontier and source of enrichment for many fields within the humanities. Of course, this perspective requires that we be open to new ideas generally and not just to new ideas within the comfortable boundaries of our usual disciplinary concerns.

Wilber (1996) argued that contemplative disciplines, with their unique methods, insights, and processes of verification, are a much-needed complement to our scientific, philosophical, or rationalist methods of understanding. Epstein (1995) went even further in maintaining that without contemplative understanding to complete our ways of interpreting our existence, we cannot experience genuine, lasting integrity and life meaning. But where do contemplative methods fit within the current milieu of the humanities? How do we learn these methods?

SPIRITUAL DEVELOPMENT

In the view of spirituality presented here, full enlightenment is the ultimate in spiritual development. But it would be a mistake to assume that progress toward enlightenment is linear or predictable or that enlightenment is always total. Many people describe their spiritual journeys in terms of alternating periods of crystal clear enlightenment and periods of struggle. But a person who has experienced absolute enlightenment, however briefly, *knows* that enlightenment is a real possibility in a way that those who only think about or aspire to enlightenment cannot.

Enlightenment has two important aspects: a capacity to be intensely present without preconceptions or judgments, and constant awareness of ourselves as being permeated by the ground of all being. Such experiences underlie the description of Enlightenment as "being *in* the world but not *of* the world." *World* here means the phenomenal world experienced by our senses and the thoughts we have about that world.

In 1944, Aldous Huxley published *The Perennial Philosophy,* in which he offered persuasive evidence that basic views about the nature of human spirituality espoused by the mystical strains of each of the major faith groups, eastern or western, could be traced to a common underlying set of understandings about the human spirit that originated in India thousands of years ago. This basic understanding spread West from India through the Middle East to Europe and eventually to European colonies and East from India through Tibet and Indochina to China and Japan. He briefly summarized the elements of the perennial philosophy in his introduction to Prabhavananda and Isherwood's (1944) classic translation of the Bhagavad-Gita:

> At the core of the Perennial Philosophy we find four fundamental [understandings].
>
> First: the phenomenal world of matter and individualized consciousness—the world of things and [humans] and even gods—is the manifestation of a Divine Ground within which all partial realities have their being, and apart from which they would be nonexistent.
>
> Second: human beings are capable not merely of knowing about the Divine Ground by inference; they can also realize its existence by a direct intuition, superior to discursive reasoning. This immediate knowledge unites the knower with that which is known.
>
> Third: [humans possess] a double nature, a phenomenal ego and an eternal Self, which is the inner . . . spirit, the spark of divinity within the soul. It is possible for a [person] . . . to identify . . . with the spirit and therefore with the Divine Ground.
>
> Fourth: a [person's] life on earth has only one end and purpose: to identify . . . with [his or her] eternal Self and so to come to unitive knowledge of the Divine Ground. (Huxley, 1944:13)

Thus, according to this view, personal realities are always incomplete pictures of spirituality; intuitive, mystical connection with the ground of being is superior to merely thinking about the ground of being; the human spirit has a divine nature and a person can come to identify with that universal Self rather than with the personal ego; and the ultimate purpose of spiritual development is to experience no separation from the ground of being.

Thus, spiritual development can be defined in terms of movement toward ultimate possibilities, and the highest regions of spiritual development occur in the development of a capacity that allows consciousness to transcend the boundaries of body, language, reason, and culture (Alexander et al., 1990; Atchley, 1997a; Wilber, 1996). Movement toward ultimate possibilities means movement from simple imitative and dependent spiritual thought and consequent behavior toward a personal cognitive picture of spiritual issues that integrates both inner and outer life experiences of spirituality; toward subtle, contemplative, and transcendent understanding of the common ground of both inner and outer life experiences; toward being fully united with the ultimate ground of all being. Spiritual development is a process of transcendence that could be seen as a continuing spiral of increasingly broad understanding of oneself and the universe.

Some students of spiritual development emphasize the continuing nature of spiritual development. For example, Zen master Joko Beck sees spiritual development as something that grows out of the daily

practice of sitting meditation and bringing present-moment consciousness to everyday life. "Enlightenment is not something you achieve. It
is the absence of something. All your life you have been going forward
for something, pursuing some goal. Enlightenment is dropping all that.
But to talk about it is of little use. The practice has to be done by each
individual. There is no substitute. We can read about it until we are a
thousand years old and it won't do a thing for us. We all have to practice, and we have to practice with all of our might for the rest of our
lives" (Beck, 1989, p. 5). "Attention is the cutting, burning sword, and
our practice is to use that sword as much as we can" (Beck, 1989, p.
32). In this view, the process is the focus, not progress or achieving levels of spiritual understanding.

Others view spiritual development as having identifiable stages. For
example, Fowler (1981) conceived of adult spiritual development as
having the following developmental stages: an individual-reflective
stage in which the self begins to turn away from external sources of
spiritual authority toward the development of an internal moral and
spiritual orientation that has personal meaning for the individual; a
conjunctive stage characterized by greater acceptance of paradox and
ambiguity, a deepening sense of understanding, disillusionment with
the overreliance on logic and rational thought that typifies the individual-reflective stage, and a more open attitude toward religions or views
of spirituality other than one's own; and a universalizing stage involving a rare willingness to give up oneself and one's life to make spiritual
values a reality in the social world. Fowler felt that there was a link
between life stage and spiritual development, with the individual-
reflective stage being likely in young adulthood and the conjunctive
stage developing in midlife and later. He did not think that many people reached the universalizing stage.

Wilber (1996) saw spiritual development as progressing from an
emphasis on sensory knowing in childhood through various levels of
rational knowing in adulthood, to contemplative knowing, beginning
in midlife. For example, children often have their first mystical experiences through sensory sources such as communing with nature or
listening to sacred music or seeing an awesome sunset. Later on,
adults can experience tremendous inspiration through their minds,
from written and spoken words, scarcely aware that the silence between
and around those words may be crucial to their feeling of spiritual
connection. As people continue on their spiritual journey, most develop some sort of discipline, a repetitive activity that allows them to
transcend their self-consciousness to experience the true serenity of
their inner being.

Alexander and his colleagues (1990), Wilber (1996), and Atchley (1997a)
described stages of spiritual development in terms of increasingly

transcendent levels of consciousness. The first experiences of transcendence occur within conventional ego-consciousness. Through taking the role of observer, a more abstract aspect of the ego awareness can broaden consciousness and transcend ego-centered thought, which tends to operate at a lower level of abstraction (Pascual-Leone, 1990). Ego-based transcendence can create a useful perspective and some degree of detachment from the desires and fears of the ego, but a more powerful transcendence is achieved when the ego is transcended altogether in what is called *transpersonal* consciousness.

For our purposes, two levels of transpersonal consciousness are useful in conceiving of spiritual development. The first is called bare attention or mindfulness. The key to mindfulness or wakefulness is to develop the discipline to pay attention to the present and to simply observe, without subvocal comment or emotional reaction, what happens in consciousness. Mindfulness involves learning to transcend the ego by letting go of ego-based preconceptions, standards, and judgments. In the famous meditation manual, *The Cloud of Unknowing*—the first description of Christian mystical practice written in the English language (Johnston, 1973)—the anonymous author states that during contemplative prayer all things created by humans, including our ego selves, must be "buried beneath a cloud of forgetting." By learning to stay intensely present without constant subvocal analyzing and self-talk, the meditator learns to experience a level of consciousness that transcends verbal thought. This level of consciousness is characterized by an experience of clearness, of equanimously seeing the world as it is, not as we might wish it to be. Although there are many other pathways to mindfulness—such as chanting, reading sacred texts, or devotion to a teacher—meditation or meditative prayer is emphasized in most sacred mystical traditions.

The second level of transpersonal consciousness is nonpersonal consciousness. As the witness of that which experiences bare attention or mindfulness, nonpersonal consciousness is even further removed from ego-awareness and thus provides a source of the quality we call wisdom, the essence of which depends on clear seeing and broad nonpersonal perspective, in which the observer sees his or her personal needs as having no more priority than the needs of the many. Nonpersonal consciousness develops out of and is sustained by mindfulness, which itself is sustained by disciplined spiritual practice. Again from *The Cloud of Unknowing* (Johnston, 1973), we are urged to "dwell between distraction and oblivion." This means that in meditation, we must let go of the world by letting it enter the "cloud of forgetting" but we must continue to concentrate our attention to remain awake as we approach "the cloud of unknowing," what Huxley (1944) called the divine ground of being.

Moody and Carroll (1997) described five stages of spiritual development: the call, the search, the struggle, the breakthrough, and the return. The call occurs when we experience an inner yearning for connection, or deeper connection, with our spiritual Self. The call may initially be a feeling that there is an empty part of ourselves; later it may be a feeling that the spiritual aspect of ourselves is not yet fully developed. The search involves finding and exploring a spiritual path. The search may occur in the context of a traditional religion or it may involve an exploration and sampling of many sacred traditions. The struggle often involves overcoming the ego's resistance to meditative or contemplative practices aimed at transcendence. Beginning meditators often experience profound discomfort from the countless objections and obstacles the mind creates to prevent the experience of a quiet mind. Breakthroughs occur when the obstacles or objections to transcendence have been overcome, even if the overcoming is temporary. However, once people experience pure mindfulness and nonpersonal consciousness, they are likely to remain motivated in their intention to continue experiencing these qualities as part of their consciousness.

When people develop transcendent awareness, they do not typically drop out of the world. They continue on in their customary lives, but their perspective on everyday life has changed. The return involves bringing the spiritual insights gained through transcendence back into the world. The form such service takes depends in large part on the spiritual path chosen. A path of devotion can lead back to being an exemplar of devotion. A path of insight and understanding may come back in the form of being a teacher or a leader. One characteristic that all who have broken through share is the capacity to see the world from a nonpersonal perspective, which is open, unselfish, honest, trustworthy, compassionate, and clear-minded, among many other qualities. Quietly bringing these qualities to all that we do in life can be a powerful result of the return.

Moody and Carroll's progression is not meant to imply that there is just one course to complete and then we are enlightened. Rather, it is a cyclic process through which we become more and more enlightened by going through the entire process they describe whenever we experience a call for deeper development.

Silence plays a vital role in spiritual development, according to spiritual texts from a wide variety of traditions. Indeed, a profound inner silence—consciousness free of attachment to the verbal mind and physical body—IS the ground of being. It is as close as we can get in human experience to that vast principle out of which we came and to which we will return. As soon as we attempt to describe or analyze or react to that experience, we move further away from our goal of undivided connectedness.

One of the great paradoxes of spiritual development is that we cannot achieve it. We must be open to connection with the ground of being, but we cannot produce this connection. We are not in control of the process. We can only do our spiritual practices and, as the Quakers say, "wait upon the Lord." But if we have no earnest interest in mystical experience, it is very unlikely that we will have one. Spiritual development leads to a focus on the journey itself, not the outcome. We are never finished. Just when we think we understand everything, we learn more. Buddhists refer to this as "a journey without a destination."

But how do we know that our spiritual experiences are authentic? After all, the human mind is quite skillful in leading us to misperceive all manner of phenomena. First, millions of men and women over thousands of years and in a wide variety of historical eras and cultures have reported having an experience of a universal presence as a part of themselves. This inner experience is reported as a direct connection that bypasses the verbal mind and therefore is less susceptible to personal or cultural bias. Second, spiritual communities serve an important function by collectively reflecting on individual spiritual experiences. Sharing of spiritual experiences and insights within a spiritual community is an important protection against mistaking a subtle ego-agenda for spiritual realization. "Eldering" is the term Quakers use to describe a process of very gently and patiently and respectfully counseling those who seem to have lost the way.

The Buddhists say, " I take refuge in the Buddha. I take refuge in the Dharma. I take refuge in the Sangha." These are the "three jewels" of Buddhism (Thich Nhat Hanh, 1987). Taking refuge in the Buddha means knowing that enlightenment in this lifetime is a real possibility. Taking refuge in the Dharma means that following the pathway of Buddhist meditation and life principles derived from meditation increases the possibility of enlightenment. Taking refuge in the Sangha means relying on a religious community to point the way when we take a wrong turn. Thus, democratic feedback from others is an important source of assurance that spiritual realizations are indeed authentic.

THE RELATION OF AGE AND LIFE STAGE TO SPIRITUAL DEVELOPMENT

Aging does not inevitably bring spiritual development, but aging and the cultural concepts of what is appropriate or expected in later life stages do alter the conditions of life in ways that can heighten awareness of spiritual needs and that can stimulate interest in a spiritual journey. Of course, physical and mental aging are not unitary phenomena. Different individuals can experience quite different age patterns in terms of what changes occur, at what age, and at what rate. Differences in genes, environment, and culture combine to produce a staggering variety of individual experiences of physical and mental aging.

Popular stereotypes of aging portray it as a process of decline, but for most people, at least prior to age 80, aging is a relatively neutral balance of gains and losses, and aging is experienced as a gentle slowing down that never causes them to alter their preferred lifestyle (Atchley, 1999). What does change significantly is interest in an inner journey. Numerous scholars have observed that middle and later life involve an experience of increasingly transcendent aspects of inner life (Alexander et al., 1990; Erikson et al., 1986; Kogan, 1990; Thomas, 1994, 1999; Wilber, 1996). Achenbaum and Orwoll (1991) tied the development of wisdom to an increasingly transcendent attitude toward oneself, toward relationships with others, and toward worldly aims. Tornstam (1994) found that a majority of his representative sample of Danes age 75 or older perceived themselves as having increased in transcendent attitudes. They took more delight in their inner world, were less fearful of death, and felt a greater connection to the entire universe. Atchley (1997b) presented similar findings from a study of Americans age 70 or older.

A study of active spiritual seekers among a representative sample of people born during the baby boom found that 62% of active seekers were middle-aged or older, and most felt that "People have God within them, so churches aren't really necessary" (Moody & Carroll, 1997, pp. 133–134). These findings affirm the ancient wisdom among groups as diverse as the Navaho and the Jewish Kabbalists that a person must be age 40 to begin serious spiritual study. Many spiritual traditions assign special significance to age or life stage in terms of an increased receptivity to spiritual development.

Social aging is mainly an experience of release from the heavy responsibilities of midlife. Launching one's children into adulthood and retirement are seldom experienced as life crises; instead they are experienced as newfound freedom, and many elders use this freedom as an opportunity for increased spiritual reflection. As age increases, individuals live an increasingly quiet lifestyle conducive to contemplation.

By late middle age, most adults have long since found out that the traditional prescriptions for life meaning—materialism and social achievement—are empty promises. They do not meet the needs of the soul. Shifts in later adulthood toward less competition and more affiliation and toward less self-centeredness and more generativity have been documented by several scholars (Atchley, 1999; Clark & Anderson, 1967; Guttman, 1987; Maehr & Kleiber, 1981). By late middle age most adults have also struggled with the challenge to life meaning that can come with the death of people with whom they had close personal

relationships. If materialism, social achievement, and social relationships are not predictable sources of meaning in life, what is? This type
of meaning question is more common and becomes more salient as
people move into the last half of life (Moody & Carroll, 1997; Moody &
Cole, 1986). The lack of reliable social answers to meaning questions
can be a powerful impetus for an inner, experiential quest for meaning—for a spiritual journey.

Although a large proportion of aging adults report being on a spiritual journey (Atchley, 1999; Koenig, 1994), by no means all aging
people follow this pattern. Some have a philosophy of life based in
everyday humanistic principles and see little need for spiritual or religious validation. They feel no call toward a spiritual journey but are
vital and involved elders. Others are so overhabituated (Kastenbaum,
1993), so stuck in their habits of thinking and behaving, that there is
little chance for the kind of openness that is a prerequisite for a spiritual journey.

Evidence that spiritual growth is common in later life includes gradual increases with age in the prevalence of: self-acceptance and perceptions of one's life as having integrity (Gadow, 1983; Scott-Maxwell,
1979; Tobin, 1991); service to others, especially in the form of providing long-term caregiving to family and friends (Dwyer & Coward, 1992;
McGrew, 1991; Stegner, 1991); and patience with and interest in the
young (Erikson et al., 1986). These data come from studies of earlier
cohorts who have passed through the stages of later life. Increased
interest in transcendent spirituality was also found in studies that followed the same individuals over time (Atchley, 1999). With their exposure to the recent heightened cultural interest in spirituality, upcoming
cohorts of elders may be even more interested in spiritual journeys as
a focal point of later life.

Increased perceptions of life meaning and integrity, service to others, and generativity all require an attitude of transcendence and a
measure of selflessness. They suggest that growing older can represent
a return home to the silence from which we came and that on the way
home, a nonpersonal state of consciousness may be uncovered gradually by conditions common in later life: a quiet mind, a simplified daily
life, and a let-be attitude toward the world. The deepening spirituality
of later life is often subtle and nondeliberate; it may occur naturally
and spontaneously as a result of the physical, mental and social
processes of aging. Thibault (1996) described the conditions under
which many people experience aging as a "natural monastery."

Despite, or perhaps because of, widespread ageism and age discrimination, a large number of elders, often unknowingly, follow the ancient
mystical path of spiritual growth laid out in the Hindu scriptures
(Radhakrishnan, 1989). With increasing independence and self-reliance,

aware elders can see the world clearly, just as it is. They are less likely to be blinded by idealism. Dispassionate observation can lead to detachment—involved disinvolvement—and a diminished identification with personal and social agendas. Detachment can quiet the mind and create space in consciousness for nonpersonal consciousness, an experience that more clearly indicates right action by reducing ego-driven distortions of perception. The results of right action affirm the value of mindfulness and nonpersonal consciousness, which have as their center a massive, serene silence. The peace of nonpersonal consciousness gradually becomes an intimate companion and guide (Row, no date). To become enlightened is to become aware that mindfulness and nonpersonal consciousness have been with us all along and to identify with them more than with the personal body-mind. Of course, as Alan Watts (1957) was fond of pointing out, these words are merely the menu. The dinner must be experienced first-hand because the essence of spirituality is in experience, not in concepts, however well intended or cogently argued.

An important task for the humanities is to engage more elders in dialogues about these subjects. Elders who have been on a conscious spiritual journey can tell us a great deal about how aging and spiritual growth interact. This chapter provides a viewpoint about the essence of spirituality, while identifying individual and social aspects of aging that might cause an increased interest in and opportunity for spiritual growth. What we have learned so far indicates that these are promising avenues for further inquiry, but much work remains to be done.

REFERENCES

Achenbaum, W. A., & Orwoll, L. (1991). Becoming wise: A psychogerontological interpretation of the Book of Job. *International Journal of Aging and Human Development, 32,* 21–39.

Ahmadi, F., & Ahmadi, N. (1995). *Iranian Islam and the concept of the individual.* Uppsala, Sweden: Uppsala University.

Alexander, C. N., Davies, J. L., Dixon, C. A., Dillbeck, M. C., Druker, S. M., Oetzel, R. M., Muehlman, J. M., & Orme-Johnson, D. W. (1990). Growth of higher stages of consciousness: Maharishi's Vedic psychology of human development. In C. N. Alexander & E. J. Langer (Eds.), *Higher stages of consciousness* (pp. 286–341). New York: Oxford University Press.

Armstrong, K. (1993). *A history of God: The 4,000-year quest of Judaism, Christianity, and Islam.* New York: Ballantine Books.

Atchley, R. C. (1997a). Everyday mysticism: Spiritual development in later adulthood. *Journal of Adult Development 4, 2,* 123–134.

Atchley, R. C. (1997b). Working with the Gero-Transcendence scale in the U.S. paper presented at the Annual Meeting of the Gerontological Society of America, Cincinnati, Ohio, November 17.

Atchley, R. C. (1999). *Continuity and adaptation in aging.* Baltimore, MD: Johns Hopkins University Press.

Baldwin, C. (1990). *Life's companion: Journal writing as a spiritual quest.* New York: Bantam Books.

Beck, C. J. (1989). *Everyday Zen: Love and work.* New York: HarperCollins.

Bianchi, E. C. (1992). *Aging as a spiritual journey.* New York: Crossroad.

Brinton, H. H. (1972). *Quaker journals: Varieties of religious experience among friends.* Philadelphia: Pendle Hill.

Chodron, P. (1994). *Start wherever you are: A guide to compassionate living.* Boston: Shambhala.

Clark, M., & Anderson, B. (1967). *Culture and aging.* Springfield, IL: Charles C Thomas.

Cole, T. R. (1992). *The journey of life.* New York: Cambridge University Press.

Cole, T. R., & Winkler, M. G. (1994). *The Oxford book of aging.* New York: Oxford University Press.

Dilthey, W. (1977). *Descriptive psychology and historical understanding.* (R. Zaner & K. Heiges, Trans.) The Hague: Niijhoff. (Original work published in 1894).

Dunn, J. (1982). *Seeds of consciousness: The wisdom of Sri Nisargadatta Maharaj.* New York: Grove Press.

Dwyer, J. W., & Coward, R. T. (Eds.) (1992). *Gender, families, and long-term care.* Newbury Park, CA: Sage.

Epstein, M. (1995). *Thoughts without a thinker.* New York: Basic Books.

Erikson, E. H, Erikson, J. S., & Kivnick, H. Q. (1986). *Vital involvement in old age.* New York: Norton.

Falkner, T. M., & de Luce, J. (1989). *Old age in Greek and Latin literature.* Albany, NY: SUNY Press.

Fischer, C. T. (1996). A humanistic and human science approach to emotion. In C. Magai & S. H. McFadden (Eds.), *Handbook of emotion, adult development, and aging* (pp. 67–82). New York: Academic Press.

Fischer, D. H. (1978). *Growing old in America* (expanded edition). New York: Oxford University Press.

Fowler, J. W. (1981). *Stages of faith.* San Francisco: Harper & Row.

Frydman, M. (Ed.). (1973). *I am that: Conversations with Sri Nisargadatta Maharaj.* Bombay: Chetana.

Gadow, S. (1983). Family and strength: The dialectic in aging. *The Gerontologist, 23,* 144–147.

Goldman, C., & Mahler, R. (1995). *Secrets of becoming a late bloomer.* Walpole, NH: Stillpoint.

Guttman, D. (1987). *Reclaimed powers: Toward a new psychology of men and women in later life.* New York: Basic Books.

Hixon, L. (1978). *Coming home: The experience of enlightenment in sacred traditions.* Garden City, NY: Anchor Press.

Huxley, A. (1944). Introduction. In S. Prabhavananda & C. Isherwood (Eds.), *The song of God: Bhagavad-Gita* (pp. 11–22). New York: Penguin Books.

Johnston, W. (Ed.). (1973). *The cloud of unknowing.* New York: Doubleday.

Kabat-Zinn, J. (1994). *Wherever you go, there you are: Mindfulness meditation in everyday life.* New York: Hyperion.

Kastenbaum, R. (1993). Habituation: A key to lifespan development and aging?

In R. Kastenbaum (Ed.), *Encyclopedia of adult development* (pp. 195–200). Phoenix, AZ: Oryx Press.

Kimble, M. A., McFadden, S. H., Ellor, J. W., & Seeber, J. J. (1995). *Aging, spirituality and religion: A handbook.* Minneapolis: Fortress Press.

Koenig, H. G. (1994). *Aging and God.* New York: Haworth Pastoral Press.

Kogan, N. (1990). Personality and aging. In J. E. Birren & K. W. Schaie (Eds.), *Handbook of the psychology of aging* (3rd ed., pp. 330–346). New York: Academic Press.

Leder, D. (1997). *Spiritual passages: Embracing life's sacred journey.* New York: Jeremy P. Tarcher.

Levin, J. S. (Ed.). (1994). *Religion in aging and health.* Thousand Oaks, CA: Sage.

Maehr, M. L., & Kleiber, D. A. (1981). The graying of achievement motivation. *The American Psychologist, 36,* 787–793.

McFadden, S. H., & Levin, J. S. (1996). Religion, emotions, and health. In C. Magai & S. H. McFadden (Eds.), *Handbook of emotions, adult development, and aging* (pp. 349–365). New York: Academic Press.

McGrew, K. B. (1991). *Daughters' decision making about the nature and level of their participation in the long-term care of their dependent elderly mothers: A qualitative study.* Oxford, OH: Scripps Gerontology Center.

McKee, P. L. (Ed.). (1982). *Philosophical foundations of gerontology.* New York: Human Sciences Press.

Mitchell, S. (1989). *Enlightened heart: An anthology of sacred poetry.* New York: Harper & Row.

Mitchell, S. (1991). *Enlightened mind: An anthology of sacred prose.* New York: HarperCollins.

Moody, H. R., & Carroll, D. (1997). *The five stages of the soul.* New York: Anchor Books.

Moody, H. R., & Cole, T. R. (1986). Aging and meaning: A bibliographic essay. In T. R. Cole & S. Gadow (Eds.), *What does it mean to grow old?* (pp. 247–253). Durham, NC: Duke University Press.

Pascual-Leone, J. (1990). Reflections on life-span intelligence, consciousness, and ego development. In C. N. Alexander & E. J. Langer (Eds.), *Higher stages of human development* (pp. 258–285). New York: Oxford University Press.

Payne, B. P., & McFadden, S. H. (1994). From loneliness to solitude: Religious and spiritual journeys in late life. In L. E. Thomas & S. A. Eisenhandler (Eds.), *Aging and the religious dimension* (pp. 13–27). Westport, CT: Auburn Press.

Powell, R. (1996). *The experience of nothingness.* San Diego, CA: Blue Dove Press.

Prabhavananda, S., & Isherwood, C. (1944). *The song of God: Bhagavad-Gita.* New York: Penguin Books.

Radhakrishnan, S. (1989). *Indian philosophy.* London: Unwin Hyman.

Ram Dass (1971). *Be here now.* San Cristobal, NM: Lama Foundation.

Ram Dass (1978). *Journey of awakening: A meditator's handbook.* New York: Bantam Books.

Row, G. K. D. (no date). *Sadguru Nisargadatta Maharaj: Life and teachings.* Bangalore, India: Narendra Memorial Committee.

Schacter-Shalomi, Z., & Miller, R. (1995). *From age-ing to sage-ing.* Los Angeles: Time Warner.

Scott-Maxwell, F. (1979). *The measure of my days.* New York: Penguin Books.

Smith, H. (1991). *The world's religions: Our great wisdom traditions.* New York: Harper Collins.

Stegner, W. (1991). *Crossing to safety.* New York: Penguin USA.

Surya Dass (1997). *Awakening the Buddha within.* New York: Broadway Books.

Thibault, J. M. (1996). Aging as a natural monastery. *Aging and Spirituality, 8,* 3 and 8.

Thich Nhat Hanh (1987). *Being peace.* Berkeley, CA: Parallax Press.

Thomas, L. E. (1994). The way of the religious renouncer: Power through nothingness. In L. E. Thomas & S. A. Eisenhandler (Eds.), *Aging and the religious dimension* (pp. 51–64). Westport, CT: Auburn House.

Thomas, L. E., & Eisenhandler, S. A. (Eds.). (1994). *Aging and the religious dimension.* Westport, CT: Auburn House.

Thomas, L. E., & Eisenhandler, S. A. (1999). *Religion, belief, and spirituality in late life.* New York: Springer Publishing Co.

Tobin, S. S. (1991). *Personhood in advanced old age.* New York: Springer Publishing Co.

Tornstam, L. (1994). Gero-transcendence: A theoretical and empirical exploration. In L. E. Thomas & S. A. Eisenhandler (Eds.), *Aging and the religious dimension* (pp. 203–229). Westport, CT: Auburn House.

Trungpa, C. (1973). *Cutting through spiritual materialism.* Boulder, CO: Shambhala.

Vardey, L. (1995). *God in all worlds: An anthology of contemporary spiritual writing.* New York: Pantheon Books.

Watts, A. W. (1957). *The way of Zen.* New York: Vintage Books.

White, J. (1995). *What is enlightenment? Exploring the goal of the spiritual path.* New York: Paragon House.

Wilber, K. (1996). *Eye to eye* (3rd ed.). Boston: Shambala.

17

Narrative, Death, and the Uses of Anthropology

Sharon R. Kaufman

T his chapter is about narrative and death. Narrative is conceived here as an interpretive mode of thinking about people and events and an analytic method for portraying human agency, moral worlds, power relations and cultural forms. Death—more specifically, how death occurs in the American hospital, the subject of the author's research—is approached as a cultural practice, with multiple and even contradictory features, that are both shaped by and embedded in social and historical contexts.[1]

Contemporary interest in narrative in fields outside of the traditional humanities, for example, cultural anthropology and medicine, is a product of the "interpretive turn" in the social sciences and in trends in intellectual reformulation more generally since the late 1960s and 1970s (Rabinow & Sullivan, 1979). Geertz, both a leader and observer of this trend, has examined the tasks of 'knowing,' truth-making, and representing the cultural Other and summarized the central tension in contemporary anthropology created by the turn from fact-finding to interpretation, from assuming that some kind of 'objectivity' is possible to articulating the impact of literary processes on the understanding of cultural phenomena. Geertz notes the difficulty of "constructing texts ostensibly scientific out of experiences broadly biographical" (1988:10): ethnography is a record "of being there" that aims both to establish authority about the way things are and to acknowledge the subjective terrain of the ethnographic encounter. The challenge to the discipline today, says Geertz, is to create work that is "supposed to be at one and the same time an intimate view and a cool assessment." The pull between intimacy and objectivity he cogently describes as "a scientistic worry about being insufficiently detached" and "a humanistic worry about being insufficiently engaged" (1988:15). The goal of much anthropological writing today is to balance the poles of the tension Geertz articulates.

The various uses of narrative in ethnographic writing—and for this essay I use the term in a restricted yet well-recognized sense: accounts from informants that portray their subjective experience, including a sense of intention, explanation, and emotion—are methodological and textual strategies employed by authors to grapple with that tension in the representation of the Other. Those uses have been subjected to a great deal of scrutiny in the past decade or so as anthropologists and other ethnographers attempt to deal, in their writing, with the pull between the kinds of truths represented by the idea of science on the one hand and by literature and the humanities on the other. Thus there are many works which experiment with the portrayal of informants' voices and authorial presence and which reflect on uses of narrative theory from philosophy, linguistics, history, and psychology and employ it in original and thoughtful ways to frame data collected during participant-observation.[2]

For example, in the great surge of experimental writing in anthropology (Clifford & Marcus, 1986; Marcus & Fischer, 1986) narrative forms of first person accounts have sought to give voice to persons or communities who are low-status within a particular social world and system: the poor, chronically or terminally ill, elderly, disenfranchised, or those otherwise silenced through popular or dominant cultural representation (for example: Balshem, 1993; Behar, 1993; Bourgois, 1995; Farmer, 1992; Jackson, 1996). Narrative has been used in those works to address questions of human agency, to explore the feelings, thoughts, and intentions of social actors. Narrative has been viewed as a useful, expansive tool by those scholars wishing to articulate, from details of the native's point of view, how individuals construct meaning and negotiate their worlds. This approach to research method and ethnographic writing, in which the goal is to portray "local knowledge" (Geertz, 1983) or a certain kind of 'truth,' is in contrast to expository forms that seek to *know* 'truth,' that is, which seek to transcend the particular by reaching for abstraction through logic and deduction (Bruner, 1986). Advocates of narrative in the social sciences argue that, as method, it captures and constitutes both lived morality and experience and the dynamics of social practice and convention, thus revealing an open, richer field of cultural understanding than objectivist perspectives allow. In medical anthropology and sociology specifically, the by now large literature on illness and clinical narratives offers multiple ways to think about relationships among illness, medicine, culture, and experience. The intent of many of those works is to make explicit personal, experiential, and moral dimensions of illness in order to heal and authenticate the narrator (Becker, 1997; Frank, 1995); to provide medical practitioners with the subjectivity of the patient's perspective (Good et al., 1992; Kleinman, 1988); to understand health practitioners' worlds (Hunter, 1991; Kaufman, 1993, 1997; Mattingly, 1998) and to inject the instrumental rationality of clinical medicine with a broader and more humane purpose (Brody, 1987; Good, 1994; Kleinman & Kleinman, 1991; Young, 1997). Narrative conceptualizations and representation of aging, illness, and dying, for example, provide a way to explore the multiple meanings, truths, and voices that are expressed during life course transitions and liminal moments.

While advocating the use of narrative structures and properties and experimenting with narrative form, scholars who collect, analyze, and create narratives generally do not engage in wider academic debates about the shortcomings, as well as the attributes, of the narrative approach to cultural representation or truth-making (Phillips, 1994: Polkinghorne, 1998). Much ethnographic writing has embraced narrative as a data-gathering tool, expository method, theoretical frame, and/or textual structure, yet, for the most part, it has not been critical of narrative either as an analytic strategy or as a mode of thinking (Atkinson, 1997). Because narrative constructs are the fulcrum between experience and representation and have become a powerful convention for shaping knowledge, it is worthwhile to consider some criticisms of narrative in order to be aware of its limitations as a mode of understanding and representation. For narrative "encourages blind spots" (Simpson, 1995) in its reliance both on the 'experience' of the ethnographer and the 'experience' of those persons whom it seeks to illuminate. Two critiques are especially pertinent to the narrative of death which follows.

Wikan (1995), in her work on the construction and experience of "self," suggests that the use of narrative in anthropology has become a "privileged source in the analysis of selfhood" (p. 263), a mode of understanding identity and the lifeworld that has replaced or muted all other modes. She echoes Bruner (1990) in arguing that it is through acts, rather than talk, that people fashion a self and construct and understand their worlds, and she points out that anthropologists have not subjected their work on narrative to the same kind of methodological scrutiny that informs the study of cultural models, for example. Through ethnographic examples drawn from her studies in Bali and Cairo, she shows how the struggle to form and express the self emerges from "the multitude successes and defeats of action" (p. 269), from conditions of urgency and necessity in which one must act. It is misplaced, she suggests, to privilege narrative in the expression and understanding of self. Wikan posits that anthropologists gravitate toward narrative in their desire to portray the personal experience of muted groups and individuals and are reluctant to recognize the importance of necessity and action for two reasons. First, there is a freedom from urgency and necessity both in the work and in the lives of professional anthropologists which distorts the epistemological basis for acknowledging the power of circumstances beyond the self to shape identity. Second, coherence, wholeness, and self have emerged as central problems among a "Western or Eurocentric academia" (p. 274), reflecting the peculiar North American idea—now exported to other parts of the world—that individuals can create and re-create the self, that history and circumstance are not as salient as the process of becoming one's own person. These two features of anthropologists' lives and thought, Wikan argues, have skewed our interpretations of lives in the world.

Following Bruner (1986) in analyzing narrative as a "mode of thought," Young (1997) points out that persons and their lives are constructed narratively "by being enclosed in a trajectory given a narrative shape by the ethnographer" (p. 140). The resulting *narrative* selves, she points out, are not the same as the *persons* whose lives are represented through the narrative as text. Thus writing about the Other "contracts the presentation of a person to its narratable aspect" (p. 141). This limitation of narrative is not always acknowledged by ethnographers, who, in their writing at least, sometimes blur the distinction between self and story, between person and identity created through narrative. The claim, Young notes, that narrative texts, scenes created in narrative writing, *represent* a cultural or phenomenological world "rides on the Aristotelian assumption that language imitates reality" (p. 141). The problem, of course, is that the realm of the Other is not known directly through ethnographic writing, rather it is *constituted* by such writing. Writers have power, Young suggests, over the "characters" they constitute and because of this, questions can be raised by readers about bias, elaboration, mistakes, and inventions. Many ethnographers tend not to articulate a reflexivity in their texts about the writing conventions they use "to sustain an impression of objectivity" (p. 143). The result may be for the reader to wonder: Whose story is being told here? (Steedly, 1993:18). Thus the constraints of narrative in anthropological writing—that it mutes the centrality of action and contracts and constitutes persons and lives—are as important as the meanings it can express and generate.

Though death is a universal biological fact, the dying process, like all life course passages, is culturally patterned. Today in the United States, most deaths occur in the acute care hospital (Institute of Medicine, 1997), where a relatively large proportion occurs following intensive-care-unit treatments and high technology interventions (SUPPORT Investigators (see McCullough), 1995). The idea that death in America at the end of the millennium is 'problematic' is a response to cultural conventions of where and how death occurs. In this particular historical moment the end of life is conceived largely (though not entirely) in a medical idiom that seeks to diagnose disease *while* dying occurs and to prolong life for as long as possible with the best technology available. Indeed, the largest and most recent study ever conducted on the process of dying in the hospital concluded that the quality of the dying transition was not satisfactory for patients and their family members. Forty-three hundred patients were followed in the first phase of that study which found: only 47% of physicians knew when their patients wanted to avoid cardiopulmonary resuscitation (CPR); 38% of patients who died spent 10 or more days in an intensive care unit (ICU) preceding death; 46% of "Do-Not-Resuscitate" (DNR) (see McCullough) orders were written within 2 days of death even though 79% of the patients had a DNR order; for 50% of conscious patients, families reported moderate to severe pain at least half the time in the 3 days preceding death. The second phase of the study, a 2-year intervention aimed at improving physician-patient communication and physician knowledge of prognosis and patients' end-of-life wishes, did not change the practice of medicine regarding the use of ICU treatments, timing of DNR orders, avoidance of CPR, or pain relief, nor did those interventions alter the quality of patient and family experience. The study concluded that even where a focused and concerted effort was made to reduce pain and to respect patient wishes regarding end-of-life care, no overall improvement in care or outcomes was made (Moskowitz & Nelson, 1995; SUPPORT Investigators (see McCullough), 1995). The notion of 'death with dignity,' a counter-cultural production of the last decade or so, is a response to high-technology hospital medicine and the dissatisfaction it causes. Grassroots efforts to provide palliative care and home and hospice care without technologies for life prolongation are by now a well-articulated rebellion against the pervasiveness and dominance of a medico-cultural model perceived to have run amok.

This chapter provides a description and exploration of the hospitalization and death of one person in order to exemplify both the 'problem' of death in America and the challenges of narrative representation. The following discussion is intended to illustrate how one anthropologist approaches her work and approaches the problem of how to talk about or 'analyze' death in the hospital. I am interested in exploring first, ways in which specific actors are engaged in systems of power and normalizing strategies; second, how cultural knowledge about death and the dying transition is produced for the actors involved; and third, ways in which a narrative approach can capture the 'strangeness' of contemporary hospital practices surrounding the end of life. For although hospital routines are normalized and taken for granted by many, they are not 'natural.' Here, the task of my narrative is to expose that taken-for-grantedness and to present a cultural world as the subject for analysis and critique.

There are many ways in which death occurs in a hospital, for example: suddenly or after weeks of technological support; with or without the presence of family; with or without pain or consciousness; in an environment considered hostile or supportive. These ways are defined, substantively and morally, by positioned actors whose experience of 'the facts' is framed by gender and education, location in the structures of medical knowledge and power, and familiarity with the language of medicine and the routines of the hospital world. Moreover, a study of 'how death occurs in the hospital' is not about one thing (age, technology, ethics, etc); such a topic cannot be tidily conceived through only one unit of analysis nor summarized by one stance or viewpoint. Explication of one case in some detail is intended to reveal the particularity of death while at the same time emphasizing its cultural and multifaceted nature. Additionally the narrative offered below can be viewed skeptically: as only one version of events, as one construction, how is it problematic?

AN ETHNOGRAPHY OF DYING

The following example is drawn from a larger ethnographic study of how dying and death are approached and understood by health professionals, patients, and families, and how dying and death occur among older adults in one community hospital. The study is based on the collection of data by participant-observation on the adult wards in one mid-size, urban community hospital and by conversations and interviews with physicians, nurses, social workers, chaplains, patients, and family members. Over a 12-month period (calendar year 1997) I observed the course of events surrounding hospitalization, decline, and death for 80 individuals age 50 and above. Thirty-one of those deaths occurred in the intensive care unit, where one-third of all hospital deaths occurred that year.[3] I have selected the following case because it is not routine; it is considered problematic by the actors I observed. The story took place in the ICU.

THE PROBLEMATIC OF ETHNOGRAPHIC REPRESENTATION

The narrative constructed below is my reconstitution of events and perspectives that unfolded around one patient and it is based on my observations of patient, family, and staff, discussions with medical staff and family members, verbatim notes of a family conference, and medical chart notes. It may be considered as both a case study and social drama (Turner, 1974) and includes what I consider to be the main topical points of the patient's hospital course as well as events, words, and interactions that serve as windows onto the ways in which death in the hospital occurs. This narrative is not to be confused with *real events,* that is, what actually occurred in the messy and undifferentiated flow of clinical work, urgent situations, personal suffering, and everyday hospital activity. Rather, it is words created from activity, as Wikan observes. And it contracts the dying process (in the case of one woman) to its narratable features, as Young indicates.

Making a narrative is a generative process. I created the following narrative from scenes I observed and tales I collected as well as from my limited perspective of the unfolding of events. There is never just one story to be told about a particular person's decline; there are always a variety of viewpoints, different kinds of knowledge and interpretive frames brought to bear on the telling of a tale and the understanding of a set of events. The narrative below represents one choice out of many potential options. It is based on the way I positioned myself in the hospital to collect data in the first place. I chose to learn the perspectives of many actors—doctors, nurses, support staff, patients, and families—rather than conduct a study of 'patients' or 'nurses,' for example. While my time spent with and thus experience of multiple players perhaps gave me a more superficial understanding of the experience of dying in the hospital for one group, it enabled me to gain a broader understanding of interaction, social process, and decision making. I certainly did not observe all events or all interactions surrounding this particular case. My version of what happened is thus limited by the amount and kind of evidence—data—I collected, as well as how I chose to present it to readers. Because my goal was to portray the incommensurability among actors' *lifeworlds* in the hospital setting and the tension it evokes, I chose to fashion a multivocal account. Though many points can be made using the data I collected, I was motivated to illustrate how the 'problem' of death in America arises: through multiple views of what is at stake near the end of life. Thus I have organized the text to present a variety of voices—nurse, doctor, patient, family, medical chart—so the reader has a sense of contrasting viewpoints, ideology, and emotion. I deliberately constructed the narrative to highlight the discrepancies between medical and lay knowledge and commitments.

The patient's voice is absent here. Her verbal viewpoint was not available to me because she was extremely ill and sedated, asleep, or unable to communicate during much of her ICU stay and during most of the (few) moments when I was at her bedside. She did, however, make her wishes known during critical moments as the narrative reveals.

A NARRATIVE OF DYING

(ICU Nurse:) I learned about Carol Jones,[4] age 54, from one of the intensive care unit nurses who informed me that the patient had been on the unit for 2 weeks. She said Mrs. Jones had come into the hospital for exploratory surgery. When the surgeons opened her up they found her "full of cancer, spread everywhere; there was nothing they could do." They could not extubate her (that is, remove her from the mechanical ventilator that was enabling her to breathe, and thus to survive), the nurse added, so she had to come up to the ICU. A few days later the ICU physicians did succeed in removing the ventilator and replacing it with an oxygen mask, a less invasive and more comfortable technology. Over the weekend, the nurse continued, Mrs. Jones pulled the mask off or one of the tubes became blocked and she vomited and aspirated. The result was that the patient stopped breathing and "coded" [required emergency measures to sustain life]. The staff remedied the situation with intravenous medication; they did not need to perform full-blown cardiopulmonary resuscitation. The nurse concluded her quick summary of events by remarking that she did not know how much Mrs. Jones's husband knew about her prognosis and extent of the illness. She did not know what the oncologists were telling him. I asked about the possibility of a different scenario: could the surgeons, following the discovery of very extensive cancer, inform the family that the patient is dying and move the patient to a room on the medical floor for palliative care? Yes, that route is sometimes taken, she replied. But in this case, because the patient probably would have died shortly or even immediately following surgery and extubation, and because surgeons try to avoid that outcome, the decision was made to send her to the ICU to "give her a chance."

(Patient's Sister:) Later the nurse introduced me to the patient's husband and sister. The sister had recently arrived from another state and spoke with me at length about Mrs. Jones's condition and the way in which events had unfolded. She told me she had learned of the seriousness of the illness 2 weeks earlier when her brother-in-law called to tell her that Carol had been to see the doctor, a gallon of fluid had been drawn from her abdomen, and cancer cells had been found in the abdominal fluid. Then came the surgery to try and diagnose and treat the problem. After a few days on the ventilator, Carol was extubated. The sister informed me that the patient, an articulate, strong-minded woman, was thrilled to have the ventilator removed. "That was Friday. She wants to live," the sister said.

On Saturday, the sister continued, she and Carol's husband were getting ready to come to the hospital for a visit when someone from the hospital called and said, "Come right away." Carol's mask had come off and her heart had stopped. The staff started it with medications; no chest compressions were needed. But Carol needed to be re-intubated. The sister wanted to know how long Carol had been without oxygen. She told me she was assured no brain damage had occurred. There were questions about the mask, she said, and then she began to cry. Carol insisted the mask fell off. A nurse claimed the patient had pulled it off. The sister noted that the nurse had given Carol some morphine "right before this incident." Perhaps Carol had a dream and pulled the mask off, she mused. She told Carol that she needed to be re-intubated immediately; she needed the oxygen to survive. Carol understood and gave permission. The sister told me they didn't have much time and they should have re-intubated her 10 minutes before they did. She said the patient wants to fight for her life.

She continued her story. Carol's husband, Al, was told by the doctors that the prognosis was poor. After the mask had come off but before Carol was re-intubated, one of the ICU doctors suggested to Carol and Al that instead of being put back on the ventilator [which would temporarily save her life and prolong her dying] she could be sedated, kept comfortable, and die. Al and Carol talked, and Carol told Al that the doctors were going to "off" her. Al can't believe she is going to die and wants to have a conference with the cancer doctors about whether or not they can treat her.

(Family Physician:) The next day, while I waited for the start of the conference that the husband had requested, I met the patient's family doctor in the ICU. I asked his view about talking to the patient and family about the nearness of death once metastatic cancer was discovered. He replied, "You never like to let a patient think there isn't any hope." He told me that before the surgery, but after he had withdrawn the abdominal fluid full of cancer—a sign that the disease had spread to other organs—he did not think it was appropriate to talk to the family about death. After the surgery he "pulled back from the case" and did not say anything to the patient, although it was clear to him that she was going to die.

(Conference with Family:) One of the ICU physicians arranged the conference for the family in order to answer the husband's questions about treatment and to press for clarity and direction from the family because the patient was deteriorating. Present were the ICU and family physicians, an oncologist, a surgeon, and the patient's husband, sister, and adult son. The family doctor began by summarizing Mrs. Jones's medical history immediately preceding the discovery of cancer. The oncologist discussed his talks with Mrs. Jones before the surgery

regarding the question of the primary site of the cancer: locating the site would make a difference regarding prognosis and treatments. He stated that tests did not reveal the source and neither did the surgery. The surgery did, however, reveal how extensive the cancer was and the impossibility of removing any organs. The husband asked about the usefulness of chemotherapy. The oncologist explained that drugs could not treat the extent of her disease, "a type of cancer that spread very rapidly through the peritoneal cavity." Verbatim excerpts from the dialogue among family and medical staff follow:

Husband: And her prognosis with the cancer?

Oncologist: I never want to take away someone's hope, but there is nothing we can do. She is going to die.

Son: You've never seen someone come back?

Oncologist: Like one in a million?

Son: Okay, so no one comes back.

ICU MD: Her prognosis is less than one in a million. She wouldn't survive the chemo, she's so compromised. We don't know if we can get her off all this support. She needs sedation to die. The body as a whole is a problem. We have to support her with blood products and proteins and despite all these efforts, we're doomed to failure. What's difficult for me is that she is responsive. She is not in a coma. I didn't discuss any of this with her.

Sister: Carol is a fighter.

ICU MD: In terms of the cancer, it's going to get worse. All functions of the body are being compromised by the tumor. I've never seen anyone with this extensive a tumor survive.

Family MD: There's no such thing as perfect knowledge. If at this point you all feel we should continue what we're doing, we'll respect that, and go on a day-by-day basis. If, on the other hand, you feel you want to let her go so she doesn't suffer, that's okay too. And you don't have to decide right now or today.

ICU MD: As a bridge, we maybe have the option of extubating, to let her communicate her wishes. It's a risk, with a mask she wouldn't be breathing as well as she is now.

Husband: Since her last extubation and reintubation, she's psychologically gone downhill.

Husband to surgeon: You're really important to her. You're her teammate. What's your current optimistic view?

Surgeon: She was alert, wanting to keep going after the surgery. Now we have the added insult of this pneumonia on top of the emergency problem that we've had over a week. What required her to be reintubated was not that mask falling off, but that she was so marginal. Her lung function was not in the normal range. She did not continue to improve as we had hoped. Things seem to have taken a turn for the worse, all over. She has a fever; that means infection. She has lots of strikes against her: malnourished, kidneys, cancer, pneumonia, poor lung function. Never able to get water off the lungs. Not absorbing anything in her gut. And now her heart. We're using medications that we only use in cardiac-arrest patients. These are major problems . . . So we're stuck between a rock and a hard place as we can't treat her cancer.

Husband: Say they cut the drugs down so she can communicate . . .

Family MD: This is a complex situation. I don't know if they will be able to, and there is very little hope for a meaningful recovery. We can't just extubate and ask her.

Husband: The philosophic problem is, do we want to ask her?

Surgeon: We can try to take the sedatives away. But we are not in the place we were a week ago, when she could respond. We may not get the same Carol we had a week ago. I don't know if she can make a choice. There is too much going on with her.

Husband: Even if she could, do we want her to go through this?

Sister: She can't make an informed decision.

Surgeon: I think you have to be involved. This is the 90s, not the 30s or 40s or 50s when doctors just decided everything. And you have to make a decision. We can discontinue antibiotics . . .

Family MD: If you do decide to let go, you can talk with [ICU MD], if you do decide to accept the inevitable . . . another way to say it is to give her dignity.

Surgeon: As her primary surgeon, I need from you the code status. She is being resuscitated right now with drugs. Should she be shocked? defibrillated? We need to know 'yes' or 'no.' You can say don't go higher on the drugs. We could dial them down. For me, the main issue is shocking the heart. It's not active, it's just saying if her heart stops, you wouldn't want to do this. I'd like a decision from you before this conference is over.

Son: We need time to think about that and we'd like to consult with you (breaks down and cries.)

Sister to Husband: Are you comfortable with a 'No Code?'

Husband: Yes.

Surgeon to Son: Are you?

Son: No, not yet.

Family MD: We respect that. You don't have to make that decision now . . .

The meeting concluded with no resolution about whether or not to perform cardiopulmonary resuscitation if the patient suffered a cardiac arrest, or whether to allow her to die by withdrawing technological and pharmaceutical support.

(Surgeon:) Later in the day, the surgeon told me that his philosophy is never to take away hope and that he realizes that families take lots of time for "things to sink in." Even if one family member does not agree about code status, he said, it is best to wait so that that family member does not feel railroaded into making a decision that he "killed the patient." He does not want that to happen in this case.

(ICU Nurse:) The next day, I learned from Mrs. Jones's nurse that the son came to the patient's bedside, teary, a few hours after the conference. The nurse asked if he would like some time alone with the patient and he said that he would. She drew the curtain and left. He only stayed at the bedside about 15 minutes, she reported, but shortly afterwards, the surgeon called to say that the patient had been made "No Code." The nurse told me, "I guess that was a good idea to give him time alone with her. He was able to process that much." But, she remarked, that was the only decision that was made. The patient was still receiving full ventilator and vasopressor medication support in order to survive. Three days after the family conference, 20 days after her admission to the ICU, Carol Jones was moved into the corner room on the ICU, to give the family more privacy, I was told by staff, as they prepare for and face her death.

(ICU Physician:) Yet at morning rounds in the ICU several days later, I learned that the medical staff was trying again to extubate Carol Jones. One intensive care physician told me that she was completely alert in spite of her extensive disease and bad prognosis and that there was now a "window of opportunity to wean her" from ventilator support. He told me he wanted to make it clear to the patient that the short-term prognosis is uncertain and that she is not going to get better. He noted that the patient was now "a bit paranoid." She wanted to see all medications, wanted to know everything that was being done to her, wanted to see her x-rays. He commented that he has never had a patient in the ICU ask to see an x-ray. The nurse caring for her most during this period wondered aloud to me what that was all about: Is she worried that someone, or the medical staff, wants to hasten her death? The intensive care physician had conferred with the respiratory therapists; the patient was strong enough to breathe on her own. But if they extubate, he does not want to re-intubate if necessary.

After rounds, I went with the physician to Carol Jones' bedside. He held her hand while he told her that now there was a window of opportunity, a chance she could breathe on her own for awhile. He explained that they don't want to leave the breathing tube in because there are complications from doing that, pneumonia, etc. Because of the underlying disease, for which there is no cure, if problems occur when the tube is out, we don't want to put it back in. "Does that make sense to you?" he asked. The patient, very alert and focused at that moment, shook her head "No" and motioned for a pad and pencil to write with. She tried to write something but it was indecipherable. The physician asked if she needed to talk to her husband about this and she nodded "yes." He replied, "That's good. Talk to him and then we'll talk later."

Later that day, I observed a conversation between the ICU physician and the husband. Al was noncommittal as to what his wife would want but he certainly did not support pulling out the breathing tube with no "safety net." The physician responded that it was now three weeks postsurgery. "Most people would say they had had enough," he said. "But a tracheotomy is an option if you want to buy more time."

(ICU Nurse:) Toward the end of the afternoon, I met briefly with Carol's nurse, who was looking exhausted. She said the oncology folks had come in and done some tests because the patient has been hospitalized for 3 weeks and "she's at risk for deep vein thrombosis." Sure enough, they found a blood clot in one of her legs. So now they have to treat it with anticoagulants. The nurse, very frustrated about this latest development, called the ICU physician, who was also frustrated and who responded, "She's a 'No Code' and they do these tests, and they found something, so now we have to treat it." The nurse told me that with terminal cancer and 'No Code' status, they never should have done the tests. So she was working on what kind of orders she needed to get from which physicians in order to treat the problem.

(Husband:) Three days later, when I met up with the husband in the hospital elevator, he told me, "Now she has 'ICU psychosis.'"[5] He said it was very hard to communicate with Carol. Her writing was not making sense, and "if her writing isn't making sense, nothing is." A tracheotomy was scheduled for that afternoon, to give the patient more comfort and potentially enable her to speak. Al said that for the first time in a long time he was in a more hopeful period. "Maybe she'll do better now, have a period of time she'll be able to go outside, get out of here."

(ICU Physician:) Several days later, a full month after Carol Jones arrived on the ICU, one of the intensive care physicians told me that he and another physician had spoken with the husband and told him, though not exactly in these words, that "She needs to die and she needs to die now." He said they had started a morphine drip.[6] He noted that Al responded, "I guess we shouldn't increase the dopamine," thus

concurring with their view. [Dopamine was maintaining her blood pressure and therefore, keeping her alive.]

(ICU Nurse:) The nurse caring for Mrs. Jones that day told me that the husband was finally "ready to let her go." He had said, "I don't want to see her suffer anymore." She remarked that the family members were as prepared as each of them was going to be.

(Medical Chart:) The death was planned. The 'progress notes' in Mrs. Jones's chart on the day of her death read: "further decline. T[emperature] = 102. Assessment: Terminal state. Discussed withdrawal of rx [treatments] with husband last nite. He talked to rest of family and they concur. Will keep on 4 mg ms [morphine sulphate] for comfort. Will increase as needed. Stop TPN [artificial nutrition], antibiotics. Start dopamine wean when family arrives. Rediscussed with husband this a.m." The 'doctor's orders' in the chart read: "9:30 am. Wean dopamine over 4 hours after family arrives." The nurse informed me that Mrs. Jones died about 5 hours later with all her intravenous lines and the ventilator still in place.

(ICU Physician:) When the ICU physician arrived on the scene about 2 hours later (4:30 pm) the nursing shift had changed and a nurse who hadn't been with the patient and family during the last moments of life was beginning 'postmortem care,' the procedure for preparing to send a body to the morgue. The physician asked the nurse when the patient died and if the family was present. Then he went immediately to dictate the 'death pronouncement' note for the chart. When I spoke with him a few minutes later, he told me that he had talked with the husband the night before. Al said he was finally ready and that the doctor could begin to let her die. Al knew that when the amount of dopamine was reduced, his wife would die and he was prepared.

INTERPRETING CULTURAL PROCESS

How can this multivocal narrative contribute to an understanding of 'the problem' of death in America? What can the intersecting viewpoints and contradictory processes within this case study/social drama tell us about death in the hospital as a cultural process? I want to suggest that a detailed, multivocal portrayal of one dying trajectory is useful both for teasing apart the multiple threads that constitute "end-of-life issues" and for understanding how these threads act as a cultural force in determining the practice of death in the American hospital. Through this narrative we can identify at least six cultural processes at work.

First, structures of power, ideology, and economics within hospital culture define appropriate moments and contexts for death to occur.

For example, it is not 'good' for patients to die during or immediately following surgery regardless of age or medical condition. Such a death tarnishes both individual and institutional reputations. On the other hand, it is considered appropriate by physicians and nurses to withdraw support so death can occur after a patient has spent hours to weeks in the ICU.[7] In this pervasive social *and* moral system individual clinicians do not act as autonomous and unencumbered players to make decisions about the timing of death. Various ethnographers have shown how the locus of responsibility for moral choice-making, especially around death, is embedded in structural features of medical practice and in institutional priorities (Anspach, 1993; Bosk, 1992). In addition, one large survey of health professional views of life-sustaining treatment found that clinicians were deeply frustrated with a system that did not meet their own standards for care and was thought to overtreat patients (Solomon et al., 1993). The story of Mrs. Jones unfolded within a particularly American moral-structural hospital context in which death immediately following exploratory surgery is to be avoided but death one month later is considered desirable or even mandatory.

Second, the issue of 'code status'—determining whether or not a patient wishes to have cardio-pulmonary resuscitation attempted in the event of cardiac arrest—looms large in hospital policy and practice. Current policy seems to dictate that in the event of cardiac arrest, resuscitation will be attempted unless the patient or patient's surrogate specifies otherwise.[8] Most physicians I spoke with usually do not choose to initiate discussions of a "Do-not-resuscitate" order with patients or families in the hospital setting. Some consider 'code status' determination to be an artifact of hospital bureaucracy in a litigious society and irrelevant to treatment decision making. Some think discussions of 'code status' with very ill patients and anxious family members are anathema to hope and a productive doctor-patient or doctor-family relationship. Sometimes physicians do not bring up the topic until (a) they are prodded to do so by nurses, who generally are quick to consider the negative outcome and suffering that a resuscitation attempt frequently causes or, (b) a patient is, in their opinion, very close (hours or days) to death. In the latter case doctors may press for a "Do-not-resuscitate" order from family or patient as part of an overall change in direction of treatment—from aggressive disease intervention to palliative care.

The family of Mrs. Jones was urged at the conference to make a decision about 'code status,' that is, to designate the patient "Do-not-resuscitate" in case of cardiac arrest. From the family's point of view, hospital rules, especially those regarding the need to designate a code status, are usually outside their world of experience. Most families I observed had never conceptualized, let alone discussed with their relative, the notion of choice surrounding a resuscitation attempt. Very few families had discussed the possibility of or desire for resuscitation or intubation, specifically, with their relative before hospitalization.

Third, there is a fundamental incommensurability between lay and medical worlds of understanding. While medicine has become the dominant lens through which to view the problems of old age and death (Estes & Binney, 1989; Kaufman, 1994), and though the 'technological imperative' of hospital care is widely shared by health professionals and health consumers alike, at least several areas of knowledge are not shared by medical practitioners and the lay public. For example, detailed knowledge about human physiology and disease processes, the ways in which particular technologies actually work on the body, and hospital rules regarding the designation of resuscitation orders are not similarly understood by health providers, patients, and families. Diagnoses themselves are often ambiguous from a patient's point of view (Rapp, 1993). Patients and families often are entirely unprepared for the kinds of active decision making that critical illness in the contemporary hospital context imposes. Faced with the prospect of intubation or its withdrawal or an intensive care stay with an unknown outcome, families generally do not know *what to want,* other than the general recovery of their relative. They do not know what 'life support' entails operationally. And they are not always concerned with pain and suffering when they fear immanent death and hope for survival. The point here is that the 'choices' patients and families face in the ICU are created for them by institutional directives, late 20th-century hospital culture, and the technological imperative. They do not arise from the patients' worlds of experience.

Fourth, the national conversation that so dominates contemporary cultural discourse in the United States—about the tension between "aggressive treatment" versus "comfort care"—is shown to be overly simplistic in the context of a detailed example of multiple perspectives, conflicting wishes and treatments, and perhaps most important, ambiguity about the goals of medical practice in the face of death. Though Mrs. Jones was actively dying, and her doctors articulated that fact, they continued to provide more interventions as her condition deteriorated because she was responsive and was able to express her desire for life-sustaining care and her fear about being put to death prematurely. Few would deny continued life-prolonging treatment, even as death approaches, to a competent patient.[9] Thus great energy was spent trying both to manage the discrete medical and psychological problems that kept arising, and to make it easier for the patient to breathe by suggesting, first, a mask, and later, a tracheotomy. At the same time, however, the medical team tried to convince the patient and family that death should be allowed to occur. Adding to an already confused course of action, one physician's diagnosis of deep vein thrombosis dictated treatment despite the patient's terminal status, thus further frustrating the medical team.

Not until one month of intensive care interventions to stave off death had passed did physicians convince the husband that 'it was time' for Mrs. Jones to die. Various observers have noted the lack of clarity about medical goals at the end of life (Brody, 1992; Callahan, 1993). The conflicts produced by coexistence of the broad value of patient autonomy and patient- and family-centered care, hospital rules about treatments and resuscitation, and the legally based need for patients and families to be the decision makers regarding withdrawal of life support all contribute to an uneasiness about the relationship of medical goals to practitioner responsibility and to the prolongation of dying.

Fifth is the issue of this particular dying trajectory. Given the combination of desires of this patient and family, physician approaches toward 'hope,' 'options,' and family involvement in decision making, and the moral and structural rules of the contemporary hospital world, could this scenario have unfolded differently? Could this death have been 'improved'? What would that have entailed? It could be argued, first of all, that different decisions by individual players would have resulted in a different outcome. But it is important to note that individual behaviors that foster a certain kind of death occur in and are shaped by a broader context of culture, ideology, and institutional imperatives. For Mrs. Jones to have had a different kind of death at least two things would have had to be different. First, radical change in hospital ideology and practice would be required (Lo, 1995; Reiser, 1994; Solomon et al., 1993) including a reconsideration both of life-extending technology use in the face of terminal illness and unspoken yet powerful rules about the timing and location of 'appropriate' and 'inappropriate' deaths. Second, a general cultural acceptance of death in the context of advanced terminal illness would be needed (Callahan, 1993). The widespread cultural conversation about 'death with dignity' fails to consider these multilayered forces at work. It is the ongoing interaction of these forces that makes some hospital deaths, particularly those that occur in intensive care units, unfold in a particular way.

Sixth is the issue of age. Would the narrative have been different if the patient were 84 instead of 54? In light of my observations of 31 individuals between ages 50 and 89 in one ICU, I suggest not. Treatments in the ICU are most often age blind (Schecter, 1994) and, ironically, that feature of hospital practice contributes to the cultural 'problem.' In that setting care is determined largely by physiological function and the response of bodily systems to aggressive interventions, not by age per se. Physiological decline has come to be reimagined as something that can be treated, managed, and potentially reversed. And death is viewed as perhaps not inevitable right now. Perhaps there would have been stronger hospital pressure to stop life supporting technology if Mrs. Jones had been 84, yet it is unlikely that medical staff would override a patient's (or family's) clear request at any age. In the ICU, the 'choice' to continue life-prolonging treatment is available to all patients, even when the practice of life prolongation in the very old is considered bad medicine.

The case of Mrs. Jones makes us ponder the 'difference'—at least in the ICU setting—between someone age 54 and someone over 70 or 80 or 90, for instance. How and where does one apply the designation 'old,' and is this a meaningful category when considering both hospital ideology and moral practice? Although Carol Jones was 54, her physical decline resembled that of an older person. Most important, she exhibited a key feature of many older persons who become institutionalized: her own voice was largely unavailable. She was an object of attention in a world where routine and ideology generally mute biography (Cole et al., 1995; Diamond, 1992). Others needed to speak for her. In this case, the patient was deemed competent and her desire to continue life-sustaining treatment was honored until her physiologic decline became more powerful than the combined medical treatments. But her competency would have been honored at age 84 or beyond as well.

THE USE OF NARRATIVE

My construction of this particular multivocal narrative emerged from first, my field experience and the type of data I collected including what conversations and events I was privy to, what actors I was able to meet and engage, what I wanted to 'see.' Second, it was fashioned with a deliberate intent: to identify the cultural processes that perhaps contribute to, or lie at the source of, the 'problem' of death in America. What distinguishes anthropological uses and constructions of narrative from those of other disciplines in the humanities are *data*.[10] Grounded in the real world and the flow of time and events, data are, above all, *observed* social processes, not discrete or objective 'facts.' Ethnographers watch what people do, hear what they say, engage with them in conversation and debate, all in natural settings that contain and produce conflict, ambiguity, urgency, contradiction, and lack of closure. Informants come and go. The politics of situations change. Ethnographers are sometimes denied and sometimes permitted access to spaces, rituals, events, people. Through all of this, we write down only something of what we see and hear and what we think happens. Ethnographic narrative is produced from this flux. Later, in our articles, reports, and ethnographies we sometimes acknowledge and articulate our standpoint and personal agenda in the 'seeing,' collecting, and representing of 'the data.'

Thus 'how death occurs in the hospital' can be viewed in infinite ways, as the explosion in experimental and critical writing and the blurring of genres indicates. The story presented here is not authentic, that is, it does not reproduce the 'truth' about the death of Carol Jones. The voices within it are selected from the flow of events and are only verbal responses to deeply felt experience. In addition, it could be argued that I omitted important material, misrepresented various players, or was 'biased' in a variety of ways. Another ethnographer certainly would have written another kind of story. Yet any anthropological presentation of this particular death, I believe, would reveal how social processes unfold and where struggles over 'the moral' are located. From an anthropological perspective, narratives constructed by the researcher to portray multiple voices serve as *cultural documents* (Becker, 1997; Good et al., 1990; Gordon, 1994; Kaufman, 1997) and, in this case, they reveal how medical and hospital activity are reflected on after the fact, the social construction of patient and family 'choice' and hospital staff constraints, and how Americans practice death.

CONCLUSION

In the construction of this narrative, I have prioritized the details of everyday hospital practice and juxtaposed multiple voices in order to illustrate conflict, resistance, ambivalence, and the complexity of one hospital death. It is hoped that this kind of humanistic portrayal moves away from normalizing and generalizing accounts of hospital practices that precede death and instead captures the positioned, subjective content of various perspectives as well as the contexts of knowledge, power, and practice in which they occur. A narrative such as this reveals only a particular 'truth' about the *lifeworld,* "that domain of everyday, immediate social existence and practical activity, with all its habituality, its crises, its vernacular and idiomatic character, its biographical particularities, its decisive events and indecisive strategies" (Jackson, 1996). Yet it offers a guide to the *multiple* meanings of how death in the hospital occurs. It shows us, as well, how the 'problem' of death in America today is specifically embodied, practiced, and known and that the 'problem' cannot be reduced to single oppositions—of palliative care versus aggressive treatment, control versus powerlessness, choice versus inevitability—if we are to seriously grapple with it.

ACKNOWLEDGMENTS

The study on which this chapter is based was funded by the National Institute on Aging, grant #AG13636, Sharon R. Kaufman, P.I. I am deeply indebted to the hospital staff, patients, and families who participated in this project. Many thanks to Co-P.I. Guy Micco for his insights about hospital practice, policy, and ethical issues in end-of-life care which I have incorporated in this chapter. Additional thanks go to project staff Karen Van Leuven and Chris Wood. Robert Kastenbaum and Steve Weiland provided astute comments on an earlier draft and Gay Becker, Tom Cole, Gelya Frank, and Steve Weiland have engaged me in lively conversations about the role of narrative in anthropology. I am grateful to them all.

NOTES

[1] My work 'stands on the shoulders' of the early sociological studies of dying in the hospital (Strauss, 1965, 1968; Sudnow, 1967). As those works are situated in the scholarship of their time to reflect concerns of social structure and organization, interaction, work roles, and knowledge about dying, my study, too, is historically and academically situated in debates about bioethics and subaltern experience, as well as in a milieu of 'experimental writing.'

[2] See Becker (1997) and Mattingly (1998) for recent reviews of the uses of narrative in anthropological writing.

[3] Specific data collection procedures throughout the hospital consisted of the following activities: (1) attendance at multidisciplinary rounds in which the cases of patients, including their diagnoses, prognoses, treatments and treatment plans, family dynamics, and discharge options were discussed; (2) conversations with health professionals about those patients who were near death; (3) where possible, discussions with patients and their family members; (4) review of patient charts; and (5) attendance at conferences in which various health professionals discussed with family members the patient's condition, possible and preferred treatment plans, prognoses, the possibility of death, and choices—from the medical standpoint—that family members where confronting. In all these activities data were collected by descriptive note-taking including verbatim notation during some conversations and conferences.

[4] All names have been changed to protect anonymity.

[5] "ICU psychosis" is a disorientation that occurs in people who are confined to intensive care units. It results both from sensory deprivation of the normal, orienting world and from overstimulation of noise, lights, machinery, and unfamiliar procedures. Some people exhibit hallucinations and delusions.

[6] Morphine is frequently given to patients preceding a planned death. It provides respiratory comfort and pain reduction.

[7] This length of time is variable and depends on the particular doctor or nurses involved and the patient's age and severity of medical problems.

[8] It was brought to my attention that hospital 'policy' regarding the matter of "Do Not Resuscitate" orders is not clear-cut and is under discussion by hospital staff continually. Policy on this matter is, in fact, a fuzzy and protean matter. The ethics committee at this hospital frequently reviews its policy in an attempt to offer a clear guideline for physician action. In general, a family decision regarding code status trumps physician opinion.

[9] Moreover, few would deny life-prolonging treatment in the face of family member or surrogate demands.

[10] I am indebted to Gay Becker for conversation about this topic.

REFERENCES

Anspach, R. R. (1993). *Deciding who lives: Neonatal care.* Berkeley: University of California Press.

Atkinson, P. (1997). Narrative turn or blind alley? *Qualitative Health Research, 7,* 325–344.

Balshem, M. (1993). *Cancer in the community.* Washington: Smithsonian Institution Press.

Becker, G. (1997). *Disrupted lives.* Berkeley: University of California Press.

Behar, R. (1993). *Translated woman.* Boston: Beacon Press.

Bosk, C. (1992). *All God's mistakes.* Chicago: University of Chicago Press.

Bourgois, P. (1995). *In search of respect.* Cambridge: Cambridge University Press.

Brody, H. (1987). *Stories of sickness.* New Haven: Yale University Press.

Brody, H. (1992). *The healer's power.* New Haven: Yale University Press.

Bruner, J. (1986). *Actual minds, possible worlds.* Cambridge: Harvard University Press.

Bruner, J. (1990). *Acts of meaning.* Cambridge: Harvard University Press.

Callahan, D. (1993). *The troubled dream of life.* New York: Simon and Schuster.

Clifford, J., & Marcus, G. E. (1986). *Writing culture.* Berkeley: University of California Press.

Cole, T. R., Thompson, B. L., & Rounds, L. (1995). In whose voice? Composing an ethics case as a song of life. *Journal of Long Term Home Health Care, 14,* 23–32.

Diamond, T. (1992) *Making grey gold.* Chicago: University of Chicago Press.

Estes, C. L., & Binney, E. A. (1989). The biomedicalization of aging: Dangers and dilemmas. *The Gerontologist, 29,* 587–597.

Farmer, P. (1992). *Aids and accusation.* Berkeley: University of California Press.

Frank, A. W. (1995). *The wounded storyteller.* Chicago: University of Chicago Press.

Geertz, C. (1983). *Local knowledge.* New York: Basic Books.

Geertz, C. (1988). *Works and lives: The anthropologist as author.* Stanford: Stanford University Press.

Good, B. (1994). *Medicine, rationality and experience.* Cambridge: Cambridge University Press.

Good, M. J. D., Good, B., Schaffer, C., & Lind, S. (1990). American oncology and the discourse on hope. *Culture, Medicine and Psychiatry, 14,* 59–79.

Good, M. J. D., Brodwin, P. E., Good, B., & Kleinman, A. (Eds.). (1992). *Pain as human experience.* Berkeley: University of California Press.

Gordon, D. R. (1994). The ethics of ambiguity and concealment around cancer. In P. Benner (Ed.), *Interpretive phenomenology* (pp. 279–317). Thousand Oaks, CA: Sage.

Hunter, K. M. (1991). *Doctors' stories.* Princeton: Princeton University Press.

Institute of Medicine. (1997). *Approaching death: Improving care at the end of life.* Washington, DC: National Academy Press.

Jackson, M. (Ed.). (1996). *Things as they are: New directions in phenomenological anthropology.* Bloomington: Indiana University Press.

Kaufman, S. R. (1993). *The healer's tale.* Madison: University of Wisconsin Press.

Kaufman, S. R. (1994). Old age, disease, and the discourse on risk: Geriatric assessment in U.S. health care. *Medical Anthropology Quarterly, 8,* 76–93.

Kaufman, S. R. (1997). Construction and practice of medical responsibility: Dilemmas and narratives from geriatrics. *Culture, Medicine and Psychiatry, 21,* 1–26.

Kleinman, A. (1988). *The illness narratives.* New York: Basic Books.

Kleinman, A., & Kleinman, J. (1991). Suffering and its professional transformation. *Culture, Medicine and Psychiatry, 15,* 275–301.

Lo, B. (1995). Improving care near the end of life. *Journal of the American Medical Association, 274,* 1634–1635.

Marcus, G., & Fischer, M. J. (1986). *Anthropology as cultural critique.* Chicago: University of Chicago Press.

Mattingly, C. (1998). *Healing dramas and clinical plots.* Cambridge: Cambridge University Press.

Moskowitz, E. H., & Nelson, J. L. (Eds.). (1995). *Hastings Center Report,* Special supplement, November–December, S2–S36.

Phillips, D. C. (1994). Telling it straight: Issues in assessing narrative research. *Educational Psychologist, 29,* 13–21.

Polkinghorne, D. (1988). *Narrative knowing and the human sciences.* Albany: State University of New York Press.

Rabinow, P., & Sullivan, W. M. (Eds.). (1979). *Interpretive social science.* Berkeley: University of California Press.

Rapp, R. (1993). Accounting for Amniocentesis. In S. Lindenbaum & M. Lock (Eds.), *Knowledge, power & practice* (pp. 55–76). Berkeley: University of California Press.

Reiser, S. J. (1994). The Ethical Life of Health Care Organizations. *Hastings Center Report,* November–December, pp. 28–35.

Rosaldo, R. (1989). *Culture and truth.* Boston: Beacon Press.

Schecter, W. P. (1994). Withdrawing and withholding life support in geriatric surgical patients: Ethical considerations. *Surgical Clinics of North America, 74,* 245–249.

Simpson, D. (1995). *The academic postmodern and the rule of literature.* Chicago: University of Chicago Press.

Solomon, M. Z., et al. (1993). Decisions near the end of life: Professional views on life-sustaining treatments. *American Journal of Public Health, 83,* 14–23.

Steedly, M. M. (1993). *Hanging without a rope.* Princeton: Princeton University Press.

The SUPPORT Principal Investigators. (1995). A controlled trial to improve care for seriously ill hospitalized patients. *Journal of the American Medical Association, 274,* 1591–1634.

Turner, V. (1974). *Dramas, fields, and metaphors.* Ithaca & London: Cornell University Press.

Wikan, U. (1995). The Self in a world of urgency and necessity. *Ethos, 23,* 259–285.

Young, K. (1997). *Presence in the flesh.* Cambridge: Harvard University Press.

18

Positive Development in Later Life

Gisela Labouvie-Vief

A s their colleagues from the humanistic disciplines, psychologists of this century have been engaged in a thorough reevaluation of the process of adult development and aging. Major theories of development that arose around or shortly after the transition from the 19th to the 20th century had primarily addressed youth, and described the apex of development: the ability for rational thought, for internalizing society's demands, and for regulating one's behavior and emotions in accordance with both. Yet, 20th century changes in longevity, health, and psychological well-being made obvious that individuals maintain vitality throughout most of their life spans. As a consequence, to formulate more positive accounts of the "second half of life" has become ever more urgent. Indeed, it has defined a major endeavor of psychologists interested in adulthood and aging during the second half of this century.

In this chapter I provide a brief discussion of these approaches. I suggest that many of them have uncovered strengths that can be associated with the advance of age. Yet they also were driven by a sense of youthful idealism that replaced predominantly negative views of late life with somewhat romantic notions of the older person as a wise and generative leader of society. As Erikson (1984) suggested, the equation of the notions of "elder" and "elderly" may be more idealistic than realistic. In actuality, the picture appears to include both of these extremes, and to encompass the full range of variation between either end of the continuum.

Views of what constitutes positive development in later life, then, are not uniform. Indeed, I suggest that across different traditions and approaches, individuals have addressed what are essentially two different core strategies or processes inherent in positive development. First, as a response to older rationalist versions of the individual, positive development has been defined as the integration of the rational with the nonrational and emotional to yield more integrative and complex structures (e.g., Chinen, 1985; Jung, 1931; L-V, 1997, 1998). For other writers, in turn, positive aging has primarily implied the ability to achieve a sense of peace and even well-being in the face of life's negative and tragic aspects, such its suffering, loss, death, and decline. Often, these two visions are treated as different versions of the same underlying process of aging. However, much recent evidence suggests that in actuality, they are driven by somewhat different processes and form rather different versions of what is meant by 'positive development.'

COGNITION-EMOTION INTEGRATION

The first vision of positive development as increasing emotion-cognition integration arose out of critiques of the two grand developmental theories born early in this century, those of Freud and Piaget. Probably no single theory more that Freudian psychoanalysis argued that all of human behavior, including advanced forms of rationality, ultimately are to be placed in the context of important emotional systems. For Freud (Freud, 1911/1957), development is based on the tension and balance between two modes of being and of defining reality. One is primary process, an organic mode in which an inner world of desires and wishes prevails. The other is secondary process, a conceptual mode no longer directed by the inner reality of wish fulfillment and fantasy. Rather, this mode strives to find out what is objectively true, what holds in the outer world.

The ideal of such a balance between the rational and the organismic was also a basic of Piaget's (Piaget, 1967) theory. Paradoxically, however, neither theorist carried that notion to its logical conclusion. Freud's theory, for example, is less aimed at a harmonious balance between inner and outer reality, but more at a fairly complete victory of the secondary process over the primary process principle. Indeed, the former is called 'reality principle,' while the latter is termed 'pleasure principle.' Thus, Freud defines education ". . . as an incitement to the conquest of the pleasure principle, and to its replacement by the reality-principle." Similarly, the ideal of the adapted individual is the scientist who ". . . comes nearest to this conquest" (Freud, 1911/1957, pp. 43–44).

The result of this view of maturity as the triumph of ego control over biology and instincts was a widespread tendency to view adulthood in terms of deterioration—decline of ego functions and regression. For example, Freud held that adulthood brought a threat of ego disintegration (see Riegel, 1973). In turn, early views of aging derived from Piaget's theory proposed that aging implied a loss of higher-order functioning. However, such decline-oriented views were thoroughly revised, from both psychodynamic and cognitive perspectives.

Transcendence of the Rational

One major theorist to define a new way of looking at adulthood was Jung (Fordham, 1966; Jacobi, 1962; Whitmont, 1969). Jung's famous break from Freud was motivated out of his belief that Freud, though in one sense liberating primary process from tabu, in another sense had continued to imprison it in a rationalist perspective. For Jung, the broad organismic heritage expressed in story, myth, and visual symbol was not merely a primitive mode of processing displaced by the ascent of reason, but potentially was a rich and highly advanced mode in processing and thinking in its own right. Beyond the capacities of reason, it revealed a larger context that constrains reason, a context of universal biological heritage—of the enduring emotional patterns relating to birth, death, sexuality and love, and generational succession.

From a life span perspective, Jung's (Jung, 1933) major contribution was to emphasize that functions of the ego might play different roles at different points in the life span. Early, in the process of forming a primary adaptation based on conscious ego control, the individual disowns many emotional experiences that are not congruent with the ideals of culture. Nevertheless, these rejected self-aspects strive for expression in distorted ways, as in processes of dissociation and splitting. Jung believed that the unique potential of adult development consisted in healing these splits and in forming a more integrated structure. In that process, there is also a reevaluation of the ego and rational processes, with the realization that they are undergirded by these powerful 'archetypal' patterns.

Jung suggested that out of confronting the dialectical tension between these two systems—ones I refer to as logos and mythos in my recent book, *Psyche and Eros* (Labouvie-Vief, 1994)—the individual can eventually form a new structure—the "Self"—that transcends either system, yet blends both within higher-order forms of experience. This transcendent way of relating to the world, according to Jung, reconceptualized the world from an ordinary sense of objective reality to one in which the opposites of reason and emotion, self and other, or masculine and feminine are blended into a new experience of reality. That reality is defined by universal aspects of the *psyche* or *soul* as it tends to be experienced through times and cultures. This view is essentially

a spiritual one, repeated in many religious traditions, and often represented by the union of two contrasexual figures in a 'divine marriage'
(Fordham, 1966; Jacobi, 1962).

Jung's view of positive development in later life has influenced
several writers. Among the first to put his notions of a midlife transformation to the test were Gould (1977) and Levinson et al. (1978). Both
of these authors reported that their samples reflected the kinds of
changes Jung had proposed: an inward turn and heightened interest
in the nonrational, an increasing openness to examine life's negative
and disappointing aspects, a heightened interest in exploring paradoxical polarities such as good and evil, young and old, masculine
and feminine.

More recently, Chinen (1985) pointed out that the notion of transcendent structures of the psyche is evident not only in individuals'
experience, but is mirrored in fairy tales around the world, especially
those that address later life issues. While fairy tales of early life often
stress the importance of forming a persona and adjusting to a reality
defined by the existing social system, those dealing with mid- and late
life reveal a turning away from conventional roles, a blending of
notions of gender, and the emergence of an inner-oriented self. Thus,
such tales help define unique roles of the older individual that differ
from those of younger ones. The older individual, accordingly, is seen
as a spiritual leader, and as an expert in the realm of emotion rather
than technique. Older women often are displayed in heroic roles
reserved for men in tales of younger protagonists, while older men are
confronted with experiences of suffering, empathy, and nurture.

In a similar vein, research by Adams and Labouvie-Vief (Adams,
Labouvie-Vief, Hobart, & Dorosz, 1990; Jepson & Labouvie-Vief, 1992)
suggests that mature and older individuals, in contrast to young adults,
render different readings of stories such as those of fairy tales, myths,
and parables. While college age individuals often interpret such stories
in terms of their overt detail and the sequence of actions and events,
older individuals are more likely to focus on the inner and psychological meaning of the information: what it reveals about the general condition of being human, and about spiritual and transcendent principles
that allow us to accept misfortune and injustice.

Findings such as these also are reminiscent of Erikson's (Erickson,
1984) view that later life is a period in which issues of integrity come
to the fore. That is, faced with issues of approaching death and time
limitations, the elderly need to reexamine their lives with its positive
and negative dimensions and come to accept it as a structure that overall, is meaningful and whole. Following Erikson, several authors (e.g.,
Tornstam, 1989) proposed that this process requires a transcendent
focus away from preoccupations with one's body, one's ego, and one's

personal self and toward the general human condition. Tornstam (1989) has referred to this process as one of 'gerotranscendence.'

Cognitive Complexity and Transcendence of Convention

Mostly, however, Jung's influence has been only less directly felt in academic psychology. Yet the notion that mature development brings a transcendence of objectively based views of reality and the emergence of one that is based on a more general vision of what life could and should be also arose out of more cognitively based accounts, such as those of Piaget. As already stated, Piaget's theory, like that of Freud, was based on a duality of organismic and rational processes, and like his theory, it maintained the rationalist bias of early psychoanalysis.

As a consequence, one major impetus to searching for continued growth in later life has come from the cognitive-developmental expansions of Piagetian notions, such as those of Loevinger (1993) and Kohlberg (1984) (for a review, see Labouvie-Vief, 1994). Both of these theorists suggested that as individuals acquire cognitive structures that are more complex and powerful, they move beyond conventional and institutional interpretations, rules and roles. Instead, they develop modes of thinking that expose both a more differentiated and individuated self. They attempt to locate that self within broader, supra-individual structures within which that self can be validated and justified. Thus, the notion of postconventional forms of thinking has a decidedly Jungian ring! However, it is also important to note that these postconventional or postconformist forms ultimately remain rooted in rational principles, in contrast to Jung's view which was much more mythos driven. This is especially true of Kohlberg (1984) who remained committed to a view of rational principles of justification that might motivate the search for postconventional principles.

The last two decades have seen a plethora of attempts to extend Piagetian structures of youthful thinking into mature adulthood. Proponents of this approach suggest that formal operations are not the final stage of cognitive development, but that a qualitatively new form of thinking emerges during adulthood which is often referred to as "postformal" or "dialectical thinking" (Riegel, 1973). This new form of thinking goes beyond the decontextualized, abstract formal reasoning observed during adolescence and young adulthood, and involves a higher use of reflection and the integration of contextual, relativistic, and subjective knowledge. This approach has resulted in an array of studies concerned with postformal or wisdom-related aspects of knowledge (King & Kitchener, 1994; Kitchener & King, 1981; Kramer & Woodruff, 1986) or important real-life knowledge such as the processing of text, decision making in conflict situations (Kitchener & King, 1994;

Kuhn, Pennington, & Leadbeater, 1983), or the representation of and reflection on self, emotions, and values (Commons et al., 1984; Labouvie-Vief, DeVoe, & Bulka, 1989; Sinnott, 1989).

All of the above proposals indicate that rational processes on the one hand, and processes related to self and emotions on the other, are profoundly interconnected. Even though this is true of all of the life span, however, it appears to be only at relatively advanced levels that individuals are able to represent and understand these relationships and integrate them within single, nonconflicting systems. This ability to bridge the tensions between the universal and the contextual, the theoretical and the pragmatic, and the rational and emotional is often referred to as wisdom (Baltes & Staudinger, 1993; Clayton & Birren, 1980; Labouvie-Vief, 1990; Staudinger & Baltes, 1994, 1996).

While all of the work discussed above related to processes of wisdom, the most detailed research project thus far has attempted to provide a specific operational definition of 'wisdom.' According to Baltes and his colleagues (Baltes, Smith, & Staudinger, 1992; Baltes & Staudinger, 1993), wisdom, defined as expert knowledge with regard to important but uncertain matters of life, can be characterized by several components. Individuals receive ratings on each of these components, and an overall 'wisdom score' is derived. As is true of the studies reported in this section, Baltes and his collaborators found that although age in itself was not a sufficient condition for the development of wisdom, older adults were somewhat more likely to be nominated as wise, and those nominated in fact produced the highest wisdom scores. But in general, there was no evidence for a strong link between age and wisdom.

One possibility is that this lack of association is due to the particular criterion of wisdom used in Baltes's research project. That criterion remains rather strongly embedded in a cognitive perspective that retains a high degree of relativism but does not emphasize the general principles that structure emotional realities and that, ultimately, are to be integrated with cognitive perspectives as implied in Jung's work (Labouvie-Vief, 1994). As Kitchener and King (1982) suggested, such principles of integration can refer to structures of communication that can guide the process of inquiry but that do not guarantee the static 'truth' of facts. Instead, individuals commit themselves to a *process* of critical inquiry in which notions of 'objectivity' are relocated into the intersubjective domain. In my own work, I refer to this form of thinking as 'hermeneutical thinking' (Labouvie-Vief, 1994).

Together with my colleagues and students, I have adopted this latter approach and applied it directly to an examination of individuals' thinking about their emotions and their self. For example (Labouvie-Vief, DeVoe, & Bulka, 1989), we demonstrated that younger individuals described emotions in terms of outer appearance, conventional standards, relatively static impulse monitoring, and an emphasis on control and the ideal. In contrast, those older or of higher ego level conveyed a keener sense of differentiation of self from norms, of vivid felt experience, and of an individuality that is distinct, historically formed, and subject to change and transformation, and of complex psychological transactions both within the self and between self and others. Similar changes also were evident in individuals' descriptions of their self and their parents (Labouvie-Vief et al., 1995a, b). This work is also consistent with other writings on emotion (Blanchard-Fields, 1997), the self (Kegan, 1982; Noam, 1988), and religion (Fowler, 1981).

What about early notions that these types of changes might reveal late life structures of thinking? In actuality, our data suggest that the apex of thinking in terms of complex cognition-emotion integrations is not in late life, but rather around midlife. Individuals past the age of 60 were rather similar to those in the adolescent to young-adult age groups. They were more likely to describe emotions in simple, conventional, and relatively undifferentiated terms. Since subsequent work showed that cognitive-emotional integration was strongly related to other forms of conceptual complexity and intelligence, these findings suggest a parallel between declines in the domain of intellectual functioning (see Schaie, 1994) and the ability to think in complex emotion-cognition integrations.

Another surprising finding was that our levels of cognition affect integration correlated differentially with cognitive and affective variables. Levels of integration were strongly correlated with other cognitive variables. However, these levels were not related, or less related to a number of variables indicating positive emotional adjustment. For example, such emotion-related variables as depression, positive and negative affect about the self, and attachment status and family climate were strongly intercorrelated and formed, in fact, a single factor. However, they did not predict complexity of integration, nor were they related to other variables of cognitive complexity.

These data may suggest that measures based on considerations of cognitive-affective complexity and ones related on positive adjustment actually represent quite different components of positive development. One refers to emotional development in the sense to which Jung, for example, referred: an increasing sense of individuation, i.e., shedding the masks of social convention and identifying a unique sense of self that transcends those conventions; an increasing exploration of the tension between the rational and the nonrational and use of that tension in the interest of creativity; and an increased openness to new experiences. That notion is also congruent with cognitive-developmental approaches such as those of Kohlberg, Kegan, and myself, and with Loevinger's ego level approach. Affectively, this approach stresses individuals' ability to integrate positive and negative affect into structured wholes. This integration does not imply an overall positive affect. It is this component that shows a curvilinear relation to age. Another notion of positive development is not based on cognitive-affective differentiation and integration but rather on individuals' maintenance of positive affect and a positive self-concept. This component seems to be positively correlated with age, or, in some samples, unrelated to age.

POSITIVE DEVELOPMENT AND WELL-BEING

The notion that there may be different components or criteria of positive development in adulthood is not a new one in the history of the field. For example, Loevinger has long maintained that ego level is not a predictor of adjustment (see also Noam, 1988). More specifically, Helson and Wink (1987) proposed that what we define as "adult maturity" or "adult adaptation" actually reflects two quite different theoretical criteria and also different empirical relationships. These authors differentiated between 'Ego Level' and 'Competence' or, as I prefer to call the second dimension, "Adjustment." Ego Level in that context refers to development as increasing individuation (in the Jungian sense), including the working out of an individual personal integration and a sense of one's values and meaning. It is, in essence, synonymous with the kinds of complex integrations discussed in the previous section. In Helson's work this form of development was primarily defined in terms of intrapsychic differentiation and marked by variables indicative of growth in cognitive complexity, tolerance of ambiguity, and flexible affect regulation. This form of maturity was related to measures of individuality and creative expressiveness, including such variables as recognition for work, interest in self-understanding, and philosophical and religious interests. The second form of maturity, 'competence' or adjustment, was defined as the ability to align with social norms and to regulate behavior by reducing friction and obtaining rewards in social life. This form of maturity was positively related to variables such as emotional security, confidence, and lack of defensiveness, and it was negatively correlated with use of drugs and medications. Similar results were also reported by Vaillant and McCullough (1987) who found that ego level was part of a cluster of conceptual and creative complexity that was marked by variables such as articulateness, intuition, citation in *Who's Who in America,* and frequent use of sublimation as a coping strategy. In contrast, the cluster of psychosocial maturity included as marker variables healthy adult adjustment, maturity of defense mechanisms, lack of alcoholism, no visits to psychiatrists, and a warm childhood environment.

That there may be somewhat separate processes or strategies of positive development makes good theoretical sense. Much recent research on the relationship between cognition and emotion suggests that the two systems do, in fact, constitute somewhat different structures with different neuroanatomical pathways and different mechanisms of learning (Damasio, 1994; LeDoux, 1995). Thus these structures can act independently of each other, suggesting that the notion of integration of cognition and emotion may be a somewhat idealistic developmental scenario.

The significance of such findings is that later-life positive development does not necessarily imply the kinds of complex integrations discussed in the previous section. Rather, other routes to a relative sense of well-being may be based not so much on complex cognitive-affective integrations but rather on ones that operate more directly on the economy of positive and negative affects. That this is so is suggested by widely repeated observations that older individuals, even those that are faced with a degree of cognitive decline, appear to be quite resilient and display a uniformly positive pattern of well-being. This suggests that even in the face of declining resources, there are unique, resilient ways of adaptation in later life (see Staudinger, Marsiske, & Baltes, 1995).

Coping and Emotion Regulation

The observation that older individuals overall display a pattern of well-regulated behavior is compatible with a host of studies that have examined age-related differences in patterns of coping and affect regulation (for a review, see Labouvie-Vief, 1997). This literature consistently indicates that older individuals are less likely to regulate their behavior through relatively impulsive strategies such as hostile acting out, projection, and turning against others. In contrast, they are more likely than younger individuals to use strategies such as reinterpreting situations, avoiding conflict, accepting negative events, and appealing to general norms and principles (see Blanchard-Fields, 1997; Labouvie-Vief, 1997). Thus in general, older individuals are typically found to present a picture of well-being, good adjustment, and well-regulated behavior. Interestingly too, there is evidence that this pattern of age differences in part reflects the role of cultural change, since older individuals have been socialized into stricter rules of emotion regulation (Magai & Passman, 1997).

Age differences showing overall more well regulated behavior in the older individual may tap a particular aspect of development. That aspect is different from the flexible control mechanisms discussed in the previous section. Instead, it indicates that some forms of development do not necessarily bring increasing expansion and flexibility of emotional experience, but rather are aimed at reducing social friction by adhering to the rules and norms of the social system. Indeed, available data suggest that the good coping picture displayed by the elderly does not necessarily reflect a pattern of flexibility, but rather one of the gating out of negative experience. This notion is in line with two general proposals. First, many authors (see Lawton, 1996, for a review) have noted that although older individuals are good at transforming negative affect, they also tend to do so at the expense of avoiding negative experience, even in vital interpersonal situations. Second, older individuals' regulation strategies rely primarily on greater norm orientation, at the same time as they experience decreases in flexibility (see also Helson & McCabe, 1994). Such findings suggest that as individuals experience changes in a variety of cognitive and emotional resources, they restrict their focus from an exploratory and open mode to one that is narrower and more self-protective. This observation also is in line with a recent proposition by Heckhausen and Schulz (1995). These authors suggest that with increasing age, individuals shift their mode of self-regulation from one aimed at 'primary' control through direct action. They now focus on 'secondary' modes of control that disengage from action and adopt 'inner' means of adjusting to a reality that is manipulated through cognitive means such as interpretation (Heckhausen & Schulz, 1995).

Assimilative and Accommodative Shifts

A somewhat similar perspective has been proposed by Brandstädter (Brandstädter & Greve, 1994). Brandstädter notes that impairments and losses are an inevitable fact of aging. We are faced with a decline of adaptive reserves of various kinds; we experience a shrinking of the temporal horizon and begin to experience ourselves as mortal; we increasingly experience bereavement and loss, failing health, and the restriction of more youthful roles, dreams, and ideals. From such evidence one might expect a picture of lowered self-esteem and identity problems in old age. Yet quite to the contrary, older individuals maintain a good sense of well-being. Indeed, rather than experiencing increasing rates of depression, older people even may be buffered from high rates of depression.

Brandstädter proposes that this emotional resilience of the elderly can be accomplished by a shift from an 'assimilative' to an 'accommodative' mode of self-regulation. Assimilation, in that view, is aimed at strategies that attempt to realize or maintain desired self-aspects. For example, individuals may make great efforts to enhance health or fitness, maintain physical or interpersonal attractiveness, maintain levels of competence. All of these strategies are assimilative activities.

Accommodation, in contrast, involves adjustments in normative self-representations that are aimed at buffering the experience of loss. For example, realizing that our resources are failing, we can adjust to such losses by rearranging our values, rescaling our goals, and adjusting aspirations so that they fit with given situations. In addition, we may engage in a variety of 'immunizing' strategies—strategies that are aimed not so much at experiencing the full range of such losses, but that rely of such self-protective processes as palliative interpretations, putting negative experience in a rosy light, and so forth.

Research by Brandstädter and his colleagues shows strong support for his theory over an age range from young to old adulthood. There are nearly linear declines in assimilation, with corresponding linear rises in accommodation. Yet, this switch in strategies is related to the recovery and maintenance of a positive view of self and personal development in later life. Thus, accommodative strategies should be distinguished from 'coarser' processes of distortion of reality, such as denial and fragmentation. Further, the critical factor in such accommodative changes is not age per se, but rather a host of psychological, psychological, and social changes that usually are accompany change over time, but that are conceptually different from age.

Social Networks and Emotions

One theory that also has addressed the older individual's resilient emotion regulation is Carstensen's social selectivity theory (Carstensen et al., 1997). Rejecting views that consider the older person as bereft of resources and roles, Carstensen suggests that older individuals have become experts at investing their resources into optimizing the experience of positive aging. They do so by actively arranging their social environments so as to guarantee optimal well-being.

Carstensen's work is supported by studies that show that across the life span, individuals tend to gradually interact with fewer people; yet, she argues, this restriction shows an adaptive pattern as they deliberately withdraw from social contact in peripheral relationships, while maintaining or increasing involvement in relationships with close friends and family. This selective narrowing functions to maximize gains and to minimize risks in social and emotional domains—and indeed, the restriction to a smaller but more intimate network, trading quantity for quality, is related to adaptive outcomes and consistent changes through the life span. Younger individuals tend to have larger and more peripheral social networks, while those of older individuals are restricted to the more central contacts. At the same time, older individuals are more satisfied with their social networks than younger ones, and less likely to want more friends.

Carstensen maintains that these changes constitute truly positive forms of development rather than merely forming a pattern of compensatory changes in response to the challenges of increasing age and nearing mortality. Yet it is also possible that her data can be explained by the already reported tendency on the part of the elderly to emphasize the positive and normative. What is not known, at this juncture, is whether these individuals truly have optimized their environments as opposed to having learned to adjust to and accept their environments, whether or not they truly present optimal and functional conditions. This question is an extremely important one for future research to address.

In sum, one important line of thinking focuses on the notion that older individuals have resilient strategies for coping with losses; indeed, that adaptive aging (in the sense of maintaining a sense of well-being) requires such optimization strategies. Individuals may become more self-protective and restrict their interactions to those that are not too disturbing. Still, a consideration that has not been highlighted in this class of interpretations is the general interpersonal and cultural consequence of this pattern of social restriction. What are the costs of this restriction for family and caregivers, and for culture at large?

DISCUSSION AND CONCLUSIONS

In this chapter I have suggested that notions of positive aging actually contain two different general visions of development. One of these visions is guided by the notion of openness to oneself and others alike. The goal here is to achieve maximum complexity by opening ourselves to all forms of human experience, whether positive or negative, whether in self or others. This goal is achieved through widening our emotional horizons to achieve fuller intersubjective partnership between individuals, and between individuals and institutions and cultures. The criterion for studying aging thus is placed in a social framework in which consideration is given not only to the well-being of the self, but also to that of others and culture at large. This view of development thus highlights the need for creativity and transformation rather than closure and stability at all points of adulthood, even into late life. In such a view, a unique role can accrue to elders, who due to their broad integration of reason and emotion can become mentors for younger generations, teaching them about the broad and central conditions of the human condition.

The second vision, in turn, is based on the view that *individual* adaptation is optimized by achieving an overall positive affect. In this view, optimal aging is not so much defined by the more general location of the individual in culture as by inner processes that maximize individual well-being. Yet evidence suggests that well-being can be achieved at the expense of increasingly gating out experiences and individuals that disturb one's equilibrium.

In the end, I suggest these two views form the endpoints of what is a continuum, and future research will need to be aimed at describing aging as some form of balance individuals achieve on this continuum. From that perspective, individual aging can take on a number of outcomes. On one hand, restriction of resources will inevitably narrow individuals' focus; on the other hand, whether such a restriction is met with an increasing focus on the well-being of the self or a widening concern with that of culture remains a question that should invigorate future inquiries into the process of development in adulthood and later life.

REFERENCES

Adams, C. (1991). Qualitative age differences in memory for text: A life-span developmental perspective. *Psychology and Aging, 6*(3), 323–336.

Adams, C., Labouvie-Vief, G., Hobart, C. J., & Dorosz, M. (1990). Adult age group differences in story recall style. *Journal of Gerontology, 25,* 17–27.

Baltes, P. B., Smith, J., & Staudinger, U. M. (1992). Wisdom and successful aging. In T. B. Sonderegger (Ed.), *Nebraska symposium on motivation 1991: Vol. 39. Psychology and aging* (pp. 123–167). Lincoln, NE: University of Nebraska Press.

Baltes, P. B., & Staudinger, U. M. (1993). The search for a psychology of wisdom. *Current Directions in Psychological Science, 2,* 75–80.

Blanchard-Fields, F. (1997). The role of emotion in social cognition across the adult life span. In K. W. Schaie & M. P. Lawton (Eds.), *Annual review of gerontology and geriatrics, 17* (pp. 238–265). New York: Springer Publishing Co.

Brandstädter, J., & Greve, W. (1994). The aging self: Stabilizing and protective processes. *Developmental Review, 14,* 52–80.

Carstensen, L. L., Gross, J. J., & Fung, H. H. (1997). The social context of emotional experience. In K. W. Schaie & M. P. Lawton (Eds.), *Annual review of gerontology and geriatrics, Vol. 17* (pp. 325–352). New York: Springer Publishing Co.

Chinen, A. B. (1985). Fairy tales and transpersonal development in later life. *Journal of Transpersonal Psychology, 17,* 99–122.

Clayton, V. P., & Birren, J. E. (1980). The development of wisdom across the life span: A Reexamination of an ancient topic. In P. B. Baltes & O. B. Brim, Jr. (Eds.), *Life-span Development and Behavior* (Vol. 3, pp. 103–135). New York: Academic Press.

Commons, M. L., Richards, F. A., & Armon, C. (1984). *Beyond formal operations: Late adolescent and adult cognitive development.* New York: Praeger.

Damasio, Antonio, R. (1994). *Descartes' error: Emotion, reason, and the human brain.* New York: G. P. Putnam.

Erikson, E. H. (1984). *The life cycle completed.* Boston, MA: Norton.

Fordham, F. (1966). *An introduction to Jung's psychology.* New York: Pelikan.

Fowler, J. W. (1981). *Stages of faith: The psychology of human development and the quest for meaning.* San Francisco: Harper & Row.

Freud, S. (1911). Formulations regarding the two principles in mental functioning. In J. Rickman (Ed.), (1957), *A general selection from the works of Sigmund Freud* (pp. 43–44). Garden City, NY: Doubleday.

Gould, S. J. (1977). *Ontogeny and phylogeny.* Cambridge, MA: Belknap Press of Harvard University Press.

Heckhausen, J., & Schulz, R. (1995). A life-span theory of control. *Psychological Review, 102,* 284–304.

Helson, R., & McCabe, L. (1994). The social clock project in middle age. In B. F. Turner & L. E. Troll (Eds.), *Women growing older: Psychological perspectives.* Thousand Oaks, CA: Sage Publications.

Helson, R., & Wink, P. (1987). Two conceptions of maturity examined in the findings of a longitudinal study. *Journal of Personality and Social Psychology, 53,* 531–541.

Jacobi, J. (1962). *The psychology of C. G. Jung.* New Haven, CN: Yale University Press.

Jepson, K., & Labouvie-Vief, G. (1992). Symbolic processing in youth and elders. In R. West & J. Sinnot (Eds.), *Everyday memory.* Hillsdale, NJ: Lawrence Erlbaum.

Jung, C. G. (1931). The stages of life. In J. Campbell (Ed.), *The portable Jung* (Trans. R. F. C. Hull). New York: Viking Press.

Jung, C. G. (1933). *Modern man in search of a soul* (Trans. W. S. Dell & C. F. Baynes). New York: Harcourt, Brace & World.

Kegan, J. (1982). *The evolving self.* Cambridge, MA: Harvard University Press.

King, P. M., & Kitchner, K. S. (1994). *Developing reflective judgement.* San Francisco: Jossey Bass.

Kitchner, K. S., & King, P. M. (1981). Reflective judgement: Concepts of justification and their relationship to age and education. *Journal of Applied Developmental Psychology, 2,* 89–116.

Kohlberg, L. (1984). *Essays on moral development: Vol. 2. The psychology of moral development.* San Francisco: Harper & Row.

Kramer, D. A., & Woodruff, D. (1986). Relativistic and dialectical thought in three adult age-groups. *Human Development, 29,* 280–290.

Kuhn, D., Pennington, N., & Leadbeater, B. (1983). Adult thinking in developmental perspective. In P. B. Baltes & O. G. Brim, Jr. (Eds.), *Life-span development and behavior* (Vol. 5, pp. 158–195). New York: Academic Press.

Labouvie-Vief, G. (1990). Wisdom as integrated thought: Historical and developmental perspectives. In R. J. Sternberg (Ed.), *Wisdom: Its nature, origins and development.* Cambridge: Cambridge University Press.

Labouvie-Vief, G. (1994). *Psyche and Eros: Mind and gender in the life course.* New York: Cambridge University Press.

Labouvie-Vief, G. (1997). Emotional integration in later life. In P. M. Lawton & K. W. Schaie (Eds.), *Emotions in Adult Development.* New York: Springer Publishing Co.

Labouvie-Vief, G. (1998). Emotions in later life. In V. Bengston (Ed.), *Theories of adult development and aging.* New York: Springer Publishing Co.

Labouvie-Vief, G., Chiodo, L. M., Goguen, L. A., Diehl, M., & Orwoll, L. (1995a). Representations of self across the life span. *Psychology and Aging, 10,* 404–415.

Labouvie-Vief, G., Devoe, M., & Bulka, D. (1989). Speaking about feelings: Conceptions of emotion across the life span. *Psychology and Aging, 4,* 425–437.

Labouvie-Vief, G., Diehl, M., Chiodo, L. M., & Coyle, N. (1995b). Representations of self and parents across the life span. *Journal of Adult Development, 2,* 207–222.

Lawton, M. P. (1996). Quality of life and affect in later life. In C. Magai & S. H. McFadden (Eds.), *Handbook of emotion, adult development, and aging* (pp. 327–348). San Diego: Academic Press.

Ledoux, J. E. (1995). In search of an emotional system in the brain: Leaping from fear to emotion and consciousness. In M. S. Gazzaniga (Ed.), & E. Bizzi et al. (Section Eds.), *The cognitive neurosciences* (pp. 1049–1061). Cambridge, MA: MIT Press.

Levinson, D. J., Darrow, C. N., Klein, E. B., Levinson, M. H., & McKee, B. (1978). *The seasons of a man's life.* New York: Ballantine.

Loevinger, J. (1993). Measurement of personality: True or false. *Psychological Inquiry, 4,* 1–16.

Magai, C., & Passman, V. (1997). The interpersonal basis of emotional behavior and emotion regulation in adulthood. In K. W. Schaie & M. P. Lawton (Eds.), *Annual review of gerontology and geriatrics, Vol. 17* (pp. 104–137). New York: Springer Publishing Co.

Noam, G. G. (1988). The self, adult development, and the theory of biography and transformation. In D. K. Lapsley & F. L. Power (Eds.), *Self, ego, and identity: Integrative approaches.* New York: Springer Publishing Co.

Piaget, J. (1967). *Six psychological studies.* New York: Random House.

Riegel, K. F. (1973). Dialectical operations: The final period of cognitive development. *Human Development, 16,* 346–370.

Schaie, K. W. (1994). The course of adult intellectual development. *American Psychologist, 49,* 304–313.

Sinnott, J. D. (1989). Life-span relativistic postformal thought: Methodology and data from everyday problem solving studies. In M. L. Commons, J. D. Sinnott, F. A. Richards, & C. Armon (Eds.), *Adult development: Vol. I. Comparisons and applications of developmental models* (pp. 239–278). New York: Praeger.

Staudinger, U. M., & Baltes, P. B. (1996). Interactive minds: A facilitative setting for wisdom-related performance? *Journal of Personality and Social Psychology, 71,* 746–762.

Staudinger, U. M., Marsiske, M., & Baltes, P. B. (1995). Resilience and reserve capacity in later adulthood: Potentials and limits of development across the life span. In D. Chcchetti & D. J. Cohen (Eds.), *Developmental psychopathology: Vol 2. Risk, disorder and adaptation* (pp. 801–847). New York: Wiley.

Tornstam, L. (1989). Gerotranscendence: A reformulation of the disengagement theory. *Aging: Clinical and Experimental Research, 1,* 55–63.

Vaillant, G. E., & McCullough, L. (1987). The Washington University Sentence Completion Test compared with other measures of adult ego development. *American Journal of Psychiatry, 144,* 1189–1194.

Whitmont, E. C. (1969). *The symbolic quest: Basic concepts of analytical psychology.* Princeton, NJ: Princeton University Press.

19

Creativity and the Arts

Robert Kastenbaum

I probably am a little more trustful in unconscious instincts than I was before. I'm not as rigid as I was. And I can feel this in the quality and texture of the poems themselves. They are freer metrically, they're freer in general design. The earliest poems that I wrote were almost rigid in their eagerness not to make any errors. I'm less worried about that now.
—Anthony Hecht (quoted by Czikszentmihalyi, 1996, p. 215)

From the age of six I have had a mania for sketching the forms of things. From about the age of fifty I produced a number of designs, yet of all I drew prior to the age of seventy there is truly nothing of any great note.
—Katsushika Hokusai (quoted by Baker, 1995, p. 189)

I'm changing my style, getting modern in my old age, with a head full of ideas.
—Grandma Moses (quoted by Kallir, 1982, p. 148)

The spark of artistic creativity often reveals itself early in life. What happens thereafter does not follow such a simple rule, as we will see. The situation becomes especially complex when we consider creativity over the course of a long life. What will become of that boy who runs wildly across the fields, his arms widespread, his voice shouting improvised verse into the wind?

And what of that other lad to whom everything is rhythm but who especially delights in upsetting respectable people by making rude sounds with a hand "performing" inside his armpit? Look at that little girl who spends hours constructing an imaginary household under an apple tree, complete with "a shingle boat in a dishpan lake, and doll people for whom she stitched little clothes" (Lisle, 1986, p. 10). Will she become a clever housewife, a fantasy-dwelling isolate, or a creative artist?

We do know that Alfred Lord Tennyson made something of himself as a poet, and wrote memorable verses into his eighth decade (e.g.,

Crossing the Bar). Igor Stravinsky would go on to stimulate and disturb listeners throughout his long life, variously in and out of favor with the critics. Georgia O'Keeffe would create images even more enduring than her own phenomenal life becoming, by the end, herself a distinctive O'Keeffe creation. Others, though, seem to leave their creativity behind as they grow up, and others, as they grow old. There are also remarkable instances of creative renewal and—a major topic of exploration in this chapter—of transformation of style, purpose, and thrust. In other words, we know just about enough to realize that we don't know nearly enough about the fate of creativity across the lifespan.

In this chapter we focus on some of the most intriguing unresolved questions regarding creativity and the arts within a life-span perspective. Fortunately, there is a useful foundation on which to build from the humanities, the sciences, and the somewhat unclassifiable. I did take on these questions in the first edition of the Handbook (Kastenbaum, 1992) and am concerned not to repeat too much of what was previously said. Accordingly, there will be a number of references to the earlier chapter and occasional summaries. It is intended that both this and the previous chapter can stand independently.

We begin with a nod to ancient gods and scheming alchemists, and then move to observations by humanists and findings of behavioral and social sciences that will reward our attention. In the later sections we will be in position to re-examine the central issues.

"DIVINE ALCHEMY," OR "YOUNG AGAIN AND FOREVER"

Then as now, people sometimes felt inspired and did astounding things with great enthusiasm. In other words, a small wisp of the breath of God was inhaled—in-spired—and something of the divine essence remained within: en-theos-iasm. A state of being marked by elation, energy, and envisionings would be attributed to this occasional spark from the gods; exceptional deeds also indicated that the spirit was with us.

But beware—the spirit was far from innocuous and beneficent. Prometheus knew he was playing with fire and at least had no Kafka-like doubt about why he was forced to endure such cruel punishment. The spark might also come spontaneously at the whim of the gods, but more often it was a very brave or very foolish mortal who reached for this mixed blessing. Most instructive for gerontologists was Tithon, a Trojan prince who became the consort of Aurora, the goddess whose rosy fingers brought dawn. She could not bear the thought of her love toy perishing as all mortals must. Zeus, worn down by her entreaties, agreed to grant Tithon eternal life. Good work, Aurora! She had not read the small print, however. Tithon was doomed. As Tennyson had him say:

> And after many a summer dies the swan.
> Me only cruel immortality consumes. . . .

The rumor, not yet confirmed, is that Tithon grew so very old and so very decrepit that he was transformed into a cricket who lives in a matchbox, pathetically chirping away an eternity that was not what the lovers had imagined.

This cautionary tale was not lost either on the ancients or the alchemists who combined myth, lore, and ambition with what proved to be the makings of modern science. The ancients came up with scary ritualistic ordeals and concoctions that were intended to assure continued youth or rejuvenate the old. These interventions could be counterproductive: madness or death were possible outcomes. Alchemists generally devoted themselves either to the transformation of base metals into gold or to the even more thrilling possibility of transforming age into youth (Gruman, 1966). Gender bias was overwhelming. By the 19th century we had occasional images in literature and drama of women who might live forever, but throughout most of history, and certainly in the more remote (pre-Viagra?) past, it was the man who sought urgently to restore his strength and virility and maintain his power.

This emphasis on rejuvenation is one of our deepest links with the relatively modern concept of creativity. There was not much talk of creativity in myths and legends or during the centuries that were dominated by theology but teeming with alchemists and other would-be miracle workers. Either directly or indirectly, the exaltation of experience and the ability to accomplish great things depended much on the favor of the gods. Today the concept of inspiration remains familiar, although most artists seem to give more credit to hard work, discipline, and the occasional bit of luck that result in a breakthrough. There is also a frequently expressed feeling that what one seems to be creating actually is more of a translation or mediation. For example, a poet with several books and numerous awards to his credit confided to me that he "tunes in" to words and images that already had an existence "out there, in a kind of spirit-space." Reports of this kind are fairly common and suggest that creative artists may still have a sense of connection with the divine or the mysterious.

Nevertheless, creativity is no longer firmly subsumed under the category of a gift from the gods. The rejuvenation theme remains robust in our society, transformed to some extent by the improved conditions of later adult life and a variety of other sociotechnological developments

(Kastenbaum, 1995). Moreover, there is a lively enough market for youth-resembling or dissembling potions. Creativity has taken its own pathway, though, distinct from rejuvenation. What, then, is so compelling about creativity for artists who do not place their faith in God, nor expect miracles to restore youth or elude death?

I suggest the following (incomplete) set of influences:

1. Talent requires its exercise. People are likely to see the opportunity to use and develop their most outstanding skills. Freud's nearly forgotten concept of Lustfunktion—the intrinsic pleasure in doing—comes to mind here.

2. Creativity brings rewards. People who deal with problems and opportunities in a creative manner may achieve success and win admiration and status. These positive outcomes serve as reinforcers for subsequent creative approaches.

3. Creativity recreates the self. Intense acts of creation may involve both the loss and rediscovery of the self. The person is somehow transformed through the painting, the poem, the music, the choreography.

4. Creativity is the last light and breath before the dark silence. "From childhood's hour, I have not been as others were," wrote Poe. Both the brooding Mahler and the exuberant Bernstein felt death's hand on them throughout their lives. Creative artists often seem keenly aware of time's winged chariot in the midst of life. Whether tinged more by serene acceptance or by desperation, the creative person may have an urgent need to shape and express images before the last light fades and the last breath expires.

These influences are by no means mutually inconsistent, nor are they necessarily ordered in the same priorities, even within the same person in a different situation. Furthermore, all have their downside. A talent may be exercised in such a way or in such a situational context that it reaps scorn and abuse. Once or twice burned, young people may shy away from further explorations of their talents. Mozarts are few. We do not know how many people put aside their creative impulses because their early efforts were crude or misunderstood. Fortunately, some revisit their earlier interests in the later adult years when they own a more secure sense of self. Even outstanding creativity may bring not rewards but frustration or punishment. The cliché of "starving artist" was not cobbled together from moonbeams. The biographies of creative artists in all domains often repeat the basic melancholy tale of disinterest, rejection, and struggle for the bare necessities.

The act (or process) of creativity can also unmake the self. There is the risk of anxiety, depression, a descent into the deepest crevices of despair. When the creative process seems to have failed, the consequences can vary from a mild funk to a resolute suicide attempt. The dialectic between creation and destruction can extend to the creator as well as the created. The elderly Monet zestfully kicked his foot through one of his paintings he considered to be stupid, and Brahms throughout his life destroyed one composition after another that did not come up to his elevated standards. Other creative artists, however, have destroyed themselves.

Keen awareness of the swiftness of time and the sureness of death has evoked a variety of magnificent artistic creations in all the modalities. Obvious examples in music include the moving but very different requiems and masses composed by Schutz, Haydn, Mozart, Beethoven, Brahms, Fauré, and Britten, as well as practically anything by Mahler (perhaps most painfully beautiful in his Kindertotenlieder). Set aside all poetry that focuses on death and one would set aside probably the greater portion of affecting and memorable verse. Nevertheless, some creative artists fall silent as they contemplate loss and death. Holocaust experiences, for example, left some survivors almost mute with horror, while others burned with the need to testify in words or images. Those who engage death in a close artistic encounter also run the risk of ostracism from a society that prefers to look away.

The experience of aging (both direct and vicarious) makes it increasingly difficult to ignore the inexorable limits of life. "See how frail grandmother has become." "I guess I'd better really get to that will—and that living will." Even those of us most skillful in avoiding hard realities cannot help but realize that the road ahead is shorter than the road behind. Somebody needs to face this challenge—if not us, then the artists, writers, and composers whose own flesh and bones are drifting out with the same tide (Jacques, 1965; O'Connor, 1979; Pollock, 1989)

CREATIVITY UNDER THE MICROSCOPE: WHAT HAVE WE LEARNED FROM RESEARCH?

Exceptional talent is still often referred to as a gift from the gods, but the modern temperament is more attuned to the measurement of creativity as a human ability that, like any other ability, is distributed throughout the population at various levels of endowment. In practice, researchers have usually inferred level of creativity from products such as paintings, sculptures, poems, novels, compositions, and scientific discoveries and inventions. Several pioneer investigators believed that the study of products was only an indirect and inconclusive way to understand the essence or bedrock of creativity. The difficulties of a more direct approach can be illustrated by a student of the new-fangled "science" of phrenology who engaged in a little bribery to obtain the head of his recently deceased friend, Franz Joseph Haydn (Geiringer, 1982). Carl Rosenbaum intended to go beyond phrenological skull readings: he wanted to peer into the brain itself to see where all those quartets, symphonies, and oratorios had been coming from. Rosenbaum did not reach that phase of his research (and Haydn's head was rejoined with his body, though not until 1954).

Two generations later a physician reflected on creativity as an occasional escape from the horrors he encountered as a physician in the Civil War. George Beard was much more qualified than Rosenbaum to explore the mysteries of creativity and the brain—but he also had a much more realistic appraisal of the situation. He was aware that a true neuroscience was still in the future; it would be a useless exercise to explore around in the brain with the limited techniques and knowledge base of his own time (Beard, 1874). The idea that creativity might be explained by reference to brain structure and activity has been with us for many years. The tremendous advances that are being made in neuroscience today with vastly improved research techniques will no doubt be brought to bear on the question of creativity. It would be too speculative a digression to consider the possible outcome of future brain creativity research here. One may note, however, that epistemological as well as empirical questions remain to be answered. Would creativity be "explained" by establishing neural correlates? Or would the neural correlates themselves become meaningful as enablements for creative thinking? The entire matter of levels of discourse and their interrelation requires more attention than is usually received by our empirically oriented research establishment. Furthermore, when we have more refined investigations of the neural side of creativity and an improved understanding of explanatory strategies, we will still need to factor in age-related changes at the neural, psychological, and sociocultural levels.

It is not surprising, then, that most of the research has taken the commonsense approach of doing what one can do with what is available.

Francis B. Galton (1869) provided a broad foundation for the measurement of human abilities and introduced the concept of "genius" into our vocabulary. (He later rejected this term as misleading, but it had already gained what proved to be enduring popularity.) Galton was working with the assumption that heredity is the primary source for the distribution of abilities, an assumption that heavily favored the status quo (all those rich and powerful families deserve their goodies because they inherit and pass along high-quality genes). Galton not only set the abilities measurement movement into action but also put the spotlight on the distinguished few, the men (and, more rarely, the women) of excellence.

Creative Production Declines with Advancing Adult Age

Humanists, advocates, and a number of researchers often contest the assumption of age-related decline. This resistance clearly has merit when we are discussing the value of a person or the meaning of a life. The sphere of creative achievement, however, offers more of a challenge to those who see aging in a positive light. Dean Keith Simonton (1997b) credits Adolphe Quetelet (1835/1968) as the first person to have conducted methodologically sound research on creative achievement and age. Quetelet discovered a pattern of age-related decline—and so did the next two investigators, George Beard (1874) and Harvey Lehman (1953). More recent studies have given us significant new information, but have not reversed the basic finding of age-related decline.

Beard's study is worth describing again. The young neurologist—studying human achievement as a counterbalance to his stressful duties as a Civil War physician—compiled a list of a thousand famous people and the ages at which they had made their major contributions (a substantial task in the precomputer era). He found a strong curvilinear connection between age and achievement, as represented in his characterization of the adult years as follows:

The golden decade	Between 30 and 40
The silver decade	Between 40 and 50
The brazen decade	Between 20 and 30
The iron decade	Between 50 and 60
The tin decade	Between 60 and 70
The wooden decade	Between 70 and 80

This parade of decades is not as fanciful as it might appear. The pattern is based on Beard's statistics. We see that youth does not completely steal the show. The brazen 20-year-old is a reasonable candidate for making an outstanding creative achievement, but 10 years later he is much more likely to make a breakthrough contribution, and he is still in the prime zone 15 or 20 years later. Lehman's (1953) research nearly a century after Beard was fairly similar in method and result. Subsequent studies that bear on age and achievement are also generally confirmatory as to the overall pattern.

These studies did not escape several flaws and limitations. One obvious limitation is the focus on "men of distinction." The gender bias of Euro-American culture both reduced opportunities for women to make creative contributions and led to dysvaluation or neglect of the contributions they did make. The relative influence of restricted opportunity and failure to acknowledge women's achievements cannot readily be determined, even today. The definition of what constitutes a major

achievement is also subject to controversy. Numerous other methodological issues have been raised (Dennis, 1966; Kastenbaum, 1992).
Although these criticisms have merit, one hesitates to reject the major
finding of age-decline without having substantial findings to the contrary. It seems more useful to recognize the limits of the foundational
studies and press further ahead—which is pretty much what has been
happening in current research.

Age Does Not Mark the End of High-Quality Creativity

Much of what has been learned about age and creativity in recent years
comes from the work of Dean Keith Simonton (1994; 1996; 1997a; 1997b).
His quantitative research has introduced a new level of sophistication
to this area. It is worth noting that, like other quantitative researchers
before him, Simonton does not dismiss the qualitative side nor the
personality and sociocultural contexts within which creativity either
flourishes or flounders. In a summary of his findings up to that point,
Simonton (1991) offered the following conclusions:

1. Individuals vary immensely in their creative potential—quite
apart from their age. Therefore, we know only part of the story, and not
necessarily the most important part, when we focus on age.

2. There is always a ratio of "hits" and "misses" among the products
of a creative artist. Even the best have had their potboilers and failures.
This ratio seems to continue right through into the later adult years.
"Older creators may be indeed producing fewer hits, but they are . . .
producing fewer misses as well. . . . an individual's creative powers
remain intact throughout the life span" (p. 15).

3. The age decrement in creativity differs across domains. The
decline is rather severe in pure mathematics and lyrical poetry, for
example, but scholars tend to show little if any drop-off even in their
most advanced years. It is more useful, then, to compare people within
the same domain of creativity.

4. There can be a substantial renaissance in the last years of life, a
second wind, or as Simonton puts it, a secondary peak. One of Simonton's most interesting studies found that aging composers with death
on their minds "began to create compositions with simpler and more
restrained melodic lines; yet these compositions scored extremely well in
esthetic significance, as judged by musicologists, and eventually joined
the popular mainstays of the classical repertoire." This finding is well in
keeping with the hypothesis that the most profound creativity may be
evoked by the awareness that time's winged chariot is hurrying near.

5. The people who were creative when they were young are those
most likely to be creative in their later adult years.

These findings enrich our knowledge of creativity across the life-span. Meanwhile, other investigators have been looking into factors that either encourage or discourage the exercise of creativity throughout the life span.

Person, Situation, Gender, and the Creative Artist

Both familiar routines and exceptional acts of creativity occur within a fabric of person, situation, and relationship. Intelligence and personality have been the most frequently studied correlates of creativity (although one cannot say that any topic has been exhaustively studied). It was once assumed that intelligence and creativity are almost interchangeable concepts. This assumption has been disconfirmed (Robinson & Stern, 1997). The IQ score does not tell us how creative a person is or might become. There are people who can function intelligently within closed systems, but who seldom come up with a new alternative, fresh idea, or original image. Creativity in the arts and other spheres seems to require a level of intelligence in the "bright normal" range, but higher IQ test scores do not correlate strongly with originality and productivity. Allowing for exceptions, it appears that creative people are intelligent, but that intelligent people are not necessarily creative. Furthermore, a person may demonstrate a special endowment in one domain (e.g., linguistic processing) while having only moderate talent in another (e.g., visual-spatial imaging). One can observe many profiles of creative functioning, from those with a single area of proficiency to others who bring skill and originality to everything they touch.

J. P. Guilford, a psychologist who himself displayed a broad range of interests and talents, made major contributions to the conceptualization and measurement of both personality and higher cognitive functions. His systematic research extracted several factors that were characteristic of creative adults. As compared with other people of similar age and general intelligence level, creative people excelled in divergent thinking: the ability to take an idea some place else and see how far they can go with it, as well as to explore alternatives and demonstrate mental flexibility as distinguished from staying relentlessly on the same track (Guilford, 1957). He believed there was also a role for convergent thinking in the overall creative process, particularly in the evaluation of the one's own product.

Guilford clarified some of the major cognitive and personality characteristics of the "creative person" without simplifying or reducing them to a formula. The creative person was open to experience and capable of divergent thinking, but also fluent in coming up with words, images, symbols, and solutions. Fluency itself was not sufficient. These thought products also had to have an element of originality. Although it will probably always be difficult to define "originality" to everybody's satisfaction, Guilford made a useful beginning in assessment strategies. After coming up with original thoughts, one still had to do something with them, crossing the border from the cognitive to the public sphere. The creative act was not complete until one also showed the ability and the willingness to critique the product. Those without the discipline to evaluate the painting, poem, or invention through the critic's eye might well fall short of their creative potential. According to Guilford, creative people also showed considerably more tolerance for ambiguity and more preference for complexity than most other people (Guilford, 1959). These conclusions have since received support from longitudinal research as well (McCrae, 1987).

Fluency, flexibility, preference for complexity, and tolerance for ambiguity are not characteristics that are usually attributed to elderly people. In fact, there is a body of theory and research that has suggested that fluid intelligence (Raymond B. Cattell's concept, 1963) declines rather precipitously with advancing adult age. Abstract and flexible thinking are also among the "don't hold" components of the Wechsler Adult Intelligence Scale for people who are either of advanced age or afflicted with a neural syndrome. It might appear, then, that the cognitive skills and personality traits that are most conducive to creativity do fade with time, quite in keeping with Beard's decades and other studies that have correlated age and achievement.

This conclusion would be premature, however. There is abundant biographical and case history evidence that some people demonstrate the highest (and deepest) levels of creativity throughout a very long life. This observation is consistent with psychometric studies of personality that focus on the same person at various points of measurement across the life span. People do change to some extent, but within the compass of their own personality structures: the open, energetic, fluent, and productive young person is likely to be the open, energetic, fluent, and productive elder. The overall question of cognitive functioning throughout life requires more consideration than can be given here and, most of all, requires continued research that is up to the challenge of accounting for the role of opportunity, stress, health and sociocultural shift. Fluency, flexibility, and tolerance for ambiguity are among a number of valuable concepts in our attempts to understand creativity across the life span, but more attention needs to be paid to the sociocultural manifold in which these abilities manifest themselves.

The situation of the aging creative person has received some attention from interpretive scholars and from elders themselves, as will be touched on in the next section. There has been little systematic research, however. Maduro's (1981) study of aged painters in India suggests what might be learned with more concerted efforts. He found a strong connection between the refined creativity of the oldest artists and cultural expectations based on a life-span model in which one is expected to become more spiritual rather than less competent or useful with advancing age. These artists were fulfilling a cherished cultural value by continuing to cultivate their spiritual development. (One must bear in mind that this situation, highly conducive to creativity for aging Brahmins, did not extend to the entire population across sociocultural and gender lines.)

Hendricks (in press) has called for more attention to the social and institutional relationships that influence individual creativity. He takes the position that creativity itself must be considered as an interactive product. For example, "As Baby Boomers age, the structure of their careers and their lives will reflect the impact of the size of their cohort. . . . Given that the shape of careers may undergo change and opportunity structures will be altered by demographic imperatives, the distribution of economic activities, norms governing retirement and a prolongation of the healthy years will also change, and thereby affect patterns of creativity." Many hypotheses worth pursuing could be generated by a systematic approach to the sociocultural context of aging and creativity.

Gender is not simply one variable among others, but rather a theme that plays out in all domains and situations. It has already been noted that the pioneering studies of creativity and other higher-level human abilities focused on men. This extraordinary exclusion of half the human race was simply in keeping with the prevailing discriminatory assumptions, stereotypes, and practices in society at large. More recent investigators have been working to redress this imbalance. A valuable resource here has been the famous Stanford University longitudinal study of gifted children which still yields information today as the surviving "Termanities" move even deeper into their late years. These women continued to showed outstanding "generativity," the ability to foster the success of other people and of community organizations. This might also be described as a broader and perhaps more sublimated form of nurturance. Their creativity often was centered outside the home. The most creative women were those who were not burdened with care-giving roles and either had supportive husbands or no husbands (Vaillant & Vaillant, 1990). Interestingly, the researchers also noted that there was often a keen enjoyment of life. This observation might serve to remind us that creativity is not just a matter of accomplishment, but also an intrinsic source of pleasure and meaning.

Women were included in a series of studies conducted by Birren and his colleagues (Crosson & Robertson-Tchabo, 1983; Ruth & Birren, 1983). The somewhat complex results are well summarized by Rodeheaver, Emmons, and Powers (1998). Perhaps the most provocative finding was that the age-creativity relationship differed for artists and nonartists. A negative relationship was found for a general community sample, but "older female visual artists were as likely to be creative as their younger counterparts." Males tended to show more flexibility on tasks measuring cognitive flexibility, but there were not marked gender differences in performance across the entire array of procedures.

Through the centuries and into our own time, fewer women have come into prominence as creative artists in various domains. This differential has stimulated numerous explanations, most of which can be reduced to lack of opportunity and/or more burdens and hardships. Rodeheaver et al. note that "Becoming an artist depends first on survival. When women's life expectancy was shortened by female infanticide or by death in childbirth, the number of women who could be artists, especially late life artists, was obviously diminished. Likewise, being an artist was difficult when marriage occurred at an early age. Finally, the average number of children, size of household, and nature of family responsibilities affect artistic inclinations. . . . It may even be the case that the often-noted increase in women artists in the 19th century was related to a decline in the birth rate and to an increase in the number of unmarried women."

One might expect to see a continuing growth, perhaps even a quantum leap, in creativity among elderly women, considering the general aging of society, improved health and fitness programs, and a less discriminatory sociocultural attitude. There still may be a long way to go on the latter count, though Hira and Faulkender (1997) asked if age and gender played a part in the perception of wisdom. Their research findings were in the affirmative. Older women were perceived as being less wise than either males or young women on the basis of video-taped presentations. It is probable that perceptions of creativity would follow the same pattern, although such a study has yet to be reported.

Nevertheless, it should not be too quickly assumed that interpersonal or societal recognition of creative potential is altogether a favorable influence. Holahan and Holahan (in press), also working with elders participating in a longitudinal study, determined at what age they had been told of their special intellectual abilities. Those whose "giftedness" had been acknowledged at an earlier age were more likely to feel despondent and unfulfilled in later life: they never seemed able to do enough to come up to their own standards, no matter how well their creative achievements were received by others. Clearly, there is much more to learn about societal influences on creativity throughout the life span.

Helson (1985; 1987; 1990; 1998) is on the trail of the development of creative potential in women from the early to the middle adult years with a continuing series of studies and commentaries. She has been able to distinguish between women with varying productivity trajectories (always, early, late, and never) on the basis of their performances on a Q sort task and the California Psychological Inventory. The scores obtained at an earlier age helped to predict creativity at a later age. This overall finding is consistent with a number of major studies that have documented a consistency of personality throughout the adult years. The implication is that one should not expect all women to show the same trajectory of creativity throughout their lives, but, rather, to move within the individual orbits they have established for themselves in early adulthood, if not before. It also follows that a woman who does not quickly establish herself as creative at one point in life may do so at a later time.

Several concepts that guide Helson's studies also appear promising for the study of age and achievement in men, e.g., engaging in a de facto moratorium during a particular period of life, or focusing on an emotionally intense search for meaning and expression. Helson's line of research has promise for further useful distinctions among the ways of life chosen by creative people of either gender, thereby taking us well beyond global generalizations.

CREATIVITY SPEAKS FOR ITSELF: NARRATIVE AND INTERPRETIVE APPROACHES

Much can be learned from the testimonies of creative artists themselves and from scholars who interpret their lives and work. Consider, for example, the brief quotations that open this chapter.

Poet Anthony Hecht describes an increasing sense of inner freedom that he could not or at least did not allow himself in his younger days. This liberated approach shows up in the poetry itself. Hecht is far from alone in making such an observation. The aged artists interviewed by Maduro (1981), for example, also expressed a freedom to follow their own spiritual promptings or whims, as the case may be. Composer Ernst Toch was driven by time urgency as his health rapidly declined; nevertheless, he also experienced an opening of possibilities and a transcendence of the highly disciplined classical approach that had characterized his music throughout his life. We might expect creative people to become more narrow and less flexible in their later years, but many testimonies offer quite the opposite view, as does the evidence of the products themselves.

Falstaff, Verdi's late-life farewell to opera, is a dazzling departure from the main body of his compositions. There is wit and merriment that he did not fully allow himself to express in earlier works, yet with an enhancement rather than a falling away of his creative powers. In his

84th year, Ralph Vaughan Williams completed his eighth symphony—almost. The night before the premiere he took one of the only seats still available for a performance of Puccini's opera, Turandot: that meant listening to a lot of gongs very close up. Delighted, Vaughan Williams immediately added three gongs to the orchestration of his symphony, which he had already loaded with extra percussion "including all the 'phones and 'spiels known to the composer," as he confessed. The result was a symphony unique in its sheer delight in sound while at the same time reaffirming his mastery of the symphonic form. Like Hecht, Toch, Verdi, and many others, the aged Vaughan Williams could relax and allow himself some fun without worrying about precedent and propriety.

Hokusai (1760–1849) went so far as to describe himself as "The old man crazy about painting." He was not crazy, of course, but exuberant. Yet he was not just exuberant but also gifted with the ability to bring life and immediacy to detail work that in other hands would have come across as merely ornamental. It should not be overlooked that in the joy of creativity experienced and expressed by aged masters there is also a further deepening of insights, accompanied by the ability to shape their productions in accord with their new perceptions. Hokusai testified that:

> at the age of seventy-three I finally came to understand somewhat the nature of birds, animals, insects, fishes—the vital nature of grasses and trees. Therefore at eighty I shall have made great progress, at ninety I shall have penetrated even further the deeper meaning of things, and at one hundred I shall have become truly marvelous, and at one hundred and ten, each dot, each line shall surely possess a life of its own (Baker, 1995, pp. 189–190).

Similarly, one of Goya's last sketches depicts a feeble old man, precariously walking on two sticks. The caption below: "Still learning." Beatrice Wood, entering her ninth decade, expressed a similar feeling when she showed her most recent painting to Connie Goldman (a work she could barely see herself because of failing eyesight). "You know what, Connie? I think I'm finally starting to get the hang of it."

Anna Mary Robertson Moses—better known as Grandma Moses—was also succinct in her disclosure that she was now changing her style, "getting modern in my old age, with a head full of ideas." Indeed, many (though by no means all) long-lived creative artists had even more ideas, experiments, and projects in mind after completing what turned out to be their final works. Vaughan Williams, for example, went on to write a ninth symphony (just as remarkable in its own way as any of its predecessors and the first symphony by any composer to add a fluegelhorn and a trio of saxophones). He had his next symphony in mind as well as a host of other ideas. Tennyson, that lonely child running through the wind and sprouting wild verses, tried to retire from writing poetry, but kept breaking through with new works in his last years of life, and Georgia O'Keeffe remained a font of energy and enthusiasm until her body finally gave way at age 98.

If one can generalize at all from such a diversity of people working in such a diversity of domains within so many sociocultural frames, long-lived artists seem to be endowed with more energy and stamina than the average person. They tend to show signs of their special interests and talents early in life, although later in some domains (e.g., writing) than others (e.g., music). Their actual creative trajectory may have little relationship with recognition by fellow artists, critics, and society. Grandma Moses, for example, became an "overnight success," "that old woman who just took up painting"—but in fact she had been creating art out of available materials since early childhood. Although she had little time for herself through her years as wife, mother, and grandmother, art was a natural and enduring part of her life that she finally could give the attention it deserved.

Creative artists are not necessarily warm, fuzzy, and compliant people. If another generalization may be permitted, they really like to have their own way, at least so far as artistic matters are concerned. There is little basis for assuming that there is a single type of artistic personality, although many show the divergent thinking, tolerance of ambiguity, and openness to experience that has already been noted. Nevertheless, those creative artists who survive the risks and tribulations of youth often seem to develop protective strategies. What are they protecting? Most often, they protect their time, working space, and products, but also their artistic integrity. Tactfully or boorishly, they try to fend off distractions, interruptions and other impositions. This toughness seems to be an indispensable part of thriving as a creative artist through a long life and its roller-coaster ride of plunges and ascensions. Some creative artists—Wagner and Picasso spring readily to mind—became notorious for their abusive and manipulative treatment of other people. O'Keeffe is more typical, however: a person who enjoyed other people and could be delightful company, but who also knew how to draw the curtain firmly when it was time to make herself scarce and get back to work.

"Late Style" and Its Implications for Life-Span Human Development

The question of "late style" has been discussed for many years without a clear consensus having been reached. One could find illustrative material either to support or dismiss this concept, depending on choice of person, domain, and sociocultural setting. If there is a clear change of style, does this represent an intrinsic change within the artist, or a response to what is happening on the current social and artistic scene? Or is it perhaps futile even to try to differentiate between so-called intrinsic and exogenous influences? Aging artists have experienced many years of interacting with their sociophysical environments: who can say, for example, how much of Dali is Catalonia and how much of Catalonia is Dali? And who can say whether Munch's "electrifying new colors" (Stang, 1979, p. 271) represented the aging artist's shift to a bold new style, or a compensation for his failing eyesight? Students of life-span development never have an easy time in establishing the relative contributions of person, physical status, time, place, and situation, not to mention the interpretive haze that tends to envelop all the foregoing.

A key contribution to the late style debate was Alfred Einstein's (1937) concept of the Opus Ultimum which, in turn, drew upon the earlier tradition of the "swan song." Some aging artists do not simply produce a work that turns out to be their last. Instead, they create a farewell to life and art. This ultimate creation is a kind of summing up of what has gone before, yet it may also include features that are new to the artist and perhaps new to the art. The examples selected by Einstein are persuasive as far as they go, and certainly enhance our awareness that a final creation might possess a special level of meaning, a last message before the silence.

There is much that is appealing about this concept, and there is also little doubt that some final creations do represent the artist's swan song.[1] Haydn, for example, actually referred to his last (unfinished) composition as a swan song. Nevertheless, there are practical and conceptual difficulties with the Opus Ultimum (Kastenbaum, 1992) that should lead to caution.

The concept of late style goes beyond the swan song. In the previous edition of this Handbook I wrote that "The late style often is characterized by an economy of means, a conciseness of expression in which the essence is communication without a superfluous brush stroke, word, or note" (1992, p. 302). This trait was found in the work produced by the aged artists of Northern India (Maduro, 1981) and in the creations of many other masters in all domains who find they can say more with less. It was also suggested that underlying late style is the attempt to integrate strong competing impulses. This desire to reconcile opposing elements can be observed in the creative process itself, as in calling upon the fugue as a stringent organizing technique for musical materials that are themselves of diverse and wide-ranging character.

At another level, these artistic integrations may represent the working out of personal dualities. Depending on the individual, we may see more of the tightly disciplined person becoming freer, or more of the rhapsodic creator becoming more focused and restrained. As suggested by his own words, Hecht counterbalanced his previous cautious and painstaking approach with a freer and more intuitive creation of poetry in his later years. By contrast, the Richard Strauss who composed extravagant tone poems in his early prime completed his orchestral oeuvre with the restrained, pristine beauty of Metamorphosen.

Cohen-Shalev (1998), however, offers a provocative alternative view. He suggests that the late styles of long-lived creative artists involve the playing out of themes and conflicts that have been with them since their earliest days. In this regard, Cohen-Shalev's interpretations are consistent with the view already presented, i.e., artistic and personal conflicts are being addressed through the same holistic process. However, Cohen-Shalev challenges the idea that creative masters are keen to integrate opposing elements in their art and lives. Instead, he offers examples in which contrary elements are allowed equal opportunity for expression. There is no winning or losing element. There is no approved or disapproved element. It is as though the aged creative artist has achieved a new perspective from which the glories and follies of life can be addressed from a greater remove.

Cohen-Shalev musters the argument that creative artists find their "voice" or style somewhere in the midlife zone and thereafter continue to work from within their distinctive style. This approach, though, binds them to one polarity or one sector of the total artistic and human possibilities. In their later years at least some creative artists break from the patterns they have made their own, "defying the artistic and philosophical principles they had so diligently perfected." Mondrian is one of Cohen-Shalev's most instructive examples. He became the unique and celebrated Mondrian around age 40 and elaborated upon his experiments with form for another three decades. To the surprise and dismay of his followers, however, Mondrian eventually introduced vivid color and a new sense of vitality and movement, even whimsy. *Broadway Boogie Woogie,* for example, is every inch a Mondrian, but (as a new New Yorker) it is also an audacious work that spins away from his main corpus.

Cohen-Shalev's contribution is worth consideration by life span developmentalists as well as artists and humanities scholars. Perhaps it is the part of creative wisdom not to elevate thought over feeling or vice versa. Perhaps one does not have to choose between reality and fantasy, or even between good and evil, or life and death. Ambitious, stressed, achievement-oriented people in a competitive, fast-paced society may have to take their stand and remain firm and self-protective for much of their lives. So much of one's experiences and interactions seem to be in conflict, therefore conflict-resolution becomes a high priority. In the later years of life some people may be able to set aside rather than settle the whole rigmarole of dichotomies and conflicts. "Here it is," the artist may be saying, "undressed, unresolved. I can live with it now. Can you?"

SOME CONCLUDING THOUGHTS

We do not have a well-established theory of creativity in general, and perhaps never will (Simonton, 1996). The study of aging and the aged has its share of guiding models but, again, no one theory to command allegiance and inspire breakthrough research. Not surprisingly, then, we do not have a satisfactory theory of creativity throughout the life span. It might be well, however, to keep our eyes on the one if we hope to understand the other. When deep and sustained creativity results in identifiable products, it is also likely that there is a process of personal creation and re-creation in operation.

What might we do next?

It would be useful as well as refreshing to include creativity as a major focus for all subsequent longitudinal studies, and for in-depth retrospective studies as well. There should be no barrier to combining qualitative and quantitative methods unless one has become captive of worn out doctrines and sluggish habits.

In particular we might want to learn more about the ways in which the creative imagination enables people to be where they are, while also being some place else. Time-place-person displacement is sometimes derided as daydreaming or fantasy, but this precious human ability to employ both engrossment and perspective and "visit" past and potential selves and situations can have profound benefits for both the individual and society (Kastenbaum, 1965; 1989).

Specialists in gender issues may find it illuminating to explore both underlying similarities and the perhaps fundamental differences in creativity across the life span. It would be easy to laugh out of court the notion that men are motivated for creative achievements because they cannot grow babies. One may also prefer to ignore the cross-research of Gutmann (1987) with its suggestion that men become more "feminine" and women more "masculine" in the second half of life. More productive than laughing or ignoring, however, might be a healthy curiosity about possible influences on gender-related creativity.

Those whose concerns center on mental health and illness might find valuable clues by exploring the antecedents and consequences of thwarted creativity. People who do not have the opportunity to develop and express their sparks of creativity are apt to become deeply frustrated. This is a more stressful situation than is commonly realized, contributing to impaired relationships and deteriorated health. Viewed in this light, creativity is a central rather than a peripheral element in living a meaningful life through a great many years.

NOTES

[1] It was once commonly believed that all swans are mute—not true. This belief was the foundation for the romantic notion that the swan sings only once in its life: when it is dying.

REFERENCES

Baker, J. S. (1995). *Japanese art.* London & New York: Thames & Hudson.

Beard, G. (1874). *Legal responsibility in old age.* New York: Russell.

Cattell, R. B. (1963). Theory of crystallized intelligence: A critical experiment. *Journal of Educational Psychology, 54,* 1–22.

Cohen-Shalev, A. (1998). *Both worlds at once: Art in old age.* Unpublished manuscript.

Crosson, C. W., & Robertson-Tchabo, E. A. (1983). Age and preference for complexity among manifestly creative women. *Human Development, 26,* 149–155.

Csikszentmihalyi, M. (1996). *Creativity.* New York: HarperCollins.

Dennis, W. (1966). Creative productivity between the ages of 20 and 80 years. *Journal of Gerontology, 21,* 1–8.

Einstein, A. (1937). Opus ultimum. *Musical Quarterly, 22,* 269–286.

Galton, F. B. (1869). *Hereditary genius.* London: Macmillan

Geiringer, K. (1982). *Haydn: A creative life in music.* Berkeley: University of California Press.

Gruman, G. J. (1966). *A history of ideas about the prolongation of life.* Philadelphia: The American Philosophical Society.

Guilford, J. P. (1957) Creative abilities in the arts. *Psychological Review, 64,* 110–118.

Guilford, J. P. (1959). Traits of creativity. In H. H. Anderson (Ed.), *Creativity and its cultivation* (pp. 142–161). New York: Harper.

Gutmann, D. (1987). *Reclaimed powers: Toward a new psychology of men and women in later life.* New York: Basic Books.

Helson, R. (1985). Which of those young women with creative potential became productive? Personality in college and characteristics of parents. In R. Hogan & W. H. Jones (Eds.), *Perspectives in personality* (Vol. 1, pp. 49–80). Greenwich, CT: JAI Press.

Helson, R. (1987). Which of those young women with creative potential became productive? II. From college to midlife. In R. Hogan & W. H. Jones (Eds.), *Perspectives in personality* (vol. 2, pp. 51–92). Greenwich, CT: JAI Press.

Helson, R. (1990). Creativity in women: Outer and inner views over time. In M. A. Runco & R. S. Albert (Eds.), *Theories of creativity* (pp. 46–58). Newbury Park, CA: Sage.

Helson, R. (1998). Ego identity and trajectories of productivity in women with creative potential. In C. E. Adams-Price (Ed.), *Creativity and aging: Theoretical and empirical approaches.* New York: Springer Publishing Co.

Hendricks, J. (1999). Creativity over the life course: A call for a relational perspective. *International Journal of Aging & Human Development.*

Hira, F. J., & Faulkender, P. J. (1997). Perceiving wisdom: Do age and gender play a part? *International Journal of Aging & Human Development, 44,* 85–102.

Holahan, C. K., & Holahan, C. J. (1999). Being labeled as gifted, self-appraisal, and psychological well-being: A life-span developmental perspective. *International Journal of Aging & Human Development.*

Jaques, E. (1965). Death and the midlife crisis. *International Journal of Psychoanalysis, 46,* 502–514.

Kallir, J. (1982). *Grandma Moses: The artist behind the myth.* Secaucus, NJ: Wellfleet.

Kastenbaum, R. (1965). Engrossment and perspective in later life: A developmental approach. In R. Kastenbaum (Ed.), *Contributions to the psycho-biology of aging* (pp. 3–18). New York: Springer Publishing Co.

Kastenbaum, R. (1989). Old men created by young artists: Time-transcendence in Tennyson and Picasso. *International Journal of Aging & Human Development, 28,* 81–104.

Kastenbaum, R. (1992). The creative process: A life-span approach. In T. R. Cole, D. D. Van Tassel, & R. Kastenbaum (Eds.), *Handbook of the humanities and aging* (pp. 285–306). New York: Springer Publishing Co.

Kastenbaum, R. (1995). *Dorian, graying. Is youth the only thing worth having?* New York: Baywood.

Lehman. H. C. (1953). *Age and achievement.* Princeton, NJ: Princeton University Press.

Lisle, L. (1986). *Portrait of an artist: A biography of Georgia O'Keeffe.* New York: Washington Square Press.

Maduro, R. (1981). The old man as creative artist in India. In R. Kastenbaum (Ed.), *Old age on the new scene* (pp. 71–101). New York: Springer Publishing Co.

McCrae, R. (1987). Creativity, divergent thinking and openness to experience. *Journal of Personality and Social Psychology, 52,* 1258–1265.

O'Connor, F. V. (1979). Albert Berne and the completion of being: Images of vitality and extinction in the last paintings of a ninety six year-old man. In David D. Van Tassel (Ed.), *Aging, death, and the completion of being* (pp. 255–289). Philadelphia: University of Pennsylvania Press.

Pollock, G. H. (1989). The mourning process, the creative process, and the creation. In D. R. Dietrich & P. C. Shabad (Eds.), *The problem of loss and mourning* (pp. 27–60). Madison, WI: International Universities Press.

Quetelet, A. (1968). *A treatise on man and the development of his faculties.* New York: Franklin. (Original work published 1835).

Robinson, A. G., & Stern, S. (1997). *Corporate creativity.* San Francisco: Berrett-Koehler.

Rodeheaver, D., Emmons, C., & Powers, K. (1998). In C. E. Adams-Price (Ed.), *Creativity and aging: Theoretical and empirical approaches.* New York: Springer Publishing Co.

Ruth, J., & Birren, J. E. (1985). Creativity in adulthood and old age: Relations to intelligence, sex, and mode of testing. *International Journal of Behavioral Development, 88,* 99–110.

Simonton, D. K. (1994). *Greatness.* New York: The Guilford Press.

Simonton, D. K. (1996). Creativity. In J. E. Birren (Ed.), *Encyclopedia of gerontology* (pp. 341–351).

Simonton, D. K. (1997a). Achievement domain and life expectancies in Japanese civilization. *International Journal of Aging & Human Development, 44,* 103–114.

Simonton, D. K. (1997b). Creative productivity: A predictive and explanatory model of career trajectories and landmarks. *Psychological Review, 104,* 66–89.

Stang, R. (1979). (Translated by Geoffrey Culverwell). *Edvard Munch.* New York: Abbeville Press.

Vaillant, G. E., & Vaillant, C. O. (1990). Determinants and consequences of creativity in a cohort of gifted women. *Psychology of Women Quarterly, 14,* 607–616.

PART IV
Reflections

20

Reflections on the Gerontological Handbook

Stephen Katz

Handbooks are one of the most unique products of the evolution of books. As both commonsensical works of reference and innovative conceptual toolkits, their appeal has as much to do with their everyday usefulness as with their special status within academic traditions. This power of handbooks to span "high" and "low" literary cultures derives, in part, from their history. Known at first as "manuals" (from Latin *manualis* for "fitting the hand") handbooks began in the 13th century as portable, personal supplements to the Christian clergy's weighty medieval lectern and desk volumes. *Le Manuel des Péchés,* an Anglo-Norman penitential manual from the period, says of itself: "This is called a manual because it is held in the hand" (Bennett, 1988, p. 166).[1] Through the centuries, the handbooks and manuals of "high" culture were joined by guidebooks, primers, pamphlets, bulletins, readers, and brochures, to form a constellation of utility texts written to teach and train ordinary people in the pragmatic arts of living. In a countermovement emerging since the Enlightenment and growing during the 19th and early 20th centuries, however, some of these popular texts became once again primary intellectual resources, in those realms where the practical arts were transformed into secular professions. Handbooks on childcare, schooling, medicine—and eventually gerontology—became state-of-the-art purveyors of newly professionalized knowledges.

Gerontological handbooks, in addition to providing handy synopses of current research on aging and old age, can thus be seen as part of the wider cultural development of textual practices in western society. As such they present us with two interesting questions about knowledge-production and scientific disciplinarity in gerontology. First, how is it that gerontological handbooks have become authorities on the myriad of issues and problems surrounding the aging process—especially in the United States? Second, outside of the handbook's constituent parts—chapters, themes, topics, and contributors—what other textual activities inherent in the handbook define and configure the field of aging studies as a professional enterprise? To address these questions, this chapter proposes a critical interpretive approach to gerontological handbooks that highlights their stylistic, literary, and rhetorical features.

It is worth noting, first, that this is an essay on handbooks in a handbook on the humanities and aging. In the first edition of *Handbook of the Humanities and Aging* coeditor Thomas R. Cole remarks that "a 'handbook' in the humanities and aging certainly has its ironic side" (1992a, p. xii). On the one hand, gerontology handbooks are the fundamental texts by which the profession has identified itself as a scientific endeavour. On the other hand, Cole asserts that a humanities handbook on aging is different: It must be "less scientific and instrumental, more historical, more concerned with the limits and conditions of its own knowledge, and more focussed on questions of representation, meaning, and value than traditional handbooks in gerontology" (p. xii). Thus situated at some distance from mainstream gerontology, the first edition of *Handbook of the Humanities and Aging* promoted the methodological strengths of the humanities: interpretation, reflection, and criticism, along with an emphasis on experience, narrative, and dialogue. The double goal of the first humanities handbook, therefore, was to become "a standard reference for academic and clinical gerontologists, as well as a stimulus for future work in the humanities and aging" (p. xiv).

It is instructive to look back, from the viewpoint of this second edition of *Handbook of the Humanities and Aging,* at the first edition's mapping of the conceptual encounters between the science of gerontology and the ingenuity of the humanities. The examination of gerontological textuality was central to this mapping, as the first edition's contributors explored the historical, spiritual, and literary dimensions of aging. Although the first edition did not include a study of handbooks, such as this present essay, it did, in staking out its challenging position as a different kind of handbook with an 'ironic side,' imply a critique of the handbook genre itself. It is this implied but absent critique in the first edition, therefore, that serves as this chapter's point of departure in the second edition. Specifically, I wish to introduce four overlapping reflections on the handbook as: 1. a genealogical document, 2. a gerontological standard, 3. a disciplinary practice, and 4. a public philosophy.

THE HANDBOOK AS A GENEALOGICAL DOCUMENT

A cursory check on the subject of handbooks in the *sociofile* search catalogue produces 726 entries; the *Humanities Index* has 168 entries. These entries comprise handbooks themselves as well as critiques of them. They show that handbooks today are not limited to professional texts but also continue as popular guides to the art of living. The critical commentary embraces both streams: prosaic and largely forgotten handbooks are transformed into rich archival documents by researchers who trace the historical discourses through which human conduct has been shaped and regulated. For instance, Carol Auster's examination of 20th-century Girl Scout Handbooks is a marvelous glimpse at the world of domestic expectations for girls in the period between 1913–1984 (1985). Likewise, Yvonne Schutze looks at German medical handbooks to analyze the construction of "mother-love" and childrearing practices since the mid-18th century (1987). A broader cross-cultural impetus motivates Deborah Best and Nicole Ruther's astute survey of developmental psychology handbooks published between 1931-1993 (1994).

These studies and others of supposedly minor and mundane texts have, in part, been influenced by the work of Michel Foucault and attest to one of the great strengths of his *genealogical* method (inspired by Nietzsche's *On the Genealogy of Morals*). By "genealogical method," its many users mean a multidisciplinary technique for discovering the contingent historical trends that underpin contemporary society's structures, discourses, and practices. For Foucault, the documentary history of western cultures is not to be found in the "great" texts that various traditions have established as their canons. Rather, events are to be found, via the genealogical method, "in the most unpromising places, in what we tend to feel is without history." In Foucault's characterization, "genealogy is gray, meticulous, and patiently documentary. It operates on a field of entangled and confused parchments" (1977, p. 139).[2]

In using the genealogical method then, we are avoiding "the canons" and looking instead for the history resident in the "confused" archive of codebooks, rulebooks, underground writing, diaries—and handbooks—that has been deposited in the present but which is routinely denied importance in reconstructions of the past. The genealogical method, in recovering this archive for historical analysis, enables us to ask via the archive's documents why certain discourses, vocabularies, and knowledges took on the status of truth at specific historical junctures, while others were marginalized or disparaged. As the next section shows, genealogy is an effective tool for uncovering the role of handbooks in establishing the truths of old age in the middle of the 20th century.

I am suggesting that the ideas of Foucault generally, and of the critics of handbooks in other fields specifically, are valuable for a critique of the gerontological handbook archive, because they lead us to reconsider it as a body of historical documents that is socially significant in ways often overlooked by their authors and readers. In other words, it becomes possible to go beyond the overt purposes of the gerontological handbooks to discover them as chronicles of the development of the field's professional, multidisciplinary, and scientific codes. A genealogical approach also brings the handbooks into the interpretive realm of the humanities, where it is as important to understand the politics and practicalities of text-making as it is to explicate the texts' contents and authorships.

THE HANDBOOK AS A GERONTOLOGY STANDARD

The genealogical approach usefully frames an intriguing question: given the great variety of texts that can be written about aging and old age, why is the handbook a gerontological standard? Beginning with the publication of Edmund V. Cowdry's *Problems of Ageing* (1939, more fully discussed below), professional handbooks have assumed the dominant textual lineage in gerontology in a growing publication market. Cowdry's text went through two further editions, and by the time of the third edition in 1952 gerontological textbook production and research began to expand rapidly along the lines set out in Cowdry's collections.[3] In the late 1950s and early 1960s the Inter-University Training Institute in Social Gerontology, under the directorship of Wilma Donahue at the University of Michigan, sponsored a trio of formative handbooks that emphasized the nonbiological dimensions of aging in multidisciplinary formats (see Donahue, 1960): *Handbook of Aging and the Individual: Psychological and Biological Aspects of Aging*, edited by James Birren (1959); *Aging and Society: Handbook of Social Gerontology*, edited by Clark Tibbitts (1960); and *Aging in Western Culture: A Survey of Social Gerontology*, edited by Ernest Burgess (1960). These handbooks, in turn, stimulated further research, framed educational programs, and gave shape to the disciplinary discourse of gerontology, especially as it developed through the multiple editions of three predominant handbooks with James E. Birren as editor-in-chief: *Handbook of the Biology of Aging, Handbook of the Psychology of Aging*, and *Handbook of Aging and the Social Sciences*. These were published together with four editions each (1976/1977, 1985, 1990, 1996), the first two by Van Nostrand Reinhold and the latter two by the Academic Press. The handbooks' editors, all major figures in the field, largely remained the same through the different editions, while topics, emphases, and contributors have changed with the times.[4]

As these handbooks remain predominant, others have been published as well, especially since the 1980s as gerontology developed increasingly more subfields; for example, *Handbook of Geriatric Psychiatry* (E. Busse & D. Blazer, Eds., 1980), *International Handbook on Aging* (E. Palmore, Ed., 1980), *Handbook of Mental Health and Aging* (J. Birren, Ed., 1992), *Handbook of Nutrition in the Aged* (R. Watson, Ed., 1994), *Handbook on Ethnicity, Aging, and Mental Health,* (D. Padgett, Ed., 1995), *Handbook of Communication and Aging Research* (J. Nussbaum & J. Coupland, Eds., 1995), *Handbook of Aging and the Family* (R. Blieszner & V. Bedford, Eds., 1995), and *Handbook on Women and Aging* (J. M. Coyle, Ed., 1997).

Supplementing gerontology's handbook corpus has been a host of book reviews and critiques from within the gerontological community. Often reviewers point out what is missing in a particular handbook, such as Elizabeth A. Kutza's complaint in *The Gerontologist* that the policy chapters in the final section of the 1996 edition of *Handbook of Aging and the Social Sciences* lack the theoretical rigor and political acumen developed in earlier chapters (1996, p. 828). Others cite handbooks as embodiments of the unimaginative, scientific rationalism that pervades gerontology. For instance, Haim Hazan, in his introduction to *Old Age: Constructions and Deconstructions* (1994), disapprovingly observes that the table of contents of the second edition of *Handbook of Aging and the Social Sciences* (1985) "is a fine example of the attempt to preserve the distance of so-called scientific language from the categories enunciated by the subject of its study" (p. 9). "The calculated vocabulary is evident" (p. 10). Likewise, in his philosophical analysis of subjectivity in aging studies, Ronald Manheimer invents a new category, the "handbook self," to poke fun at the empiricist, behavioral tradition in gerontological texts (1992).

Alan Walker, in an earlier review (1987) of the second edition of *Handbook of Aging and the Social Sciences,* made several penetrating criticisms that might apply to other handbooks as well. He wrote that many of the contributions make the text too advanced to be pitched at an introductory level (p. 236). Walker's most telling criticism, however, was that the handbook is overwhelmingly American in content and approach, an ethnocentricism that belied the claim put forward by the title to general coverage of the subject. Walker asked: "what does the handbook reveal about the current state of gerontological research in the USA?" (p. 237). His stark conclusion was that the absence of critical structural thinking in the handbook reflected the lack of these features in American gerontology itself at that time. Although the next two editions of *Handbook of Aging and the Social Sciences* (1990, 1996) included more materials on structural relations, the political economy of aging, and international scholarship and authors, Walker's concern about the Americanization of aging studies remains an important point, but not necessarily because, as he suggested, "a handbook with a similar title produced in Europe would have a significantly different content" (p. 240).[5] Rather, Walker's critique points to the contextual nature of handbooks and the social relations of knowledge evident both inside and outside the text. Thus a progressive reviewer like Walker is criticizing the very embeddedness of the handbook genre in the specifics of American gerontological politics despite the genre's claim to transcend context and create a dispassionate science of gerontology.

More introspective reviews have been published by scholars who have themselves contributed to the handbooks. Edward J. Masoro, who wrote on "metabolism" for the second edition of *Handbook of the Biology of Aging* (1985), remarked that the 1996 edition of the handbook had several problems, among which was "the fact that each chapter is a free-standing review article" (1996, p. 828). This led Masoro to ponder two interesting questions: first, "why [are] collections of such articles . . . published in books when their publication over time as review articles in the leading journals of biological gerontology would probably better serve the field?" (pp. 828–829); and second, why doesn't a handbook on the biology of aging generate a consensus on what *aging* actually means as a biological phenomenon? (p. 829). Appropriately, Masoro titled his review, "What are we Talking About?"

W. Andrew Achenbaum, in his contributions to the second and fourth editions of *Handbook of Aging and the Social Sciences* (1985, 1996) and the first edition of *Handbook of the Humanities and Aging* (1992), and elsewhere (1995), has written extensively on the gerontological handbook. He has also been one of its most outspoken critics and on several occasions reviewed the biology, psychology, and social sciences handbooks in tandem (1991, 1993, 1996). Achenbaum criticized the handbook editions published in 1990 because, in his view, they provided no unifying themes, they typified the insularity of American gerontology, and their claim to multidisciplinarity was compromised by overspecialized chapters (1991). He called "for more critical handbooks" (p. 134) that would also hark back to the spirit of innovation and dialogue that characterized Cowdry's classic volumes. Similarly, Achenbaum noted in his review of the most recent handbook editions (1996) that a lack of cross-referencing to earlier volumes and bridge-building among disciplinary communities meant that the "editors deliver fresh ideas, but leave it to readers to make connections" (1996, p. 826).

Achenbaum is right to expect handbooks to fulfill gerontology's promise as a multidisciplinary, comprehensive, and accessible enterprise, one that provides its practitioners with state-of-the-art research and "gerontologic maps" to forecast the prospects of aging and the problems of old age. The limitations of the gerontological handbook may have less to do with the contents, the contributors, or the currency of the research, however, as the reviewers above suggest, than with the structure of the handbook genre itself. Rather than expect the handbook in all of its variations to accomplish the multidisciplinary ideals set forth by its mandate, perhaps we should detect in its lack of unity and thematic imbalances the patterns by which gerontological knowledge has been reproduced—a lack and an imbalance resulting from the handbook's nature as an "itinerant" text produced pragmatically to meet local shifting conditions. Judgments of gerontological handbooks based on positivist criteria of sufficiency and rigor or critical assessments of biases and scientism miss the point that handbooks are *productive* relays between authors, subjects, institutions, and worldviews. Further, such patterns involve more than just research models and data collections—however significant these may be—because the handbook also draws together the institutional practices of funding agencies, university programs, teaching curricula, relations of prestige, and the organization of expertise, as Walker's review above suggests. While the gerontological handbook's status as a standard appears to derive from its intellectual strengths, its real character comes from the burden placed on it to represent, in textual form, the disparate social and intellectual resources that have been brought to bear on the aging process. Gerontology's texts, like gerontology itself, therefore, should be seen as part of a struggling, indeterminate, and ultimately incomplete exercise to make old age a knowable feature of modern life. Revisiting the gerontological handbook with these issues in mind, along with earlier reflections on the handbook as a genealogical document, moves us closer to the rhetorical aspects of gerontological knowledge and takes up the question of the handbook as a disciplinary practice with particular reference to Cowdry's foundational text.

THE HANDBOOK AS A DISCIPLINARY PRACTICE IN GERONTOLOGY

At a general level, scientific texts discipline knowledge; they not only organize research problems in professionally legitimating ways, but also enfold their historical contingencies and social values into narratives of progress and objectivity. Further, as Bazerman and Paradis put it, authors and texts are "produced by a complex of social, cognitive, material, and rhetorical activities"; in consequence, written texts both construe knowledge and represent it. As expressions of disciplinary practice, they also "dialectically precipitate the various contexts and actions that constitute the professions" (1991, p. 4). Thus, texts are practical events that do things beyond what their authors say they do and beyond their designated roles in academic fields. Thinking of texts as practical events also prompts us to discover that texts might rework what they supposedly represent and critically counteract their academic status. As Dominick LaCapra says, "The apparent paradox is that texts hailed as perfections of a genre or a discursive practice may also test and contest its limits" (1985, p. 141).

How might we reinterpret anatomy professor Edmund V. Cowdry's *Problems of Ageing* in this critical light? Thus reconsidered, it can be seen as not only an innovative text, but as a practical event and a complex of rhetorical activities around multidisciplinarity and state-of-the-art scientific thinking that set the stage for the gerontological handbooks that followed. Further, a critical interpretation of Cowdry's work may demonstrate its value as a resource to "test and contest" the limits of gerontology.[6] Specifically, as I shall show below, as a multi-authored, multidisciplinary text Cowdry's handbook proclaimed the scope of the enterprise. The prefaces and forewords of its various editions, and the featuring of authors' professional credentials in a textbook-style list of contributors served to assert the existence, coherence, and scientific merit of a field of knowledge that was not yet either coherent or scientific, and was merely in the process of coming into existence. And finally, in using the handbook as the textual vehicle for launching the enterprise, Cowdry established at the outset the hegemonic form of gerontological knowledge-production—scientifically accredited multidisciplinary research framed as a practical guide for professionals—that has shaped the field ever since.

The idea of a multidisciplinary handbook in the early 20th century was already central to other professions, especially child studies. Indeed, Cowdry had already published a handbook on the problem of arteriosclerosis in 1933 and a multidisciplinary text with the (irksome) title, *Human Biology and Racial Welfare* in 1930. Within this context, Cowdry published the first edition of *Problems of Ageing* in 1939, with a second edition in 1942. In the Preface, Cowdry establishes the text's professional credentials: it was based on research presented at the Woods Hole Conference (Mass.) in 1937 (one of the first major scientific conferences on aging), and sponsored by The Josiah Macy Jr. Foundation, the Union of American Biological Societies, and the National Research Council. Cowdry tells us in the handbook's preface:

> Abstracts and complete manuscripts have been circulated widely among the contributors. Consequently, the opportunity to bring to bear on the problem the experience and points of view of many specialists, working together in a constructive way, has been unrivaled. But each contributor is personally responsible for his chapter. There are, as one would expect, some differences of opinion. These foreshadow progress since they will stimulate further investigation. The style is as simple as possible consistent with scientific accuracy. (Preface to 1st edition reprinted in Cowdry, 1942, p. iii.)

In the Preface to the second edition (1942) Cowdry adds that "our principle of mobilizing and integrating the knowledge and experience of specialists in different fields has been widely followed as is evidenced by the arrangement of symposium after symposium on the subject of aging" (p. iv). He then follows with a list of symposia and new interventions by foundations and national agencies between 1940 and 1941. In the second edition's Foreword, Lawrence K. Frank—who would go on to become a leader in American gerontology—corroborates Cowdry's scientific optimism. He says, "It is evident that the problem of the ageing process is multi-dimensional and will require for its solution not only a multidisciplinary approach but also a synoptic correlation of diverse findings and viewpoints, toward which this volume offers a highly significant contribution of facts and of theoretical formulations" (p. xv). Here the multidisciplinary theme is fully enunciated as the solution to the "problem" of the ageing process.

Hence, the Prefaces and the Foreword in *Problems of Ageing* persuade the reader of the text's legitimacy by dissolving three tensions: (i) Although there are differences between researchers, they are united by a common disciplinary imperative as a community of scholars. (ii) Although much more needs to be known about the aging process, the contributions stimulate further research. (iii) Although the problems of aging are complex and hardly containable in one text, scientific methods can elaborate the reasonability of the aging process. The introduction to *Problems of Ageing* was written by American philosopher John Dewey, who further authenticates the multidisciplinary ambitions of the text. Dewey, elderly himself at this point, saw in the study of aging the opportunity to link biological and cultural explanations as a way of creating a new form of knowledge, where "science and philosophy meet on common ground in their joint interest in discovering the processes of normal growth and in the institution of conditions which will favor and support ever continued growth" (in Cowdry, 1942, p. xxxiii).

Following Dewey's introduction is a listing of the many contributors and their credentials, a feature of textbook construction designed specifically to strengthen the text's authority through the rhetoric of the lists' entries. The bulk of the text consists of 34 chapters, each with a standard summary, that illustrate how aging occurs in the evolutionary worlds from protozoa to humans. In their combination, the chapters of *Problems of Ageing* appropriate scientific modeling in their construction of old age. For example, they expand the usages of medicalizing terms such as "senile" to characterize a broad range of human behavior. Book chapters are often organized according to anatomical models; comprehensive inventories and tables catalogue the special circumstances of old age; and the research pursuits of the book's contributors are legitimized through referral to work and authors in other already established scientific fields, such as pediatrics. The latter part of the second edition of Cowdry's text includes two chapters on the psychological aspects of aging. The first, by Yale psychology professor Walter R. Miles, discusses perception, intelligence, motivation, and personal interests, thus enhancing gerontology's psychological profile. The second chapter, by New York consulting psychologist George Lawton, on individual adjustment, endeavors to situate the psychology of aging as a rigorous analytical subject rather than a mere practical tool for eldercare. The author warns that "all of us working in this field will do the science of gerontology an ultimate disservice if we confuse our desire to ameliorate with our desire to describe"; scientific gerontology must be separated from "pseudo-healing cults" and "quasi-psychological literature" (p. 791). In insisting that the psychology of aging is a science that must be must be separated from older prescientific knowledges about the aging process, Lawton makes a substantive contribution to the certification of gerontology as a scientifically grounded profession. Lawton predicts that in the future communities will have "schools for older people" and Old Age Centers (p. 792), while expert gerontologists would be "social engineers" of imagination, "who will manipulate community resources, and when necessary, devise new instrumentalities" (p. 808).

The last two chapters of the second edition of *Problems of Ageing* reiterate the importance of multidisciplinarity and professionalism to the project of gerontological knowledge-production. In the penultimate chapter medical professor Albert Mueller-Deham delineates the varieties of physical problems in old age, remarking that "the senile body is a pathological museum, an equation with not merely one, but several unknown quantities" (p. 863). In order to know this body, "geriatrics will develop by specialization within Internal Medicine, not as an isolated structure, but only as a central station where many cables meet" (p. 887). In the final chapter Edward J. Stieglitz—who as a physician conceived the idea of social gerontology—attempts to give a coherency to the concept of multidisciplinary gerontology via a metaphorical linkage between the human body and the "body politic." Dividing gerontology into three categories of problems, biological, clinical and socioeconomic, Stieglitz proposes that: "As the cell is the unit from which the elaborate structure of the human body is constructed, so are individual men and women the basic units of collective society, the body politic. It is these socio-economic problems which have become so acute that now the need for knowledge in gerontology is a matter of true urgency" (p. 895).

The rhetorical practices of Cowdry's text—the contributors list, the authoritative Preface, the progressive chapter order, the multidisciplinary agenda, the emphasis on professional credentials, and the scientific vocabularies—bring the rationalities and aspirations of modern science to the problems of aging. In producing a text of this kind, Cowdry wedded the promise of gerontological knowledge to the handbook genre, and he has been praised by gerontologists for doing so ever since.[7] Indeed, if we look again at some of the recent handbooks, the same rhetorical practices are evident and they continue to serve the same kind of disciplinary function—to promote and shape the professional, multidisciplinary, and scientific status of gerontology.

CONCLUSIONS: THE HANDBOOK
AS A PUBLIC PHILOSOPHY

One of the first outcomes of the deconstruction I have just advocated may be to recover the promise of gerontology as a kind of "public philosophy" in the sense of the term used by Robert Bellah in his appendix to *Habits of the Heart* (1985) entitled "Social Science as Public Philosophy." Bellah's lament on the loss of the "public philosophy" tradition in the social sciences in the wake of their professionalization in modern institutions is particularly apt when applied to gerontology with its highly strategic professionalizing tendencies. In Bellah's view, this tradition merits restoration because professional social science has distanced itself from public concerns while harboring a narrow vision of the social "whole" (p. 300). The transdisciplinary agenda of social science as a public philosophy, however, is to open up the "arbitrary boundary between the social sciences and the humanities" and to remake social science into "a form of social self-understanding" (p. 301). But how to convert gerontology handbooks—the dominant textual forum for gerontological knowledge—to such purposes? And what role might handbooks, given their *raison d'être* as professional development tools, play in furthering the public philosophical prospects of gerontology?

The present volume proposes one answer to these questions: To cite Thomas R. Cole again, we should develop handbooks with a "difference" (1992a, p. xii) and look to the humanities for guidance in transforming the handbook genre. But this may be only a partial solution, if, as I have argued here, the handbook's legacy as a scientific, disciplining structure is left out of the critique of professional gerontology. A second response would be to recall the original, historical purpose of the handbook as a nomadic and public text, a manual that linked scholarship with commonsense and wisdom with instruction. Gerontology might be reconstructed through the forging of these links as "a form of social self-understanding."[8]

NOTES

[1] *Le Manuel des Péchés* survives in several manuscripts, but the one Bennett discusses here is itself one example of the genre. I thank my colleague Professor John Andrew Taylor for pointing out these aspects of handbook history.

[2] Accordingly, Foucault identifies numerous documents as genealogical expressions of the dilemmas of modernity, such as Jeremy Bentham's late 18th-century plan for the imprisoning *Panopticon* (1979), the memoirs of 19th-century hermaphrodite Herculine Barbin (1980), and a "minor" periodical publication by Immanuel Kant in 1784 called "What is Enlightenment?" (1984). An excellent example of a genealogical study of psychology is Rose (1989).

[3] Birren and Clayton estimate that the literature on aging published between 1950 and 1960 equals all that had been published in the previous 115 years (1975, p. 74).

[4] Besides gerontological handbooks, multiple editions are a feature of many other gerontological texts. For example, at the time of this writing there are four editions of *Later Life: The Realities of Aging* (H. Cox), and *Social Gerontology: A Multidisciplinary Perspective* (N. R. Hooyman); five editions of *Death, Society, and Human Experience* (R. Kastenbaum); and six editions of *Social Forces and Aging* (R. Atchley). Researchers in critical perspectives in gerontology have also gathered their ideas into recent readers. Examples are *Images of Aging: Cultural Representations of Later Life* (M. Featherstone & W. Wernick, 1995), *Critical Gerontology: Perspectives from Political and Moral Economy* (M. Minkler & C. Estes, 1999) and, *Figuring Age: Women, Bodies, Generations* (K. Woodward, 1999).

[5] Victor Marshall, editor of two distinguished editions of *Aging in Canada: Social Perspectives,* acknowledges the existence of national distinctions in gerontological scholarship by noting that, "Canadian theory about aging is more structural, collectivist and historically grounded than the predominantly attitudinal, individualist and consensually oriented theorizing found south of the border" (1987, p. 4). Lawrence Cohen goes further to elaborate the international impact of western gerontology texts with an illuminating focus on India (1998).

[6] Historical gerontologists W. Andrew Achenbaum (1995), Thomas R. Cole (1992b), Carole Haber (1983), and David G. Troyansky (1989), among others, have pioneered the analysis of gerontological literature as a vibrant dimension of contemporary historical scholarship. See Richard Harvey Brown (1992) for examples of deconstruction and social science texts.

[7] Why other texts did not become as foundational as Cowdry's is an important question. For example, psychology professor G. Stanley Hall's *Senescence: The Last Half of Life* (1992), written during his retirement from Clark University, is a *tour-de-force* that surveys not only the sciences of old age but also poetry, fiction, religion, ethnography, and autobiographies. In contrast to Hall's earlier influential work on adolescence, *Senescence* is regarded as too speculative, scattered, and unscientific. In his ambivalence about scientific explanations of aging (Achenbaum, 1993; Cole, 1993), however, Hall poses new questions in *Senescence* that gerontology is still challenged to answer.

[8] I explore the possibilities of gerontological "undisciplining" elsewhere (Katz, 1996). One interesting example of a more traditional handbook hidden

among contemporary ones is *Handbook of Aging: For Those Growing Old and Those Concerned With Them* (1972), written by retired American academic Elliot Dunlap Smith. His promise in the Preface to make "the book short, partly to make it easy for elderly people to hold, but mainly because it is not a book of extensive particularization to be skimmed through quickly" (viii), is borne out in this slender volume which would not be out of place in the hands of an aging medieval cleric.

REFERENCES

Achenbaum, W. A. (1991). The state of the handbooks on aging in 1990. *The Gerontologist, 31*(1), 132–134.

Achenbaum, W. A. (1993). One way to bridge the two cultures: Advancing qualitative gerontology through professional autobiographies. *Canadian Journal on Aging, 12*(2), 143–156.

Achenbaum, W. A. (1995). *Crossing frontiers: Gerontology emerges as a science.* New York: Cambridge University Press.

Achenbaum, W. A. (1996). Handbooks as gerontologic maps. *The Gerontologist, 36*(6), 825–826.

Auster, C. J. (1985). Manuals for socialization: Examples from Girl Scout handbooks 1913–1984. *Qualitative Sociology, 8*(4), 359–367

Bazerman, C., & Paradis, J. (1991). Introduction. In C. Bazerman & J. Paradis (Eds.), *Textual dynamics of the professions* (pp. 3–10). Madison: University of Wisconsin Press.

Bellah, R. N. (1985). Social science as public philosophy. In R. N. Bellah, R. Madsen, W. M. Sullivan, A. Swidler, & S. M. Tipton (Eds.), *Habits of the heart: Individualism and commitment in American life* (pp. 297–307). Berkeley: University of California Press.

Bennett, A. (1988). A book designed for a noblewoman: An illustrated manuel des Péchés of the thirteenth century. In L. L. Brownrigg (Ed.), *Medieval book production: Assessing the evidence* (pp. 163–181). Los Altos Hills: Anderson-Lovelace and Red Gull Press.

Best, D. L., & Ruther, N. M. (1994). Cross-cultural themes in developmental psychology: An examination of texts, handbooks, and reviews. *Journal of Cross-Cultural Psychology, 25*(1), 54–77.

Birren, J. E., & V. Clayton. (1975). History of gerontology. In D. S. Woodruff & J. E. Birren (Eds.), *Aging: Scientific perspectives and social issues* (pp. 15–27). New York: D. Van Nostrand.

Brown, R. H. (Ed.). (1992). *Writing the social text: Poetics and politics in social science discourse.* New York: Walter de Gruyter.

Cohen, L. (1998). *No aging in India: Alzheimer's, the bad family, and other modern things.* Berkeley: University of California Press.

Cole, T. R. (1992a). The humanities and aging: An overview. In T. R. Cole, D. Van Tassel, & R. Kastenbaum (Eds.), *Handbook of the humanities and aging* (pp. xi–xxiv). New York: Springer Publishing Co.

Cole, T. R. (1992b). *The journey of life: A cultural history of aging in America.* New York: Cambridge University Press.

Cole, T. R. (1993). The Prophecy of *Senescence:* G. Stanley Hall and the Reconstruction of Old Age in Twentieth Century America. In W. K. Schaie & W. Andrew Achenbaum (Eds.), *Societal impact on aging: Historical perspectives* (pp. 165–181). New York: Springer Publishing Co.

Cowdry, E. V. (Ed.). (1930). *Human biology and racial welfare.* New York: Paul B. Hoeber.

Cowdry, E. V. (Ed.). [1939] (1942). *Problems of ageing: Biological and medical aspects.* Baltimore: Williams and Wilkin.

Donahue, W. (1960). Training in social gerontology. *Geriatrics, 15*(11), 801–809.

Foucault, M. (1977). Nietzsche, genealogy, history. In D. L. Bouchard (Ed.), *Language, counter-memory, practice* (pp. 139–164). Ithaca: Cornell University Press.

Foucault, M. (1979). (Tr. A. Sheridan). *Discipline and punish: The birth of the Prison.* New York: Vintage Books.

Foucault, M. (Ed.). (1980). (Tr. R. McDougall). *Herculin Barbin: Being the recently discovered memoirs of a nineteenth-century French hermaphrodite.* New York: Pantheon.

Foucault, M. (1984). What is enlightenment? In P. Rabinow (Ed.), *The Foucault reader* (pp. 32–50). New York: Pantheon Books.

Haber, C. (1983). *Beyond sixty-five: The dilemma of old age in America's past.* New York: Cambridge University Press.

Hall, G. S. (1922). *Senescence: The last half of life.* New York: D. Appleton.

Hazan, H. (1994). *Old age: Constructions and deconstructions.* Cambridge: Cambridge University Press.

Katz, S. (1996). *Disciplining old age: The formation of gerontological knowledge.* Charlottesville: University Press of Virginia.

Kutza, E. A. (1996). The maturation of an interdisciplinary discipline. *The Gerontologist, 36*(6), 827–828.

LaCapra, D. (1985). *History and criticism.* Ithaca: Cornell University Press.

Manheimer, R. J. (1992). In search of the gerontological self. *Journal of Aging Studies, 6*(4), 319–332.

Marshall, V. W. (2d ed. 1987). Introduction: Social Perspective on Aging. In V. W. Marshall (Ed.), *Aging in Canada: Social perspectives* (pp. 1–7). Markham, Ont.: Fitzhenry and Whiteside.

Masoro, E. J. (1996). What are we talking about? *The Gerontologist, 36*(6), 828–830.

Rose, N. (1989). *Governing the soul: The shaping of the private self.* Routledge.

Schutze, Y. (1987). The good mother: The history of the normative model "motherlove." *Sociological studies of child development, 2,* 39–78.

Smith, E. D. (1972). *Handbook of aging for those growing old and those concerned with them.* New York: Barnes and Noble.

Troyansky, D. G. (1989). *Old age in the old regime: Image and experience in eighteenth century France.* Ithaca: Cornell University Press.

Walker, A. (1987). Ageing and the social sciences: The North American Way. *Ageing and Society, 7*(2), 235–241.

21

Afterword

W. Andrew Achenbaum

"Throughout the 1970s and early 1980s, interest in gerontology (the study of aging) and geriatrics (health care of older persons) was fueled by recognition of the social, economic, and health care consequences of the unprecedented aging of America's population," observe John W. Rowe and Robert L. Kahn (1998: xi) in their foreword to *Successful Aging*. Standard bibliographic reference works documented that the number of articles and books on aging-related research was growing exponentially. Graduate schools and community colleges across the nation were launching certificate programs to train people to work with the aged. "Despite this energy, the progress of gerontology began to stall in the mid-1980s" (ibid.).

Rowe and Kahn do not explain why advances in gerontology slowed down during the 1980s, but it is not difficult to imagine what they might have had in mind (Achenbaum, 1995). Federal funding priorities changed during Reagan's presidency. The National Institute on Aging was investing more and more heavily into basic research on the causes of Alzheimer's disease. Training grants and dollars for social services for the elderly funded through the Administration on Aging were cut at the same time. Meanwhile, it was proving harder to attain the research objectives than an earlier cohort of gerontologists had anticipated. Biomedical investigators had not found a "magic bullet" to postpone or cure the vicissitudes of senescence. In the mid-1980s social and behavioral scientists lacked a theoretical construct as interesting and controversial as (the now discredited) disengagement theory had been.

In order to enliven a field that many scientific advisers and opinion makers felt would only rise in importance, the John D. and Catherine T. MacArthur Foundation assembled a group of scholars in 1984 to lay the intellectual and methodological foundations for a "new gerontology." Sixteen well-known investigators were drawn from prominent research programs, including U.S.C.'s Andrus Gerontology Center (3),

Harvard's medical and public health schools, Michigan's Institute for Social Research; those at Duke, Penn State, Irvine, Johns Hopkins's Mind/Brain Institute, Virginia, Minnesota, Wisconsin, and the Russell Sage Foundation.

The group was as disparate in disciplinary training as the institutes were in geographical location. John Rowe had made his mark as a geriatrician and physiologist; Bob Kahn was a renowned social psychologist. Others selected were epidemiologists, geneticists, neurobiologists, psychologists, and sociologists. For good measure the MacArthur Study also tapped a psychiatrist, neurologist, and a neuropsychologist. It is worth noting that only one participant, Caleb Finch, identified himself as a gerontologist—although nearly everyone else chosen had done significant research on aging.

The Foundation wanted a team of researchers who could interact with colleagues from different disciplines. For the MacArthur network to succeed, members had to know how to work with peers who pursued complementary interests with orientations that were not necessarily compatible (Kahn, 1996). The investigators hoped that computer technologies and a common research design would result in the creation of interchangeable tools and a large data base. The goal seemed feasible. Several members of the MacArthur team had migrated to new areas of inquiry over their careers: Eight of the 16 specified two distinctive scientific specialties in their self-descriptions. After a decade of collaboration the breadth and depth of productivity generated by the scientists fulfilled the expectations of a foundation "committed to an interdisciplinary research program" (Rowe & Kahn, 1998: xii).

THE SCHOLARLY AND SCIENTIFIC CULTURES DIVERGE

It is telling but not really surprising that experts in the humanities were not invited to join the MacArthur study. The vitae of the researchers invited to investigate the dimensions of "successful aging" had at least one trait in common: all had subscribed to disciplinary-specific modes of *scientific* inquiry in advancing knowledge. To them, gerontology's future successes depended on the rigorous application of laboratory-based principles. Scientific theories and methods, to be sure, vary over time. Nevertheless, assumptions about how to do science have proven quite resilient. For this reason, the paradigm and procedures laid out in *Successful Aging* would have been readily understood by the biomedical researchers and few social scientists tapped in the 1930s by Edmund Vincent Cowdry to explore the *Problems of Ageing* (1939). In both projects "hard" science prevailed.

That experts in the humanities were not included in the MacArthur project says something about the state of contemporary gerontology. Stars in "our" camp are as bright and productive as the luminaries in the MacArthur network. But novelists, critics, and philosophers by and large employ a different set of tools and methods. They usually work alone. The scholars who I think might have leavened discussions under the Foundation's aegis tend to be more reflexive about how they go about their business than the men and women who joined forces to study *Successful Aging*. We have not arrived at a stage of cross-disciplinary discourse that would satisfy John Dewey's dream that "science and philosophy meet on common ground" intellectually and methodologically (Cowdry, 1939; xxvi–xxvii). Gerontological investigators typically belong to one tribe or the other: they are scholars or scientists, rarely both. And within this division are nodes of scholarly activities (as well as projects involving both basic and applied research) without parallel in the other camp. Some alliances in the respective cultures have been strategic, others serendipitous.

The second edition of the *Handbook of the Humanities and Aging* manifests excellence in research that both resembles and differs in important ways from what is found in successive editions of the *Handbook of the Biology of Aging,* the *Handbook of the Psychology of Aging,* or the *Handbook of Aging and the Social Sciences.* Articles in all of these gerontologic handbooks are becoming narrower and narrower. We know more and more about less and less. Like its biomedical, behavioral, and social science companions, this second edition of the *Handbook of the Humanities and Aging* strikes me as less comprehensive than the 1992 volume. Paradoxically, however, it is richer in detail. Its contributors seem more assured in making their assessments with an eye to disciplinary-specific conventions—even though they realize that the canons that used to govern humanistic inquiry are in flux.

Through the mid-1980s virtually *all* humanistic works on aging seemed fresh to mainstream gerontologists. Scientists knew that poets did not write like philosophers, but it really did not matter as long as they added something to research on aging. Humanistic perspectives attracted the attention of social scientists, clinicians, and social workers (Achenbaum, 1992). Gerontologists cited articles and monographs by literary and art critics, dramatists, philosophers, theologians, ethicists, and historians. Contributions from scholars in the humanities were considered accessible supplements to mainstream research in aging—in part because the newcomers knew how to write jargon-free English. Philosophers and critics were invited to scientific conferences. Once there, they invariably met a geriatrician who had majored in English, an epidemiologist who read history. There were, in short, possibilities for bridging areas of expertise.

In contrast to the sputtering occurring in gerontology's established quarters, moreover, the relative novelty of humanistic perspectives on aging gave the domain an aura of liveliness. Perhaps as important as the networking between the scientific and scholarly cultures was the rise of constructive disputes over interpretations and methods that started to break out within (sub)disciplines of the humanities. Controversies raged in many domains; skirmishes were particularly vocal among social historians and bioethicists. Scholarly debates about the validity of "modernization" theory, the priority to be accorded "autonomy" in long-term-care settings, and how to contextualize "Self" in late-life memories (Achenbaum & Stearns, 1978; Cole & Gadow, 1986) served their purpose. They were evidence of genuine intellectual excitement, signs that the passionate engagement could be sustained. For historians of aging, the fights of the mid-1980s marked a step toward maturation, which is conveyed in the revisionist tone of Carole Haber's balanced assessment of America's elders in "Beyond Modernism" (infra).

To look at the contents of the first and second editions of the *Handbook of the Humanities and Aging,* in sum, is to observe the history of gerontology unfolding into several mini-histories. At the very moment that Rowe and Kahn claimed that research on aging in the social, behavioral and biomedical sciences was beginning to stagnate, work in the humanities and aging was coming of age. And since the mid-1980s humanistic gerontology has continued to take on new forms.

THE EXPANDING FRONTIERS OF THE HUMANITIES

The domain's broadening repertoire can be fathomed by analyzing the lists of subjects covered and authors tapped in the first and second editions of the *Handbook of the Humanities and Aging.* Both editions have roughly the same number of articles (20 and 21, respectively). Yet only eight articles deal with basically the same topic—both editions include separate chapters on aging in the Jewish and the Christian traditions, as well as chapters that focus on U.S. history and literature and aging. Only six authors (including me, who presumptuously requested the last word) contribute pieces to both editions. Thomas Cole, Ruth Ray, and Robert Kastenbaum invited new voices to join the conversation. They selected experts who might be well positioned to assess developments occurring at the interstices of traditional modes of inquiry.

By recruiting advocates of cutting-edge scholarship, the editors deliver ample proof that the boundaries which once enclosed the realm of the humanities and aging are bursting. Innovations are taking place everywhere. Seasoned scholars, trained in traditional disciplines, are shifting gears. Some try to amalgamate a lifetime of intellectual interests as they begin to study late-life wisdom or express their feelings and ideas in poetic meter. Similar to writers who advanced feminist perspectives in scholarship or who were fleshing out the lines of queer theory, well-known scholars are redesigning the traditional modes of humanistic discourse. Peter Laslett, for instance, had gained international acclaim for his demographic analyses of the elderly. Now, in retirement, he is applying his expertise to cultural and social history to provide educational opportunities for men and women who, like him, are in the third age. Kathleen Woodward's analyses of the late-life styles of Frost, Eliot, and Pound brought her recognition early in her career. Lately, she has been utilizing ideas by Lacan and other Continental thinkers to reinterpret bodily and psychological images of older people.

Such self-consciously mature scholars did not gain new appreciation into the faces and feelings of age simply by borrowing from the ideas of a Pierre Bourdieu or Jane Gallup. They learned by coming to terms with their own aging. Their personal experiences affected the way they write, what they choose to study. They themselves embody the principles of age studies. One sees in their work a process that Margaret Morganroth Gullette limns here and elaborates in *Declining to Decline.* It is a revisionist stance that rejects self-defeating notions of loss due merely to the passage of years. Rather, it opts for a constructive mode, animated by the sheer intellectual vitality of knowledge building.

Various contributors to the *Handbook of the Humanities and Aging* confirm the point being made here. The first sentence in Anne Wyatt-Brown's essay (infra) attests to how "dramatically" the field of literary gerontology has grown in the brief 7 years since her careful, exhaustive critique of the field was published in 1992. In an essay on "literary history," new to this second edition, Teresa Magnum shows that exploring literary and cultural narratives are generating truly interdisciplinary critiques of empirical data. The editors of the second edition and their advisers, several of whom pursue contemplative paths in their private hours, include here a chapter on late-life spirituality. Significantly, they disentangle its focus from the analyses offered on how religious traditions and institutions affect and support the elderly. Tom Cole and his colleagues chose to write the chapter on spirituality about one of gerontology's master synthesizers, Robert Atchley, who is now devoting more of his time to soul-making. Author of several editions of the country's best-selling gerontology textbook, Atchley moves deftly from grand themes of eastern and western traditions to nuanced descriptions of mundane aspects of spiritual practices. A careful sociological methodologist, Atchley seems liberated by the scope of this volume to speak clearly. The "logical, interpretive, and experiential methods of the humanities," he claims, are more amenable than the "hard sciences" to the contemplative nature of spirituality. Other contributors to the *Handbook of the Humanities and Aging,* as we shall see, reach a similar conclusion.

New foci insinuate themselves throughout the second edition of the *Handbook.* Although the 1992 volume moved beyond "texts" to embrace artistic expressions, the editors here offer an even broader range of relevant media wherein humanistic perspectives on aging are to be found. Robert Yahnke, for instance, offers a fascinating critique of aging-related themes and characterizations of late life that appear in films and videos especially since the 1970s. Like virtually every contributor to this volume, Yahnke's discussion of gerontological issues is informed by his disciplinary training and vice versa: thus it would be hard for me to say whether I value his observations more for their fairmindedness as movie reviews than I do for their insights into the dynamics of senescence in their own right.

I learned a lot of new information reading all the articles in this second edition of the *Handbook of the Humanities and Aging.* I was astounded by the number of books listed at the end of chapters that I did not know, though I do look forward to savoring them eventually. Let me mention one other important indicator of the intellectual ferment evident among these experts in the humanities: a voracious consumer of research across several domains, I gauge the extent to which I have been surprised by a contributor's argument and evidence. I do not wish to slight any author, but the prize for "surprising me the most" goes to Anne Davis Basting. I expected Cole, Ray, and Kastenbaum to include in this edition of the *Handbook* at least one assessment of cultural studies in gerontology; cultural studies is a "hot" field. And I would have been disappointed had historical studies been excluded. But the phrase "performative studies" caught me short. I did not know that it was a specialty, much less an interdisciplinary field that brought together folklorists, anthropologists, social scientists and theatre specialists.

Anne Davis Basting insists that the emergence of performative studies is linked to postmodernism in academic culture. Merely stipulating this context is instructive. It reminds me that new fields often result from broad intellectual currents, which are transforming the intellectual landscape. New nexi of academic exchanges produce bold ways of thinking, ones I surely did not imagine until they were brought to my attention. And because of my own insecurities, I probably would have resisted their message earlier in my career. Even now I questioned whether Basting was right. Would this particular combination of disciplines not have been evident in ancient Greece, Shakespeare's day, or even in the Harlem Renaissance? The rumination afforded me an occasion to mull over what "performative studies" embraces and excludes.

It forced me to think harder about what "postmodernism" entails, for it remains an elusive term in my mind. Hence it helped when Basting made critical turns from texts to the phenomenonological: in "turning" from one direction to another, she represented a *modus operandi* that I am more inclined to associate with scholarship in the humanities than results from a laboratory or scientific survey. And when I feared that I would get hopelessly lost in her argument, Basting's allusions to theoretical works by people I admire—such as Bob Kastenbaum and Barbara Myerhoff—reoriented me. So, too, did her references to performative studies of age by the likes of Victor Turner and Marc Kaminsky. My goodness, I thought, Basting must be on to something. Performative studies, clearly, is an exciting field that already has enriched the gerontologic corpus through an unusual cross-disciplinary amalgam.

REFINING IDEAS AND METHODS IN THE HUMANITIES AND AGING

By creating new possibilities for crafting holistic descriptions of what it means to grow older, experts in the humanities are blazing gerontologic frontiers. And the entire venture thus far has been remarkably cost-effective—a few favorable tenure decisions, a well-timed conference, subventions to university presses to publish worthy manuscripts. Compare that to the cost of doing Big Science these days. According to Rowe and Kahn, the MacArthur Foundation invested "well over ten million dollars in support" to emphasize "the *positive aspects of aging* [sic.]—which had been terribly overlooked" (1998: xii). Was *Successful Aging* worth the outlay? If so, why: what were its major results and immediate impact?

Rowe and his MacArthur colleagues sought to get beyond definitions of later life based on chronological age. They investigated a wide battery of genetic, biomedical, behavioral, and social factors that enabled older men and women to maintain their vitality, possibly enhance their life experiences. Setting a truly enviable standard for interdisciplinarity, members of the 16 research groups agreed to be in regular communication; they met several times a year over more than a decade to compare work in progress. Beginning with a very influential piece by Rowe and Kahn in *Science* (1987), the MacArthur network produced nearly a hundred scientific papers. *Successful Aging* was sent gratis to every member of the Gerontological Society, among others. Results from the MacArthur project influenced the latest national blueprint for research on aging issued by the Institute of Medicine (ibid., xiv). Given the sums spent on other scientific enterprises, the Foundation undoubtedly got its money's worth.

That said, if the MacArthur network had reviewed the scholarship being generated by people trained in the humanities, it might have resulted in a more subtle understanding of successful aging—one that went beyond featuring its "positive" and "negative" dimensions. Experts in the humanities as well as bench scientists often deploy dualisms to organize complex data. Characterizing aspects of the human condition as "positive" or "negative" provides a way of differentiating one cluster of ideas and traits from another. Insofar as making sharp distinctions—between light and dark, good and evil—helps to clarify thinking in everyday life, so too dualisms often facilitate efforts to make technical material accessible, to underscore points.

But dualisms must be used with care. Not much worth saying about aging or human development boils down to "positive" or "negative" characteristics. For the most part personalities and circumstances fall along a multidimensional continuum. Hence categorizing late-life growth simply in terms of "normal" aging or "pathological" aging fails to capture the realities felt by someone suffering from a genetic defect or experiencing the onset of a chronic illness. This is why Gisela Labouvie-Vief, in "Positive Development in Later Life," underscores the lack of uniformity in trajectories as she emphasizes analysts' need to balance the impact of innate resources and environmental restraints in elders' individual choices. Other contributors to this second edition of the *Handbook of the Humanities and Aging* agree: with Labouvie-Vief they get beyond either/or distinctions, and posit more than two ways of perceiving reality.

Consider the message of the first two essays in this second edition. "Variety" and "heterogeneity" are keywords in Pat Thane's survey of aging in western civilization. Although she notes that the elderly's conditions remained fairly stable until the 20th century, Thane does not depict a monolithic past. Gender, class, and age always have affected an elderly person's relative status. The portrait of "Aging in the East," drawn by Leng Leng Thang, complements Thane's. The aged in the Orient were not invariably revered. Eastern customs and practices for millennia actually have made growing older a process fraught with ambiguities. The reasons for conflicted attitudes and ambivalent statuses vary from place to place. History and culture have created conditions in China that diverge from what exists in Japan or elsewhere. The aged's place in oriental societies has changed over the past 50 years. Like analysts in western civilization, policymakers in Singapore, Tokyo and East Asia are perplexed by aging as a "social problem." No wonder Thang argues that there may actually be greater convergence between East and West since World War II than existed before.

In stressing varieties and ambivalences, experts in the humanities have not wholly eschewed dualisms. But if one compares the polarities that appear in the first edition of the *Handbook of the Humanities and Aging* with the ones invoked in this edition of the multidisciplinary volume, there appears to be more explicit sensitivity in distinguishing between previous dualisms that worked and those that did not. In the process several authors manage to create a dialectic within their own dualistic framework. Perhaps three examples will suffice.

Steve Weiland entitles his contribution "Social Science Toward the Humanities," brilliantly (and perhaps a bit slyly) noting the double meaning of the preposition. Invoking the works of such scholars as Jay Gubrium and Sharon Kaufman, Weiland shows that social scientists interested in studying the lives of the aged are beginning to seize on the freedom accorded by methodological pluralism. They move "towards," insofar as they adapt what lies at the heart of the humanities—interpretation, rhetoric, and narrative—and are themselves transformed by the interaction. In a similar vein, Gisela Labouvie-Vief plays off the mythic and empirical images of wisdom accorded by visions of the life course in the humanities and the fruits of scientific psychology. More than most contemporary commentators who study pathways to growing wiser with advancing years, she underscores the central place of suffering in both traditions. Finally, Stephen Katz seizes on the ironies that turn on the encounter between what he calls "the science of gerontology" and "the ingenuity of the humanities" in a handbook of this sort. He moves from dualisms to a four-part schema that gazes at the handbook as a genealogical document, gerontological canon, disciplinary practice, and public philosophy. Katz concludes that the text of handbooks, like the field itself, is indeterminate, struggling to contextualize old age in its contemporary milieu.

In several successfully executed essays, contributors deploy dualisms as part of their revisionist aims. They seek to advance knowledge by building on (and off) ways of organizing ideas in the past; in this mode of analysis, scholars restate notions they presume to be familiar to readers in a manner that they hope will yield a more precise, rigorous, and insightful understanding of an issue. Sometimes the revisionist exegesis falls largely within disciplinary confines. Thus the essay by Carole Haber on continuities and changes in the elderly's place in U.S. history, seeks to amplify the revisionist thesis that she and Brian Gratton published in an article (1993a) and book (1993b). By engaging in exercises in comparative religion, Gene Thursby in his essay is able to show variations in the perceptions and treatment of older people in faith traditions that share common geographical territories. Elsewhere, "orthodoxy in geriatrics and gerontology" is challenged through skepticism over the conventional wisdom that arises in an area such as bioethics. Hence in "Bioethics and Aging," Larry McCullough revisits issues of autonomy and justice, which dominated the literature in the

1980. He believes that geroethics contributes to the development of health-care policy by formulating concepts of justice that would apply to the entire population (not just the aged). In the process he warns against an eclectic approach to framing issues that would result in intellectual instability as proposals are made into laws.

Sometimes prevailing gerontologic ideas are called into question by invoking multiperspectivism. Melvin Kimble achieves this effect in "Aging and the Christian Tradition" by illustrating continuities and changes in Christian theologians' views of aging, suffering, and death over the centuries. McCullough tried to sharpen debate by limiting his focus on bioethics. In contrast, Harry Berman creates a hermeneutic circle that plays off the relationship between parts and the whole as it explores the dynamics between the knower and the known. Berman assembles many voices (novelists, anthropologists, philosophers, literary critics, psychologists, even Ronald Reagan) to distinguish between representation and what is being represented. He argues that diaries and autobiographies help people to imagine the range of experiences possible in the future. Sharon Kaufman, like Berman, creates a multivocal narrative in her ethnography of death. Her careful ordering of details in a hospital, her prioritizing of the viewpoints of patients and their families and of physicians and nurses demonstrates the incommensurability between the lay and medical worlds of understanding the nature of disease, old age, and death. There are, Kaufman concludes, no "single oppositions," but clusters of contested perspectives concerning care, control, and choice.

This brief overview does not do justice to the diversity of ideas, the richness of details, the outpouring of publications that have been generated by recent work in the humanities and aging. In my opinion, they provide a richer portrait of the paradoxes, variety, ironies, and coincidences that characterize the human condition in later years. To put it bluntly: *Successful Aging* gives us a reliable baseline for comprehending positive features of growing older that we hitherto may have underestimated; the latest *Handbook of the Humanities and Aging* enables us to see additional ways to transform the potentials of advancing years, without denying the pitfalls associated with age. In the spirit that pervades this volume, let me revise (but only slightly) the central themes of my Afterword to the first edition so that they reflect more accurately the current state and future prospects of the humanities in gerontology.

THE STATE OF THE FIELD

The 20 essays in this handbook attest to the intellectual vitality of a field no longer fledgling, yet not quite mature. Good work is being done. Books like *Journey of Life* (Cole, 1992) and *Five Stages of the Soul* (Moody, 1997) have reached a worldwide audience. They are being read thoughtfully and incorporated into the thinking of scholars in the humanities as well as bench scientists and practitioners. Appropriate efforts are being made to link narratives of aging with the theories and data produced by social and behavioral scientists. There are more outlets for scholarship. Experts in the humanities have been instrumental in launching *Contemporary Gerontology,* which fashions itself to be a *New York Review of Books* for researchers on aging, and a recent addition, *The Journal of Aging and Identity.* The *Journal of Aging Studies* remains a primary vehicle for interdisciplinary inquiries that build on history, literary criticism, and philosophy. Coeditor Robert Kastenbaum regularly offers space in the *International Journal of Aging and Human Development* to "our" group. The University Press of Virginia has launched a successful series of monographs in the humanities and aging. Pine Forge Press solicits proposals from historians and philosophers geared to undergraduate audiences.

All that said, I am somewhat more pessimistic about proximate developments than I was in 1992. Four longstanding obstacles continue to bedevil the field. First, I share the conviction of Anne Wyatt-Brown (infra) and David D. Van Tassel (1995) that we have yet to create a critical mass of scholars interested in studying the meanings and experiences of aging and old age using insights, methods, and styles drawn from the humanities. Many of us who were completing our PhDs, writing dissertations on a topic in this area, and then struggled to get tenure in the 1970s and 1980s are aging fairly productively. But there were not many of us in the pool then, and we have not managed to train very many men and women who can be said to constitute the next wave(s) of scholarship. The situation is perplexing. I sometimes think that ageism must be more virulent among graduate students than sexism, racism, or homophobia. I shepherd three or four students a year through qualifying exams, but they rarely follow my advice in selecting a dissertation dealing with an aging topic. Apparently we have failed to demonstrate the advantages of a "practical" thesis in a tight job market. Gero-humanities may not be unique in this regard: after considerable flurry "applied" history languishes nowadays.

If we cannot get enough undergraduates in the humanities' traditional areas interested in studying old age, then we should deepen relationships with fellow travelers trained in other domains. We need more cross-disciplinary models like the ones produced by Jay Gubrium (1993) and Jay Sokolovsky (1997), works by creative minds who have profitably utilized qualitative methods in their inquiries. We desperately require the input from polymaths such as Robert Kastenbaum. His essay on "creativity and the arts" (infra) playfully invokes the collective wisdom of Albert Einstein, Francis Galton, Jon Hendricks, Adolphe Quetelet, and Keith Simonton. Here is brilliance executed with a knack for looking at an issue from various perspectives. So perhaps we should concentrate on "converting" gerontological researchers in neighboring disciplines. Historians nowadays work so closely with sociologists and anthropologists that the lines dividing their specialties seem fuzzy. And as this *Handbook* indicates, the possibilities for fruitful exchanges of ideas are limitless. No game plan is necessary, but the urgency to collaborate has become more compelling.

The lack of sufficient numbers of people working in the field has resulted, second, in a paucity of information in (so) many areas. I agree with Robert Yahnke that in too many cases we rely on the "well-worn formula." Margaret Morganroth Gullette is correct in declaring that aging remains "an impoverished concept," particularly "because of its undertheorized relation to 'the body.'" Since the publication of the first edition of the *Handbook of the Humanities and Aging,* we have not made much progress in studying ideas about aging and the treatment of the elderly in Africa or South America. In North America, we have a better sense of how sex and gender shape choices in later years, but there has not been much work done on race and ethnicity. In an era in which AIDS has shaken our acceptance of medical paradigms of disease, the relationship between disability (especially chronic mental and physical maladies) and aging remains little studied.

Third, experts in the humanities still have not figured out how to reach a public audience that extends much beyond organizations interested in listening every once in a while to entertaining "experts" talk about aging. We can claim no Betty Friedans or Ken Dychtwalds, though they like to incorporate our research into their speeches. That is fine as far as it goes: at least some of our scholarship is getting circulated beyond the seminar table. Still, how frustrating when *Newsweek* or the *Washington Post* persist in calling only on the usual suspects— physicians, biologists, government officials, an occasional political scientist or demographer—for opinions about the latest findings in aging research. Gerontology is not an arcane science, but that is how it is perceived by the press and our enlightened citizenry. Apparently few grasp that philosophers, critics, or artists might have something to say that goes beyond the usual scope of their training.

And this is why, fourth, I worry about whether scholars in the humanities will ever secure a place at the gerontological table. I used to think that we would be invited under the banner of "interdisciplinarity." I no longer am so sanguine. After all, when physicists and engineers interact, deans and provosts rightly deem their work to be interdisciplinary. Better yet, the collaboration generally yields large indirect costs and results worthy of Big Science. So who needs a historian or theologian? Commitments to experts in the humanities too often prove rhetorical, sadly abandoned amidst budget tightening, when the priorities of departments perforce take precedence over the health of cross-disciplinary programs and centers on aging.

The future of the humanities and aging remains more uncertain than its recent accomplishments would seem to warrant. So it goes. Aging scholars should perhaps take solace in several of the major themes that pervade this *Handbook of Humanities and the Aging.* Paradoxically, because the next stages of intellectual development are unstructured, we should let our minds roam as they wish. Experts in the humanities no longer have anything to prove. Excellence remains its own reward, as does the sheer delight in imagining how our future selves may continue to mature in ways that give pleasure in days of light and comfort in moments of darkness.

REFERENCES

Achenbaum, W. A. (1992). Afterword: Integrating the humanities into gerontologic research, training, and practice. In T. R. Cole, D. D. Van Tassel, & R. Kastenbaum (Eds.), *Handbook of the humanities and aging* (pp. 458–476). New York: Springer Publishing Co.

Achenbaum, W. A. (1995). *Crossing frontiers: Gerontology emerges as a science.* New York: Cambridge University Press.

Achenbaum, W. A., & Stearns, P. N. (1978). Old age and modernization. *The Gerontologist, 18,* 307–313.

Cole, T. R. (1992). *The journey of life.* New York: Cambridge University Press.

Cole, T. R., & Gadow, S. (Eds.). (1986). *What does it mean to grow old?* Durham: Duke University Press.

Cowdry, E. V. (Ed.). (1939). *Problems of ageing.* Baltimore: Williams and Wilkins.

Dewey, J. (1939). Introduction. In E. V. Cowdry (Ed.), *Problems of ageing.* Baltimore: Williams and Wilkins.

Gratton, B., & Haber, C. (1993b). In search of 'Intimacy from a Distance.' *Journal of Aging Studies, 6,* 51–69.

Gubrium, J. (1993). *Speaking of life.* New York: Aldine deGruyter.

Haber, C., & Gratton, B. (1993a). *Old age and the search for security.* Bloomington: Indiana University Press.

Kahn, R. L. (1996). Interdisciplinary in the MacArthur Project. Seminar at the Institute of Gerontology, University of Michigan.

Moody, H. R. (1997). *Five stages of the soul.* New York: Anchor.

Rowe, J. W., & Kahn, R. L. (1987). Human aging: Usual and successful. *Science, 237,* 143–149.

Rowe, J. W., & Kahn, R. L. (1998). *Successful aging.* New York: Partheon.

Sokolovsky, J. N. (Ed.). (1997). *The cultural context of aging* (2nd ed.). Westport, CT: Bergin and Garvey.

Van Tassel, D. D. (1995). Unpublished paper. Gerontological Society annual meeting.

Index

("i" indicates an illustration; "n" indicates a note)

⑤ *Springer Publishing Company*

Ageism, 2nd Edition
Negative and Positive
Erdman B. Palmore, PhD
Foreword by **George Maddox,** PhD

"Erdman Palmore has provided a portrait of older people in America that is both scientifically impeccable and extremely readable...Palmore's approach is forthright in calling attention to ways in which individuals, social groups, and social isntitutions undervalue older people."

-M. Powell Lawton, PhD, Philadelphia Geriatric Center

In this updated edition, Palmore provides a comprehensive review of many different forms of ageism - including the interesting notion of positive ageism, which projects onto the elderly as a group of traditional virtues like wisdom and thrift. He discusses both the individual and social influences on attitudes towards the aged; analyzes institutional patterns of ageism; and explores ways to reduce the impact of ageism on the elderly. This book is a valuable resource for students and professionals interested in the sociology of aging in our society.

Contents: Foreword by George Maddox • Preface • Part I: Concepts • Introduction and Basic Definitions • Types of Ageism • The Meaning of Age • Part II: Causes and Consequences • Individual Sources • Social Influences • Cultural Sources • Consequences • Part III: Institutional Patterns • The Economy • The Government • The Family • Housing and Health Care • Part IV: Reducing Ageism • Changing the Person • Changing the Structure • Strategies for Change • The Future • Appendix A: The Facts on Aging Quizzes • Appendix B: Ageist Humor • Appendix C: Annotated Bibliography • References • Index

1st Edition: Japanese Translation
1999   280pp   0-8261-7001-3   hard   0-8261-7002-1   soft
www.springerpub.com

536 Broadway, New York, NY 10012-3955 • (212) 431-4370 • Fax (212) 941-7842

SP *Springer Publishing Company*

The Self and Society in Aging Processes

Carol D. Ryff, PhD and Victor W. Marshall, Editors

"How do social structures make a difference in how we age? Is the changing nature of work producing differences in our later years? Such issues are explored by this timely and thoughtful volume, with emphasis on the self and its relation to changing lives and times. Essential reading for all who wonder about how society influences the way we age."

— **Glen H. Elder**, PhD, The University of North Carolina at Chapel Hill

Ryff and Marshall construct a "macro" view of aging in society by bridging disciplines and assembling contributors from all the social sciences. The book is organized into three sections: theoretical perspectives, socioeconomic structures, and contexts of self and society. Leading psychologists, anthropologists, gerontologists, and sociologists present theoretical and empirical advances that forge links between the individual and the social aspects of aging. For gerontology researchers and graduate students in human development, psychology of aging and other social aspects of aging.

Partial Contents: Part I: Theoretical Perspectives on Self and Society Linkages • Linking the Self and Society in Social Gerontology • Social Perspectives on Self in Later Life • Neoteny, Naturalization, and Other Constituents of Human Development • Continuity Theory, Self, and Social Structure • Identity and Adaptation to the Aging Process • Self-Development in Adulthood and Aging • Part II: Socioeconomic Structures and the Self • Practical Consciousness, Social Class, and Self-Concept • Educational Attainment and Self-Making in Later Life • Forging Macro-Micro Linkages in the Study of Psychological Well-Being • Income and Subjective Well-Being Over the Life Course • Part III: Contexts of Self and Society: Work and Family • Structure and Agency in the Retirement Process • Gender and Distress in Later Life

1999   504pp.   0-8261-1267-6   hard   www.springerpub.com

536 Broadway, New York, NY 10012-3955 • (212) 431-4370 • Fax (212) 941-7842

Springer Publishing Company

Psychological Issues in Biblical Lore

Explorations in The Old Testament

A.I. Rabin, PhD

"...Rabin identifies several current pychological issues, finds parallel concerns in the Old Testament, and compares modern psychological understanding with that of the ancient Hebrew writers. As a comparison of old and new perspectives, his text is very interesting."

Readings: A Journal for Reviews and Commentary in Mental Health

Dr. Rabin, an eminent scholar of the psychology of personality and well versed in Hebrew, reviews the chronicles of the Old Testament through the lens of modern psychology. The topics established by the author follow familiar themes such as life course, family, gender, sexuality, and special states. The biblical accounts provide abundant "case examples" for these aspects of psychology and amply resemble our modern universe of human behavior and personality issues, including family problems, violence, rivalry, and greed.

This book opens doors to historical, timeless themes that will surprise, enlighten, and inspire psychologists as well as readers of any background.

Contents:
Preface
The Bible and Psychology
The Life Course: Childhood to Senescence
Sexuality
Aspects of the Biblical Family
Building the Family
Male and Female
Special States of Consciousness
Biblical Psychological Themes

1998   232pp.   0-8261-1212-9   hard   www.springerpub.com

536 Broadway, New York, NY 10012-3955 • (212) 431-4370 • Fax (212) 941-7842

Listening to Life Stories
A New Approach to Stress Intervention in Health Care
Bruce Rybarczyk, PhD and **Albert Bellg**, PhD

"Listening to Life Stories gives a refreshing, enriching, and useful approach to unifying the science and art of medicine."

> **-Herbert Benson**, MDChief, Division of Behavioral Medicine,
> Deaconess Hospital President, Mind/Body Medical Institute,
> Associate Professor of Medicine, Harvard Medical School

"This useful book presents a practical introduction to understanding, planning and implementing narrative reminiscence programs, particularly in the hospital setting. I recommend the book for those interested in a low-cost but highly effective narrative approach to enhancing the quality of life of patients in a variety of settings."

> **-Martita Lopez**, PhD, Director of Clinical Training
> Rush-Presbyterian-St. Luke's Medical Center

"An important contribution to the literature in both geropsychology and behavioral medicine. This is an essential book for anyone interested in medical care, rehabilitation or counseling of older adults. I predict it will be seen as a classic in years to come."

> **-Jon Rose**, PhD, Geropsychologist,
> Geriatric Research Educational and Clinical Center
> VA Palo Alto Health Care System

"The authors have done an excellent job of presenting the personal, psychological, and spiritual benefits of sharing life stories for both storyteller and listener. This book is filled with helpful, concrete suggestions and illustrations for conducting effective interviews."

> **-George Fitchett**, Associate Professor
> Rush-Presbyterian-St. Luke's Medical Center

1997   168pp.   0-8261-9570-9   hard   www.springerpub.com

536 Broadway, New York, NY 10012-3955 • (212) 431-4370 • Fax (212) 941-7842

Aging and Biography
Explorations in Adult Development

James E. Birren, PhD, **Gary M. Kenyon,** PhD, **Jan-Erik Ruth,** PhD, **Johannes J. F. Schroots,** PhD, and **Torbjorn Svensson,** PhD, Editors

Personal life narratives can serve as a rich source of new insights into the experience of human aging. In this comprehensive volume, an international team of editors and contributors provide effective approaches to using biography to enhance our understanding of adult development. In addition to providing new theoretical aspects on aging and biography, the book also details new developments concerning the practical use of different biographical approaches in both research and clinical work. This landmark volume advances the use of narrative approaches in gerontology.

Contents: Biography in Adult Development and Aging • The Meaning/Value of Personal Storytelling •Emotionality and Continuity in Biographical Contexts •Studying Older Lives: Reciprocal Acts of Telling and Listening • Narrative Knowing and the Study of Lives • Competence and Quality of Life: Theoretical Views of Biography • The Fractal Structure of Lives: Continuity and Discontinuity in Autobiography • Narrating the Self in Adulthood • The Complexity of Personal Narratives • Ways of Life: Old Age in a Life History Perspective • Experienced Aging as Elucidated by Narratives • Beyond Life Narratives in the Therapeutic Encounter • Restorying a Life: Adult Education and Transformative Learning • Life Review and Reminiscence in Nursing Practice • Biographical Assessment in Community Care • Autobiography: Exploring the Self and Encouraging Development

1995   368pp.   0-8261-8980-6   hard   www.springerpub.com

536 Broadway, New York, NY 10012-3955 • (212) 431-4370 • Fax (212) 941-7842